MARRIAGE AND THE FAMILY

Diversity and Strengths

THIRD EDITION

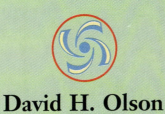

David H. Olson
University of Minnesota

John DeFrain
University of Nebraska

Mayfield Publishing Company
Mountain View, California
London • Toronto

This book about families
is dedicated to our families

Copyright ©2000, 1997, 1994 by Mayfield Publishing Company

Library of Congress Cataloging-in-Publication Data

Olson, David H. L.
    Marriage and the family: diversity and strengths / David H. Olson, John DeFrain.—3rd ed.
        p.   cm.
    Includes bibliographical references and index.
    ISBN 0-7674-1209-5
    1. Family—United States—Psychological aspects. 2. Marriage—United States—Psychological aspects. 3. Circumplex Model of Marital and Family Systems. 4. Family assessment—United States. I. DeFrain, John D. II. Title.
    HQ536.046 1999
    306.8'0973—dc21   99-22761
                                                        CIP

Manufactured in the United States of America
10   9   8   7   6   5   4   3   2

Mayfield Publishing Company
1280 Villa Street
Mountain View, CA 94041

Sponsoring editor, Franklin C. Graham; developmental editor, Kathleen Engelberg; production editor, Carla White Kirschenbaum; manuscript editor, Andrea McCarrick; text designers, Gary Head and Jeanne M. Schreiber; cover designer, Jean Mailander; art editor, Amy Folden; photo researcher, Rennie Evans; illustrator, Lotus Art; manufacturing manager, Randy Hurst. The text was set in 10/12 Janson Text by York Graphic Services and printed on 45# Somerset Matte by R. R. Donnelly & Sons.
Cover art by Pascol Milelli.

Brief Contents

Contents

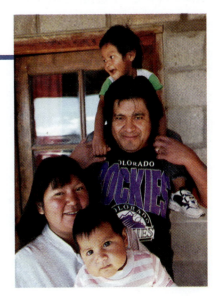

PART II   Developing Intimate Relationships   119

PART IV Stages of Marriage and Family Life   359

PART V Challenges and Opportunities 453

ABOUT THE AUTHORS

David H. Olson, Ph. D., is professor of family social science at the University of Minnesota, where he has been for more than 25 years. He is founder and president of Life Innovations; a past president of the National Council on Family Relations (NCFR); a past president of the Upper Midwest Association for Marriage and Family Therapists (UMAMFT); a fellow and clinical member of the American Association for Marital and Family Therapy (AAMFT); and a fellow of the American Psychological Association (APA). Olson is also a member of the editorial boards of six family journals. He has received numerous awards, including the Distinguished Contribution to Family Therapy Research Award from both AAMFT and the American Family Therapy Association (AFTA). Olson has written or edited more than 20 books, including *Building Relationships, Families: What Makes Them Work, Circumplex Model, Power in Families, Treating Relationships,* and 10 volumes of the *Inventory of Marriage and Family Literature.* He has published more than 100 articles with the theme of bridging family research, theory, and practice. Olson and his colleagues at the University of Minnesota have developed the Circumplex model of Marital and Family Systems and a variety of couple and family assessment tools, including PREPARE, ENRICH, FACES, PAIR, and AWARE. He is happily married to Karen Olson, who has provided companionship and support throughout this and numerous other projects. They have three terrific children (Hans, Amy, and Chris), a great son-in-law (Daniel) and daughter-in-law (Shelly), and four wonderful grandchildren (Adrienne, Evan, Chelsea, and Alex). Olson has been blessed with a fun-loving and caring family that continues to sustain and support him.

John DeFrain, Ph.D., is a professor of family science at the University of Nebraska-Lincoln and has focused his professional and personal energy for the past 28 years in better understanding how families learn to live happily together. He received his doctorate from the University of Wisconsin-Madison in 1975 and has been on the faculty of UNL for more than 20 years. He has experience as a newspaper reporter and a preschool and kindergarten teacher; has codirected a graduate training program in marriage and family therapy; was cofounder of the National Symposium on Building Family Strengths; and has been a consultant to courts, universities, churches, agencies, and individual families on marriage, parenting, grief, divorce, and child custody issues. DeFrain has co-authored three dozen professional articles on family issues and 17 books, including *Secrets of Strong Families, Sudden Infant Death: Enduring the Loss, Stillborn: The Invisible Death, On Our Own: A Single Parent's Survival Guide, Parents in Contemporary America: A Sympathetic View,* and *Good Families.* He and his wife and best friend, Nikki DeFrain, M.S., are the parents of three daughters: Amie, 30, Alyssa, 23, and Erica, 20. Nikki was especially important in the development and writing of this textbook, offering support in innumerable areas of the project and expertise in her own areas of study: life-span human development in a family context and, especially, older people. The DeFrains are very interested in the understanding of family strengths and challenges from a global perspective. They are currently working with the University of Newcastle on a national study of Australian family strengths.

Preface

Our colleague and friend, the late Dr. David R. Mace, once said, "Nothing in the world could make human life happier than to greatly increase the number of happy couples and strong families." Our goal in writing *Marriage and the Family: Diversity and Strengths*, Third Edition, is to provide students with knowledge about marriage and family relationships that will help them move toward Mace's goal.

Three distinctive themes have guided our efforts in writing this book. First, we stress that the growing *diversity* of couples in our society is a positive, enriching trend. Second, we express our belief that couple and family *strengths* help people maintain themselves and weather the inevitable storms of life. And third, we emphasize the concept that marriage and families are *systems* of relationships, functioning both within themselves and with other systems beyond themselves, such as society at large.

Our intent, further, is to make the concepts and ideas presented in this book useful and meaningful enough to students that they will want to apply them to their own lives. We hope to help students integrate intellectual ideas and personal experiences, thereby enriching both. Numerous features of the book, ranging from personal stories related by real people to student activities at the ends of chapters, are designed to help students see the relevance of the material to their lives. And although the text deals with complex ideas and materials, it is written in a style accessible both to students new to the field of family studies and to the more experienced reader.

Diversity and Strengths

Diversity is a key theme in this book. Wherever possible, we consider how concepts, research, and theories about the family apply to couples and families of diverse ethnic and cultural backgrounds. We also focus on the diversity in structure that characterizes families today, looking at the many different forms that "family" can take. Diversity in sexual orientation—gay and lesbian relationships and families in our society—is a third type of diversity we explore. The theme of diversity is introduced in Chapter 1, "Perspectives on Intimate Relationships," and discussed in detail in Chapter 3 "Cultural Diversity: Family Strengths and Challenges." As a prominent characteristic of our society and the world, diversity is integrated into discussions throughout the book.

Marital and family strengths is another key theme in this book. The family strengths perspective is based on the premise that if you approach relationships from a "problem" perspective, you will find problems. If you look for strengths, you will find strengths. Growing numbers of family educators and family therapists are using this approach today, helping families recognize their own strengths and use them as a foundation for positive growth. In Chapter 1, we identify a number of strengths that have been found to be present in healthy marriages and families all over the world. Throughout the book, we show how these strengths help families provide healthy settings for the growth of individual family members, face challenges, and solve problems.

Although diversity and strengths are integrated throughout the book, three chapters focus especially on these themes: Chapter 3 highlights the couple and family strengths of diverse ethnic and cultural groups; Chapter 15, "Family Stress and Coping," examines how families can use their strengths to manage crisis and stress; and Chapter 18, "Strengthening Marriages and Families" looks at how families and societies can work together to build healthier societies in the future.

Family Systems and Family Strengths

We present many theories of family in this book, but we focus especially on family systems theory. Recognizing that the family unit is a system of interdependent parts, we look at how families maintain themselves and yet change, how family members can be separate and yet connected, and how communication facilitates the processes of change and growth. We focus on communication and conflict resolution skills as essential tools for creating healthy intimate relationships. We also look at how families can learn to function well within the larger systems of community and society.

The family strengths perspective, developed by Nick Stinnett, John DeFrain, and many colleagues across the country, is also used throughout the text as a model for understanding and evaluating families. It identifies and focuses on six key qualities of healthy families: commitment, appreciation and affection, positive communication, time together, spiritual well-being, and the ability to cope with stress and crisis. The research driving this model has involved thousands of family members in the United States and around the world.

The Couple and Family Map, an assessment tool developed by David Olson and colleagues, is based on concepts from family systems theory. Focusing on the three dimensions of cohesion, flexibility, and communication, the Couple and Family Map has been used in hundreds of studies to help researchers understand and evaluate families. The map is introduced in Chapter 4, "Understanding Marriage and Family Dynamics," and studies that have used the map as a theoretical base are reported throughout the text. An ongoing family case study project is described in *The Resource Book* to help instructors show students how the Couple and Family Map is applied.

Changes to the Third Edition

A good textbook is like a healthy couple or family; It grows and changes in positive directions over the years. Although the second edition of *Marriage and the Family: Diversity and Strengths* was published just three years ago, this third edition incorporates a number of improvements, many of them based on the suggestions of students and instructors. Changes include the following:

- The field of family science continues to grow dramatically. This edition of *Marriage and the Family* includes the newest research and latest statistics available. Cutting-edge literature has been included from such sources as the *Journal of Marriage and the Family, Family Relations, Journal of Family Psychology, Child Development, Family Process,* and *Journal of Marital and Family Therapy.* We used several family science, psychology, sociology, and humanities databases to locate new journal articles, books, and other resources. Treatment of many topics has been substantially updated and revised.

- A new Chapter 2, "Social Environment Impact on Couples and Families," has been added to describe the importance of social factors on relationships. Some of the diverse social forces addressed in this chapter include issues related to the mass media, violence, the Internet, drug use, increasing levels of stress, sexuality issues, and the global economy.

- More than 60 "personal stories" have been included in this edition to bridge the gap between concept and "real life." The voices of real people are heard as they describe their family relationships, their struggles and achievements, their disappointments and hopes. These stories, drawn from the authors' files, illustrate family dynamics in a variety of situations, settings, and life stages. They touch on such issues as single parenting, sexual intimacy, family violence, managing money, dividing chores, expressing difficult emotions, adjusting to the death of a family member, and many more. One of our goals in including these stories is to help students realize how much they share with families everywhere.

- New material on couple and family strengths has been added to this edition and integrated throughout. Chapters 4, 12, and 18 in particular offer current views on these topics and personal strategies for strengthening couple and family relationships.

- A new addition to many chapters is recent research completed in 1999 from a national survey of married couples done by Olson and colleagues. Using a national sample of over 27,000 married couples, the results focus on major areas for couples including communication, conflict resolution, sexuality, and roles. For each chapter, the major strengths of happy versus unhappy couples are identified on that topic and the major issues for married couples in that area are described.

Content and Organization

This textbook has been written for students who are interested in learning more about themselves, their family, and their close relationships. Each chapter provides a comprehensive and up-to-date look at salient issues. Each chapter contains a chapter outline, a chapter summary, activities, a list of terms, and suggested readings.

An awareness of how the textbook is organized is a prerequisite to using it successfully. Due to the growing complexity of the marriage and family field, the four chapters in Part I, "Social Context of Intimate Relationships," emphasize the critical themes of diversity and strengths and their centrality of the subject of marriage and family. Chapter 1 presents "Perspectives on Intimate Relationships," including the realities of marriage and family life today; defining marriage and family; trends in marriage and the family; and family science as an emerging field. Chapter 2, "Social Environment Impact on Couples and Families," describes the important role of the social context on relationships. Some of the important social forces addressed include the Internet, mass media, increasing stress levels, lack of time, drug use, and violence in our society. Chapter 3, "Cultural Diversity: Family Strengths and Challenges," discusses the nature of cultural diversity; family strengths, stereotypes, and challenges in various ethnic and cultural groups; and issues in cross-cultural family studies. In Chapter 4, "Understanding Relationships in Marriage and Family Dynamics," the various conceptual frameworks used in the field are reviewed. The major focus is on family systems and family strengths but other frameworks are also described including family development, symbolic interaction, social construction, and the feminist framework. In addition, the importance of three family system dimensions of cohesion, flexibility, and communication are described.

Part II, "Developing Intimate Relationships," provides a foundation for understanding how individuals pair up and move toward intimate and committed relationships. Chapter 5 "Friendship, Love, and Singlehood" explores the differences between friends and lovers; how people move from intimate experiences to intimate relationships; intimacy games people play; and the pros and cons of being single. Chapter 6, "Dating, Living Together and Mate Selection," begins with an overview of the American dating system and the limitations of this system for selecting a mate. The growing prevalence of living together is addressed along with a review of its impact on marriage. Various theories of mate selection are described with a concluding section on violence in dating. In Chapter 7, "Sexual Intimacy," the focus is on sex and society; American sexual behavior as uncovered by various surveys; sex education; premarital sexual behavior; marital and extramarital sexual behavior; and how couples can move toward sexual health.

In Part III we emphasize the "Dynamics of Intimate Relationships." Chapter 8 is a discussion of "Gender Roles and Power in the Family," beginning with traditional and contemporary views of gender roles; continuing on to theories of gender-role development and change; and ending with a discussion of power in families. In Chapter 9 the subject is "Communication and Intimacy," beginning with perspectives on communication and using communication to develop and maintain intimacy. Chapter 10, "Conflict and Conflict Resolution," outlines the hierarchy of conflict in intimate relationships; notes the relationship between intimacy and conflict; and discusses ways to resolve conflict successfully. Chapter 11, "Managing Economic Resources," discussed the stresses related to family financial issues; why finances cause family problems; family income and expenses; the process of family financial resource management; and uses and abuses of credit in our society.

In Part IV, "Stages of Marriage and Family Life," we begin with Chapter 12 "Marriage: Building a Strong Foundation," which has been expanded to include more research on the positive benefits of marriage. The chapter provides a formula for a successful marriage, explores positive and negative reasons for marrying, and describes the importance of premarital education. The challenges of the newlywed years are described along with a new typology of couples. Chapter 13 "Parenthood," begins with a discussion of the challenge of parenthood and ends with a discussion of various important issues in parenting. Styles of parenting are described along with the consequences of these styles. The important issue of discipline is discussed in more depth. Chapter 14, "Midlife and Older Couples," discusses family life in the middle years, including sexuality, middle-aged marriage, empty or spacious nests, the sandwich generation, and grandparenthood; the discussion of family life in the later years focuses on definitions of old age, conventional wisdom about aging, retirement, family dynamics and the aging couple, and losing a spouse.

In Part V the focus is on "Challenges and Opportunities." Chapter 15 "Family Stress and Coping," looks at cultural perspectives on family stress; the curvilinear nature of stress; stressors families face; family stress theory; family coping strategies; the biopsychosocial approach and family problems; medical care and the family; and the family's influence on health behaviors. Chapter 16, "Divorce and Family Problems," begins with a description of our divorce culture and the impact it is having on individuals, particularly children, and society. The trends in divorce are described and the process of adjusting to divorce is presented. An overview of family problems includes focus on physical abuse and violence in addition to neglect. The chapter ends with a discussion of alcoholism and abuse of other drugs. Chapter 17, "Single-Parent Families and Stepfamilies," looks at the changing picture of the family; single-parent families from a strengths perspective; and stepfamilies from a strengths perspective. Chapter 18, the concluding chapter of the text, is entitled "Strengthening Marriages and Families." We discuss the future of families from a global perspective and present some thoughts about the future of families. The chapter then focuses on personal strategies to strengthen marriage and family relationships, and ends with recommendations for making every year an International Year of the Family, and how we can work together in our communities and the community of nations to help families succeed in life's most important task: creating healthy, satisfying close relationships.

The goal of a marriage or of a family must be more than simply to survive; it must be to thrive. Couples and families must be proactive rather than reactive in dealing with ongoing relationship issues. Strong relationships, strong marriages, and strong families require time, energy, and commitment. The rewards of these investments include an enhanced and healthy emotional and physical life for every family member. Finally, strong families also provide the foundation for a strong and caring society.

Ancillary Materials

This textbook is accompanied by a 10-segment custom video. The teaching package also includes *The Resource Book: Teaching with Marriage and the Family*, a computerized text bank using Chariot software for Windows and Macintosh, and a student *Study Guide*.

For each chapter of the textbook, *The Resource Book* includes a chapter outline, learning objectives, a summary, key terms for most chapters, lecture notes, activities, and suggested readings. *The Resource Book* contains descriptions of and suggestions for using the videotapes with specific textbook topics and chapters, strategies for using Family Quads in class, and instructions for the Family Case Study assignment. *The Resource Book* also includes 63 transparency masters. A test bank with answer key is available separately and contains about 1,550 items, including multiple-choice, true/false, short answer, and essay questions. Hundreds of the items included have been classroom tested.

The *Study Guide to Accompany Marriage and the Family: Diversity and Strengths* has been written by Dr. Jeanne Kohl of the University of Washington. It includes review materials to help students master the concepts in each chapter of the textbook, prepare for examinations with practice tests, assess their personal attitudes and beliefs, and apply their knowledge to real-life situations. To further the assessment and application objectives, each chapter of the *Study Guide* concludes with a Personal Involvement Assessment and a Knowledge in Action exercise. The Personal Involvement Assessment gives students the opportunity to examine in some depth one of the important issues discussed in the textbook (for example, stereotyping, attitudes about money, accepting criticism). Knowledge in Action exercises highlight key research studies on important topics. Each exercise is designed to encourage students to apply what they have learned to real-life situations involving others. Projects include content analyses, interviews, and surveys.

Acknowledgments

We wish to thank the following people for their thoughtful reviews of the manuscript: Judith Bordin, California State University at Chico; Jeanne Kohl, University of Washington; JoAnn Nicola, California State University at Sacramento; and Bernita Quoss, University of Wyoming.

PART I

Social Context of
Intimate Relationships

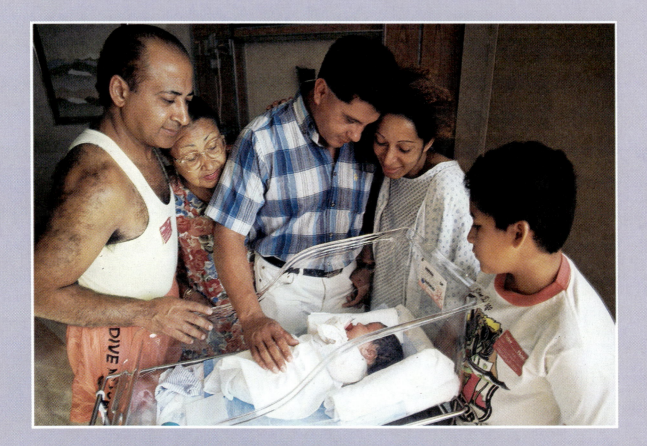

CHAPTER 1

Perspectives on Intimate Relationships

Marriage and family life are microcosms of life itself. They can bring both great joy and excruciating pain. A healthy marriage and family can be a valuable resource during difficult times. Conversely, unhealthy or dysfunctional relationships can create problems that may persist from one generation to the next.

Marriage and family are perhaps society's oldest and most resilient institutions. From the beginning of human life, people have grouped themselves into families to find emotional, physical, and communal support. Although in recent years social commentators have predicted the demise of both marriage and the family, they not only survive but continue to change and evolve. Family structures may vary around the world, but the value of "family" endures.

Marriage and family life are not always easy. This is perhaps because human beings are much like porcupines—we find it necessary to sleep close together to keep warm, but our prickliness also makes living at close quarters perilous. Marriage and family can provide intimacy and closeness, but with them come disagreement and conflict.

"We sure have our ups and downs in our family," Rachel, a 22-year-old college student in Ohio noted. "But I think we're a good family. Scratch that, I think we're a great family. We bicker sometimes and Dad's so conservative, but when you're in trouble, the family is always there to help.

"It was terrible when Mom and Dad divorced. I was 12 at the time and I hated Dad for 3 years. But today I can see things a bit differently. Maybe it's better they're apart. They were staying together the last several years just for us kids, and that wasn't working out for anybody very well. They went to counseling for a long time, but in the end they separated.

"It's a lot better today. I even get along with Dad pretty well. He's been a great help for me. I wouldn't be here at the U without him.

"Sometimes I don't let my family know how much I really care for all of them, but I do. I plan to get married some day, and I'll probably have a child or maybe two. And my family will not really change through all of it. It will only get bigger. We'll still look at the world differently, and I suppose Mom will always be there trying to smooth things out between us. We'll just go on and on and on.

"Because we're Family!"

If you had a happy family life when you were growing up, you should feel fortunate. Such an experience provides an important foundation and model for developing a happy family of your own. If you grew up in a troubled family, the task of building a strong family of your own will be more difficult, but it will be possible. Countless individuals have transcended adverse family experiences and created healthy, new families for themselves and their loved ones.

This book provides a realistic portrayal of marriage and the family today. Its purpose is to help individuals become more aware of important personal and relationship issues and to provide the tools to develop and maintain satisfying intimate relationships.

Realities of Marriage and Family Life

Most human beings search for intimate experiences and intimate relationships throughout their lives. Although most individuals are able to establish some type of intimate relationship, it is not uncommon for individuals to have difficulty either maintaining and/or increasing their levels of intimacy over time. As a direct result, many people experience marital problems, and many marriages end in divorce. A major review of trends in marriage and divorce by David Popenoe and Barbara Whitehead (1999) indicated that:

> Key social indicators suggest a substantial weakening of the institution of marriage. Americans have become less likely to marry. . . . And married couples face a high likelihood of divorce. . . . Unmarried cohabitations and unwed births have grown enormously, and so has the percentage of children who grow up in fragile families (Popenoe and Whitehead, 1999, pg. 3).

Marriage and the Family Are Changing

What are marriage and the family like today? Current trends include fewer marriages, later age of marriage, fewer children, more divorce, more single-parenting families and stepfamilies, more working mothers, a greater need for day care, more child abuse, more spouse abuse, and less connection to kin networks (Popenoe and Whitehead, 1999).

Statistics on divorce, domestic violence, and alcohol and other drug abuse, as well as stories of families in crisis, paint a negative picture of marriage and family life today. These snapshots of troubled families may be newsworthy, but the situations they describe are not new. For decades, many respected social scientists have predicted that the institutions of marriage and the family would not survive. For example, in 1927, psychologist John B. Watson predicted, "In 50 years, unless there is some change, the tribal custom of marriage will no longer exist." He believed marriage would disappear because family standards had broken down. In 1937, Pitirim Sorokin, a respected Harvard sociologist, wrote, "The family as a sacred union of husband and wife, of parents and children, will continue to disintegrate." Ten years later, Carl Zimmerman, also a Harvard sociologist, noted, "There is little left now, within the family itself or the moral code, to hold the family together" (Bernard, 1970, p. 42).

Although some professionals emphasize the decline of marriage and the family, others see them as being in a state of transition. As Ernest Burgess stated in 1953, "Certainly marriage and the family in the U.S. are in the process of rapid change. But is it change for the worse? Perhaps it may be for the better" (Bernard, 1970, p. 43). In a similar vein, David and Vera Mace, pioneers in the marriage and family enrichment movement in Great Britain and the United States, argued that "marriage has not failed—it is simply in transition" (Mace & Mace, 1980, p. 260). Skolnick and Skolnick (1977), in their classic study *Family in Transition*, clearly illustrated the dramatic changes in family life over the centuries. In fact, one of the salient characteristics of the family is its ability to adapt to changing times and new challenges.

Pessimists and optimists disagree about how to interpret these trends and what to do about them. The pessimists see recent changes as an indication that

Marriage and the family as institutions have many strengths, one of which is their ability to adapt to changing social, economic, and political conditions. American families today reflect various current trends in our society. High divorce and remarriage rates, for example, have led to more families like this one, in which one or both partners bring children from a previous marriage and then have another child together.

marriage and family are in serious trouble and are declining in their significance to society. They believe we need to return to a more traditional value system to curtail these negative trends. The optimists, on the other hand, see recent changes as a reflection of the flexibility of marriage and family and the ability of these institutions to adapt to the increasing stresses of modern life. They believe marriage and the family will survive and thrive. (For a look at how family patterns in the United States have evolved over the course of our history, see Box 1.1.)

In fact, marriage and the family *do* continue to survive, despite all the predictions of their imminent collapse. Moreover, marriage remains the most popular voluntary institution in our society, with about 85% of the population marrying at least once (Popenoe and Whitehead, 1999).

BOX 1.1

Family Types Over Time

Families don't exist in isolation; they are embedded in a particular society, a particular culture, a particular historical period. Thus, they evolve over time and reflect the beliefs and values of the larger society. Family patterns in turn influence how individuals and their family systems operate.

William Doherty, of the University of Minnesota, has developed a useful framework for understanding changing family patterns (Doherty, 1992). The four family types he identifies are the institutional family, the psychological family, the pluralistic family, and the intentional family. Each type represents a cultural ideal of family life in the United States in a broadly defined historical period. (There is some overlap between time periods as the new type emerges and the earlier type recedes.) Characteristics of the four types follow.

Institutional Family: Pre-1925

This family type is organized around economic production, with the father as the authority. The kinship network is strong, and the family has many community connections.

- *Marriage:* Functional partnership.
- *Important aspects:* Family loyalty, family tradition, and solidarity.
- *Chief value:* Responsibility.

Psychological Family: 1925–1975

This family type is more nuclear, more mobile, less tied to kin networks, and less connected to the broader community than the institutional family.

- *Marriage:* Friendship, love, and attraction.
- *Important aspect:* Personal satisfaction of family members.
- *Chief value:* Satisfaction.

Pluralistic Family: 1975–1990

This family type encompasses a diversity of family structures, including single-parent families, stepfamilies, and never-married families. Gender equality and personal freedom are increasingly important themes. Women become more independent as they work outside the home and see marriage as less necessary. Other variations include dual-career families and gay-male and lesbian families. There is no broad cultural consensus on the ideal type of family structure.

- *Marriage:* Changing forms.
- *Important aspects:* Diversity and tolerance.
- *Chief value:* Flexibility.

Intentional Families: 1990 and Into the Future

Families of the future will combine elements of the psychological and pluralistic family types. Couple and family relationships will be more intentional, and interest in maintaining quality relationships will grow.

- *Marriage:* Changing forms.
- *Important aspects:* Equality and diversity.
- *Chief values:* Flexibility and responsibility.

Why Do So Many Marriages End in Divorce?

Although marriage is popular, it is not necessarily lasting. Based on current trends, about 50% of all recent U.S. marriages are likely to end in divorce (U.S. Bureau of the Census, 1997). And even though 50% survive, the quality of some of those marriages may be poor (Popenoe and Whitehead, 1999). In many lasting marriages, one partner is unhappy; typically, it is the wife who is more unhappy than the husband. A respected sociologist, Norval Glenn (1996), predicted that after ten years of marriage only about 25% of the couples will still be happily married, which is a substantial decrease from the past.

Why are there so many divorces and unhappy marriages in our society? First, many people enter marriage with unrealistic expectations. Second, many marry the wrong person for the wrong reasons. Third, marriage is a very difficult type of relationship, even if one chooses a partner wisely. Fourth, little time or effort is put into developing the relationship skills needed to maintain a strong marriage.

In intact marriages, intimacy and quality often decline over time. Couples face many challenges together, including disagreements over money, difficulties communicating, questions regarding past friendships with members of the other sex, the complexities of blending two family systems together and dealing with in-laws, sexual relations, the question of whether to have children, and decisions about how to divide household tasks.

Even newlywed couples face serious problems during the first year of marriage. A study of several hundred newlywed couples found that 63% had serious problems related to their finances, that 51% had serious doubts about their marriage lasting, that 49% had significant marital problems, that 45% were not satisfied with their sexual relationship, that 42% found marriage harder than they had expected, and that 35% felt their partner was often critical of them (Arond & Pauker, 1987).

Many couples cannot handle the major problems in married life. They simply are not mature enough, sufficiently committed to the relationship, or creative enough in their problem-solving abilities. We will discuss these issues and challenges in detail later in the book.

Defining Marriage and Family

Few people today live in the so-called traditional family, with a dad at work and a mom at home with the kids—only about 25% of all families in the United States match this model. In addition to the diverse types of family structure, families may vary in cultural or ethnic background, income, size, and longevity. Today, there are many possible family structures rather than one "right" way for a family to be organized.

What Is Marriage?

Marriage is by nature a multifaceted institution. We define **marriage** as the emotional and legal commitment of two people to share emotional and physical intimacy, various tasks, and economic resources. Although people typically think of marriage as a union of a man and a woman, same-sex couples are also interested in marriage. The definition of marriage used in this text can be applied to same-sex couples, except that there is no legal commitment. Marriage licenses for same-sex relationships are not currently issued by any state in the United States. However, several states (including Hawaii) are considering bills that would make same-sex marriages legal.

The following nine characteristics of marriage were identified by Carlfred Broderick (1984). A former president of the National Council on Family Relations, Broderick found these characteristics to be common across income levels, educational levels, and ethnic groups in the United States:

- *Marriage is a demographic event.* Each marriage creates a social unit in society.

- *Marriage is the joining of two family and social networks.* When individuals marry, they marry not only each other but their partner's family and friends. Their social network may comprise friends of both partners, but only those friends liked by both partners tend to remain friends of the couple.

- *Marriage is a legal contract between the couple and the state.* Each state specifies the rights and responsibilities of the partners.

- *Marriage is an economic union.* A married couple usually becomes a single financial unit for most purposes. As a group, married couples are probably society's most important financial decision makers—buying, selling, borrowing, and sharing resources as one.

- *Marriage is the most common living arrangement for adults.* Few people choose to live alone. Marriage is by far the most popular living arrangement for adults.

- *Marriage is the context of most human sexual activity.* Most married couples rate sexual activity positively, especially in the early years.

- *Marriage is a reproductive unit.* Most married couples become parents and see parenting as an important goal and a valued purpose in their lives.

- *Marriage is a unit that socializes children* (although children can also be raised by single parents, extended families, grandparents, and other caregivers).

- *Marriage is an opportunity to develop an intimate, sharing relationship.* Although many marriages fail, many others provide a supportive context in which people develop and maintain intimacy.

What Is a Family?

As mentioned, family life in the United States is changing. Before we turn to the more technical definitions of family, read this poem by Gerhard Neubeck (1999).

> *The family of yore*
>   *is no more.*
> *Tradition is upended*
>   *when the family is blended.*
> *There is the single mother,*
>   *unwed couples living with one another.*
> *A single father doing his bit*
>   *rearing by himself his little kid.*
> *There is the same gender marriage*
>   *not exactly the thing that went with carriage.*
> *Children adopted from many places*
>   *of many nationalities and races.*

BOX 1.2

Some Definitions of Family

A family is any two or more persons related by birth, marriage, or adoption and residing together.

U.S. BUREAU OF THE CENSUS, 1997 (p. 6)

Family is a group of people who love and care for each other.

ASSOCIATED PRESS, RANDOM SAMPLE OF 1,200 PEOPLE

A family is defined as two or more persons who share resources, share responsibility for decisions, share values and goals, and have a commitment to one another over time.

AMERICAN ASSOCIATION OF
FAMILY AND CONSUMER SCIENCES

Families provide emotional, physical, and economic mutual aid to their members. Ideally such families are characterized by intimacy, intensity, continuity, and commitment among their members.

FAMILY SERVICE OF AMERICA
(definition provided by a network of 300 families)

The definition of a family "should not rest on fictitious legal distinctions or genetic history" but instead should be based on the functional and psychological qualities of the relationship: the "exclusivity and longevity" of relationship; the "level of emotional and financial commitment"; the "reliance placed upon one another for daily family services"; and how the couple (members) "conducted their everyday lives and held themselves out to society."

NEW YORK STATE SUPREME COURT

A family is . . . cohabiting groups of some duration composed of persons in intimate relations based on biology, law, custom or choice and usually economically interdependent.

FAMILY POLICY IN THE 1980s: CONTROVERSY AND CONSENSUS by Joan Aldous and Wilfried Dumon, published in the *Journal of Marriage and the Family*, November 1990

Divorced mates remarrying
  and carrying
on like they never split
  and making it.
Yes, this new world indeed is brave.
  Great Grandpa and Grandma
  are turning around in their grave.

Family can be defined in many ways. One dictionary offers four definitions:

> 1. A fundamental social group in society consisting of a man and woman and their offspring. 2. A group of persons sharing a common ancestry. 3. Lineage, esp. distinguished lineage. 4. All the members of a household under one roof. (*American Heritage Dictionary*, 2nd College Ed., 1985)

Any definition of family should be broad enough to encompass a range of family structures, dynamics, and functions. Our definition of **family** is two or more people who are committed to each other and who share intimacy, resources, decision-making responsibilities, and values. This definition is inclusive rather than exclusive and allows for diversity in family structure, family values, and ethnic groups.

Other definitions of family are given in Box 1.2. Although these definitions vary, they tend to emphasize emotional connections, commitment, and the sharing of resources between people. In many cases, the importance of family increases when individuals need emotional support. In Robert Frost's (1946) words, "Home is the place where, when you have to go there, they have to take you in."

"I get pretty fed up with people putting down single parents," said Clinton, a 23-year-old college student from a small town in North Carolina. "Sometimes the way people talk, it's as if a family with only one parent isn't even a family at all.

"Well, I come from a family. A really strong family. My mom worked two jobs to keep us fed and clothed. She's a great person and [chuckling] tough as nails. She didn't take any stuff from any of us boys. There were six kids in our home—four boys and two girls—when I was growing up.

"Dad's an alcoholic. He beat Mom bad when I was 14 or 15, and she took us and left. It's good she did. Somebody might have gotten killed. Maybe Dad [smiling]. I was just getting big enough to put up a good fight.

"Mom yelled at us and loved us and kept us in order. I'm the first ever in our family to be graduating from college, and three of the other kids are in college right now, too. They'll make it for sure, and we'll all be able to take care of Mom when she gets old. She's had a real hard life and deserves our support after what she's done for us.

"One kid, Andrew, he got in trouble as a teenager and spent some time in a detention center. he got in with a bad group, and Mom couldn't stop him. But I'm going back home when I graduate, and I'll be working in a family-service agency. I'll be able to help other families like ours, and I'll be able to keep on Andrew's case till he gets his life straightened out also."

Trends in Marriage and the Family: Change and Continuity

The number of marriages in the United States has continuously decreased over time and has reached its lowest level in our country's history. The rate has steadily declined from a high of 68% in 1970 to 62% in 1980 and 59% in 1990 (U.S. Bureau of the Census, 1997). Currently, about 60% of all people over the age of 18 are married, but the percentage varies by ethnic group. As shown in Figure 1.1, 63% of Caucasians are married, as compared to 58% of Hispanics and 42% of African Americans.

The number of unmarried and divorced people continues to increase, partly accounting for the decreasing number of married persons in the United States. About 26% over the age of 18 are not married. In the 25- to 34-year-old age group, about 34% (14 million) have never been married, and that rate increases for African Americans: 39% of African Americans have never married, as compared to 30% of Hispanics and 21% of Caucasians (see Figure 1.1). In terms of divorce, almost 20 million Americans—about 9.8% of the population—are currently divorced (U.S. Bureau of the Census, 1997). So the increasing number of divorced people and singles has contributed to the decreasing percentage of married couples today.

Figure 1.1 Marital Status of U.S. Population (Persons 18 Years and Older). *Source:* U.S. Bureau of the Census (1997, table 58, p. 55).

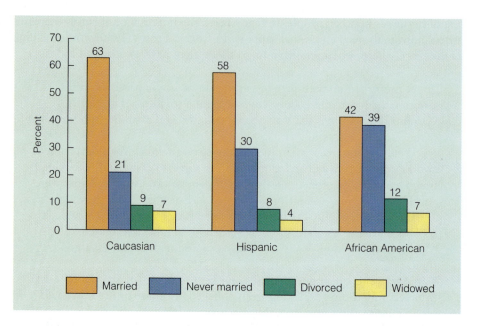

The emergence of a greater variety of family structures has been prompted primarily by high rates of divorce and remarriage. Variety in the family structure is also occurring because of the growing number of women who have chosen to have children without being married.

There are also many teenage mothers who have chosen not to get married and this number varies considerably by ethnic groups. The percentage of teenage mothers who are unmarried is nationally 75%, but it is only 5% for Chinese Americans, 9% for Japanese Americans, 25% for Caucasians, 45% for Mexican Americans, 57% for Native Americans, and 70% for African Americans (U.S. Bureau of the Census, 1997, p. 74).

According to the U.S. Bureau of the Census (1997, p. 73), the percentage of all births to teenagers is about 15% nationally, and it has been slowly decreasing over the last 5 years. These rates also vary by ethnic group: 24% for African Americans, 21% for Native Americans, 12% for Caucasians, and only 2% and 3% for Chinese Americans and Japanese Americans respectively.

Additional statistics reflect the change in types of family structures. Fifty percent of U.S. families are currently headed by couples in their first marriage; 30% are single-parent families; and 20% are headed by remarried couples (U.S. Bureau of the Census, 1997).

Family structure is also becoming more complex through remarriage, which creates new kinship relationships. New family terminology is needed to describe these complex relationships, but as yet, little progress has been made in clarifying or adequately defining these new structures. Even less has been done in describing the complexity of family dynamics in these new relationships.

Trends in Marriage and Cohabitation

As mentioned earlier, marriage continues to be one of the most popular voluntary institutions; more than 85% of all American adults marry at least once. The number of persons getting married over the age of 15 has continued to decrease from

Table 1.1 Percentage of Persons Married Over 15

		MALES			FEMALES	
YEAR	Total	Caucasians	African Americans	Total	Caucasians	African Americans
1998	**58**	60	41	**55**	58	36
1990	**61**	63	45	**57**	59	40
1980	**63**	65	49	**59**	61	45
1970	**67**	68	57	**62**	63	54
1960	**69**	70	61	**66**	67	60

Source: U.S. Bureau of the Census, Current Population Report, Series P20-514: *Marital Status and Living Arrangements.* March 1998.

about two-thirds in 1960 to a little more than half in 1998 (Table 1.1). In 1960, about 69% of males and 66% of females were married. In 1998, 58% of males were married and 55% of females were married. The decrease in the percentage of married persons was even more dramatic for African Americans. Although about 60% of African Americans were married in 1960, the percentage dropped to 41% for males and 36% for females by 1998.

- More individuals delay marriage until their late 20s. Currently, the median age for first marriage is 26.7 years for men and 25 years for women, the oldest in American history. Age at marriage has been on the increase for three decades. In 1960, the median age for first marriage was 22.8 years for men and 20.3 years for women (Glick, 1989).

- More than half of all couples cohabit before marriage, and cohabitation is becoming more acceptable (Bumpass and Lu, 1998). The rate of cohabitation has increased eight-fold since the 1960s, with fewer than 500,000 cohabitating. The rate increased to about 2.5 million couples living together in 1988, 3.5 million couples cohabiting in 1993, and more than 4 million couples currently cohabiting (U.S. Bureau of the Census, 1998).

- More than 50% of cohabiting adults have never been married (U.S. Bureau of the Census, 1994). Because of the increased rate of cohabitation among both previously unmarried and divorced individuals, cohabitation has gained acceptance in many segments of our society. (See Chapter 6 for a detailed discussion on cohabitation.)

Trends in Divorce and Remarriage

The divorce rate climbed during the 1960s and 1970s, however, it has stabilized in the 1990s at about 50%. About 75% of those couples who divorce will later remarry, and at least 50% of those who remarry get divorced again. Because of this marriage-remarriage cycle, marriage patterns in our society are increasingly moving toward what anthropologist Margaret Mead originally described as serial monogamy.

BOX 1.3

The Statistics of Marriage and Divorce

- About 90% of all Americans marry at some time in their lives.

- In 1996, there were 2.3 million marriages and 1.2 million divorces.

- People marrying today have a 50% chance of divorcing (Popenoe and Whitehead, 1999).

- The median age for first marriage is 26.7 for men and 25 for women.

- The median duration of marriage is 7 years.

- The average age of remarriage for men is 36 years and for women, 33.

- First marriages for both the bride and groom account for only 54% of the marriages each year.

- Most divorces involve children, and more than 1 million children are affected by divorce each year in the United States.

- Most divorced individuals eventually remarry. For younger divorced individuals, this remarriage occurs within 5 years of the divorce.

- Over 4 million couples currently are cohabiting.

Source: U.S. Bureau of the Census (1997), unless otherwise indicated.

Only 54% of those who marry each year are doing so for the first time. In 23% of marriages, both the bride and the groom have been married before, and in the remaining 23%, it is the first marriage for one partner and a remarriage for the other person (U.S. Bureau of the Census, 1997, p. 102).

After divorce, men tend to remarry more quickly and more often than do women. The majority of younger divorced men and women, however, do remarry. According to one survey, 72% of recently divorced women remarried (Glick, 1989), but the rate of remarriage decreased as the number of children increased. About 81% of divorced women with no children remarried, 73% of women with one or two children remarried, and only 57% of women with three or more children remarried. In other words, the more children a woman has, the less likely she is to remarry. Box 1.3 provides some statistics on marriage and divorce trends.

Trends in Family Structure

The following trends illustrate the changes in family dynamics in the latter part of the 20th century in the United States:

- Single-parent families with children under the age of 18 are increasing in number dramatically. In the 1970s, only 12% of children lived in a single-parent home. In 1980 this number had increased to 22%, and in 1990, to 28%. By 1998, the rate was approaching 30% (U.S. Bureau of the Census, 1998). The family structure with children under 18 varies by ethnic group (Figure 1.2). A majority of Caucasian and Hispanic children live in two-parent homes (79% and 69%, respectively), but less than half

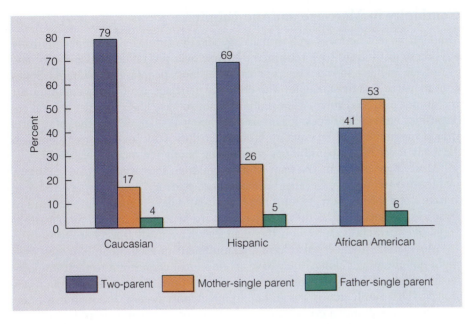

Figure 1.2 Family Structures With Children Under 18. *Source:* U.S. Bureau of the Census (1997, tab. 76, p. 64).

of all African American children (53%) live in two-parent homes. Over half (53%) of all African American families are headed by a single mother, whereas roughly 26% of all Hispanic families and 17% of all Caucasian families are headed by a single mother. A small but growing number of families (4% to 6% of families across ethnic groups) in the United States are headed by a single father. Social scientists predict that 60% of children who are 2 years old will have lived in a single-parent household by the time they are 18 years old.

- The number of **stepfamilies**—families in which one or both of the partners have children from a previous marriage—is growing. Rising divorce and remarriage rates are the primary reason for the increase in the number of stepfamilies. About 75% of those who divorce eventually marry again. Today, about 20% of all U.S. families are stepfamilies. The percentage will probably increase to about 25% by the year 2000.

- Families are having considerably fewer children, except for certain ethnic groups. In 1970, more than 50% of 40-year-old women had three or more children; by 1994 the number had dropped to less than 30%. In 1989, couples with no children or with one child represented one third of all families. Currently, the average number of children per family in the United States is 1.7.

- In many families, both partners work. In the 1950s in more than 70% of families, the father worked and the mother stayed at home. Today, only about 33% of U.S. families are characterized by this pattern (U.S. Bureau of the Census, 1997). In nearly 30% of U.S. families, both parents work full-time. In many others (16%), the father works full-time and the mother works part-time.

Continuity in Marriage and the Family

Although we tend to focus on how marriage and the family have changed, in many ways these institutions have remained the same over several decades and continue to provide stability in our lives. For example, most people in the United States want to marry, and most couples who do so see marriage as a lifelong commitment and do not plan to divorce. Many couples want to have an egalitarian marital relationship, but equality does not mean that they will share exactly the same roles around the house. Rather, equality means that they work together to accomplish the many tasks and responsibilities required by family life on a regular basis.

Most couples who marry want to have children. Parenthood is an important goal for many couples, a fact that becomes more evident when a couple is not able to have a child. Most parents want their children to have a good education and to be at least as successful as they, the parents, are in society. In fact, most parents would like their children to do better than they have in all aspects of life.

Most family members also have a commitment to each other, although they might not always get along. They have an emotional connection to their immediate and extended family network, and feel it is appropriate to call on them in times of need. This family network is an important support system, although it is often taken for granted until a crisis arises. In other words, the family is an interdependent system of people who are emotionally connected to each other.

Most families also have a value system that encompasses spiritual beliefs that provide the foundation for their attitudes and behaviors. These values become even more important to couples after they have children or in times of crisis. There is an ongoing commitment and connection between parents and their children, even after divorce. This is particularly true if the parents are given joint custody of their children. Most people also feel that the family is the most effective and efficient way of socializing children.

In summary, marriage and family provide significant continuity in our society. Unfortunately, emphasis on marriage and family problems often overshadows the stability and continuity these intimate relationships offers us in our daily lives.

Family Science: An Emerging Profession

Family science is growing rapidly, as a profession and as a social science. In recent years, research on the family has improved in both quality and quantity. Family researchers use many of the same methods as other social scientists, but they tailor these methods to their own interests and purposes. This section describes several research methods, including questionnaires, interviews, case studies, and observational approaches.

A Knowledge Explosion

Family science is a multidisciplinary field; that is, many disciplines contribute to the understanding of families (Table 1.2). Over the past 20 years, this science has emerged as a genuine discipline unto itself. Its primary goal is to achieve a better understanding of families in order to enhance the quality of family life. Professionals whose main interests are research, theory, and the development of

Table 1.2 Disciplines Contributing to Family Science

DISCIPLINE	TOPICS IN FAMILY SCIENCE
Anthropology	Cross-cultural studies; kinship; diversity in families
Biology	Conception and reproduction; growth, development, and aging
Child development	Development of infant and child; interpersonal skills
Economics	Family finances; consumer behavior
Education	Family life education; marriage preparation
English	Families in literature (present and past)
History	Historical perspectives on the family throughout time
Human ecology	Ecosystem perspective on family, nutrition, housing, clothing
Law	Marriage and divorce laws; child custody laws
Medicine	Families and health
Psychiatry	Family therapy
Psychology	Family psychology; assessment of couples and families
Social work	Treating problem families; family policy
Sociology	Marriage and divorce statistics; sociological theories about families

programs for families tend to call themselves *family scientists*. Those who develop educational programs for couples and families call themselves *family life educators*. Those who work clinically with troubled families are called *marital and family therapists*.

Family scientists have backgrounds in a wide variety of disciplines: human development, family science programs, human ecology, home economics, social work, nursing, educational psychology, psychology, sociology, psychiatry, and anthropology. Family scientists may be researchers, professors, teachers, family life educators, family therapists, ministers, nurses, social workers, or attorneys. Box 1.4 describes how you can do family research yourself.

Research Methods

The whole of science is nothing more than a refinement of everyday thinking.
—ALBERT EINSTEIN (in *National Geographic*, 1983)

It is primarily through research that new ideas and facts are discovered. The word *research* is derived from the Middle French word *recherche*, meaning "to investigate thoroughly." Science, in the final analysis, is an examination of events or information in an attempt to make new discoveries.

It has been argued that the family is the most difficult institution in human society to study. The reason for this is that families tend to be closed to outsiders; they often "put their best foot forward." To study important issues and to solve family problems, researchers and practitioners have to get below the surface and deal with both the positive and negative aspects of family life.

Family researchers have a creative mix of tools and techniques for learning more about family realities, using both "insider" and "outsider" perspectives. An

BOX 1.4

Family Science Research—Past and Present

Research on families, which has a long history, has expanded rapidly in recent years. In the 1960s, Reuben Hill and Joan Aldous began their pioneering work at the University of Minnesota in developing a database for marriage and family research going back to 1900. The first reference work they published, *The International Bibliography of Research in Marriage and the Family*, contained 12,610 research articles that had been published between 1900 and 1964. Volumes 3 through 12, representing research done between 1975 and 1987, were compiled by David Olson and colleagues at the University of Minnesota. Volume 12 alone lists 2,636 articles written by 3,156 authors and published in 750 journals (Olson & DeRubeis, 1987). This series of reference works is called the *Inventory of Marriage and Family Literature (IMFL)* and is published by the National Council on Family Relations (NCFR), the pre-

dominant national and international organizations of family scientists and family life educators. Students can use these *IMFL* reference books at their local university library to identify research studies and locate relevant articles.

The data from all the volumes of the *IMFL* are now contained in an integrated computerized **Family Studies Database,** which contains more than 235,000 articles and is available at most university libraries.

Students or researchers can access the Family Studies Database to do a computer search of published research on hundreds of family topics and to obtain references and abstracts with little cost or effort using this system. An undergraduate student thus has access to much of the same information available to academic researchers and can even learn how to conduct his or her own research using a personal computer.

insider perspective is provided by family members when they describe how they see their relationships. An **outsider perspective** is provided by researchers or therapists observing and describing the activity from their point of view. Methods that tap the insider perspective are questionnaires, interviews, and case studies. Outsider perspectives are obtained through observational approaches. Family researchers often use only one method in a particular study, but there are advantages to a multimethod approach that uses both insider and outsider perspectives.

Research methods also have to be suitable for the population being studied. Written questions, for example, are inappropriate for people whose culture is predominantly oral. For more on adapting to cultural differences, when conducting research, see Box 1.5.

Questionnaires   Perhaps the most common method of studying families is the questionnaire. The researcher carefully prepares a series of questions based on a review of previous research on the topic. *Fixed-response questions* require an individual to pick his or her response from a selection of possible responses; *open-ended questions* allow the individual to respond in her or his own words. A questionnaire might contain either or both types of questions.

Developing a questionnaire is a challenge. What questions one asks and the manner in which the questions are phrased can greatly influence the results of a study. Researchers are wise to do a trial run with a small sample of families to see whether the questions are clear and precise. Next, the process of **validating** a survey instrument—ensuring that the instrument measures what it is intended to measure—often takes researchers several months or even a number of years, depending on the complexity of the problem they are studying.

BOX 1.5

Research Methods in Cross-Cultural Studies

Research of families in cultures outside the United States offers challenges and opportunities for American family researchers. One such researcher, John DeFrain, traveled to the South Pacific to study the strengths and challenges of South Pacific families. Upon arrival in Fiji, two things became exceedingly clear. First, the South Pacific is a huge geographic area with lots of water, little land, and few people. Fiji has only about 715,000 people, but they are scattered over about 80 islands. Travel from island to island can be very expensive, time-consuming, and sometimes dangerous.

Second, from a Westerner's perspective, everything about Fiji culture is different; nothing is familiar or easy. It was therefore tempting for DeFrain to focus on the differences—in the language, the food, the landscape, the sports, and the family customs—which were at times overwhelming and disorienting.

It soon became apparent that the approaches used in U.S. family research would not work in Fiji; questionnaires were a failure. Realizing that the families have a strong oral tradition of story telling, DeFrain asked people to talk about important stories in their families. Many of the stories were about holidays, birthdays, and other occasions when families got together. Individuals also told stories about family strife and pain: about beatings, extramarital affairs, attempted murder of family members, and drug abuse. These stories made clear the importance of family during difficult times.

This researcher discovered that when the barriers of the initial differences in other cultures are overcome, similarities tend to emerge. It was through the use of methods appropriate to the culture that cross-cultural commonalities were revealed.

After the questionnaire is deemed satisfactory by the research team, it is distributed to a sufficiently large sample of family members. A number of factors determine the size of the sample, including how much money the research team has to spend on the project, how important the topic is to the researchers, and how difficult it is to find a group of families who are willing to participate in the study.

In the past, it was quite common for family researchers to limit their studies to what mothers thought was going on in their families. Fathers and children were often ignored. Researchers assumed that one individual could speak for the family as a whole. Furthermore, researchers favored this approach to studies of multiple family members because the latter were much more time-consuming, expensive, and difficult to analyze. Today most researchers recognize that fathers, mothers, and children often differ in their perceptions of family life and that a good study demands information and perceptions gathered from multiple family members (LeMasters & DeFrain, 1989).

Interviews   The interview—whether face-to-face or by telephone—is another family-research method. Some investigators believe that interview data are more valid than data from questionnaires because the researcher can ask follow-up questions and get more information. On the other hand, some research has found that people are more honest on questionnaires. Furthermore, interviews tend to take more time, cost more money, and thus reach fewer people than is possible with questionnaires. Variation from one interviewer to another may also taint the results; questionnaires, of course, are standardized. Perhaps the best approach is to use both questionnaires and interviews. The results can then be compared with each other to provide **cross-validation.**

Case Studies   Some of the most emotionally gripping research findings have come from family therapists using the case study method. A **case study** is detailed description of a person or family whose interactions illustrate some specific idea, concept, or principle of family science. Using this method, researchers record in narrative form and analyze the painful complexities of family dynamics. Great care is taken to protect the privacy and anonymity of the family members, in part by concealing their names and disguising any identifying family characteristics.

The major problem with case studies is that the families described are probably not representative of all American families. For example, if a researcher were to analyze the case of a stepfamily in treatment at a counseling agency, the researcher might conclude that stepfamilies have numerous problems. This conclusion would be biased, however, because it was based on a family who had come for help. If the researcher were to question stepfamilies by randomly telephoning people in the community, the result would be a more **representative sample**—that is, a random selection—of stepfamilies and probably a more positive description of interactions in this type of family.

Observational Approaches   Social psychologists who study families and family therapists who deal with problem families tend to work by observing family interactions in natural settings, such as the home. Observational approaches, which tap the outsider perspective, have both strengths and limitations. One strength is that the researcher does not have to rely on family members' self-reports of their own behavior. One major limitation is that the presence of a stranger (the therapist or researcher) influences family members' behavior, making it less natural. Researchers also need to consider whether families who volunteer for such studies differ in some ways from families who do not. These are important issues in any research study, but they are more problematic in observational studies.

Sometimes a family is brought into a research laboratory for a study. Often the laboratory is set up like a living room or a dining room, and the family is asked to perform a particular task together, such as playing a game. The researchers videotape the interaction and later study the video to analyze and evaluate the family members' communication styles. Many families are not willing to participate in such studies, of course, and those who do may act differently than they do when behind closed doors. Despite the difficulties associated with observational research, however, many creative observational family studies have contributed significantly to the field of family science.

Historical and Multicultural Studies   Studies of families from earlier generations are often useful and interesting to us today. As historians point out, we cannot know where we are going in the future unless we know where we have been. Historical research, which often relies on diaries and historical statistics about families, can help us understand families in the past.

Feminists argue that much of what has been presented as family history in the past has focused on the lives of men (*his*-story) and has neglected the lives of women (*her*-story). The history of the family, in many cultures traditionally the domain of women, has received little attention from historians (who have for the most part been men). But in recent decades, a resurgent feminist history movement has begun to look at the past from women's perspectives.

Similarly, multicultural studies of families can contribute rich insights into family life and family interactions. The United States has innumerable family cultures: African American, Caucasian, Latino, Italian American, Chicago suburban, inner-city Boston, gay-male, lesbian, middle-class, upper-class, rural, urban, and so forth. Family life is different in each of these cultures. A family in the commuter culture of Los Angeles, for example, lives a life quite different from that of a family in rural Iowa. Diversity in families is discussed in greater detail in Chapter 3.

Research Designs

Researchers are often interested in how particular families grow and change over time. Three types of research design that take the passage of time into consideration are longitudinal studies, cross-sectional studies, and cross-sectional cohort studies.

Longitudinal Studies   In a longitudinal study, the researcher interviews or observes a family several times over a period of months or years. This approach obviously takes a fair amount of time, effort, and money. For those reasons, only a small proportion of family research is longitudinal. The results of such projects, however, are often well worth the effort because they provide valuable information about long-term processes, such as the effect of the birth of a child on a marriage.

One longitudinal study focused on couples who took a premarital inventory—called PREPARE—3 months before marriage and were followed up 3 years after marriage (Larsen & Olson, 1989). PREPARE is a 125-item questionnaire that focuses on 12 important areas of a couple's relationship, including communication, conflict resolution, role relationships, and sexual intimacy. Couples who were separated or divorced at the 3-year follow-up were compared with couples who remained happily married. The scores on the PREPARE inventory were found to predict with about 80% to 85% accuracy which couples would later divorce and which would be happily married. The findings indicate that problems experienced by couples before marriage can lead to more serious problems after marriage. This study also demonstrates the predictive validity of PREPARE and the value of longitudinal research.

Cross-Sectional Studies   In a cross-sectional study, a researcher selects couples or families at various stages of the family life cycle and compares the differences between the various stages. For example, a researcher could compare four stages of the life cycle by selecting some newlywed couples, some couples with young children, some couples with adolescents, and some older couples whose children had left home. The aim of this approach is to describe the similarities and differences between couples and families at these four stages.

The advantage of the cross-sectional design is efficiency: Data can be collected from all four groups at about the same time and then immediately compared. A disadvantage of this type of study is that it is not possible to know if identified similarities and differences are due only to the stage of the life cycle or to the characteristics of these specific families—a question that could only be answered by a longitudinal study that followed the same families over time. Furthermore, cross-sectional studies cannot reveal whether the historical context for each group (past experiences, crises, etc.) has influenced the findings.

Cross-Sectional Cohort Studies   Because of the problems with both longitudinal and cross-sectional studies, researchers have designed a shortcut known as the cross-sectional cohort study. Using this approach, researchers do not follow a group of families for many years; instead, they study various families at different stages of the family life cycle for shorter periods. They might, for example, study one family with a 10-year-old, another with a 12-year-old, a third with a 14-year-old, and a fourth with a 16-year-old. If they followed these families for 5 years, they could analyze changes from age 10 to 15, 12 to 17, 14 to 19, and 16 to 21. The result would be an overview of an 11-year period (age 10 to age 21) achieved in only 5 years of research.

A Final Word About Research

No single study can provide definitive answers to important questions in family science. In fact, each study almost invariably raises new questions that are complex and difficult to answer. The advancement of scientific knowledge is a slow and painstaking process. People researching a particular topic in family science have to examine data from many related studies on the topic.

Sometimes studies produce findings that conflict with the results of other studies. These discrepancies may be due to variations in the type of questions asked, the method of research used, or the specific sample studied. For example, a sample of families drawn from the Midwest may look at gender-role issues in families somewhat differently from a sample of families drawn from Latino families living in California. Likewise, two-parent traditional American families may have a different way of looking at certain issues than do single-parent families.

Although studies on similar topics may have differing results, good studies tend to complement each other. When dozens of researchers from various parts of the United States look at a problem from many different theoretical approaches, using different research methods and different statistical analyses, a fairly comprehensive picture emerges. When the findings are similar in spite of all the differences in sample, method, and analysis, the results are more conclusive and help to build more valid findings and theories about couples and families.

Summary

- The family today is not in danger of extinction, but it is changing. The American family is more diverse today, in terms of family structure and ethnicity, than ever before.

- About half of the people marrying today will probably divorce at some time in their lives, often because they enter marriage with unrealistic expectations, marry the wrong person, marry for the wrong reasons, or have few skills to deal with the many challenges of marriage.

- Marriage is the emotional and legal commitment of two people to share emotional and physical intimacy, various tasks, and economic resources. A family is two or more people who are committed to each other and who share intimacy, resources, decision-making responsibilities, and values.

- Some of the major trends in family structure, marriage, divorce, and remarriage are the following: There are both more families headed by single women and more stepfamilies today than there were in the 1950s and 1960s; families are smaller today; women are more likely to work outside the home after marriage; both men and women are marrying at a later age; cohabitation before marriage has increased eightfold; the divorce rate increased but has now stabilized at about 50%; and about 75% of those who divorce later remarry.

- Researchers use a variety of tools and techniques in their work, including questionnaires; interviews; case studies; observation; historical and multicultural studies; and longitudinal, cross-sectional, and cross-sectional cohort studies.

Key Terms

marriage	Family Studies Database	cross-validation
family	insider perspective	case study
stepfamily	outsider perspective	representative sample
family science	validation	

Activities

1. In small groups, write down your own definition of family. Share your responses within the group, and compare how your ideas are similar and/or different.

2. Are human beings *really* all that different from each other? In this exercise, sit down and talk with a person from another sexual orientation or another cultural or ethnic group. List the similarities and the differences between your families (attitudes, beliefs, behaviors, customs, and so forth). How many of the differences can be attributed to the different cultures your families come from, and how many of these differences are simply differences between two unique families?

3. Interview a grandparent or a great-grandparent (or another older person you would like to get to know better) about family life in "the old days"—both positive and negative aspects. Some interesting areas to explore might be (1) growing up in a family, (2) a "woman's place" in the world 50 or more years ago, (3) gender roles, (4) the Great Depression of the 1930s, (5) World War II, (6) major family crises, (7) religion, and (8) philosophies of childrearing.

Suggested Readings

Boss, P., Doherty, W. J., LaRossa, R., Schumm, W. R., & Steinmetz, S. K. (Eds.). (1993). *Sourcebook of family theories and methods: A contextual approach.* New York: Plenum. An excellent source for in-depth information regarding theories and research methods used in the marriage and family field.

Popenoe, D. and B. D. Whitehead (1999). *The state of our unions.* New Jersey: National Marriage Project. Excellent summary of key social indicators of marriage and family in the United States.

Stinnett, N., Stinnett, N., DeFrain, J., and DeFrain, N. (1997). *Good families.* New York: Doubleday. Explanation of the family strengths conceptual framework emphasizing six qualities, based on studies with over 16,000 family members.

CHAPTER 2

Social Environment Impact on Couples and Families

Ecological processes are not only more complex than we think. They are more complex than we can ever think.

—Michael Crofoot (1996)

Human beings do not live and love in a vacuum. Just as we are connected to the special people in our lives—our friends and loved ones—so we are inextricably embedded in our social environment. The **social environment** comprises all the factors, both positive and negative, in society that impact individuals and their relationships, such as mass media, the Internet, changing gender roles, and growing urban crowding. As individuals we have a modest influence on the society, yet society clearly shapes our personal attitudes and behaviors and ultimately our couple and family relationships.

We may be drawn to the Western ideal of rugged individualism—going boldly where no man or woman has gone before—but the reality of our lives is probably closer to the East Asian notion that each of us is but a drop of water in the ocean of life. Cultural norms and expectations have a powerful impact on us, especially if we try to behave against these norms. Visiting another culture is one way to experience the pervasive influence the social environment has on our lives, as the following story illustrates.

"When my husband and I were living in China, everything was so different from what we were used to: the language, the food, the music, the dress, everything. Now this is a hard thing to explain to someone who has not already experienced it, but being out of my own culture, my own environment, I started to feel after a few months in China like my identity as a person was disappearing.

"It was like I was shrinking. Without my family and my friends at home, without our dog Jessie, without my music, without my food, without our crummy old car, I felt so disconnected, so insignificant. One day I would have given $50 for a cheeseburger. It sounds crazy talking about it now.

"We both finally did adjust pretty well to China. After about a year or so I kind of turned an emotional corner. And after two years I felt like an old hand at surviving culture shock. Today, I love China. But we also love home. And I learned something very important from all this: the social environment I'm used to is very, very important to me. I felt like a fish out of water for a while when taken away from what's familiar to me. I'm not the great individualist I thought I was."

In general, the social environment shapes us much more than we can shape the social environment. However, we are not puppets of the social environment. Growing up in an alcoholic family is not an excuse for being an alcoholic. Similarly, being abused as a child does not justify abusing one's own children. Countless people grow up in violent families but are able to rise above those life experiences. Individuals can make positive choices in their life, regardless of their pasts.

In this chapter we will discuss the many aspects of the social environment that can prove challenging to couples and families today. But before we begin, it is important to address the difficult issue of how to evaluate American society.

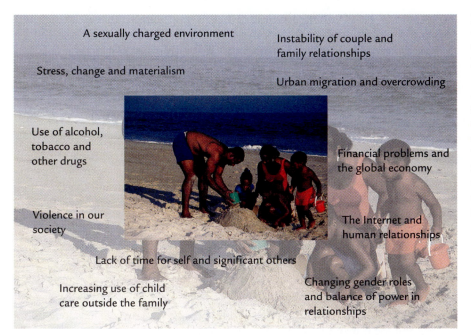

A sexually charged environment

Instability of couple and family relationships

Stress, change and materialism

Urban migration and overcrowding

Use of alcohol, tobacco and other drugs

Financial problems and the global economy

Violence in our society

The Internet and human relationships

Lack of time for self and significant others

Increasing use of child care outside the family

Changing gender roles and balance of power in relationships

Figure 2.1 Elements of the Social Environment that Affect Couples and Relationships

Although families work and play together to create a haven in a sometimes bewildering world, countless elements in the social environment can challenge a family's drive for balance and stability.

In essence, we live in a complex society with both negative and positive influences. On a daily basis the media shower us with negative stories, including many about couples and families. We hear about domestic abuse, family violence, child abuse, and other distressing reports. Rarely do we hear anything positive about how couples and families have effectively dealt with a problem (such as a car accident or a diagnosis of cancer in a family member) or had fun together. Take heart, though. These stories do exist. Surveys indicate that the majority of Americans think their marriages and their families are doing well.

Social Environment Challenges to Marriages and Families

There are many elements in our social environment today that pose difficult challenges for couples and families. In this section, we will discuss a variety of issues that affect our close relationships (Figure 2.1).

Stress, Change, and Materialism

Stress is directly related to change; the greater the change, the higher the level of stress. There are so many new developments that add stress to our lives. In addition to regular mail (snail mail), we now have voice mail and E-mail. Not only has this increased the volume of information we receive and must respond to, but the time in which we are expected to respond has been shortened—from a few days to return a letter to a few hours to return an E-mail.

As a society, we also have a great appetite for material possessions—for *stuff*. To illustrate our tendency toward excessive consumption, consider the class exercise assigned by one teacher. The teacher asked his students to go home and count the number of T-shirts they each owned. The average number owned by each student was 27! Now, what exactly does one do with 27 T-shirts?

Combined, technology and materialism increase our level of stress in all areas of life. We feel pressured to do more—and to run faster while we're doing it. The first casualty in such an environment is our individual sense of well-being.

Lack of Time for Oneself and Significant Others

According to family researchers, one of the most difficult qualities to develop in many American families is the ability to spend enjoyable time together. Not only do we find ourselves challenged by a busy and competitive social environment outside the home, but once we return home, we need time to unwind from a hectic day before reconnecting with others (Stinnett, Stinnett, DeFrain, and DeFrain, 1997).

In today's society, the boundaries between the home and work are being blurred. As sociologist Arlie Hochschild (1997) has observed, work becomes more like home and home becomes more like work. Caught in the time bind, the more time we work, the more stressful home life becomes. The more stressful home life becomes, the more we want to escape back to work. Hochschild argues that we must challenge the economic and social system that invites or demands long hours at work and focus investing less time in the job and more time in one's couple and family relationships.

Increasing Use of Child Care Outside the Family

What do we do about our kids when both parents work outside the home? This is one of the most challenging questions our society faces today. In 1940, only 10% of American children lived with a mother who was in the labor force. By 1990, nearly 60% of American children lived with an employed mother. This sixfold increase of mothers in the workplace over a fifty-year period (Hernandez, 1997) fueled the steady increase of child care outside the family and the extended family, even for infants.

The most recent figures indicate that there are nearly 21 million children under five years of age in this country who are not enrolled in school. According to statistics, parents regularly care for about 40% of these children; 21% are cared for by other relatives; 31% attend child-care centers; 14% are enrolled in family day-care centers, and 4% are cared for by sitters in the child's home. These figures total more than 100% because 9% of the children receive more than one manner of care during a typical day, such as going to preschool in the morning and being with a parent in the afternoon (Hofferth, 1996).

Among the child-care issues we must face as a society are the following:

- Is child care in America primarily meant to serve the needs of working parents, with little regard for the education of preschoolers?

- Will families not on welfare receive government support for child care?

- Will regulations imposed on licensed care make center care so costly that most parents are forced to use unregulated care in homes? Or, will state regulations become so lax that American child care will be little better than custodial warehousing (Scarr, 1998, p. 106)?

Mothers and fathers, surrounded by the swirling controversy over child care, ask their own very personal questions:

- Do I really need to work outside the home? Is employment essential for our family's well-being? for my well-being? And how will it effect our child's well-being?

- Will I be able to develop a bond with my child if she spends so much time away from me?

- Will I spend more money on child care, extra clothes, lunches, and transportation than I make on the job?

- How will the stresses of the job affect me personally? our family? Can all this be balanced effectively?

- How will our child adapt to outside care? Will he receive good care? Will it be as good as the care we can give him?

- Will we be able to pass on our values to our child if she spends so much time in a child-care program? Or will outside values and behaviors change her in undesirable ways?

- Will he enjoy being with other children? Will his social development be enhanced by these opportunities?

For parents, finding satisfactory answers to these and countless other child-care-related questions is a considerable challenge.

Instability of Couple and Family Relationships

Many observers have argued that our fast-moving and competitive social environment is directly responsible for the high rate of marital dissolution and the increase in single-parent families and stepfamilies. Although personality conflicts and troubles within a marriage clearly contribute to marital breakdown, societal factors and values also influence our intimate behavior.

Rather than come home from work and sit on the front porch to talk with family and neighbors, we often hide behind closed doors in a cocoonlike atmosphere, plopped down in front of the television or a computer. As a result, many of our personal impressions come from the media. We may know more about our favorite actor's marriage than we know about how the couple is doing next door. Perhaps we are choosing to live like this, of course, in the name of personal privacy. But married life on television and in the tabloids is far different from the average couple's life. It can be argued that the steady diet of extramarital affairs and marital conflict we receive from the media helps to create a "culture of divorce" in this country.

In fact, everything has to be new, if we were to believe media sales pitches: we need new cars, new houses, new clothes, perhaps a new nose. The business world is brimming with stories of corporate takeovers and downsizing. Companies come and go every day, and workers are cast off like old furniture. In this kind of social environment, it's not such a stretch to imagine that finding a new partner should also be easy.

But aligned against our throw-away culture are voices counseling fidelity, time together, and kindness: "Don't be reckless with other people's hearts. Don't put up with people who are reckless with yours," Mary Schmich (1997) advises.

Violence

Violent and abusive behavior continues to be a major cause of death, injury, and stress in our country. Suicide and homicide result in over 50,000 deaths each year, and more than 2 million people are victimized by violence annually (U.S. Department of Health and Human Services, 1997).

In *This Noble Land*, one of James Michener's last books before his death in 1997, Michener argued that America is becoming more and more violent. "The most instructive proof of our nation's increasingly vigorous move toward a macho society can be seen in our unique fascination with guns, our insistence on having them and our willingness to accept murder as a result of the huge number we allow and even encourage private citizens to own" (1996, p. 176).

Another observer, columnist Bob Herbert, argues that "We are the murder capital of the world" (Herbert, 1994). Most gun-related fatalities result from the use of handguns. In 1992 handguns were used in the murders of 33 individuals in Great Britain, 36 in Sweden, 97 in Switzerland, 128 in Canada, 13 in Australia, 60 in Japan, and 13,220 in the United States. In the same year, 38,317 Americans were killed by firearms of all kinds. This was more than the total number of American troops killed in battle during the Korean War.

Reports of family violence in recent years have increased dramatically, causing researchers to ask if we are indeed becoming a more violent society. Or are people simply becoming more aware of abuse and thus more readily reporting suspected problems in a family? Or does the increase in the reporting of family violence represent a lowered threshold in the popular perception of what is abusive behavior in our society (Emery & Laumann-Billings, 1998)?

Those who believe that there has been a real increase in child abuse in recent years argue that the number of moderate cases of child abuse remained stable between 1986 and 1993 but that the number of serious cases quadrupled from 142,000 to 565,000 (Sedlak & Broadhurst, 1996). If the rise was due only to increased public awareness or "definitional creep," then it is logical to think that moderate cases of child abuse would also have increased dramatically.

Researchers who believe there is a rise in the number of cases of serious child abuse in this country attribute the growing problem to a variety of societal factors: illegal drugs, greater poverty, increased overall violence in the United States, and the disintegration of communities (Garbarino, 1995; Lung & Daro, 1996; Sedlak & Broadhurst, 1996).

A Sexually Charged Society

Sex pervades the American social environment. It's the topic on the radio, on television, on billboards, in movies, at the mall, in the classroom, at the office, in the pulpit, in our daily conversations, in Congress, in the White House, and *sometimes* even in the bedroom.

Philip E. Simmons, a college English teacher, has an interesting take on sex:

> As for sex, here animals clearly have us beat. Almost all of them have the good sense to want it only at certain times of the year. In other seasons, they live free of the tormenting urges that in one way or another account for most of our gross national product. You would think, by the way, that with all our interest in sex we would enjoy it more than we do. As the poet Howard Nemerov puts it, "We think about sex constantly, except during the act itself, when our minds tend to wander."

Sex has been big business in American culture for some time, but today it has reached the status of a national obsession. This is curious, indeed, because the average American is more a sexual amateur than a sexual Olympian. (See Chapter 7 for a detailed discussion on sexual intimacy.)

Now that many elementary school children are familiar with the term (if not the meaning of) oral sex, it is logical to conclude that sexual values in America are changing. We are clearly more open in our discussions of sexuality today than we were 30 years ago. Our new openness about sexuality has encouraged research on the topic that has increased in breadth, depth, and sophistication. Researchers today tell us, for example, that:

- 49% of women in this country will have at least one unplanned pregnancy between the ages of 15 and 44, and, at current rates, 43% of American women will have had an abortion by age 45 (E. Goodman, 1998; U.S. Department of Health and Human Services, 1997).

- Problems associated with poor family planning include low birthweights, high rates of infant mortality, and inadequate monetary and family support for the child (U.S. Department of Health and Human Services, 1997).

- By the time they reach their early 30s, almost half the U.S. population will have cohabited at some time (Nock, 1995).

- Adolescent pregnancy, a long-standing social concern in the United States, has been one of the most frequently cited examples of perceived societal decay in this country over the last decade (U.S. House of Representatives, 1996). And yet the rate of births to teenagers is lower today than it has been throughout much of the 20th century (Coley & Chase-Lansdale, 1998).

- There are increases in the rates of sexual activity and illegitimacy and in the receipt of welfare benefits among adolescents (Coley & Chase-Lansdale, 1998).

- Extramarital sexual relationships are estimated to range from 30% to 50% for men and 10% to 40% for women (Laumann, Gagnon, Michael, Michaels, & Kolata, 1995; Pittman, 1993a, 1993b).

What does all this interest and discussion about sex portend for couples and families? For couples it will mean trying to create a loving and committed relationship in a social environment fascinated by sex and full of temptation and hypocrisy. For parents it will mean developing open and honest communication with their children on a subject that few of us are really very good at talking about. Although many professionals are making a concerted effort to improve the quality of sex education in our schools, places of worship, and homes, we appear to be losing the battle as the mixed messages of the mass media continue to dominate the images of sexuality that bombard Americans today.

Use of Alcohol, Tobacco, and Other Drugs

Our social environment today is dominated by advertising and a consumption-oriented approach to living. Complex issues are reduced to sound bites; the sitcom family's problems are resolved in a half hour (that is, 22 minutes of dialogue serving as a grabber for 8 minutes of commercials).

The advertising world has succeeded over the years in making alcohol and tobacco use look fun, sophisticated, and sexy to countless young people who are lured to these dangerous drugs every day. But the dark side of these socially accepted and legal drugs is rarely portrayed. In fact, illegal drugs receive much more media attention, even though alcohol and tobacco kill approximately 20 times as many people as illegal drugs each year in this country. An estimated 12 million men, women, and children suffer from alcoholism, and 16 to 19 million adults are problem drinkers. About 100,000 people die each year as a result of alcohol misuse (National Council of Alcoholism, 1989). Similarly, 500,000 smoking and non-smoking Americans die each year from diseases related to legal cigarette smoking. Compare those figures with an estimated 30,000 who die each year from illegal drug use (Whelan, 1995).

While the media focus on crack in the ghetto and methamphetamine use among the young, the advertisers promote the use of alcohol and cigarettes. We live in a social environment of denial, one that points the finger at the young, the poor, and minorities for their alleged overindulgence in illegal drugs and that overlooks the "more acceptable" self-indulgences of the majority culture, namely alcohol and tobacco.

The Internet and Human Relationships

In our continuous quest to market technological solutions to human problems, much has been made of the computer's potential for connecting human beings. In the movie *You've Got Mail*, Meg Ryan and Tom Hanks fall in love via E-mail. It is a charming notion, but one study tells a different story. Researchers at Carnegie Mellon University have found that individuals who spend even a few hours a week on-line experience higher levels of depression and loneliness than those who spend less or no time on the Internet (Harmon, 1998). They also found that individuals who use the Internet more tend to decrease their communication with other family members and reduce the size of their social circle. This $1.5 million research project found that Internet use itself appeared to cause a decline in psychological well-being. According to Robert Kraut, a social psychologist, "We are shocked by the findings, because they are counterintuitive to what we know about how socially the Internet is used." He noted that "we are not talking here about the extremes. These were normal adults and their families, and on average, for those who used the Internet most, things got worse" (Harmon, 1998).

CATHY   BY CATHY GUISEWITE

Changing Gender Roles and the Balance of Power in Couple Relationships

As mentioned earlier, there has been a dramatic increase in the number of mothers working outside the home. This development has helped fuel an ongoing discussion of the roles of women and men in America and how power should be allocated in society as a whole and between household partners in particular.

Although women have served as leaders of more than twenty countries around the world, a woman has yet to serve as president of the United States (Porter, 1999). Nevertheless, women are serving as associate justices in the Supreme Court, as senators and representatives of Congress, and in countless other positions of power and influence in both government and the business world.

With the emergence of women in traditionally male roles, particularly in positions of power, **gender roles** (the traits and behaviors assigned to males and females in a culture) are being redefined. Some observers argue that there is a "masculine culture," which thrives on competition and the achievement of dominance, and a "feminine culture," which aims at connection and the creation of community. In their relatively new roles of authority, women are being encouraged to be more assertive and to let others know exactly where they stand. In contrast, males are being urged to be less aggressive and more honest and open about their feelings. Society today is questioning both the images of the "strong and silent male" and the "shrinking-violet female."

Just as "supermoms" struggle to find a meaningful balance between work and family, so too men are challenged by their own changing world. Years ago, a man's home was *his* castle; today it's an "equalitarian haven." Just how fairly power and work should be shared in American households is a topic of considerable discussion today. Some observers suggest that men still have a long way to go before true equality is reached in the home.

Many maintain that women have been the true pioneers of the gender revolution, arguing that wives have more quickly changed their roles *outside* the home than men have changed their roles *inside* the home. Still others question how equal we really want males and females to be in our society. They assert that females and males are biologically different and that wives should stay at home to better socialize our children. Regardless of one's position, it's impossible to deny that gender roles and relationship power balances are evolving in today's society.

Urban Migration and Overcrowding

"The history of American agriculture," according to Rex Campbell, a rural sociologist at the University of Missouri at Columbia, "is the history of technology in rural areas" (cited in Graham, 1998, p. 9). When farmers depended upon animals for work and transportation, small towns dotted the rural landscape in the heartland about six miles apart. Eventually, trucks and tractors replaced horses and mules, farms got bigger, and the number of farmers and farm families declined steadily over the years. Small towns also shrank in size.

Cyclical waves of economic difficulty took their toll, and during the 1980s, when an especially difficult farm crisis hit the Midwest, three fourths of the towns in Nebraska suffered a reduction in population. In Kansas, more land is classified as "frontier" today than a hundred years ago. Since the 1930s, South Dakota has seen a major decline in the number of communities and their populations, with the farm crisis in the 1980s bringing that state's rural population to an acutely reduced level (Graham, 1998).

What do we lose when a small town vanishes? What do we lose when the kids grow up and leave the farm or ranch for the city? A realist, focusing solely on harsh economic forces, might say that the young person is leaving the farm to find work and a more stable life in an urban environment. An idealist might argue that we lose a little bit of the fabric of America, a small piece of the American dream. American rural societies tend to be caring environments in which many honest and hard-working individuals live and join together to help each other and their communities to succeed.

But technological change is not likely to slow down in the United States any time soon, and few predict a resurgence of population in most rural areas, especially those beyond commuting distance from larger cities. The dream of living in a caring community for most Americans will have to be realized in an urban area.

Although it may take a village to raise a child, a villagelike atmosphere can be created in an urban neighborhood, in an apartment building, or among relatives and friends scattered about a city. The impersonal forces of urban living can be countered by the creation of villagelike social structures in the neighborhood, in the workplace, in religious institutions, and in community settings.

Financial Problems and the Global Economy

Financial issues are the most common stressors couples and families face, regardless of how much money they make. Researchers have consistently found that economic distress and unemployment are detrimental to family relationships (Gomel, Tinsley, Parke, & Clark, 1998). One out of four children in this country is now living in poverty (Carnegie Task Force, 1994), and 40% of all poor people are children (Corbett, 1993). Estimates of the number of homeless people in our country range from 230,000 to as many as 750,000 (Cohen & Tharp, 1999).

Many Americans today are doing exceedingly well financially, and yet many other Americans live close to the edge, lacking savings and chronically spending more than they earn. Easy credit lines in a materialistic society have contributed to mounting debt, especially credit-card debt, which carries extraordinarily high interest rates. Debt threatens not only individuals but also the well-being of the lenders and, eventually, the economy as a whole.

The economic game is played on an uneven playing field. Some individuals come to the field with enormous advantages, enjoyed since birth: the advantages of being born into an affluent and sheltered social class, of being a member of the dominant ethnic group, and of growing up in a prosperous family and secure environment, with good nutrition, adequate rest and exercise, and access to excellent schools, health-care facilities, and other social services. Other individuals, however, come to the playing field at a considerable disadvantage, and yet they compete effectively through sheer intelligence, perseverance, and courage.

The Children's Defense Fund reports that over the past two decades, family incomes in most age groups have held their ground, economically speaking, but that incomes for parents under age 30 dropped by one third ("Study says economy hurts young parents," 1997). "Twenty years ago, young families typically had $10,000 more income than they do now, adjusting for inflation, and far more of them could afford to rent homes or even to buy a home," says Arloc Sherman, author of the study. The reason for this trend is that there are many more single-parent families today, and single parents as a group have always had lower incomes than two-parent families. Furthermore, wages for less-educated workers have dropped over the past 20 years.

The number of children living in poverty is highly related to living in a single-parent versus a two-parent household in the United States but less so in other countries (Figure 2.2). In the United States, nearly 60% of the children from single-parent households live in poverty, as compared to only 11% of children from two-parent households. The unfortunate fact of single parenthood in the United States is the lack of government support for these families that other countries provide. (In Chapter 11, we will address the many ways the economic environment in our country today affects couples and families.)

It is important, however, to point out here that although economic survival is challenging for many people in the United States, residents of many countries around the world are in far worse straits. Nonetheless, their economic problems do not exist in isolation; as business commentators and politicians frequently point out, we are living in a global economy. The strength of the American economy is inextricably linked in complex ways to the economies of many other nations. Thus, the employment situation in Asia, Europe, or Latin America not only influences marriage and family relationships in those corners of the world but in this country as well. If, for example, American farmers can't find markets for their produce in the United States or elsewhere, they aren't going to be able to buy American cars, Japanese televisions, or shirts crafted in Malaysia. Likewise, if the Japanese or Malaysians can't find markets for their products at home or abroad, income and employment will drop in those countries and Malays won't be going to college in California and Japanese won't be vacationing in Hawaii.

To illustrate our economic interconnectedness another way, suppose that Koreans can make steel cheaper than Americans. A steel mill in Seattle shuts down, laying off hundreds of workers and causing untold hardship in many homes. Each

Figure 2.2 Percentage of Children Living in Poverty by Family Structure. Adapted from "Family decline and child well-being: A comparative analysis" by S. K. Houseknecht and J. Sastry, 1996, *Journal of Marriage and Family, 58,* 734.

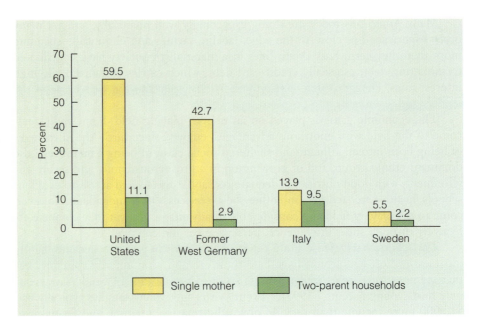

affected family's standard of living falls dramatically as bills go unpaid, creditors make demands for payment, and arguments within the family increase as the stress of the situation mounts.

It can be argued that couples and families feel the impact of the ups and downs of the global economy most severely. Social problems tend to filter down. Even though individuals are not responsible for creating global problems and certainly do not have the power to fix them, couples and families end up feeling the effects.

Positive Responses to the Social Environment

Without a global revolution in the sphere of human consciousness, nothing will change for the better in the sphere of our being as humans, and the catastrophe toward which we are headed . . . will be unavoidable.

—Vaclav Havel

Human beings have sought the shelter of their loved ones and families for countless generations. The family often is a haven in a heartless world where one can feel safe, secure, accepted, and loved. But today's social environment stretches far beyond the cozy bounds of the neighborhood, the community, the state, or the nation. We now live in "an entangled web of global economic, political, social, and environmental events and forces," according to psychologist Anthony Marsella (1998, p. 1282). "Global events and forces are now local events and forces!" Whether we like it or not, our world has become the fabled "global village" that Marshall McLauhan (1968, 1989) first wrote about more than three decades ago.

Dr. Martin Luther King, Jr., once stated what he believed to be "life's most persistent and urgent question: What are you going to do for others?" (King, cited by Clinton, 1999). But there are so many problems in the global village. If I want to be a part of the solution rather than part of the problem, where do I start? How do I pick a way to invest my life? And is it in my best interests as an individual to worry about all this? It's hard enough to take care of my own personal problems and help my friends and loved ones. An anonymous observer once described the dilemma in a more humorous way: "Some days I wake up and want to make a lot of money. Some days I wake up and want to save the world. This makes it hard to plan my day."

Fortunately, there are countless ways to provide for oneself and one's family and at the same time help to make the world a better place. There are types of work that not only provide financial security but also emotional satisfaction and the comfort of knowing that one's life actually makes a difference. The following account illustrates the reciprocal value of giving to others. This is what Raedene, 20, an undergraduate student and volunteer in a big brother/big sister program, had to report:

"I felt it was my job as a college student as well as a citizen to give something that I had always received, a little love and attention. I signed up for training in the program and was contacted by one of the organizers. After attending many long hours of training, I wondered if I had gotten myself into something more than I had bargained for. They required me to spend at least five hours a week with my match. I didn't think that I possibly had time but decided to give it a shot.

"About five days after training, I received a phone call that I was going to be matched with a little 5-year-old girl. I met my supervisor at the home of Elizbeth, my new little friend. A little nervous, I walked into their home. It was really strange. The minute I sat down, Elizbeth jumped up on my lap like she had known me for years. 'Could you read this book to me? . . . Watch this! . . . Come into my room!' She just couldn't stop talking.

"I did know from that minute on that this young child needed my love and attention more than five hours a week. I felt a sense of warmth come over me. To think that I was second-guessing five hours a week to give to a child who needed me. We clicked instantly. We played for a couple hours until her mom felt comfortable with the match. I told Elizbeth that I would phone her Monday. Her response was, 'Don't forget.' When I left all I could do was smile. I knew I was in for some fun.

"Even though we spend a lot of time together, we never have a dull moment. She's always saying something funny. I see the excitement in her eyes when I go to pick her up. We have done everything we had planned, plus much more. Often times I have trouble taking her home when it's time.

"Over the semester I have seen much growth in her, socially and intellectually. She's in kindergarten and is always telling me how much she likes it, and I always try to reinforce how much fun school is. I understand what she talks about, and I listen to what she has to say. I feel she has gained so much trust in me over the past four months. Sometimes I wonder if it's too much.   *(Continued. . .)*

(. . .Continued)

"I am able to communicate openly with her mother. I offer suggestions to her on many topics. I am very honest with her mother, and her mother trusts me a lot, too. I have learned how difficult a time their family has dealing with finances, stepparents, and stepsiblings. I have seen much growth in their family over the past four months. I am very happy that I chose to volunteer my time. I wish everyone would volunteer because not only does the child benefit from the experience, but you do, too."

Betty Friedan, a pioneer in the latest wave of the feminist movement believes that "People's priorities—men's and women's alike-should be affirming life, enhancing life, not greed." Friedan, at age 77, says she never thought of herself as a religious person but recently has "recognized a dimension of religiousness" in her life. She predicts that "We're on the cusp of a paradigm shift: We're the richest, most powerful nation in the world, and nobody is addressing the larger philosophical question of what values we should have for the future" (Selle, 1998, p. 51). As individuals, and as a society we cannot afford to ignore this question.

Because the social environment in which we live poses many problems for couples and families, it is important that we work together in our society to find solutions to these problems so that we all benefit. Fortunately, in spite of all these challenges, most couples and most families do reasonably well in creating a nurturing environment for themselves.

Summary

- Human beings do not live and love in a vacuum. Besides being connected to special people in our lives, we are inextricably embedded in our social environment. As individuals, couples, and families, we have little influence on society, but society has a great deal of influence on our personal attitudes and behaviors.

- Although society influences us in many ways, we do not have to be puppets of the social environment. We should take responsibility for our own lives.

- There are many elements in our social environment that pose difficult challenges for couples and families, including stress, change, and materialism; lack of time for oneself and significant others; the increasing use of child care outside the family; instability of couple and family relationships; violence; a sexually charged society; the use of alcohol, tobacco, and other drugs; the Internet and human relationships; changing gender roles and the balance of power in intergender relationships; Urban migration and overcrowding; and financial problems and the global economy.

- Surveys over the years indicate that the majority of Americans think their marriages and families are doing pretty well and that their lives are generally satisfying.

- Because the social environment in which we live brings many problems, it is important to work together to find solutions.

Key Terms

social environment

stress

gender roles

Activities

1. What are the stressors in your social environment? How do you meet these challenges?

2. How many T-shirts do you own? Go to your closet and check.

3. Do you agree with Arlie Hochschild's argument that many parents flee home and kids for work?

4. Visit a child-care center and observe the interaction between the children and the caregivers.

5. What personal skills do you have that could make a difference in your community?

Selected Readings

Coley, R. L., & Chase-Lansdale, P. L. (1998). Adolescent pregnancy and parenthood: Recent evidence and future directions. *American Psychologist, 53* (2), 152–166. Provides a comprehensive review of research on this topic.

Emery, R. E., & Laumann-Billings, L. (1998). An overview of the nature, causes, and consequences of abusive family relationships. *American Psychologist, 53* (2), 121–135. Thoroughly reviews critical issues regarding abusive family relationships.

CHAPTER 3

Cultural Diversity: Family Strengths and Challenges

The United States is a meeting place of many cultures. Each cultural group that has come here has surrendered some of its past in an effort to build a new life in a new land. But the United States is not so much a "melting pot," in which these distinct cultures meld together, as it is a salad bowl, in which each of the ingredients retains its distinct flavor. The United States can also be likened to a symphony and its various cultural groups to instruments. Each instrument has its distinct part to play—its distinct contribution—but all must work together to produce beautiful music. One Midwest teacher expresses his appreciation for the diverse instruments in the symphony of his life as follows:

"I have friends from so many different cultures and ethnic groups that it makes my life really interesting. One woman I know is part–Lakota Indian and part–African American. Her perspective on life in the United States is fascinating. She likes to tease me: 'White boy, you just don't get it!' she says. Sometimes, I think she's right. My experience still is pretty narrow, but I'm learning.

"Another friend is part–Polynesian from the South Pacific and part–White American. She grew up with her mom, a Polynesian, and identifies culturally more with her than with her father from the United States. Then there's my friend Edie, who is a lesbian. She and her friend Tasha are working with a medical doctor right now so they can have a baby together via artificial insemination.

"My friend Paul is a Czech American from a small farm town in South Dakota. He drives a diesel truck and keeps me attuned to the male blue-collar world he lives in. Xia Wen is a friend from China. She's working on her doctorate in computer science. Ali comes from Istanbul in Turkey and is married to my friend Mary, who comes from a suburban Milwaukee family. My buddy Frank is a refugee from ethnic strife in Romania. Our family friend Enid is an Indian/African mix from Tobago in the Caribbean. She married Edward, a Kiwi from New Zealand. Mark, an all-American boy from Chicago, is never home because he's always wandering the world. He just recently got married in Israel to a Jewish woman from France.

"The news on television has a personal impact on me almost every evening because I have friends from so many different backgrounds. How boring my life would be if the only people I hung out with were chubby middle-aged White guys like me."

One's cultural identity is an important aspect of being human. **Cultural identity** evolves from the shared beliefs, values, and attitudes of a group of people. It embodies standards of behavior and the ways in which beliefs, values, and attitudes are transmitted to the younger generation. Cultural identity also entails the ways in which kinship relationships and marital and sexual relationships are structured. Examples of the vast array of cultural identities in the United States include Anglo American, Italian American, African American, and Asian American—to name just a few.

Cultural identity transcends **ethnic identity,** or ethnicity, which refers to the geographic origin of a minority group within a country or culture, and **race,** which commonly refers to the physical characteristics of a particular group of people. Most cultures contain subgroups called **cocultures,** distinct cultural or social groups living within the dominant culture but also having membership in another culture, such as gay men and lesbians.

In this chapter we will describe the nature of cultural diversity in the United States and examine family strengths in a variety of ethnic and cultural groups. We will look at some of the issues family researchers explore, such as ethnocentrism and racism, and discuss the challenges ethnic families face in the United States.

The Nature of Cultural Diversity

The United States today is one of the most culturally diverse nations in the world. (For a global perspective on cultural diversity, see Box 3.1). Although the dominant culture of the United States is Anglo American, this country is home to many other ethnic and cultural groups. The major ethnic **minority groups** that are usually distinguished in the United States are African Americans (or Blacks), Latinos (or Hispanics), Asian Americans, and Native Americans. When discussing ethnic and other minority groups, however, it is important to remember that tremendous diversity exists among the people who are commonly grouped together.

In this section we will focus on the mythology of race and the problems that arise in classifying people by particular ethnic and cultural labels. We will also explore a variety of terms that help describe the range of marital, family, and kinship relationships among various cultural groups in the United States.

B O X   3 . 1

Global Diversity

The United States is a culturally diverse nation. To put cultural diversity in a global perspective, however, consider the following figures:

If the earth's population were shrunk to a village of 100 people, the composition of the village would be:

57 Asians

21 Europeans

14 North and South Americans

8 Africans

And they would have the following characteristics:

51% would be female; 49% would be male

70% would be non-White; 30% would be White

70% would be non-Christian; 30% would be Christian

80% would live in substandard housing

70% would be unable to read

50% would suffer from malnutrition

1% would have a college education

0% would own a computer

50% of the world's wealth would be in the hands of only 6 people, and all 6 would be citizens of the United States

Source: World Citizen Update, Winter, 1998.

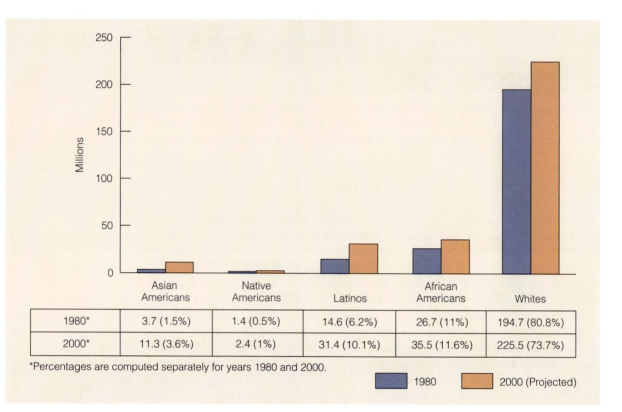

	Asian Americans	Native Americans	Latinos	African Americans	Whites
1980*	3.7 (1.5%)	1.4 (0.5%)	14.6 (6.2%)	26.7 (11%)	194.7 (80.8%)
2000*	11.3 (3.6%)	2.4 (1%)	31.4 (10.1%)	35.5 (11.6%)	225.5 (73.7%)

*Percentages are computed separately for years 1980 and 2000.

■ 1980   ■ 2000 (Projected)

Figure 3.1 Changing Ethnic Composition in the United States, 1980–2000. *Source:* U.S. Bureau of the Census (1997, p. 14).

A Changing Picture: Demographic Trends in the United States

As shown in Figure 3.1, the ethnic composition of the U.S. population is changing. Whites, numbering 225.5 million, represent about 74% of the total population. Although Whites comprise the largest ethnic group (that is, the majority), their percentage in terms of the total population decreased between 1980 and 2000—as compared to African Americans, Latinos, Native Americans, and Asian Americans, whose percentages in terms of the total population all increased over the same time period.

African Americans, numbering 35.5 million, are the largest minority group and represent about 12% of the total population. Latinos, the second largest minority group, numbering 31.4 million, make up about 10% of the total population. Latinos are very diverse and include Mexican Americans, Puerto Rican Americans, and Cuban Americans, as well as smaller numbers of individuals from Central or South American and Caribbean backgrounds.

Asian Americans, the fastest growing ethnic group, number more than 11 million and currently represent nearly 4% of the total population. Asian Americans comprise people of Japanese, Chinese, Vietnamese, Laotian, Cambodian, Korean, and Filipino descent; Samoans, Native Hawaiians, and other Pacific Islanders are included in this group.

Native Americans, including Alaskan Native Americans, are the smallest minority group, numbering about 22.2 million; they represent approximately 1%

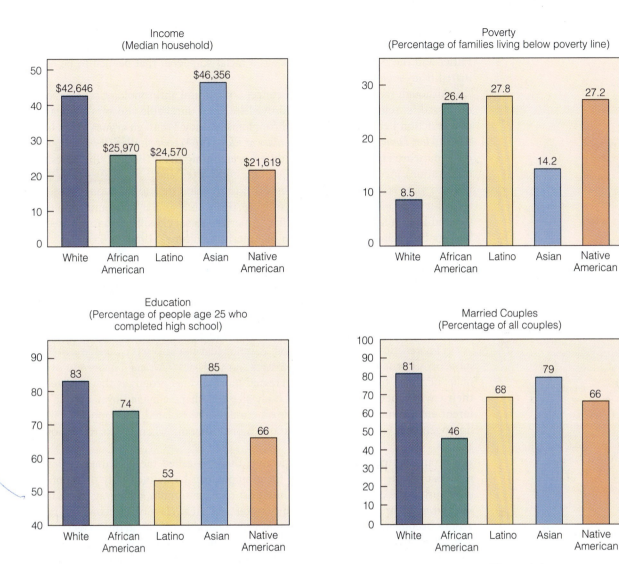

of the total population. Most members of this group embrace a tribal identity, such as Navaho, Hopi, or Sioux, rather than identifying themselves as Native Americans.

Asian Americans have the highest median household income as compared to Whites, African Americans, Latinos, and Native Americans (Figure 3.2). Greater percentages of African Americans, Latinos, and Native Americans live below the poverty line than do Asian Americans and Whites. Figure 3.2 summarizes data on income level, percentage living in poverty, level of education, and percentage of married couples for these five ethnic groups.

Figure 3.2
Characteristics of Families from Various Ethnic Groups, 1997.
Source: U.S. Bureau of the Census (1997, tab. 49, p. 49; tab. 52, p. 51; tab. 53, p. 52).

The Mythology of Race

The concept of race originally arose as a way to explain the diversity of the human population worldwide. As such, "race is a social, cultural, and political creation, a product of human invention" (Cameron & Wycoff, 1998, p. 279). Race has often been used as a psychologically and emotionally divisive tool, such as when Hitler and the Nazis identified Jews as a racial scapegoat that needed to be eliminated from society.

Although race was once a core concept of cultural anthropology, scholars have dismissed its relevancy because it proved to be an unreliable and invalid measure of distinction between people. Anthropologist Ashley Montagu argues in his book *Man's Most Dangerous Myth: The Fallacy of Race* (1964) that similarities among ethnic groups are far greater than the differences among them (Box 3.2 illustrates this observation). According to Montagu, "the term 'race' itself, as it is generally applied to man, is scientifically without justification, and that as commonly used, the term corresponds to nothing in reality" (p. 351). In a similar vein, anthropologist Conrad Phillip Kottak points out that "American racial classification isn't based on biology but is an arbitrary creation of American culture" (1989, p. 45).

In the field of genetics, the term has also been dropped because there is so little (less than .001%) difference in all human beings in their genetic code. In fact, there is more genetic difference between two Europeans than there is between one European and an Asian or an African (Cameron & Wycoff, 1998). In medicine, genetic differences between all people are so small that in many cases a Black donor can be a much better match for a White patient than can another White person.

The genetic theory of evolution assumes that humans were a genetically homogeneous group that began in one area of the world—Africa. This group of humans migrated to other lands and created more diverse groups as they adapted to their environment. Skin color and body size and shape changed over time in different environments. As these groups became more isolated, they appeared more homogeneous within their groups and more different when compared to other groups.

From a strictly scientific perspective, then, so-called racial characteristics do not exist (Root, 1992). Skin color for example, can be defined only on a continuum, just as the colors black and white exist on a continuum, with gray in the middle and no clear-cut distinctions in between. As such, classifying people by racial groups becomes rather arbitrary. For example, consider the child of an Irish American mother and a Japanese American father. The child may have a skin color like her mother's and eyes like her father's. Genetically and aesthetically, she is an expression of both her father's and her mother's characteristics. Toni Morrison, the Nobel Prize–winning author of such novels as *Song of Solomon, Beloved, Tar Baby,* and others puts it this way: "Race is the least reliable information you can have about someone. It's real information but it tells you next to nothing" (cited in Gray, 1998, p. 67).

In spite of scientific findings disputing the relevancy of race, the U.S. government has continued to classify people into four racial categories (American Indian/Alaskan Native, Asian/Pacific Islander, Black, and White) and two ethnic categories (Hispanic and non-Hispanic). The confusion created by racial designations was underscored by the 1990 census, in which people claimed membership in more than 300 different racial or ethnic groups.

The use of the term *mixed race* has not been approved by the federal government, even though it would probably be the most accurate classification. Before 1989, according to the National Center for Health Statistics, a person could only

BOX 3.2

There Are More Things That Link Us Than Set Us Apart

Kristine M. Holmgren

Syl Jones

We are female and male, black and white, rural and suburban. We grew up in segregated sections of large cities. The differences between us are obvious. Because of them, we may not always see the world the same way, or share the same point of view. . . .

Twelve days ago, a jury in Los Angeles found O. J. Simpson not guilty of the murders of his ex-wife and her friend Ron Goldman. Like some of you, we were both surprised at the verdict. . . .

Although the verdict allows Simpson to walk away from his jail cell, he will forever be branded as a wife-battering drug abuser. But we are not going to let the evil that surrounded O. J. Simpson, the trial, and the attendant media circus turn us against each other. We still believe it is possible to live in separate worlds, have different views, and find common ground. . . .

Simpson's triumph came at great cost to everyone. The two families who grieve over their murdered loved ones feel no sense of justice. Likewise, it is also wrong to stew in a vat of anger and insult an entire race by implying that group-think took over the jury. . . .

We think it is time to get on with the difficult work ahead in racial and gender matters.

- We deplore the mistreatment of women and believe that the increasing violence against women around the world must be addressed.

- We agree that racial injustice is endemic, and we stand against it with others in our communities.

- We see the wealthy being well-served by the courts of our nation while the poor suffer, and we abhor the corruption of a system that encourages such unequal justice.

Despite our different skin colors, the values we share are as similar as the color of our blood. We will hold out for peace.

Kristine M. Holmgren of Northfield, Minnesota, is a writer and Presbyterian pastor. Syl Jones of Excelsior, Minnesota, is a playwright, journalist, and communication consultant.

A successful intercultural marriage can be an important mechanism for helping to bring cultural groups together. Fortunately, the elements that are identified as core family strengths are common to all cultures.

be White if both parents were White. As of 1989, a person's race is determined by the race of the mother. Indeed, many children today are born to parents who are unclear about their ethnic/racial identity or classification. As such the confusion regarding ethnicity increases to the point of absurdity.

For the reasons just mentioned, we will not use the term *race* again in this book; rather, we will use the terms *culture* (or *cultural group*) or *ethnicity* (or *ethnic group*) when referring to different groups of people. A **cultural group** is a set of people who embrace core beliefs, behaviors, values, and norms and transmit them from generation to generation. An **ethnic group** is a set of people who are embedded within a larger cultural group or society and who share beliefs, behaviors, values, and norms that are also transmitted from generation to generation. Ethnicity "plays a major role in determining what we eat and how we work, relate, celebrate holidays and rituals, and feel about life and death and illness" (McGoldrick, Giordano, & Pearce, 1996, p. ix).

Due to the great diversity within groups, however, even calling them *ethnic* or *cultural* groups can be misleading. Jews, for example, are often classified as an ethnic group, but doing so stretches the imagination considerably, for a number of reasons: (1) Jews hold a wide variety of religious views, from very conservative to very liberal—some are Orthodox believers, and others are atheists; (2) Jews speak a variety of languages, and many Jews today cannot speak Hebrew, the language of tradition; (3) Jews are of many nationalities as a result of Judaism's expanding influence worldwide over the centuries; and (4) Jews exhibit a variety of physical characteristics, ranging from very dark skinned, black-haired African Jews to light-

Family and kin relationships are becoming more complex as people get divorced and remarried, forming blended families. Family gatherings help family members get connected with each other and learn more about their larger extended family.

skinned, blue-eyed, blond European Jews. From a cultural viewpoint, a nomadic Jewish shepherd in Ethiopia has much more in common with other Africans than he does with a Jewish dentist in suburban Chicago.

Perhaps the key issue in determining membership in an ethnic or cultural group is whether the individual *believes* he or she is a member of that group. Human beings are diverse. Classifications cannot be based solely on religious views, language, ancestry, or physical characteristics.

Kin Relationships Across Cultures: Concepts and Terms

Most of us learn about kinship early in our lives, with little or no theoretical explanations. We learn, for example, about brothers and sisters and about aunts, uncles, and cousins; but we identify with them as people rather than focus on specific kinship principles. We know who Uncle Jack and Aunt Libby are long before we understand the concepts of "mother's brother" or "father's sister."

All cultures recognize **kinship,** the relatedness of certain individuals within a group, and have norms and expectations that structure and govern kin behavior. The diversity of these norms is wide-ranging. These kinship concepts describe kinds of kinship groups and the norms that govern marital forms, family structure and organization, inheritance, authority, and residence.

Kinship groups range from nuclear families to various forms of extended families and may even include symbolic relationships. The **nuclear family**—the smallest, most elementary kinship unit—usually consists of two parents and their dependent children. Even in societies in which the nuclear family is embedded within a larger group, it is recognized as a distinct entity. The nuclear family is a **conjugal family system,** one that emphasizes the relationships formed through marriage. Typically, a conjugal system comprises only two generations and is relatively transitory, dissolving when the parents die or the children grow up and leave. Because nuclear families are comparatively small and short-lived, they are less likely to develop traditions that are handed down through the generations.

Many family functions are better performed by composite family groups, or **consanguineal family systems,** which emphasize blood ties more than marital ties. In consanguineal systems, married couples and their children are embedded in a larger kinship group of three or more generations related by blood. Consanguineal systems can include extended families or families resulting from plural marriages. An **extended family** consists of a nuclear family and those people related to its members by blood ties, such as aunts, uncles, cousins, and grandparents. A **plural marriage,** or **polygamy,** is a marriage in which a man has more than one wife (**polygyny**) or, more rarely, a marriage in which a woman has more than one husband (**polyandry**). In **monogamy,** a man or woman has only one mate. Although people from monogamous societies often perceive potential hazards in plural marriages, family patterns appear to operate smoothly in groups in which plural marriages are the norm.

A third kind of kinship group is a **pseudo-kin-group,** in which relationships resembling kinship ties develop among unrelated individuals. Relationships within these groups range in intensity, from close friendships to godparent-godchild connections to individuals living together and caring for each other without any legal or blood relationship. In the words of one 35-year-old woman:

"I don't really have a biological family anymore. I have a real family, though. I call it my psychological family. You see, my father was an alcoholic and died in an automobile accident. My mother was mentally ill and died several years ago in an institution. I didn't have any brothers or sisters, but when I was in high school a family in the parish knew how bad our family was doing and kind of took me in like a lost lamb.

"They've been my real family since then. I celebrate all the holidays with them, and Alf, the father, calls me the daughter his wife, Nancy, never gave him. Nancy returns the joke, calling me the daughter Alf was incapable of giving her. So I've got a dad and mom and two big brothers. It's a very special family to live in, and they're always there for me in a pinch."

Cultural norms influence family structure, but they also influence concepts of **lineage,** or lines of descent; of who holds authority in a family; and of where newly married couples should reside. Lineage is important in determining membership in a particular kinship group, patterns of inheritance, and kinship obligations or responsibilities. In some societies, descent is traced by gender: **matrilineal societies** trace descent through females, and **patrilineal societies** trace descent through males. In a matrilineal society, for example, a man inherits group membership through his mother; lines of descent through his sister(s) are also important. Although a man may live with his wife or wives, he perceives the households of his mother and sisters as his true home. In a patrilineal society, a man's sister will be in his descent group but her children will not; they belong to their father's descent group.

Bilateral descent is common in many Western societies, with children tied equally to relatives of both the mother and the father. In this "family tree" approach to descent, in which ancestors and descendants multiply geometrically, true descent kinship groups are not formed unless limited by generation or to particular ancestors and descendants.

Norms for lines of descent may or may not be linked to lines of authority within a kinship group. If females exercise the authority, a kinship group is considered a **matriarchal group.** If males are dominant and exercise the authority, the kinship group is considered a **patriarchal group.** Note that these terms emphasize femaleness and maleness rather than motherhood and fatherhood. In a patriarchal group, for example, the grandfather is likely to wield more authority than the father of a nuclear family. But the criterion of gender always supersedes that of age in matriarchal and patriarchal kinship groups.

In **equalitarian groups,** such as those found in the United States, the ideals of democracy suggest that the rights and perspectives of both genders and all generations be respected. A given family's structure and interactions may lean toward the patriarchal or matriarchal, but the norms of the group would most likely be considered equalitarian.

Norms of residence for newly married couples can also be categorized by a society's emphasis on biological sex. In a **matrilocal society,** newly married couples normally live with or near the wife's kin, especially her mother's kinship group. Newly married couples in **patrilocal societies** are expected to live with or near the husband's kin, usually his father's kinship group. In a **neolocal society,** norms encourage newly married couples to establish a separate, autonomous residence, independent of either partner's kinship group.

Although a society may have norms regarding marital and family organization and interaction, diversity is generally also evident within that society's families and kinship groups. Understanding the concept of kin relationships, however, enables observers to compare and analyze the structure and dynamics of a broad range of kinship groups.

Family Strengths, Stereotypes, and Challenges in Various Ethnic Groups

It has been hypothesized that strong families, whatever their ethnic identification or country of origin, share three major clusters of qualities: cohesion, flexibility, and communication (Gorall & Olson, 1995; Olson, 1996; Walsh, 1998). These three broad clusters (Figure 3.3) encompass the six qualities of strong families identified by the family strengths framework, as described in Chapter 4. **Family cohesion** involves commitment and spending time together. Commitment to the

Figure 3.3 Sociocultural Context and Family System Characteristics

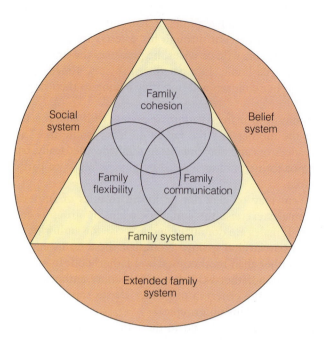

family includes trust, honesty, dependability, and faithfulness. Spending time together means committing a considerable amount of quality time to sharing activities, feelings, and ideas and enjoying each other's company.

Family flexibility relates to dealing effectively with stress and having helpful spiritual beliefs. Coping abilities include using personal and family resources to help each other, accepting crises as challenges rather than denying them, and growing together by working through crises. Spiritual well-being includes happiness, optimism, hope, faith, and a set of shared ethical values that guide family members through life's challenges.

Family communication focuses on positive communication and on appreciating and having affection for family members. Positive communication includes having open, straightforward discussions, being cooperative rather than competitive, and sharing feelings with one another. Appreciation and affection include kindness, mutual caring, respect for individuality, and a feeling of security. (To help you become more aware of the strengths in your family, complete the short inventory provided in Box 3.3.)

Douglas Abbott and William Meredith (1988) studied over 500 successful families from five American ethnic groups—Native Americans, Hmong refugees, African Americans, Mexican Americans, and Caucasians—focusing on the three clusters (cohesion, flexibility, and communication) and on the family strengths items developed earlier by David Olson, Andrea Larsen, and Hamilton McCubbin (Olson, McCubbin, et al., 1989). The study revealed more similarities than differences across the five groups. In fact, there were significant similarities among all the groups, with correlations in the range of .60–.85, except between the Hmong and the Native Americans and between the Hmong and the Caucasians. All five groups agreed that strong families (1) use effective communication and listening skills, (2) are trusting and trustworthy, (3) are affirming and supportive, and (4) teach a sense of right and wrong behavior. Other common strengths were teach-

BOX 3.3

Rate Your Family's Strengths

This Family Strengths Inventory was developed by researchers who studied the strengths of over 3,000 families. To assess your family (either the family you grew up in or the family you have formed as an adult), cir-cle the number that best reflects how your family rates on each strength. A 1 represents the lowest rating and a 5 represents the highest.

1. Spending time together and doing things with each other	1	2	3	4	5
2. Commitment to each other	1	2	3	4	5
3. Good communication (talking with each other often, listening well, sharing feelings with each other)	1	2	3	4	5
4. Dealing with crises in a positive manner	1	2	3	4	5
5. Expressing appreciation to each other	1	2	3	4	5
6. Spiritual wellness	1	2	3	4	5
7. Closeness of relationship between spouses	1	2	3	4	5
8. Closeness of relationship between parents and children	1	2	3	4	5
9. Happiness of relationship between spouses	1	2	3	4	5
10. Happiness of relationship between parents and children	1	2	3	4	5
11. Extent to which spouses make each other feel good about themselves (self-confident, worthy, competent, and happy)	1	2	3	4	5
12. Extent to which parents help children feel good about themselves	1	2	3	4	5

Scoring Add the numbers you have circled. A score below 39 indicates below-average family strengths. Scores between 39 and 52 are in the average range. Scores above 53 indicate a strong family. Low scores on individual items identify areas that families can profitably spend time on. High scores are worthy of celebration but shouldn't lead to complacency. Like gardens, families need loving care to remain strong.

Source: Secrets of Strong Families (pp. 167–169) by N. Stinnett and J. DeFrain, 1985, Boston: Little, Brown.

ing respect for others, spending time doing things together, and feeling a sense of shared responsibility. Table 3.1 details the responses from the various ethnic groups.

In summary, Abbott and Meredith noted that the most striking finding was the consensus among all five ethnic groups on the traits they considered most important to healthy family functioning. The researchers concluded that strong families are those that are high in family cohesion, family flexibility, and family communication. These traits of strong families, according to Abbott and Meredith, "extend beyond ethnic boundaries" (1988, p. 146).

In describing successful families, we have emphasized family system characteristics, but it is also important to consider the sociocultural context in which families live. Figure 3.3 includes the family system characteristics of cohesion, flexibility, and communication and also illustrates the connection of the extended-family system, the social system, and the belief system.

Table 3.1 Family Strengths in Various Ethnic Groups

		ETHNIC GROUP				
FAMILY TRAIT	Caucasian $N = 210$	African American $N = 103$	Mexican American $N = 105$	Hmong $N = 80$	Native American $N = 57$	CHI SQUARE[a]
Communicates and listens	88%	67%	86%	81%	60%	36.2**
Trusting and trustworthy	87	69	88	73	51	46.7**
Is affirming and supportive	86	70	82	75	51	13.2*
Teaches a sense of right and wrong	85	77	78	76	81	16.6*
Teaches respect for others	73	58	85	76	61	48.0**
Shares leisure time	67	41	51	41	74	47.4**
Is responsible for family welfare	65	52	51	43	23	15.5*
Has a sense of play and humor	58	55	35	18	53	47.9*
Respects privacy of family members	57	57	72	56	37	17.9*
Shares religious beliefs	56	30	32	15	39	50.9**
Has two parents living at home	46	39	63	24	32	34.6**
Values family traditions	41	38	45	73	30	29.9**
Seeks help with problems	40	36	36	41	35	N.S.
Encourages individuality	38	27	26	14	23	22.0*
Financial security	36	51	42	35	17	N.S.
Has a base of parental rules	34	41	28	41	40	N.S.
Respects elders	34	35	66	54	18	60.4**
Shares similar values	32	27	30	38	79	N.S.
Allows for negotiation of family rules	31	14	20	20	21	17.5*
Values a college education	29	28	45	64	35	42.3**
Prays together	26	36	34	39	23	N.S.

Note: Traits reported in this table had to be considered important by at least two thirds of the parents in at least two ethnic groups.

[a] Chi square is a statistic that compares the frequencies or percentages in two or more groups to determine if their differences are significantly greater than the differences expected by chance. In the Chi Square column, * indicates $p < 01$, ** indicates $p < 001$, and N.S. indicates nonsignificant differences between rankings.

Source: "Characteristics of Strong Families: Perceptions of Ethnic Parents" by D. A. Abbott and W. H. Meredith, 1988, *Home Economics Research Journal, 17* (2), p. 144. Copyright 1988 by American Home Economics Association. Reprinted by permission.

The **extended-family system,** which encompasses relatives, kin, and other family members connected to the family system, is a particularly important resource for families of color (McAdoo, 1997). The **social system** is also an important resource for families; it covers economic resources and educational and related opportunities. Families of color are often at a disadvantage in the social system because they are likely to be of middle or lower socioeconomic status. Because of their relative lack of both education and economic resources and because of discrimination against them in various settings, the social system is often more a liability than an asset to families of color. The **belief system** refers to a family's spiritual beliefs and a certainty that family members on their own and as a unit can deal with the challenges that confront them. Families of color often have a solid belief system that helps them maintain a strong and successful family.

The summary figures that follow identify some of the stereotypes, strengths, and challenges of several ethnic and cultural groups in our society. The text emphasizes each group's strengths.

One important characteristic of strong families is that they have fun together and enjoy doing things as a family. These family times provide positive memories when times are more challenging.

Unfortunately, most of what people know about ethnic and cultural groups other than their own is based on **stereotypes**—standardized, oversimplified, often foolish and mean-spirited views. When a person from one group describes people from another, the description is often a stereotype. **Prejudice,** which literally means prejudging, is also closely linked with stereotyping; both attitudes reinforce each other. As a society we need to move beyond stereotypes and focus on each group's strengths and challenges. Recognizing others' strengths helps reduce prejudice.

Strengths of White Families

Much of the early research on family strengths focused on White families and resulted in the family strengths framework of Nick Stinnett and John DeFrain (1985; see Chapter 4 of this text). In a study of 1,000 couples and families throughout the family life cycle, Olson and his colleagues identified strengths that helped families at each stage maintain high levels of marital and family satisfaction (Olson, McCubbin, et al., 1989). Because these strengths will be described in detail in

Figure 3.4 Stereotypes, Strengths, and Challenges of White Families

Stereotypes	Strengths	Challenges
• Prejudiced against other cultures, racist • Wealthy, greedy • Powerful, aggressive • Materialistic, values possessions over people • Extremely conservative or reactionary; narrow-minded • Lacking in family values; only cares about self; puts older people in nursing homes rather than care for them in the family • Elevate the individual over the community; "me" instead of "us" • Egotistical; think their way is the only way	• Commitment to the family • Time together • Ability to cope with stress and crisis • Spiritual well-being • Positive communication • Appreciation and affection	• Balancing work and family • Maintaining physical and emotional health • Creating healthy relationships in a society that glorifies winning, money, and things • Learning about other cultures and being sensitive to the needs of those who are not in positions of power and authority • Preserving the natural environment in an economic system that is fueled by consumption

Chapter 4, we will simply summarize them here (Figure 3.4):

- *Commitment to family.* Strong White families are very committed to one another and are able to give all family members the freedom and support they need to achieve their individual goals.

- *Time together.* White families that remain strong throughout the family life cycle find ways to spend time together and enjoy each other.

- *Ability to cope with stress and crisis.* Although all families encounter marital and family stress, strong families see stress as a challenge and deal directly with issues as they occur.

- *Spiritual well-being.* Strong White families have spiritual beliefs and values, often including religious beliefs, that help them deal with ongoing life issues.

- *Positive communication.* One of the most important characteristics of healthy White families is that they feel good about their communication with one another.

- *Appreciation and affection.* Sharing the positive feelings they have about one another helps keep relationships positive in strong White families.

Strengths of African American Families

A number of family researchers have been interested in African American family strengths for more than two decades (Boyd-Franklin, 1989; McAdoo, 1993; Willie, 1988). The picture they have developed of healthy African American families is similar to the picture of healthy White families. One of the earliest studies was conducted by Marie Peters (1981), who reviewed her own work in addition to that of other African American family investigators and identified six strengths of

Stereotypes	Strengths	Challenges
• Lower class; on welfare • Less intelligent • Criminal • Poorly educated • Athletic • Gifted as entertainers • Religious • Promiscuous • Absent as fathers	• Strong kinship bonds • Strong work orientation • Flexibility in family roles • Strong motivation to achieve • Strong religious orientation • Caring parenting • Egalitarian marriages	• Being judged as a financial risk • Feeling powerless • Building self-esteem • Facing a high risk of being killed as a young man • Overcoming discrimination • Achieving higher levels of education • Violence against each other • Identifying male role models

Figure 3.5 Stereotypes, Strengths, and Challenges of African American Families

African American families (Figure 3.5):

- *Strong kinship bonds.* The extended family is very important to many African American families, and African Americans tend to take relatives into their households (Hunter, 1997; Padgett, 1997).

- *Strong work orientation.* Dual-job households are common among strong African American families.

- *Flexibility in family roles.* Role flexibility serves as an effective coping mechanism in healthy African American families. Because it has been necessary for many mothers to work outside the home, Black mothers tend to have more power in the family. The typical strong African American family is not matriarchal or patriarchal but is equalitarian in style. African American families have a longer tradition of equalitarian marriages than White families; compared with African American couples, White couples as a group are relative newcomers to the dual-job arena (McAdoo, 1993).

- *Strong motivation to achieve.* African American parents believe education is important, and many would like to see their children go to college.

- *Strong religious orientation.* African American churches provide emotional, spiritual, and intellectual satisfaction to African American families. Church work provides meaning and purpose for many African Americans. Dr. Martin Luther King, Jr., for example, achieved "greatness . . . through the leadership developed and cultivated in the African American church" (Azubike, 1987, p. 99).

- *Caring parenting.* Researchers have studied rates of corporal punishment (slapping and spanking) across all income levels of African American and White families. Murray Straus, a nationally known family researcher who has focused on violence in families, reports that 78% of White parents hit their 4-year-old children in a given year as compared to 70% of parents of color (1994). In families having 16-year-old adolescents, 48% of White parents hit their teenagers as compared to 39% of parents of color. When

Caring parenting has been identified as a particular strength of African American families. When parents take the time to share recreational activities with their children, as this couple is doing, they make an investment in both the emotional development of their children and the future stability of the family.

facing economic stress and social disadvantage, African American parents are apparently better than White parents at staying cool. This is especially noteworthy in light of the fact that African American parents, being members of a minority group, must also contend with racism.

Researchers at Howard University (Gary, Beatty, & Berry, 1986) studied 50 strong African American families in Washington, D.C., and found that the strengths these families exhibited were very similar to the strengths reported in a study of strong families who were predominantly White (Stinnett, Sanders, & De-Frain, 1981). If indeed there are differences between healthy families in these two groups, a review of various studies of African American and White family strengths suggests that religious values and kinship ties are somewhat more important in African American families than in White families (Lee, Peek, & Coward, 1998; Peters, 1981). See Box 3.4, which discusses Kwanzaa, a holiday celebrating Black principles and values.

BOX 3.4

Kwanzaa Holidays Celebrate Black Principles, Unity

In many homes in our community, from December 26 through the new year, African American families and individuals practice a unique, non-heroic observation called Kwanzaa.

The word *Kwanzaa* is from the Kiswahili language, which is noteworthy because Kiswahili is a non-ethnic trading language used throughout Africa and not tribal specific. Kwanzaa is derived from the expression "matudnad ya Kwanzaa," which means "first harvest" or "first fruits," and the ritual/observance bears similarity to community celebrations which follow the harvest in many African cultures.

Kwanzaa was initiated in this country by Malauna Ron Karenga, a small group of African American adults, and seven children in Los Angeles, in 1966. Karenga is widely respected as a scholar, social activist, critical thinker, founder of "US" (United Slaves) and the "Soul Patrol," and as the originator of the "Nguzo Saba," which literally translated means "seven foundations" or "seven principles" of blackness, on which Kwanzaa is based and which form the bedrock of "Kawaida," the black value system.

Regrettably, when explaining what Kwanzaa is, it is often most helpful to explain what Kwanzaa is not. Kwanzaa is not—and should not be considered—a "black Christmas." The emphasis in Kwanzaa is earth-based—not mystical, commercially exploitative, or based on people traveling through the clouds. Kwanzaa stresses our African roots; it seeks to narrow and deny the differences between black people throughout the world and to demonstrate and define our historical and cultural unity, while facilitating its acceptance.

Kwanzaa is primarily a practice of gathering and celebration among black people, and its reinforcing gestures (often called rituals) are practiced or observed during the seven-day period from December 26 to January 1. It was created to strengthen our collective self-concept as black people, honor our past, critically evaluate our present, and commit ourselves to a fuller,

more productive future. While Kwanzaa does involve gifts for children and one another (preferably items we have created or cultural and educational gifts), again, the primary force or focus of Kwanzaa revolves around children and the Nguzo Saba, or seven principles, with each day of the Kwanzaa observance dedicated to one of the principles.

The Nguzo Saba are as follows:

1. *Umoha (unity):* To strive for and maintain unity in the family, community, nation, and race.

2. *Kujichagulia (self-determination):* To define ourselves, name ourselves, create for ourselves, and speak for ourselves.

3. *Ujima (collective work and responsibility):* To build and maintain our community together and make our sisters' and brothers' problems our problems—to be solved together.

4. *Ujamaa (cooperative economics):* To build and maintain our own stores and other businesses and to profit from them together.

5. *Nia (purpose):* To make our collective vocation the building and developing of our community, to restore our people to their traditional greatness.

6. *Kuumba (creativity):* To do always as much as we can, in order to leave our community more beautiful and beneficial than we inherited it.

7. *Imani (faith):* To believe with all our heart in our people, our parents, our teachers, our leaders, and the righteousness and victory of our collective struggle.

Again, Kwanzaa is primarily intended for children, the hope of our future, and is not a mere seven-day observation but a model to live by for African Americans. Happy Kwanzaa!

Source: "Kwanzaa Holidays Celebrate Black Principles, Unity" by Y. Mgeni, Dec. 27, 1992, Minneapolis *Star Tribune*, p. 4. Copyright 1992 by the Minneapolis *Star Tribune*. Reprinted by permission.

Strengths of Latino Families

As mentioned earlier, Latinos encompass people from numerous Spanish-speaking cultures. About two thirds are Mexican Americans, but even within this group there is diversity:

> Scholars Mario Garcia and Rodolfo Alvarez suggest that people of Mexican descent in the United States constitute several rather than a single demographic group (Shorris, 1992, pp. 95–100). Two such reference groups are Mexican Americans and Chicanos/Chicanas. The Mexican American group comprises people who immigrated to border states, such as California and Texas, following World War II. People who consider themselves Mexican Americans are generally older and more conservative than those who identify themselves as Chicanos or Chicanas, who are younger and more militant.
>
> Chicanos and Chicanas came of age in the 1960s and gained some attention in the 1970s. They perceived Mexican immigrants who wanted to assimilate with the predominant Anglo culture as sellouts. To distinguish themselves from the Mexican American group, Chicanos and Chicanas adopted specific patterns of behaving, including their own code words. (Brydon & Scott, 1997, p. 262)

Although this kind of diversity is real, there are still cultural commonalities that allow us to refer, in general terms, to the Latino population of the United States. (*Hispanic* is the term most often used in studies and statistics, including those published by the U.S. government, for Latino populations.) But always keep in mind that commonalities are broad and general; every individual and every family is unique.

Latinos in the United States have managed to preserve a strong family system in spite of the difficult challenges they face. Latinos place a high priority on the family as a source of identity and support. Family encompasses the immediate family unit (*la casa*), the extended family (*la familia*), and godparents (*los compadres*). In Latino culture, the well-being of the entire family system has priority over individual goals. Box 3.5 highlights common stereotypes of Latino Americans. Rather than focusing on such stereotypes, however, this chapter emphasizes family strengths.

In one extensive overview of the strengths of Latino families, William Vega (1995) identified the six most important characteristics, which are very similar to those identified for families from other cultures in the United States (Figure 3.6):

- *Familism.* The family is a major priority; it is highly valued. There is a strong emotional commitment to the family.

- *High family cohesion.* Strong Latino families have very high cohesion, or closeness, although cohesion decreases across generations somewhat among Latino families living in the United States.

- *High family flexibility.* There is considerable role flexibility in Latino families, in contrast to the stereotyped view in which the male is seen as dominant.

- *Supportive kin network system.* The large kin network system of most Latino families is very important as a supportive resource and is a strong tradition.

BOX 3.5

Getting Beyond Latino Myths

According to the stereotype, Latino Americans are a monolithic interest group. Among other myths about Latinos are that they prefer liberal immigration policies, favor the Spanish language over English, and tend to vote in political blocs. A [1992] study [has] shatter[ed] those beliefs and should help Americans move beyond wholesale descriptions of population groups based on race and ethnicity.

The Latino National Political Survey discovered that Latinos share a driving commitment to be part of American society. That dedication often eclipses ethnic loyalties among the three largest groups, Mexican Americans, Puerto Ricans, and Cuban Americans.

Yet for decades the media and the federal government have generalized from the most visible part of the Latino population. The resulting stereotypes alienated Latinos from the mainstream.

The Census Bureau, for example, has tried to classify Latinos by color. In 1940, Latinos were categorized as "black" or a "racial" nonwhite group. In 1950 and 1960, the Census used the category of "white persons of Spanish surname." In 1970, the classification was changed to "white persons of Spanish surname and Spanish mother tongue." Then, in 1980, the expansive "nonwhite Hispanic" [was introduced]. Because the Census uses "white" and "black" to classify residents, it has shuttled Latinos back and forth between the two extremes. In each case, the principle behind the label is the perceived presence or absence of color.

In reality, the mirror that Latinos hold up to America reflects many opportunities to move beyond a system of racial distinctions. Latinos often prefer to juggle two languages, or two cultures or national heritages, even if the resulting syntheses seem messy or dangerous. To those conditioned to tidy ethnic compartments, Latino ambiguity is indeed threatening. A people who violate boundaries of race, language, and culture upset myths of a nation-state based on borders and exclusion.

But in a nation increasingly transformed by global restructuring, and collapse of some mythic categories that once defined its identity, Latinos may be the vanguard. Their seemingly discordant virtues—ethnic identities and faith in America—can be a source of celebration and strength. Latinos can help America move closer to a future in which all its citizens will be accomplices in a multiracial kinship and culture.

Source: "Getting Beyond Latino Myths," editorial, December 26, 1992, Minneapolis *Star Tribune*, p. 10A. Copyright 1992 by the Minneapolis *Star Tribune*. Reprinted by permission.

Stereotypes	Strengths	Challenges
• Poorly educated • Prone to having large families • Mostly migrant workers • Macho males/machismo • Superstitious • Religious • Predominantly illegal aliens • Prone to alcohol abuse • Traditional in terms of gender roles	• Familism • High family cohesion • High family flexibility • Supportive kin network system • Equalitarian decision making • Strong ethnic identity	• Remaining family centered • Maintaining traditions • Gaining financial resources • Overcoming the language barrier • Overcoming economic discrimination • Handling relocation issues • Achieving higher levels of education • Acculturating across generations

Figure 3.6 Stereotypes, Strengths, and Challenges of Latino Families

In every ethnic group, fathers can make a very important contribution to the well-being of the family by being active in household tasks, and can enjoy themselves thoroughly at the same time.

- *Equalitarian decision making.* Increasingly, families share roles more equally; decision making is equalitarian.

- *Strong ethnic identity.* The importance of the Latino culture and values binds families together and helps give them a strong ethnic identity.

Many Latino families are going through transitions similar to those that Anglo (non-Latino White) families have experienced through the generations. Alfredo Mirandé (1977, 1979) outlines how social scientists' views of Chicano (Mexican American) families have evolved over the years. Historically, social scientists

BOX 3.6

Cultural Conflicts for a Female Chicana College Student

I am a Chicana graduate student who wants to complete a Ph.D. in family studies so I can teach at the college level and help the family field be more inclusive and up-to-date regarding Chicano families. Fortunately, the choices I've made are not in conflict with my family of procreation.

It was very difficult for my family of origin initially to understand why I wanted or needed to go to school for so long. Since my grandparents and parents struggled just to provide for adequate housing, food, and clothing, they find it difficult to see why education is so important. They were also somewhat threatened by the fact that I wanted to study families because I might learn too much.

Another conflict was regarding my interest in my own development versus their emphasis on the whole family. They felt I was focusing too much on myself and not giving back enough to the family. Also, they felt this was making me more competitive and less cooperative, which is a quality valued highly. Another issue is the use of the Spanish language and whether I would use both Spanish and English in my home. Since we decided to raise our children using English only, some family members viewed that choice as rejecting our heritage. Also, as my years of college education increased, my relatives tended to distance themselves more from me.

Fortunately, my husband, who is also Chicano, is totally supportive and is a house husband for our two small children. He takes care of the children, and I am the primary wage earner. This is not the traditional family model for most Chicanos, and so it does challenge some of our other family members and kin.

While I was not initially aware of the importance of my mother's support, I have lately become even more appreciative of her encouraging words. I have finally been giving her more credit for her support. She also served as a positive role model since she began working full time when I was young. She also has strongly encouraged me to work outside the home and even to try to seek a career.

In general, I have made it because I am determined to have a professional career and have the strong support of my husband and my mother. My other relatives are less understanding and supportive since they question my goals and values. In spite of it all, education is necessary for me to help advance myself and my family.

Source: Unpublished manuscript by Julie Palacio, 1992, former graduate student in Family Social Science, University of Minnesota, St. Paul, MN. Reprinted by permission.

have tended to disagree on the nature of these families. After reviewing research on Mexican American families, Mirandé (1979) concludes that the dominant pattern of decision making and action is not male dominated and authoritarian but equalitarian—that is, power is shared among relative equals. Most husbands and wives share not only in decision making but in the performance of household tasks and child care. Although many have assumed clear gender-role segregation, Mirandé found this pattern to be the exception rather than the rule (Box 3.6).

Researchers have found that Mexican American families and Anglo families share two strengths. Using an assessment scale called FACES (Family Adaptability and Cohesion Evaluation Scales), William Vega and colleagues (1986) studied cohesion (togetherness) and adaptability (flexibility) in a group of low-income Mexican American parents and a group of middle-income Anglo parents. The researchers expected to find differences between the two groups, based not so much on culture but on social class. In short, they hypothesized that money helped family life run a bit more smoothly. They were surprised to find that even though the

A tradition of hard work, discipline, high regard for education, and commitment to the family has translated into a valuable and important strength for many Asian American families. This graduate honors his family with his achievement, but he has probably also enjoyed their wholehearted support and encouragement as he worked toward it.

Mexican American families had the additional challenges that come with low income, their group scored no differently on cohesion and adaptability than the middle-income Anglo families.

Another study focused on immigrant Puerto Rican families in New York City. Lloyd Rogler and Rosemary Santana Cooney (1984) interviewed 100 intergenerational families, each consisting of an older married couple in the parent generation and a younger married couple in the children generation. As expected, ethnic identity—identification with Puerto Rican rather than American culture—was stronger in the parent generation, but it remained relatively strong in the children generation. Those who had arrived in New York City from Puerto Rico at a younger age were less likely to have an exclusively Puerto Rican identity. Younger people appeared to be more adaptable and more readily influenced by the host society. They were more willing to take on a dual identity—saying, in effect, "I am both Puerto Rican and American."

Conflicts between generations are a common family problem in many ethnic and cultural groups. The case of a Chicana student whose extended family was threatened by her struggle for a graduate school education and personal success illustrates this point (see Box 3.6). But the case also shows the transitions many Chicano families are undergoing—and the strengths they possess. Because of the support of her Chicano husband and her mother, this young woman was able to overcome hostility and lack of support from other family members.

Strengths of Asian American Families

Families of Asian descent are another very resilient group in this country. Although Asian Americans have faced prejudice and discrimination throughout their history in the United States, they have fared better than other ethnic minorities economically and have managed to preserve their family ties, traditions, and values (McLeod, 1986; Schwartz, Raine, & Robins, 1987). A period of disruption oc-

Stereotypes	Strengths	Challenges
• Submissive women • Highly intelligent • Obedient children • Competitive • Hard working • Unemotional • Academically motivated	• Strong family orientation • Filial piety • High value on education • Well-disciplined children • Extended family support • Family loyalty	• Relaxing personal expectations • Maintaining ties with kin • Overcoming emotional vulnerability • Overcoming stigma against seeking help • Trusting those outside the group • Relaxing focus on work

Figure 3.7 Stereotypes, Strengths, and Challenges of Asian American Families

curred in the 1940s. Following the bombing of Pearl Harbor, fear of further attacks by Japan led the U.S. government to resettle Japanese Americans—even those born in this country—in what were essentially prison camps until the war ended. Four decades later, the federal government agreed to modestly recompense surviving family members for the ill-treatment they suffered.

Although Asian Americans probably do not face the same level of discrimination that African Americans face in the workplace, a report by the Commission on Civil Rights was forced to conclude that "anti-Asian activity in the form of violence, vandalism, harassment and intimidation continues to occur across the nation" (Schwartz et al., 1987). Even today there is a degree of discrimination against Asian Americans, fueled by a fear of competition from the economies in East Asia. Many Asian immigrants have come to this country in search of economic progress, which was unachievable in their homelands. Having reached their goals through hard work, many Asian Americans pose a threat to those who have lived in this country longer and have settled into a comfortable, more easygoing life.

Many Asian Americans share a cultural heritage that values discipline, family commitment, hard work, and education (Blair & Qian, 1998). Young people reared in such an environment become challenging competitors in a society such as ours, which values competition and individual initiative.

Asian American families are very diverse, but they commonly share many of the strengths of other cultural groups. Following are the six major strengths of Asian American families, which are summarized in Figure 3.7:

- *Strong family orientation.* Both the nuclear and the extended family are very important historically and today.

- *Filial piety.* The great respect Asian American families have for their elders is noteworthy. It helps explain the high level of mutual support each generation receives from the other generations.

- *High value on education.* Asian American families emphasize the importance of education, from nursery school through college.

- *Well-disciplined children.* Traditionally, children are expected to be quiet, well behaved, and somewhat passive.

BOX 3.7

A Life History Approach to Understanding Families From Southeast Asia

To better capture the family dynamics in families that came to the United States from Vietnam, Cambodia, and Laos, Daniel Detzner used the life history approach. The focus of his research centered on the question: How does forced relocation to another culture change family structure, dynamics, and rituals? The life history approach was considered relevant to the study of Asian elders because storytelling and sharing of oral traditions were part of the culture. Elders were also held in high esteem as advisors and wise people.

In field-testing his survey questions, Detzner found denial of any family conflict or even disagreement. This is understandable because the traditional teachings of Confucius and Buddha describe conflict as shameful. Reworking the questions to focus on family rules and the consequences when rules were broken revealed more than 200 cases of conflict. With the help of a translator, Detzner then conducted in-depth, semi-structured interviews with the oldest generation in each household. He then computer-coded the responses for analysis.

Detzner was surprised to find that despite the reluctance of those interviewed to discuss conflict directly, the indirect approach revealed conflict in almost every life history case, across the cultural groups and at every stage of the family life cycle. So conflict was seen as normative and was rather frequent, even though as an issue it was avoided and even denied. A related finding was that the elders felt their traditional power was disappearing and they were no longer respected by the younger generation, many of whom were rebelling against traditional practices.

Source: From "Life Histories: Conflict in Southeast Asia Refugee Families" by D. F. Detzner. In *Qualitative Methods in Family Research*, pp. 85–102, edited by J. Gilgun, K. Kaly, and G. Handel, 1992, Newbury Park, CA: Sage. Copyright © 1992 by J. Gilgun and D. F. Detzner. Adapted by permission of the publisher.

- *Extended family support*. Financial and emotional support is provided by the extended family when the nuclear family needs it.

- *Family loyalty*. Family members support each other and protect each other's privacy.

Recent immigrants from Southeast Asia (Vietnam, Cambodia, and Laos) have had a more difficult time adjusting to American culture than earlier immigrants from Japan, China, and Korea did. Although many recent arrivals have been farmers from rural areas, these immigrants often find themselves in poor inner-city neighborhoods, where their traditional values are challenged, making the adjustment to American culture difficult. To better understand the acculturation process of these families, one researcher used a method called the life history approach, in which elders told their stories rather than responding to questionnaires (Detzner, 1992). The findings are described in Box 3.7.

Strengths of Native American Families

There are approximately 1.5 million Native American families in the United States, representing roughly 400 tribes. About half live on reservations (Carson, Dail, Greeley, & Kenote, 1990). The tremendous degree of diversity among tribes contributes to the difficulty researchers have in studying Native American families, leading one investigator to conclude, "What we know, then, about Indian families

Stereotypes	Strengths	Challenges
• Lazy • Unmotivated • Irresponsible • Passive • Nonexpressive • Easily influenced by alcohol	• Extended family system • Traditional beliefs • High family cohesion • Respect for elders • Bilingual language skills • Tribal support system	• Dealing with the conflicting values of the tribe and U.S. society • Maintaining family traditions • Staying cohesive and connected • Identifying role models • Achieving higher levels of education

Figure 3.8 Stereotypes, Strengths, and Challenges of Native American Families

is fragmented, anecdotal, descriptive, and often overpowered by poor understanding of the particular cultures being studied" (Stauss, 1986, p. 345).

Six important strengths of Native American families are listed here and summarized in Figure 3.8:

- *Extended family system.* The extended family is very strong in Native American families.

- *Traditional beliefs.* The belief system of Native American tribes focuses on harmony with nature and the value of contentment.

- *High family cohesion.* The connectedness of the family is important. The family is broadly defined to include the nuclear family, the extended family, and the tribal community.

- *Respect for elders.* Elders are the most respected individuals in traditional Native American tribes, and the family reinforces this attitude.

- *Bilingual language skills.* Most Native Americans work hard to maintain their native language, but this objective is becoming more difficult because the children attend school off the reservation and are increasingly exposed to television and other mass media.

- *Tribal support system.* Many Native Americans rely on their tribal support system for all types of problems. Only when that is inadequate do they turn to outside support.

Although Native American families are characterized by diversity (Stauss, 1986), some investigators have asserted that the family remains the basic unit of the Native American community and that the Native American family can be characterized as having traditional beliefs, practices, and languages and a unique history and lifestyle. Native American families derive support from both individual family members and the clan or tribal group to which they belong (R. Lewis, 1981).

Studies have found that many Native American tribes emphasize mutual dependence among tribal members, responsibility, respect for others, courage, optimism, and contentment. This contentment comes from an identification with the cosmos (feeling one with the world), a spiritual orientation to life, and traditional

Native American families have many strengths, but society tends to focus on their problems as they try to strike a balance between maintaining their culture and fitting in to contemporary society.

religious practices. Living in harmony with nature and with other human beings is of utmost importance, nature being a powerful learning tool for family members and the tribe (R. Lewis, 1981; J. S. Olson & Wilson, 1984).

The extended family is still a source of strength for many Native Americans, but this is changing as more family members leave the reservation to seek opportunities elsewhere. Native American youths may have a wider array of people to whom they are attached than do non–Native Americans. In times of crisis, support from both the extended family and the tribal community helps people survive (Robbins, 1987). Nuclear families are important, but the tribal community also acts as a safety net, assuming a great deal of responsibility for the welfare of its individual members. Many fathers actively care for their own children along with the mothers and serve as father substitutes for children whose fathers have died or deserted the family (Staples & Mirandé, 1980; Carson et al., 1990).

How an individual behaves, in both positive and negative ways, reflects upon the individual's family and tribe (Carson et al., 1990). The group is in part collectively liable for the transgressions of its individual members, so the group provides a collective conscience and consciousness that emphasize individual responsibility. Respect for elders is common among Native American tribes, and grandparents often hold a unique position, helping to pass on cultural values and beliefs to their grandchildren and educating the young about the physical, social, and spiritual world. Social shame (that is, embarrassment) is a common tool for disciplining children. In general, physical punishment is not encouraged or condoned. Parents usually praise their children only for special accomplishments. The young are not socialized to expect praise, and it is not given lightly (Burgess, 1980).

A number of tribes stress marriages based not only on an attraction between two people but on the consensus of their relatives and the tribal community (Medicine, 1981). This approach to marriage recognizes the fact that an individual marries not only another individual but also that person's family and cultural community. Research suggests that these officially sanctioned marriages are more stable than those not recognized by the couple's family members or the tribe (Stauss, 1986).

The bilingual childrearing seen in some tribes and families is also identified as a strength of Native American families (Carson et al., 1990). Although most Native Americans learn English for survival in a White-dominant culture, they often find strength in sharing their own common language. The family strengths and culturally adaptive patterns of Native Americans deserve more extensive study in the years ahead (Carson et al., 1990).

Issues in Cross-Cultural Family Studies

Cross-cultural family studies tend to focus on two interrelated questions. First, how are families in the United States different from those in other parts of the world? Second, how are they similar? At first glance, people are often struck by the obvious differences between family cultures. Clothing styles, food preferences, religious beliefs, housing, music, education—all these aspects of culture vary from one society to another. When visiting a new culture, people often look for the differences between it and their own culture. Eventually, they also begin to see the similarities. When learning about another culture, then, the key is to emphasize similarities rather than differences.

Cross-cultural family studies focus on how particular cultural contexts influence a wide variety of issues: family values and behaviors, courtship patterns and weddings, marital and parent-child communication, power and gender roles, work and the family, ethical and religious values, childrearing patterns, sexuality, the role of grandparents and the extended family, and the role people outside the immediate family play in helping families in crisis.

Ethnocentrism

We are all ethnocentric to some extent; we see others through unique lenses that are shaped by our own culture. **Ethnocentrism** is the assumption that one's own culture is the standard by which other cultures should be judged. Our ethnocentricity influences the extent to which we judge other people, families, and cultures to be similar to or different from us. Tolerance of the traditions and values of other cultural and ethnic groups is the first step in transcending our overconcern with human differences. Understanding other ways of looking at life and the world around us can lead to genuine, mutual appreciation among people of different backgrounds.

Related to the issue of ethnocentrism is what anthropologists have called *perspective*. When one looks at a society from the outside, or from an **etic perspective,** one sees its characteristics in isolation rather than as they relate to the

The movie *Do the Right Thing*, directed by Spike Lee, reveals the absurdity—and the reality—of ethnic hatred and violence in the United States. In the movie, escalating arguments among ethnic groups lead to violence that foreshadows the real-life Los Angeles riot of 1992.

structure of the society as a whole. On the other hand, when one looks at a society from the inside, or from an **emic perspective,** one analyzes behaviors in terms of the internal structural elements of the society. The etic perspective tends to focus on and exaggerate differences, whereas the emic perspective makes it easier to see similarities between cultures.

Family researchers attempt to combine these two perspectives, recognizing the differences between cultures but also trying to identify similarities. Researchers from one culture can never completely discard their personal lenses. They can, however, try to become more open to new ideas and behaviors by submerging themselves in another culture, even learning that culture's language and living within that culture.

Racism

Racism is closely related to ethnocentrism and may even be a by-product of it. All the various "isms" tend to distance human beings from each other by accentuating differences and ignoring fundamental similarities, which in turn leads to tension and conflict. **Racism** develops when the most powerful group in a society creates an elaborate mythology (a set of beliefs that grossly distort reality) about a minority group. These prejudices often endure because of the need of the dominant group to feel superior to others.

Racist myths focus on a wide variety of issues. The minority group may be said to lack intelligence, eat strange foods, play weird music, be extremely violent and dangerous, or take dreaded drugs. The men of the minority group are often reputed to be sex starved, lusting after the women of the majority group. These fears are powerful and can increase prejudice and discrimination against minority-group members.

In sheer numbers, a minority group may actually outnumber the majority. For example, African Americans outnumber Whites in many counties in the South and in Washington, D.C.

Because minority-group members are often the victims of prejudice and discrimination, they may develop prejudices against the "other" group. Unfortunately, this reduces both groups to the charge of stereotyping. In effect, "We have met the enemy, and they are us."

Spike Lee did a fine job of portraying hatred in his film *Do the Right Thing*, which focuses on three groups who have experienced discrimination. In the climactic scene, an argument among African Americans, Korean Americans, and Italian Americans ends in a neighborhood riot. The scene is both stunningly funny in the grotesqueness of the combatants as they display their prejudices and also terrifying in its potential for being realized. Lee holds a mirror up to society, but what we see is not appealing. Indeed, a great deal of progress has been made in improving the rights of various minorities in the United States, but one does not have to look far to see examples of the dark undercurrent of bigotry that still stains the fabric of American society.

Challenges for Ethnic Families

Ethnic families in the United States face many challenges. Among them are intercultural marriage, the issue of assimilation, and relationships between men and women and between parents and children. Ethnic families do not experience the "advantages of being in the majority" that Whites in the predominant culture do (Box 3.8).

Marriage Outside the Group

In many countries throughout the world, marriage is seen primarily as an agreement between two families. An alliance through marriage between two successful families can enhance the power, prestige, and well-being of all the members of both families. In this sense, one marries not just an individual but also that person's family.

Because American culture stresses individuality, the importance of a good "fit" between families is often overlooked, and individuals who wish to marry often purposely ignore advice from family members. Sometimes that advice is based on ignorance of the proposed partner's personal strengths and/or on prejudice toward the cultural group from which the proposed partner comes. The greater the differences between the two families, the more likely the chance for conflict.

As our society becomes more ethnically diverse, marriage across ethnic groups has increased and, in turn, expanded ethnic diversity. Asian Americans have the highest rate of **intercultural marriage**—marriage between people from two different cultural or ethnic groups—of all U.S. groups. The rate of intercultural marriage is 34% among Japanese Americans, 31% among Korean Americans, and 16%

BOX 3.8

The Advantages of Being in the Majority

If you're a member of the predominant culture in any society, there are innumerable benefits that accrue to you. You receive these benefits every day of your life, regardless of whether you worked for them—and, thus, "deserve" them—or didn't do anything at all to gain them. They are a birthright, like being born into a wealthy family.

If you're a member of the majority culture, you take these benefits for granted. In fact, you hardly ever think about them. One of the few times they come to mind is when members of a minority express their desire to have the same benefits. When this happens, the response of the majority culture member is relatively predictable: the majority culture is likely (1) to feel a bit guilty and ashamed and want to share these advantages with the minority culture, (2) to deny that this is the case and refuse to listen, or (3) to get outright angry and defensive.

We're not just targeting American culture here; we believe this is a cross-cultural phenomenon. Many countries throughout the world have a dominant culture. The dominant culture does not necessarily have to comprise the largest population, but it does hold most of the power.

As one cynic observed, the group that has the most guns dictates which language people speak in the society. Basically, the dominant culture creates rules, customs, and agencies that best serve the needs of the dominant culture. Some people might argue that this is only natural: if there are more of your particular group, or if your particular group is in command, you will almost without thinking create a world good for your group.

The problem with this thinking, of course, is that most societies in the world are not composed of only one culture but a collection of diverse cultures. To favor one culture over another is simply unfair. Minority cultures—that is, those who do not hold the most power—rarely ask that the majority culture change completely to accommodate them. Rather, members of minority cultures generally tend to ask for a more level playing field, in addition to respect, sensitivity, and consideration—the basic rights that members of the majority culture also demand. Only when minority cultures feel pushed up against the wall do they demand a revolution, and this usually happens when the dominant culture has turned a deaf ear on their feelings.

What, in essence, are we talking about here? If you're a member of the majority culture:

- People speak the same language you speak.

- The educational system is patterned after your ways of thinking and honors your history, your beliefs, and your values.

- The job market is more open to you because you are the "right" color, gender, religion, sexual orientation, political affiliation, or social class, and you don't have a disability that makes the majority culture uncomfortable.

- People will not discriminate in renting an apartment to you or selling you a house in their neighborhood.

- The laws, the police, and the courts all are sensitive to your cultural values and tend to deal with you in a relatively open-minded fashion.

- Religious and spiritual values of the culture are ideals that you can agree and live with.

- Music, literature, movies, and art reflect your tastes and values.

The list of advantages accruing to those in the majority culture is almost endless. What advantages can you add to this list?

among Chinese Americans. African Americans and Latinos have the lowest rates of intercultural marriage, at 2% and 12%, respectively (S. M. Lee & Yamanaka, 1990).

Family therapists have questioned whether some young people "fall in love" with someone from another cultural group as a way of rebelling against their parents. Such a strategy may work in the short run, but it is a weak foundation upon which to build a long-term relationship. Movie director Spike Lee points out in his film *Jungle Fever* that some intercultural partners may be attracted to each other's unique cultural mystiques. In the movie, the lead male character says that his affair with a White woman was a matter of simple curiosity: "You were curious about Black. . . . I was curious about White." After filming the movie, the actress who played the female lead told an interviewer that "within the cast there were some very, very different points of view about whether or not interracial love was acceptable or healthy" (Kroll, 1991, pp. 44–45).

When same-culture and intercultural marriages are compared statistically, intercultural couples are somewhat more likely to divorce. Lack of support from parents and other family members probably contributes to this higher divorce rate. This is not to say that intercultural marriages cannot succeed, but couples in such marriages do need the support of their family and friends.

Black-White Marriages

Black-White relationships and marriages are not common among Americans; in 1997, out of a total of 56 million married couples in the United States, only about 450,000 consisted of one Black partner and one White partner (U.S. Bureau of the Census, 1997). One study found that Black-White couples experienced more negative reactions and discrimination than either African American couples or European American couples.

To gather information about Black-White couples, Paul Rosenblatt, Terri Karis, and Richard Powell (1995) conducted a study of 21 multiracial couples (*multiracial* was the term the couples preferred). Terri Karis, a White woman, and Richard Powell, a Black man, who are themselves a couple, interviewed all of the couples in the study. In 16 of the 21 couples, the man was African American; in the other 5 couples, the woman was African American. This percentage is similar to the national sample. Of the 21 couples, 19 were married, and most were between the ages of 20 and 50. The couples were generally well educated.

Most of these multiracial couples said they became interested in each other because they were so alike in values and interests. Similar findings were reported in a 1993 study of 29 Black-White couples (Kouri & Lasswell, 1993). Most of these couples said they had much in common and felt like "soul mates."

Most of the multiracial couples in the Rosenblatt, Karis, and Powell study experienced opposition from the family of the White partner. Fathers and other kin are often more opposed than mothers. These families typically will not discuss with other family members or friends that their White daughter is involved with a Black man. The White partner often grows distant from family members who are not supportive of the relationship.

Rosenblatt et al. (1995) identified six principal objections to the multiracial relationship raised by family members of the White partner. First, they worried about disapproval from other family members, friends, and society in general. Second, they expressed concern about the safety and well-being of their adult child. Third, they pointed to the alleged clannishness of African Americans. Fourth, they worried about problems the children of the couple might have. Fifth, they expressed concern about the likelihood of a poor economic future for the couple. And sixth, they foresaw other problems that were often not specified. The White partners' reaction to the parents' opposition was often complicated; some said their feelings were a "blend of pain, anger, frustration, desperation, [and] determination" (p. 81).

In contrast, the African American family was often more accepting of the multiracial relationship than was the White family (Kouri & Lasswell, 1993). The mother was generally more accepting than the father and other kin. About half of the Black families did have some objections, including concerns that their child was marrying outside the group, perhaps marrying "down" in terms of education or status, or "sleeping with the enemy."

All the multiracial couples hoped that they would not experience racism. They hoped others would see them as any other couple and not relate to them on the basis of racial stereotypes. One person said, "I want the larger society to know that interracial relationships or not, people are people. All races of people require the same thing . . . we all need love and affection" (Rosenblatt et al., 1955, p. 278). Another person felt that "interracial couples . . . aren't good or bad because of being interracial. . . . It is what that relationship becomes that determines its goodness or badness, but it has nothing to do with the complexion of the people" (p. 281). And a third person suggested that the biggest difference between partners in a Black-White marriage was not their race but their gender—something that most couples have to deal with, no matter what their skin color (pp. 294–295).

Relationships Between Men and Women

Regardless of nationality or cultural background, friction occurs between men and women in intimate relationships. Although couples strive for mutual love and caring, different socialization processes and biological inheritances produce misunderstanding and conflict. Women in developed countries, due to greater education and more employment opportunities outside the home, tend to have more options. If they are dissatisfied with their marriage and can support themselves, they are not as likely to stay in the marriage. Women in rural areas and in developing countries have fewer options, even though they may be just as unhappy as their divorcing counterparts in developed countries. As a result, divorce rates tend to be higher in industrialized, urban-oriented societies around the world and lower in less-developed, agrarian societies. But the lower divorce rates in the more rural societies do not necessarily indicate happier marriages.

Relationships Between Parents and Children

Children often develop into adults much like their own parents. In the process of growing up, however, children and parents often experience much conflict. The younger generation strives to create a relatively independent life, and the older generation tries to maintain control of the children. These struggles are played out in most cultures around the world. Family power structures in various cultures seem to change gradually over time, as societies move from agriculturally oriented economies to industrialized economies. In an agriculturally oriented family, the father, who is responsible for making sure the farm runs smoothly, has more control over his children. In the city, the father's influence lessens, and the influence of others (peers, school) increases. Rural societies generally emphasize respect for the authority of the dominant males. In more modern societies, the rights of the individual receive more weight because the family is more likely to succeed if all its members become well educated and find good jobs.

When a family moves from one culture to another, parent-child relationships can be especially strained, as the youngsters struggle to fit into the new culture and inevitably lose touch with past traditions. Nicole, a 35-year-old woman who married an American and emigrated to the United States from France, explains why it is important for their children, born in France but being raised in the United States, to be able to speak not only English but her native language as well:

> "Of course, they need to know English. They're going to end up being Americans. That's obvious. We aren't going back to France to live, only to visit.
>
> "It's hard for them. They speak English in school and in the neighborhood, but in the home we speak French. They get confused sometimes and mix languages. Sometimes the neighbor kids tease them about it. It's especially difficult for Jared, our son, but Emily is doing great. I think they'll both catch on and see why it's important in the long run.
>
> "I want them to appreciate their roots, to remember the wonderful civilization they come from. And, most important, I want them to know me, their mother. I live in the United States but probably always will be French deep down, because that's where I grew up. I can't help it. That's home. The language of emotion, the language of love is your native language. How can I show my true emotions, my true love for my children if they cannot understand my French? How can they really know me?"

It will be a delicate balancing act for the family to maintain connections to both French and American cultures, but the benefits of such an accomplishment can far outweigh the difficulties.

Assimilation, Acculturation, or Segregation

Newcomers to any society face a difficult set of choices: Should they swiftly reject their former life and the culture from which they came? Should they downplay their ethnic origins in an effort to fit the mainstream view? Or should they build their own ethnic enclave and try to create a safe microworld that reflects their cultural heritage? These questions are extremely difficult to answer, and minority-group members often disagree on how to proceed. Some families are torn apart by controversies of this nature.

There are three important processes that help explain what happens when a cultural group from another country encounters the dominant culture of the new country. **Assimilation** is the process in which old cultural traits and values are relinquished and replaced by those of the dominant culture. **Acculturation** is the process whereby cultural traits and values from one ethnic group become intermeshed with those of the dominant culture. **Segregation** is the process in which an ethnic group isolates itself or is forced into isolation within the dominant culture. All three of these processes can occur in an interactive way as a family adapts to living in another culture.

Ethnic identity is more a social construction than a biological fact. The children in this family are of mixed Anglo and Asian heritage; their ethnic identity depends not on their physical characteristics but on the tradition within which they are being raised.

Members of the majority culture whose families have been in the United States for two, three, or more generations sometimes do not understand why immigrants are hesitant about assimilation—adopting the values of the dominant culture. But it is clear that immigrants are in a difficult psychological position. They see and are attracted by the strengths of American culture, especially its abundance of economic resources. But they also see the weaknesses of American culture—materialism, competitiveness, wasteful exploitation of the natural world, a fast-paced and often impersonal existence. Immigrants are in some ways in a better position to see America's strengths and weaknesses than are Americans, for they have another culture with which they can compare this one.

Appreciating Diversity

Understanding American families with their wide-ranging cultural variations is challenging. Trying to understand families around the world is probably even more difficult, given both the closed nature of family life and the greater degree of cultural variations worldwide. Nevertheless, it is useful for all of us to learn to appreciate diversity.

One way to increase our appreciation of diversity is to seek out opportunities to talk with people who have ethnic backgrounds different from our own. Sharing feelings about one's cultural heritage with someone from another ethnic group can be a mutually rewarding experience, an opportunity to learn more about others and their unique cultures.

Summary

- Kin relationships—the structure of marital and family relationships—vary considerably across ethnic and cultural groups.

- Although a great deal of diversity exists both within and across cultural and ethnic groups, there are also common family strengths. Strong families share the traits of cohesion, flexibility, and communication.

- The strengths of White families in the United States include commitment to the family, time spent together, ability to cope with stress, spiritual well-being, positive communication, and appreciation of and affection for other family members.

- The strengths of African American families include strong kinship bonds, strong work orientation, flexibility in family roles, strong motivation to achieve, strong religious orientation, and caring parenting.

- The strengths of Latino families include familism, high family cohesion, high family flexibility, a supportive kin network system, equalitarian decision making, and strong ethnic identity.

- The strengths of Asian American families include strong family orientation, filial piety, high value on education, well-disciplined children, extended family support, and family loyalty.

- The strengths of Native American families include an extended family system, traditional beliefs, high family cohesion, respect for elders, bilingual language skills, and a tribal support system.

- Cross-cultural family studies tend to focus on two broad, interrelated questions: How are families in various ethnic groups different? How are they similar?

- Such studies can be hindered by ethnocentrism and racism.

- Intercultural marriage can be challenging for families, but it can also be the source of considerable learning and personal growth.

- Male-female relationships and parent-child struggles are common issues in families from a variety of ethnic groups.

- The issues of assimilation, acculturation, and segregation must be faced by any new ethnic or cultural group.

Key Terms

cultural identity	polyandry	extended-family system
ethnic identity	monogamy	social system
race	pseudo-kin-group	belief system
coculture	lineage	stereotype
minority group	matrilineal society	prejudice
cultural group	patrilineal society	cross-cultural family study
ethnic group	bilateral descent	ethnocentrism
kinship	matriarchal group	etic perspective
nuclear family	patriarchal group	emic perspective
conjugal family system	equalitarian group	racism
consanguineal family system	matrilocal society	intercultural marriage
extended family	patrilocal society	assimilation
plural marriage	neolocal society	acculturation
polygamy	family cohesion	segregation
polygyny	family flexibility	
	family communication	

Activities

1. Make a list of your family's strengths. How do they compare with the strengths identified by family researchers?

2. For a week, observe and collect examples of racism in American society. Jot down in a notebook all the examples you find of prejudice and discrimination. Also collect examples of cooperation and appreciation expressed between different ethnic groups. Share these examples with others in a small-group discussion.

3. Telling racial and ethnic jokes is one of the primary ways we pass our prejudices from one generation to the next. Discuss how you feel about this type of humor and what effect it has in society.

Suggested Readings

Billingsley, A. (1992). *Climbing Jacob's ladder: The enduring legacy of African-American families.* New York: Simon & Schuster. A professor of family studies at the University of Maryland, College Park, argues that African American families are amazingly "strong, enduring, adaptive, and highly resilient."

Bornstein, M. H. (Ed.). (1991). *Cultural approaches to parenting.* Hillsdale, NJ: Erlbaum. Describes childrearing practices in a wide variety of cultures in the United States and around the world.

Bozett, F. W., & Hanson, S. M. H. (1991). *Fatherhood and families in cultural context.* New York: Springer. Discusses fatherhood from historical and cross-cultural perspectives, social class and fatherhood, religion and fatherhood, rural and urban influences on fatherhood, the future of fatherhood, and more.

Burton, M. G. (1995). *Never say nigger again! An antiracism guide for white liberals.* Nashville, TN: Winston. Provides excellent suggestions for Whites on becoming more sensitive to African Americans.

McAdoo, H. P. (Ed). (1993). *Family ethnicity.* Thousand Oaks, CA: Sage. Explores family ethnicity in five major cultural groups in the United States: African Americans, Latino Americans, Native Americans, Asian Americans, and Muslim Americans.

McAdoo, H. P. (Ed.). (1997). *Black families* (3rd ed.). Thousand Oaks, CA: Sage. Focuses on the diversity of Black families and balances the strengths of these families with the challenges they face.

Rosenblatt, P. C., Karis, T., & Powell, R. D. (1995). *Multiracial couples.* Thousand Oaks, CA: Sage. Describes the experiences of interracial couples, including opposition from both African American and White family members, racism in the workplace, and institutional racism.

Zambrana, R. E. (1995). *Understanding Latino families: Scholarship, policy, and practice.* Thousand Oaks, CA: Sage. Focuses on the strengths of Latino/Hispanic groups, the structural processes that impede their progress, and the cultural and familial processes that enhance their intergenerational adaptation and resiliency.

Understanding Marriage and Family Dynamics

There are a variety of perspectives or ways of describing marriage and family dynamics. These perspectives are like different lenses through which we can observe the various aspects of close relationships. Each perspective, or framework, is built upon different assumptions and has specific concepts that help define the relevant elements of each framework.

In this chapter we will describe the six major conceptual frameworks for describing marriage and family dynamics: the family system theory, the family strengths framework, the family development framework, the symbolic interaction framework, the social construction framework, and the feminist framework. We will also take a look at three major dimensions of couple and families dynamics that integrate many of the concepts from the six frameworks; these three central dimensions are cohesion, flexibility, and communication. To conclude, we will discuss the Couple and Family Map, which helps integrate and apply these more abstract frameworks and concepts to specific couple and family relationships.

Conceptual Frameworks for Studying Marriage and the Family

Before we begin exploring the conceptual frameworks, we will define some of the relevant concepts related to conceptual and theory development.

A **conceptual framework** is a set of interconnected ideas, concepts, and assumptions that helps organize thinking from a particular perspective. A **theory** consists of general principles that are composed of interrelated concepts and **hypotheses** (presumed relationships between variables). A **research study** is an investigation designed to test one or more specific hypotheses.

Most family professionals maintain that there are many ways of looking at families; thus they use ideas and principles from several conceptual frameworks to help them understand marriage and family life. This open-minded approach to learning and to life is often termed an "eclectic" approach, and most family researchers, family life educators, and family therapists subscribe to it.

However, professionals with an eclectic approach can sometimes be too open and accepting of contradictory ideas. This text encourages the reader to begin developing a personal set of principles and concepts that will help in understanding marriage and family life. For most family scientists, this pursuit of understanding is a lifelong task, and many find that their theoretical perspectives change with time.

Some family scientists maintain that human beings are unique and that it is therefore difficult to construct a broad conceptual framework that applies to all couples and to all families. This view has been labeled **idiographic,** meaning that it focuses on the individual or the unique. Professionals who lean in this direction are more interested in individual case studies and tend to have a clinical focus. On the other end of the theory spectrum, the **nomothetic** approach focuses on developing a theory that works for a great number of cases. Researchers using this approach try to develop a broader understanding of couples and families and to work toward a general theory. Each of these approaches has some value and usefulness, because every marriage and every family *is* unique and yet has much in common with others.

This text focuses on six conceptual frameworks that are currently considered valuable to family professionals: the family systems theory (or the family systems framework), the family strengths framework, the family development framework, the symbolic interaction framework, the social construction framework, and the feminist framework. The most popular of these perspectives is the *family systems theory*, which focuses on the family as an ongoing system of interconnected members. (Because it is a broad and comprehensive set of principles, this perspective is referred to more often as a theory than as a conceptual framework.) The *family strengths framework* is becoming more accepted because it highlights the positive aspects of couples and families rather than their problems. The *family development framework* looks at how couples and families change over time. The *symbolic interaction framework* has historically been valuable to family professionals because it examines how family members learn roles and rules in our society. The *social construction framework*, which is growing in popularity, maintains that our views as partners and family members are shaped by our social world and that each of us has a different life experience and therefore a unique view of our own close relationships. The *feminist framework* is increasingly important to the family field because it emphasizes the value of a woman's perspective on marriage and family life and on society.

The Family Systems Theory

According to the **family systems theory** (or the **family systems framework**), everything that happens to any family member has an impact on everyone else in the family because family members are interconnected and operate as a group, or **family system.** This approach to describing the family as a system has become very popular in both theory and practice, particularly with therapists working with couples and families who have problems.

Family therapist Carl Whitaker (1979) has commented that in a metaphorical sense "there are no individuals in the world—only fragments of families." In other words, individual human beings are inextricably tied to their families. How people think and behave is deeply influenced by family background, and people are best understood by understanding their families. From a family therapist's standpoint, an individual can most effectively change if his or her family also changes. If a family is in trouble, both parents and children need to become involved in the therapy.

Some people believe that a family systems approach has been a natural part of many cultures for thousands of years. Carolyn Attneave (1982), a psychology professor and Native American, believes that Native Americans have used family systems concepts and even broader approaches to healing for a long time. When an individual has a problem, not only the family but also the whole community is often involved in finding a solution, an idea echoed in the popular statement "It takes a whole village to raise a child." A family simply cannot do it all alone. Troubled families often live in troubled communities, and if individuals are to be well, the community must find a way to create health for all its members.

The family systems theory grew out of the general systems theory, a conceptual framework developed in the 1960s by Ludwig von Bertalanffy (1968). The **general systems theory,** a broad-based model used in a variety of fields, is a set of principles and concepts that can be applied to all types of systems, living and nonliving. The dictionary defines a **system** as (1) a set or arrangement of things so related or connected as to form a unity or organic whole and (2) a whole made of interacting parts.

Therapists working with troubled individuals over the years discovered through trial-and-error that working with the individual alone simply was not enough. A disturbed child might calm down and show evidence of increasing health when in a treatment center under the guidance of committed and sensitive professionals, but the same child was likely to revert to severely disturbed behavior when placed back with the family.

When a child has problems, there are often problems in the family system. For example, some family therapists believe that if there is a disturbed child in a two-parent family, a troubled marriage will likely be the root of the child's difficulties. Treating the child alone and ignoring the marriage relationship would be like replacing the motor in an automobile with an empty gas tank. The family systems framework helps therapists get to the root cause of the problem rather than simply treating symptoms.

Proponents of the family systems theory have expanded on ideas and terminology developed by general systems theorists, and family therapists use these ideas in their practice. Several concepts of the general systems theory are particularly relevant to family systems; we discuss these concepts next.

Multiple Levels   One of the most basic assumptions of the general systems theory is that systems are embedded within other systems. Whenever attention is focused on a given system, a **suprasystem** (a large system) and a **subsystem** (a smaller system) are usually also involved. In a couple, the suprasystem is the family and the subsystem consists of the two individuals. In a family, the suprasystem is the extended family and the subsystem is the couple or any other dyadic (two-person) unit, such as parent and child. Any system can be the focus of interest. That system is both embedded in other larger systems and made up of smaller systems.

Systems are both connected to and separated from other systems by **boundaries.** The notion of a boundary also implies a hierarchy of interconnected systems, each system larger than the one before it (Burr, Day, & Bahr, 1993; Day, Gilbert, Settles, & Burr, 1995; Goldenberg & Goldenberg, 1991).

Different tools and techniques are used to help focus on different system levels. A biologist might use a very powerful electron microscope to study DNA in a cell or a less powerful microscope to study the cell as a whole. Observational approaches might suffice when studying an entire animal or plant. By the same token, an astronomer could use a telescope to study the planets and stars, but acquiring more detailed information might require the use of a radio telescope or an orbiting satellite.

Human systems have many different levels that can be characterized in many different ways. These levels can be pictured as a set of concentric circles. For example, the smallest circle, at the center, would be the individual; encircling this, in graduated rings, would be the couple (a dyad, or two-person human system), the family, the local neighborhood (including businesses, schools, etc.), the town, the nation, the continent, the world, and so on. Thinking about human systems in this way is to take an ecological approach; **ecology** is the study of how all the organisms in a system relate to one another. The general systems theory assumes that all the concentric circles are connected to one another and that the people in

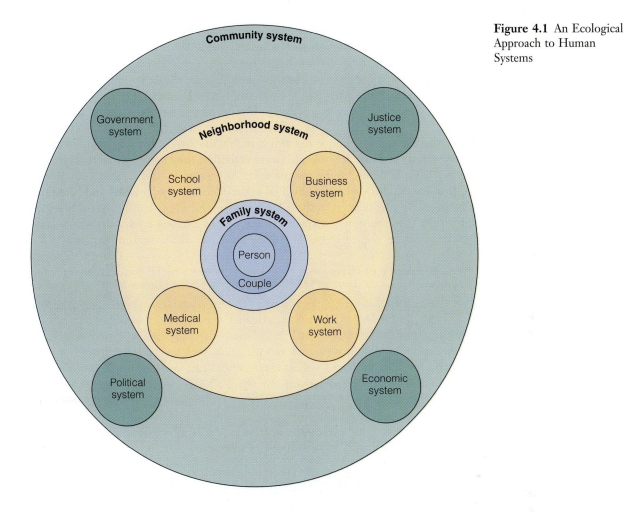

Figure 4.1 An Ecological Approach to Human Systems

each of the circles influence the people in the other circles—creating a human ecosystem (Figure 4.1). An individual family influences how the total community functions, and vice versa. Strong families help build strong communities, and strong communities support strong families. When trying to understand an individual family system, we need to consider the various system levels it influences and that influence it. Helping a middle-class, suburban family through a crisis can be a very different experience for a family therapist from helping a family living in an inner-city area or a poverty-stricken rural environment. Families do not function in a vacuum; they are part of larger systems.

Wholeness   The general systems theory includes **wholeness,** the concept that the whole is more than the sum of its parts. From a family systems perspective, the whole family is more than the total of all its individual members. You cannot know the family simply by knowing each person as an individual because you cannot predict how they will interact as a group (Day et al., 1995; Goldenberg & Goldenberg, 1991). For example, Carla, a student living in an apartment, has a certain identity related to her life at college and another identity back home with her family. An observer could study Carla very carefully in her college environment and come to a reasonably good understanding of what she is like, but when Carla goes home to visit her family for a holiday break, she becomes a different person in many ways during that time. She is transformed into a daughter, a granddaughter, a big sister, a little sister; she is part of her family in many more ways than she is while attending college away from home.

Family members regularly separate from the family to go to work, to school, or to activities with friends. Every member becomes a slightly different person outside the family and is a unique individual within the family. But when family members return from work, school, and other activities, they merge to some degree to become a whole family, and a unique entity is created by this fusion.

Just as a good cook takes individual herbs, spices, and vegetables and combines them to create a wonderful, zesty sauce, likewise, the whole family system is something more than the sum of its parts. In the case of a strong family, the whole family system can be argued to be something *greater* than the sum of its parts.

Interdependence of Parts   Another concept of the general systems theory is the **interdependence of parts:** The parts or elements of a system are interconnected in such a way that if one part is changed, other parts are automatically affected (Burr et al., 1993; Day et al., 1995). Visualize for a moment a mobile, an artistic creation suspended in midair, made up of many carefully balanced elements. Each element in the mobile is weighted and placed in such a way as to create not only an aesthetic effect but also a delicate system that can be easily set in motion by a slight ripple of wind or a soft touch. Anything stronger might knock it out of balance. Healthy families, in a sense, are like a mobile: Each member fits into the whole in a unique way and adds to the beauty of the whole. If one individual changes—for better or worse—the total creation is affected. Consider how one event changed the family in the following story:

> Julia was a single parent living with her two young children, Camille and Katy. Their life together was a hectic but satisfying round of school, work, family visits, and activities with friends. Last year Julia was involved in an auto accident and was seriously injured. She could neither work nor care for her children. The family's delicate balance was upset until Julia's mother, Eloise, her brother, Tim, her sister, Allison, and her best friend at work, Sheryl, all stepped in to help create a new sense of family balance.
>
> These four adults spent countless hours at the hospital, reassuring Julia and listening to her express her uncertainty and pain. They also worked out some new arrangements to make up for her absence. Camille and Katy temporarily moved in with Eloise. She took care of them, prepared their meals, made sure they had clean clothes for school, and took over many details of their lives. Tim, who lived nearby, drove Camille and Katy to and from school and took care of them afterward. Allison, who still lived at home, got them to bed at night and took them on outings on the weekends. Camille and Katy took on some new responsibilities themselves, like walking the dog and doing their homework without prompting. Sheryl kept things going at the office by taking on several of Julia's responsibilities herself.   *(Continued. . .)*

(. . .Continued)

After an initial period of confusion and difficulty, all these individuals became familiar with their new roles and proud of their new skills. Julia was hospitalized for several weeks and had physical therapy for several months, but eventually she regained her strength and her courage. When she returned home, the whole family celebrated. In the months that followed, she established a new balance with her children, assimilating the experiences they had all had since the accident. It was a different balance than before but one that evolved naturally out of the circumstances.

Like other families affected by sudden changes, Julia's family will probably never return to the way things were before the accident. But as Julia's case shows, the nuclear family, with the help of extended family members, is capable of establishing a more integrated family system.

Balance of Openness and Resistance to Change (Flexibility)   Systems exhibit both stability and the capacity to change, depending on the circumstances. A strong couple or family is like a flower in the wind; by being flexible and bending with the breeze, it endures. General systems theorists use the term **open system,** or **morphogenic system,** when referring to a system that is open to growth and change. A **closed system,** or **morphostatic system,** is one that has the capacity to maintain the status quo, thus avoiding change (Becvar & Becvar, 1993; Burr et al., 1993; Day et al., 1995). The key is figuring when to bend under pressure and when to stand firm, for both strategies are useful.

In their work, family therapists have discovered that many couples and families are highly resistant to change, even though they need to adapt to solve the problems they face. They are likely to want to maintain the status quo out of habit, lack of insight, or fear of something new. Jay Haley, a pioneer family therapist, argues that "when one person indicates a change in relation to another, the other will act upon the first so as to diminish and modify the change" (1972, p. 189).

As an example of a morphostatic system, consider the following story:

Ken and Katherine have been married for 15 years. Ken is an alcoholic, though he manages to hold on to his job as a floor supervisor at a printing plant. Ken has been having an extramarital affair with Winona, a co-worker at the plant, for 6 months. When Katherine discovers the affair, she tells Ken she is leaving him. He responds by begging for forgiveness and promising to give up the relationship with Winona. He wants to avoid divorce for a number of reasons: embarrassment at work, shame in his extended family, and financial consequences. Besides, although the thrill is gone from the marriage, he and Katherine have a long history together, and she is a good mother to their three children.

Katherine is skeptical about Ken's promises. She tells him that she wants him to give up drinking as well. He says he can control his drinking and just drink "socially." He doesn't really need to go "cold turkey," he argues. Katherine remains skeptical; she has heard such arguments many times before.   *(Continued. . .)*

> *(. . .Continued)*
>
> In spite of her skepticism, however, Katherine decides to forgive Ken, as she has before, and to stay. She genuinely loves him, even though she hates his drinking and, now, his seeing other women. And he provides a good income for her and the children. Katherine also fears being on her own, both socially and financially. She dreads the thought of going back into the workplace after so many years at home. Whatever she has now, she feels, is better than what she would have as a divorced mother of three.

By failing to deal openly and effectively with their relationship problems, Katherine and Ken are beginning a free fall into despair. They are an example of a morphostatic family system, unable or unwilling to change. A morphogenic system, one open to growth and change, might have been able to prevent such a scenario.

The family systems framework assumes that systems operate on a continuum from extreme morphostasis to extreme morphogenesis. In a healthy system, there is a balance between these extremes. The couple or family needs to be open to change, but not to the point of being rootless or chaotic. Conversely, it needs to be centered and stable, but not to the point of being rigid.

Balance of Separateness and Connectedness (Cohesion)   Couples and families need to find a balance between their separateness as individuals and connectedness as a system. The dynamics that help systems maintain this separateness-connectedness balance are the opposing forces of centrifugal and centripetal interactions. **Centrifugal interactions** tend to push family members apart, thereby increasing separateness; **centripetal interactions** pull family members together and increase family closeness (Stierlin, 1972).

Family therapists have found that a family crisis can spark both centripetal and centrifugal interactions. Faced with a death, one family may pull together and come out stronger as a result of the loss, whereas another may find itself torn apart by the events. The first family resolves to hold on to each other, communicate about feelings, and help each other. These centripetal interactions strengthen the bonds of love and concern. The members of the second family are afraid, cannot talk with one another, and attempt to deal with the death as individuals. They separate completely from the family and look for comfort outside it, or they bury themselves in personal despair, refusing to talk with anyone.

Family therapists agree that a healthy balance of separateness and connectedness works best for families in crisis. In the face of death, family members can draw on each other's strengths and skills for comfort and at the same time seek out positive people in the community who can be growth-enhancing for the family as a whole. If family members choose to go their separate ways as a result of the crisis, the likelihood of a positive outcome for the family as a whole lessens considerably.

Feedback Within the System (Communication)   Another basic principle of the general systems theory is that communication in the system is essential. No matter how hard one might try, one simply cannot *not* communicate (Becvar &

Many cultures embrace a form of family and community life that reflects what theorists think of as family systems. Among many Native American tribes, for example, significant life events are marked with community-wide ceremonies, and individual problems are considered problems that can only be solved within the context of the group.

Becvar, 1993). Even if we completely withdraw from our family, we are communicating an important message: that the family is not a safe, healthy, or happy place to live.

Systems provide information to their components on how the various parts of the system are functioning. Family systems function successfully when important information is regularly exchanged among the members. General systems theorists talk about information feedback loops, which can be either positive or negative (Burr et al., 1993; Goldenberg & Goldenberg, 1991). **Positive feedback** in families is intended to create change, whereas **negative feedback** is designed to minimize change and keep things the same. Feedback can come either from family members or from people outside the family. Positive and negative do not connote value judgments or indicate whether a change is good or bad but rather whether change occurs in the system or not. For example, Sandy suggests that the members of her family exchange jobs around the house to add variety and give everyone a better understanding of what the various jobs entail. If Sandy's family members accept this idea and change their routine, then Sandy's feedback to the system is considered positive; if not, it is considered negative.

In sum, balance and openness are key concepts in the family systems framework. Couples and families under stress sometimes pull inward and desperately try to prevent new information or people from coming into the system, even if these additions could be helpful. Perhaps these couples and families are simply in a state of emotional shock and are incapable of thinking openly and creatively for a while. Nonetheless, it is in every couple's and family's long-term best interest to find a dynamic balance between the need to maintain stability and the need to adapt successfully to change. Couples and families must also find a balance between the need to solve problems among themselves and to seek outside help.

The Family Strengths Framework

The **family strengths framework** focuses on how couples and families succeed rather than on why they fail. This perspective arose from the notion that strong families can serve as models for other families wanting to succeed. One advantage of the family strengths framework is that it tends to change the nature of what one finds in families. Simply stated, if one studies only problems, one finds only couple and family problems. Similarly, if researchers and therapists are interested in couple and family strengths, they have to look for them. When these strengths are identified, they can be the foundation for continued growth and change.

Family therapists and other counselors are finding the family strengths framework helpful in treating family problems. Many professionals have found that just solving problems is not enough. They need a model of healthy family development as a goal for troubled families to work toward. Identifying a family's strengths also boosts morale among family members.

> "In our child abuse treatment and prevention program here in Lincoln, we focus on the strengths of our families," Romney, a family therapist, explained. "This may surprise you, but it works really well. Sure, we also are aware that these families have lots and lots of problems. But we always try to remember their important strengths. A family I'm working with now is a good example: a mom and dad and three kids under age 7. Though they don't have much money and the little boy has severe health problems, they've got a lot going for them: They are resilient and can cope with a lot of difficulties; they are resourceful and creative; they love each other and are committed to their family. We use these strengths as a foundation to build on. We focus on their strengths and use these strengths to meet the challenges head on. *(Continued. . .)*

The family strengths framework focuses on the positive qualities of families. Apparent in this family are such strengths as warmth, caring, appreciation, affection, trust, commitment, and enjoyment of each other's company.

(. . .Continued)

"And it works. Instead of always looking at the problems, we accentuate the positive, and this gives the family a sense of optimism and courage. As a counselor I find myself being more optimistic about how much the family can accomplish with my help."

Perhaps the most extensive series of studies of family strengths were conducted by Nick Stinnett and his colleagues (DeFrain & Stinnett, 1992; Stinnett, Sanders, & DeFrain, 1981; Stinnett, Stinnett, DeFrain, & DeFrain, 1997). In over 20 years of study, the researchers have collected data on more than 16,000 families in every state of the United States and more than 25 countries around the world. Stinnett and his colleagues propose that six major qualities are commonly present in strong families, especially in Western industrial societies and in more developed countries (Box 4.1). These qualities are

- Commitment
- Appreciation and affection
- Positive communication
- Time together
- Spiritual well-being
- Ability to cope with stress

All these family strengths are interrelated, overlap to some degree, and interact. Appreciation and affection for one another make family members more likely to spend time together, and time together is enhanced by positive communication.

BOX 4.1

Qualities of Strong Families

Commitment	**Appreciation and Affection**
Trust	Caring for each other
Honesty	Friendship
Dependability	Respect for individuality
Faithfulness	Playfulness
Positive Communication	**Time Together**
Sharing feelings	Quality time in great quantity
Giving compliments	Good things take time
Avoiding blame	Enjoying each other's company
Being able to compromise	Simple good times
Agreeing to disagree	Sharing fun times
Spiritual Well-Being	**Ability to Cope With Stress**
Hope	Adaptability
Faith	Seeing crises as challenges and opportunities
Humor	Growing through crises together
Compassion	Openness to change
Shared ethical values	Resilience
Oneness with humankind	

Sources: Adapted from Stinnett & DeFrain (1985, p. 14); Olson (1996).

Communication enhances commitment, and commitment leads to spending more time together. A feeling of spiritual well-being gives people the confidence to weather a crisis, and the ability to cope with crises makes family members appreciate each other more. Family strengths are thus interconnected like a large, complex puzzle. Let's look at each strength in more detail.

Commitment   Members of strong families generally show a strong **commitment** to one another, investing time and energy in family activities and not letting their work or other priorities take too much time away from family interaction. "My wife and kids are the most important part of my life," one father said in describing commitment. Another noted that "what we have as a family is a treasure." Commitment does not mean, however, that family members stifle each other. "We give each other the freedom and encouragement to pursue individual goals," one wife noted. "Yet either of us would cut out activities or goals that threatened our time together."

Commitment includes sexual fidelity. Some of the people interviewed by the researchers admitted to having engaged in an extramarital affair earlier in the marriage. Some believed the affair precipitated a crisis that in the final analysis led to a stronger marriage. But marriages can change for the better without a crisis of such major proportions. "Being faithful to each other sexually is just a part of being honest with each other," one young woman noted. Honesty, indeed, is the best policy.

Appreciation and Affection   People in strong families care deeply for one another, and they let the others know this regularly. Many people, however, don't express **appreciation and affection** in their families. Consider the response of one spouse: "She cooked dinner every evening, but it never occurred to me to thank her for it. She doesn't thank me for going to work every day." Such an attitude is unfortunate, because expressing affection and giving and receiving sincere thanks foster a positive atmosphere and help people get along better. A pat on the back, a smile, or a hug builds a bond of caring. One member of a strong family explained it this way: "He makes me feel good about me and about us as a couple. Very few days go by without him saying something positive."

One strong family has developed an excellent technique for keeping the home a positive place: If a family member feels the need to criticize another member, the criticizer must maintain a ratio of ten positive strokes to one critical statement. "We criticize each other on occasion in our family," the father explained, "but we try to criticize with kindness. And we try to make sure that we express appreciation for something positive the person does at least ten times for each negative thing we say." Positive feelings tend to snowball. If Mom feels good about herself, she will be more likely to say kind things to Dad. And when Dad feels good, he is likely to be especially nice to the children.

People in dysfunctional families more often focus on the negative. Family therapist Herbert Otto calls these people "energy vampires," people who gain energy by feeding off the self-esteem and good feelings of others. They believe that by putting other people down they can build themselves up. The approach usually backfires, however, often producing only countercriticism.

Researchers have found that sexual behavior in strong marriages is often a form of expressing appreciation for each other. "Foreplay does not begin at 10:30 P.M. on Saturday night," one husband explained. "It begins when I take out the garbage on Wednesday morning, when I cook dinner on Friday night, and when I help Jeannie solve a problem at her work on Saturday afternoon." Sex is a natural way to express warm feelings for the partner. Another person reported, "The times when sex was best have been times when we've felt especially close and in tune with each other, when we'd solved a problem or when we were working on a project together."

Positive Communication   When people are asked to list the qualities they consider essential to a strong family, most list **positive communication,** yet many families don't spend much time talking to one another. Although successful families are often task-oriented, identifying problems and discussing how to solve them, family members also spend time talking with and listening to one another just to stay connected. Some of the most important talk occurs when no one is working at communication. Open-ended, rambling conversations can reveal important information. How does your teenager feel about sex? her grades? her future? When parents and children get comfortable with each other, important issues arise.

Communication does not always produce agreement in strong families. Family members have differences and conflicts, but they speak directly and honestly about them without blaming each other. They try to resolve their differences but may agree to disagree. Dysfunctional families, on the other hand, are either overly critical and hostile in their communication with each other or deny problems and avoid verbal conflict. Although verbal hostilities are not productive, neither is avoidance of problems.

Studies reveal that communication in healthy families has several important aspects. Members of strong families are extremely good at listening. "I'd much rather listen to other people talk," one father explained. Family members are also adept at asking questions, and they do not try to read one another's minds. Members of strong families understand that people's views of the world change.

Humor is another important aspect of healthy family communication. Strong families like to laugh. A study of 304 mothers, fathers, and teenagers revealed that humor is a valuable source of family strength. Wuerffel, DeFrain, and Stinnett (1990) reviewed the scientific literature on humor and found that humor can be used in many different positive and negative ways. Humor can reduce daily tension, facilitate conversations, express feelings of warmth and affection, lessen anxiety, point out mistakes made by others, and entertain. It can also help put others at ease and help maintain a positive outlook on life.

The study found positive correlations between the use of humor and how strong the families were based on their responses to a family strengths inventory. The stronger the family, the more likely they were to use humor to maintain a positive outlook on life, to entertain each other, to reduce tension, to express warmth, to put others at ease, to facilitate conversations, to lessen anxiety, and to help cope with difficult situations. The stronger families in the study reported negative effects, however, when humor was used to put down other family members. Put-downs and sarcasm were used less often by the stronger families.

The study concluded that families benefit from humor that points out the incongruous aspects of life—the inconsistent, bizarre, silly, illogical things that happen to people every day. Families, however, do not benefit from humor that places someone in a superior position or from sarcasm aimed at demeaning a family member. Sarcasm is often an attempt to mask anger; it is rarely used out of love.

Time Together   "What do you think makes a happy family?" a researcher asked 1,500 schoolchildren. Few replied that money or cars or fancy homes or television sets made a happy family. The most frequent response? A happy family is one that does things together and spends **time together.** Although the response seems simple enough, family therapists see many couples and families who haven't figured this out. "I don't have a lot of time with my family," many people like to say, "but I try to make it quality time."

Strong families spend time together. Whether it's a bedtime story or a picnic, the family activities that become the happiest memories are usually simple ones.

Happy memories result from quality time spent together: "I remember stories Mom and Dad told me when they tucked me into bed." "Going with Dad to work on the farm. I felt so important." "Singing together—we had an old piano, and I learned to play, and we would all sing corny old songs." "Vacation. We would go fifty miles to the lake and rent a cabin, and Dad would swim with us."

These happy memories share common threads. First, happiness often centers on activities that are shared as a family. Second, pleasurable time together often centers on simple activities that don't cost a lot of money. Strong families identified these popular family activities: meals together, house and yard chores, and outdoor recreation, including camping, playing catch and other yard games, canoeing, hiking, and picnicking.

Spiritual Well-Being Perhaps the most controversial finding of the family strengths researchers is the importance of religion or spirituality in strong families. Some families call this **spiritual well-being.** Others talk about faith in God, hope, or optimism about life. Some say they feel a oneness with the world. Others talk about their families in almost religious terms, describing the love they feel for one another as sacred. Others express these kinds of feelings in terms of ethical values and commitment to important causes.

Spiritual well-being can be the caring center within each individual that promotes sharing, love, and compassion. Spiritual well-being is the feeling or force that helps people transcend themselves. "I feel my family is a part of all the families of the world," said one respondent. Another important aspect of membership in a religious or spiritual group is the caring, supportive community it provides. When illness strikes, a baby is born, or an accident occurs, friends in the group are often quick to help each other (Stinnett et al., 1997).

Ability to Cope With Stress   Strong families are not immune to stress and crisis, but they are not as crisis-prone as dysfunctional families tend to be. Rather, they possess the **ability to cope with stress** effectively. Strong families are often successful at preventing troubles before they occur, but some stressors in life are inevitable. The best a family can do is to meet the challenge as efficiently as possible, minimizing its damage and looking for any growth opportunities in the process.

What are the most difficult family crises for strong families? Serious illness or surgery was cited as the toughest by 23% of adult respondents. A death in the family was next in order of frequency; 21% saw that as their most difficult crisis in the 5-year period preceding the study. The third most common form of crises were marital problems, most of which involved adult children, in-laws, or brothers and sisters. A child's unwanted pregnancy, delinquency, or poor adjustment in school was also occasionally listed (Stinnett et al., 1997).

Fully 96% of the strong families said they were successful in meeting these crises. Among the strategies strong families use to weather crises is pulling together. Each person, even a very young child, has a part to play in easing the burdens of the others. Additionally, strong families seek help if they cannot solve the problem themselves. Although this may surprise some people, members of strong families do get counseling in an attempt to learn better ways of coping with crisis. In contrast, truly troubled families often do not have the strength to admit they have troubles and to seek advice (Stinnett et al., 1997).

The Family Development Framework

Family development as a conceptual framework was originally designed to describe and explain the process of change in couples and families (Rodgers & White, 1993). Researchers and clinicians working from a **family development framework** are primarily interested in how partners and family members deal with various roles and developmental tasks within the marriage and family as they move through various stages of the life cycle. Table 4.1 lists those roles and the developmental tasks in a family that are both stressful and challenging. The family development framework assumes that the more efficient a family is at completing these tasks, the more successful the development of the various family members will be.

Evelyn Duvall, a major founder (with Reuben Hill) of the family development approach, has described some of the advantages of this framework (Duvall & Miller, 1985). For one thing, it focuses on development and change in individuals and the family over time. It also encourages attention to process. It approaches the family not as a static and unchanging group but as a dynamic system.

Some controversy surrounds the exact number of stages involved in the family life cycle. Duvall originally identified 8 stages; other family science professionals have identified 4 to 24 stages (Rodgers & White, 1993). The sequence of stages is clearest and easiest to apply when there is only one child in the family. The number of stages and the complexity of overlapping stages increase when there is more than one child or when the couple gets divorced and one or both partners remarry.

The family development framework has been very useful in describing family tasks; however, its static approach and its focus on stages of the family life cycle have resulted in its failure to address the complexity of today's family systems.

Table 4.1 Family Life Cycle Stages and Developmental Tasks

STAGE OF THE FAMILY LIFE CYCLE	POSITIONS IN THE FAMILY	FAMILY DEVELOPMENTAL TASKS
1. Married couple	Wife	Establishing a mutually satisfying marriage
	Husband	Adjusting to pregnancy
		Fitting into the kin network
2. Childbearing	Wife/mother	Having and adjusting to an infant
	Husband/father	Establishing a satisfying
	Infants	home for parents and infants(s)
3. Preschool	Wife/mother	Adapting to the needs of
	Husband/father	preschool children
	Daughter/sister	Coping with energy
	Son/brother	depletion and lack of privacy as parents
4. School	Wife/mother	Fitting into the
	Husband/father	community
	Daughter/sister	Encouraging children's
	Son/brother	educational achievements
5. Teenage	Wife/mother	Balancing freedom with
	Husband/father	responsibility
	Daughter/sister	Establishing postparental
	Son/brother	interests
6. Launching	Wife/mother/grandmother	Launching youth into
	Husband/father/grandfather	adulthood
	Daughter/sister/aunt	Maintaining a supportive
	Son/brother/uncle	home base
7. Middle-aged parents	Wife/mother/grandmother	Refocusing on marriage
	Husband/father/grandfather	relationship
		Maintaining kin ties with older and younger generations
8. Aging family members	Widow/widower	Coping with death and
	Wife/mother/grandmother	living alone
	Husband/father/grandfather	Selling the family home
		Adjusting to retirement

Source: Adapted from "Stages and Family Developmental Tasks" in *Marriage and Family Development* (6th ed.) by Evelyn Millis Duvall & Brent C. Miller. Copyright © 1985 by Harper & Row Publishers, Inc. Reprinted by permission of Addison Wesley Educational Publishers, Inc.

The Symbolic Interaction Framework

As the name indicates, the **symbolic interaction framework** focuses on symbols, which are based on shared meanings, and interactions, which are based on verbal and nonverbal communication. This framework helps explain how we learn through communicating with each other about various roles in our society. The family is seen as a unit of interacting personalities, which according to Ernest Burgess (Burgess & Wallin, 1943), explains the importance of family interaction in creating an ongoing group.

A **role** is the expected behavior of a person or group in a given social category, such as husband, wife, supervisor, or teacher. Every family member plays a variety of roles at different times. For example, a man can be a parent, spouse, manager at work, and coach of a baseball team. A woman can be a parent, spouse, manager at work, and chairperson of a fundraising committee. A young girl can be a daughter, student, and musician.

Roles are learned in society by **role taking,** the process whereby people learn how to play roles correctly by practicing and getting feedback from others. **Role making** involves creating new roles or revising existing roles. For example, as a couple's relationship changes from husband-led to a more equalitarian relationship, the partners need to change the way they interact with each other.

Some of the assumptions of symbolic interaction can help clarify the value of this framework for understanding family behavior (LaRossa & Reitzes, 1993). One assumption is that meaning arises in the process of interaction between people. Shared meaning helps people understand each other and learn how to play various roles. Another important concept is **definition of the situation,** developed by William Thomas: Each person subjectively interprets a given situation, and different people will interpret an interaction or situation in different ways. This helps explain why there are often different perceptions of a marriage; there can be "his" marriage and "her" marriage, as described by Jessie Bernard (1970).

Another assumption is that people learn about themselves and develop a self-concept based on their interaction with others. An early theorist, Charles Cooley (1864–1929), developed the concept of the **looking-glass self,** the idea that you learn about yourself based on the feedback you receive from others who are reacting to your behavior. In other words, your feelings about yourself are derived from how others react to you. Another important theorist was George Mead (1863–1931), who described how the self-concept emerges in childhood. The child plays out a certain role, which helps him or her learn to take the role of the generalized other—to understand and even predict the feelings of another person. This ability can be valuable in any situation because it enables a person to understand another's feelings.

The Social Construction Framework

According to the **social construction framework,** human beings are profoundly immersed in the social world; our understanding of this world and beliefs about this world are social products. Similar to the earlier thinking of the symbolic interactionists, social construction theorists argue that because the self is a product of social processes, individuality is most difficult to develop because we live in a social environment:

> We are born into and live within social settings, as members of particular social groups. Our identities are shaped over time through intersubjective experiences.

Recognition by others as a particular sort of person is a necessary part of identity formation. (Boughner, Davis, Spencer, & Mims, 1998, p. 5)

Or, in other words, "the unconstrained individual never existed anywhere" (McGowan, 1991, p. 216). One's self, one's persona, is heavily influenced by the social processes continually ebbing and flowing around the individual.

Social construction theories, which are compatible with the postmodernist and multicultural intellectual movements, are gaining attention today. **Postmodernism** has been described as a "thoroughgoing skeptical doubt in regard to questions of truth, meaning and historical interpretation" (Norris, 1990, p. 29). Rather than assuming that human reason should be or is the prime mover in developing our views of the world, postmodernist thinking emphasizes the notion that we live in a complex world and that multiple perspectives or "truths" are in constant interaction and conflict with each other. In a postmodern era, then, there is no objective, universal truth that can be seen, once and for all, and readily agreed upon; rather, there is a collection of subjective truths shaped by the particular subcultures in which we live. These multiple subjective truths are constantly competing for our attention and allegiance.

When we look at the world, we are looking through a lens colored by our own beliefs and values, which we have developed in our own particular social worlds. Any "truth statement" is a statement about the observer as well as about what is being observed (Gergen, 1982, 1985, 1991; Watzlawick, 1984). The various perspectives on life we encounter have been called *knowledge-positions*. When one knowledge-position gains more power than the others in a particular culture, it becomes dominant and its adherents sometimes refer to it as the truth with a capital *T.* Traveling around the world, however, we find that there are innumerable truths from country to country; even within a particular country or particular family there are many different brands of truth.

From a postmodernist perspective, a dominant truth in a particular cultural group is simply the most popular and widely accepted story or narrative explanation about the way life is or should be—nothing more and nothing less. This story serves two purposes: to reinforce and maintain the power and cohesiveness of the particular group and to eliminate or minimize the stories and explanations of competing groups.

But because this story or truth or knowledge-position is socially constructed, as society changes over time and countless new influences emerge, the story continuously evolves: "The truth we see is a negotiated rather than a discovered one" (Sprey, 1990, p. 22).

From an individual family's perspective, the truth about who the family is and what the family does can change as time passes. A troubled family can learn how to create a new, more positive story about who they are and where their family is going. Narrative therapy, which has developed out of social constructionist and postmodern thinking, seeks to develop a new story for the individual and the family that works better than the old approach (White & Epston, 1990). The family, as storyteller, relates the current perspective on reality that the family holds. In addition, the family therapist, in concert with the family members, helps to develop a new narrative, or story, that helps the family meet its goals in a more effective manner.

It has been pointed out that current narrative therapies have roots going back to Freud (Reeder, 1992). Indeed, all forms of therapy are, in essence, narrative therapies:

> Whatever you are doing, or think you are doing, as therapist or client can be understood in terms of telling and re-telling stories. Yet there is no "narrative therapy," there is no way of doing this. To present "narrative therapy" as a new brand-name product in the therapeutic marketplace is to misunderstand what this is all about. . . . If there is any common ground among narrative therapies, it lies in the intention to give the client every opportunity to tell his or her story, to really listen to these stories, and to allow space for the telling of new or different stories. (McLeod, 1997, p. i)

Psychotherapy, then, "is primarily a special kind of conversation that elicits clients' strengths, competencies, and solutions." The therapist's role is that of "an expert in creating conversations that reveal clients' expertise and empower them to change" (Gilligan, 1993, p. 2).

Likewise, using a social constructionist and postmodernist mode of thinking, a troubled society, through the long and arduous process of public debate and policy making, can construct a new explanation about what it values and identify an alternative direction in which it will move so that the story of the society can have a more positive ending. For example, the feminist framework (discussed in the following section) seeks to change our society's dialogue about the relationship between men and women, making it possible for individuals to sever the gender-role bonds that constrain them, if they so choose.

Finally, from a social constructionist and postmodernist point of view, this textbook represents not necessarily the truth about marriage and family today but rather the perspective of two family scholars who see the world through particular conceptual lenses and whose worldviews are shaped by the unique sociocultural context in which they live. The articles and books we choose to quote in this textbook and the personal comments we make all reflect the social environment that has heavily influenced us.

The Feminist Framework

Central to the **feminist framework** is the notion that women are exploited, devalued, and oppressed and that society should commit to empowering women and changing their oppressed condition (Osmond & Thorne, 1993; A. J. Walker & Thompson, 1984). Although the roots of the feminist movement were evident in earlier years, a wave of feminist activity began with the publication of Betty Friedan's best-selling book *The Feminine Mystique* (1963). Friedan argued that women need a more active voice in decisions that affect them and society. More recently, Friedan (1985) has proposed ways to free women from the burden of guilt they often feel because they are unable to adequately balance motherhood and a career outside the home.

Feminist theories have a common interest in understanding the subordination of women with the goal of changing it (Osmond & Thorne, 1993). Feminists assume that women's experiences are central, not less important than those of men, and that gender must be explicitly used as a central focus. **Gender** is defined as the learned behaviors and characteristics associated with being male or female in a particular culture. Feminist theories examine gender differences and how gender-based distinctions legitimize power differences between men and women.

Feminists have also challenged the definition of family that is based on traditional roles. They see the family as a dynamic, changing, and open system that does not restrict roles and opportunities. They have criticized the "structural/functional framework," which prescribed the roles of males and females. Parsons and Bales (1955) assumed that the family was most functional if the male played the **instrumental role,** being in charge of tasks, and the wife played the **expressive role,** being nurturing. Feminists maintain that both men and women can play both roles. This perspective provides couples with more flexibility because both members can play roles based on their unique skills and interests.

Even though some men today are offended and threatened by feminist thinking, feminism may have certain benefits for both men and women in family relationships. It encourages men to express their feelings, to share wage-earning responsibilities, and to focus less on their careers and more on their children. For men, the pressure of being the only wage earner is reduced when both partners are working outside the home. At the same time, working outside the home helps women to enjoy an identity separate from their role within the family. It also provides them with independent economic security. Sharing the responsibility for childrearing allows men to participate in their children's development and women to pursue professional and personal interests. When work and power are shared, both partners have more opportunity to develop their full potential.

Many feminists propose that women act in anticipation of future problems by making specific job and career plans. Social and economic realities dictate that the "homemaker" option is no longer available for many women. As difficult as it is, most woman will need to build both a career and a family at the same time.

Women's and men's roles continue to converge in American society, and distinctions between male and female activities are blurring. As this convergence continues, women and men will find more ways to work together. Betty Friedan (1985) has argued that the feminist frontier now is the family and that "the problem is how to juggle work, love, home, and children."

Although the women's rights movement has a long history in the United States, Betty Friedan's *The Feminine Mystique* triggered the wave of feminist sentiment and awareness that continues today. Friedan gave voice to the dissatisfaction felt by a generation of women whose role in life was confined to that of homemaker.

Major Dimensions of Couple and Family Systems

There is considerable agreement among theorists who have studied couples and families that the dimensions of cohesion, flexibility, and communication are central to understanding relationship dynamics. As indicated in Table 4.2, over 10 theorists have independently developed concepts related to the dimensions of cohesion, flexibility, and communication. Although the descriptive terms vary from theorist to theorist, the majority fall under the three dimensions of relationships that we will now describe in more detail.

Cohesion in Couples and Families

Cohesion is a feeling of emotional closeness with another person. Four levels of cohesion can be described in couple and family relationships: disengaged,

Table 4.2 Family Theorists' Descriptions of Major Family-System Dimensions

THEORIST	COHESION	FLEXIBILITY	COMMUNICATION	OTHER

Barnhill (1979)	Mutuality
	Clear parent-child
	    boundaries
	Individuation
		Flexibility versus
		    rigidity
		Clear roles
			Clear communications	

Beavers and
    Hampson (1990)
	Centripetal/Centrifugal
	Closeness
	Parent coalition
	Autonomy
		Adaptability
		Egalitarian power
		Goal-directed
		    negotiation
		Ability to resolve
		    conflict
			Clarity of expression
			Range of feelings
			Openness to others
			Empathic
			Understanding	

Billingsley (1986)	Strong family ties			Strong religious
				    orientation
				Educational
				    aspirations/
				    achievements

Curran (1983)	Togetherness Respect and trust Shared leisure Privacy valued Shared mealtime	Shared responsibility Family rituals	Communication Affirmation of each other	Religious love Humor/play

Epstein, Bishop,
    Ryan, Miller,
    and Keitner (1993)
	Affective involvement	Behavior control	Communication	

Kantor and Lehr (1974)	Affect	Power		

Krysan, Moore,
    and Zill (1990)
	Commitment to family
	Time together
	Encouragement of
	    individuals
		Ability to adapt
		Clear roles
			Communication
			Expressing
			    appreciation
				Religious
				    orientation
				Social
				    connectedness

J. M. Lewis (1989)	Strong marriage
	Family closeness
	Encouragement of
	    autonomy
		Shared power
		Good at problem
		    solving
		Openness to change
			Express feelings
			Good communication
				Positive values

Olson, McCubbin,
    et al. (1989)
	Strong marriage
	High family cohesion
		Good family flexibility
		Effective coping with
		    stress and crisis
			Positive couple
			    and family
			    communication	

D. Reiss (1981)	Coordination	Closure		

Stinnett, Stinnett,
    DeFrain, and
    DeFrain (1997)
	Commitment
	Time together
		Ability to cope with
		    stress and crisis
		Spiritual well-being
			Communication
			Appreciation and
			    affection	

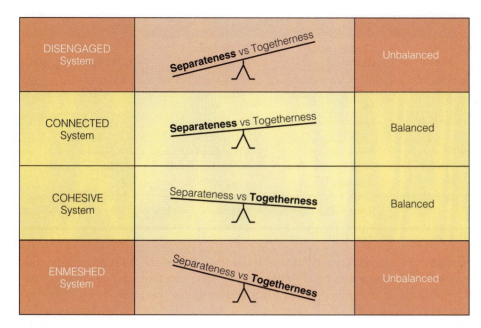

Figure 4.2 Four Levels of Family Cohesion: Balancing Separateness and Togetherness

connected, cohesive, and enmeshed (Figure 4.2). The extreme low level of cohesion is called *disengaged*, and the extreme high level, *enmeshed*. Although being disengaged or enmeshed is appropriate at times, relationships become problematic when they are stuck at one of these extremes. The two middle levels of cohesion—*connected* and *cohesive*—seem to be the most functional across the life cycle, in part because they balance separateness and togetherness. Connected and cohesive relationships are both classified as balanced family systems.

Balance Between Separateness and Togetherness   Balance between separateness and togetherness is the essence of family cohesion. Family members need to balance between being intimate with and feeling close to other family members and being independent from the family so that they can develop as individuals. The concept of balance entails both autonomy and intimacy—and the ability to move back and forth between the two. Establishing a dynamic balance between the two requires shifting back and forth on a weekly, daily, or even hourly basis.

Table 4.3 defines the four levels of family cohesion, from low to high. There is a balance between separateness and togetherness at both the connected and the cohesive levels of cohesion. *Connected relationships* place more emphasis on the individual than on the relationship. Levels of closeness are often low to moderate in a connected family system, with lower levels of loyalty; there is often more independence than dependence and more separateness than togetherness. *Cohesive relationships* place more emphasis on togetherness and less on separateness. There is some loyalty to the relationship, and there is often more dependence than independence.

Disengaged relationships (those with a low level of cohesion) emphasize the individual. There is often very little closeness, a lack of loyalty, high independence, and high separateness. *Enmeshed relationships* emphasize togetherness: very high levels of closeness, loyalty, and dependence on one another. Enmeshed

	DISENGAGED	**CONNECTED**	**COHESIVE**	**ENMESHED**
CHARACTERISTIC	(UNBALANCED)	(BALANCED)	(BALANCED)	(UNBALANCED)
Separateness-Togetherness	High separateness	More separateness than togetherness	More togetherness than separateness	Very high togetherness
I-We balance	Primarily I	More I than We	More We than I	Primarily We
Closeness	Little closeness	Low to moderate closeness	Moderate to high closeness	Very high closeness
Loyalty	Lack of loyalty	Some loyalty	Considerable loyalty	High loyalty
Activities	Mainly separate	More separate than shared	More shared than separate	Mainly shared
Dependence-Independence	High independence	More independence than dependence	More dependence than independence	High dependence

Table 4.3 Levels of Family Cohesion

relationships are often typical of couples in love. When this level of intimacy occurs between a parent and a child (for example, an enmeshed father-daughter relationship or an enmeshed mother-son relationship), the relationship often becomes problematic.

Kahlil Gibran describes a balance between separateness and togetherness in his poem "On Marriage":

> *Love one another, but make not a bond of love:*
> *Let it rather be a moving sea between the shores of your souls.*
> *Fill each other's cup, but drink not from the same cup.*
> *Give one another of your bread, but eat not from the same loaf.*
> *Sing and dance together and be joyous, but let each one of you be alone,*
> *Even as the strings of a lute are alone though they quiver with the same music.*
> *Give your hearts, but not into each other's keeping.*
> *For only the hand of Life can contain your hearts.*
> *And stand together yet not too near together:*
> *For the pillars of the temple stand apart,*
> *And the oak tree and the cypress grow not in each other's shadow.*
> *But let there be spaces in your togetherness,*
> *And let the winds of the heavens dance between you.* (1923/1976, pp. 16–17)

The relationship Gibran describes is an ideal. In the real world of loving relationships, few find this perfect balance with their partners. It is a useful goal but one that is difficult to maintain for long. It is also important to note that in intimate relationships, people can experience and even enjoy, at least for a short time, both extremes on the togetherness-separateness continuum. Couples can remain in love with each other while also enjoying being apart for periods of time.

Extreme Togetherness and Extreme Separateness   Too much togetherness can lead to relationship fusion, or enmeshment. People "in love" often feel they need each other. Although this feels good for a while, soon the enmeshment begins to prickle. After too much togetherness, lovers can get on each other's nerves.

Within every family, each member must find a balance between autonomy and intimacy. If they are like other families, these five people will experience periods of greater and lesser separateness and togetherness over the course of their lives.

Especially in the early stages of a relationship, couples enjoy being totally together. When two people are "falling in love," being away from each other for very long literally hurts. Each one aches and pines and feels pent-up emotion in the expectation of seeing the other again. Couples in this type of situation are enmeshed; being together so totally can be very exciting for a time. To expect to be totally sheltered from the storms of life by a loved one is a nice fantasy—but it *is* a fantasy. Judy Altura has expressed it poetically:

Togetherness Poem

We do everything together.
I am here to meet all your needs and expectations.
And you are here to meet mine.
We had to meet, and it was beautiful.
I can't imagine it turning out any other way. (1974, p. 20)

Two of the most common reasons an enmeshed relationship becomes troublesome are jealousy and personification. People feel jealous when they fear they might lose their partner to another person. Tied closely to jealousy is ***personification,*** the notion that everything one's partner does is a personal reflection on oneself. A person who personifies his or her partner's actions will try to control the other's behavior. This may work in the short run, but it can destroy intimacy in the long run.

Enmeshment is problematic both for the people in the relationship and for the relationship itself because it romanticizes the relationship and puts impossible expectations upon the partners. It also tends to stifle individual development. One way to improve an enmeshed relationship is for each person to develop individual interests and abilities.

Figure 4.3 Four Levels of Family Flexibility: Balancing Stability and Change

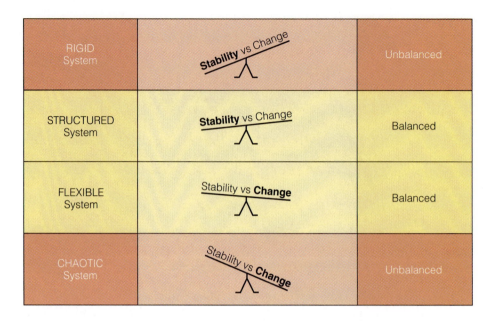

In the 1970s, one cultural theme in American society was "doing your own thing." Young people were dubbed "the me generation." This overfocus on self was problematic for relationships. "Doing your own thing" can lead to a disengaged relationship, in which there is very little emotional closeness. The ideal of extreme separateness is expressed in this prayer by psychotherapist Fritz Perls:

Gestalt Prayer

I do my thing, and you do your thing.
I am not in this world to live up to your expectations.
And you are not in this world to live up to mine.
You are you and I am I.
And if by chance we meet, it's beautiful.
If not, it can't be helped. (1969, p. 4)

Successful couples tend to be those who have figured out how to balance effectively between "I" and "we." Partners maintain both their own individuality and their intimacy as a couple.

Flexibility in Couples and Families

Flexibility is the amount of change that occurs in leadership, role relationships, and relationship rules. Like cohesion, flexibility has four levels, ranging from low to high. Those levels are rigid, structured, flexible, and chaotic (Figure 4.3). The extreme types of family systems—the *rigid* and the *chaotic*—can work well in the short run, but they have difficulty adapting over time. Conversely, the balanced types—the *structured* and the *flexible*—are more able to adapt to change over the family life cycle.

Table 4.4 Levels of Family Flexibility

CHARACTERISTIC	RIGID (UNBALANCED)	STRUCTURED (BALANCED)	FLEXIBLE (BALANCED)	CHAOTIC (UNBALANCED)
Leadership	Authoritarian	Sometimes shared	Often shared	Lack of leadership
Discipline	Strict discipline	Somewhat democratic	Democratic	Lenient discipline
Negotiation	Limited discussion	Organized discussion	Open discussion	Endless discussion
Roles	Roles very stable	Roles stable	Role sharing	Dramatic role shifts
Rules	Rules very clear, stable	Rules clear, stable	Rules clear, flexible	Rules unclear, changing
Change	Very little change	Some change	Moderate change	Considerable change

Balance Between Stability and Change   The essence of family flexibility is balancing stability and change. Families need a basic foundation that gives them stability, but they also need to be open to change when necessary. Change is particularly important when families are under stress and need to adapt in a crisis (Olson, 1993).

The two balanced levels of change are called structured and flexible. Of the two, structured relationships have more moderate levels of change, with leadership that is sometimes shared. Discipline is often democratic, and the roles are stable. In flexible relationships, there is more change. Often both the relationship between the couple and the relationships among family members are more democratic, and there is also more role sharing between the couple, as shown in Table 4.4.

The two extremes of change are described as rigid, indicating a very low degree of change, and chaotic, indicating an extremely high degree of change. Both extremes are unbalanced and problematic because families are often stuck at these extreme positions. In rigid relationships, the leadership is often authoritarian. As a result, the discipline is strict, and the roles are very stable. In chaotic relationships, there is too much change, often because there is a lack of leadership. Discipline is erratic and inconsistent, partly because there are often dramatic shifts in family roles.

Extreme Stability and Extreme Change   Families by nature tend to resist change; they are basically rigid (Haley, 1959). Most families function primarily to maintain the status quo: "When an organism indicates a change in relation to another, the other will act upon the first so as to diminish and modify the change" (Haley, 1959, p. 281).

In short, when one partner tries to make changes in a relationship, the other partner's first reaction is often to defend against the change or at least to slow it down until he or she can better understand what is happening. People often fear that the change will bring more harm than good. The family, which is maintenance oriented and conservative in its approach to change, often creates even more problems for itself. As Lyman Wynne sees it, "Families that rigidly try to maintain homeostasis [the status quo] through successive developmental phases are highly disturbed and atypical. Enduring success in maintaining family homeostasis perhaps should be regarded as a distinctive feature of disorder in families" (1958, p. 89).

Extreme stability is seen in rigid families, those in which there is little room for change. The family rules are always the same, even though the game of life outside the family continuously changes. This rigidity manifests itself in such relatively trivial matters as scheduling family meals. Family members do not permit one another to make even the slightest changes, even if they helped one or more members. The rigidity may also be evidenced by resistance to changes in family roles. For example, a mother wants to find work outside the home but the father opposes it, or a son wants to become a musician but his parents are not supportive.

On the other extreme of change are chaotic families. These families are almost completely without structure, rules, and roles. No one knows what to expect. For example:

> A young former prostitute described the family she grew up in as very chaotic, saying, "It was like a sieve. Anybody could come into it, and anybody could leave, and anybody could fall through the gaps. The family wasn't safe or reliable for anybody at all." The young woman related that her mother divorced her father and then invited another man to move in with her. This newcomer raped the young woman when she was 11 years old. When she told her mother what had happened, her mother refused to believe her and decided to let the man stay. She also decided that the 11-year-old daughter was a divisive influence on the family and chose the new lover and her younger son over her daughter. She left the daughter to fend for herself on the street, and the girl was soon involved in drugs and prostitution.

A chaotic family operates on the premise that nothing is constant in life but change. It is difficult to go through life without some change—and individuals and relationships often do better if they are open to some change over time. However, constant change is problematic for most people.

Communication in Couples and Families

Communication is the grease that smoothes frictions between partners and family members. Family communication is linear: The better the communication skills, the stronger the couple and family relationship.

The following six dimensions are considered in the assessment of family communication: listening skills, speaking skills, self-disclosure, clarity, staying on topic, and respect and regard (Table 4.5). Positive *listening skills* involve empathy and giving feedback. *Speaking skills* include speaking for oneself and using "I" statements rather than speaking for others. *Self-disclosure* entails sharing personal feelings and ideas openly. *Clarity* involves the exchange of clear messages. *Staying on topic* is another important aspect of interpersonal exchanges. Last, *respect and regard* reflect the good intentions of family members and keep communication positive.

Table 4.5 Levels of Family Communication

CHARACTERISTIC	POOR	GOOD	VERY GOOD
Listening skills	Poor listening skills	Appear to listen, but feedback is limited	Give feedback, indicating good listening skills
Speaking skills	Often speak for others	Speak for self more than for others	Speak mainly for self rather than for others
Self-disclosure	Low sharing of feelings	Moderate sharing of feelings	High sharing of feelings
Clarity	Inconsistent messages	Clear messages	Very clear messages
Staying on topic	Seldom stay on topic	Often stay on topic	Mainly stay on topic
Respect and regard	Low to moderate	Moderate to high	High

Couple and Family Map

How can we represent in a clear and compelling way the dynamics of relationships within marriage and families? The **Couple and Family Map** is one especially useful model for this purpose. The Couple and Family Map (otherwise known in the field of family research as the *Circumplex Model of Marital and Family Systems*) was developed by David Olson and his colleagues at the University of Minnesota, especially Douglas Sprenkle and Candyce Russell, who worked on the original model. It serves to identify the key characteristics of any given relationship in terms of cohesion, flexibility, and communication. For the theorist, researcher, or interested lay person, the model offers a way of mapping and understanding couple and family relationships. It can also be applied by therapists, counselors, and family members interested in changing the dynamics within a couple or family experiencing difficulties.

The Couple and Family Map is built primarily on principles and concepts from family systems theory, but it also has features in common with other frameworks. As a graphic model, it clearly represents the dimensions of cohesion and flexibility; the third dimension, communication, serves a facilitating function.

It is through communication that family members identify and work out their concerns about cohesion—issues of spending time together versus having enough separateness to retain a sense of oneself—and flexibility—issues of adapting to the demands of change versus minimizing such demands if they threaten the stability of the relationship. Communication thus helps families move between the extremes of cohesion and flexibility to find a balance that works for them. If couples or families have good communication skills, they are more likely to be able to maintain their cohesive structure, adapt to change, and work out whatever problems confront them (Olson, 1993).

There are several advantages to using *the Couple and Family Map* to understand marital and family life. First, *the model provides a common descriptive language for talking about real couples and real families—a language the expert and the lay person can use to talk with each other.* Second, *the Couple and Family Map draws on concepts and ideas from three of the major frameworks we have discussed—family systems, family strengths, and family development.* It offers a means of bringing together and applying all three frameworks to the examination of real families and their interactions. It grounds theory in examples of relationships based on intimacy and commitment.

Figure 4.4 Couple and Family Map

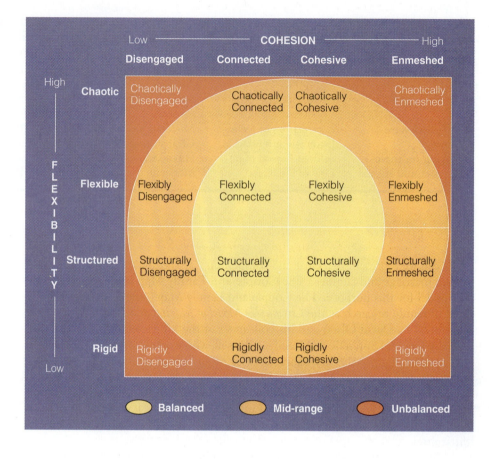

Third, *the Couple and Family Map can help describe how a couple relationship or a family changes as time passes or as stresses and challenges appear.* The relationship map provides information about the present dynamics of a couple or family's relationship and what actions are necessary to bring about change. It provides a means to visualize where one is and where one might wish to be.

Finally, *the Couple and Family Map turns concepts into working themes so one can observe and measure couple and family dynamics.* Just where is a given family on the relationship map? Is this relationship a rigid, inflexible, suffocating environment? Is it an unpredictable, unsafe, chaotic place to be? Or is it flexible and nurturing? Can family members communicate what their problems are and express what kind of family they would like to become? What changes must they make to move toward that ideal or maintain the aspects they wish not to lose as they change others?

The Couple and Family Map identifies 16 types of couple and family relationships (Figure 4.4). The logic is quite simple: The dimensions of cohesion and flexibility are broken down into four levels each, and $4 \times 4 = 16$. A marriage or family relationship can be classified according to one of these 16 types depending on how a given family or couple relationship operates.

The 16 types of family relationships can be clustered into three general types of family systems: balanced families, mid-range families, and unbalanced families. **Balanced families** are those that fit into the four central categories (yellow section) on the relationship map in Figure 4.4. Balanced families are labeled flexibly connected, flexibly cohesive, structurally connected, and structurally cohesive. **Mid-range families** (orange section) are extreme on one dimension (e.g., cohesion) but balanced on the other (e.g., flexibility). **Unbalanced families** (red section) are those that score at extreme levels on both dimensions. In the Activities section at the end of this chapter, you will have the opportunity to classify your own family using the Couple and Family Map Scales.

Balanced Versus Unbalanced Relationships   The Couple and Family Map is a valuable model because it is scientifically verifiable; in other words, researchers can validate (or invalidate) the Couple and Family Map by testing hypotheses derived from it. A few of the most important hypotheses that have been developed and tested in numerous studies are discussed in the rest of this chapter.

One hypothesis is: *Balanced couple and family systems* (those that fall under two central levels of cohesion and flexibility) *generally function more adequately across the family life cycle than unbalanced types* (two extremes on cohesion and flexibility). Families balanced on cohesion allow their members to be both independent from and connected to the family. Families balanced on flexibility maintain some stability but are also open to change. Although balanced family types are located in the central area of the model, they can experience the extremes of the dimensions when necessary to deal with a situation, but they do not typically function at those extremes for long.

Conversely, couples and families with problems are more typically found at the extremes of the dimensions; they are unbalanced types. Problem families often experience too much separateness (disengaged type) or too much togetherness (enmeshed type) on cohesion. On flexibility, problem families tend to have too much stability (rigid type) or too much change (chaotic type).

There is considerable support for the main hypothesis derived from the Couple and Family Map: *Balanced family types are healthier and more functional than unbalanced family types* (Olson, 1993). One systematic study that found strong support for this hypothesis is by Volker Thomas (Thomas & Olson, 1993). Thomas tested four groups of families with an adolescent, videotaping each family while they discussed some family topics. The four samples included 35 families with an emotionally disturbed child, 25 families in family therapy for a variety of problems, 62 healthy families with a Down's syndrome child, and 60 healthy families.

The findings strongly supported the hypothesis (Figure 4.5). As hypothesized, only 16% of the families with an emotionally disturbed child and 12% of the families in therapy were balanced types, whereas about 78% to 80% of the healthy families were balanced types. Conversely, almost half (49%) of the families with an emotionally disturbed child and 40% of the families in therapy were unbalanced. Only 8% of the healthy families were unbalanced.

Movies as Illustrations of Family Dynamics

Movies often do an excellent job of portraying couple and family dynamics. Because they tend to be more dramatically interesting, the unbalanced family types are depicted more often than the balanced types. Some movies also illustrate how families change in response to a stressor or over time as people age. In this

Figure 4.5 Degree of Balance in Problem and Healthy Families

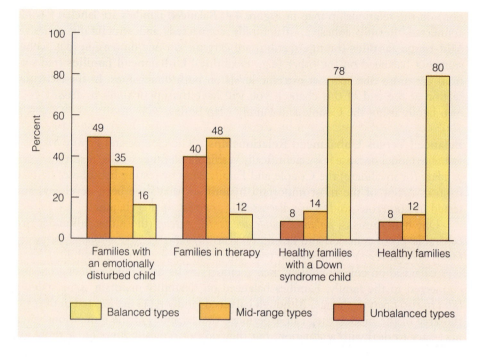

section we will take a look at some family movies that vividly depict several family types. Many classic and current movie families could serve as examples of the various family types; we chose the following selections, however, because they are particularly good examples of three family types.

What About Bob?: **A Rigidly Connected Family**

The Marvin family is headed by a prominent psychiatrist, Dr. Leo Marvin (Richard Dreyfuss), author of a popular book called *Baby Steps.* He and his wife, Fay (Julie Hagerty), have a teenage daughter, Anna, and a 9-year-old son, Sigmund. Leo is very self-confident and maintains strong control over his family. Fay is a warm and caring homemaker who tries to support her husband; both children are rather distant from their father. As a family the Marvins operate as a *rigidly connected* system because the father is so controlling and there is a low level of emotional closeness in the family. Their communication skills are poor, mainly because the father controls the exchange of information and does not let others have much say.

The family experiences a great deal of change when Bob Wiley (Bill Murray) becomes a patient of Dr. Marvin. Bob becomes so dependent on Dr. Marvin that he follows him to the family's vacation home. About the same time, "Good Morning America" contacts Dr. Marvin and arranges to interview him at his lake home. Bob becomes involved in the production because he wants to share how helpful Dr. Marvin's counsel was. During the filming of the interview, Bob is very articulate; Dr. Marvin, on the other hand, becomes so flustered and frustrated that he is often speechless.

After the "Good Morning America" show the family system changes. Bob encourages the family to express their feelings and have fun together. He helps the son, Siggy, learn to dive in the lake, something Leo had failed to do. The family becomes more *flexibly cohesive*, with good communication skills. Leo loses his total control over his family, and they enjoy the more flexible style of operating that Bob encourages. Leo becomes increasingly frustrated and disengaged from his family, which leads him to depression. Eventually he is hospitalized. But, in the end, the family changes and is more balanced as a result of Bob's becoming part of the family.

Ordinary People: A Rigidly Disengaged Family

At the other extreme of the cohesion dimension is the disengaged family as depicted in the movie *Ordinary People*. This pleasant suburban family—a mother (Mary Tyler Moore), a father (Donald Sutherland), and one son (Timothy Hutton)—is also very rigid. This family is outwardly pleasant, maintaining a good appearance to outsiders, but passively controlling.

The *rigidity* is borne in part out of the family's need to survive the loss of the first-born son in a boating accident, just a few months before the story begins. Buck was the star of the family: handsome, charming, an excellent student, a star athlete. His death has left an emptiness in the mother, to which she reacts with rigidity and disengagement. The rest of the family becomes rigid and disengaged in response. In this family, emotions are controlled, roles are narrowly defined, and there are strict (but unspoken) rules about what feelings can be discussed. The surviving son, who has attempted suicide because he feels guilty about the boating accident, cannot talk about his feelings with the family because of the implicit rules forbidding such intimate self-disclosure.

The *disengagement* in this family is painfully apparent. Distance is carefully maintained to prevent any further grief. The son and the father try to make contact with the mother, but they fail. Near the end of the movie, the mother wakes up in the middle of the night and discovers that her husband is not at her side. She goes downstairs and finds him sitting in the dark, crying softly to himself. He says he doesn't think he knows her anymore—the woman she has become—and he is not sure he loves her anymore. Without a word, she goes upstairs and begins to pack her suitcase. There is a brief moment when she gasps and nearly cries. But she regains control, finishes her packing, and leaves.

The rigidity in this family affects the degree of emotional closeness among family members. It maintains emotional disengagement and keeps feelings of grief and guilt over the loss of the oldest son from surfacing. In this family, the mother keeps her son and husband at arm's length—emotionally stiff-arming them. Although both husband and son attempt to break through this rigidity, they finally give up in despair because they cannot connect with her emotionally.

Shoot the Moon: A Chaotically Disengaged Family

The family in *Shoot the Moon* is falling apart due to a divorce. The father (Albert Finney) is having a secret affair, but his oldest daughter is suspicious and listens in on an extension to a call he makes to his lover from home. His wife (Diane Keaton) has suspected for some time that her husband might be having an affair but has not confronted him. His excuses about "working late" finally wear thin, however, and she confronts him; a dish-breaking fight ensues. He offers to leave; she says she packed his bag last night. This couple has been disengaged for a long time, and now their estrangement intensifies. When the father finally moves out, the *chaos* in the family system takes over.

To try to escape her pain, the mother sleeps late, buries her head under the pillow, and moans. Before, this woman was never tired and always had time for her four daughters. The oldest daughter, Julie, takes over her mother's role. In a scene typical of the family chaos, Julie is simultaneously trying to make breakfast, phoning to schedule a doctor's appointment for a sister who has sprained her foot, and yelling to her sisters to come downstairs to breakfast—which is burning. The sisters yell back that they don't want the breakfast that she worked so hard to prepare. She yells back that she doesn't need this, throws the frying pan of scrambled eggs into the sink, and heads out the door to the school bus.

Dad—trying both to overcome his guilt and to spend some time with his daughters—is waiting in his car at the end of the driveway to take the children to school. His daughter-turned-parent sees him, walks around his car, and gets onto the school bus without saying a word to him. As the bus pulls out, Julie can be seen looking through the window, crying.

Before the separation, the father had been *disengaged* from his daughters for some time. The mother had been close to her daughters, but now she too has become disengaged from them due to her depression and inability to function. The oldest daughter, despite taking over some of the parenting roles, still wants a mother and a father to care for her and to be in charge. All the rules and roles are up for grabs in this family.

Summary

- Conceptual frameworks help describe different perspectives on couple and family dynamics.

- The family systems theory focuses on the family as a system of interdependent parts.

- The family strengths framework focuses on the positive characteristics of healthy families and couples.

- The family development framework examines how couples and families change across the life cycle.

- The symbolic interaction framework examines the internal perceptions of family members and how they learn social rules and roles.

- The social construction framework emphasizes the importance of multiple perspectives on reality and their use in helping families meet their goals more effectively.

- The feminist framework, which focuses on the world as women perceive it, aims to empower women in all aspects of their life.

- Family theorists have identified three basic qualities that make couples and families stronger: cohesion, flexibility, and communication. These three concepts are central to the family systems theory, the family strengths framework, the family development framework, as well as other theories and frameworks.

- Cohesion focuses on the dynamic balance between the extremes of separateness and togetherness in both couple and family relationships. Balancing these two extremes entails maintaining both autonomy and intimacy but not remaining stuck at either extreme for long periods.

- Flexibility focuses on the dynamic balance between stability and change. The most functional couples and family systems have both characteristics, and they are able to move back and forth between them. Couples and families with problems over time tend to become stuck at one of the extremes, either too much stability (rigid) or too much change (chaotic).

- Communication is a facilitating dimension that can help create change in the levels of cohesion and flexibility when change is necessary.

- The Couple and Family Map is a tool for understanding couple and family relationships. It is based on the family systems theory and is structured on the three dimensions of cohesion, flexibility, and communication.

- The Couple and Family Map describes three general types of family systems—balanced, mid-range, and unbalanced.

Key Terms

conceptual framework

theory

hypothesis

research study

idiographic

nomothetic

family systems theory

family system

general systems theory

system

suprasystem

subsystem

boundaries

ecology

wholeness

interdependence of parts

open system

morphogenic system

closed system

morphostatic system

centrifugal interaction

centripetal interaction

positive feedback

negative feedback

family strengths framework

commitment

appreciation and affection

positive communication

time together

spiritual well-being

ability to cope with stress

family development framework

symbolic interaction framework

role

role taking

role making

definition of the situation

looking-glass self

social construction framework

postmodernism

feminist framework

gender

instrumental role

expressive role

personification

Couple and Family
Map

balanced families

mid-range families

unbalanced families

Activities

1. Use the Couple and Family Scales (Table 4.6) to describe your family of origin. Select a time period when you were all together (e.g., when you were in high school). Make a list of the people you are including in your family. Then do the following:

a. Review the six categories shown in the scales (Table 4.6) for assessing cohesion, flexibility, and communication.

b. On a separate piece of paper, rate your family on a scale of 1 to 8 for each of the categories in the three dimensions.

c. To determine a total score for each dimension, review the scores and select a number that represents the best average score. Record the score below, and indicate the level for each dimension (e.g., for cohesion, enter *disengaged, connected, cohesive,* or *enmeshed*).

Cohesion	**Flexibility**	**Communication**
Score: _____	Score: _____	Score: _____
Level: _____	Level: _____	Level: _____

d. Now, plot the scores for cohesion and flexibility onto the Couple and Family Map (Figure 4.6) and identify the type of family system in which you grew up.

e. After plotting your scores onto the model, consider the following questions:

- What is/was it like to live in your type of family (e.g., flexibly connected, rigidly enmeshed, etc.)?

- In what ways related to cohesion and flexibility is/was your family satisfying and in what ways is/was it frustrating?

- How did your family change on cohesion and flexibility as you were growing up?

- In what ways did communication affect your family's dynamics?

2. If you are dating someone, are engaged, or are married, both you and your partner should answer the questions on the Couple and Family Scales twice: first, in terms of your families of origin (same as Activity 1) and second, in terms of your couple relationship. Compare your partner's description of your couple relationship with yours, and discuss the similarities and differences. Then compare the descriptions of each of your families of origin with those of your couple relationship.

(For more details on using the Couple and Family Scales, see Resource Section A at the back of the book.)

Table 4.6 Couple and Family Scales

			COHESION					
CHARACTERISTIC	DISENGAGED (UNBALANCED)		CONNECTED (BALANCED)		COHESIVE (BALANCED)		ENMESHED (UNBALANCED)	
SCORE	1	2	3	4	5	6	7	8
Separateness-Togetherness	High separateness		More separateness than togetherness		More togetherness than separateness		Very high togetherness	
I-We balance	Primarily I		More I than We		More We than I		Primarily We	
Closeness	Little closeness		Low to moderate closeness		Moderate to high closeness		Very high closeness	
Loyalty	Lack of loyalty		Some loyalty		Considerable loyalty		High loyalty	
Activities	Mainly separate		More separate than shared		More shared than separate		Mainly shared	
Dependence-Independence	High independence		More independence than dependence		More dependence than independence		High dependence	

			FLEXIBILITY					
CHARACTERISTIC	RIGID (UNBALANCED)		STRUCTURED (BALANCED)		FLEXIBLE (BALANCED)		CHAOTIC (UNBALANCED)	
SCORE	1	2	3	4	5	6	7	8
Leadership	Authoritarian		Sometimes shared		Often shared		Lack of leadership	
Discipline	Strict discipline		Somewhat democratic		Democratic		Lenient discipline	
Negotiation	Limited discussion		Organized discussion		Open discussion		Endless discussion	
Roles	Roles very stable		Roles stable		Role sharing		Dramatic role shifts	
Rules	Unchanging rules		Few rule changes		Some rule changes		Frequent rule changes	
Change	Very little change		Some change		Moderate change		Considerable change	

			COMMUNICATION				
CHARACTERISTIC	POOR		GOOD		VERY GOOD		
SCORE	1	2	3	4	5	6
Listening skills	Poor listening skills		Appear to listen, but feedback is limited		Give feedback, indicating good listening skills		
Speaking skills	Often speak for others		Speak for self more than for others		Speak mainly for self rather than for others		
Self-disclosure	Low sharing of feelings		Moderate sharing of feelings		High sharing of feelings		
Clarity	Inconsistent messages		Clear messages		Very clear messages		
Staying on topic	Seldom stay on topic		Often stay on topic		Mainly stay on topic		

Figure 4.6 Couple and
Family Map

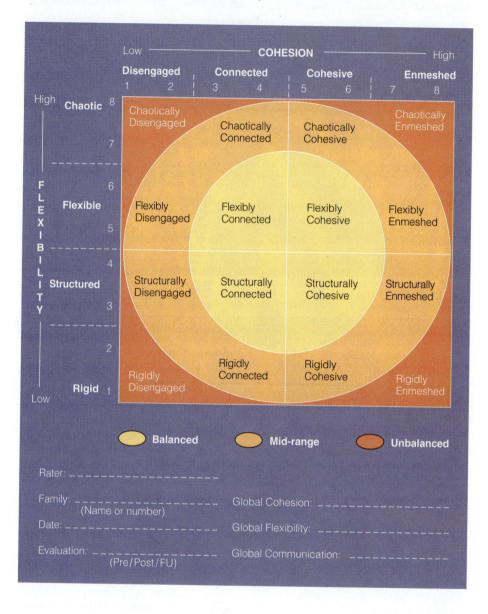

Suggested Readings

Olson, D. H., McCubbin, H., Barnes, H., Larsen, A., Muxen, M., and Wilson, M. (1989). *Families: What makes them work* (2nd ed.). Beverly Hills, CA: Sage. Describes a nationwide study, conducted at the University of Minnesota, of 1,000 intact families at all stages of the life cycle, ranging from newlyweds to retired couples. Focuses on different types of families, the stresses they encounter, the internal and external resources that help them cope, and the factors that produce marital and family satisfaction across the family life cycle.

Olson, D. H., Russell, C. S., & Sprenkle, D. H. (1989). *Circumplex model: Clinical assessment and treatment intervention with families.* New York: Haworth. Explains the use of the Family Circumplex Model (Couple and Family Map) to assess and treat family problems.

PART II

Developing Intimate Relationships

CHAPTER 5

Friendship, Intimacy, and Singlehood

Love and friendship bind society together, providing both emotional support and a buffer against stress and thereby preserving our physical and psychological health. Love is clearly much more than friendship, and thus we treat love relationships more seriously. However, the strongest love relationships have roots in friendship: Satisfying and stable love relationships come from shared interests and values. When friends fall in love, they are adding passion to the emotional intimacy we call friendship.

Love means different things to different people. Definitions of love are almost endless (Box 5.1). No other topic demands so much attention and generates so much confusion in our society. We cannot turn on the radio or TV, pick up a magazine or book, or converse with a friend for long without being confronted with words about love, thoughts of love, acts of love, or images of love. Despite the ubiquitous nature of love, it remains a mystery to many. Many regard it as a strange force that can overpower us and at times take control over our lives: People speak of being "under love's spell" or being "swept away" with passion.

Intimacy, too, is mysterious. In healthy human relationships, love and intimacy are inextricably interwoven. Intimacy is the goal of most love relationships, yet because it requires revealing one's vulnerabilities, it can be a frightening prospect for some.

In this chapter we will explore various ways of defining love and the related concept of intimacy. We will also identify a number of constructive and destructive games people play in their intimate relationships. The goal of this chapter is to help you understand love and intimacy and learn how to enhance your own intimate experiences and relationships. To conclude, we will take a close look at singlehood, which for many is a legitimate, healthy, and happy alternative to marriage.

Friends Versus Lovers

Research indicates that love and friendship are alike in many ways but that crucial differences make love both more rewarding and more volatile than friendship. After conducting several studies, Keith E. Davis and his colleague Michael J. Todd came to this conclusion:

> Typical love relationships will differ from even very good friendships by having higher levels of fascination, exclusiveness and sexual desire, a greater depth of caring about the other individual (which would be manifest in a willingness to give the utmost when needed), and a greater potential for enjoyment and other positive emotions. Love relationships will also have, however, a greater potential for distress, ambivalence, conflict, and mutual criticism. (K. E. Davis, 1985, p. 30)

Love, in short, runs deeper and stronger than friendship. And because the stakes are so high with love, the possibility of interpersonal difficulties increases, and we jealously guard this important relationship.

The Fabric of Friendship

Davis and Todd began their research by developing a hypothetical model of friendship and love (K. E. Davis, 1985). In their original profile of friendship, they first

BOX 5.1

On Love

In love the paradox occurs that two beings become one yet remain two.
—ERICH FROMM, *PSYCHIATRIST*

Love doesn't just sit there, like a stone, it has to be made, like bread; remade all the time, made new.
—URSULA K. LE GUIN, *WRITER*

Being in love isn't ever really loving, it's just wanting. And it isn't any good. It's all aching and misery.
—JAMES LEO HERLIHY, *WRITER*

Love is the history of a woman's life; it is an episode in man's.
—MADAME DE STAËL, *WRITER*

He who knows nothing, loves nothing . . .
But he who understands also loves, notices, sees . . .
The more knowledge inherent in a thing, the greater the love.
—PARACELSUS, *PHILOSOPHER*

The trouble with some women is that they get all excited about nothing—and then marry him.
—CHER, *ACTOR*

When the satisfaction or the security of another person becomes as significant to one as is one's own security, then the state of love exists.
—HARRY STACK SULLIVAN, *PSYCHIATRIST*

Chains do not hold a marriage together. It is threads, hundreds of tiny threads which sew people together through the years. This is what makes a marriage last—more than passion or even sex!
—SIMONE SIGNORET, *ACTOR*

Love is a state of perpetual anesthesia.
—H. L. MENCKEN, *JOURNALIST*

My brother refers to my husband, in his presence, as "Joan's husband." Marriage is the classic betrayal.
—JOAN DIDION, *WRITER*

---

assumed that two individuals participate in a reciprocal relationship as equals. The fabric of friendship included eight important elements:

- *Enjoyment.* Friends enjoy each other's company most of the time, although disagreements and friction occasionally occur.

- *Acceptance.* Friends accept each other for who they are and don't try to change each other.

- *Trust.* Friends assume that they will act in each other's best interest. "Even when he's hassling me, I know it's for my own good." "She would never intentionally hurt me, except in a fit of extreme anger."

- *Respect.* Friends respect each other; they assume the other has good judgment in making choices in life.

- *Mutual assistance.* Friends help and support each other; they can count on each other in times of need.

- *Confiding.* Friends share life experiences and feelings with each other.

- *Understanding.* Friends know each other's values and understand what is important to each other. "I know what makes her tick."

Love has much in common with friendship, but it is more intense and passionate. Like this man and woman, couples in love tend to be fascinated with each other, spending long moments gazing unself-consciously into each other's eyes. Like the couple on the right, they also tend to have interests in common and enjoy just being together.

- *Spontaneity.* Friends feel free to be "real" around each other. They don't feel they have to play a role or hold back their true feelings.

The Tapestry of Love

Davis and Todd assumed at the outset of their studies that romantic relationships would have the same characteristics as friendship but that they would also have additional, unique characteristics. The unique characteristics were grouped in two broad categories: the Passion Cluster and the Caring Cluster. The model of friendship and love that Davis and Todd developed is shown in Figure 5.1.

The **Passion Cluster** encompasses three related characteristics: fascination, sexual desire, and exclusiveness. Fascination is a preoccupation with the other person—a tendency to think about, look at, want to talk to, and want to be with that person. Sexual desire is the lovers' desire to touch each other and to make love, even though they may not engage in sexual intercourse for religious, moral, or practical reasons. Exclusiveness is giving the partner priority over other relationships in one's life.

The **Caring Cluster** contains two components: being an advocate for one's partner and giving the utmost. Being a champion and an advocate means defending and supporting each other, even during difficult times. Giving the utmost is easy for people in love; sometimes they give to the point of self-sacrifice.

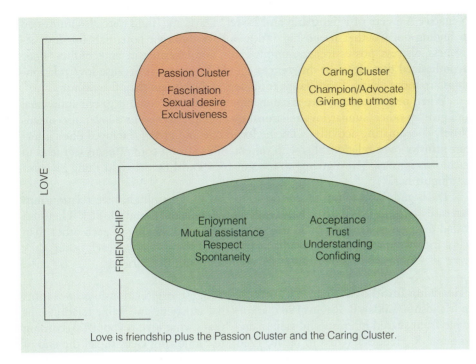

Figure 5.1 Love and Friendship. *Source:* "Near and Dear: Friendship and Love Compared" by K. E. Davis, 1985, *Psychology Today* (February), p. 24. Copyright 1985 by Sussex Publishers, Inc. Reprinted by permission from *Psychology Today* magazine.

Love is friendship plus the Passion Cluster and the Caring Cluster.

Contrasting Friends and Lovers

Davis and Todd found that love is friendship with a few added components, but they were surprised by a few other findings. In their survey of 242 friends, spouses, and lovers (two thirds students, one third community members), the researchers discovered specific similarities and differences between friends and lovers.

Positive Aspects of Friendship and Love On the Caring Cluster, best friendships are similar to spouse/lover relationships in several ways: Both show virtually identical levels of acceptance, trust, and respect and similar levels of confiding, understanding, spontaneity, mutual assistance, and satisfaction and happiness with the relationship. On the Passion Cluster, however, there is much more fascination and exclusiveness in spouse/lover relationships than in best-friend relationships.

On the Caring Cluster, Davis and Todd hypothesized that spouses and lovers would be more willing than best friends to give the utmost when needed and would be more active champions and advocates of the loved one. They were surprised, however, to find that this was the case only on the give-the-utmost characteristic. They were also surprised to find that best friendships were perceived as being more stable than spouse/lover relationships. Spouses and, especially, unmarried lovers were more concerned that their relationships might break up. As a single woman in her early 30s put it, "Lovers come and go, but I can always count on my friends." The loss of friends and, especially, loved ones can lead to illness and even suicide. Although love is much more than friendship, both kinds of relationships are important in people's lives.

Negative Aspects of Friendship and Love   Davis and Todd were also interested in finding out whether friendship and love have different potentials for destructiveness, distress, possessiveness, ambivalence, mutual criticism, and conflict. They hypothesized that clear-cut differences should be apparent because love relationships are more charged with fascination and exclusiveness than friendships.

When people enter a love relationship, they usually commit to one individual and give up other, similar love relationships. Being a spouse or a lover also means closely coordinating activities with the loved one and giving the loved one's interests priority over relationships with others. This strong commitment can lead to such questions as, "Am I giving up too much?" "Did I do the right thing by committing to her?"

Davis and Todd found that because the stakes are so high, love relationships can easily become breeding grounds for ambivalent feelings and conflict. They also found that spouses and lovers were significantly less accepting of each other than were friends. Spouses and lovers had a greater desire to change each other; they were also more willing to criticize their partners than their friends.

Friendship Into Love   It appears that the strongest love relationships have roots in friendship. Lillian B. Rubin (1985) argues that satisfying and stable relationships come from shared interests and values, and "that's what love is about." According to Susan S. Hendrick (cited in Jacob, 1986), the following clues signal the end of a beautiful friendship and the beginning of love: you are suddenly aware of your friend's wonderful smile, great body, or cute freckles; you get dressed up when you know you're going to see each other; you feel excited at the thought of meeting; and you begin to feel shy and less spontaneous when you're together.

Similarly, psychologist Robert Sternberg (1986) believes that when friends fall in love, they are simply adding passion to the emotional intimacy we call friendship. The temptation is to let oneself be swept away by romance, but Hendrick (cited in Jacob, 1986) argues that individuals should use some uncommon sense. This includes letting things develop slowly, being honest with the other person and with oneself, and keeping an open mind and a sense of humor. It is important to remember that it is easier to fall in love than to stay in love.

"I'm so happy we were friends for a long time before we became lovers," Josh, a graduate student, related. "Passion is really great, but it clutters up a relationship a great deal. You don't know what you have underneath the passion if it drains away. But the friendship shines on and on, through good times and bad times." Josh explained that he had met Jessica while doing laundry one afternoon in Berkeley. He was dressed pretty shabbily, and so was she.

"I didn't really think of Jessica in a genuinely sexual way until several months after I got to know her. She was just always that good friend down the hallway in the apartment building who I could talk to about anything. Sometimes she would counsel me on my girlfriends, and then one day I looked at her and thought, 'Wow, she ought to be my girlfriend!'"

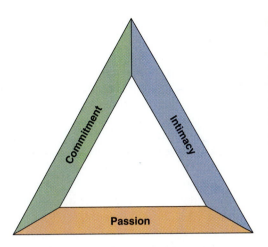

Figure 5.2 The Love Triangle. *Source: The Psychology of Love* (p. 37) edited by R. Sternberg and M. Barnes, 1988, New Haven, CT: Yale University Press. Copyright 1988 by Yale University Press. Reprinted by permission.

The Love Triangle

Although the phrase *love triangle* usually brings to mind a relationship in which one person has two lovers, another sort of love triangle was developed by Sternberg (Sternberg & Barnes, 1988). The three dimensions of the triangle are commitment (the cognitive component), intimacy (the emotional component), and passion (the motivational component; Figure 5.2).

A relationship can start off with intimacy (friendship) and develop into love. A relationship can also start off with only passion and later develop the other two components. A relationship (such as an arranged marriage) can also begin simply with a commitment between partners for economic reasons or for reasons dictated by the couple's families; even this type of relationship can later develop intimacy and passion and bloom into love (Sternberg & Barnes, 1988; Trotter, 1986).

Commitment is a cognitive attachment to another person. It develops over time, beginning slowly and increasing at a faster rate if the relationship is positive. If the relationship fails, commitment disappears. People express commitment when they move their relationship to a more advanced stage (from dating to engagement, from engagement to marriage), when they are faithful, or when they stay in the relationship during difficult times.

Intimacy involves sharing feelings and providing emotional support. It usually entails high levels of self-disclosure, the sharing of personal information not ordinarily revealed because of the risk involved. Intimacy gradually increases as closeness grows and deepens as a relationship matures. Few couples are likely to share everything with each other. People need some private space, a bit of their world that is closed to everyone else. But in a mature intimate relationship, most areas are open for discussion and sharing. By opening up, by earning each other's trust and becoming vulnerable to each other, people can build a strong emotional bond of intimacy. The paradox is that by expressing feelings of weakness and vulnerability, individuals can gain support and strength from trusted loved ones.

Passion is usually expressed by touching, kissing, and being affectionate, which are linked to physiological arousal; it is also expressed through sexual interactions. Due to its intensity, passion develops quickly but can also fade quickly. Passion is like an addiction; when it ends, a person can experience withdrawal symptoms such as irritability and depression.

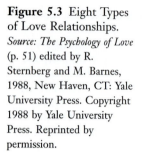

Figure 5.3 Eight Types of Love Relationships.
Source: The Psychology of Love (p. 51) edited by R. Sternberg and M. Barnes, 1988, New Haven, CT: Yale University Press. Copyright 1988 by Yale University Press. Reprinted by permission.

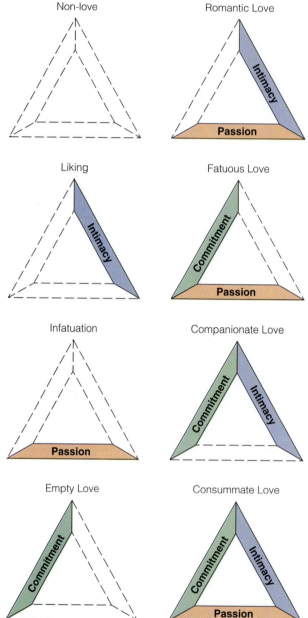

Combining the three dimensions of love in various ways, Sternberg identified eight types of love relationships: non-love, liking, infatuation, empty love, romantic love, fatuous love, companionate love, and consummate love (Figure 5.3). **Non-love** occurs when there is no commitment, intimacy, or passion. **Liking** begins when there is just intimacy, but no passion or commitment. **Infatuation** involves passion only. In **empty love** there is commitment but no passion or intimacy. **Romantic love** has both intimacy and passion, but it is lacking in commitment. **Fatuous love** occurs when a couple is committed based on passion but has not had the time to develop true intimacy. (For example, two people fall in love and, after seeing each other only on weekends for 2 months, get married.) **Companionate love** is more characteristic of couples who have been married for years. These couples have both commitment and intimacy, but they lack the passion they had when they were first married. Finally, **consummate love** is complete love, containing all three dimensions. It is the goal of most couples.

Most people have experienced several of these types of love and can recognize that each of them feels rather different. Even within one relationship, it is possible to experience two or more types of love over time. A couple, for example, may start out as close friends (liking) and then two years later become sexually involved (romantic love); a year later they may decide to live together (consummate love). However, three months later he has an affair; she finds out about it and moves out, ending the relationship (non-love).

Three Perspectives on Love

In his classic book *The Art of Loving*, Erich Fromm (1956) describes several important myths about love. He believes that too many people think love is simple; in reality, he maintains, finding the right person is difficult, requiring work and practice. Fromm believes that falling in love is very different from being in love, which involves facing the realities of living together. He also suggests that "being a loving person is the best way to be loved."

Love can also be seen as an addiction. In *Love and Addiction*, Stanton Peele (1985) suggests that, unfortunately, many people who are in love are addicted to love much as people are addicted to alcohol, tobacco, or other drugs. As with other addictions, people seek stability and comfort in the addiction and suffer withdrawal when it is not available. Infatuation generates a good deal of adrenaline in the body, causing a high that people learn to seek. When the high ceases abruptly (due to a breakup, say), people can have a sensation of "crashing," similar to the feeling people experience when certain drugs wear off. The search for this high explains why some people have dozens or even hundreds of different sexual partners during their lifetime.

Peele developed several criteria for distinguishing a mature love relationship from an addictive love relationship. Answering yes to any of the following questions indicates a mature love relationship:

- Do you each value yourself?
- Are you both better people as a result of this relationship?
- Do you both have serious interests outside the relationship?
- Is the relationship not the totality of your life?
- Is neither of you possessive or jealous of your partner?
- Are you best friends?

James Dobson offered another perspective on love in his book *Love Must Be Tough* (1983). Dobson believes that *tough love* can help couples and families overcome serious problems and develop stronger relationships. He maintains that in couple conflict, one person is often more independent than the other; the dependent person panics if the other suggests he or she is unhappy or otherwise starts to withdraw from the relationship. Rather than pursue the partner, Dobson suggests, the more dependent person should also pull back from the relationship and be "tough" by demonstrating independence and putting some realistic demands on the relationship. The tough-love concept has also been suggested for parents who are having little success dealing with troubled adolescents in more traditional ways.

Exploring Intimacy: From Experience to Relationship

Like love, intimacy is also an elusive concept. The word generally brings to mind images of physical closeness and sexuality. But it is really much more than that. Intimacy is the closeness and feelings of warmth we have with certain people. It is an ongoing process of life with other people, and it has many components. Without intimacy with other human beings, life would be boring, cold, and lonely. Many people in our culture place a high value on intimacy. Although intimacy is not restricted to marriage relationships, most of us get married in our search to find and maintain intimacy. It is considered a reward and benefit of marriage.

Intimacy Versus Isolation

Intimacy is a prominent element in Erik Erikson's (1968) eight-stage theory of human development. Erikson was a follower of Sigmund Freud but transcended the fatalism of Freud's psychoanalytic theory. He posited his own, more optimistic beliefs, which emphasized success and the flowering of human potential. Whereas Freud saw personality as being primarily established in early childhood, Erikson argued that growth occurs across the life span, from birth to death. Even older people are capable of making changes in their lives, if they choose to be flexible.

Erikson's theory focuses on psychosocial development rather than on psychosexual development, Freud's primary focus. For Erikson, the individual moves through eight predetermined steps (or stages) to become fully developed. Mastery of the developmental tasks at one stage means the individual is ready to progress to the next developmental stage. Failure or difficulty in meeting the challenges of a particular stage does not mean an individual cannot move on. Rather, progress in the next stage of psychosocial development will simply be more difficult or slower. Each stage of life brings another *psychosocial crisis*, as Erikson called it; other theorists prefer the terms *turning point* or *challenge*.

The psychosocial crisis of young adulthood is intimacy versus isolation, the challenge of developing a close, warm relationship with another human being to overcome isolation. If intimacy cannot be established with another, the risk of experiencing loneliness and isolation is greater, Erikson contended. Falling out of love is a relatively common occurrence, and many individuals find that loss of intimacy can generate considerable pain. For some individuals, the failed quest for intimacy causes such pain that they conclude the search is not worth the effort. Most people, however, continue the quest.

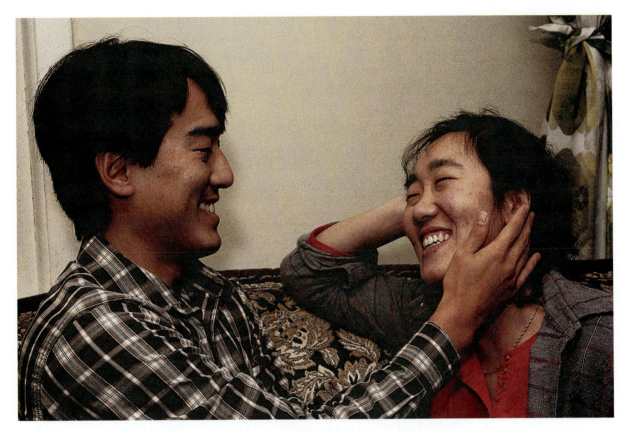

According to Erikson's theory of psychosocial development, discovering how to create and build an intimate relationship is a particular challenge of young adulthood. As this young couple demonstrates, affection and trust are integral components of such a relationship.

"I wanted to crawl in a hole and die when Jim left me," said Sheila, a 27-year-old woman living in Buffalo, New York. "And I really did withdraw for a long time. It was winter—dark and incredibly cold outside—and I spent most of my free time sleeping or just lying in bed. Then I got superinvolved in my work at the office and in volunteer activities with the YWCA. I was coordinating a support group for teen moms at the Y. Anything that kept me away from men. Finally, a friend looked me in the eye and said, 'Why are you so gun-shy?'

"I looked straight back at her and acted as if I didn't know what she was talking about. But she knew me too well, and after a long talk I decided it was time to start looking again. I knew I was being irrational. I kept thinking, 'All men are creeps!' But what I really meant was, 'I'm so afraid of falling in love with a wonderful guy like Jim again and having him leave me.' "

Intimacy and Communication

Honest communication is essential to true intimacy. We cannot feel close to another person if we are hiding or withholding important thoughts or feelings about that person, or even about ourselves. This doesn't mean, however, that we should lay bare our every thought or emotion. High self-disclosure can be detrimental to the development of intimacy at the beginning of a relationship, and it can damage a more established relationship if the "brutal truth" is too brutal. In the former case, when a relationship is just beginning, opening oneself up may threaten a partner who doesn't have the same commitment to the relationship and who therefore would not share in return. In the latter case, when a relationship is established, "honesty" may be a thin disguise for hostility or anger against the partner or spouse.

Nevertheless, open communication in appropriate doses, at appropriate times, and with good intentions can enhance a relationship and lead to greater intimacy. A couple who tries to maintain peace and stability by glossing over disputes or ignoring problems is headed for trouble. Finding a productive way of resolving differences, by meeting them head on and negotiating a workable compromise, is key. Communication in intimate relationships is the subject of Chapter 8.

Intimate Experiences Versus an Intimate Relationship

One can feel close to another person in a variety of ways and in different areas of one's life. Some of these ways include emotional intimacy, intellectual intimacy, social intimacy, recreational intimacy, and sexual intimacy.

An **intimate experience** is one in which we feel close or share ourselves with another person. For example, a deep philosophic discussion can be a very intellectually intimate experience. Working together successfully on a project can also lead to an emotionally intimate feeling. And the most commonly thought of type of intimacy is sexual intimacy. Nevertheless, people perceive experiences differently, and what one person perceives as an intimate experience may not seem so intimate to another.

An **intimate relationship** is one in which we share intimate experiences in several areas over time, with expectations that this sharing will continue. It is difficult to have and to maintain intimate relationships with more than a few people at once because intimacy is time-consuming. For example, how many really good friends, intimate friends, do you have? Probably very few.

Also, it is quite clear from research with couples that no relationship can provide intimate experiences in all areas all the time. With apologies to Abraham Lincoln, "You can please some of the people some of the time, but you can't please all of the people all of the time." This is certainly the case with love relationships. Intimate partners may be able to satisfy each other in a number of ways—emotionally, intellectually, sexually—but both partners will most likely satisfy other intimacy needs outside the relationship. We do not suggest sexual intimacy as one of these areas, because an extramarital affair can destroy intimacy in all other areas of the relationship. But both partners can have friends of either sex at work or in other areas of their lives, friends who are very special and who provide something that the mate does not or cannot. These friendships can add to each partner's happiness and thus be a positive force in the couple or marriage relationship as long as the partners can minimize feelings of insecurity and jealousy.

The Paradox of Marriage and Intimacy

Most people in our culture seek marriage in their quest for intimacy. Marriage is an important source of intimacy, but, paradoxically, intimacy too often declines, and sometimes is completely destroyed, after marriage. For many, marriage increases intimacy; for others, however, it becomes an intimacy trap and smothers the very thing the two people desperately seek to enjoy. On the one hand, marriage is extolled as the path to happiness; on the other hand, it can be a source of conflict.

The basic question remains: Does marriage provide intimacy on a permanent basis? The answer is a qualified yes. Marriage can provide intimacy, but the partners must work to make it happen. Marriage in our society has become the classic great escape. People escape into marriage to avoid loneliness and to find intimacy. Later, when the marriage feels stifling or empty, some people escape from it to maintain their sanity and independence. In the next section, we'll look more closely at how couples can develop and maintain intimacy.

Developing Intimacy

Researchers have identified ten areas of marital and family dynamics that contribute to a couple's satisfaction or dissatisfaction with their relationship (Fowers & Olson, 1989). Success in achieving intimacy in these areas increases the chances for success in the relationship as a whole. Most couples, of course, do not achieve complete satisfaction in all of these areas, but working toward a satisfactory level of intimacy in each area increases the chance of maintaining a healthy relationship.

Traits of Intimate and Nonintimate Relationships

In a large-scale study of 5,039 married couples, Blaine Fowers and David Olson (1989) looked at the relationship between level of intimacy and satisfaction with marriage. All the couples completed a comprehensive marital inventory called **ENRICH,** which contained 10 categories of questions about the issues that are important in a married couple's relationship. The inventory is scored by comparing the responses of the two partners on all questions in each category, calculating the percentage of agreement for each of the 10 categories, and then averaging the results. The couples with high scores (i.e., a high percentage of agreement) on the ENRICH marital satisfaction scale were identified as high-intimacy couples, and those with low scores were labeled low-intimacy couples.

As hypothesized, the agreement scores of couples in the high-intimacy group were significantly higher than those of the couples in the low-intimacy group in 8 of the 10 ENRICH relationship-issue categories (Figure 5.4). The categories showing the most significant differences were sexual relations, communication, and conflict resolution. These three areas have been identified repeatedly in various analyses as significant to maintaining intimacy in a relationship. It is also noteworthy that almost all (86%) of the couples in the low-intimacy group had considered divorce.

Ten Essential Couple Relationship Strengths

Ten essential areas for developing and maintaining an intimate relationship, identified by Fowers and Olson (1989), are described here:

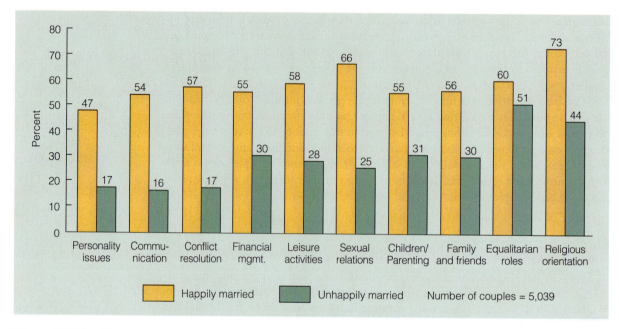

Figure 5.4 Happily Versus Unhappily Married Couples. *Source:* "ENRICH Marital Inventory: A Discriminant Validity and Cross-validation Assessment" by B. J. Fowers and D. H. Olson, 1989, *Journal of Marital and Family Therapy, 15* (1), pp. 65–79. Copyright 1989 by American Association of Marital and Family Therapy. Reprinted by permission.

Personality Compatibility   Comfort with a partner's personality is important to a healthy relationship. The more we like and accept the personality traits and habits of our partner, the more satisfying the relationship. Conversely, personality traits such as tardiness, temper, moodiness, stubbornness, jealousy, and possessiveness are a few of the many traits that contribute to negative feelings and problems in a relationship. Couples need to realize that most of these traits will not change or disappear after marriage.

Communication Skills   Although definitions of communication differ, there is considerable agreement that good communication is essential for maintaining an intimate relationship (Olson, 1992). Some people are more comfortable talking about their feelings than others, especially their feelings about their relationship. However, sharing even the most mundane thoughts or feelings can be a difficult experience for some people. Developing a satisfactory pattern of communication is critical to the development of an intimate relationship.

Conflict Resolution Skills   People have different attitudes about conflict—both acknowledging it and resolving it—in a relationship. Some partners are more open than others to recognizing and resolving issues. Others believe it is better simply not to talk about problems and to hope they will somehow disappear. Couples who do well resolve conflict rather than avoid issues.

Financial Management Skills   Finances are a key issue in any relationship, and intimacy is enhanced when a couple is in close accord on how to earn and spend money. Some people tend to be spenders; others are savers. Most are somewhere in between. Differences of philosophy about spending money can cause considerable conflict. Issues regarding whether to have separate or joint bank accounts are important to resolve.

Shared Leisure Activities We all have different ways of spending our leisure time. If one partner wants to backpack but the other prefers ballet, there is a potential for conflict in the relationship. The couple must work out a satisfactory compromise, a solution preferred by neither but workable for both. Do one or both partners believe that leisure activities should always be shared exclusively between them, or is there room for friends to become involved? Sharing leisure activities can enhance relationship intimacy, but the potential for conflict in this area is always present.

Sexual Relations Sex is an emotional thermometer of the quality of a relationship. It is also an important aspect of human relations that couples generally have a difficult time discussing. When it comes to affection and sexual expression, differences are inevitable. Couples who have a good sexual relationship are able to express their affection freely and openly with each other and respect each others' needs and desires.

Consensus on Attitudes About Children and Parenting Couples must decide whether to have children and, if so, how many. They also need to determine how they want to raise their children. Individuals have different views on the impact of children on the marriage relationship. They also differ greatly on how they prioritize children, marriage, and career. Discipline techniques vary widely, and the

Open communication is an essential component of a successful relationship, but talking about feelings—especially feelings about the relationship—can be an excruciating experience for some individuals and couples. Fortunately, communication skills can be learned.

Sharing leisure activities is one way couples can maintain and build the intimacy of their relationship. This couple has chosen an activity that allows for companionship, exercise, and adventure.

values and goals to be imparted to children can be a source of disagreement between spouses. Consensus on these issues can be beneficial to intimacy.

Good Relationships With Family and Friends   Relationships with relatives, in-laws, and friends can either strengthen or cause problems in a marriage. If the challenges of these family relationships and friendships are not handled carefully, they can compromise a couple's intimacy. Good friends, especially other couples, can be a valuable resource.

"We're friends with three other couples, and about every 6 weeks or so we get together at somebody's house for a potluck or whatever, just to talk," related Brenda, a mother of two teenage boys in Raton, New Mexico. "It's really good to hear what's happening to everybody. They're always short on money, short on time, and long on stress, just like our family. Charlie's veterinary business is extremely demanding for him, and I put in long hours, too, keeping the books.

"It's comforting to share our lives. We laugh a lot. It puts my life into better perspective. Sometimes I get whiney and think, 'Woe is me.' But everybody's got problems, and our friends have a way of cheering me up."

Consensus on Roles   Do the partners agree on leadership in their relationship? Do they agree on roles and the division of tasks? Will one partner stay home to care for the children? Who will do the dishes, the laundry, the housecleaning? Who will maintain the car and do the yard work? A key to intimacy in this area is for a couple to find the type of role relationship that works best for them, whether it be equalitarian sharing or a division of tasks and responsibilities that follows the more traditional gender-role definitions. The rigors of daily life require couples to agree on many issues.

Shared Spiritual Values   Religion often brings comfort to individuals and builds bonds among family members, but it can also drive a wedge between a couple. Some couples share spiritual values, which form a strong bond between them, but for some couples, the issue of religion is the source of long and explosive arguments. In studies of strong families, religious and spiritual values are mentioned repeatedly as an important family strength (Stinnett et al., 1997).

In sum, attaining intimacy is a process that takes time, effort, and hard work. Once achieved, it also takes effort to maintain. Couples must constantly search for ways to vitalize and revitalize their intimate relationship. Although it may be easy to fall in love, it is very difficult to stay in love. Nevertheless, achieving and maintaining intimacy is a challenge worth pursuing.

Intimacy Games

Two important aspects of any intimate relationship are honesty and straightforwardness. When one partner asks for or tells the other what he or she wants, the other partner is free to comply or not comply. But many people play **destructive intimacy games** with their partner, concealing what they really want and attempting instead to manipulate the partner into doing or giving them what they want. (As we will see later in this section, there are also constructive intimacy games.) Because destructive intimacy games tend to be effective in the short run—people often get what they want using these techniques—they can be rewarding. But in the long run, they undermine relationships. Closeness and sharing suffer, resentment grows, and the relationship may ultimately be destroyed.

Along these lines is what family therapists refer to as the **zero-sum game.** In this type of game, there is a winner and a loser. Unlike more cooperative games in which both people win by working together, the competitive zero-sum game results on one person winning what the other person loses, hence the sum is zero. In human relationships, zero-sum games usually lead to problems, especially if the rules are constructed so that the same person wins most of the time. One partner might say, for example, that he or she will make the final decisions about how the couple's money is spent because he or she works outside the home and the other spouse doesn't.

Why do people play destructive intimacy games? Sometimes people don't really know what they want from a relationship. Sometimes they're embarrassed to ask for what they want, or they assume they'll be turned down. Sometimes they perceive a situation to be so difficult that the only way they can see to handle it is

Table 5.1 Dimensions of Intimacy Games	
Characteristic	**Relevant Questions**
Name of game	What name describes the game?
Players	Who were the players/opponents? Who were the spectators? Who were the referees?
Playing field	Where was the game played? When was the game played?
Objectives	What were the short-term objectives? What were the long-term objectives?
Rules	What were the rules? Were they implicit or explicit?
Strategies	How was the game played? What strategies did the offense use? What counterstrategies did the defense use?
Communication style	Did the participants express themselves verbally, nonverbally, or both?
Rewards and penalties	What were the rewards? What were the penalties?
Outcomes	How effective was the game in the short term? in the long term? How enjoyable was the game? Was there a winner and a loser?

by playing a game. Then, because playing games often works in the short run, people tend to play them again and again.

Destructive intimacy games share many elements of such games as chess, bridge, and football: goals, players, rules, and strategies. But in football, for example, everyone knows what the goal is, who the players are, what the rules are, what the rewards and penalties are, when the game is over, and what the outcome is. In a destructive intimacy game, many of these elements are hidden or unclear. Intimacy games can be identified and defined by asking the kinds of questions listed in Table 5.1.

Constructive Intimacy Games

Although most intimacy games are destructive, **constructive intimacy games** can enhance a relationship. Too often intimates focus on what they do *not* get from each other rather than on how often they benefit from the other person. This sets up a negative cycle: As one person becomes more negative and less willing to give, the other person reciprocates. Soon neither person in the relationship is giving to the other in a positive way.

One way to reverse this type of negative interaction is to focus on the positive, on what you can do for the other person and what the other person can do for you. Giving in a positive way encourages the other person to do the same. Also, telling the other person what you want increases your chances of receiving it.

Research by psychologists has indicated that when one partner does something positive for the other, the other will respond positively in return in the short term. They found that over a period of 2 weeks, if one spouse did 10 positive things for the other, that partner would receive about the same number of positive gestures in return from the other partner. In contrast, when individuals were negative, they received negative responses, and the negative pattern repeated itself. The researchers conducted another interesting experiment in which they asked partners to double the number of compliments they gave to their spouses each day for a week. Although both spouses felt it would be strange to exchange so many compliments, they found that the recipient not only accepted the compliments but returned about the same number over the next few days. This approach developed a positive complimentary cycle. The Beatles put it more poetically when they sang, "In the end, the love you take/Is equal to the love you make."

Unlike destructive intimacy games, constructive games help develop positive cycles. In addition, constructive games have objectives that are specific, rules that are explicit, strategies that are cooperative rather than competitive, and outcomes that are mutually rewarding. A constructive intimacy game called "Giving Compliments" is described in Box 5.2. Couples who would like instruction in constructive intimacy games can enroll in a couples communication workshop. Research indicates that such training can lessen manipulative and competitive interchanges between partners (Olson, 1992). Constructive games can be especially enjoyable in intimate relationships, which allow for a greater variety of ways in which partners can reward each other and develop more positive feelings toward each other.

Destructive Intimacy Games

As mentioned, many intimacy games are destructive. Identifying and analyzing a few can illuminate their pitfalls and provide the basis for developing more contructive and positive ways of relating. Two destructive intimacy games are "I Don't Care; You Decide" and "The Ties That Bind."

"I Don't Care; You Decide" Many times, when couples are involved in decision making, one partner genuinely wants the other partner to make the decision. However, when one partner knows what he or she wants but is afraid to tell the other person, or when the partner wants to make the decision but have it appear as if the other person has made it, the decision-making process can become a game.

The initiator often begins playing this game when he or she is relatively sure the other person will make the decision the initiator prefers. The initiator often opens the game with a loaded question, such as, "Do you want to stop here for dinner?" This really means, "I want to stop here, and I hope you will know that and make that decision." When the other player says yes, however, she or he can then be held responsible if the food is bad, the service is poor, or the bill is too high.

The following dialogue illustrates another common way this game begins. Jennifer and Tom have received an invitation in the mail from a couple they haven't

B O X   5 . 2

A Constructive Intimacy Game

Name of game	"Giving Compliments"	**Strategies**	*Strategy 1:* Marty gives appropriate compliments whenever possible. *Counterstrategy 1:* Pam accepts and enjoys the compliments. *Strategy 2:* Pam focuses on giving to Marty. *Counterstrategy 2:* Marty accepts the compliments and, in turn, continues giving to Pam.
Players	Two intimates (Marty and Pam). *Spectators:* Other family members. *Referees:* None needed.		
Playing field	Any place or time players are together.		This is a cycle that feeds on positive giving and receiving.
Objectives	Short term— *Marty:* To give as many compliments to Pam as possible for at least a day; to focus on the positives rather than the negatives and on giving rather than receiving. *Pam:* To receive compliments graciously; to not question why they are given.	**Communication style**	Verbal is generally best. Doing something nice is also acceptable.
	Long term— *Marty:* To improve the relationship in a positive way; to receive compliments from Pam in turn. *Pam:* To give compliments to Marty in turn; to improve the relationship in a positive way.	**Rewards**	*Marty:* Feels good about being able to give to another. *Pam:* Appreciates compliments from another.
Rules	Explicit— *Marty:* To identify and compliment positive behavior by Pam; to not complain about not immediately receiving as much as is being given. *Pam:* To not question why so many compliments are being given.	**Penalties**	None, if the game is played correctly. However, if either Marty or Pam stops giving, he or she will also stop receiving. Also, if Pam questions or does not accept Marty's compliments, the game will stop.
	Implicit— None.	**Outcome**	If played effectively, this is a mutually enjoyable game in which both participants win. It can improve a relationship in both the short run and the long run and can be played anytime or anywhere.

seen in some time. The party-givers are primarily Tom's friends, whom he has known for years. Jennifer doesn't enjoy them because they argue so much.

TOM: What do you want to do about this party? Should we go?

JENNIFER: I don't care . . . [even though she does].

TOM: Wouldn't you like to see them again?

JENNIFER: Well . . . don't you have other things you'd rather do this Saturday?

TOM: No, I'd rather go. Okay?

Human relationships are too precious to risk by playing destructive games. Constructive interactions, positive feedback, and honest communication are the keys to successful, long-lasting relationships.

JENNIFER: Okay, but . . .

TOM: Are you sure you want to go?

JENNIFER: Yes, I guess so.

When Jennifer and Tom go to the party, Jennifer will go reluctantly and will probably be frustrated by the experience. Jennifer had hoped Tom would realize she didn't want to go to the party and would decide they shouldn't go. But by not expressing her true feelings and not actively involving herself in the decision-making process, Jennifer failed to achieve what she intended. This is one of the negative consequences of playing games.

Another negative consequence might be that when she gets home from the party, Jennifer will feel so miserable or annoyed that when Tom wants to make love, she will say quite honestly, "I don't feel like it tonight." Tom, suspecting Jennifer's playing a game, might speculate, "She didn't want to go to their house all along, and now she's punishing me by withholding sex!" The merry-go-round continues, and both people feel frustrated.

"The Ties That Bind" The parent-child relationship is also fertile ground for destructive intimacy games, especially when the children become adults. Although supposedly played in the best interest of all concerned, these games are often disguised, and the players often do not enjoy playing them. Nevertheless, there is generally some game playing between parents and their adult children. Giving up the role of parent is difficult. Although many parents would agree intellectually with Kahlil Gibran's observations on children, they often have difficulty living this philosophy:

> *Your children are not your children.*
> *They are the sons and daughters of Life's longing for itself.*
> *They come through you but not from you,*
> *And though they are with you yet they belong not to you. . . .*
> *You are the bows from which your children as living arrows are sent forth.*
> *The archer sees the mark upon the path of the infinite, and He bends you with His*
>   *might that His arrows may go swift and far.* (1923/1976, p. 24)

The degree and type of involvement parents have with their married children cause difficulty in many families. The prevalence of in-law jokes attests to the significance of this issue in marital and family relationships. Some mutually agreed-upon degree of balance is important. But it can be difficult to successfully balance the dimension of separateness as individuals with that of connectedness to our families of origin. Some parents have difficulty accepting the fact that their children are grown up and desire a more independent lifestyle, one that is free from past traditions. Parents who are frustrated by their dwindling contact with their adult children often play games, such as the one described in Box 5.3, in which the ties that bind are maintained through implicit rules and subtle strategies.

Limiting Destructive Games

Over the years, researchers and family therapists have devised a number of useful techniques for limiting gamesmanship in families and maximizing true intimacy. The four central techniques are (1) naming the game, (2) making implicit rules explicit, (3) identifying strategies and counterstrategies, and (4) discussing the disguised objectives and making them clear and specific. Each of these components is described in more detail below.

Naming the Game   Catching yourself and others playing intimacy games can be fun, as well as a way to increase intimacy in your relationships—as long as it is done in a playful and good-natured manner. A destructive intimacy game is a ploy someone uses to get something without directly asking for it. When you catch yourself or a loved one doing this, try very hard to describe what you see honestly. Encourage the loved one to be honest, too. Avoid blame or sarcasm. A matter-of-fact, caring approach is much more effective than a heavy-handed one.

Once the game playing is identified, try to give the game a catchy title. For example, everybody who has been in love is guilty at one time or another of playing the "If You Really Love Me, You'll Know What I Want" game. In this game we assume that the other person can read our mind at all times; if the loved one can't, then he or she must not care about us. Identifying and naming a game and focusing on the problem in a rational and calm manner are major steps in eliminating game playing.

Making Implicit Rules Explicit   Implicit (secret) rules are difficult to reveal, and they add confusion to the destructive intimacy game. Nevertheless, exposing implicit rules is an effective technique for destroying the destructive intimacy game.

BOX 5.3

A Destructive Intimacy Game

Name of game	"The Ties That Bind"		*Adam's counterstrategy:* Not to accept gifts, especially money.
Players	Parents (Lily and Pete) and their adult child (Adam).	**Communication style**	Usually nonverbal but sometimes by mail or phone.
Playing field	Two separate households.	**Rewards**	*Lily and Pete's:* To maintain Adam's dependency.
Objectives	Short term— *Lily and Pete's:* To influence Adam's decisions. *Adam's:* To become independent.		*Adam's:* To get help paying bills and meeting other financial needs.
	Long term— *Lily and Pete's:* To maintain Adam's dependent relationship with them. *Adam's:* To become independent.	**Penalties**	*Lily and Pete's:* Attempt fails; Adam refuses help and achieves independence. *Adam's:* Accepts help and remains dependent on parents.
Rules	Implicit— No open discussion of issues, among others.	**Outcomes**	Mutual frustration. Game works in short run but fails in long run. Feels like a win-lose game.
	Explicit— Avoided.		
Strategies	*Lily and Pete's:* To give economic support disguised as gifts.		

The most common implicit rule is "Don't directly ask for what you want." This rule assumes that if you do ask directly, you will be refused. But playing by this rule puts you in a difficult situation. You don't ask directly because you think you'll be refused, but because you don't ask directly, people have to guess what you want. If they don't guess correctly, you won't get what you want.

By being direct, you give the other person a chance to choose how and when he or she might give you what you want. This places the responsibility for action on the other person and frees that person to give to you. And giving others what they want—making them feel good—makes the giver feel good also.

Unveiling Game Strategies Withdrawing quietly and sullenly from an argument is a common strategy in destructive intimacy games. Its intent is to keep the other player in the argument from continuing on the offensive. The "opponent" may then respond with a counterstrategy, by saying, for example, "What's wrong, Dear?" And the obvious counterstrategy to this ploy is for the quiet and sullen "Dear" to respond, "[Sigh] Oh, nothing."

Unveiling game strategies like this isn't easy because, as in cards or tennis, players often try to confuse their opponent. Your intimate opponent may set you up by unveiling one game strategy, only to substitute another. Nevertheless, unveiling strategies can be an important step in building intimacy in a relationship.

Identifying Disguised Objectives   Rather than directly asking for what they want, some people disguise their objectives. The loaded question is a common technique for disguising what one really wants and for making the partner think that he or she is making the decision. For example, suppose your partner asks, "Wouldn't you like to go to this movie?" To identify the hidden objective, you can ask your partner what movie she or he wants to see.

Being Single

Marriage is still very popular; 90% of young Americans expect to marry at some time in their lives. This proportion has remained relatively stable for the past quarter century. In spite of high levels of divorce, most young people expect their marriages to last. But there has been a change in recent decades. Young people are staying single longer and getting married at a slightly older age. In 1996 there were more men and, particularly, more women who had never been married than there were in 1960 (Table 5.2).

Government figures indicate that 19.9% of women and 26.8% of men over age 18 are single (U.S. Bureau of the Census, 1997, p. 57). In 1950 only 9% of all U.S. households were occupied by a single individual. By 1993 that figure had jumped to 25% (U.S. Bureau of the Census, 1994, p. 59). In the same period, single-parent homes jumped from 7% to 30% of all households (U.S. Bureau of the Census, 1997, p. 62).

Increase in Singlehood

Many factors have contributed to the increase in **singlehood** today. For one, education and career are delaying the age at which young people are marrying. Linked to this trend is an increasing recognition in our society that singlehood can be a legitimate, healthy, and happy alternative to marriage. A. Shostak (1987) found through interviews with young people that most would be "a little" bothered if they failed to marry. Relatively few said they would be "greatly bothered" by failing to marry at some time during their lives. The mothers of these same young adults also generally acknowledged that marriage was not a "must" for their children.

Shostak also concluded that marriage continues to be more important to young women than to young men. Although more and more young women are seeking jobs and careers, they still tend to value marriage and parenthood somewhat more than young men do. This is the case even though education and work opportunities have opened up for females in recent decades; if they choose to, women can make it on their own more easily than in the past. Evidence suggests that if an individual has experienced divorce in his or her family, that person is more likely to have both negative attitudes about marriage and positive attitudes about singlehood.

Some singles have been married before but are now in transition. About two thirds of divorced people remarry, usually 2 to 3 years after they divorce. But researchers are finding that even though most people remarry after a divorce, the rate of remarriage has dropped by more than 25% (M. Coleman & Ganong, 1991). The fact that individuals are not rushing back into marriage is another indication that the single lifestyle is becoming more and more acceptable in our society.

Table 5.2 Percentage of Women and Men Remaining Single	1960	1970	1980	1996
Women remaining single				
Ages 20–24	28.4%	35.8%	50.2%	68.5%
Ages 25–29	10.5	10.5	20.8	37.6
Men remaining single				
Ages 20–24	53.1	54.7	68.6	81.0
Ages 25–29	20.8	19.1	32.4	52.0

Source: U.S. Bureau of the Census (1997, p. 56).

"I don't know, perhaps I'll never get married again," a middle-aged Alabama woman said. "At first after the divorce I was very panicky, like, 'Oh, I've got to be married, I've got to be married!' And then after several months of looking for the ideal mate, I discovered that I liked myself quite a bit and actually was quite content having my own private space in the world. I'm a dean now, and the college is developing pretty well. In a few years I might start applying for vice-chancellor jobs around the country. I think I'm capable of moving up a bit in higher education.

"Sure, it gets lonely sometimes. But I've got lots of friends, male and female. I get on the phone and call someone, and we get together and talk and laugh, and I think, 'Hmmm, it could be a lot worse. I could still be dealing with Jerome's drinking.'

[What about sex?] "Sex? Who needs it? . . . Just kidding! You can find sex without tying yourself down to a person forever. Gee, that sounds funny coming from someone who 20 years ago was so very, very conservative. But actually, I think I've got a realistic view of life now. If all I had in common with a fellow was sex, I'd be crazy to marry him."

Singlehood as an Alternative to Marriage

An increasing number of people in the United States see singlehood as a legitimate alternative to marriage. This outlook represents a major shift in our society's attitude toward marriage. Throughout most of American history, the failure to marry (note how even the terminology is loaded) was considered undesirable. Of course, not everyone married in 18th- and 19th-century America, and many married in their late 20s or their 30s. But social circumstances or pure economics probably contributed to not marrying more than personal desires did, for marriage was highly valued. *Old maid* and *spinster* were certainly not flattering descriptions for unmarried women (Degler, 1980).

In colonial times (the 17th and 18th centuries), virtually all unmarried individuals lived in a family environment of some type—either in their parents' home or as servants in another's home. Unmarried people of all ages usually stayed dependent on the families with whom they lived until they married. Only then did they become fully independent members of society.

Once considered a sad fate to be avoided at almost any cost, singlehood is today recognized as a legitimate, happy and healthy alternative to marriage. This single man in his 30s demonstrates some of the benefits of being single, including self-sufficiency and the time and space to cater to one's own tastes.

In the 19th century, the position of unmarried people began to change. They increasingly became involved in wage labor outside the family and often lived in boardinghouses. With the rise of the industrial system, many young people went to work in factories, often at some distance from the farms. The boardinghouses exercised family-type controls but were still quite different from a traditional family environment. Although attitudes toward singlehood may have improved over the 19th and early 20th centuries, social custom held that marriage was by far the preferable state, and those who remained single continued to be stigmatized (Veroff, Douvan, & Kulka, 1981).

In sum, the lifestyles of single individuals have changed in recent decades. More people are remaining single longer. Single young men and women are living together without being married—enjoying some of the benefits of marriage without the legal or religious commitments and with less stigmatization. There is at least one positive result of this trend toward longer singlehood and later marriage: The older one marries, the more likely one is to make a mature and permanent decision. Those who delay marriage until they have completed their education and found satisfying work increase their chances for marital stability.

Characteristics of Successful Singles

The adult single population today includes people who are single for a variety of reasons. One large and rapidly growing group of singles are professional and career-oriented individuals. Highly educated and achievement oriented, many of these people prefer to remain unmarried. Although employers used to believe that single professionals were less desirable employees (thinking perhaps that they could not adjust to marriage or were unstable or undependable), they are now beginning to appreciate the flexibility of "unattached" employees. Single individuals can transfer to new locations more easily than whole families, and they usually have fewer outside commitments, which can complicate a married employee's adjustment to a new locale. Single employees tend to devote more extra hours to their careers. Furthermore, they are as highly trained and capable as married employees.

Although single women have been subject to discrimination in salary and promotions (often because of employer expectations that they might marry and resign), the widespread adoption of affirmative action policies has contributed to a more equitable treatment of female employees. As a result, singlehood is losing its stigma within professional groups.

Women who remain single are likely to be high achievers of above-average intelligence. This can make it difficult for them to find an unattached man of equal status, because men often prefer to marry "down" (Macklin, 1980, p. 906). Because females outnumber males in the general population, men can choose from a larger pool of potential marriage partners. First-born girls (who are often achievement oriented) and "only" children are somewhat more likely to remain single than other children.

Although a few singles may lead the swinging lifestyle portrayed in Hollywood movies, the vast majority live very conventional lives. Career-oriented single people are likely to use the freedom their lifestyle provides to participate in a wide variety of experiences that individuals with families rarely have time for. They also like the flexibility to devote as much time as they like to career interests, to travel wherever and whenever the job demands, and to alter their lifestyle as they desire or when new opportunities arise.

One of the biggest problems singles face is developing a circle of friends and associates with whom they can share social activities. To meet this need, many churches, synagogues, and social organizations (as well as resort lodges and nightclubs) have created singles events. Most employed singles report that their social life is as active as they want it to be, and few middle-aged career-oriented singles report being lonely or isolated. Although single people may at times feel they have missed something in life by not creating a family and may perhaps fear the prospect of loneliness in old age, they often can satisfy these needs by networking with other singles.

Making Singlehood Work

Singles are an enormously diverse group; no stereotype can describe them. Individuals are single for many different reasons. In addition to younger, never-married individuals, there are divorced single people, separated single people, and widowed single people. Thus, it is very difficult to generalize about singles. A 19-year-old college student who has never been married, a 33-year-old career woman who has just separated from her husband, a 27-year-old divorced father with custody of three young children, and a 78-year-old widow whose husband has just died of cancer are a few examples of the many faces of singlehood.

As mentioned earlier, singlehood can be a happy, healthy lifestyle. Nevertheless, for many single individuals loneliness can be a challenge. John C. Woodward

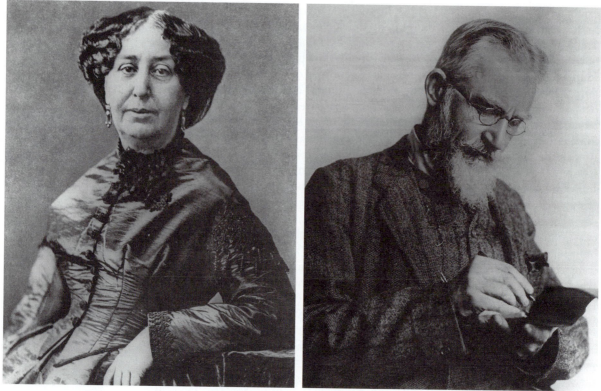

For some, singlehood affords room to develop talent without the distraction of responsibilities to a mate and children. Would novelist George Sand (1804–1876) have achieved the same degree of literary artistry had she married Chopin? Would George Bernard Shaw (1856–1950) have given us, among other works, the play *Pygmalion* (on which the musical *My Fair Lady* is based) if he had been happily married?

(1988) offers the following seven suggestions for single individuals of all types to cope with loneliness.

- *Appraise yourself.* Ask yourself what kind of investment you have in loneliness. What is the payoff for being lonely? What are the good things about yourself? If you have difficulty listing your attributes, ask some people who know you.

- *Take a chance.* To relieve feelings of loneliness, you have to reach out and take risks. You must tell people how you really feel and what you need. Say, "I'm really lonely today. I wish I just had somebody to talk to." Until you do this, people can't help you.

- *Don't expect too much.* When you go out socially, go out just to have fun. Many lonely people go out with a different motive: to find the perfect person, a lifelong friend. When they don't succeed, they soon prefer to stay home and watch television, isolating themselves even more. Convince yourself, instead, that you can enjoy relationships that are less than perfect.

- *Depend on yourself.* Looking for someone else to make you feel all right is seldom effective. You have to depend on yourself and participate in activities you enjoy.

Single people have the same basic desire for sexual intimacy that married people have, but they must take different approaches to fulfilling that need. For some, clubs such as this one offer the right mix of sociability and opportunity.

- *Rejoin your family.* Your family can be a great support. Regardless of how you treat your family or how they treat you, you still belong to that family. Families are often helpful to people coping with loneliness.

- *Find an outside interest.* Try to find something that really interests or excites you, and then work at it. If you join an organization, for example, don't just sit in the corner. Take some responsibility. Volunteer for things; really get involved.

- *Find a community.* A community can be any group in which you become a member, such as a bowling league, card club, or nature club.

In addition to loneliness, there are other aspects of singlehood that deserve attention. Margaret Adams (1976) has argued that there are three essential criteria for a successful single life:

- The capacity and opportunity to be economically self-sufficient.

- The capacity and opportunity to be socially and psychologically autonomous.

- A clearly thought-out intent to remain single by choice rather than by default.

Adams recognizes that becoming economically self-sufficient is no easy task for some singles, especially single mothers with young children. The first step to success, then, is to be able to earn a decent salary. Second, single people must develop a sense of social and psychological independence. Although singles need a good network of friends to count on, they must also have the skill and determination to stand on their own two feet. Third, those who *choose* singlehood are more successful at it than those who feel they have no other choice. Singles by choice enjoy the opportunities for solitude and for developing a wide network of friendships. Singles by choice enjoy the freedom to invest as much time in their careers as they want and the freedom to spend money as they wish.

Summary

- Love and friendship are alike in many ways, but there are crucial differences that make love both more rewarding and more volatile. Love relationships differ from very good friendships in that they have higher levels of fascination, exclusiveness, sexual desire, a greater depth of caring about the other person, a greater potential for enjoyment, and other positive emotions.

- The love triangle, developed by Robert Sternberg, has three dimensions: commitment, intimacy, and passion. Combinations of these dimensions are seen in eight different types of love relationships.

- There are three noteworthy perspectives on love. First, Erich Fromm maintains that love is difficult and requires work and practice. Second, Stanton Peele suggests that many people in love are addicted to love, just as people are addicted to alcohol, tobacco, or other drugs. Third, James Dobson argues that demonstrating some independence from a relationship (tough love) can strengthen it.

- Intimacy involves feeling close to and sharing oneself with another. Although marriage is an important source of intimacy, intimacy often declines after marriage and sometimes disappears completely. Intimacy takes a great deal of time, effort, and hard work to develop and maintain.

- Ten essential couple relationship strengths are personality compatibility, communication skills, conflict resolution skills, financial management skills, shared leisure activities, sexual relations, consensus on attitudes about children and parenting, good relationships with family and friends, consensus on roles, and shared spiritual values.

- Intimacy games can be either destructive or constructive. To minimize destructive games, it's important to identify them, make their rules explicit, determine the hidden strategies, and make the disguised objectives clear and specific.

- Young people are staying single longer and marrying at a slightly older age than in the past, partly because of their pursuit of education and career.

- An increasing number of people in today's society see singlehood as a viable alternative to marriage. This represents a major shift in thinking.

Key Terms

Passion Cluster	infatuation	intimate relationship
Caring Cluster	empty love	ENRICH
commitment	romantic love	destructive intimacy game
intimacy	fatuous love	zero-sum game
passion	companionate love	constructive intimacy game

non-love   consummate love   singlehood

liking   intimate experience

Activities

1. In a small group, discuss your friendships and how they are similar to and different from love relationships.

2. What is romantic to you? In a small group, share a description of an especially romantic time in your life. What are the similarities and differences among the descriptions group members provide?

3. Take a class survey—using anonymous written responses—to find out how many times each student has been in love. What is the average number? What is the range (lowest to highest)?

4. Try this simple exercise. (Don't tell anyone what you're doing until you've completed it.) Count the negative comments you make to a loved one and, for every negative comment, try to say at least five positive things. By simply monitoring yourself, you will make your loved one feel better about himself or herself, make that person feel better about you, and generally improve the tone of your relationship. As you focus on positive behaviors, you will find that the need for criticism will lessen because each of you will become more and more sensitive to each other's needs, and your relationship satisfaction will improve.

5. Interview a divorced or remarried person. Ask how the individual's definition of love changed as she or he went through the following phases: dating, engagement, marriage, marital dissolution and divorce, singlehood, and remarriage. To do this exercise well, spend 45 to 60 minutes with the person to get a good understanding of what happened to the marriage and why.

Suggested Readings

Bradshaw, J. (1992). *Creating love: The next great stage of growth*. New York: Bantam. By one of America's most popular lecturers on intimate relationships.

Buscaglia, L. F. (1992). *Born for love: Reflections on loving*. Thorofare, NJ: Slack/Random House. Thoughts by excellent writer and public speaker Leo Buscaglia, a professor of education at the University of Southern California, who created one of the first university courses on love in the United States.

Hendrick, S. S., & Hendrick, C. (1992). *Romantic love*. Newbury Park, CA: Sage. An engagingly written social-psychological approach to romantic love, interweaving important facts and concepts from sociobiology, philosophy, history, family science, and sociology.

Johnson, S., & Marano, H. E. (1994, March/April). Love: The immutable longing for contact. *Psychology Today*, pp. 32–35, 64, 66. Addresses our desperate need to connect and our desperate fear of connection.

Lerner, H. G. (1989). *The dance of intimacy*. New York: Harper & Row/Perennial. Examines the elaborate steps people go through to bond emotionally with each other, as identified by a clinical psychologist with the Menninger Foundation in Topeka, Kansas.

Osherson, S. (1992). *Wrestling with love: How men struggle with intimacy with women, children, parents, and each other*. New York: Fawcett Columbine. A good book focusing on men's issues; useful reading for both men and women.

CHAPTER 6

Dating, Mate Selection, and Living Together

Regardless of how intense a love relationship is, there are both good and bad reasons for getting married. Similarly, there are both good and bad reasons for remaining single. Today, marriage is a personal choice, not a social dictate. As mentioned in Chapter 5, more people are remaining single, and this choice is increasingly regarded as an acceptable alternative to marriage.

In this chapter we will examine theories that attempt to explain mate selection and the functions and stages of dating. We will focus on mate selection from a cross-cultural point of view, looking at arranged marriages around the world and comparing them with the customary "love matches" of modern developed societies. In American culture, physical attractiveness is the major factor in choosing a mate. We also tend to find mates who are like us in some way, people from our group—ethnic, religious, or socioeconomic. But many of these rules are changing as a result of our increasingly multicultural population. So-called mixed marriages are a growing phenomenon, causing many families to examine their attitudes and behaviors toward people outside their particular cultural group.

Later in this chapter we will take a close look at some serious problems in our society today: conflict and violence in dating and the relationship between premarital violence and violence after marriage. Finally, we will conclude with a discussion on the growing trend of couples living together—an arrangement that is becoming a new courtship stage but one with legal and relationship consequences.

Courtship Patterns

One of the chief reasons so many marriages fail is that the functions of a date and a mate differ radically—that of a date is to be charming; that of a mate to be responsible; and, unfortunately, the most charming individuals are not necessarily the most responsible, while the most responsible are just as often deficient in charm.

—SYDNEY HARRIS, *journalist*

All societies have created some system for matching individuals for marriage and parenthood. These systems range from the practice of bride purchase, to the selection of a mate by the village shaman according to astrological signs, to contractual systems in which a mate may serve as an indentured servant to the bride's parents, to individual choice based on personal attraction and love. In some cultures, couples are matched while they are still infants; in others, the bride or groom must prove their fertility by producing children before they are eligible for marriage. Although the customs of mate selection vary widely, all perform the necessary function of matching a couple for marriage and eventual parenthood.

Parent-Arranged Marriages

Throughout much of world history, courtships were generally brief. In most cultures, the parents of the bride and groom selected the future spouse and made most of the arrangements for the marriage ceremony. If the prospective couple were granted any freedom of choice, they were expected to complete their arrangements in a few days. The pattern common in modern industrialized nations, in which a couple spends months or even years dating and choosing a mate, developed largely over the past century.

Parent-arranged marriages, however, still occur throughout much of the non-industrialized world; up to three quarters of marriages in some cultures may be arranged (Fox, 1980). Although young adults in the United States today might view the practice as archaic and uncivilized, many people worldwide prefer parent-arranged marriages. **Parent-arranged marriages** are based on the principle that the elders in a community have the wisdom to select the appropriate spouse. Parents or elders are more likely to base their decision on economic, political, and social status considerations—to enhance the family's status and position through their choice. Considerations of lineage and family status are generally more important than love or affection in such decisions, although the parents may take the couple's preferences into account to some extent. Arranged marriages thus serve to extend existing family units rather than to create new units. They reinforce ties with other families in the community, strengthening the order and organization of the community (G. R. Lee & Stone, 1980).

Advantages of Arranged Marriages   Parent-arranged marriages are usually very stable, because it is the duty of the whole family to help the new couple get established in life. Divorce is almost unheard of—except for the reason of infertility—because of the potential disapproval a couple would receive from the parents and members of the community who were responsible for the selection. Although love between the couple before marriage is relatively unimportant, affection and respect usually grow through the years; arranged marriages are often quite harmonious. Because there is not really a courtship period, premarital intimacy is minimal or nonexistent.

In parent-arranged marriage systems, couples avoid many of the problems of "American-style" dating. There is virtually no risk of being rejected or of losing one's true love, and one does not have to determine whether one's partner is committed to the relationship. Although many people might not view these factors as advantages, they effectively ensure a stable marriage. Remnants of arranged courtship and marriage systems are still found in our culture today; for example, a limited number of professional marriage brokers still operate among urban ethnic groups. Further, as most single people know, relatives and friends are often only too eager to help find that "perfect" partner (a good example of a marriage facilitated by family and friends is provided in Box 6.1).

Patterns of Change   The world, in general, appears to be moving toward freedom of choice in marriage. This approach is sometimes referred to as the *love match*, though love is not always the goal of marriage in Western industrial societies. Murstein reviewed a number of cross-cultural studies that looked at love marriages versus parent-arranged marriages (1980, pp. 52–54). He concluded that, cross-culturally, the absence of economic means for women leads to early marriage and little individual freedom. The ability of women to work leads to the decline of arranged marriages, enhances the possibility of love matches, and may slightly diminish the marriage rate. In general, the world is also moving toward monogamous marriage, although the rate of advance varies from country to country.

The movement away from arranged marriage appears to be related to industrialization. As countries shift from more rural to urban, industrial societies, love

BOX 6.1

Mate Selection by Family and Friends

In 1998, Dave Weinlick asked his friends and family to select by election which of 29 bridal candidates—none of which he had ever dated—he should marry. They selected Elizabeth Runze. The bride and groom were married at the Mall of America in Bloomington, Minnesota. Today, Dave and Elizabeth are settled into a home and have generally worked out their roles and responsibilities around the house. By not following the typical dating process, these partners have had to work on their relationship without the benefit of past experiences. Although they report having disagreements, they have been able to handle them successfully. Dave and Elizabeth's families have found them to be well matched and doing very well as a couple. Initially, Dave's father was unhappy with Dave's method of selecting a partner, but he is pleased with the outcome, which has brought him closer to his son. Dave and Elizabeth report that their relationship is growing as they learn more about each other, both their similarities and also their differences. (See photo on page 158)

marriages become more common. One study of Turkey, a relatively rural society, found that three quarters of the marriages were still arranged (Fox, 1980). Data from Africa, India, Israel, and Malaysia indicate that love marriages are more likely among people who marry at a later age, have a higher level of education, have a higher socioeconomic status (or the promise of a higher status), and live in an urban setting. A woman who can support herself financially is more likely to want to decide for herself whom she will marry.

Cultural Variations   The ways people find marriage partners vary from culture to culture. In developing countries that are moving away from arranged marriages, the influence of cultural tradition may be combined with modern sensibilities. In India, for example, it is commonly believed that there is one predestined mate who will share life with the spouse through reincarnation. Therefore, parents believe they should supervise their children's marriage choices to avoid mistakes. But many young people are unhappy with this approach, and a compromise is often reached. Semi-arranged marriages, in which parental approval is obtained before the marriage, are becoming more common (Bumiller, 1985).

In China, a marriage law passed in 1980 dramatically changed marriage patterns: from parent-arranged marriages in which a "bride price" was paid to the bride's parents to marriages based on free choice of a partner (Yi, 1984). Because opportunities for meeting eligible partners and for dating are limited in China, young people still depend on arranged introductions by friends and relatives. Dating is often difficult. Young men and women do not know how to act in this new role, and finding a place to be alone together can be a challenge.

Japan, the industrial giant of the Pacific, has generally moved from arranged marriages to love-based marriages. The traditional *nakode*, or matchmaker, is still used in some rural areas of Japan, but the matchmaker's role has become increasingly ceremonial. As more women have entered the labor force and gained financial independence, they have moved away from marriages arranged by their parents. Japanese young people find dating very awkward and uncomfortable, however, because they often do not have much social contact with members of the other sex.

Changing courtship patterns in Japan were reflected in the 1993 marriage of Crown Prince Naruhito to Masako Owada, a well-educated and independent-minded woman without a royal lineage. Nevertheless, their wedding ceremony was steeped in mysticism and traditions dating back hundreds of years. In many cultures, there is an uneasy tension between the old and the new.

The Scandinavian countries are perhaps the most liberal in the world in regard to marriage customs. Parent-arranged marriages disappeared decades ago in Scandinavia, and cohabitation has become the most common type of relationship until after the birth of a child. Research in Sweden indicates a steep drop in the marriage rate. Associated with this decline are an increase in cohabitation and an increase in state and parental support for children born outside of matrimony.

Dating: An American Creation

Dating is a creation of young people in the United States. It symbolizes couples' efforts to take more control over the process of mate selection. Because the United States was one of the first nations to industrialize, it serves as a good example of the changes in dating behavior that occur when a society evolves from an agrarian culture.

The Emergence of Individual-Choice Courtship   Early in U.S. history, parents typically exercised considerable influence over dating and the choice of a mate. Young people were usually tied to the home and, except for the occasional community social event, had little opportunity to escape the watchful eyes of their parents. Opportunities for dating were infrequent. Courtship was a rather formal event, often conducted under parental supervision. Males were expected to get the permission of the female's parents and to initiate the acquaintance. Although the

Shown here four months after their "democratic" marriage drew international attention, Dave and Elizabeth Weinlick were settled in and thinking about children (see Box 6.1 on page 156).

couple were generally allowed the privilege of making up their own minds, family members usually announced their approval (or disapproval) before the relationship got too serious. But even then young people were granted much more freedom of individual choice than exists in a parent-arranged courtship system.

As America became more industrialized and parents began to work away from the home, young people gained considerable freedom from parental supervision, as well as the responsibility for organizing their free time. **Dating,** or individual-choice courtship, emerged as an activity in its own right, creating a new institution within the culture. (See Box 6.2 for one observer's views on the current dating system in the United States.) This pattern, with some variation, appears to be common as societies change from agrarian to industrial.

Along with the emergence of individual-choice courtship and a defined period for dating, permissive behavior also increased. The term **permissiveness** refers to the extent to which couples are physically intimate before marriage. Historically, males were permitted greater freedom and privilege than females and tended to be more experienced in intimate relations than females. However, the same basic forces that revolutionized dating customs in industrial societies also fostered a de-

Limitations of Dating

Dating has become the predominant method of finding a potential mate in the United States and other industrialized societies, yet there are numerous limitations to the current dating system. In his book *I Kissed Dating Goodbye*, Joshua Harris (1997) identifies several shortcomings of dating:

- Dating leads to intimacy but not necessarily to commitment.

- Dating tends to skip friendship, which should be the foundation of a stable relationship.

- Dating focuses on romantic attraction, so it lasts only as long as the romantic feelings remain.

- Dating focuses on enjoying love and romance solely for their recreational value.

- Dating often mistakes a physical relationship for love.

- Dating often isolates a couple from other vital relationships, leaving important friendships in disrepair.

- Dating takes a lot of time and energy, which can distract young adults from their primary responsibility of preparing for the future.

- Dating creates an artificial environment for evaluating another person's character.

Source: Excerpted from *I Kissed Dating Goodbye,* © 1997 by Joshua Harris. Used by permission of Multnomah Publishers, Inc.

cline in the **double standard**—different standards of sexual and social behavior for men than for women. As customs changed, women engaged in more sexual experimentation. The amount of sexual intimacy women experience before marriage still does not match that of men, but because female sexual involvement has increased rapidly, the difference between male and female sexual behavior is much smaller today than it was in the past. Although many females still expect males to call them, to plan dates, and to propose marriage, females are more assertive and participate to a greater extent in the dating process than they did in earlier generations.

By the 1980s, people were dating sooner—and also in a more casual fashion—than earlier generations had. Dating now commonly begins in preadolescence as a group experience, in which couples attend get-togethers as pairs. Peer-group values often advocate an individualistic approach to dating, stressing that people should "do their own thing." Steady dating is still popular, but adolescents have relaxed many of the requirements of exclusivity and commitment that were the norm in the past.

There is also evidence that young people are forming more cross-sex friendships than in earlier generations and placing more emphasis on relating to one another. Adolescents today are forming a more complete social system during the courtship period than earlier generations did, and this social system has much more influence on teenagers than parents or moral-religious systems do. On the other hand, courtship customs are less oriented toward marriage than in earlier periods; young people are less eager to become formally engaged and are delaying marriage. Divorce statistics appear to be influencing their thinking, causing them to approach marriage with more reservations. Cohabitation has become popular as a means of "testing" a relationship and exploring the nature of the marital experience.

Dating trends have changed dramatically over the years. High school and college students are likely to spend more time socializing in cross-sex groups of friends than as paired-off, exclusive couples.

Dating and Matchmaking Services   Although in an individual-choice courtship system young people make their own selections, many still want help in finding a mate. To fill this need, entrepreneurs all over the country have created a potpourri of dating services. The least expensive—and most risky—are the "Personals" or "Eligibles" sections in many newspapers and magazines (Box 6.3). For a modest fee, individuals can run a small ad describing their qualities, the qualities they seek in a partner, and the type of relationship they desire. These personals make interesting reading but they represent a less-than-safe way to find a dating partner.

Computerized dating services are a more discreet but also more expensive approach. Some services call themselves "relationship agencies," and their approach is not too much different from that used by employment services. Dating services, popular in many major cities, charge a fee, ranging anywhere from $200 to $400 or more. Applicants fill out forms, describing their traits and the traits they want in a partner; some services videotape applicants' responses. Each customer's file (coded by number, not name, to ensure some privacy) is made available to those who have paid for the privilege. If questionnaire data on "Mr. X" looks good to a woman, she might ask to see his videotape. If she is interested in learning more about him, the agency might contact him by phone or postcard, indicating the manner in which he can contact the interested woman. From that point on, what happens in the relationship is up to the individuals involved. (A selection of advertisements from several dating services appears in Box 6.4.)

The newest dating innovation is meeting people on-line, through subscription services or directly on the Internet. Some services offer chat rooms, such as

A Singles Column From a Metropolitan Newspaper

F5907

FUN LOVING

Affectionate Black Female enjoys music, sports, dancing. Slender, nice looking wants to meet attractive male with the same interests.

F5910

WANTED
THE PERFECT RECIPE

1 Athletic, cute male (aged 29–39 years); 3 cups personality; 2 cups generosity; 3&3/4lb. gregariousness; 2 large pieces intelligence. Add to confidence, imagination and a GREAT SMILE. Sprinkle with adventure and serve immediately to one gorgeous petite (5'3"-105 lbs) nurse.

F5911

31 year old single White female who enjoys spending time going to Pops concerts, movies, dining out and jogging. I'm a college educated professional somewhat conservative, who values intelligence, honesty and time spent really getting to know somebody.

F5912

LOOKING FOR STYLE

In other words, Attractive, intelligent, self-assured, sensitive, caring, stable, and between the ages of 45 and 52. Does this describe you? If so, then you are that special someone that I have been looking to meet and explore life with. I am 44, 5'4", trim, attractive and looking for a quality relationship. Variety of interests but would like to seek out as much as possible that life has to offer. Note, phone number and photo, if possible. All replies answered.

F5913

Worth getting to know, fun to dance with, interesting to talk to, politically concerned, spiritually growing. 38, 5'7" female would like to meet male with similar characteristics.

F5914

ALCOHOL AND SMOKE FREE
NOT A FANATIC

Tall, attractive woman in early 30's is looking for someone (male) to enhance social life. Tennis and eating are a few of my enthusiasms. Photo optional.

ELIGIBLES

F5921

GIVE ME A CHANCE

to make you smile! Forty-five, fun loving, free of hang ups, no children. Professional. Enjoy theatre, jazz, aerobics, travel, dancing. I am slender, very attractive, enjoy good conversation. Photo please.

F5922

WANTED ONE WOMAN MAN

Somewhat shy, warm-hearted, French/Spanish woman, 30, 5'3", 100 lbs. wishes to meet single, sincere, honest, attractive, respectable male (approximately 33–43) to enjoy life with. Note, phone (photo optional). Prefer tall and slender, no druggies, please.

F5923

Attractive, fun loving woman wishes to meet single white male, 40–55, at least 6' tall, interested in outdoor activities, concerts, plays, picnics on the North Shore. Letter, picture.

F5924

FIRST AD EVER

Hard to find, attractive 49, slender, 5'6", blonde resembling Meryl Streep, wishes to meet slender professional gentleman who is thoughtful, trim, attractive, honest, financially secure and young at heart, prefer 45–55 years, non-smoker, social drinker with hope for special relationship. Multi interests include music, hiking, dining dancing. Share interesting moments. Note, phone, photo if possible.

F5925

Anoka Country girl seeking enhancement (not completion) from a whole individual, tallish, over 40, active and not "into preferably thin."

F5926

We are sick and tired of being set-up by well-meaning friends; you know, the ones who fix you up with social misfits and "nice guys." We are two tall, dark haired, professional career women who are intelligent, attractive out-going, risk takers. You just won't believe how wonderful we are!

F5932

MY BEST FRIEND

who happens to be a man, describes me as "Gracious, elegant and feminine." I'm petite, fifty-ish, a classical violinist, teach literature at the Univ. Somewhat intense, unconventional, ethical. Looking for a man with similar interests and values, my age, older or younger, non-obese, who has the courage to risk vulnerability and commitment for true intimacy and companionship.

F5933

Hi. I'm 34, cute, fit and a good person. I'm looking for a handsome man who likes renovating, restoring, creating, enjoying life and working together towards common goals. Let's talk.

F5934

WANTED: FISHING PARTNER. I promise to bait my own hook, clean and cook the catch and provide good relaxed company. You provide the boat and knowledge where the fish bite, a sense of humor and pleasant disposition would be greatly appreciated. I am 55 but could pass for 45? Maybe. Self employed professional woman who likes the outdoors, most creatures great and small, but also all the finer things in life and comforts of home. Interested? Drop me a line or two!

F5935

Spirited Petite Blond, media professional, comfortable in denim or silk, enjoys quiet interludes to new adventures. Interested in sharing positive energy with attractive, centered and secure 35–45 professional male. Photo appreciated.

F5936

Two tall, classy, single women in their 30's are looking for male counterparts. We have put a lot of energy into our careers, and now are ready to put energy into friendship/relationship. We are warm, fun-loving and have a lot to give the right person. Please send letter and phone number. Photos appreciated.

BOX 6.4

Dating Services Advertised in a Metropolitan Newspaper

Singles
NETWORK
Dating Service
Call us about our July Special SAVE $50 on a new membership
555-1824

- **Straight or Gay Columns**
- **Correspond Anonymously**
- **Fun, Private Inexpensive**

OFFICE (9 to 5, M–F)
555-1424
COMPUTER
555-5524

Pc 2 Personal Columns On
Personal Computers
You Don't Need A Computer!

"I met a great lawyer at Introductions"
Introductions
a relationship agency
555-8488
fully complies with state law

Together
Established 1974
The Personal Introduction Service
555-3322
555-1100
555-2300

"Select-A-Date"
Let us introduce you to fun, frolic and adventure.
Be daring:
Tele: 555-0007
For Exciting Introductions

Jewish Dating Service
555-9790

America Online's "Romance Connection" and "Meeting Place" chat rooms, where strangers can get connected. As with personal ads, there are few safeguards to ensure the accuracy of the information people provide about themselves. Individuals often reveal only positive characteristics that they think will attract others to them. Although the subscription services and/or the Internet might be a simple and inexpensive way to meet someone initially, this approach to dating lacks intimacy and can be risky.

Dating Among Older People   The term *dating* has a decidedly youthful ring, but single people over 65 also date and are sexually active. The proportion of older individuals in the American population has increased dramatically since the turn of the century. In 1900, only about 4% of all Americans were 65 years of age or older; by 1990, 11% of males and 20% of females were over 65. As life spans lengthen, the percentage of older individuals is expected to increase to about 20% by the year 2030 (U.S. Bureau of the Census, 1997). People are not only living longer but are healthier and more active than in earlier generations. Also, the older they are, the less likely they are to have children at home. Subsequently, many generally healthy and active older adults are looking for meaningful relationships.

Kris Bulcroft and Margaret O'Conner-Roden (1986) explored whether older people date, fall in love, and behave romantically in ways similar to the young. While observing singles' dances for older individuals at a senior center, the researchers noticed "a sense of anticipation, festive dress, and flirtatious behavior that were strikingly familiar to us as women recently involved in the dating scene." They interviewed 45 individuals aged 60 to 92 in Minneapolis, Minnesota. One difference the investigators noted between older and younger daters was their definition of dating. The older people defined dating as a committed, long-term, monogamous relationship, similar to going steady at a younger age. Unlike many younger individuals, who "play the field," the vast majority of the older people were not casual about dating.

But one facet of dating was similar for both older and younger daters: the "sweaty-palm syndrome." The elders turned "physiological and psychological somersaults" on their dates and experienced a heightened sense of reality, perspiring hands, heart palpitations, feelings of awkwardness, the inability to concentrate, and anxiety and longing when away from the loved one. The older individuals saw romance much like younger people do—candlelight dinners, long walks in the park, exchanging flowers and candy. For older men, romance and sex were closely linked: "You can talk about candlelight dinners and sitting in front of the fireplace," a 71-year-old widower explained, "but I still think the most romantic thing I've ever done was to go to bed with her."

What older people do on dates is similar to what younger individuals do but is often "far more varied and creative," the researchers concluded. In addition to pizza, movies, and dances, older couples went camping, enjoyed the opera together, and flew off to Hawaii for the weekend. Also, the pace of dating was greatly accelerated. Older people noted that they simply did not have much time to play the field. They favored a direct, nongame-playing approach in building relationships. Sexual involvements tended to develop, and sexual intimacy enhanced self-esteem. A 77-year-old woman explained, "Sex isn't as important when you're older, but in a way you need it more." For this woman, sex reaffirmed the fact that she was alive and important to at least one other person in the world.

Another major difference between older and younger daters, the investigators noted, was their definition of passionate love. Younger people tend to equate passionate love with real love; once the intensity fades, they think love is gone. Older daters looked at passionate love differently, having learned from experience that the early intensity of passionate love simply cannot be sustained for very long. Most of the older individuals had learned through their marriages the value of companionate love—the "steady, burning fire" that endures and deepens over time. As one older man explained, "Yeah, passion is nice—it's the frosting on the cake. But

Although we usually think of dating couples as being young, today more older couples are dating.

it's her personality that's really important. The first time I was in love, it was only the excitement that mattered, but now it's the friendship, the ways we spend our time together that count."

Like younger individuals, older people face a number of dilemmas and difficulties in dating. Fear of disapproval leads many to be secretive about their dating activities. As a 63-year-old man said, "My girlfriend (age 64) lives just down the hall from me [in a retirement home]. When she spends the night, she usually brings her cordless phone just in case her daughter calls." And a 61-year-old woman reported that even though her 68-year-old boyfriend had spent three or four nights a week at her house over the past year, she had not yet told her family. "I have a tendency to hide his shoes when my grandchildren are coming over," the woman said.

Marriage is another dilemma for older people. They may initially seek a marital partner, but many decide as time goes on that they are not willing to give up their independence. Women, especially, often like the new freedom divorce or widowhood offers. Furthermore, older individuals are not involved in plans to raise a family together. Finally, many fear the burden of caring for someone in deteriorating health or being a burden themselves to someone else.

In general, family members and friends tend to support the older dater and to affirm her or his right to seek personal happiness. One 64-year-old woman summed up dating rather well: "I suppose that hope does spring eternal in the human breast as far as love is concerned. Individuals are always looking for the ultimate, perfect relationship. No matter how old they are, they are looking for this thing called love."

Criteria for Choosing a Mate

Americans tend to choose partners who are similar to them in a variety of ways—in ethnic and cultural background, age, educational and religious background, and socioeconomic status. Physical attractiveness also plays a large role in mate selection. This section discusses the criteria that influence mate selection in the United States.

Physical Attractiveness

Physical attractiveness is one of the most important components of mate selection; studies show that it is directly related to the frequency of being asked out on a first date (Berscheid & Reis, 1998). Researchers have been creative in devising rating scales to measure physical attractiveness. One method is simply to have a panel of judges rate individuals on a scale of attractiveness from low to high. Using this method, Gregory L. White (1980) measured the relative physical attractiveness of 123 couples and followed them through the various stages of their relationship (casual dating, serious dating, cohabiting, engagement, and marriage). White found that the more physically attractive a person was, the more likely she or he was to have friends of the other sex. At the same time, the more physically attractive a person was, the less likely he or she was to worry about the partner's involvement with other people.

White also found that among males, the more attractive the male, the more likely he was to desire involvements outside the relationship. According to White, this was perhaps because the attractive male's opportunities with other women were greater and he was more likely to want to capitalize on this advantage. White did not, however, find this true for women: The more attractive women did not report a greater desire for relationships with men outside the partnership than did the less attractive women. In a follow-up study 9 months later, White found that couples of similar attractiveness levels were more likely to progress deeper into the relationship than were couples in which one individual was relatively more attractive than the other. People tend to "shop around." Most of us are aware of how good-looking we are compared with other people, and we tend to use this "attractiveness capital" as a bargaining chip in our negotiations with prospective partners.

One research group studied interpersonal attraction at a commercial video-dating service (Green, Buchanan, & Heuer, 1984). The researchers developed quantitative profiles of each dating-service member, based on a point system including age, judgments of physical attractiveness, social status, humor, and warmth. They found that people who were physically attractive got more calls for dates. Physically attractive males enjoyed more popularity, and popular females tended to be younger and more attractive than their less-popular counterparts. Females tended to select males with higher social status, whereas males tended to focus on female physical attractiveness. The researchers followed up on these dating couples to see how the dating progressed. They found that although men tended to prefer younger women, they did not continue to date them. A younger date might be attractive to the man at first glance, but the age difference was a crucial factor in ending the relationship. Women tended to choose older men but also tended to be more likely to reject them after dating them for a while. Differences in maturity level can be more important than attractiveness in a long-term relationship, this study suggests.

Male-Female Differences   It is a common belief that men are more interested in physical attractiveness in a date but that women are more interested in personal qualities. Jeffrey S. Nevid (cited in Bozzi, 1985) surveyed 545 undergraduate men and women and concluded that there are some differences between the sexes in regard to the qualities they look for in a dating partner. Nevid's findings were relatively consistent with the stereotype that men are more interested in looks than women are. Nevid asked the students to rate the importance of 53 partner characteristics in terms of a purely sexual relationship and to rate the importance of the same characteristics in terms of a more meaningful, long-term relationship. The 53 characteristics included physical qualities (such as facial features, buttocks, waistline, and overall attractiveness), personal qualities (such as sensitivity, honesty, warmth, and character), and demographic characteristics (including age and ethnic background).

When men and women rated the characteristics relative to a long-term relationship, their lists were virtually identical, although in a slightly different order. For both men and women, the highest-rated personal qualities were honesty, personality, fidelity, sensitivity, warmth, kindness, character, tenderness, patience, and gentleness. When asked to rate the characteristics in terms of a sexual relationship, however, the men and women diverged. For men, the top-10 characteristics were purely physical: figure, sexuality, general attractiveness, facial features, buttocks, weight, legs, breath, skin, and breasts, in that order. The women, on the other hand, blended physical and personal qualities in their top 10: general attractiveness, sexuality, warmth, personality, tenderness, gentleness, sensitivity, kindness, build, and character, in descending order of importance. The men obviously made a big distinction between a sex partner and a long-term friend.

Physical Attractiveness, Personality, and Life Success   Research also indicates that physically attractive people are more likely to be rated by others as possessing good personal and behavioral qualities (Berscheid & Reis, 1998). Overall appearance does make a difference in one's life in a number of ways: Attractive individuals do better in school, believe they have a more promising future, and feel better about themselves than do less attractive individuals. Young people who are attractive also have lower rates of juvenile delinquency, suggesting perhaps that delinquency is lower among individuals who have a positive self-concept, good grades, and high expectations for the future. But physical appearance is not everything. Less attractive males date and interact socially just as often as attractive males. Furthermore, less attractive males are not any more angry or frustrated about life than are attractive males.

One might conclude that attractive individuals are simply living up to the positive assumptions society makes about them (Berscheid & Reis, 1998). Attractive people are believed to be more sensitive, responsive, sincere, kind, interesting, strong, poised, modest, sociable, outgoing, and exciting. They are also assumed to have more potential for social, marital, and occupational success. Because they are seen to have all these qualities, attractive people get special treatment: "Beauty affects job opportunities, for example. Even when appearance has no conceivable relationship to a person's functioning in a job, the hiring decisions of experienced

When people are physically attractive, others assume they also have positive personal qualities, such as sincerity, honesty, and warmth.

personnel consultants are significantly influenced by the applicant's physical appearance" (Berscheid, 1982).

Favorable treatment begins virtually at birth. From infancy on, attractive babies are hugged, cuddled, and kissed more often than less attractive babies. Mothers, fathers, nurses, and teachers all treat them better. Misbehavior in an attractive child is seen as a momentary slipup, whereas misbehavior in an unattractive child is seen as evidence of an antisocial personality. The classic conditions for a self-fulfilling prophecy are thus set up. We expect better things from attractive people, and they usually don't disappoint us.

The importance of physical attractiveness persists after years of marriage. Leslie Margolin and Lynn White (1987) surveyed more than 1,500 spouses who had been married for 10 or more years. They hypothesized—and found—that men, but not women, would report more sexual problems in their marriage if they believed that their spouse's attractiveness had decreased (e.g., the spouse had gained weight) while theirs had not. This study demonstrates that the male focus on physical attraction continues over time and is specifically linked to sexual satisfaction, as it is in younger men.

Age and Success

It has been estimated that in six out of every seven marriages in the United States, the man is as old as or older than the woman. Why is this the case? Physiologically, males mature more slowly than females and do not live as long. Furthermore, in the United States there are more males than females in their early 20s. Finally, there is the phenomenon social scientists have labeled the **mating gradient,** the tendency of women to marry men who are better educated or more successful than they are. Because men tend to "marry down" in terms of age and status, it can be difficult for successful older women to find an acceptable mate.

Although married men tend to be as old as or older than their spouses, the age difference between partners marrying today isn't very pronounced, especially among younger people. In the United States in the 1980s, the average male marrying for the first time was between 23 and 25 years old and the average female was between 21 and 22 years old. The average age difference between the two was 2 to 3 years. By the mid-1990s, however, the average age for males was 27.1 and for females 24.8, reducing the difference to slightly more than 2 years (U.S. Bureau of the Census, 1997). Age differences at the time of marriage are smallest between people marrying at younger ages and greater between those who marry at older ages. But in all age groups, men tend to marry younger women.

The term **sex ratio** indicates the relationship between the number of men and the number of women of a given age. Due to differences in birth and infant mortality rates, men have historically outnumbered—and continue to outnumber—women in the U.S. population. In 1910, there were 106 single men for every 100 single women; now there are 124 single men for every 100 single women. If every single man in this country wanted to marry, there wouldn't be enough women to go around. This problem is true for men across all age groups, except those 55 and older (Table 6.1).

Endogamy and Exogamy

Two other factors that influence mate selection are endogamy and exogamy. **Endogamy** is the culturally prescribed practice or tradition of choosing a mate from within one's own group. These groups might include ethnic, religious, socioeconomic, or general age groups. The principle of endogamy supposes, say, that middle-class Whites will marry middle-class Whites, Catholics will marry Catholics, and young people will marry young people.

Exogamy—the practice or tradition of choosing a mate from outside one's own group—is typically discouraged in our society. There are no laws against marrying someone of a different socioeconomic status, religion, or ethnic group; however, outside groups tend to be off-limits or less desirable as a source of marital partners.

In 1967, the U.S. Supreme Court declared miscegenation laws, which forbade interracial marriages, to be unconstitutional. Miscegenation laws sought to prevent unions between Whites and African Americans, Whites and Native Americans, and Whites and Asians. In 1945, at the end of World War II, 30 of the 48 states had miscegenation laws.

Table 6.1 Single Males and Females—Sex Ratios and Percentage Unmarried

Age	Male (Thousands)	Female (Thousands)	Sex Ratio*	Percentage Unmarried Male	Female
18–19	3,525	3,300	107	97.6	92.2
20–24	7,126	6,070	117	81.0	68.5
25–29	5,075	3,650	139	52.0	37.6
30–34	3,147	2,215	142	29.6	20.5
35–39	2,303	1,487	155	20.8	13.1
40–44	1,443	1,009	143	14.2	9.7
45–54	1,247	1,025	122	8.1	6.3
55–64	501	512	98	5.0	4.7
65–74	359	384	93	4.4	3.8
75+	167	370	45	3.3	4.4
Total:	24,893	20,022	124		

*Sex ratio indicates the number of men to women: 100 means the number is the same; a ratio above 100 indicate how many more men than women.

Source: U.S. Bureau of the Census (1997, p. 58).

Although legal prohibitions against marriage between people of different groups no longer exist, informal social codes remain. A particular community may not have a law against marrying a person of a different religion or ethnic group, but relatives and friends in the community are likely to disapprove of couples who deviate too far from the unwritten rules. There is some evidence, however, that our attitudes as a society are gradually becoming more tolerant of intercultural couples, as we will see in the following section.

Intercultural Marriages in the United States

The growing ethnic diversity in the United States and the increasing rate of marriage across ethnic groups are changing the "unwritten rules" regarding exogamy. This change reflects a common belief that in the United States all ethnic and cultural groups can live and work together. This belief is true to a certain degree—we have developed a relatively stable society and share certain democratic values—but the United States is by no means a blended and homogeneous society, as discussed in Chapter 3. Although the ethnic and cultural mix often works rather well, the elements that make it up remain distinct. Ethnic values and identifications endure for generations. When people marry out of their ethnic group, problems can arise; the difficulties inherent in intercultural marriage often intensify if the partners do not anticipate them. We confuse the idea that we are all created equal with the belief that we are all the same.

The marriage rate between members of different ethnic groups is difficult to assess accurately because the concept of race is elusive, and many people cannot be easily classified (see Chapter 3). The U.S. Bureau of the Census does, however, ask people to state their ethnic identity and thus has a means of calculating Black-White marriages, among other things. In 1993, the number of Black-White

Marriages between individuals of different ethnic backgrounds involve special challenges. Partners must acknowledge and appreciate differences and make them a strength of the relationship rather than a source of conflict.

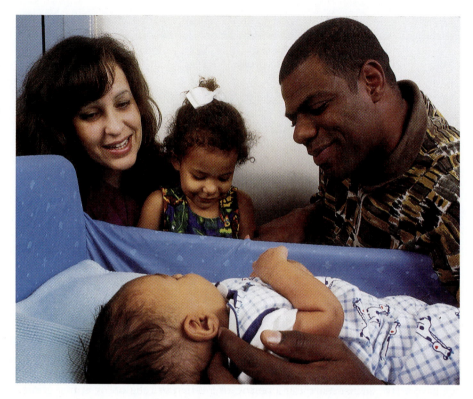

marriages increased from 65,000 in 1970 to 242,000 (U.S. Bureau of the Census, 1994). Of those 242,000 couples, 75% were Black male–White female couples, and 25% were White male–Black female couples.

Parents are often hesitant to bless an intercultural marriage. They may be aware of the problems their children will face, both within the relationship and in our society. They may also think the young partners are naive, idealistic, or blinded by love and need the guidance of their more experienced elders.

Some of these concerns are legitimate. When people marry, they are often idealistic in their beliefs. One common—and unrealistic—belief is that love conquers all. Another is that true love means that the couple either has few differences or that one partner can change the other after marriage. In the words of one family therapist, "Spouses tend to perceive their cultural differences as failings—either badness or madness. With insight, people are able to get some distance from their hurt feelings and stop taking inevitable differences personally" (Pearce, 1980). Although differences can be a source of strength in a marriage, they can also cause problems.

Ethnically mixed couples are more likely to divorce and to have a variety of marital and family problems, researchers suggest (McGoldrick & Preto, 1984). Children of intercultural marriages have more personal and relationship problems than children from ethnically homogeneous families.

The greater the ethnic differences between individuals, the less likely they are to marry, McGoldrick and Preto maintain. After marriage, the greater the differences, the greater the difficulty the couple will have adjusting to each other. These two family therapists identify eight factors that they believe most influence the degree of adjustment:

Joseph and Quinzola have been married for 15 years and have three children. Joseph is European American and Quinzola is African American. "I think Joseph and I have a pretty special relationship," Quinzola said. "He is a wonderful man, and I've always loved him. Sure, there was trouble with our families at first. Both families. And that took some working out between us.

"Joseph's parents grew up and lived in a small, White town all their lives. The biggest cultural difference they had in the whole town was fighting between Catholics and Lutherans. Joseph and I met at college in Cincinnati. When we went home to meet his parents for the first time after going out for a year, I felt you could cut the tension in the living room with a knife.

"But I have to admit my parents weren't much better. My dad was worse than my mom. He never has liked White people, in general. I'm sure he was convinced Joseph was after me just for sex. But after a while—Joseph would say it was a long while—my dad and Joseph became pretty good friends. I think they actually respect each other. Now his Aunt Wilson, I'm not so sure about her [chuckles]. I think she'll always hope for the return of slavery!"

- *Values.* The greater the discrepancy in values between the cultural groups, the more difficulty the couple will have. For example, a Puerto Rican–Italian couple will probably have less difficulty due to disparity of values than will an Irish-Italian couple.

- *Acculturation.* The greater the difference in the levels of acculturation of each partner, the greater the probability of conflict. For example, a couple is likely to have more difficulty if one is a recent immigrant and the other a fourth-generation American.

- *Religion.* Adding religious differences to cultural differences can compound adjustment difficulties. An Irish-Italian couple will probably have an easier time adjusting to marriage than an Irish-Jewish couple because the Irish and Italian partners are likely to share a common Catholic heritage. This is one less area for misunderstandings.

- *Race (McGoldrick and Preto's terms).* Interracial couples are the most vulnerable of all couples, sometimes feeling isolated from both groups. The children of an interracial union are also sometimes subject to discrimination from both groups. As interracial children become more commonplace, however, this discrimination may decline.

- *Sex and sex roles.* Because women are generally reared to talk more about their feelings, an Irish wife, for example, will probably have an easier time adjusting to a Jewish husband than a Jewish wife would have adjusting to an Irish husband. Why? Because Jews are traditionally more verbal, and the family therapists presume that matching a verbal Irish wife and a verbal Jewish husband would work out better than matching a verbal

Family Therapy for a Troubled Ethnic Intermarriage

Mike, a 28-year-old Irish-Catholic lawyer, who had been married for three years to a Jewish social worker, suddenly left his wife, which precipitated her seeking therapy. Susan said she was not alone in being totally mystified by his suddenly leaving her and refusing to discuss it. Susan said she knew little of her husband's background, as he did not like to talk about it and she had always thought her family was a welcome replacement for him. She said his own father had deserted the family when he was eight and he had become the "man in the family." He had been a very responsible son, burying his bitterness about his father's desertion. Although his mother was very religious, he turned against religion from that time on.

Mike worked his way through law school, and from the time he met Susan had only occasional visits with his mother, who disapproved of his marrying a Jew. He had no contact with other relatives because of a cut-off that occurred at the time of his father's desertion. Six months prior to the separation he had received word through his mother that his father was still alive and had written that he was ill with cancer and wanted to see his son. Mike went to visit his father. Three weeks after the father's death, Mike announced he was leaving, and the next day he packed his bags and left. Susan became infuriated, but the more she raged, the more he withdrew. By the time she sought therapy, their communication had almost ceased, except for brief conversations about money.

The therapist, sensing that Mike had touched on long-buried cultural issues, requested permission to contact Mike. After some probing by the therapist, Mike indicated that he realized his marriage had been a sham. In spite of the warmth and expressiveness of his wife's family, he felt there was an unbridgeable chasm between them. He had tried to cover it up over the years with his jokes and friendliness, but reconnecting with his father had made him appreciate something about his own identity. He began to realize how he had hurt his mother by excluding her from his life because he could not find a way to integrate her into his wife's Jewish family. A resolution that would bring Mike back into Susan's family seemed impossible, but he was able to begin talking to her about feelings. The difference between the Irish difficulty with emotional expression and the Jewish need to articulate feelings about every experience was a major factor here. Susan gradually came to realize that, unlike her, Mike had been a great talker but had kept his real feelings hidden, even from himself.

It is interesting that within three years, both Mike and Susan had remarried, this time within their own ethnic groups. On follow-up four years later, both Mike and Susan said that it was only with the comfort of the cultural similarity in their second marriages that they had become aware of the depth of the differences between them that had made their divorce inevitable. One can speculate that if Mike and Susan had worked out their relationship with their families before their first marriages, the divorce might have been avoided.

Source: Excerpted from "Ethnic Intermarriage: Implications for Therapy" by M. McGoldrick and N. G. Preto, 1984, *Family Process, 23,* pp. 347–364. Copyright 1984 by *Family Process.* Reprinted by permission.

Jewish wife and a relatively less verbal Irish husband. (See Box 6.5, which relates one of McGoldrick and Preto's case studies.)

- *Socioeconomic differences.* Partners from different socioeconomic circumstances have added difficulties adjusting to each other. The financial issues with which couples must content can become even more problematic if the partners have different life experiences and expectations regarding them.

- *Cultural familiarity.* Partners who have some experience with each other's culture before marriage are more likely to understand and adjust to each other. Couples who live in a multiethnic neighborhood after marriage are also less likely to experience pressure and negative reactions from others.

- *Extended-family agreement.* If kin of both partners are supportive, the couple has a greater chance of success. If a couple feels forced to elope or if one partner's family refuses to attend the wedding, this can indicate future difficulties.

McGoldrick and Preto point out that every ethnic group has its own unique heritage, values, and behaviors that make it special. It is important for those who marry someone from a different group to be aware of these differences and to work toward making them an asset rather than a liability.

Theories of Mate Selection

Family researchers have developed a number of theories over the years to explain how and why individuals choose a particular partner. No single theory appears to answer these questions completely, but several shed light on the subject.

Homogamy Versus Complementarity

Family theorists have maintained that people tend to marry others like themselves (Burgess & Wallin, 1943). This tendency to marry someone of the same ethnic group, educational level, socioeconomic status, religion, and values is called **homogamy.** But the fact that exceptions occur—African Americans marry Whites and Catholics marry Jews—indicates that there is much more to the mate selection process than simple homogamy.

Robert Winch (1958) spurred debate among social theorists when he proposed that people are attracted to those whose personalities are very different from their own. Winch called his idea the **complementary needs theory** because it asserted that opposites attract—that people are attracted to someone whose personality complements their own. He proposed, for example, that a dominant person and a submissive person would be attracted to each other.

Many family researchers tried to resolve the two theories—homogamy and complementary needs—and found very little support for Winch's ideas. Although there is evidence that people are attracted to those with similar background characteristics, there is little evidence one way or the other that speaks to the influence of personality on mate selection (Murstein, 1980). Perhaps one of the first to describe the importance of focusing on both similarities and dissimilarities was O. S. Fowler in his 1859 book *Matrimony*. Fowler advised, "Wherein, and as far as you are what you ought to be, marry one *like* yourself; but wherein and as far as you have any marked *excesses* or defects, marry those *unlike* yourself in these objectionable particulars" (cited in Murstein, 1980, p. 259).

Bernard Murstein (1980) argued that all the studies cited earlier are consistent with a theory that synthesizes the "opposites attract" and the "birds of a feather flock together" theories. After reviewing the studies, he reported that individuals with high self-esteem or high self-acceptance perceive themselves to be similar to their partner and that people with low self-acceptance are significantly lower in

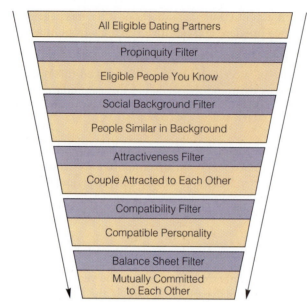

Figure 6.1 The Filter Theory of Mate Selection

both perceived and actual similarity to their spouse. Murstein also argued that although complementarity of personality does describe some marriages, it is not typical of most marriages. "The only support of Winch's theory," he concluded, "was the work of Winch (1958) himself." Murstein and others believe that, in general, similar qualities and characteristics tend to attract people to each other. Very dissimilar people do not usually marry, and if they do, they are often among the couples who are likely to divorce.

The Filter Theory

Under the law, a person of legal age can marry any unrelated person he or she chooses.* Nevertheless, an analysis of mate selection suggests that people tend to go through a filtering process to narrow the pool of possible mates to a few prospective candidates. This idea was originally proposed by A. C. Kerckhoff and K. E. Davis (1962).

Figure 6.1, a graphic representation of the filter theory of mate selection, shows how the pool of prospective partners contracts as individuals are filtered out because of differences of one sort or another. The influence of **propinquity,** or nearness in time and space, is the first filter. In other words, the pool of available partners consists of those living within the same geographic area or people with whom one is likely to come in contact. Years ago, the choice of a marriage partner was limited by the difficulty of traveling long distances; more than half of the

---

*State laws forbid marriage between parents and children, brothers and sisters, grandparents and grandchildren, and children and their aunts and uncles. Many states also forbid marriage between stepparents and stepchildren and between a man and his father's former wife or his son's former wife. Legal marriage between people of the same sex is forbidden by state laws, though many gay men and lesbians decry these laws.

In the past, the pool of eligible partners was often limited by the difficulty of traveling long distances. Today, the Internet allows people from across the country to chat online, making the pool of potential partners less restricted by physical proximity. As in any dating situation, there are both rewards and risks associated with cyberdating, of course.

people married someone who lived only a few miles from their home. Although people now travel more extensively and have a broader range of social contacts, the pool of eligible partners is still influenced by the social circles we move in, the school or place of worship we attend, the job we hold, and the type of activities we choose to engage in.

The Internet is, however, changing the pool of possible dating partners. The potential pool is now less restricted to those physically nearby. A growing number of people are chatting on-line through subscription services or directly on the Internet and connecting with others of similar interests from across the country. This trend will increase as on-line commercial dating services and other Internet services help people meet a broader cross-section of potential partners.

The social background filter determines the ethnic group, socioeconomic status, and age of potential partners. Individuals who believe marriage outside their own socioeconomic group is unacceptable will eliminate people who are not of their group from the pool of eligibles. As discussed earlier, an individual's physical attractiveness is important in selecting a date but less critical in choosing a mate. People tend to date individuals who are equally or more attractive than they are. Next, compatibility in personality, interests, and values acts as another filter in the mate selection process. At this more advanced stage, individuals select from a smaller pool of eligible partners, which increases the possibility of finding an acceptable partner. Finally, people use the balance sheet filter: They evaluate what they are giving and what they are getting in the relationship. If the give-and-take is balanced, they often move on to a mutually committed relationship.

The Stimulus-Value-Role Theory

A third theory of mate selection is known as the stimulus-value-role (SVR) theory. Murstein (1987) theorized that people are attracted to each other by an initial *stimulus* and then test their suitability for establishing a permanent relationship by comparing their *value* orientations and agreement on *roles*. In response to critiques by others in the field, Murstein has updated his SVR theory so that its three components are not distinct stages but rather work together to move a couple toward a committed relationship (Surra, 1991). Let's take a look at Murstein's description of these three components:

- *Stimulus.* People are attracted to each other initially by a particular stimulus, such as an attractive physique or popularity. Each person evaluates how attractive the prospective partner is and how attractive he or she perceives himself or herself to be. The stimulus may act as a form of magnetism that draws the couple together, and that magnetism may be variously interpreted as love at first sight, magic, destiny, or infatuation. Whatever it is, the stimulus tends to energize the relationship beyond the bounds of simple friendship.

- *Value complementarity.* After a successful exchange during the stimulus stage of attraction, the partners begin to advance to the value stage of the relationship, in which they assess the compatibility of their basic beliefs and values. They often compare (in a very indirect, conversational mode) basic religious and political philosophies; attitudes toward money, work, and people; preferences for lifestyle and leisure activities; and feelings about character and personality. Although physical attraction is very important in drawing a couple together, it cannot overcome the strain of disagreement on many issues. Thus, value complementarity becomes more important than physical attraction in selecting someone for an enduring relationship.

- *Role complementarity.* While comparing value complementarity, the partners also begin assessing role complementarity, or the extent to which they can establish a cooperative role relationship. Through interaction with each other, they discover each other's feelings and behaviors in terms of power and authority (who is going to be the boss), the division of labor (who will perform what tasks), and the expectations each has for the other in the relationship. Initially, each partner's separate values and roles emerge, but eventually negotiation may be necessary to achieve a workable balance.

  Role complementarity can be tested only to a limited extent during courtship; the real test begins with marriage. Cohabitation can provide some indications of a person's style, but jointly dealing with important issues makes each partner's style more apparent. Everyone has different needs. Further, needs tend to change throughout life. A mate who might meet one's essential needs at age 20 could be incapable of meeting them at age 40. For example, one woman may desire a man who is assertive and dominant to "take charge" of her and their children; another might prefer an equalitarian mate who would support her professional career. Some men want their wives to be submissive; others admire an independent spirit of individualism. There is no end to the possible personality types that people seek in a partner. Each couple must determine if their combination is a workable one.

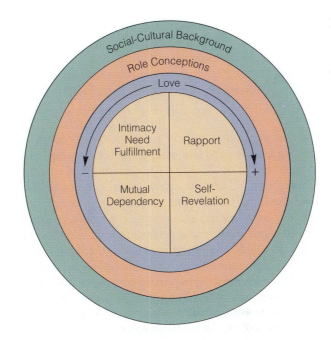

Figure 6.2 Reiss's Wheel of Love. *Source:* Adapted from *Family Systems in America* (4th ed.) (p. 103) by I. L. Reiss and G. R. Lee, 1988, New York: Holt, Rinehart & Winston. Copyright 1988 by Holt, Rinehart & Winston. Adapted by permission of the publisher.

The three components of SVR theory serve to help individuals evaluate a dating relationship and determine whether to continue or end it. When a potential relationship ends, one or both parties may observe, "It just didn't work out." Often, there was attraction, but value or role complementarity could not be achieved.

Reiss's Wheel Theory of Love

Another theory of how a love relationship begins, is nurtured, and grows is Ira L. Reiss's wheel theory of love (Reiss & Lee, 1988). This theory features four important components: rapport, self-revelation, mutual dependency, and intimacy need fulfillment. **Rapport** refers to the process of communication in which two people develop understanding and a sense of closeness. Two people have rapport when they are "on the same wavelength." Some people are quite skilled at building rapport with different types of people. They tend not to be excessively judgmental about others, and they listen so they can understand others. Good rapport between two people often leads to **self-revelation,** which is the disclosing of personal information about oneself. Self-revelation, of course, is a two-way street. When two people first meet, they are usually very cautious and reveal little. Gradually, one person lets a few "secrets" slip out, and the other person often reveals something very personal in return. Reiss notes that rapport encourages self-revelation, which in turn builds up what he calls **mutual dependency,** a relationship in which each person wants and needs the other person. This process takes time and can change over time. The fourth and final process in the development of love is what Reiss calls **intimacy need fulfillment,** the satisfaction one receives from having personal needs fulfilled, which leads to greater intimacy.

Reiss's wheel of love is graphically represented in Figure 6.2. Reiss describes his theory as a "wheel theory" of love because its four components are interdependent; that is, a reduction in any one of the components retards the development of a loving relationship. If, for example, a couple has an argument, self-revelation will diminish for a time. And if self-revelation diminishes in the relationship, the dependency and intimacy-need-fulfillment components will also diminish. The four components can also flow back and forth—even in the strongest of love relationships. In his model, Reiss indicates the movement of love in a positive direction (+) and a negative direction (–). Every relationship has its rocky times; love ebbs and flows. But in healthy relationships that survive and develop, the flow generally moves in a positive direction, toward increasing intimacy.

Surrounding the four components of the wheel of love are an outer ring, which Reiss labels "Social-Cultural Background," and an inner ring, which he labels "Role Conceptions." The four interpersonal components do not develop in a vacuum. Social-cultural background influences role conceptions, which in turn influence the four components, because role conceptions are how we define what we expect in a love relationship and determine what we do to meet these expectations. Our religious values, our educational background, the family values we grew up with— all these influence how we think about love relationships, and our thinking influences our actions. It is important to keep in mind how tremendously diverse role conceptions can be within love relationships. Views differ greatly from one part of the world to another and also among different cultural groups in the United States. In other words, we all are influenced by the society and cultural values around us.

Reiss notes that the wheel model applies not only to love relationships but also to other primary (close, intimate, face-to-face, and durable) relationships. It is useful for examining friendships, relationships with parents or children, and even casual relationships with colleagues, classmates, or roommates.

Conflict and Violence in Dating

Over the past two decades, researchers have looked at the issues of conflict and violence in dating relationships. Jealousy and differences in level of commitment are only two of numerous causes for conflict between dating partners. These conflicts sometimes result in violent behavior, which can then lead to spouse abuse.

Conflict Issues

Ten common sources of relationship problems were identified in one study of 960 students (Springer, Fournier, & Olson, 1985). These students reported 2,320 problems (an average of 2.5 problems per student) in their current relationships. Table 6.2 lists the 10 most frequently cited issues, from highest to lowest, at various stages of relationship development.

The most common sources of conflict for the students were personality issues, of which jealousy was the prime conflict issue. This finding is not surprising because commitment differences were the third most frequent source of conflict; these differences were particularly problematic in the early stages of dating. As couples approached marriage, jealousy was cited slightly less often as a source of relationship conflict, whereas parents were cited more frequently. Although they are a relatively minor source of conflict for couples at other stages of the relationship, parents are the second most frequent source of conflict for engaged cou-

Table 6.2 Top 10 Areas of Conflict Across Stages of Relationships

Conflict Areas	Overall Ranking n = 960	Friend n = 154	Casual Dating n = 167	Serious Dating n = 171	Steady Dating n = 214	Cohabiting n = 44	Pre-engaged n = 89	Engaged n = 45	Married n = 95
Personality (jealousy, esteem, moodiness)	1	2	4	1	1	2	1	1	2
Not enough time together	2	3	2	3	2	5	2	3	3
Commitment differences	3	1	1	2	3	7	6	7	9
Values (money, goals, lifestyle, gender roles)	4	8	6	4	7	1	7	5	1
Communication (disclosure, listening, honesty)	5	5	3	5	4	4	8	6	7
Background (different interests, religion, cultural, education)	6	7	5	6	5	3	3	4	6
Power (control, dependency, competition)	7	4	8	7	8	9	9	8	5
Parents	8	10	10	9	6	6	4	2	4
Sex (moral question, relative importance)	9	9	9	8	9	10	5	9	8
Friends	10	6	7	10	10	8	10	10	10

Conflict is an inevitable part of every relationship, but areas of conflict change as partners become more committed to each other. In the early stages of a relationship, jealousy and other personality issues are the greatest sources of conflict; later, conflict arises from such issues as differences in background, the balance of power in the relationship, and parent relationships.

ples. This is probably because the couple's parents become more actively involved in the relationship as it moves toward marriage—offering advice, visiting, giving parties and showers, and paying for the wedding. As might be expected for students, the second most frequent source of conflict was insufficient time to be together.

Conflict issues are different at each stage of the relationship, as Table 6.2 shows. Commitment differences were the most frequent source of conflict at the friendship and casual dating stages and the second most frequent source of conflict at the serious dating stage. But commitment differences decreased in importance across the remaining relationship stages, most likely because commitment increases with each successive stage.

Values (such as how to handle money and gender-role issues) became more problematic as couples moved toward marriage. Communication, background, and power issues were rated across the stages as the 5th through 7th issues. Friends were the 10th most frequently cited issue across all stages.

Courtship Violence

Violence between dating high school and college students is an area that was previously neglected by researchers (Cate & Lloyd, 1991). Professional findings now indicate that dating and courtship relationships are more violent than initially expected. Few individuals completely accept the traditional romantic accounts of courtship relationships in America today. But popular songs, films, books, and television continue to depict premarital heterosexual relationships in an overly positive light. Young couples are shown as overcoming obstacles and achieving

Table 6.3 Types of Conflict in Dating

| | CONFLICT USED (%) | | CONFLICT RECEIVED (%) | |
	Men	Women	Men	Women
Reasoning	100	100	100	99
Verbal aggression	87	93	87	89
Minor violence	22	38	32	29
Severe violence	3	19	16	8

Note: Sample = 272.

Source: "Contextual Factors Surrounding Conflict Resolution While Dating: Results from a National Study" by J. E. Stets and D. A. Henderson, 1991, *Family Relations, 40* (1), p. 32. Copyright 1991 by National Council on Family Relations, 3989 Central Ave. N.E., Ste. 550, Minneapolis, MN 55421. Reprinted by permission.

successful relationships; the stresses and strains inherent in these relationships are minimized, and aggression and violence are rarely mentioned.

In a study of aggression in 272 dating people, Stets and Henderson (1991) found the rate of physical aggression was highest in dating couples who were younger, were of low socioeconomic status, and had been drinking. Respondents ranged in age from 17 to 26 years and included Whites (74%), African Americans (13%), Latinos (7%), Asian Americans (3%), and Native Americans (3%). Participants were asked about four approaches for dealing with violence: reasoning (discussing issues), verbal aggression (insulting, sulking, threatening), minor violence (pushing, slapping), and severe violence (kicking, hitting, choking). The results appear in Table 6.3. In terms of handling conflict, all males and females (100%) used reasoning, and most (87% to 93%) used verbal aggression. In terms of physical violence, more men (32%) than women (29%) were on the receiving end of minor violence. This concurs with the fact that fewer men (3%) than women (19%) reported using severe physical violence. Men are less often hurt than women in violent encounters, however, because women are generally not as physically able to cause serious injury as men.

One of the earliest studies of courtship violence among high school students was done by June Henton and colleagues (Henton, Cate, Koval, Lloyd, & Christopher, 1981). In surveying 644 students, they confirmed the existence of violence among teenage partners and observed that "adolescents do, indeed, experience violence in their dating relationships with considerable frequency and intensity" (p. 477). Some of their findings are particularly disturbing. For example, 27% of the victims of date violence interpreted the violence as an act of love; 31% of the perpetrators of the violence agreed, saying they had become angry only because they cared so much about their victim. In contrast, only about 5% of the victims and 3% of the perpetrators saw hate as the motive for the violent acts. According to the researchers, "Many adolescents are, thereby, constructing a topsy-turvy world for themselves where hate becomes love and violence indicates romantic passion" (p. 479). Adolescent victims and perpetrators often define abuse as love and assume the romantic notion that if problems arise, they will go away and that violence can be tolerated without undue stress. In short, the victim and the perpetrator conspire to pull the wool over each other's eyes by believing that violence is a consequence—if not proof—of intense love.

Young men often place the blame for violence on their partner. Most of the young women described their partner's acts of violence as being impulsive, spontaneous, or out of control or said that the male acted out of fear or sadness. These interpretations indicate that the young women felt sympathy or pity for their assailants. The females often also conspired with the males by failing to let the secret out (Henton et al., 1981). Almost 25% of the violent incidents were not reported to anyone, and when victims did report the violence, they commonly told friends (67%). But friends are not in a very good position to do anything about the violence, and most friends did nothing with the information.

> "I thought it would get better after the wedding. We had planned so long and carefully for it, and I knew the wedding would be wonderful," said Ronni from Chicago. "But even on the day of the wedding, Marty slapped me in the face. I don't know. He was frustrated about something my brother said or something. I don't know.
>
> "After we got married, it really got bad. He would stay out with his friends till all hours and when he came home, if I said even one word about it, he would hit me. Hard. I stayed with him 2 years, but when he pushed me down when I was 7 months pregnant, I couldn't stand it anymore and I left for the domestic violence program shelter. He would have hurt the baby, and I would never have forgiven myself. I ended up leaving town, moving to my sister's in Indianapolis. I didn't have hardly anything . . . Alexis's baby clothes and her toys, my clothes, a small stereo system.
>
> "I didn't have anything, really, but I was free and that was what counted."

Courtship Violence and Later Spouse Abuse

Another research team was curious about the relationship between courtship violence and later spouse abuse (Roscoe & Benaske, 1985). Were abused wives likely to have been abused during courtship? In fact, 51% responded that they had been physically abused in a dating relationship at some time; however, 49% had not been abused during courtship. This means that for many women, physical abuse will come as an unpleasant surprise after the wedding. Violence in dating relationships was associated with the degree of involvement between partners; the higher the level of intimacy, the greater the likelihood of violence. The causes of violence were similar in courtship and in marriage: jealousy, alcohol, money, children, drugs, and sexual denial (in descending order of frequency).

It is clear that if an individual is violent during dating, it is most likely this behavior will continue after marriage. In general, a violent date is a poor marriage risk. Violence breeds violence and quickly destroys an intimate relationship. It is important, especially for women, to watch for warning signals that a partner might become more abusive as the relationship becomes more serious. See Box 6.6, which lists several very useful warning signals.

In summary, it is important for people to trust their own feelings regarding abuse from their partner and to not confuse abuse with love. Following are

How to Tell If Date or Mate Is a Potential Batterer

Dear Ann: Please print this list of warning signals to help women determine if a mate or date is a potential (or actual) batterer:

- Jealousy of your time with coworkers, friends and family.

- Controlling behavior. (Controls your comings and goings and your money and insists on "helping" you make personal decisions.)

- Isolation. (Cuts you off from all supportive resources such as telephone pals, colleagues at work and close family members.)

- Blames others for his problems. (Unemployment, family quarrels—everything is "your fault.")

- Hypersensitivity. (Easily upset by annoyances that are a part of daily life, such as being asked to work overtime, criticism of any kind, being asked to help with chores or child care.)

- Cruelty to animals or children. (Insensitive to their pain and suffering, may tease and/or hurt children and animals.)

- "Playful" use of force in sex. (May throw you down and hold you during sex. May start having sex with you when you are sleeping or demand sex when you are ill or tired.)

- Verbal abuse. (Says cruel and hurtful things, degrades and humiliates you, wakes you up to abuse you verbally or doesn't let you go to sleep.)

- Dr. Jekyll and Mr. Hyde personality. (Sudden mood swings and unpredictable behavior—one minute loving, the next minute angry and punitive.)

- Past history of battering. (Has hit others, but has a list of excuses for having been "pushed over the edge.")

- Threats of violence. (Says, "I'll slap you," "I'll kill you" or "I'll break your neck.")

- Breaking or striking objects. (Breaks your possessions, beats on the table with fists, throws objects near or at you or your children.)

- Uses force during an argument. (Holds you down or against a wall, pushes, shoves, slaps or kicks you. That type of behavior can easily escalate to choking, stabbing or shooting.)

Please tell women that help is as close as the telephone. Any woman who sees herself in this column should call the nearest women's crisis line and tell someone what is happening. She will be provided with support and safety options.

Identifying the warning signs is the first step in breaking the cycle of violence.

—**Portland, Ore.**

Ann says: Some women do not realize they are being abused until someone points it out to them. They have been made to believe that abusive treatment is what they deserve and that most women are treated that way.

I hope the women who see themselves in today's column will check out the nearest women's shelter and keep the phone number handy. They can also call the National Domestic Violence Hotline at 1-800-799-SAFE (TDD: 1-800-787-3224). It could save their lives.

Source: "How to Tell If a Date or Mate Is a Potential Batterer" by A. Landers, June 3, 1997, p. 16. Reprinted with permission.

four relevant questions to seriously consider before committing oneself to a relationship:

Does your love "turn you on" or "turn you off"?

Does your love "tune you in" or "tune you out"?

Does your love "make you sing" or "make you shout"?

Does your love "light your fire" or "put it out"?

Figure 6.3 Percentage of Cohabitation and Parents' Marital Status. *Source:* Amato, P. R. & A. Booth (1997) *A Generation at Risk: Growing up in an Era of Family Upheaval.* (p. 112). Copyright © 1997 by the President and Fellows of Harvard College. Reprinted by permission of the publisher.

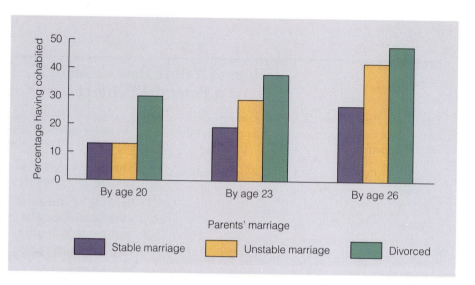

Living Together

For many people, marriage is no longer considered a prerequisite for living with a romantic partner. **Cohabitation** is defined by the federal government as two unrelated adults of the opposite sex sharing the same living quarters. A broader definition would include same-sex couples who have an emotional and sexual relationship.

Between 1970 and 1996, the number of unmarried couples living together increased eightfold from 500,000 to 4 million couples (U.S. Bureau of the Census, 1997). Among cohabiting couples, about half (54%) the partners had never been married, about one third (37%) had been divorced, and the rest were widowed.

The rate of cohabitation generally increases with age, but it is also related to the quality of an individual's parents' marriage. In a study of young people and their parents by Paul Amato and Alan Booth (1997), cohabitation increased as young adults got older. At each age level, the rate of cohabitation was lowest for adult children from stable families and was highest for adult children of divorced parents (Figure 6.3). More specifically, only 13% of the 20-year-olds from stable homes were cohabiting, whereas 30% of those from divorced families were cohabiting. For 26-year-olds, the rate was 30% for those from stable homes and 48% for those from divorced families.

The rate of living together is also related to religious orientation, according to James Duke (1999), professor of sociology at Brigham Young University. Based on several studies, Duke found that Mormons are the least likely to cohabit outside of marriage, with a cohabitation rate of 8.2%, as compared to 20% to 24% for Protestants, 23% for Catholics, 32.5% for Jews, and 44.8% for nonreligious Americans.

It is safe to say that cohabitation is becoming more common in America. It is also true that cohabitation has sparked a good deal of controversy. Numerous studies have evaluated this phenomenon, but the results are somewhat difficult to interpret. Marriage is a risky proposition: Conflict is inevitable, and the likelihood

of divorce is high. For these and numerous other reasons, more people are deciding to live together rather than marry.

People cohabit for many reasons and have various types of cohabitation
arrangements. In a highly instructive review of research and the observations of
counselors, Carl Ridley, Dan Peterman, and Arthur Avery (1978) identified four
common patterns of cohabitation: Linus blanket, emancipation, convenience, and
testing.

- **Linus blanket.** Named after the character in the comic strip "Peanuts"
  who carries a security blanket with him, the Linus-blanket cohabiting
  relationship occurs when one partner is so dependent or insecure that he
  or she prefers a relationship with anyone to being alone. The insecure
  partner often finds the open communication on which a successful
  relationship thrives to be difficult, and the stronger partner does not feel
  that he or she can criticize the more "fragile" partner. After shouldering
  the planning and decision-making burdens for too long, the stronger
  partner often becomes frustrated and leaves the relationship. When the
  relationship ends, the insecure partner's fragile self-esteem falls even
  lower, and the departing partner feels guilty.

- **Emancipation.** Some people use cohabitation as a way to break free from
  their parents' values and influence. Women who grew up in very
  conservative religious traditions sometimes seek sexual emancipation not
  permitted by their parents or their faith through cohabitation. Guilt often
  overwhelms these women, however, and they break off the relationship.
  But because the business of emancipation is not finished, they often enter
  into another cohabiting relationship. The partner suffers in this type of
  situation because the individual seeking emancipation brings too much
  unfinished business to the relationship and is trying to gain independence
  at another's expense.

- **Convenience.** Relationships in which one person is the giver and the
  other is the taker are often relationships of convenience. Cohabiting
  relationships of this type may involve a man who is in the relationship
  mainly for sex and to have a housewife (although women may cohabit for
  economic, sexual, and social reasons also). The woman supplies loving
  care and domestic labor—and hopes, but dares not ask, for marriage. It is
  obvious what the man gets out of the relationship. The woman gains a
  few hard-earned lessons: that unconditional giving can go unreturned and
  that reciprocity is essential for the long-term survival and ultimate success
  of a relationship. The partners usually part company, older and wiser.

- **Testing.** Cohabitation can be a true testing ground for marriage if the
  partners are relatively mature and clearly committed to trying out their
  already mutually satisfying relationship in a situation more closely
  resembling marriage. If the test goes well, they marry; if not, they
  separate and go their own ways.

Men have as much to gain from egalitarian relationships as women do. The quest for power, money, and material success in which so many men are immersed is accompanied by higher levels of stress, higher rates of heart disease, and shorter life spans.

Living Together as a Courtship Stage

The growing rate of cohabitation among couples adds a new step in the mate-selection and courtship process. Many counselors have severely criticized traditional courtship because it emphasizes recreation and avoids conflictual issues. Also the strong erotic needs of premarital couples tend to decrease their interest or ability to deal with problematic issues in their relationship. As one husband said in counseling, "When you're in love, you're willing to compromise on anything. Many believe that traditional courtship provides partners with idealized views of each other, making early marriage a period of more severe and difficult adjustments for most couples. In a cohabiting relationship, however, couples are able to experience the realities of life together before they decide to tie the knot.

Just as cohabitation has its supporters, so it has its detractors. Some argue against cohabitation on moral, religious, and philosophical grounds. Others question whether cohabitation is an effective predictor of marital success; because it is not truly a marriage, they contend, it cannot serve as a test of marriage. In the opinion of many observers, it is only "playing house"; to test marriage, they say, you need to actually get married.

Nonetheless, living together won't keep partners from experiencing pain and misery if the relationship breaks up. For some couples who have cohabited, dealing with the hurt of a broken relationship can be as difficult as it would have been if they had been legally married.

One of the earliest studies of cohabitation was done by Robert Watson (1983), who surveyed 87 Canadian couples in his efforts to find out if cohabitation is, indeed, "a new stage of courtship which, in replacing dating, may provide a more realistic basis for the selection of a mate" (p. 139). He found that about two thirds (64%) of the couples studied had engaged in some form of cohabitation before marriage. Watson was interested in seeing if couples who had cohabited before marriage would display a higher level of adjustment during the first year of marriage than couples who had entered marriage in a more traditional manner.

Watson was surprised to find that noncohabitants were better adjusted during the first year of marriage than those who had previously cohabited. What might account for this difference? Watson offered two possible explanations. First, researchers know that the first decade of marriage is characterized by consistently declining marital satisfaction. As the years go by, happiness with the relationship tends to diminish. The cohabitants had been living together longer than the noncohabitants. Therefore, the cohabitants' satisfaction scores would probably tend to be lower because the excitement and romance of early marriage had already worn off. The cohabitants were simply farther down the path than the noncohabitants.

Researchers have found that cohabitation is associated with a greater risk of marital dissolution than noncohabitation (DeMaris & Rao, 1992; Hall & Zhao, 1995). A comparison of couples who did and did not cohabit before marriage revealed that those who had cohabited experienced lower-quality marriages, a lower commitment to the institution of marriage, more individualistic views of marriage (wives only), and a greater likelihood of divorce than those who had not (Thomson & Colella, 1992).

Robert Schoen (1992) sheds even more light on the issue of cohabitation. He found that cohabitation is generally associated with a higher risk of marital dissolution but that the differential is smaller in comparisons of recent cohabitants and noncohabitants than it is between those whose experiences took place some years ago. Cohabitation was a highly controversial proposition 25 years ago and perhaps was an attractive option for a small group of people who were also rather different from the norm in other ways. Those characteristics may have made them more likely to divorce after marriage. Today, cohabitation is relatively commonplace. Schoen hypothesizes that as cohabitation has become more common over the years, the relatively "select nature of those who cohabited" may have largely disappeared. Perhaps the difference between cohabitants and noncohabitants will shrink even more in the future as cohabitation becomes more and more statistically normal.

Angela and George had been living together for a little over 3 years. He was a 26-year-old computer salesman; she was a 26-year-old quality control manager at a competing firm. They had met through mutual friends nearly 5 years earlier. Now they shared a condominium in Los Angeles and two Irish setters.

One evening as they were lying in bed, Angela rolled over and gave George a big kiss on the cheek. "Honey," she said, "what do you think about getting married?"

George looked at the ceiling for a few long seconds and said, "Angie, what would you say if I said 'Maybe'?"

Angela rolled over and looked at the wall. George rolled over and looked at the other wall. After a long time, George rolled over and hugged Angela as she looked at her wall. "Angie, will you marry me?" he asked, pleading ever so slightly.

"Yes!" she responded, rolling toward him and giving him a big kiss. "Of course!"

Living Together and Relationship Satisfaction

In a comprehensive review of cohabitation, David Popenoe and Barbara White-head (1999) reported that more than half of couples marrying today have already lived together—a trend they foresee as continuing. Cohabitating relationships are, however, short-lived for many couples. An estimated 40% do not result in marriage. In their report *Should We Live Together?*, Popenoe and Whitehead discovered that most couples believe it is a good idea to cohabit in order to decide if they should get married. Couples maintain that cohabitating enables them to share expenses and learn more about each other.

Nonetheless, Popenoe and Whitehead (1999) concluded from their review of many studies that cohabitation is detrimental to marriage and increases the probability to divorce. According to these researchers, living together increases the risk of domestic violence for women and the risk of physical and sexual abuse for children. Cohabiting is also potentially detrimental for children since the risk is high that the cohabiting couple will break up, thus making it difficult for the children to establish a close relationship with another adult. Also, women with children have higher levels of depression. Furthermore, cohabiting couples have lower levels of happiness and well-being than married couples.

In response to these findings, Larry Bumpass, a leading sociologist, feels that there are multiple causes of marital problems and divorce in our society. Bumpass (1999) states: "It is inappropriate and simplistic to treat cohabitation as the major factor affecting divorce. The trend in divorce stretches back over the last hundred years, so clearly it wasn't caused by cohabitation" (p. 61). In fact, he maintains, cohabitation could have lowered the divorce rate by discouraging some couples from marrying who might eventually have divorced.

In a study of 4,271 engaged couples, Kenneth Stewart and David Olson (1990) found that cohabiting couples had a less satisfying premarital relationship than engaged couples who lived apart (Figure 6.4). To determine engaged couples' levels of satisfaction, a total sample of 17,025 couples completed a comprehensive premarital inventory called PREPARE, which evaluated their satisfaction in 14 aspects of their relationship. From the total sample, the most satisfied (numbering 2,124) and the least satisfied (numbering 2,147) were selected (total = 4,271) for comparison. Of the couples selected, about one third (31%) were cohabiting; in another third (34%), one person lived with her or his parents and the partner shared housing with others. In one fifth (22%) of the couples, both partners lived with their parents; in only 13% of the couples did both partners live alone.

In this study, cohabiting couples had the lowest level of premarital satisfaction, whereas premarital couples in which both people lived alone had the highest level of premarital satisfaction. About two thirds of the cohabiting couples fell into the low-satisfaction group, and about two thirds of the couples with both partners living alone fell into the high-satisfaction group (see Figure 6.4). Furthermore, engaged couples with both partners living alone were more satisfied than couples in which one or both partners still lived with their parents.

Three possible explanations for these findings have to do with the way in which the couples became independent from or remained dependent on their families of origin. First, for some couples, cohabitation may have been a way of rebelling against their families. Second, couples in which both partners lived with their parents might have been too dependent on their parents. And third, those engaged

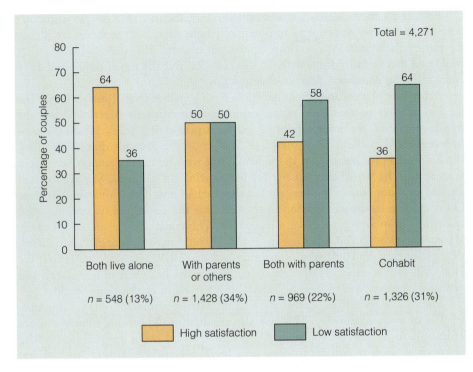

Figure 6.4 Living Arrangement and Premarital Satisfaction. *Source:* From *Predicting Premarital Satisfaction on PREPARE Using Background Factors* by K. L. Stewart and D. H. Olson (1990) (p. 17), unpublished manuscript, Prepare/Enrich, Inc., Minneapolis, MN. Copyright © 1990 Prepare/Enrich. Used by permission of the publisher.

couples who were both living alone might have achieved a more satisfactory degree of independence from their families of origin.

A recent study by Susan Brown (1998) found that women in a cohabiting relationship that did not result in marriage were more depressed and had lower life satisfaction than a matched group of women in married relationships. This was particularly true for women of cohabiting couples with children. The exception to this finding was for cohabiting couples without children who had plans to marry.

Legal Issues and Living Together

In the minds and spirits of the cohabiting couple, they may be married, but in the eyes of the law, the matter is more complicated. To some people, the most important aspect of marriage is the spiritual and religious dimension—the melding of two kindred souls. To other people, the psychological and emotional aspects—the development of intimacy—are the most important.

But marriage is also a legal contract. Couples should consider the legal issues carefully before entering into a cohabitation arrangement. As long as the living arrangement goes well, there is not a whole lot to worry about. But what about separation? Cohabitants are no more stable in their relationships than married people; in fact, they are probably less stable. So when a cohabiting couple breaks up, they have issues to resolve. Problems can arise in the areas of personal property, wills and estates, and income earned while cohabiting. Attorney Barton Bernstein concludes that "individuals choosing to cohabit should consider the ramifications of cohabitation prior to or early in the development of their relationship in order to avoid devastating legal complications" (Bernstein, 1977, p. 361).

Bernstein's rhetoric may sound a bit melodramatic to young people who don't have a lot of money or property to potentially fight over. But the stakes are higher for some cohabitants. At one time, unmarried couples who were living together could end their relationships without legal hassles. But the much-publicized 1976 court ruling in *Marvin v. Marvin* changed this.

Actor Lee Marvin and Michelle Triola lived together from 1964 to 1970. Triola adopted her partner's last name, calling herself Michelle Marvin. When the couple separated, the actor supported her for a period of 2 years. When the support ceased, Michelle Marvin sued Lee Marvin on the grounds that he had broken his verbal promise to her: If she would live with him and abandon her career as an actress, he would support her for life, sharing his earnings. She argued that she had kept her part of the bargain but that he had not. The California Supreme Court made a landmark decision in the case, for the court had no existing legal guidelines from which to make a judgment. The court set a value on Michelle Marvin's services in the relationship so that it could make a property settlement. When the first round of legal maneuvering ended in 1979, Ms. Marvin was awarded $104,000. This money was to compensate her for the lost years of her career, and part of the money was to help her reestablish herself in the working world.

Michelle Marvin thus became the first unmarried woman to obtain "equitable relief"—in a sense, alimony. This suit also resulted in the coining of a new term: **palimony.** As a result of *Marvin* v. *Marvin* and related issues, lawyers now advise couples who wish to cohabit to draw up a legal agreement to protect themselves. If the relationship ends, the agreement serves as a guide for the rational and orderly division of property. The document should cover such issues as future earnings, the custody of any offspring, and responsibility for child support.

In one legal arrangement called *contract cohabitation*, one cohabitant in essence hires the other as a live-in companion. The agreement specifies each partner's rights and obligations and is especially useful for middle-aged couples with considerable financial assets. The contract cohabitation agreement may be canceled at any time. The "employer" is thus protected from having to pay palimony or having to divide up his or her property, as might be required without such a contract.

Questions to Consider Before Living Together

Professionals are just beginning to answer some of the basic questions about cohabitation. Cohabitation works for many people, but others remain opposed to it. Happy marriages have been developed by those who lived together before marriage and by those who did not. Before cohabiting, it is important for partners to discuss questions such as those listed in Box 6.7. Ridley, Peterman, and Avery (1978), the authors of the discussion points, also offer some guidelines for assessing respondents' answers—"good" signs and "bad" signs—to determine whether living together is a positive step.

Clearly, there are a number of things for a couple to consider before deciding to cohabit. In many ways, cohabitation is just as complicated a relationship as marriage. And it is probably no buffer against the painful decisions people must make in their lives regarding loved ones. Eventually, individuals must make choices about how committed they are to their partner. Whether one is married or not, the decision can be very difficult.

BOX 6.7

Is Living Together the Right Choice for You?

1. *How did each of you come to the decision to live together?*
   Good signs: Each individual has given considerable thought to the decision, including both pros and cons.
   Bad signs: One or both partners hasn't thought much about it.

2. *What do you think you will gain from living together?*
   Good signs: Both people want to learn more about themselves and each other.
   Bad signs: One or both wish to live together for convenience only, or they seek independence from peers or parents.

3. *What responsibilities do you have to each other? What are your expectations of each other?*
   Good signs: Expectations are compatible between partners.
   Bad signs: One or both have given little thought to this, or they disagree.

4. *Identify your partner's primary physical and emotional needs, and estimate how well you are fulfilling those needs.*
   Good signs: Each has a clear understanding of the other's needs and is willing and capable of meeting them to a good degree.
   Bad signs: One or both are not fully aware of the other's needs or are unwilling to or incapable of satisfying them.

5. *What makes the relationship important to you? How do you feel about your partner?*
   Good signs: Partners care deeply for each other, and there are many significant elements bonding them together.
   Bad signs: There is an emotional imbalance, with one partner more committed than the other. Or neither partner is deeply committed.

6. *What will your family and friends think?*
   Good signs: Both people are aware of how the other intimates in their lives will react. The family and friends are either supportive of the cohabiting relationship, or the partners have carefully considered how they will deal with opposition.
   Bad signs: One or both individuals are not aware of their families' or their friends' reactions, or families and/or friends are not supportive of the couple's decision to cohabit.

7. *How open are you with each other in terms of honestly sharing feelings?*
   Good signs: Each individual usually can open up to the partner.
   Bad signs: One or both partners have a difficult time being honest.

8. *Can each of you discuss the other's strengths and weaknesses together? How much are you trying to change your partner?*
   Good signs: The partners know each other's feelings about strengths and weaknesses, and there is little effort on either's part to mold the loved one into something different.
   Bad signs: The partners have trouble accepting each other for who each one is.

9. *How do you manage conflict?*
   Good signs: The partners express their differences and mutually work out solutions. There is evidence of give and take on both sides.
   Bad signs: One or both partners have difficulty expressing their feelings. They avoid problems rather than making a genuine effort to solve them.

Source: Adapted from "Cohabitation: Does It Make for a Better Marriage?" by C. A. Ridley, D. J. Peterman, and A. W. Avery, 1978, *Family Coordinator* (April), pp. 135–136. Copyright 1978 by the National Council on Family Relations. Adapted by permission.

Summary

- Parent-arranged marriages remain common—and are effective—in many nonindustrialized cultures today, but in the United States, individual-choice courtship is the norm.

- Research on dating reveals that older individuals experience the same emotional effects as young people but that their dates are often more creative than those of younger people. Older couples do become sexually involved, but they look at sexual intimacy in a more realistic manner.

- Factors that influence mate selection are physical attrativeness, personality, age, life success, and the principles of exogamy and endogamy. The rise in ethnic diversity in the United States is changing the unwritten rules regarding mixed marriages.

- Theories about mate selection include (1) the homogamy theory, which proposes that people are attracted to others who are like themselves, and the complementary needs theory, which suggests that opposites attract; (2) the filter theory, which describes the process people use to narrow the field of eligible partners; (3) the stimulus-value-role (SRV) theory, which holds that after the initial attraction (stimulus), value and role compatibility determine mate selection; and (4) the wheel theory of love, which explains the four interdependent components in the development of a love relationship—rapport, self-revelation, mutual dependency, and intimacy need fulfillment.

- Courtship violence, a formerly neglected area of research, has come under careful scrutiny in the past few years. Research shows that violent dates are likely to become violent mates.

- Cohabitation is increasing in popularity; in 1996 over 4 million couples were living together, as compared to 500,000 in 1970. Most couples see living together as a way to help them decide if they should get married. Experts disagree about the impact of cohabitation on the quality of a couple's subsequent marriage and whether it increases the chances for divorce. Living together is not a good predictor of whether a couple will have a good marriage or whether they will be at higher risk for divorce. There is, however, considerable evidence that married couples are healthier physically and emotionally and are happier than unmarried couples.

Key Terms

parent-arranged marriage

dating

permissiveness

double standard

mating gradient

sex ratio

endogamy

exogamy

homogamy

complementary needs theory

propinquity

rapport

self-revelation

mutual dependency

intimacy need fulfillment

cohabitation

Linus blanket

emancipation

convenience

testing

palimony

Activities

1. Share your thoughts on these questions in a small group: What forces are pushing you toward marriage? What forces are pulling you toward marriage? What is pushing you toward singlehood? What attracts you to singlehood?

2. What initially attracts you to another person? Rank the following traits from 1 to 5 (1 being the highest and 5 the lowest): physical attractiveness, popularity, social status, personality, and character. Discuss your rankings in a small group.

3. Do opposites attract? Or do birds of a feather flock together? In a small group, discuss the theory of homogamy and the theory of complementary needs as they relate to friendships and love relationships.

4. Using Reiss's wheel theory of love, think about one intimate relationship in your life. Describe that relationship as it developed over time in terms of the four components contained in the wheel of love.

5. Discuss violence in dating as a small group. Be sure to address these questions, among others: How frequently have you experienced abuse? What was your reaction to it? What can be done to reduce courtship violence?

6. Find an older person (60 years or older) who is dating or has recently married. Ask this individual about his or her recent courtship experience and how it differs from his or her courtship experiences as a young adult.

7. What are the pro's and con's of living together? Make a list of five advantages and five disadvantages.

8. Does cohabitation increase marital satisfaction and decrease the probability of divorce? Discuss this question in small groups.

Suggested Readings

Cate, R. M., & Lloyd, S. A. (1991). *Courtship.* Newbury Park, CA: Sage. Good, recent research on "going out," which is hard to find; a useful guide for understanding the courtship process.

The mating game. (1993, July 19). *U.S. News & World Report*, pp. 57–63. Traces the sophisticated courtship strategies of modern men and women back to the Stone Age; concludes that women are more concerned about whether mates will invest time and resources in a relationship, and that men care more about a woman's physical attractiveness, which in ancient times reflected her fertility and health.

Popenoe, D., & Whitehead, B. D. (1999). *Should we live together? What young adults need to know about cohabitation before marriage.* New Brunswick, NJ: National Marriage Project, Rutgers University.

Sexual Intimacy

S ex is everywhere in our society. Television dramas, music videos, and advertising abound with sexual images and innuendo. The average American child, who watches about 20 hours of television a week, is thus subjected to an implicit sex education. Those who use sex to sell products and increase program ratings are by and large in charge of sex education in this country, whereas the people who should be leading the way—parents, teachers, professors, religious educators—are often too embarrassed or otherwise ill-equipped to deal with the topic directly. The issue clearly is not whether to have sex education in the United States but rather what kind of sex education we as a society want for our young people and what the source should be.

The purpose of this chapter is to present a reasoned and factual approach to sexuality, especially those issues central to the development of sexual intimacy in human relationships. We will present an overview of sex and society, including historical and cross-cultural perspectives, current trends in sexual behavior in the United States, and sex education. Following this, we will take a look at premarital sex, sexual satisfaction within marriage, extramarital sexual relations, sexual problems, achieving sexual health, and various approaches to sex therapy.

To begin this chapter (and several other chapters), we will take a look at results from a national survey of 26,442 married couples who completed a couple inventory called ENRICH (Olson, Fye, & Olson, 1999). Some of the couples took ENRICH as part of a couple enrichment program, and others took it while seeking marital therapy. The total sample of 26,442 couples was divided into three groups: (1) couples in which both the husband and wife were happily married ($n = 7,116$), (2) couples in which both persons were unhappily married ($n = 13,421$), and (3) couples in which one spouse was happy and the other was unhappy ($n = 5,905$).

Responses from the entire sample of 26,442 couples were used to identify specific issues for married couples in terms of their sexual relationship (which we will discuss in this chapter), gender roles (Chapter 8), communication (Chapter 9), conflict resolution (Chapter 10), personal finances (Chapter 11), and parenting (Chapter 13). These researchers further identified couple strengths in each of these six areas by focusing only on two of the three previously mentioned groups: happy couples (in which both partners were happily married) and unhappy couples (in which both partners were unhappily married).

As we will see in this chapter, the quality and quantity of a couple's sexual relationship is an emotional barometer of the relationship's health. This conclusion is demonstrated most clearly by the following results from the national survey of married couples.

Couple Strengths and Issues in Sexual Relationships

A major strength for a happily married couple is the quality and quantity of their sexual relationship. In a nationwide survey of married couples researchers revealed distinct differences between happy couples and unhappy couples in terms of their sexual relationship (Olson et al., 1999). Most of the happy couples (80%) reported being satisfied with the amount of affection they received from their partner,

Table 7.1 Sexual-Relationship Strengths of Happy Versus Unhappy Married Couples

STRENGTH	PERCENTAGE OF COUPLES IN AGREEMENT	
	Happy Couples (n = 7,116)	Unhappy Couples (n = 13,421)
Are satisfied with the amount of affection they receive from their partner.	80	56
Have no concerns that their partner is disinterested in their sexual relationship.	72	25
Have no concerns that their partner is interested in having an affair.	80	33
Feel their partner does not use sex in an unfair way.	76	33
Are satisfied and fulfilled by their sexual relationship.	68	27

Source: Adapted from Olson, Fye, & Olson (1999).

whereas only 56% of unhappy couples reported being satisfied (Table 7.1). Almost three times as many happy couples (72%) as unhappy couples (25%) did not have concerns about their partner's disinterest in their sexual relationship. Likewise, most happy couples (80%) were not concerned about their partner's being interested in having a sexual relationship outside of their marriage, as compared to one third (33%) of unhappy couples. Happy couples were more likely (76%) than unhappy couples (33%) to agree that their partner does not use or refuse sex unfairly. Happy couples also agreed much more (68%) than unhappy couples (27%) that their sexual relationship is satisfying and fulfilling.

In this same study the total sample of 26,442 married couples revealed that one partner's interest in sex tended to be greater or less than the other partner's; of the couples surveyed, 69% reported this as an issue in their relationship (Table 7.2). Almost two thirds of the couples (64%) reported that they are not completely satisfied with the amount of affection they receive from their partner. About half (49%) of the couples were concerned that their partner may not be interested in them sexually, and almost half (48%) had difficulties talking about sexual issues with one another. Finally, 46% of the couples reported having trouble finding ways to keep their sexual relationship interesting and enjoyable.

Sex and Society: An Overview

A person's sexual identity is an important part of who she or he is. A number of factors, including biology and culture, influence sexual identity. In this section, we will discuss these factors, look at historical and cultural perspectives on sexuality, and explore the ways in which Americans receive information on sexuality.

Sexuality, Sex, and Gender

The formation of a person's sexuality is a complex process, involving continuous interaction among a wide variety of biological influences, family and cultural

Table 7.2 Top Five Sexual Issues for Married Couples	
ISSUE	PERCENTAGE OF COUPLES WITH PROBLEMS SURROUNDING ISSUE (N = 26,442)
Have differing levels of interest in sex.	69
Are dissatisfied with the amount of affection they receive from their partner.	64
Are disinterested in each other sexually.	49
Have difficulty discussing sexual issues.	48
Have difficulty keeping sexual relationship interesting and enjoyable.	46

Source: Adapted from Olson, Fye, & Olson (1999).

influences, and each individual's relatively unique set of personality characteristics. **Sexuality** is a broad term that encompasses the set of beliefs, values, and behaviors that defines each of us as a sexual being. One aspect of an individual's sexuality is whether a person identifies himself or herself as **heterosexual, homosexual, bisexual** or **transgender.** This identity is otherwise known as one's **sexual orientation.** Other aspects of sexuality include a person's interest in having a variety of sexual partners or only one and a person's preference for specific types of sexual acts. There are countless beliefs, values, and behaviors associated with sexuality. Therefore, individuals vary widely in how they define themselves as sexual beings.

In our society, the term **sex** can refer either to being biologically female or male or to sexual activity. The term **gender** refers to the learned characteristics and behaviors associated with being male or female in a particular culture.

Historical Perspectives on Sex and Society

Throughout history, people's sexual behavior and thinking about sex have been guided by religious teachings and cultural beliefs. Many religions, Christianity among them, have attempted to regulate sex outside marriage by condemning it as sinful. Some religions, such as Islam, while also condemning sex outside of marriage, allow men to take more than one wife. Other ideas about sex evolve out of, and are part of, general cultural beliefs. For example, Western male-dominated culture has held the idea that women have little interest in sex. Other cultures—for example, that of the Inuit—consider female sexual activity to be on a par with male sexuality.

Advances in science as early as the 17th century led to a more technical approach to sex. Little was known about the biological aspects of sexuality until Dutch microscopist Anton van Leeuwenhoek (1632–1723) and his student John Ham discovered sperm swimming in human semen. Oscar Hertwig was the first to observe fertilization of the egg by the sperm in sea urchins in 1875, yet the human ovum was not directly observed until the 20th century.

In the late 19th century, the psychological aspects of sex also came under the scrutiny of the scientist. Freud proposed that sexuality is central to the human experience, that even infants are sexual beings, and that human psychological and personality development proceeds through several stages in which the crucial experiences are essentially sexual.

Briefly, Freud proposed that individuals pass through five psychosexual stages:

1. *Oral stage.* Birth to 18 months, the period when an infant's pleasure-seeking activities involve the mouth.

2. *Anal stage.* From about 1½ to 3 years of age, when the infant's pleasure seeking is centered around the anus and the function of elimination.

3. *Phallic stage.* From 3 to 6 years of age, when the child's pleasure seeking involves the genitals. This is also the time, according to Freud, when the child competes with the parent of the same sex. This phenomenon is called the Oedipus complex (named for the character in Greek mythology who unknowingly killed his father and married his mother).

4. *Latency stage.* From age 6 to puberty, a period when the child represses sexual thoughts and engages in activities that develop social and intellectual skills.

5. *Genital stage.* From puberty through adulthood, a time of renewed interest in sexuality, which the individual fulfills through relationships with others.

Freud proposed his theories about psychosexual stages in a strict, repressive era in which sexuality was denied, especially for women. His ideas, at first considered scandalous, were gradually accepted. According to historian Peter Gay, it was "a devious and insincere world in which middle-class husbands slaked their lust by keeping mistresses, frequenting prostitutes, or molesting children, while their wives, timid, dutiful, obedient, were sexually anesthetic and poured all their capacity for love into their housekeeping and their child-rearing" (1984, p. 6). Freud's ideas continue to spark controversy today as his supporters defend his theories with perhaps as much energy as they did a century ago while his detractors argue that he is little more than a historical artifact.

Today, we have a great deal of scientific knowledge about sex—about conception, contraception, and sexual functioning, as well as about how to treat infertility and sexual dysfunction. We talk openly about sex and are complacent about the ubiquity of sexual images in our society. Yet religion still plays a role in many people's sexual attitudes and behavior, and there is still conflict between those who espouse an open, objective, scientific, informational approach to sex and those who wish to regulate people's sexual behavior and their access to information on moral grounds.

Some observers have concluded, however, that the influence of organized religion on sexuality is declining. In 1989, the Christian Broadcasting Network commissioned the Gallup organization to interview 539 college students. The survey was conducted at 100 two-year and four-year campuses, and the sample of students was statistically representative of students nationwide. Nearly 80% of the students said that religion was important in their lives but that their faith had relatively little impact on their sexual attitudes and behavior. About two thirds (69%) of the students said they did not believe nonmarital sex was wrong, and more than half (56%) approved of living together in trial marriages (Gallup, Inc., 1989).

In our society, most information about sexual behavior and intimate relationships comes from the media. Not surprisingly, many people have misconceptions and distorted ideas about both the physical and the emotional dimensions of sexuality.

Sexuality Across Cultures

Attitudes toward sexuality and sexual behaviors vary markedly from one culture to another, and ethnocentrism encourages people to believe that their culture's thinking and practices are the only "right" or "natural" way to live. An important generalization cross-cultural researchers make about sexuality is that all societies regulate sexual behavior in some way, although the regulations vary greatly from culture to culture (Hyde & DeLamater, 1997). Sex is a powerful force, and societies around the world have found it necessary to develop some rules regarding sexual behavior. For example, **incest taboos,** which prohibit intercourse between parents and children and between siblings, are nearly universal; most societies also condemn forced sexual relations, such as rape (Hyde & DeLamater, 1997).

Standards of Attractiveness Cultural standards of sexual attractiveness vary widely. In many non-Western cultures, a plump woman is considered more attractive than a thin woman. But in the United States, the ideal woman has a slim body, well-developed breasts, and long, shapely legs; the ideal man is tall and moderately muscular, with broad shoulders and narrow hips. Physical attributes are often more important for women in Western societies because women tend to be judged by their appearance, whereas men are judged by their accomplishments.

In some cultures, the shape and color of the eyes are most important; other cultures value good-looking ears. The Nawa of Africa value elongated labia ma-

jora (the pads of fatty tissue on either side of the vagina), and Nawa women reportedly tug on them to enhance their length. Although the specifics vary, most cultures identify certain physical traits as attractive and valuable (Hyde & DeLamater, 1997).

Sexual Behavior   Gender roles in sexual behavior differ considerably across cultures. In a few societies, including the Maori and the Kwoma of the South Pacific, females generally initiate love affairs. Although rape in American society is primarily committed by men, the anthropologist Bronislaw Malinowski (1929) reported groups of Trobriand Island women in the South Pacific who regularly raped and sexually humiliated male strangers who were unfortunate enough to wander through the area near their village.

Standards for physical attractiveness, which we take for granted, are actually culturally determined. Although these two women are very different from each other in appearance, each is considered beautiful in her culture.

Sexual techniques also vary considerably from culture to culture (Hyde & De-Lamater, 1997). Kissing is common in most societies; however, when the Thonga of Africa first saw Europeans kissing, they were amused and could not believe the Europeans were sharing saliva. In some societies, one partner inflicts pain on the other partner during lovemaking. Apinayean women of South America have been known to bite off bits of their partner's eyebrows; Trukese women in the South Pacific poke fingers in the man's ear when sexually excited; and partners in some societies draw blood and leave scars as a result of sexual passion.

The frequency of sexual intercourse varies from society to society (Masters, Johnson, & Kolodny, 1995). American society today is about average when compared with other cultures. The range of frequency of intercourse for married couples runs from a low of about once a month among the Keraki of the South Pacific to a high of a few times a night for young couples among the Aranda of Australia and the Mangaians of the South Pacific.

Sexual Attitudes   Attitudes toward **masturbation,** the self-stimulation of the genitals, vary widely from culture to culture. It is tolerated among children and adolescents in some societies but condemned at any age by other societies. Most societies tend to disapprove of adult masturbation; if it is discovered, the consequences range from mild ridicule to punishment (Gregersen, 1983).

Similarly, attitudes toward homosexuality vary widely from culture to culture. Although some cultures tolerate same-sex sexual activity among children, they disapprove when adults engage in it. Other societies force homosexual behavior on all their male members, most often during puberty rites. Despite variations in attitudes from culture to culture, investigators believe at least four generalizations can be made: (1) homosexuality is universal, occurring in all societies; (2) homosexuality is more common among males than among females; (3) homosexuality is never the predominant form of sexual behavior for adults; and (4) only about 5% or less of the population of any culture tends to practice homosexuality (Whitam, 1983).

Cultural Change   Cultural beliefs and attitudes regarding sexuality change, often dramatically, over time. In China, for example, economic and social reform has spawned a new sexual permissiveness. The Shanghai Sex Research Center conducted a national survey of 23,000 people and found that the Chinese are having more sex outside marriage and are becoming increasingly adventurous in the ways they make love. The researchers also found an erosion of the strong tie between sex and marriage in the world's most populous nation. Of those surveyed, a vast majority of the people (86%) and about two thirds (69%) of married people approved of extramarital affairs. In the past, large families were revered in China, but today, China has a one-child policy (Burton, 1990).

American Sexual Behavior Surveyed

There have been several significant sex surveys in the United States since Alfred Kinsey's landmark study in the early 1950s. These surveys reveal, among other things, information regarding the frequency with which Americans engage in sexual activity and the kinds of sexual activities they engage in.

The University of Chicago Study

In 1994, findings from perhaps the most extensive study of sexual behavior in the United States were reported. The research was based on face-to-face interviews with 3,432 American women and men between the ages of 18 and 59. Researchers looked at how age, gender, and marital status are related to sexual behavior; how women's and men's sexual lives and attitudes are similar and different; and how social factors including education, ethnicity, and religion affect sexual behavior (Laumann, Gagnon, Michael, Michaels, & Kolata, 1995).

Although our country is awash in sexual images that suggest we live in a very promiscuous society, this study indicates that, in general, our sexual behavior does not measure up to those images (Cole, Dickerson, & Smilgis, 1994). The researchers found that although 17% of American men and 3% of American women had had sex with at least 21 partners since the age of 15, the sex life of the aver-

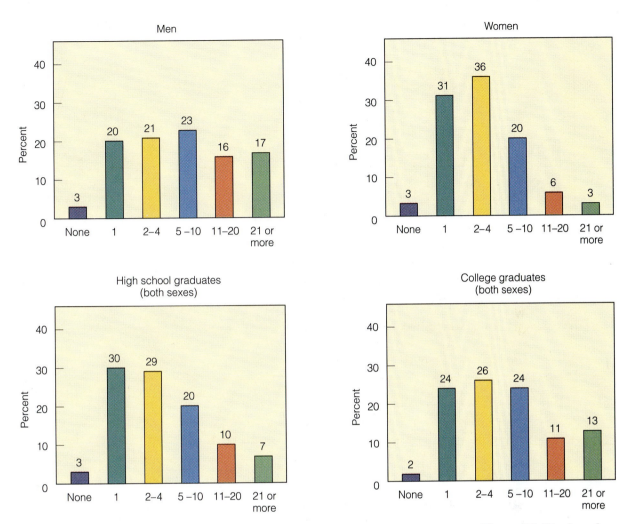

age American is more mundane (Figure 7.1). As the mass media put it, "The sex lives of most Americans are about as exciting as a peanut-butter-and-jelly sandwich" (Cole et al., 1994, p. 64).

Here are some of the results reported in the Chicago study:

- People fall into three groups: One third have sex twice a week or more, one third a few times a month, and one third a few times a year or not at all.

- People are largely monogamous. The majority (83%) have one or zero sexual partners a year. Over a lifetime, the average man has six partners, and the average woman two partners.

- Married couples, compared with single people, have more sex and are more likely to have orgasms when they do have sex. Nearly 40% of those married reported that they had sex twice a week, whereas only 25% of singles said they had sex twice a week.

Figure 7.1 Number of Sex Partners Among American Men and Women, 1994. *Source:* From *Sex in America* by Robert T. Michael et al. Copyright © 1994 by CSG Enterprises, Inc., Edward O. Laumann, Robert T. Michael, and Gina Kolata. By permission of Little, Brown and Company.

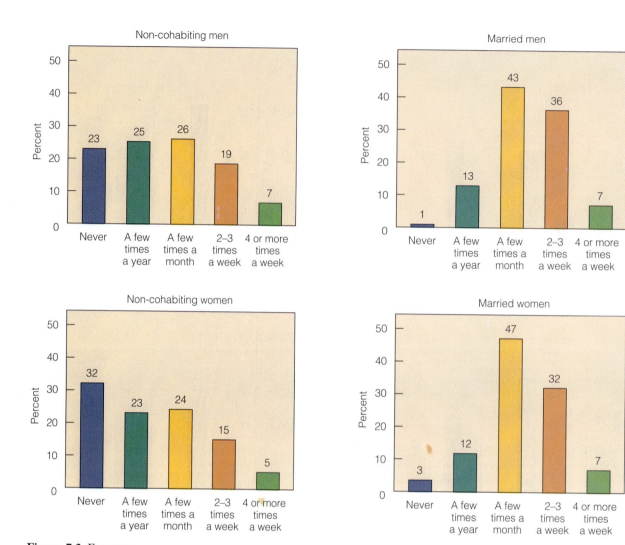

Figure 7.2 Frequency of Sexual Activity in the United States, 1994. *Source:* From *Sex in America* by Robert T. Michael, et al. Copyright © 1994 by CSG Enterprises, Inc., Edward O. Laumann, Robert T. Michael, and Gina Kolata. By permission of Little, Brown and Company.

- Vaginal sex was ranked the most popular sex act (96% found it "very appealing" or "somewhat appealing"); watching a partner undress was ranked second in popularity; and oral sex was a distant third.

- Adultery is the exception, not the rule. Nearly 75% of the married men and 85% of the married women told interviewers they had never been unfaithful. Among the married people in the study, 94% said they had been faithful over the past year.

- Only 2.7% of the men and 1.3% of the women reported to the interviewers that they had had a same-sex sexual experience over the past 12 months.

Figure 7.2 indicates the frequency of sexual activity as reported in the study.

The study sparked a wave of controversy. The most common counterargument suggested that the results were relatively conservative because people are likely to lie in face-to-face interview about their sex lives. This U.S. study, though, mirrored recent studies in France and England that reported low rates of both homosexual behavior and extramarital sex.

Although most observers felt the research was well done, the University of Chicago research team admitted that the findings will remain debatable. First of all, 4,369 people were scientifically sampled for the study, but many were reluctant to participate. The 220 interviewers were trained to persist in trying to gain people's participation; some individuals were visited 15 times before being persuaded to cooperate. In the end, 79% of those randomly selected for the research actually participated.

Second, even though people agreed to participate, they may not have told the truth. "There is no way to get around the fact some people might conceal information," team member Stuart Michaels noted. For example, some gay men and lesbians might not have disclosed their sexual orientation to an interviewer: "This is a stigmatized group. There is probably a lot more homosexual activity going on than we could get people to talk about" (Cole et al., 1994, p. 66).

Figure 7.3 summarizes the various sexual practices reported in the study. Some of the other findings of the Chicago study included the following:

- The 1960s and the 1970s were a time of free love, compared with other decades; 40-something baby boomers were more likely to have had 21 or more sex partners, compared with respondents in other age groups.

- AIDS has changed sexual behavior to some degree. Among those who were especially active (five or more partners in the past year), 76% had decided to slow down, use condoms faithfully, or get tested for HIV.

- The people who masturbate the most tend to be the people who also have sex the most. In team member John Gagnon's words, "If you're having sex a lot, you're thinking about sex a lot."

- Both men and women prefer receiving oral sex to giving it. White, college-educated men were more likely to have performed oral sex (80%) than Blacks (51%).

- Among women, 29% reported that they always have an orgasm during sex.

- Of women who had had an abortion, 72% had had only one.

- Fifty-four percent of men said they think about sex every day or several times a day; 67% of women said they think about it only a few times a week or a few times a month.

- Twenty-two percent of women said they had been forced by men to do sexual things they didn't want to do, but only 3% of men admitted to ever having forced themselves on a woman.

Perhaps humorist Garrison Keillor has the last word on the University of Chicago study:

Despite all you may have read lately, there is an incredible amount of normality going on in America these days, and it is good to know. Our country is not

Figure 7.3 Sexual Practices Among American Men and Women, 1994. *Source: From Sex in America* by Robert T. Michael, et al. Copyright © 1994 by CSG Enterprises, Inc., Edward O. Laumann, Robert T. Michael, and Gina Kolata. By permission of Little, Brown and Company.

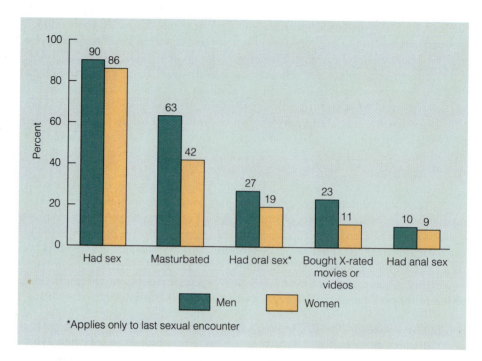

obsessed with sex. To the contrary. We wear ourselves out working, we are surrounded with noise and distraction and all manner of entertainment, we indulge our children as they run roughshod over our lives, the ghosts of old aunts and beady-eyed preachers lurk in the shadows watching us. Considering what the American couple is up against, it's astounding to think that once a week or once a month or maybe just on Memorial Day and Christmas or whenever the coast is clear, they are enjoying this gorgeous moment that is, despite its secrecy and long, shuddering climax, essentially the same experience as everyone else has had. It's almost worth all the misery of dealing with real estate people, bankers, lawyers and contractors—to have a home that has a bedroom where the two of you can go sometimes and do this. It is worth growing up and becoming middle-aged to be able to enjoy it utterly. (Keillor, 1994)

The *Janus Report*

In an excellent comprehensive survey of sexual behavior, Samuel Janus and Cynthia Janus (1993) compiled the *Janus Report*, which surveyed 2,765 Americans age 18 to over 65. This in-depth survey found that sexual activity was somewhat greater for men than for women across the life cycle but that it decreased for both as they got older. However, sex continued to be rather common even for people in their 60s (Table 7.3). The researchers also found that sexual activity had begun earlier in life for members of each age group than it had for the next-oldest group among both males and females and that the age of first sexual intercourse has become progressively younger over the years (Janus & Janus, 1993). The most dramatic difference was between people currently (i.e., at the time of the study) 18 to 26 and those over 65. Of males in the younger age group, 91% had had sex by age 18;

Table 7.3 Sexual Activity Across the Life Cycle Among American Men and Women, 1993

FREQUENCY	AGE (YEARS)									
	16–26		**27–38**		**39–50**		**51–64**		**65+**	
Sample:	**M**	**F**	**M**	**F**	**M**	**F**	**M**	**F**	**M**	**F**
Numbers:	**(254)**	**(268)**	**(353)**	**(380)**	**(282)**	**(293)**	**(227)**	**(230)**	**(212)**	**(221)**
Daily	15%	13%	16%	8%	15%	10%	12%	4%	14%	1%
Few times a week	38	33	44	41	39	29	51	28	39	40
Weekly	19	22	23	27	29	29	18	33	16	33
Monthly	15	15	8	12	9	11	11	8	20	4
Rarely	13	17	9	12	8	21	8	27	11	22

Source: Adapted from *The Janus Report on Sexual Behavior* (p. 25) by S. S. Janus and C. L. Janus, 1993, New York: Wiley. Copyright 1993 by S. S. Janus and C. L. Janus. Adapted by permission of John Wiley & Sons, Inc.

only about 60% of the males 65 and older had had sex by that age. More differences were reported for women. By age 18, 83% of the 18- to 26-year-olds had had sex; of the women 65 and older, only 41% had had sex by the age of 18. It is clear that younger people are having sex earlier than the group just ahead of them in age.

The *American Couples* Study

In a major study of sexual behavior among couples, Philip Blumstein and Pepper Schwartz (1983) surveyed 5,945 couples (11,890 individuals), of whom 3,574 (60%) were married couples, 642 (11%) cohabiting couples, 957 (16%) gay-male couples, and 772 (13%) lesbian couples. The results of their study were published in their book *American Couples.* The couples interviewed were primarily White. About 40% had professional or technical careers; about 20% were managers and administrators; and the remaining 40% had a range of occupations. The value of this study lies both in its carefully conceived methodology and in the useful perspective it offers on various types of couples.

In terms of initiation of sex, about 50% of the husbands but only 12% of the wives felt they initiated sex more often than their partner. Thirty-three percent of the husbands and 40% of the wives felt they were about equal in initiating sex. The pattern was about the same for male and female cohabitants. Gay men and lesbians had very similar patterns, with 37% feeling that both partners initiated sex about equally, 31% feeling that they initiated more often, and the remaining 32% feeling that their partner was more often the initiator.

Sexual frequency was generally higher during the first 2 years of a relationship, with 45% of married couples having sex three times a week or more. In years 2 to 10, frequency dropped, with only 27% having sex three or more times a week. After 10 years of marriage, only 18% maintained that degree of frequency. Thirty-eight percent of couples married less than 2 years had sex one to three times a week. After 2 to 10 years of marriage, almost half (46%) of the couples dropped to this level. Cohabiting couples and gay-male couples who had been together less than 2 years were the most sexually active, with 61% and 67%, respectively, having sex three or more times a week. Again, as with married couples, frequency

Research indicates that young people are becoming sexually active at an earlier age than in previous generations, and they also tend to have more sexual partners. More recently, however, there seems to be a trend toward more conservative sexual behavior, perhaps due to the threat of sexually transmissible diseases.

dropped after 2 years together. Lesbians were the least sexually active, and their frequency also dropped after 2 years in the relationship. Figure 7.4 shows frequency of sexual activity for all four groups during the time frames examined by the study.

In all of the couples, there was a direct relationship between sexual satisfaction and frequency of sex. Also, couples who were more satisfied with their relationship had sex more frequently. Couples who fought about things like parenting, household responsibilities, or how to spend money tended to have a less satisfying sexual relationship.

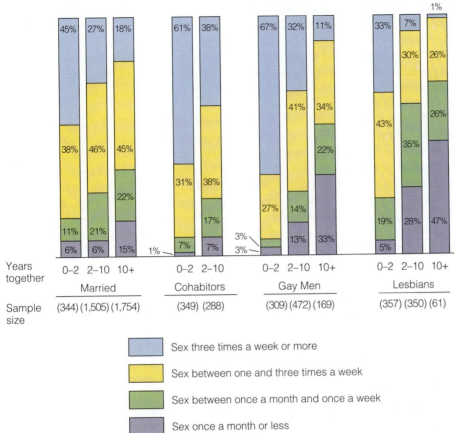

Figure 7.4 Frequency of Sexual Activity Among American Couples, 1983. *Source: American Couples* (p. 196) by P. W. Blumstein and P. Schwartz, 1983, New York: William Morrow. Copyright © 1983 by Philip Blumstein and Pepper Schwartz. Reprinted by permission of William Morrow & Co., Inc.

Sex three times a week or more

Sex between one and three times a week

Sex between once a month and once a week

Sex once a month or less

Gay-Male and Lesbian Sexual Behavior

The Chicago study, the *Janus Report*, and the *American Couples* study all report different and sometimes contradictory data about lesbians and gay men. There are probably several reasons for these inconsistencies. One is the issue of definition and identity: Are you gay if you have one same-sex interaction? Or are you gay only if you identify yourself as gay?

Another issue is the stigmatization of homosexuality in our culture. Gay people are frequently the target of prejudice and sometimes violence. Gay men and lesbians often experience discrimination in the employment and housing markets, and in most communities they hold little political power. Physical force is often used against them: Gangs of teenagers and young adults have terrorized homosexuals, and stories of brutality against gays by police and military personnel are not uncommon.

Because of the stigma and the danger attached to "coming out," many gay men and lesbians choose not to reveal their sexual orientation to their families, friends, or co-workers—and certainly not to a stranger taking a survey. It is probably impossible to determine precisely what percentage of people in our society have engaged in homosexual behavior or consider themselves to be gay or lesbian; however, studies by Kinsey and his associates found that by middle age, 50% of all males and 20% of all females had had some type of overt sexual experience with one or more members of the same sex (Kinsey, Pomeroy, & Martin, 1948). Furthermore, between adolescence and the later years of life, 37% of the men and 13% of the women had engaged in at least one sexual experience that culminated in orgasm with someone of the same sex. Four percent of the men and 2% of the women in Kinsey's studies reported that they were exclusively oriented affectionately only to members of their sex.

A study that appeared in 1989 reanalyzed data from a 1970 study of men and concluded that a minimum of 20% of the males had had sexual contact to orgasm with another male at least once in their life. About 7% had had such contact in adulthood; approximately 2% had had such contact in the previous year. The researchers emphasized that these findings should be viewed as minimum estimates because people are likely to conceal such behavior (Fay, Turner, Klassen, & Gagnon, 1989). As we saw earlier, the Chicago study reported that only 2.7% of the men interviewed and 1.3% of the women said they had had a homosexual experience in the previous 12 months.

Despite the prevalence of same-sex contact and despite the absence of evidence to support common stereotypes, society continues to discriminate against gay men and lesbians. For some people, aversion to homosexuals and homosexuality has developed into a phobia: **homophobia.** Many therapists and gays believe that people who are homophobic may be unconsciously or consciously hiding fears about their own sexual orientation. For example, many gay men who have come out (i.e., those who are open about their sexual orientation) admit to having participated in "gay-bashing" incidents in the past, to convince others and themselves that they were straight.

In nearly all ways, gay-male and lesbian relationships are like heterosexual relationships. In general, gay men and lesbians have increasingly moved toward developing and maintaining ongoing relationships with one person. Because they have had to struggle with coming out and have often experienced considerable rejection by their families, gay men and lesbians, like other groups, frequently develop skills and strengths that are valuable in relationships. These include an ability to connect emotionally with other people of both sexes, flexible role relationships and an ability to adapt to a partner, an ability to negotiate and share decision-making power, caring and effective parenting among those who choose to become parents, psychological perceptiveness, and effective communication skills.

Many gay-male and lesbian couples build satisfying relationships (Peplau, Cochran, & Mays, 1997; Peplau, Veniegas, & Campbell, 1996; Veniegas & Peplau, 1997). One study compared relationship satisfaction among comparable samples of gay-male, lesbian, and heterosexual couples and found no significant differences. All three groups rated their relationships highly satisfying (Peplau, Padesky, & Hamilton, 1981). Emotional expressiveness—"being able to talk about my most intimate feelings"—was cited by both heterosexual and homosexual women as very important. Lesbians placed a high value on equality in relationships; the most satisfying relationships were those in which both partners were equally committed, equally "in love," and equal in power (Peplau & Amaro, 1982).

Same-sex couples share other characteristics with heterosexual couples. For example, the frequency of sexual activity declines over time among gay-male, lesbian, and heterosexual couples. Like heterosexual couples, gays and lesbians sometimes have problems over who initiates sex. Although among heterosexuals the man is typically the initiator, in same-sex couples, the more emotionally expressive partner usually initiates sex (Blumstein & Schwartz, 1983).

Sex Education

To the young people of this nation
Who must find their way to sexual health
In a world of contradictions.
Where the media scream "Always say yes,"
Where many adults admonish, "Just say no,"
But the majority just say . . . Nothing.
                              —PEGGY BRICK (1989)

Where do Americans get their sex education? Unfortunately, the *Janus Report* found that most people learn about sex "on the street" from their peers. Home ranked second as a source of sex education, followed by school and, rarely, church (Janus & Janus, 1993).

Consequences of Inadequate Sex Education

Because so little of our sex education is adequate, we have become a country with major sexual and parenting challenges, such as AIDS and adolescent motherhood. The United States leads the world in rates of teenage pregnancy and abortion (U.S. Bureau of the Census, 1997). Adolescent pregnancy in the United States could be described as epidemic: The rate is twice that of France, England, and Canada; three times that of Sweden; and seven times that of the Netherlands. Each year in the United States over 1 million unmarried women become pregnant, and of those, 10,000 are girls 15 years of age or younger. In 1995, 32% of all births were to unmarried women; the rate for Whites was 25% and for African Americans 70% (U.S. Bureau of the Census, 1997). Clearly, compared with other Western nations that have similar standards of living, levels of industrial development, and forms of government, the United States has a much higher rate of teenage pregnancy. This higher rate can be attributed to the irregular and ineffective use of contraception by American adolescents (Chase-Lansdale & Brooks-Gunn, 1995; Coley & Chase-Lansdale, 1998).

The rise in adolescent pregnancy in this country has a multitude of negative consequences. The problems associated with "children having children" are enormous. The father usually disappears from the picture, and the young mother ends up rearing the child alone. This often places an extra burden on the grandparents, forcing many into a second—often unwelcome—"parenthood." And although the young mother needs a decent education, she may find it difficult to continue in school. Young mothers often experience serious financial problems, inadequate housing, lack of transportation, loneliness, poor nutrition, physical health problems, and a cluster of other stressors that commonly foster child neglect and abuse (Barratt, Roach, Morgan, & Colbert, 1996; Coley & Chase-Lansdale, 1998; Frost & Forrest, 1995; Higginson, 1998; Mulsow & Murry, 1996; Whiteside-Mansell, Pope, & Bradley, 1996).

"My parents were intelligent, sensitive individuals, and yet they treated the subject of sex like it was the plague," said Joyce, a 45-year-old single mother of three. "All I knew for sure was this must really be something if it was such a big secret! What happened with my brothers and sister (and me) was there were a lot of misconceptions and a lot of guilt.

"As a parent, what kind of message did I give my children? In my head I knew what I wanted to give them, but in my gut I was still at war with my own sexuality. So I, too, gave mixed messages to my children about sex. It wasn't until I went back to college full-time after my divorce and got into a human sexuality class that the shift really came for me internally. I began to stop feeling self-conscious and began to relax—to enjoy being human. I still have one child living at home, and I'm able to talk openly and honestly with him about any subject regarding sex.

"I feel strongly about good sex education for our children. Two years ago I would have been floored by the idea of showing films on sexual intercourse, masturbation, and gay and lesbian lovemaking to 12-year-olds and their parents in a church setting. Today, I would support it 100%. I wish sex education could be available to all children and their parents at least by the time kids are 12 years old."

Sex-Education Programs

The high rate of adolescent pregnancy and the long list of problems it causes in families have led to the development of a wide variety of sex-education programs across the country. (To find out how good your sex education has been, take the quiz in Box 7.1.) A survey of 802 American adults indicated that a little more than half of the respondents had taken a sex-education class at some time in their life. Sixty-eight percent of the younger adults, those between the ages of 18 and 24, had taken such a class. Classes are commonly held in public and private schools and in churches and synagogues (Allen-Meares, 1989).

More than 80% of American adults favor sex education (Janus & Janus, 1993). According to the Janus survey, 86% of the population supports sex education, and 89% want courses for children age 12 and older to deal with birth control information. About 75% of the adults want the courses to talk about homosexuality and abortion. Planned Parenthood, a national private nonprofit organization, has developed a wide variety of presentations and materials to benefit young people. A sample of the organization's materials, displayed in Box 7.2, lists some common misconceptions young people have about sex—"ridiculous ideas" that can lead to trouble.

Sex Education and Parents

Although people disagree about sexuality, there is agreement on one issue—that education about sexuality should begin in the home (Gordon & Snyder, 1989; Jaccard, Dittus, & Gordon, 1998; Koop, 1988; Raffaelli, Bogenschneider, & Flood, 1998). The reason that schools, religious institutions, and agencies such as Planned

BOX 7.1

Testing Your Knowledge About Sex

For more than 40 years, the Kinsey Institute at Indiana University has been a pioneer in the scientific study of human sexuality. In a Roper poll conducted for the Kinsey Institute, 2,000 adults in the United States were asked a series of true-or-false and multiple-choice questions about sex. Only 45% of those tested answered more than half the questions correctly. See how you do on this sample of the questions.

CIRCLE
TRUE OR
FALSE

T   F   1. Most women prefer a sex partner who has a large penis.

T   F   2. Menopause does not cause a woman to lose interest in having sex.

_____   3. When does the average American first have sexual intercourse?

_____   4. Of every 10 women in the United States, how many would you estimate have ever masturbated?

T   F   5. More than 25% of American males have had a same-sex sexual experience.

T   F   6. Anal intercourse between uninfected people can cause AIDS.

T   F   7. Most husbands have extramarital affairs.

_____   8. What percentage of women engage in anal sex?

T   F   9. Problems with erections are most often started by a physical problem.

T   F   10. Almost all erection problems can be successfully treated.

_____   11. What do you think is the average length of a man's penis?

T   F   12. Lubricants like Vaseline Intensive Care or baby oil can cause microscopic holes in a condom or diaphragm.

T   F   13. Homosexuality is usually difficult to tell just by people's appearance or gestures.

T   F   14. A woman can get pregnant if she has sex during her menstrual period.

T   F   15. A woman can get pregnant even if the man withdraws his penis before ejaculating.

Answers: 1. F; 2. T; 3. age 16 or 17; 4. 6–8; 5. T; 6. F; 7. F; 8. 30–40%; 9. T; 10. T; 11. 5–7 inches; 12. T; 13. T; 14. T; 15. T

Source: Adapted from *The Kinsey Institute New Report on Sex* (p. 45) by J. Reinisch and R. Beasley, 1994, New York: St. Martin's. Copyright © 1994 by The Kinsey Institute for Research in Sex, Gender, and Reproduction. Reprinted by permission.

Parenthood have become involved in sex education is that most parents feel incapable of or uncomfortable about talking seriously with their offspring about sexual matters. A subtle conspiracy of silence exists between parent and child. Parents tell themselves that they are willing to answer any questions their children might have about sex, but children sense that their parents really do not want to talk about these sensitive issues. Because both feel uncomfortable talking about sexuality, they avoid the subject.

Few children receive direct instruction from their parents in the areas of sexuality, sexual intercourse, or birth control (Miller & Moore, 1991). This is sad because good parental communication about sex might forestall or postpone a child's sexual activity. Among those daughters who are sexually active, parental communication appears to help promote more effective contraceptive practices on the part of the adolescent. An interesting study of family interaction patterns in homes with

BOX   7 . 2

Ten Ridiculous Ideas That Will Make You a Parent

- You can count on your partner to use birth control.

- Men have stronger sex drives than women do.

- Men need to have sex with different women to learn to be better lovers.

- If a woman uses birth control, then she has probably been sleeping around.

- A woman would do anything to keep from getting pregnant.

- It is easy for a woman to get on the pill.

- If a man hasn't gone all the way by the time he's 16, then something is wrong with him.

- Condoms are *not* cool.

- When a woman says no, she really just wants to be talked into it.

- I could never talk to my partner about birth control.

Source: Adapted with permission from the brochure "Ten Ridiculous Ideas That Will Make a Father Out of You," © 1984, Planned Parenthood of Central Oklahoma, 619 N.W. 23rd Street, Oklahoma City, OK 73103.

teenagers found that adolescents who experienced open communication and satisfaction with family interaction also reported having received more sex education in the home (Baldwin & Baranoski, 1990).

Sol Gordon and his colleagues concur that parents who accept their children's sexuality and help them learn to cope with it have a better chance of raising healthy and sexually responsible children than parents who avoid the issues. Gordon urges parents to become "askable," positing that young people who can talk freely with their parents about sex will be stronger and more able to make wise choices as they grow to adulthood. Surveying more than 8,000 students, Gordon found that fewer than 15% had received a meaningful sex education from their parents. Girls were usually told about menstruation; the balance of their teaching, however, could be summed up in one word: *don't.* And except for the occasional or single prepuberty talk with Dad, who used vague birds-and-bees analogies and ended by mentioning the use of a condom, the boys were on their own (Gordon & Gordon, 1990; Klein & Gordon, 1992).

Brent Miller and his colleagues studied how strictness of parenting was related to adolescents' sexual attitudes and behaviors (Miller, McCoy, Olson, & Wallace, 1986). These researchers hypothesized and found a curvilinear relationship between flexibility in parenting and sexual behavior. Sexual promiscuity and the experience of intercourse were highest among teenagers who saw their parents as not being strict or as not having any rules (chaotic on the Couple and Family Map; see Chapter 4), lowest among those teens who reported that their parents were moderately strict (flexible on the Couple and Family Map), and intermediate among teenagers who saw their parents as being very strict and having many rules (rigid on the Couple and Family Map). The results of this study suggest that if parents are concerned about adolescent sexual behavior, they can err in two directions: by being either too lenient (chaotic) or too strict (rigid). The more balanced levels

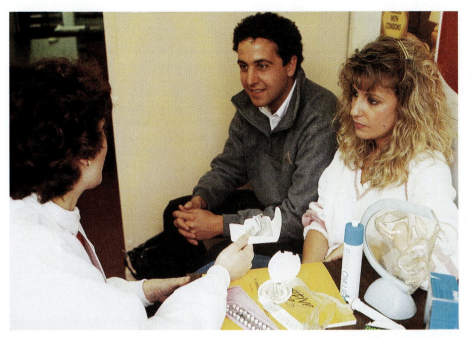

Because parents tend to be poor at providing their children with clear, useful information about sex, the responsibility for sex education in our society has fallen largely to schools and communities. Sex education is more effective when combined with access to a health clinic where contraceptives are available.

(being structured or flexible on the Couple and Family Map) are related to more responsible sexual behavior on the part of adolescents.

> "It's very difficult finding the right balance with our kids," James, a middle-aged father in Cleveland, Ohio, noted. "I think we're doing okay, but you never know for sure until they're grown up and have made it safely through the difficult years of adolescence and young adulthood. We try to give them guidance, some things to think about when it comes to sexuality.
>
> "But we try not to be too strict or moralistic because we know that can backfire. And really, they're going to do what they want to anyway, no matter what we say. We can only cross our fingers and hope their judgment is reasonably good.
>
> "My own judgment as a young person was pretty good. I did make some mistakes, but I learned from them. I know my kids will make some mistakes, too, and I suspect they'll learn from them. I just hope the mistakes aren't irreversible."

Is Sex Education Effective?

Do sex-education programs work? After a 7-year study of nine programs around the country, a six-volume analysis by Mathtech Inc. concluded that certain conditions must be met if sex-education programs are to be effective (Leo, 1986). First, two of the nine programs were very successful because they had strong backing from parents and the local community. Second, the use of birth control increased

BOX 7.3

A New Approach to Sex Ed

A recent approach for discouraging adolescent girls from getting pregnant is an 8-pound doll called Baby Think It Over. The doll looks innocent enough, but if you put it down for any length of time, it emits a high-pitched cry that sounds like a real baby. The shrieks occur at random intervals day and night. The only way to stop them is by inserting a key in the doll's back and holding it for 20–30 minutes, the average time it takes to feed a real newborn.

Teenage girls who have taken Baby Think It Over home for 3 days come back to school looking like they have been the subjects of a sleep-deprivation experiment. In other words, they look like real moms.

"I'm going to wait at least 10 years," said one exhausted San Diego high school student after her stint with the doll.

Source: From "Teens Need Dolls' Drastic Lessons" by David Grimes, 1994, Sarasota *Herald-Tribune.*
Copyright © 1994 by David Grimes. Reprinted by permission of the Sarasota *Herald-Tribune*, Sarasota, FL.

only when the sex-education program was coupled with ready access to a health clinic. Graduates of sex-education programs were less permissive about nonmarital sex than young people in control groups.

A Minnesota-based program recorded 40% lower birth rates in schools with health clinics (Stark, 1986). Of the adolescent mothers who used the clinics, 80% stayed in school, and repeat pregnancies were almost nonexistent. Follow-up contact was necessary in such programs, however, because teenagers are poor at remembering to use birth control (Leo, 1986). This supports other studies reporting that only 14% of teenage girls used contraceptives the first time they had intercourse.

Most Western nations try to reduce adolescent pregnancy through programs that emphasize abstinence but also offer the alternative of effective contraceptives to those who choose to remain or become sexually active. In the United States, "Just Say No" programs are promoted heavily, but there is little research evidence to conclude that they are very effective (Christopher, 1995; Christopher & Roosa, 1990; St. Pierre, Mark, Kaltreider, & Aikin, 1995). As in Europe, the most effective American programs encourage abstinence but also offer an alternative for those who are already or who choose to become sexually active. Box 7.3 describes a clever approach to discouraging teenage pregnancy.

Premarital Sexual Behavior

In the 1960s, about two thirds of American adults felt premarital or nonmarital sex was wrong, according to a Gallup poll. By the late 1980s, adults in this country were about evenly split, with half saying it was wrong "for a man and a woman to have sex relations before marriage" and about half saying it was not wrong. The pollsters believed this to be a dramatic turnaround in attitudes (Gallup, Inc., 1989).

Sexual Behavior Among Adolescents

Young people have their own ideas about nonmarital sex, of course, and their behavior often does not square with adults' attitudes. A 1990 government survey, conducted by the Centers for Disease Control (CDC), found that 54% of the nation's high school students in grades 9 through 12 had had sex (Kolbe, 1992). Of that number, 39% said they had had sex in the 3 months before the survey. Among 9th graders, 40% of those surveyed said they had had sex. Among 10th graders, the figure rose to 48%. By 11th grade, it was 57%, and by 12th grade, 72%. This survey of 11,631 students, conducted in 1990, was the first the government had made.

Students were asked to identify the birth control method they or their partner had used to prevent pregnancy the last time they had had sex. Forty-five percent reported using condoms, 33% reported using another method of contraception (e.g., birth control pills, withdrawal), and 22% reported not using any birth control (Kolbe, 1992).

Pregnancy is not the only concern for sexually active teenagers. They also risk contracting a sexually transmissible disease (STD), such as herpes or HIV infection. According to the government survey, 1 in 25 students reported having had an STD (Kolbe, 1992).

The CDC now surveys health-risk behaviors among young people in the United States on a regular basis. The latest data indicate a decline in the percentage of high school students who say they are sexually active: from 54% in 1991 to 48% in 1997 ("More High Schoolers," 1998). Data also indicate that condom use (during the respondent's last sexual intercourse) also increased from 46% in 1991 to almost 57% in 1997. Dr. Lloyd Kolbe, director of the CDC's Division of Adolescent and School Health, said the findings are evidence that teaching teenagers about safe sex hasn't resulted in more promiscuity. He also noted that the findings show that teens who are virgins shouldn't feel like outcasts.

"It is an important milestone," he argued, "because students who have not engaged in intercourse can say that they're in the majority." Kolbe attributed the declines in risky sexual behavior to vigilant efforts by parents, schools, and health officials to educate young people about safe sex and the risks of teen pregnancy, AIDS, and other STDs.

Sexual Behavior Among College Students

Research on the sexual behavior of college students indicates that permarital intercourse has continued to increase consistently (Robinson, Ziss, Ganza, Katz, & Robinson, 1991). Ira Robinson and his colleagues surveyed students about nonmarital sexual behavior every 5 years for more than 20 years (1965, 1970, 1975, 1980, 1985). They found that nonmarital sexual activity among college males increased 14.2% and that female nonmarital sexual activity jumped 34.3% between 1965 and 1985. As indicated in Table 7.4, the percentages of both males and females who had experienced intercourse increased from one time period to the next in almost every instance.

In addition to concluding that nonmarital sex has become more common over the years, Robinson and his colleagues (1991) also concluded that differences between male and female attitudes regarding sex decreased over the years. They did,

Table 7.4 Sex Among American College Students, 1965–1985

YEAR	MALES		FEMALES	
	Percentage	Number	Percentage	Number
1965	65.1	129	28.7	115
1970	65.0	136	37.3	158
1975	73.9	115	57.1	275
1980	77.4	168	63.5	230
1985	79.3	208	63.0	257

Source: From "Twenty Years of the Sexual Revolution, 1965–1985: An Update" by I. E. Robinson, K. Ziss, B. Ganza, S. Katz, and E. Robinson, 1991, *Journal of Marriage and the Family, 53*, p. 217. Copyright © 1991 by the National Council on Family Relations. Reprinted by permission.

however, note a certain contradiction in values: Although more college students were engaging in sexual intercourse, the percentage of those who thought non-marital sex was immoral and sinful also increased. The old double standard gave males greater license for sexual behavior than females. The "new" double standard (reflected by the contradiction in attitudes) imposes greater sexual restrictions on others than on oneself.

Marital and Extramarital Sexual Behavior

Surveys indicate that most young people have intercourse before marriage; in fact, premarital relationships are often highly sexual. After marriage, the sexual relationship gradually changes. Some people have jokingly asked, "Is there sex after marriage?" Research indicates there is.

Sex Within Marriage

When newspaper columnist Ann Landers asked her readers, "Has your sex life gone downhill since you got married?" 82% of the 141,210 people who responded said yes, sex after marriage was less exciting (A. Landers, 1989). However, intimacy—feelings of warmth and closeness between two people who love each other—does not appear to diminish with time. Within the intimate environment of a happy marriage, sexual experiences can become more satisfying and meaningful—and retain their excitement—over time.

The *Janus Report* indicated that married couples have higher levels of sexual activity than divorced people and single people, as shown in Table 7.5 (Janus & Janus, 1993). More specifically, 44% of the married couples reported having sexual activity at least a few times a week, compared with 32% of singles and 33% of divorced people. Conversely, only 7% of married people rarely had sex, whereas the figure was 19% for singles and 22% for divorced people. In other words, married couples across the life cycle are even more active sexually than singles.

A hectic life often gets in the way of an active sex life. Long hours on the job, caring for children, continual interruptions, and countless other stresses tend to

Table 7.5 Sexual Activity Among American Married, Divorced, and Single People, 1993

FREQUENCY	MARRIED (n = 1,552)	DIVORCED (n = 246)	SINGLE (n = 815)
Daily	14%	9%	11%
Few times weekly	44	33	32
Weekly	27	26	21
Monthly	8	10	17
Rarely	7	22	19
TOTAL	100	100	100

Source: Adapted from *The Janus Report on Sexual Behavior* (p. 159) by S. S. Janus and C. L. Janus, 1993, New York: Wiley. Copyright 1993 by S. S. Janus and C. L. Janus. Adapted by permission of John Wiley & Sons, Inc.

tire people out and decrease their sexual activity. For those couples with two jobs, the phenomenon has been called the **DINS** (double income, no sex) **dilemma.** Therapists have labeled it *inhibited*, or *hypoactive*, *sexual desire*. In addition to sheer fatigue, boredom is also a factor for some individuals. Most of the time couples can resuscitate the sexual relationship with some tender care and concern, such as having dinner out together, seeing a movie, or going to bed early. Consulting a marriage and family therapist or a sex therapist may be useful for persistent sexual problems. The preeminent sex researchers and therapists William Masters and Virginia Johnson, along with Robert Kolodny (1988), argued in *Masters & Johnson on Sex and Human Loving* that half of all American couples are troubled by some type of sexual distress, ranging from disinterest to genuine sexual dysfunction. Some couples need therapy, but many others can benefit simply by heeding the 16 ideas outlined in Box 7.4.

For many people, sex is not the most important thing in life. A nationwide survey of 815 men found that the most important thing in a man's life is not sex, career, fame, or fortune, but marriage, according to 75% of the married men in the sample (Hellmich, 1990). About 90% of these husbands called their wife their best friend. Friendship, based on trust and sharing of responsibilities, becomes more important as life's challenges mount and sexual energy decreases (Hellmich, 1990).

Couples commonly reported that the number of times they had sex decreased somewhat as their years together passed. In a study of 100 happily married couples, one third said they have intercourse about three times a month (Woodman, 1986). In some surveys, sex ranks low among the most rewarding aspects of life. In fact, sex ranked fifth—after love, health and fitness, friendship, and children—in the study of 100 happy couples (Woodman, 1986). Many family and sex therapists agree that some couples have happy, stable marital relationships with little sex. However, without sex, the relationship may develop a kind of coolness, and one or both partners may feel unfulfilled.

Although sex is clearly not everything, it is important to an intimate relationship. David Knox, director of the marriage therapy program at East Carolina University, explained it succinctly, "When sex goes well, it is 15 percent of a relationship, but if it goes badly, it's 85 percent." Sex is more than a simple physical need;

BOX 7.4

Advice From Masters and Johnson on Sexual Health

- Always remember that good sex begins while your clothes are still on.

- Take time to think about yourself as a sexual being.

- Take responsibility for your own sexual pleasure.

- Talk with your partner about sex.

- Make time to be together regularly.

- Don't let sex become routine.

- Use fantasy—you'll find it's one of the best aphrodisiacs.

- Understand that working at sex doesn't work.

- Don't carry anger into your bedroom.

- Realize that good sex isn't just a matter of pushing the right buttons.

- Nurture the romance in your life.

- Don't make sex too serious.

- Don't always wait to be "in the mood" before agreeing to have sex.

- Realize that you and your partner don't have to see eye to eye sexually.

- Don't be afraid to ask for help.

- Try to keep your sexual expectations realistic.

Source: Adapted from *Masters and Johnson on Sex and Human Loving* (pp. 452–461) by W. H. Masters, V. Johnson, and R. C. Kolodny, 1988, Boston: Little, Brown. Copyright © 1982, 1985, 1986, 1988 by William H. Masters, M.D., Virginia E. Johnson, and Robert Kolodny, M.D. By permission of Little, Brown and Co.

"it represents identity, desirability, an affirmation of one's self. We attach many important psychological needs to our sexuality. That's why it's such a revealing area." In a similar vein, Gene Abel noted, "Anyone can say I care about you, and you may believe it or not. But during sex we naturally evaluate how our partner seems to feel about us. If loving feelings are there, they come through. If they are lacking, that comes through, too" (cited in Woodman, 1986, pp. 130–131).

Different people have different needs for sexual intimacy, and those needs affect how they perceive their sexual behavior. For this reason, couples must communicate clearly about sex if they are to maintain a satisfying relationship. The movie *Annie Hall* depicts two lovers with different perceptions of their sexual relationship. When a therapist asks them (separately) how often they have sex, the character played by Woody Allen answers, "Hardly ever, maybe three times a week"; the character played by Diane Keaton replies, "Constantly, three times a week."

Overall, it appears that in many marriages sex is very important for long-term happiness. It has powerful symbolic value in a successful marriage, reaffirming the bond between the individuals. It is an indication that everything is still okay despite wrinkles, sags, and love handles. To keep the spark in their lovemaking, married couples need to keep the relationship alive through communication and sharing. It is very difficult to have a successful sexual relationship if each partner does not feel good about himself or herself or about other aspects of the relationship.

"Our sexual relationship is great today," noted Serena, a middle-aged woman living in St. Louis. "It's a lot better than it was early in our marriage. I don't know why exactly, but I think we're more used to each other, more comfortable with each other. Perhaps we really love each other more. As the years pass, you look back and see a long-term tradition of commitment and kindness, and recognize that you have really created a wonderful marriage together.

"That's very special, and it makes you feel so very close to each other. It's hard to explain, but we do have a very sexy relationship with each other. Perhaps not as often as before, but it sure can be full of fire and tenderness."

Extramarital Sex

Where there is marriage without love, there will be love without marriage.
—Benjamin Franklin (1733/1980, p. 347)

Extramarital friendships are common in American society. As one husband put it, "It doesn't make a whole lot of sense to deny friendships across-the-board to half the human race. If I enjoy talking with a person at work, it doesn't make sense to lose this friendship just because she's a female." Ideally, couples should allow each other the freedom to develop relationships outside the marriage. But if they are not properly handled, friendships with members of the other sex can harm a marriage. These friendships can sometimes develop into extramarital sexual relationships, which are commonly cited as one reason for divorce. Opinion is divided on whether men and women can be friends—loving, affectionate, accepting, and so on—without becoming sexually involved.

A national survey of sexual behavior in 1994 found that about 21% of men and 11% of women had an extramarital affair at least once in their life (National Opinion Research Center, 1994). The rate of infidelity ranged from about 7% to 37% for men and from 11% to almost 20% for women (Figure 7.5). Because the survey focused on the incidence of extramarital affairs across one's lifetime, it is natural that the frequency increased for both men and women with age. The only exception was for women ages 54 to 63, for whom the incidence of affairs was less than for the previous age group of women. This finding is probably due to the stronger religious and moral values held by this group of women.

Recall that the 1994 University of Chicago study, cited earlier, found that about 25% of the husbands and 15% of the wives had been unfaithful at least once. The results of any study of the incidence of extramarital sex are highly debatable. The likelihood of underreporting is great because, as family therapist Frank Pittman notes, "if people would lie to their own husbands or wives, they would lie to a poll taker" (Pittman, 1993a, 1993b, 1997; Pittman & Wagers, 1995).

Pittman, who has spent 30 years counseling people who have committed adultery, notes that affairs can be *very* different in terms of duration and intensity. According to Pittman affairs seem to fall into four broad categories: the most common, accidental infidelity (unintended and uncharacteristic acts of carelessness that really did "just happen"); romantic infidelity (falling in love, "the craziest and most

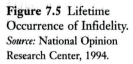

Figure 7.5 Lifetime Occurrence of Infidelity. *Source:* National Opinion Research Center, 1994.

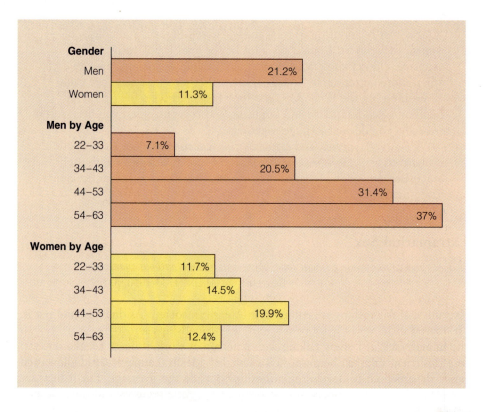

destructive form of infidelity"); marital arrangements (calling in marital "aides" to keep one company while failing to deal positively with a deficient marriage); and philandering (although there are female philanderers, this is a predominantly male activity, in which infidelity is a hobby; Pittman, 1993a, 1993b).

Pittman (1993a) identifies seven major myths about infidelity:

- *Everybody is unfaithful—it's a normal, expectable behavior.* Actually, we don't know how many people are unfaithful, but Pittman believes that most people are faithful most of the time.

- *Affairs are good for you; an affair can revive a dull marriage.* An affair can shake up a petrified marriage, and sometimes things work out, but in reality, an affair can "blow the hell out of a marriage."

- *People have affairs because they don't love their marriage partners.* Pittman observes that "it routinely turns out that the marriage was fine before the affair happened and the decision that they were not in love with their marriage partner was an effort to explain and justify the affair."

- *People have affairs because they are oversexed.* Pittman argues, to the contrary, that "most affairs consist of a little bad sex and hours on the telephone." Most affairs are really about secrets: secret telephone calls and furtive lunches. "Affairs generally involve sex, at least enough to create a secret that seals the conspiratorial alliance of the affair, and makes the relationship tense, dangerous, and thus exciting."

- *Affairs are ultimately the wife's fault.* In a patriarchal society, it is assumed that when a man is unfaithful, it is because of the wife's aesthetic, sexual, or emotional deficiencies. But Pittman argues that "there is no point in holding the cuckold responsible for the infidel's sexual behavior unless the cuckold has total control over the sexual equipment that has run off the road. . . . Only the driver is responsible."

- *It's best to pretend not to know.* Silence fuels an affair, which can survive only on secrecy. "Adulterous marriages begin their repair only when the secret is out in the open, and the infidel does not need to hide any longer."

- *After an affair, divorce is inevitable.* With therapy, "most adulterous marriages can be saved, and may even be stronger and more intimate than they were before the crisis."

Emily Brown, a social worker, offers a different perspective on affairs. She identifies six stages in the process of infidelity (Brown, 1991). The first stage occurs when a climate develops in which infidelity can germinate, such as a couple's allowing hurt, dissatisfaction, and differences to go unresolved. Betrayal occurs in the second stage. The more dissatisfied spouse "slides" into the infidelity. The unfaithful spouse denies it is happening, and the other spouse may collude by ignoring obvious signs. In stage three, the infidelity is revealed. At this stage both partners realize they will never be able to picture themselves or their marriage again in the same way. According to Brown, this stage requires a lot of time for partners to process; both need to experience the shock and fury of what happened, why it happened, what it means, and what the underlying issues might be. The impact can be as severe as the revelation of sexual abuse. The fourth stage involves admission of a crisis in the marriage. Brown believes that too often the infidelity itself is seen as the crisis rather than the problem she believes underlies the infidelity. In the fifth stage the partners make a decision either to address all of the issues involved or to bury them and get on with rebuilding the marriage. The sixth and final stage involves forgiveness. Brown believes this can take place only if the preceding five stages have been successfully addressed and resolved.

Family therapists counsel couples dealing with the crisis of infidelity and try to help them work through the situation in a cautious and rational manner. A professional therapist can be very helpful by encouraging spouses to be calm and honest in disclosing their motives. Infidelity can signal the end of a relationship, or it can be a catalyst for dramatic and positive growth in a marriage.

Toward Sexual Health

Sex is an important part of human life, health, and happiness. It's a crucial ingredient in individual well-being and in intimate relationships, especially marriage. Problems in sexual functioning therefore need to be addressed if people are to have successful relationships.

A survey of common sexual problems identified the most frequent problems for women and men (Laumann, Gagnon, Michael, & Michaels, 1994). About one third (33.4%) of women reported a lack of interest in sex, as compared to only

Sexual interactions can be a source of frustration, disappointment, and anger in a relationship, but they can also be a source of happiness and great joy. A satisfying sexual relationship is a crucial ingredient in a healthy intimate relationship.

15.8% of men (Figure 7.6). The second most frequent issue for nearly one quarter of the women surveyed was an inability to reach orgasm (24.1%) and to find sex pleasurable (21.2%). In contrast, roughly one quarter of the men reported that they reached climax too early (25.5%) or had anxiety about their sexual performance (17%). These symptoms are very similar to the common complaints heard from married couples in which the male feels the female is not interested in him sexually—often because he climaxes too early and does not satisfy her needs.

Sexual Problems and Dysfunctions

When is sex a problem in one's life? In the words of sexologists Mary Calderone and Eric Johnson:

> Sex and human sexuality are not—or should not be—problems unless we human beings make them so. When and how do they become problems? In general terms, when they are used or expressed in ways that are harmful to any person or persons; when people are unable to express them in ways that they find satisfying and creative; and when they become associated with such negative feelings as anger, jealousy, fear, and guilt. (Calderone & Johnson, 1989, pp. 154–155)

Among the most common sexual problems are, for men, the inability to achieve and/or maintain an erection and, for women, the inability to reach orgasm. Many sexual problems arise from beliefs and attitudes about sex that are narrow or incorrect. Calderone and Johnson (1989) summarized a variety of general problems,

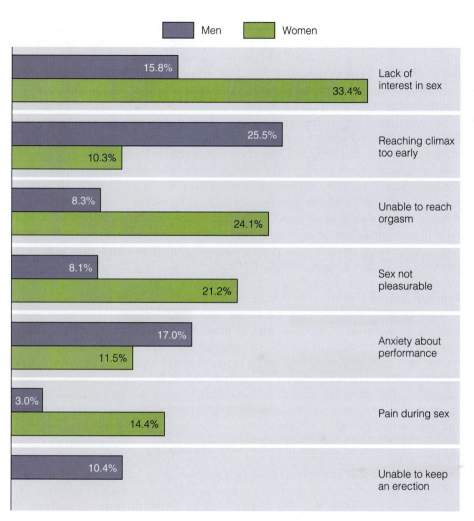

■ Men   ■ Women

	Men	Women
Lack of interest in sex	15.8%	33.4%
Reaching climax too early	25.5%	10.3%
Unable to reach orgasm	8.3%	24.1%
Sex not pleasurable	8.1%	21.2%
Anxiety about performance	17.0%	11.5%
Pain during sex	3.0%	14.4%
Unable to keep an erection	10.4%	

Figure 7.6 Frequency of Sexual Problems. *Source: The Social Organization of Sexuality: Sexual Practices in the United States* (pp. 370–371) by E. O. Laumann, J. H. Gagnon, R. T. Michael, and S. Michaels, 1994, Chicago: University of Chicago Press.

including the beliefs that sexuality is limited to the genitals, that sex equals intercourse, and that one's performance must be flawless. Unrealistic expectations about sex also played a role.

It is estimated that, at some time in their marriage, 50% of all married couples have sexual dysfunctions (Masters et al., 1995). Masters and his colleagues define **sexual dysfunction** as a state in which sexual behavior or the lack of it causes anxiety, anguish, and frustration, which can lead to unhappiness and distress in a couple's relationship.

What Causes Sexual Dysfunction?   There are two causative categories for sexual dysfunction, according to Masters and his colleagues (1995). **Organic sexual dysfunctions** are related to physiological factors; **psychosocial sexual dysfunctions** are related to psychological, developmental, interpersonal, environmental, or cultural factors. The researchers note that it may not be possible to identify the precise cause of a particular form of dysfunction and that some dysfunctions may have multiple causes. Organic factors cause 10% to 20% of all cases of sexual dysfunction and contribute to the dysfunction in another 15% of all cases, the researchers estimate. For example, a man may have difficulty achieving or maintaining an erection as a result of numerous medical conditions, including diabetes and alcoholism. Prescription medicines (e.g., drugs for high blood pressure) and street drugs (e.g., amphetamines, barbiturates, and narcotics) can also cause erection difficulties (Masters et al., 1995).

Psychological factors that can result in sexual dysfunction are numerous. Developmental factors include troubled parent-child relationships, negative family attitudes toward sex and sexuality, traumatic childhood or adolescent sexual experiences, and conflict over one's gender identity (one's sense of being male or female). Personal factors include a variety of fears: of poor sexual performance, of pregnancy, of venereal disease, of rejection, of pain, of becoming close to someone, of losing control, or even of success. Interpersonal factors that can be related to sexual problems include poor communication and frequent power struggles between partners; hostility, distrust, and deceit; lack of mutual physical attraction; and gender-role conflicts (Masters et al., 1995).

Types of Sexual Dysfunction   Male sexual dysfunction is expressed in a variety of ways. **Erectile dysfunction** (formerly called impotence) is the inability to achieve or maintain an erection that is firm enough for intercourse. (Isolated episodes of the inability to achieve or maintain an erection are nearly universal among men.) **Premature ejaculation,** or rapid ejaculation, is difficult to define precisely, although it is a common sexual dysfunction. It causes problems in a sexual relationship when the woman is dissatisfied because the man reaches orgasm much more quickly than she does. **Retarded ejaculation,** the opposite of premature ejaculation, describes a dysfunction in which prolonged and strenuous effort is needed to reach orgasm. **Ejaculatory incompetence** is a man's inability to ejaculate in his partner's vagina despite a firm erection and a high level of sexual arousal. **Painful intercourse,** often believed to be a problem only for women, can also affect men. Pain can be felt in the penis and/or testicles or internally; the pain is often related to a problem with the seminal vesicles or the prostate gland (Insel & Roth, 1998; Masters et al., 1995).

There are also various female sexual dysfunctions. **Vaginismus** is a condition in which the muscles of the outer third of the vagina respond with involuntary spasms to attempts at penetration, preventing intercourse. **Anorgasmia** is the inability to have an orgasm. **Rapid orgasm,** reaching orgasm too quickly, is the much-ignored female counterpart to male premature ejaculation. And painful intercourse, including burning, sharp or searing pain, or cramping, is also a common problem in women (Insel & Roth, 1998; Masters et al., 1995).

Sexual dysfunctions are generally something people are uncomfortable admitting to themselves and discussing with others. We can laugh and leer about sex, but our culture has a difficult time talking honestly and openly about it.

Sex Therapy

Many people with sexual difficulties go without help for a long time. This is unfortunate, because most **sex therapy** is simply a process of education. Sex therapists instruct clients (people who seek sex therapy are not called patients) in the gentle art of lovemaking.

Reputable professional sex therapists are trained in the subjects of sex and sexuality and have experience working with many different people regarding sexual needs and dysfunctions. A national organization, the American Association of Sex Educators, Counselors, and Therapists (AASECT), has established criteria for certifying sex therapists who have met its training standards. AASECT has also developed ethical principles for the practice of sex therapy. For a small fee, the AASECT will provide by mail a list of certified counselors and sex therapists.*

Sex educators typically work with relatively large groups of people and teach general information and principles that are useful to a variety of individuals. **Sex therapists** typically work with individuals, couples, or small groups of individuals and couples and focus more on individual concerns and problems. Based on content alone, a sex-therapy session can be difficult to discern from a sex-education session. The two approaches overlap considerably, so much so that some professionals do not distinguish between sex education and sex therapy.

Solving Sexual Problems   Sex therapy can involve a number of different components, including the following:

- Learning more about basic anatomy.

- Learning what one's true feelings are about the body.

- Learning what one's basic attitudes toward sex and sexuality are.

- Learning to relax with a partner and to get in a sexually responsive mood.

- Learning to sense one's own body and how the setting affects the body's responses.

- Learning sexual techniques.

- Exploring one's own and one's partner's body.

- Developing new sexual attitudes and techniques and maintaining them over time.

Sex therapists are quick to point out that couples with sexual problems should not rush into intercourse but should take time to enjoy each other's company and to touch each other in a variety of loving ways. The Masters and Johnson Institute, for example, allowed no intercourse at all in the first weeks of sex therapy. Instead, couples were taught that the art of touching is pleasurable in itself (Cohen, 1987).

Therapists assert that a sure way to decrease lovemaking pleasure is to set intercourse and orgasm as its goals. Sex therapists Susan Dean and Adele P. Kennedy advise:

> When you are goal-oriented you are no longer in the present. You interrupt your responses when you try to anticipate the next step. Stay focused on the moment so that you receive all that is being offered. Touch is, in and of itself, the pleasure.

---

* AASECT, P.O. Box 238, Mt. Vernon, IA 52314; (319) 895-8407; E-mail: AASECT@ worldnet.att.net

Any by-product is coincidental to the experience, although it is to be enjoyed and appreciated. The motivation is to sensitize your body to its intrinsic capacity. (cited in Cohen, 1987, p. 87)

The PLISSIT Model   One classic approach to sex therapy, developed by Jack Annon, is the **PLISSIT Model** (Annon, 1976). PLISSIT applies four levels of treatment, from the relatively simple to the more in-depth, in an ordered progression: permission (P), limited information (LI), specific suggestions (SS), and intensive therapy (IT). At the first and simplest level, clients receive *permission* from an authority or another respected individual to engage in certain sexual behaviors. For example, many people in our society view sex negatively; they may need reassurance that a particular behavior is relatively harmless—for example, "Yes, masturbation is normal."

The second level is *limited information*, during which a client gathers information or feedback on a given sexual problem. For example, a young man might be depressed and feel inadequate because he believes his penis is too small; this, in turn, may affect his sexual behavior. Through discussion with a friend, attendance at a course on human sexuality, or reading, the young man might learn that comparisons of penis size should not be made when the organ is in the flaccid state (that seen in the locker room) because erect penises differ less in size than do flaccid ones. He might also learn that there is no correlation between penis size and a woman's sexual satisfaction. With this information, the young man will likely feel better about himself and may become more sexually responsive. Without this information, his fears and feelings of inadequacy may develop into more serious sexual problems.

The third level, *specific suggestions*, involves behavioral exercises or suggestions for reducing stress. If the first two levels of treatment do not resolve a sexual problem, this third level, focusing on brief therapy with the help of a counselor, may be necessary. Developing a history of the client's sexual problem may be the initial step at this level.

The fourth level in the PLISSIT Model is *intensive therapy* with a trained and certified sex therapist or counselor. Only about 10% of clients with a sexual dysfunction need this level of help. The sexual problem a person is dealing with today may have roots in the person's past, and the distress resulting from the past needs to be resolved before progress can be made in the present. Specific suggestions regarding sexual technique may not get at the heart of the problem but rather simply treat the symptom.

Other Approaches and Techniques   Two of the most common self-help techniques for overcoming sexual problems are body exploration and masturbation. Clinicians have found that masturbation exercises are helpful for treating orgasmic dysfunction in women and lack of ejaculatory control in men. Once a woman learns how to reach orgasm through self-stimulation, she can teach her partner the best ways to bring her to orgasm through intercourse. Self-help techniques that help men slow down during masturbation often help them delay ejaculation while making love with a partner (Kelly, 1998).

Behavioral exercises may also be prescribed to help couples enrich and expand their sexual awareness and enjoyment. These exercises include sensate focus, the stop-and-go technique, and the squeeze technique.

- *Sensate focus.* This technique teaches couples what gives each partner pleasure without expecting anything in return. The goal is not sexual arousal or intercourse but education. Each partner directs the other, showing her or him what kinds of touches are the most enjoyable and where the sensitive places are. The exercise helps people learn to communicate better sexually.

- *The stop-and-go technique.* This technique teaches men how to control ejaculation and orgasm. The man's partner manually or orally stimulates his penis until he is just about to ejaculate. Then, the partner stops the stimulation, resuming it only when the man is in control. Stimulation and rest may be alternated several times in a session before orgasm and ejaculation are triggered. Repeated sessions over weeks or months help men control rapid or premature ejaculation.

- *The squeeze technique.* In this variation on the stop-and-go technique, when the partner stops stimulating the man's penis, the partner immediately applies pressure to the penis, squeezing it with the thumb and two fingers until there is a tolerable degree of pain. This pattern is repeated seven or eight times until the man learns to tolerate intense stimulation while delaying ejaculation. The squeeze technique further shortens the time it takes to resolve the problem of premature ejaculation (Hyde & DeLamater, 1997; Masters et al., 1995).

Does Sex Therapy Work?   Masters and Johnson treated more than 2,300 clients at their St. Louis clinic between 1959 and 1985. The researchers have written that 84.4% of men and 77.8% of women reported long-term cures to problems ranging from impotence and premature ejaculation to anorgasmia (Alpern, 1988).

At the Masters and Johnson Institute, whether the problem lies with the man or the woman, both partners are treated together for two weeks. Couples are tested for underlying physical conditions and are seen repeatedly by a male-female therapist team to discuss emotional problems. They are then sent back to their hotel room with suggestions on how to develop comfort and intimacy with each other. Fees run up to $10,000, based on the ability to pay. (Cost of treatment is often covered by medical insurance.) The therapists at the institute treat not only sexual dysfunction but also cases of sexual compulsion, abuse, and incest (Alpern, 1988). The approach developed by Masters and Johnson has been expanded, modified, and used by sex therapists throughout the country.

In a review of a wide variety of sex-therapy approaches, Joseph LoPiccolo and Wendy E. Stock (1986) pointed out that many people are helped by sex therapy even if they do not become fully functional sexually. At minimum, the therapy improves people's ability to understand their problems and to communicate with their partners about their needs and feelings.

Summary

- According to a national survey, happily married couples reported that they were satisfied with the affection they receive from their partner, did not have concerns about their partner's interest in sex, were not concerned that their partner was interested in having an affair, felt their partner did not use sex unfairly, and had a more satisfying and fulfilling sexual relationship as compared to unhappily married couples.

- The most commonly reported issues for married couples in terms of their sexual relationship were differing levels of interest in sex between husband and wife, dissatisfaction with the amount of affection received from one's partner, sexual disinterest between partners, difficulty talking about sexual issues, and an inability to keep the sexual relationship interesting and enjoyable.

- A scientific approach to the subject of sexuality began in earnest during the Victorian era in the late 19th and early 20th centuries. This work included the theories of Sigmund Freud, who proposed five psychosexual stages of development.

- Attitudes toward sexuality, including sexual attractiveness and sexual behaviors, vary markedly from one culture to another.

- Sex surveys—such as the University of Chicago study, the *Janus Report*, and the *American Couples* study—reveal useful information about the sexual behaviors of Americans.

- Sex-education programs encouraging abstinence but also offering an alternative for those who are already or choose to become sexually active are among the most effective.

- Few children in the United States receive direct instruction from their parents on sexuality, sexual intercourse, or birth control. However, studies have shown that parental communication may forestall or postpone a child's sexual activity.

- Although sexual activity often decreases after marriage, this decline is not inevitable. Key elements in keeping the sexual relationship vital include communication, commitment, and investing time to enjoy each other.

- According to the 1994 University of Chicago study, about 25% of husbands and 15% of wives reported having had an extramarital sexual affair. Infidelity can signal the end of a marriage, but it can also be a catalyst for dramatic and positive growth in the relationship.

- Types of male sexual dysfunction include erectile dysfunction, premature ejaculation, retarded ejaculation, ejaculatory incompetence, and painful intercourse. Female sexual dysfunctions include vaginismus, anorgasmia, rapid orgasm, and painful intercourse.

- Sex therapy involves a number of different components, including learning more about basic anatomy, learning what one's true feelings are about the body, and discovering one's basic attitudes toward sex and sexuality.

Key Terms

sexuality	sexual orientation	homophobia
heterosexual	sex	DINS dilemma
homosexual	gender	sexual dysfunction
bisexual	incest taboo	organic sexual dysfunction
transgender	masturbation	

psychsocial sexual dysfunction	ejaculatory incompetence	rapid orgasm
erectile dysfunction	painful intercourse	sex therapy
premature ejaculation	vaginismus	sex educator
retarded ejaculation	anorgasmia	sex therapist
		PLISSIT Model

Activities

1. Is sex truly everywhere in our society? For a day, keep a log, noting what, when, and where you see or hear something with a sexual theme. Several people in the class can work together and report their findings to the larger group.

2. In small groups, discuss the following situation: You are the parent of a 15-year-old son. He is interested in your views on nonmarital sex. What would you tell him?

3. What are your personal beliefs about nonmarital sexual behavior? Write a brief essay articulating and supporting your views.

4. Compare and contrast the results of Activities 2 and 3. How did your "advice" for the adolescent differ from your personal views? In what ways were the two messages the same?

Suggested Readings

Berzon, B. (1990). *Permanent partners: Building gay and lesbian relationships that last.* New York: Plume/Penguin. Suggestions by a psychotherapist specializing in same-sex relationships for resolving conflicts over power and control, jealousy, differences in sexual desire, money, and family demands.

Boston Women's Health Book Collective. (1998). *Our bodies, ourselves for the new century: A book by and for women.* New York: Touchstone/Simon & Schuster. The latest edition of a classic that has helped countless women understand their physical and emotional health for a quarter century.

Clark, D. (1997). *Loving someone gay* (3rd ed.). San Francisco: Celestial Arts. A positive manual written by a credentialed gay professional for gay men and lesbians and those who love them.

Gullotta, T. P., Adams, G. R., & Montemayor, R. (Eds.). (1993). *Adolescent sexuality.* Newbury Park, CA: Sage. Examines historical and theoretical perspectives; anatomy, physiology, and gender issues; heterosexual behavior; lesbian, gay-male, and bisexual youths; teenage pregnancy and parenting; aberrant (incestuous or involuntary) sexual experiences; sexually transmissible diseases; and sexual responsibility.

Laumann, E. O., Gagnon, J. H., Michael, R. T., & Michaels, S. (1995). *The social organization of sexuality: Sexual practices in the United States.* Chicago: University of Chicago Press. Perhaps the most extensive study of sexual behavior ever conducted in this country. A thinner companion volume for lay readers, *Sex in America: A definitive survey* (Boston: Little, Brown, 1995), was written with journalist Gina Kolata.

Masters, W. H., Johnson, V. E., & Kolodny, R. C. (1995). *Human sexuality* (5th ed.). New York: HarperCollins. An outstanding encyclopedic text covering an enormous number of topics in the area of human sexuality; an invaluable reference.

Mathes, P. G., & Irby, B. J. (1993). *Teen pregnancy and parenting handbook.* Champaign, IL: Research Press. A practical handbook with a matter-of-fact tone, appropriate for its target audience, teenage girls.

Miller, B. C., & Moore, K. A. (1990). Adolescent sexual behavior, pregnancy, and parenting: Research through the 1980s. *Journal of Marriage and the Family, 52* (November), 1025–1044. A very useful review that distills the extensive research in this area.

Ortiz, E. T. (1989). *Your complete guide to sexual health.* Englewood Cliffs, NJ: Prentice Hall. A readable, practical guide.

Pittman, F. (1993). *Private lies: Infidelity and the betrayal of intimacy.* New York: Norton. The reflections of a therapist following 30 years of helping people "clean up the mess" created by their affairs.

Rosenheim, M. K., & Testa, M. F. (Eds.). (1992). *Early parenthood and coming of age in the 1990s.* New Brunswick, NJ: Rutgers University Press. A volume of interdisciplinary essays for families, educators, public health practitioners, and policy makers.

Wincze, J. P., & Carey, M. P. (1991). *Sexual dysfunction: A guide for assessment and treatment.* Treatment Manuals for Practitioners Series. New York: Guilford Press. An excellent overview of sex therapy today.

PART III

Dynamics of Intimate Relationships

CHAPTER 8

Gender Roles and Power in the Family

All animals are equal, but some animals are more equal than others.
—GEORGE ORWELL (1951)

Contemporary models of intimacy stress gender equality in marriage and other types of partnerships. Equalitarianism is the trend among many couples making a serious commitment to each other. But if women continue to make less money for the work they do outside the home and if men continue to avoid child care and household labor, the fabric of intimate relationships is threatened. The fragile bonds of intimacy can easily be damaged when one spouse is subordinate to the other, has more power than the other, or receives less respect and dignity in society.

Despite the influence of feminism for more than three decades in this country, gender-based segregation of labor is alive and well in many families. This is especially true in the home, where men continue for the most part to do "men's work" and women to do "women's work." The problem with this arrangement is that the traditional roles also involve a disparity in power. Men's work receives more respect and better pay in our society than women's work; thus men tend to hold the upper hand in both the workplace and the home. Why this persists is the subject of ongoing debate. It is clear, however, that rigidly categorizing people and dictating their behavior in traditional masculine and feminine terms stifle individual creativity and diminish the potential for achievement in both the world of work and the world of intimacy.

In this chapter we will look at gender roles and their origin and discuss how many of the behavioral differences between men and women stem not from biology but from culture. We will also examine four major theories about gender-role development. Finally, we will explore power in families, and, in particular, how couples establish and maintain a balance of power in their relationships.

To begin, let's revisit the national survey of married couples (Olson et al., 1999) described earlier in Chapter 7. In the following section we will look at the portion of the survey that focused on couple strengths and issues in terms of role relationships.

Couple Strengths and Issues in Gender Roles

The nationwide survey that focused on the strengths of married couples revealed that happy couples agreed more often (51%) than unhappy couples (30%) that the husband's occupation should not be regarded as more important than the wife's occupation (Olson et al., 1999; Table 8.1). More happy couples (66%) than unhappy couples (54%) believed the woman should be able to work outside the home, even if it was not financially necessary. Happy couples agreed more often (60%) than unhappy couples (49%) that women's roles should not be restricted. Happy couples also agreed more often (35%) than unhappy couples (24%) that women should be allowed to work outside the home even if there are young children in the family. Finally, this survey found more sharing of housework among happy couples (57%) than among unhappy couples (49%).

Based on the national sample of 26,442 married couples, the major role relationship issue that couples faced (58%) was the notion that a wife should accept the husband's judgments on important issues (Table 8.2). Half of the couples (51%)

Table 8.1 Role-Relationship Strengths of Happy Versus Unhappy Married Couples

STRENGTH	PERCENTAGE OF COUPLES IN AGREEMENT	
	Happy Couples (*n* = 7,116)	Unhappy Couples (*n* = 13,421)
Place equal value on the husband's and the wife's occupations.	51	30
Feel a wife should be able to work outside the home, even if the income is not needed.	66	54
Place no restrictions on the wife's roles and opportunities.	60	49
Feel a wife and mother of young children should be able to work outside the home.	35	24
Share more of the housework, especially if the wife works outside the home.	57	49

Source: Adapted from Olson, Fye, & Olson (1999).

disagreed about whether a wife and mother of young children should work outside the home and about whether a husband's occupation should be regarded as more important than the wife's. Thirty-three percent of married couples had issues with the wife's being primarily responsible for doing the housework, even if she worked outside the home. And about one third (32%) of married couples had issues surrounding the notion that a woman's place is in the home.

Gender Roles

The different ways in which men and women behave are linked to, but not necessarily determined by, their biological sex. Individuals are identified as male or female on the basis of physical structures, which are determined by chromosomes, gonads, and hormones. This labeling occurs at birth and is the first step in the process of developing **gender identity**—a sense of being male or female and what that means in one's society (Cook, 1995, 1997).

Although nature determines an individual's sex, culture determines the attitudes and behaviors appropriate for an individual on the basis of her or his sex. In each culture, individuals learn to adapt to these expectations as they shape their personal and professional lives. **Gender roles** are expectations about people's attitudes and behaviors in life based on whether they are male or female. When a child is born, **gender-role stereotypes** come into play. People comment, for example, that he is "a strong, healthy boy" or she is "a darling, adorable girl."

Labeling affects a child's psychological development in a variety of ways. The child begins to adopt personality traits, attitudes, preferences, and behaviors considered appropriate to his or her sex, and these affect how he or she walks, talks, eats, exercises, thinks, and later makes love. The gender-role patterns assigned to males and females influence all our roles in life.

Masculinity is the gender-linked constellation of traits that have been traditionally associated with men; **femininity,** the traits associated with women. In our

Table 8.2 Top Five Role Relationship Issues for Married Couples

Issue	Percentage of Couples With Problems Surrounding Issue (N = 26,442)
The notion that the wife should accept the husband's judgment.	58
Disagreements regarding a wife and mother of young children working outside the home.	51
Greater value placed on the husband's occupation than on the wife's.	57
Responsibility for housework resting primarily on the wife.	33
Restrictions on the wife's roles and opportunities.	32

Source: Adapted from Olson, Fye, & Olson (1999).

society, the qualities stereotypically associated with masculinity include aggressiveness, independence, dominance, competence, and a predisposition for math and science. Qualities stereotypically associated with femininity include passivity, dependency, sensitivity, emotionality, and a predisposition for art and literature. These stereotypes are destructive because they imply that all males, and only males, have the so-called masculine qualities and that all females, and only females, possess the so-called feminine qualities. Obviously, any human being can have any of these qualities. Socially imposed gender-role stereotypes create inequality by prescribing—based on whether a person is male or female—certain qualities, behaviors, and opportunities and prohibiting or discouraging others.

Language is one of the most powerful tools people use both deliberately and inadvertently to establish and maintain rigid gender roles. The subtle ways we talk about people of the other sex reinforce stereotypes and segregate people by sex. We talk about men and women as being members of the "opposite" sex, reinforcing the notion that men and women are opposites and accentuating the differences rather than affirming the similarities. We thereby continue a hierarchical tradition in our culture that often places men on top and women on the bottom. It is more appropriate to talk in terms of the "other" sex, rather than the "opposite" sex. Box 8.1 illustrates how gender-biased language reinforces the misguided notion that men are more competent and rational than women.

An International Survey of Male and Female Traits

In an international survey of 22 countries, the Gallup Poll (1996), found conventional stereotypes of women and men. Women were perceived as more affectionate, emotional, talkative, and patient than men. In the United States, 76% of those surveyed considered women to be the more affectionate sex; only 6% named men the more affectionate. When asked which sex is the more emotional, 88% said women and only 4% said men. Men were perceived across cultures as being more aggressive, ambitious, and courageous than women. In most cultures, women and men were perceived to be equally intelligent.

BOX 8 . 1

Gender-Biased Language

He	She	He	She
discussed	chattered	has character lines	has wrinkles
reminded	nagged	is assertive	is pushy
networked	gossiped	was tired	was depressed
complained	bitched	was upset	was emotional
is forgetful	is an airhead	dressed nicely	dressed "to kill"
is confident	is conceited	was friendly	was flirting
is careful	is picky	was upset	was moody
is articulate	is talkative		

Source: Based in part on *Sex Differences in Human Communication* (p. 131) by Barbara Westbrook Eakins and R. Gene Eakins. Copyright © 1978 by Harper & Row, Publishers, Inc. Reprinted by permission of Addison Wesley Educational Publishers, Inc.

Although none of the 10 traits surveyed were seen solely as male or female, the trait considered predominantly male was aggressiveness. The country with the highest margin was China, where 81% identified aggression as most characteristic of men and only 3% as most characteristic of women, a difference of 78 points. The differences favoring men were 58 points for the United States and 60 points for Canada and Britain. Both men and women across most of the 22 countries surveyed tended to agree with the opinions reported here.

Traditional Versus Contemporary Views of Gender Roles

In the traditional view of gender roles in our society, males are assumed to be superior to females and to have characteristics that are more desirable. The contemporary view holds that neither males nor females are superior; both have desirable—and undesirable—traits not based specifically on sex.

A Traditional View   The traditional view of gender roles in our society grew out of our male-oriented culture, but specific theories have been put forth in its support. One of the best known is that of sociologist Talcott Parsons (1955, 1965), whose theory of the family assumed that highly contrasting gender roles were essential for families and society. For nearly two decades, Parson's theory dominated sociology. This theory was in part developed as a response to earlier observers who had argued that in urban industrial societies the family had lost its functions and was on the decline. Parsons countered that "the modern family" was an organized and functional unit that, instead of losing its value, was more important than ever.

Parsons believed that, in this modern family, society required that men be "instrumental" and women be "expressive." The man's instrumental role was to be

A person's sex is biologically determined, but the abilities, behaviors, activities, social roles, and other characteristics that are considered appropriate for males and females are determined by one's culture.

the breadwinner, the manager, and the leader of the family. The woman's expressive role was to take care of the emotional well-being of the family through nurturing and comforting (Parsons, 1955, 1965). Parsons saw these two roles as separate, one to be performed by the husband and the other by the wife.

Parsons's theory, which has been attacked by numerous critics, is no longer a predominant family theory. His critics charged that it was a mistake to assume that the traditional family structure was both a universal and necessary social institution—that only this traditional family structure could fulfill the needs of the individuals within the family and of the greater society. They further argued that Parsons's theory focused on the positive aspects of this traditional family structure but deemphasized potential problems; that is, it emphasized stability rather than change, focused on harmony rather than conflict, and identified function but ignored dysfunction. Parsons's theory also tended to stereotype masculine and feminine traits, reinforcing differences and denigrating women.

A More Contemporary View   Today, it is more commonly assumed that both sexes are capable and can be successful in a variety of roles at home and at work. Women can be independent, strong, logical, and task oriented; men can be nurturing, sensitive, cooperative, and detail oriented. However, men and women can benefit by learning from each other: Men can learn the value of being more sensitive and caring from women; women can learn the value of independence from men; and both can learn to work together and become interdependent.

Women may be at an advantage in this more cooperative approach to living. Traditional culture has encouraged them to be good listeners, to be empathic, understanding, helpful, and supportive. These caring values fit well with the more cooperative approaches to group decision making that are gaining strength at home and at work.

Androgyny Life confronts us daily with situations in which both resiliency in the face of difficulty and sensitivity to other human beings are valuable traits. **Androgyny** refers to a blending of traditional masculinity and traditional femininity in the same individual. "Androgyny is a newly discovered old concept," according to Ellen Piel Cook (1985, p. 18). One definition of androgyny explains it this way:

> A condition under which the characteristics of the sexes—and the human impulses expressed by men and women—are not rigidly assigned. . . . [An androgyne is] a creature for whom . . . anatomy is not destiny; for whom the capacities to respond and make and be are irrelevant of gender. (Rosenstein, 1973, p. 38)

The concept of androgyny bridges the gap between masculinity and femininity, suggesting that individuals are free to create a personality based on their own personal needs and beliefs. Psychologist Carl Jung argued that both masculinity and femininity are inherent in everyone and emphasized the need for people to recognize and integrate both capacities. Jung believed the integration of masculinity and femininity was essential to the development of personal wholeness (L. Olds, 1981). Sandra Bem (1993, 1995) pioneered the development of a method for measuring psychological androgyny. Studies have found that people who have a good balance of both masculine and feminine characteristics are more loving than those who are stereotypically "macho" or feminine (Stark, 1985).

Dina Safilios-Rothschild (1976) speculated that gender-typed men and women tend to see members of the other sex as people to be manipulated rather than as partners in a give-and-take relationship. To maintain control, macho men learn not to express their feelings or to let themselves become dependent on others. Highly feminine women, on the other hand, often believe that the only way to relate successfully with men is to flirt, tease, and use other so-called feminine wiles to gain power. A successful love relationship requires a combination of traditional masculine and traditional feminine characteristics in each partner.

The androgynous model of the mentally healthy person is not mostly masculine in nature, as earlier models have been. Rather, this model is based on a workable mix of masculinity and femininity. Women's ways of knowing and living are treated with the same respect and dignity as men's ways of operating.

Soon after the term *androgyny* resurfaced in the early 1970s, discussions began on how to create a society without gender-role differentiation. An androgynous parent, for example, would be one who could be both expressive-affectional when the situation demanded it and instrumental-adaptive at other times (DeFrain, 1975, 1979).

The idea of androgyny came as a breath of fresh air to many people in the early 1970s, because many women felt overworked and underappreciated in the home and longed for contact with other adults and recognition in the working world. Countless women pointed out how demanding motherhood can be, involving round-the-clock, 7-day-a-week, year-in year-out responsibility. Many feminists called for men to become more active in childrearing. Influenced by these voices, a number of men responded with criticisms of conventional American fatherhood. They argued that fathers suffer from the inattention and emotional sterility of a life consumed by "careerism" at the expense of family and described the dreariness of the working world for fathers. "The guy who wins the rat race is still a rat," William Sloan Coffin pointed out (DeFrain, 1974).

Gender-role stereotypes limit people's choices by dictating what they are believed to be able to do. Despite the prevalent stereotypes in our society, this man demonstrates that males can be sensitive, nurturing, patient, and capable of caring for children.

Beyond Androgyny In 1993 Bem published another book on gender roles and relationships, *The Lenses of Gender: Transforming the Debate on Sexual Inequality.* Although she was instrumental in advancing the discussion of psychological androgyny in the 1970s and early 1980s, Bem argues in this book that the concepts of masculinity and femininity ought to be dropped altogether. The focus on androgyny, she claims, has merely heightened the focus on so-called masculine and feminine traits. This focus reinforces **gender polarization,** "the organizing of social life around male-female distinctions" (p. 192) and the linking of all aspects of human experience to sex and gender. The premise underlying gender polarization is not simply that men and women are different, she points out, but that men are superior to women.

Bem envisions a society in which gender polarization has been completely dismantled except for the purpose of reproduction. This vision is unrealistic, she acknowledges, because it challenges both the traditional belief that men are inherently dominant and the contemporary feminist focus on a woman-centered view of experience (Bem, 1993, 1995).

B O X   8 . 2

Contemporary Versus Traditional Dating and Marriage Patterns

Contemporary	Traditional
Both women and men initiate dates.	The man initiates dates.
The woman keeps her maiden name after marriage.	The woman takes the man's last name.
The partners cohabit before marriage.	The partners live apart before marriage.
Premarital sex is expected.	Premarital sex is not an option.
Both partners continue their education.	The wife supports the husband through school.
The birth of a child might precede marriage.	Children are conceived after marriage.
Both partners work, and both may have careers.	The husband's work is the priority.
Roles are flexible.	Roles are rigid.
Both partners share child care.	The mother is responsible for child care.
Both partners initiate sex.	The husband initiates sex.
Both partners select the couple's friends.	The husband's friends become the couple's friends.

The Move Toward More Equalitarian Roles   American society in many ways is moving away from male dominance and toward **equalitarian roles** (also called *egalitarian roles*)—social equality between the sexes. The process of change has been long, and fraught with controversy. The struggle occurs not only in society but is also played out each day in close relationships. Box 8.2 highlights some differences between traditional dating and marriage patterns and more contemporary practices. Looking back through the generations of one's own family illustrates how dramatically times have changed.

One of the most telling indexes of change is the decline of the double standard, the social convention allowing men more sexual and social freedom than women. Women are claiming more freedom for themselves, although some don't realize or acknowledge they are doing so. A number of social scientists have commented that today many women shy away from calling themselves nontraditional or feminist but are clearly living very different lives than their mothers or grandmothers. What is apparently happening is that as women's roles change, the definition of *traditional* also changes.

Household Tasks Left for Women   Despite many changes in gender roles, old patterns persist (Pittman & Blanchard, 1996; Pyke & Coltrane, 1996; Sanchez & Kane, 1996; Thorn & Gilbert, 1998). American couples still tend to exhibit gender-role family work patterns. In the home, men tend to do "men's work," and women tend to do "women's work." One research team found that for families to achieve gender equality in the division of labor, "American males would have to reallocate 60 percent of their family work time to other tasks" (Blair & Lichter,

Relationships tend to be more equalitarian today than in the past. This young woman has many more options and opportunities than her mother or grandmother did, both in her relationships and in other life choices.

1991, p. 91). In a similar vein, other researchers have found that women carry a larger share of the responsibility for the children than do men.

In his book *Chore Wars*, James Thornton (1997) clearly identifies the struggles couples have with household tasks. In surveying 555 married people, Thornton found that household tasks are a major source of conflict, usually because women do most of the work. In his survey, two thirds of the women reported doing most to all of the housework as compared to only 13% of the men surveyed. Conversely, almost half (45%) of the men said they did about a quarter or less housework, whereas only 9% of the women reported doing that little housework.

Women not only do most of the housework, but men are significantly less involved in the overall aspects of housework. As shown in Table 8.3, about 80% to 90% of the women reported having taken care of in the previous week such typical household chores as cleaning the toilet and cleaning the refrigerator. Only about 50% to 60% of the men reported having done these same tasks.

What is more telling about the distribution of household tasks are the findings related to the survey item labeled "Husband Never Does." There are considerable differences between women's and men's responses to this question. For example, 17% of the men reported they had never cleaned the toilet, yet 59% of the women reported their husband never completed this task. It is difficult to know if the men are overreporting how often they perform tasks or the women are underreporting the husband's contribution. Probably both of their reports are biased.

There are at least two common gender differences related to housework. First, women often have a higher standard for housework than men. Men often feel that women have such high standards that they cannot complete the task in the "right way." For example, John might try to clean the bathroom, but Mary feels he does such a poor job that she needs to repeat the task. She feels that asking him to do it is a waste of time because he doesn't do it well.

Table 8.3 Gender Differences in Household Tasks

HOUSEHOLD TASK	COMPLETED IN THE LAST WEEK		HUSBAND NEVER DOES	
	Women	Men	Women	Men
Cleaned toilet	89%	46%	59%	17%
Vacuumed house	84	60	27	7
Changed sheets	93	57	53	15
Cleaned refrigerator	86	54	68	24

Source: Thornton (1997).

Second, women often feel household tasks are their responsibility, and men consequently assume the less-demanding role of "helping out." This often means that the man has to be told what to do. Thus, the male often assumes the passive role and fails to feel responsible for doing most jobs around the house.

These two gender differences set the stage for many ongoing conflicts regarding household tasks. Men are, however, becoming more aware of their need to do household tasks and are more willing to be "trained" to complete certain jobs according to an acceptable standard. Nonetheless, housework continues to be an area in which participation and responsibility vary greatly between husband and wife, even when the wife works full-time outside the home.

An Anthropological Perspective

Perhaps the classic description of how gender roles are rooted in culture comes from anthropologist Margaret Mead. In *Sex and Temperament in Three Primitive Societies*, Mead (1935) looked at "maleness" and "femaleness" in three New Guinea tribes: the Arapesh, the Mundugumor, and the Tchambuli. In American society, two traditional attributes of females are gentleness and unaggressiveness. Among the Arapesh, Mead found both the women *and* the men to be unaggressive. Not far away, among the Mundugumor tribe, Mead found that both males and females displayed an aggressiveness that Americans would characterize as traditionally masculine. In both the Arapesh and the Mundugumor tribes, Mead found little contrast in temperament between the sexes.

The third New Guinea tribe Mead studied provided further evidence of cross-cultural differences. Among the Tchambuli, both men and women behaved in ways that are opposite to traditional behavior in Western societies. Tchambuli women were independent and aggressive, acting like traditional Western men; Tchambuli men were gentle and sensitive, like traditional Western women. Mead's conclusion was that the varieties in temperament she observed among these three "primitive" societies were not dictated by biology but were largely the creations of the societies.

Mead's conclusion has been vigorously debated since it was published. Psychologist David Buss believes, for example, that innate biological differences between males and females have more to do with the differences in their social behavior than does the culture in which they live. He devised a questionnaire asking people to describe their ideal mate in five categories: earning capacity, industriousness, youth, physical attractiveness, and chastity. Buss then administered the

SALLY FORTH   BY GREG HOWARD

Copyright 1991 by Greg Howard. Reprinted with special permission of King Features Syndicate.

questionnaire to 37 groups of men and women in 33 different societies around the world. Even though they came from different geographic and cultural areas, the people Buss surveyed consistently expressed the same patterns of preference. Females placed greater value on wealth and ambition, and males were more interested in signs of youth and fertility. Finding a mate who was a "good financial prospect" was more important to females in 36 of 37 groups. "Good looks" were more important to males than females in all 37 groups (cited in Cowley, 1989, p. 56).

Evolutionary theory, focusing on the notion that gender traits are to some degree transmitted through the genes, predicts that different cultures will have certain gender-role similarities due to the similar biological makeup shared by all males and that shared by all females. According to anthropologist John Tooby and psychologist Leda Cosmides, "The assertion that culture explains human variation will be taken seriously when there are reports of women war parties raiding villages to capture men as husbands" (cited in Cowley, 1989, p. 57).

Cross-cultural studies have found that women have been the primary caretakers of children in almost all known societies, whereas men have been much more likely to assume leadership roles in the economic and political arenas (Cowley, 1989). This division of labor by sex has almost always meant that women have found themselves in positions subordinate to men. Why do women provide most of the child care from culture to culture? Biology is frequently cited: Women give birth to children, breast-feed them, and then continue in the role of a nurturing parent.

American society shows a clear trend toward establishing more equalitarian roles. However, the debate over nature, nurture, and gender differences has not been resolved and probably never will be. If men take more responsibility for child care and housework, women will have more opportunity for access to the economic and political world, likely resulting in a more even distribution of power in our society.

An International Perspective

In its comprehensive survey of gender roles and the family, the Gallup Poll (1996) surveyed men and women in 22 countries with a combined population of 3.05 bil-

BOX 8.3

Gender Roles in Japan

To understand the complex topic of power and gender roles in families in Japan, it is necessary to understand both the social system and the family system. The following overview, which applies to middle- and upper-class urban Japanese families, is provided by Shuji Asai (1996), a Japanese family therapist.

At the societal system level, Japanese culture is patriarchal. The male dominates; he plays the instrumental role in society and tends to be married to his work. Although women make up about 40% of the labor force in Japan, they face discrimination in terms of wages, assignments, and promotions.

Although Japanese society is patriarchal, the Japanese family is more of a matriarchal system, with the mother dominating. This is particularly true of child-rearing and finances. Although the husband brings home the money, the wife controls it, often deciding how much spending money the husband receives each month. The woman's financial power also entails making decisions about when and where to invest and how much to pay for a house or remodeling.

In most Japanese families, family cohesion and family communication are also controlled by the mother. Japanese mothers often develop a very strong emotional connection with their children and serve as the communication link between the children and the father; the father may remain disengaged from the family. As a result, the mother dominates the family system, and the father emphasizes his role at work.

Today, more Japanese women are seeking professional careers, and more are delaying marriage and even remaining single. These changes are moving Japan toward a more equalitarian society and are demanding that men and women renegotiate their traditional gender roles at work and at home.

lion, or 53% of the world's population. The survey included countries in North America, South America, Europe, and Asia. The sampling error in the results is within 3 percentage points (plus or minus).

Residents of nearly two thirds of the countries polled felt that their society was biased toward men. In 15 countries, either a majority or a plurality of those surveyed said that society favors men over women. Countries in greatest agreement that society favors men are Japan (78%), Germany (76%), Iceland (76%), France (76%), the United States (73%), and Britain (72%). In 7 countries, including El Salvador (63%), China (53%), and Thailand (52%), the consensus leaned more toward the belief that men and women are treated equally.

The survey showed some potential for change, however, because in 5 countries, about half those surveyed resented the gender-role expectations their society placed on them (Gallup Poll, 1996). Those countries are Germany (52%), Japan (52%), Thailand (52%), Chile (46%), and Panama (46%). In those 5 countries, at least half the women and more than 40% of the men expressed resentment. (See Box 8.3, which focuses on Japan's traditional yet evolving gender roles.)

The Gallup survey (1996) also demonstrated lessening support for the traditional family structure, in which the father is the breadwinner and the mother is the homemaker. In only 6 of the 22 countries did a majority or near majority of the population support the traditional roles: Hungary (66%), Chile (49%), the United States (48%), France (46%), and Japan (46%). Least supportive of the traditional family roles were Thailand (25%), Taiwan (26%), Spain (27%), India (28%), Germany (28%), and Lithuania (28%). These 6 countries were more supportive of the idea that both parents should work outside the home.

Multicultural Perspectives on Gender Roles in the United States

It is commonly believed that gender roles do not spring from innate characteristics individuals possess; rather, they are learned behaviors, rooted in the social context of the particular culture in which people live. The gender roles women and men play vary widely from culture to culture. This section examines some examples of cultural gender-role differences in the United States.

Mexican American Culture

Mexican American males are often stereotyped as being *macho*. Male exhibitions of aggressiveness—*machismo*—include bossing women around, being abusive to them, and having numerous extramarital affairs. But this macho attitude is not supported in the research literature (Vega, 1991, 1995). Even though some Mexican American males act macho, this is not the predominant pattern for this group. Researchers have found that warm, nurturing, and equalitarian male behavior is more likely in marriages in which the wife is employed, although it is also demonstrated in many, more traditional marriages.

There are different interpretations of why some Mexican American males display machismo. One viewpoint holds that machismo is an unconscious attempt to overcompensate for feelings of inferiority, powerlessness, and inadequacy. This inferiority springs from the fact that the man's Mexican ancestors were conquered by Spaniards (Whites), producing a "hybrid Mexican people having an inferiority complex based on the mentality of a conquered people" (Baca-Zinn, 1980, 1995). Intermingling of the various cultures over the centuries produced a nation of mostly *mestizo* (mixed-"race") people.

An alternative explanation asserts that the macho behavior is a conscious reaction to the socially inferior position Mexican American males have been put in:

> Men in certain social categories have had more roles and sources of identity open to them. However, this has not been the case for Chicanos or other men of color. Perhaps manhood takes on greater importance for those who do not have access to socially valued roles. Being male is one sure way to acquire status when other roles are systematically denied by the workings of society. (Baca-Zinn, 1980, p. 39)

Men in a variety of ethnic groups are capable of exhibiting a macho, or aggressive, attitude as a way of asserting their need for respect and dignity. Macho behavior becomes less acceptable when it attempts to deny the inherent rights of other family members, particularly women.

African American Culture

African American men may have an advantage over White men in developing and integrating the "feminine" qualities that foster equalitarian relationships with women. According to one African American scholar, displaying dominant, aggressive behavior in the greater society carries considerable risk for African American males. As a consequence,

Black male socialization includes a range of very positive results that young white men do not typically experience. From peers, for instance, young black men learn the concepts of "brother" and "blood"—a deep sense of identification with other black men that cuts across age, class, and geography. . . . From the women who raise us, black men learn firsthand to respect the strength of so-called feminine qualities—intuition, warmth, cooperation, and empathy. (C. W. Franklin, 1989, p. 278)

Is a strong women's movement that pushes for changes that benefit all women still needed in the United States? A recent poll found that African American women were more likely (85%) than White women (64%) or Latino women (76%) to respond in the affirmative (Cowan, 1989, p. 11). But many African American women see feminism from a different perspective than do White women. African American women have rarely served only in the housewife role because economic circumstances have dictated that they work outside the home. African American women are also acutely aware of the disadvantages African American men have faced over the years, making it difficult for them to adopt a wholeheartedly feminist agenda. The dilemma: Am I more oppressed as a woman or as an African American? Because these two factors converge for African American women, life can be especially difficult for them.

Many African American women are hesitant about committing themselves to feminist goals that lead to conflict with African American men because, as Black psychiatrist Alvin Poussaint has said, "being a black man in American society is a high-risk adventure" (1982, p. 37). The U.S. Bureau of the Census bears out this statement. The average life expectancy of African American males is about 8 years less than that of White males, 9 years less than that of African American females, and almost 15 years less than that of White females. Furthermore, African American males have a higher infant mortality rate than African American females. They have a high adult death rate from various illnesses and from homicide, a high unemployment rate, and a high rate of imprisonment. African American males also have relatively high rates of hospitalization for mental illness, alcoholism, and other drug abuse (U.S. Bureau of the Census, 1997).

Native American Culture

Native American women confront many of the same problems that African American women face in American society, including a lack of political power that dates from the reorganization of Native American life in the 1920s. Native American cultures in the United States vary widely, but some are identified by a matrilineal tradition in which women owned or still own houses, tools, and agricultural land. Over the past two decades, there have been signs that Native American women are beginning to regain some of the power and prestige they had historically. In 1985 a woman was elected chief of the Cherokee nation, signifying "a revitalization of the role of women" in that tribe. In the 1986 Navajo elections, women won 72 of 327 local offices, and 62% of Navajo tribal scholarships were awarded to women (Robbins, 1987).

Many Native American families also face racism, unemployment, poverty, and the abuse of alcohol and other drugs (Robbins, 1987). Native American women play an important role in keeping the family and the tribe together. Some tribal

Wilma Mankiller, former chief of the Cherokee Nation, was the first woman ever elected to that position. Her election reflected the growing power of women in some Native American tribes.

traditions make it difficult for Native American women to attain leadership roles, and some tribes have religious beliefs against both contraception and abortion. But it has also been argued that tribal traditions are a source of strength for Native American women. In many cases, by upholding tradition Native American women have preserved tribal life despite the devastations of modern life. "If it wasn't for the women, their intestinal fortitude in keeping our traditions going, we would have disbanded as a tribe a long time ago," claims Alfred Benalli, Navajo director of an alcoholism program (cited in Robbins, 1987). The traditions unite tribal members, and from this sense of oneness comes strength.

Cultural values and family life among Native Americans and the many other minority groups in American society offer fascinating comparisons and contrasts with the dominant culture. Although valid generalizations are difficult, the basic similarities between groups seem to outweigh the differences.

Theories About Gender-Role Development and Change

Theorists interested in gender roles have focused on how children acquire gender-role identity during the early years of life and how changes in gender-role identity occur. Some observers believe that changes in gender-role identity are possible after early childhood, but it is generally assumed that once gender-role iden-

and rhetoric, but when she expresses her views, her parents react emotionally. "Are you telling me my life has been worthless?" her more traditional mother asks. "Those damned feminists!" her father sputters. Her mother becomes defensive because she has made a career of her children and her marriage. Her father becomes defensive because he felt he had done the right thing by supporting his wife and children.

Family systems that are balanced (on the Couple and Family Map) tend to be more open to change and are more supportive of independence in family members (Tiesel, 1992). In contrast, some types of unbalanced family systems, particularly rigidly enmeshed types, are resistant to change and restrict independence in family members.

The Feminist Framework

Traditional gender-role patterns—stressing the differences between men and women, masculinity and feminity—have been criticized by many observers of American society since the 1960s, including feminists. The gender-role constraints under which men and women traditionally have lived have been revised considerably. Many women are doing things their mothers would not have deemed possible. Many men are also gaining the freedom to function outside the traditional boundaries of masculinity. Making these profound changes in life is a struggle, and it would be difficult—if not impossible—for many people to go back to the traditional patterns.

Feminist scholars have focused on a variety of concerns (A. J. Walker & Thompson, 1984; Thompson & Walker, 1995). They have worked to document the contributions women have made in the world. Feminists point out that although women have made countless contributions to culture and to human life, the omission of these achievements from the historical record reflects the low status in which women have been held in society. Feminists point out that women have been exploited, devalued, and oppressed. In addition, as a result of their own experiences, feminists tend to be sensitive to other oppressed people.

Another focus of feminists is a commitment to change the conditions of women. Feminists strive to empower women by documenting oppression so that people recognize it when they see and experience it. Feminists take an affirming stance toward women, challenging the status quo of devaluation (see Box 8.4, which describes one woman's struggle against gender inequality). This affirmation of women does not imply a rejection of men or all things masculine. Instead, both men and women are accorded equal respect and value.

Feminists have found traditional gender-role theories to be highly suspect. They argue that Talcott Parsons's concept of instrumental and expressive activities falsely assumes that the two are mutually exclusive—that an individual cannot blend both. They point out that Parsons acknowledged the primacy of the father over the mother, which he felt was linked to the Western emphasis on achievement and instrumentality, and they criticize Parsons for not questioning male dominance (Thorne, 1982). According to feminists, the boxes males and females are put in are too simple and too idealistic. In practice, many individuals—both men and women—feel stifled by the roles they have been assigned and have sought a way to transform the traditional family. The following poem by Nancy R. Smith sums it up nicely:

BOX 8.4

A Woman's Struggle for Gender Equality

I am not a female suffering from "delusions." I am not "unstable," "psychotic," or "schizophrenic."

I was Minnesota's Business Woman of the Year in 1988. I was a delegate to the White House Conference on Small Business in Washington, D.C., in 1986. I was named one of *Corporate Report Minnesota*'s Outstanding Women in Business in 1989.

But 10 years ago, in 1981, I was a divorced mother of two struggling with a small business. I made an appointment to meet with a traveling Small Business Administration representative about available loan programs. When I asked for an application, he rifled through his briefcase, then said, "I must have left that particular application in my motel room. Why don't you meet me there at 5 o'clock to fill it out?" It was clear what he meant. . . .

Let me try to make it easier for men to understand the social conditioning on females to keep their mouths shut.

Reverse the roles—and imagine growing up as a male in a world where everyone who has power is female: the president, Supreme Court, Congress, governors, judges, police, legislators, doctors, dentists, lawyers, school administrators, clergy. . . .

As you go through school, your female counselors steer you into the secondary positions; you can be the dental hygienist, but not the dentist. If you protest, you are told you are "unmanly" to want women's jobs. In this world, men earn 59 cents for every dollar women earn and rarely make it to the top, as the "glass ceiling" is firmly in place. Men—no matter how old or what their job—are still called "boys."

As a teacher, you are paid less than female colleagues with the same experience. You then start your own business—and are humiliated when you have to get your wife's permission for a bank loan even though she doesn't need your permission. You buy insurance through your business, and are appalled when the policy is issued in your wife's name and you are listed with the children under "dependents."

Not a pretty picture, is it? *Yet all of the above happened to me* and many women of Anita Hill's generation. These are not things that happen to men, which is why they cannot imagine the intimidating, fearful effect of society's long-term conditioning on women when they are treated like children and second-class citizens with little legal rights. No, baby, we have not come a long way.

Source: "No, Baby, American Women Have Not Come a Long Way" by L. Kraft, November 5, 1991, Minneapolis *Star/Tribune*, p. 6. Copyright 1991 by the Minneapolis *Star/Tribune*. Reprinted by permission of the publisher.

For every woman who is tired of acting weak when she knows she is strong,
There is a man who is tired of appearing strong when he feels vulnerable.
For every woman who is tired of acting dumb,
There is a man who is burdened with the constant expectations of "knowing everything."
For every woman who is tired of being called an "emotional female,"
There is a man who is denied the right to weep and be gentle.
For every woman who feels "tied down" by her children,
There is a man who is denied the full pleasures of shared parenthood.
For every woman who takes a step toward her own liberation,
There is a man who finds the way to freedom has been made a little easier.

Power in Families

The fundamental concept in social science is Power, in the same sense in which Energy is the fundamental concept in physics.

—BERTRAND RUSSELL

The words *family* and *power* are inextricably linked. Power, control, and authority are continuously exercised in families, and struggles for personal power in families are exceedingly common. Tradition has dictated that considerable power go to the males in the family, but women often have more power than they or anyone else admits.

Power is defined as the ability (potential or actual) of an individual to change the behavior of other members in a social system (Olson & Cromwell, 1975, p. 5). Extending the above definition to families, **family power** is the ability of one family member to change the behavior of the other family members.

Many of the characteristics of power in close relationships were summarized by Kathleen M. Galvin and Bernard J. Brommel (1986, p. 123). Power is a system property—a feature of a family system—rather than a personal characteristic of any one family member. Power is an interactive process involving one family member who desires something from one or more other family members; these members may affect all other members in the system. Power is also a dynamic process, not a static one. It creates reciprocal causation (i.e., family members react to power attempts) in which one move leads to another, which leads to another, and so forth. Power also changes over time, particularly when the family is under stress. Power has both perceptual and behavioral aspects: The same power issue may be perceived differently by each family member.

A Family Power Model

Many disciplines have attempted to understand power, but it has proven to be a complex and elusive concept. "In the entire lexicon of sociological concepts, none is more troublesome than the concept of power. We may say about it in general only what St. Augustine said about time, that we all know perfectly well what it is—until someone asks us" (Bierstedt, 1950).

David Olson and Ronald Cromwell (1975) posed a series of relevant questions about power:

- Is power the actual ability to influence another person's behavior, or is it just the potential ability to do so?

- Is power an intentional or an unintentional process?

- Is power both overt and covert?

- Is power who decides or who does an activity?

- Is power who decides, or is it who decides who decides?

- Is power a process or an outcome?

- Does a power struggle mean there is a winner or loser, or is it possible for both individuals to win or lose? (1975, p. 5).

Olson and Cromwell (1975) have divided family power into three areas: bases of family power, family power processes, and family power outcomes.

Bases of Family Power   Interest in the study of family power by family-focused social and behavioral scientists was sparked by Robert Blood and Don Wolfe's clas-

Educational level, occupational prestige, and income are all sources of power in our society—and in relationships as well. This college graduate is very likely to have more power in a marriage relationship than a high school graduate who chooses the role of full-time homemaker and mother.

sic study *Husbands and Wives* (1960), which developed a **resource theory of family power.** The researchers argued that the balance of power in a marriage is related to the relative resources each spouse has in that relationship. Blood and Wolfe focused on the resources of money, educational level, and occupational prestige and found that these were statistically related to the extent of the husband's perceived power in the marriage. In short, whoever has the most resources in the relationship has the most power.

Blumstein and Schwartz (1990) also found that money is an important resource that can affect the balance of power in a relationship. The sociologists studied heterosexual couples, gay-male couples, and lesbian couples. They found that money helped establish the balance of power among heterosexual couples and gay-male couples but not among lesbian couples. Husbands had greater power over wives when the male-provider role was accepted. In more than 30% of the marriages in which the husband earned at least $8,000 more than the wife, the husband was perceived to have more power. When the spouses' incomes were equal, however, the husband was more powerful in the relationship in only 18% of the cases.

Similarly, in gay-male couples, the individual who had the larger income was more likely to dominate. But among lesbian couples this was not true because the partners tended to avoid dependence on one another. Among cohabiting heterosexual couples, a woman's income helped her establish equality in the relationship. Blumstein and Schwartz also found that money often means different things to men than to women. For men, money tends to represent identity and power. For women, money tends to represent security and autonomy (Blumstein & Schwartz, 1990).

Some social scientists have argued that power in families is a function of more than income, education, and occupation. People find value in many different things, including intelligence, pleasing personality traits, personal appearance, skill in various areas of endeavor, social prestige, a sense of humor, and interpersonal skills (C. R. Berger, 1980). One husband, speaking of his intelligent, well-educated, professionally successful wife, half-jokingly admits that a big part of the power she has over him stems from her personality. The wife, on the other hand, says that one of her husband's most powerful resources is his sense of humor: "He's crazy, I admit. But he sure is entertaining!" The ability to make a partner laugh often translates into power in a relationship.

An important nonmaterial resource that needs to be considered in any discussion of power is the individual's interest in maintaining the relationship. This *principle of least interest* was described by Waller (1951), who believed that the individual who is least interested in maintaining the relationship has the most power. If one person is more dependent than the other or is more concerned about keeping the relationship alive, the most-interested partner is likely to defer to the least-interested partner. In short, the least-interested partner will have more power. Even if the least-interested partner does not exploit the situation, he or she will be more powerful, and this is likely to be demonstrated in a variety of subtle and not-so-subtle ways.

Other researchers have approached the bases of family power in a somewhat more abstract way (Cromwell & Olson, 1975). Raven, Centers, and Rodrigues (1975) identified six bases of power. *Legitimate power*, also called authority, is based on an individual's legitimate or normatively prescribed right to change another's behavior. Legitimate power stems from one person's acceptance of a role relationship, believing that the other person has the right to request compliance. *Reward power* is the ability to provide rewards for desired behavior changes. *Coercive power* is based in the perception that punishment will occur if the desired behavior does not happen. *Referent power* is based on identification with or attraction to another; people with referent power are role models or are physically attractive to others. *Informational power* is an individual's ability to use explanations and other persuasive communication to change someone else's behavior. The individual with informational power has carefully and successfully explained the necessity for change. *Expert power* is based on the perception that one person has superior knowledge or ability within a given area, the understanding and skill to lead another to the best outcome. Table 8.4 lists examples of these six bases of family power.

Family Power Processes   Family power processes are those interaction techniques that occur during general family discussions, decision making, problem solving, conflict resolution, and crisis management. *Assertiveness* and *aggressiveness* refer to ways in which people attempt to change the behavior of others. People are being assertive when they express what they want or desire: "I would like you to pick up your clothes." People are being aggressive when they demand that others comply with their requests: "Pick up those clothes, or I won't fix dinner tonight." *Control* refers to the effectiveness of these attempts to change the behavior of others. The more often others are willing to comply with a person's request, the more control that person has.

Table 8.4 Six Bases of Family Power

TYPE	RESOURCE	DEFINITION	EXAMPLE
Legitimate power	Authority	Having the right to make a decision	A single woman's right to decide whether to have an abortion
Reward power	Rewards	Being able to reward for appropriate behavior	Praising a child for helping with household chores
Coercive power	Punishment	Being able to punish for inappropriate behavior	Punishing a child for staying out late
Referent power	Respect and/or love	Having others' trust following	Following one's parents' advice about how to handle their funerals
Informational power	Knowledge	Having specialized knowledge	Following a husband's advice on buying a car because he has carefully researched the topic
Expert power	Experience in an area	Having experience and respect in a field	Following a wife's advice about finances because she is a financial counselor

Source: Adapted from "The Bases of Conjugal Power" (pp. 217–232) by B. H. Raven, R. Centers, and A. Rodrigues. In *Power in Families,* edited by R. E. Cromwell and D. H. Olson, 1975, Sage Publications. Copyright © 1975 by David H. Olson.

Family Power Outcomes   The third area of family power—outcomes—centers on who makes decisions and who wins. There are several ways of measuring power outcomes. When doing observational research on power in families, researchers typically count the number of assertive statements individuals make and record how others respond to those statements. For example, in a family with two parents and an adolescent, if the husband makes 10 assertive statements and 8 of them are accepted by the rest of the family, the researchers calculate the husband's effective power in the family as 80%. If the wife makes 8 assertive statements but only 2 of them are accepted by the other family members, her effective power is 25%. If the adolescent makes 14 assertive statements and only 2 of them are accepted, the adolescent's effective power is 14%. On the basis of these observations, one could conclude that the husband in this family has more effective power than the wife or the adolescent.

Types of Power Patterns

According to one classic model (Herbst, 1952), the power balance in a marriage can be characterized in four basic ways: a **husband-dominant power pattern,** in which the man is basically the boss; a **wife-dominant power pattern,** in which the woman is basically the boss; a **syncratic power pattern** (in essence, "to decide together"), in which authority is shared and decisions are made on a joint basis in most areas of endeavor; and an **autonomic power pattern,** in which each spouse has about equal authority but in different areas of life and essentially makes decisions in her or his particular domain independent of the other. These patterns are illustrated in Figure 8.1.

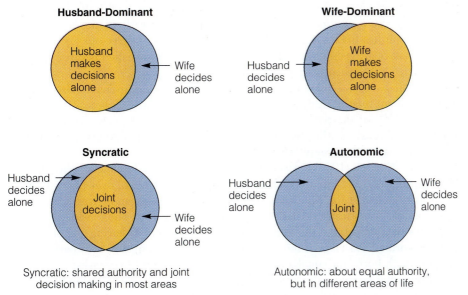

Figure 8.1 Power Patterns in Marriages. *Source:* Adapted from "The Measurement of Family Relationships" by P. G. Herbst, 1952, *Human Relations, 5,* pp. 3–35. Used by permission of Kluwer Academic/Plenum Publishers.

In the early stages of a relationship, there can be a great deal of instability as the individuals struggle to work out the balance of power. As time passes, the partners assert themselves to establish some power in the relationship. A male- or female-dominant relationship, with one person leading and the other following, is difficult to maintain. Eventually the dominant one may tire of leading and the submissive one may tire of following. The result may be a change to another type of power sharing.

In a syncratic relationship, the sharing of decisions and tasks affords the family system a better power balance. The partners are relatively equal, and couples with children often encourage some sharing of power, especially as the children become older.

In an autonomic relationship, one spouse may have most of the power in one area, such as inside the home, whereas the other spouse may have most of the power in another area, such as outside the home. Both perceive the relationship to be relatively equal in power on the whole, because both domains of endeavor are perceived to be important.

Power, Marital Satisfaction, and Mental Health

Certain power arrangements tend to be related to higher marital satisfaction and mental health. Ramon Corrales found that high marital satisfaction occurs most frequently among equalitarian (syncratic or autonomic) couples. Husband-dominant couples are less likely to have a high level of marital satisfaction than are equalitarian couples, and wife-dominant couples rank third (Corrales, 1975).

Corrales found that many women do not seem satisfied in wife-dominant marriages. In a study of wives who perceived that they dominated the marriage, the women had relatively low scores on marital satisfaction. Corrales believed that these wives often exercised power by default, to compensate for a weak or ignoring husband. Husbands in these wife-dominant marriages reported that they were not as dissatisfied with the relationship as their wives were. Kolb and Straus (1974) suggested a *role incapacity theory* to help explain the wives' dissatisfaction. When a man relinquishes his traditional leadership role or fails to carry out his part of an equalitarian relationship, the wife is likely to become dissatisfied because she feels she married a less-than-competent man (p. 761).

A similar study of the relationship of power to marital satisfaction also revealed wife-dominant relationships to be problematic. Raven and colleagues (1975) found that only 20% of the partners in wife-dominant marriages were "very satisfied" with the relationship, whereas more than two thirds of the partners in other types of power relationships were "very satisfied."

M. E. Madden (1987) measured power in 37 couples, looking at who made final decisions and the extent to which each spouse had control over the tasks he or she was responsible for. She found that for both husbands and wives, marital satisfaction was statistically related to perceived control over one's tasks. Who performed what task around the house was not so important as having a choice about who performed the tasks. The most satisfying relationship for both partners was one in which both had equal and moderately high control over tasks.

Premarital couples who are equalitarian in terms of roles also tend to have a more satisfying relationship. Alan Craddock (1984) studied 100 premarital couples who took the premarital inventory called PREPARE, which asks questions about roles, communication, conflict resolution, and other relevant topics. He compared four groups of couples: those in which both partners were equalitarian, those in which both partners were traditional, couples in which the male was equalitarian and the female traditional, and male-traditional/female-equalitarian couples. As predicted, premarital couples in which both were equalitarian were happier than the other three groups in terms of communication, conflict resolution, personality compatibility, leisure activities, and family and friends. The least satisfied were those couples in which the male had a traditional role orientation and the female had an equalitarian orientation. Marriages with an unequal division of decision-making power were also associated with high levels of depression in both spouses as compared to more equitable relationships (Ross, Mirowsky, & Goldsteen, 1991).

In summary, power is a vital issue in intimate relationships. Sensitive use of power and the creation of a balance of power are two important keys to relationship satisfaction and mental health.

"In my parents' marriage, my mother always acted like my father had the power, but you could tell that she was constantly figuring out ways to manipulate him into thinking something was his idea," said Emily, a young woman living in Northampton, Massachusetts. "I realize she felt that, in the culture of her time, that was the best way she could ensure a reasonable measure of power in the family. It was the 1950s. Dad was a minister and everyone expected him to act like God, and he did.

"Today, I like how my own marriage works better. The assumption in society leans more toward equality, even though I think men still hold most of the cards. But in our family, the assumption is pretty much that

(Continued. . .)

(. . .Continued)

power will be balanced out. We don't say this in so many words, but it's quite clear that when a decision is made, it's a shared decision. I wouldn't have it any other way, and I think David is pretty much in agreement on this, also.

"If we didn't do it this way, somebody would be pretty cranky pretty quick, until things got worked out fairly."

Communication and Power Dynamics

Researchers who study communication have identified several ways in which spouses exert power in their interactions with each other or avoid the use of power in communication (Fitzpatrick, 1988, pp. 116–117). Conversations can be either symmetrical or complementary. A **symmetrical interaction** is one in which partners send similar messages that are designed to control how the relationship is defined. Researchers further divide symmetrical interactions into three types: competitive, submissive, and neutralized. The three are similar in that both spouses adopt the same tactic: both compete, both submit, or both are relatively neutral in the search for a solution to the issue. They differ in the tactic used and in the results.

In **competitive symmetry,** the conflict between partners escalates. He says, "I don't want to go to your relatives' birthday party. I'm real tired from work." She says, "You may be tired, but the real reason you don't want to go is you simply don't like my relatives. You never have." He says, "Well, I don't. They're boring and bigoted, and I've heard everything they ever had to say years ago." The discussion becomes a competition in which both aim to defeat the other. This win-lose approach sets the stage for escalating hostilities.

In **submissive symmetry,** both spouses try to give control of the situation to the other. He says, "Look at the checkbook. How will we ever get out of debt?" She says, "I don't know. We never seem to have enough money." He says, "I'm afraid they'll reposses the new car if we don't send in the payments on schedule." She says, "It would be a shame. I love that car. . . ." Both partners avoid taking control of the situation, attempting to win by passing responsibility to the other.

In **neutralized symmetry,** spouses respect each other and try to avoid exerting control over each other. She says, "I noticed the toilet has a little leak again. I have a meeting this evening, but tomorrow after work I can fix it." He says, "You're better at figuring out mechanical things than I am, but I could pick up the parts." She says, "That would free us both up by 6:30 to go out to dinner together." These spouses have avoided a power struggle over the toilet by offering ideas in a gentle spirit, approaching the matter as equals on the same team instead of as boss and servant. Each gives a little, and both come out ahead. This win-win approach ensures that partners will have time to enjoy each other instead of fighting.

A **complementary interaction** differs from a symmetrical interaction in that the participants adopt two different tactics: One is dominant and one is submissive. He says, "Would you iron my shirt? I've got an important meeting tonight." She says, "Sure." If a relationship is to remain vital, it is important that partners try not to exert power over each other but, instead, work together for mutual benefit. Equality nurtures intimacy.

Suggestions From Family Therapists

Richard B. Stuart (1980) offers several useful principles for couples interested in keeping a balance of power in their relationship. Remember that power is a characteristic of relationships, not of people. Power is always relative, changing, and useful only to the extent that it is legitimate. Many of the conflicts that cause relationship stress are struggles over the power process (the way decisions are made) rather than disagreements about a specific issue. The person holding the authority to make each decision must have the responsibility for following through on the decision. Decision making should be balanced by the value of the areas each partner controls, not by the number of areas each has. It is more efficient and more realistic to assign each partner primary responsibility for making decisions in certain areas, whether or not the other has veto authority, than to make all decisions a matter of mutual agreement.

Men may think they have a lot to lose by giving up some of their power over women and children, but in fact they have a great deal to gain. Men tend to die younger than women, often from a variety of illnesses related to stress and poor

The quest for power, money, and material success in which so many men are immersed is accompanied by higher levels of stress, higher rates of heart disease, and shorter life spans.

lifestyle choices. A macho, "win-at-all-costs" attitude is commonly thought to contribute to men's health problems. "Having to continually prove oneself by out-performing others, and being fearful about losing, can become an obsession that leads only to anxiousness and uncertainty," according to family therapist Larry Frahm (1987). Rigid gender roles may have afforded men more power in our culture, but it is lonely at the top. The path toward intimacy is best walked side by side.

Summary

- According to a national survey, happily married couples agreed more often than unhappily married couples that the husband's and wife's occupations are equally important, that the wife should be able to work outside the home, that women's roles should not be restricted, that mothers of young children should be free to work outside the home, and that housework should be shared by both partners.

- The most commonly reported issues for married couples in their role relationship were the following: the notion that the wife should accept the husband's judgment on important issues; disagreements about the wife's working outside the home, especially when she is the mother of small children; the notion that the husband's occupation is more important than the wife's; responsibility for housework resting primarily on the wife; and restrictions on the wife's roles and opportunities.

- Gender roles—the expectations every society has about people's attitudes and behaviors based on whether they are male or female—are rooted in biology but heavily influenced by culture.

- Sociologist Talcott Parsons espoused a traditional view of gender roles. His theory of family roles assumed that men should be "instrumental" and women "expressive." Parsons's theory has been vigorously challenged and is no longer accepted.

- In many ways, American society is moving away from male dominance toward equalitarian gender roles. The concept of androgyny refers to a blend of traditionally masculine and feminine personality traits in one person. Recent perspectives on gender appear to be moving the discussion beyond androgyny; critics argue that the concepts of masculinity and femininity are cultural constructs rather than biological realities. It makes little sense, they declare, even to talk about "maleness" and "femaleness" because individuals are all so different.

- Persistent gender-role patterns in marriage mean that women do much more of the housework in the family than men do, which often leads to relationship conflict.

- In Mexican American, African American, and Native American cultures, as in White society, men have often been dominant in their families, but signs of change are also apparent in these cultures.

- Historically prominent theories of gender-role development include the social learning theory, which is concerned with how individuals learn the behavior patterns considered appropriate for their sex; the cognitive development theory, which links the progressive acquisition of gender-typing to the general maturation of the child's thinking processes; the family systems theory, which holds that the entire family must change when an individual member changes; and the feminist framework, which argues that women are exploited, devalued, and oppressed and affirms their equality with men.

- Family power is the ability of one family member to change the behavior of other family members. Researchers have looked at three areas of family power: bases of power, power processes, and power outcomes. Power in a family is related to how much money an individual earns, to educational level, and to occupational prestige, among other things.

- The power balance in a marriage can be characterized in four basic ways: a husband-dominant pattern; a wife-dominant pattern; a syncratic pattern, in which authority is shared; and an autonomic pattern, in which each spouse has about equal authority but in different areas of life.

- One way power is exerted or avoided in families is through patterns of communication. The most successful relationships appear to have a relatively even balance of power between the partners.

Key Terms

gender identity	cognitive development theory	syncratic power pattern
gender role	power	autonomic power pattern
gender-role stereotype	family power	symmetrical interaction
masculinity	resource theory of family power	competitive symmetry
femininity		submissive symmetry
androgyny	husband-dominant power pattern	neutralized symmetry
gender polarization	wife-dominant power pattern	complementary interaction
equalitarian roles		
social learning theory		

Activities

1. In small groups, discuss whether American society will ever evolve into one in which one's sex is relatively unimportant, except in relation to reproduction. How far can we go in removing the old gender-role stereotypes? How far do you, as an individual, want society to go? Report what you decide to the larger group. Did you reach any consensus on these issues?

2. Study Box 8.2, "Contemporary Versus Traditional Dating and Marriage Patterns." If you are in an intimate relationship, decide which aspects from the "contemporary" list and which from the "traditional" list apply to your relationship. Have your partner do the same exercise, and compare your answers.

3. In small groups, discuss family power: How was power distributed in your family of origin? How do you know? (Give examples.) How do you want power to be distributed in the family you hope to create in the future? Do you think this will be possible? How? Report your findings to the larger group.

Suggested Readings

Barnett, R. C., & Rivers, C. (1996). *She works/he works: Two-income families are happier, healthier, and better off.* New York: HarperSanFrancisco/HarperCollins. A discussion of the rewards and concerns associated with women's and men's experiences as employees, marital partners, and parents and how these relate to mental and physical health.

Bem, S. L. (1993). *The lenses of gender: Transforming the debate on sexual inequality.* New Haven, CT: Yale University Press. An important theorist discusses how we can move beyond masculine and feminine to human.

Cook, E. P. (1985). *Psychological androgyny.* New York: Pergamon. An excellent overview of research and theory on the notion that human beings can be both masculine and feminine, tough and tender.

Crose, R. (1997). *Why women live longer than men: . . . and what men can learn from them.* San Francisco: Jossey-Bass. A gerontologist's perspective on how much of the difference in life expectancy (an average of seven years) between women and men can be attributed to traditional, masculine high-risk behaviors that men could change if they wanted to.

Gilmore, D. D. (1990). *Manhood in the making: Cultural concepts of masculinity.* New Haven, CT: Yale University Press. Explores what it means to be a man in many cultures around the world.

Goodrich, T. J. (Ed.). (1991). *Women and power: Perspectives on family therapy.* New York: Norton. Excellent discussions from a feminist perspective on the empowerment of women in family therapy.

Knudson-Martin, C., & Mahoney, A. R. (1996). Gender dilemmas and myth in the construction of marital bargains: Issues for marital therapy. *Family Process, 35,* 137–153. Examines how couples often work out an implicit but unfair bargain with each other, what the authors call "the myth of equality." In their efforts to preserve the relationship the couple buys into this myth, when in fact the reality is that one (usually the male) has more power than the other (usually the female). The authors urge couples to find other, more workable solutions in their efforts to create fair and equitable relationships in the family.

Lips, H. (1997). *Sex and gender.* (3rd ed.). Mountain View, CA: Mayfield. An encyclopedic text explaining the biological and psychosocial processes of becoming male and female, masculine and feminine.

Schwartz, P. (1995). *Love between equals: How love peer marriage really works.* New York: Free Press.

Taylor, R. J., Chatters, L. M., Tucker, M. B., & Lewis, E. (1991). Developments in research on Black families. In A. Booth (Ed.), *Contemporary families: Looking forward, looking back* (pp. 275–296). Minneapolis: National Council on Family Relations. A very good review of research on African American families, packed with useful ideas and directions for study and understanding.

Thompson, L., & Walker, A. J. (1991). Gender in families: Women and men in marriage, work, and parenthood. In A. Booth (Ed.), *Contemporary families: Looking forward, looking back* (pp. 76–102). Minneapolis: National Council on Family Relations. An excellent reviews of research on gender roles in families.

Vega, W. A. (1991). Hispanic families in the 1980s. In A. Booth (Ed.), *Contemporary families: Looking forward, looking back* (pp. 297–306). Minneapolis: National Council on Family Relations. Reviews research on Hispanic families and gives direction for future studies.

CHAPTER 9

Communication and Intimacy

Communication is at the heart of intimate human relationships—it is literally the foundation on which all else is built. **Communication** is the way humans create and share meaning, both verbally and nonverbally. The ability to communicate is one of a handful of essential skills individuals must master if they are to enjoy close relationships. In fact, the ability and the willingness to communicate have been found to be among the most important factors in maintaining a satisfying relationship.

In this chapter we will look at the art of interpersonal communication, focusing on several important principles of communication, as well as gender and cultural differences in communication styles. We will examine ways for people to become more aware of their communication patterns and styles. Finally, we will explore various approaches and techniques people can use to improve communication in their relationships, thereby increasing the level of intimacy they enjoy with friends, partners, and family members.

Because communication is the key to a successful couple relationship, we will open this chapter with some findings from the national survey (Olson et al., 1999) described earlier in Chapter 7. In the following section, we will look at couple strengths in terms of communication, comparing happy couples with unhappy couples. Next we will review the five most common communication issues as identified by the total sample of 26,442 couples.

Couple Strengths and Issues in Communication

In a national study (Olson et al., 1999) comparing the major communication strengths of happy couples with those of unhappy couples, researchers found that happy couples were more than six times more likely (68%) than unhappy couples (10%) to agree that they are very satisfied with how they talk to each other (Table 9.1). Happy couples had significantly less trouble (74%) than unhappy couples (23%) in believing things their partner tells them to be true. Over half (57%) of

Table 9.1 Communication Strengths of Happy Versus Unhappy Married Couples

STRENGTH	PERCENTAGE OF COUPLES IN AGREEMENT	
	Happy Couples (*n* = 7,116)	Unhappy Couples (*n* = 13,421)
Are very satisfied with how they talk to each other.	68	10
Have no trouble believing their partner.	74	23
Feel their partner does not make comments that put them down.	57	11
Are not afraid to ask their partner for what they want.	57	12
Find it easy to express their true feelings to their partner.	55	11

Source: Adapted from Olson, Fye, & Olson (1999).

Table 9.2 Top Five Communication Issues for Married Couples	
ISSUE	**PERCENTAGE OF COUPLES WITH PROBLEMS SURROUNDING ISSUE (N = 26,442)**
Feel their partner does not understand how they feel.	86
Feel their partner does not share feelings.	78
Are afraid to share negative feelings because their partner will get angry.	75
Receive the silent treatment from their partner.	67
Receive comments from their partner that put them down.	65

Source: Adapted from Olson, Fye, & Olson (1999).

happy couples agreed that they do not make comments to put each other down, whereas only 11% of unhappy couples felt this way. Happy couples were significantly less afraid (57%) to ask their partner for what they want than were unhappy couples (12%), and happy couples found it easier (55%) to express all their true feelings than did unhappy couples (11%).

Table 9.2 lists the findings of the total sample of 26,442 married couples surveyed by Olson and colleagues (1999). The top communication issue reported by a majority of couples (86%) was having a partner who does not understand how they feel. Seventy-eight percent indicated that they wished their partner would share his or her feelings more often, and 75% said they were afraid of sharing negative feelings, which might anger their partner. About two thirds (67%) of the couples surveyed reported that their partner gives them the silent treatment (67%) and makes comments that put them down (65%). In general, this survey demonstrates the major communication issues for married couples and in many ways reflects what marital therapists often hear from couples seeking help for their marital problems.

Perspectives on Communication

Communication difficulties often arise when participants have divergent communication styles. This section sheds light on the two most significant sources of communication-style differences: gender and culture.

Gender Differences in Communication Style

Common gender-related differences in communication often cause conflict between men and women. It sometimes seems that there are two separate styles of communication: a masculine style and a feminine style. A better understanding of the differences between these styles can reduce some of the friction between men and women.

Jane Tear (cited in Meier, 1991) summarizes what many authorities believe to be common differences between male and female communication styles (Box 9.1).

BOX 9.1

Conversational Style and Gender

Listening Style

Male	Female
Irregular eye contact	Uninterrupted eye contact
Infrequent nodding	Frequent nodding
Infrequent use of "uh-huh"	Frequent use of "uh-huh"
May continue another activity while speaking	Usually stops other activities while speaking
Interrupts in order to speak	Waits for pauses in order to speak
Questions are designed to analyze speaker's information	Questions are designed to elicit more information

Speaking Style

Male	Female
Few pauses	Frequent pauses
May abruptly change topic	Connects information to previous speaker's information
Speaks until interrupted	Stops speaking when information is delivered
Speaks louder than previous speaker	Uses same volume as previous speaker
Frequent use of "I" and "me"	Frequent use of "us" and "we"
Personal self-disclosure rarely included	Personal self-disclosure often included
Humor delivered as separate jokes or anecdotes	Humor interwoven into discussion content
Humor often based on kidding or making fun of others	Humor rarely based on kidding or making fun of others

Note: This chart was developed by Jane Tear, a New York City–based consultant who specializes in gender dynamics in the workplace. She stresses that although most people have a speaking style fairly typical of their sex, each person's individual style reflects gender-typical tendencies to a greater or lesser extent.

Source: "War of the Words: Women Talk About How Men and Women Talk" by P. Meier, January 6, 1991, Minneapolis *Star/Tribune (First Sunday)*, p. 8. Copyright 1991 by Minneapolis *Star/Tribune*. Reprinted by permission.

Men often use conversation in a competitive way, perhaps to establish dominance in the relationship, whereas women tend to use conversation in a more affiliative way, hoping to establish friendship. Females tend to use good listening behaviors (such as making eye contact, nodding frequently, focusing attention on the speaker, and asking relevant questions), whereas men seem less focused on listening and more focused on responding. Men also tend to talk more but to disclose less personal information about themselves. Women tend to speak as a way to connect with people and ideas.

Deborah Tannen's work complements Tear's synthesis of communication styles. In her book *You Just Don't Understand: Women and Men in Conversation*, Tannen (1990) reported a conversation between a couple in their car. The woman asked, "Would you like to stop for a drink?" Her husband answered truthfully, "No," and they didn't stop. He was later frustrated to learn that his wife was annoyed because she had wanted to stop for a drink. He wondered, "Why didn't she just say what she wanted? Why did she play games with me?" The wife was annoyed not so much because she had not gotten her way but because her husband had not considered her preference. From her point of view, she had shown concern for her husband's wishes but he had shown no concern for hers.

Tannen believes that in this instance the spouses had used different but equally valid styles of communication and that both need to learn how to decipher each other's approaches to communication:

> In understanding what went wrong, the man must realize that when [his wife] asks what he would like, she is not asking an information question but rather starting a negotiation about what both would like. For her part, however, the woman must realize that when he answers "yes" or "no" he is not making a non-negotiable demand. (1990, p. 22)

Competition Versus Connection   Men are generally socialized to be competitive; they live in a hierarchical world in which each encounter with another person is seen as a challenge to their position. When the match is over, the man often evaluates himself as one-up or one-down. Male conversations are almost symbolic struggles in which the competitor tries to gain the upper hand, protect himself from threatening moves, and not allow himself to be pushed around. Men are therefore more uncomfortable talking about feelings than women are, because feelings can be interpreted as signs of weakness.

Women tend to approach the world not as competing, independent individualists but as individuals intimately interconnected with one another. Women tend to "network"; men tend to "compete." Tannen argues that for women, conversations are "negotiations for closeness in which people try to seek and give confirmation and support, and to reach consensus" (1990, p. 25). Women tend to seek out a community and to work to preserve intimacy and avoid isolation. Although they are also concerned with achieving status and avoiding failure, these are not their major focuses in life.

Although we all apparently need to have both a sense of independence from others and a sense of intimacy with others, men lean toward independence and women lean toward intimacy. The greater the difference in communication style between a man and a woman, the greater the potential for misunderstanding. A woman, needing closeness, will naturally want to tell her spouse where she's going, whom she'll be with, and when she'll return. A man, needing independence and control, may find it more difficult to see why it is important to share this information.

Similarly, a woman, being more concerned with building a close relationship, will want to tell her spouse about every purchase she would like to make—even those that are relatively inexpensive. Her husband may resist seeking permission from her for every little purchase, seeing any lessening of control over the family purse strings as a loss of control in life (Tannen, 1990, p. 26).

Gender differences in conversational style can lead to misunderstandings if people are not aware of them. Women tend to view conversation as an opportunity to connect with another person; men tend to view conversation as an arena for establishing dominance. These young women are probably able to communicate with each other more easily than with a member of the other sex.

Communication in an intimate relationship involves a continuous balancing of competing needs for intimacy and independence. Tannen points out that intimacy implies that "we're close and the same," whereas independence implies that "we're separate and different." Independence can also be the foundation of a hierarchy in a relationship—that is, "If I'm independent of you, and you're dependent on me, I'm higher on the totem pole. I'm in power." Perhaps that is why men, socialized to pursue power and control, tend to place more emphasis on independence than women do. Independence fits better into the world in which men have been trained to live (Tannen, 1990, p. 28).

Tannen explains women's "nagging" by arguing that it comes from a different approach to living. Women are inclined to do what people ask them to do, whereas men tend to resist even the slightest hint that someone else—especially a woman—has the authority to tell them what to do. Women tend to repeat their requests of men—to "nag"—because they assume men think like they think. "He would, of course, want to do what I'm asking if he only understood what I want."

So who's at fault? Neither. Both are simply reflecting masculine and feminine gender roles in their conversational styles. Tannen is careful to point out that women also value freedom and independence but tend to emphasize interdependence and connection more. Similarly, men find comfort in closeness but are socialized to see independence as more important.

Affiliation Versus Action   Women are often seen as the "talkers" in the family, whereas men may play the "strong and silent" role. This phenomenon also springs from differences between masculine and feminine gender roles. Women, seeking to affiliate, do so by talking. Men, being competitive, tend to be careful about talking. So when men go out with their friends, they are likely to do things together rather than to just talk. Women, on the contrary, tend to seek social situations centered around conversation, such as having lunch together. A good heart-to-heart talk builds intimacy and warm feelings. (Many gay men also favor a conversational style that focuses on building intimacy.)

In groups of people, men tend to be the talkers, but much of this talk is performance oriented, an attempt to establish dominance. When the topic is politics, sports, or other controversies that can be vigorously disputed, men lead the discussion. This performance-oriented talking is not really about establishing intimacy but about clarifying who has the power.

Men also tend to focus on solutions to problems, whereas women focus on sharing what they are feeling about problems. Because of this difference in focus, men often feel that women "only talk" about problems, and women often feel frustrated and misunderstood.

Male and female gender roles begin to influence boys and girls at a young age. Boys generally play outside more, in larger, hierarchically structured groups. Girls tend to play more in small groups or pairs, and their life often revolves around a best-friend relationship. For girls, intimacy is an essential ingredient of a relationship (Tannen, 1990, p. 43). During adolescence, males and females struggle to integrate with each other. Although they are attracted to each other, they have difficulty understanding each other. These difficulties continue throughout dating and into marriage. It is logical to argue that gender-role differences contribute to the unhappiness many people experience in marriage.

Tannen (1990, 1993) concludes that both sexes could learn from each other. Women could learn to accept some conflict and difference without considering it a threat to intimacy; men could learn from women that interdependence is not a threat to personal freedom. Tannen believes that the "best" style of communication is a flexible one: finding that delicate balance between separateness and connectedness. To determine your gender communication quotient, take the quiz in Box 9.2.

Tannen's work has generated a good deal of controversy. According to Elizabeth Aries (Tannen & Aries, 1997), the most common counterargument to Tannen's research is that Tannen unnecessarily polarizes the differences between men and women, de-emphasizing the fact that men's and women's styles of communication overlap considerably. This argument is similar to the one that Sandra Bem makes in regard to gender roles: The differences between individual women and the differences between individual men are greater than the differences between women as a group and men as a group. In effect, even though men and women as groups may differ, there are countless individuals within each group who defy the stereotypes. The key is to recognize that the sexes do seem to differ to a modest degree on average but that averages do not tell the whole story by any means. As a friend of ours likes to say with a wry smile, "The meanest, toughest, most insensitive person in my office is . . . a woman!"

BOX 9.2

Your Gender Communication Quotient

How much do you know about how men and women communicate with one another? The 20 items in this questionnaire are based on research conducted in classrooms, private homes, businesses, offices, hospitals—places where people commonly work and socialize. The answers appear at the bottom.

	TRUE	FALSE
1. Men talk more than women.	___	___
2. Men are more likely to interrupt women than they are to interrupt other men.	___	___
3. There are approximately ten times as many sexual terms for males as females in the English language.	___	___
4. During conversations, women spend more time gazing at their partner than men do.	___	___
5. Nonverbal messages carry more weight than verbal messages.	___	___
6. Female managers communicate with more emotional openness and drama than male managers.	___	___
7. Men not only control the content of conversations, they also work harder at keeping conversations going.	___	___
8. When people hear generic words such as "mankind" and "he" they respond inclusively, indicating that the terms apply to both sexes.	___	___
9. Women are more likely to touch others than men are.	___	___
10. In classroom communications, male students receive more reprimands and criticism than female students.	___	___
11. Women are more likely than men to disclose information on intimate personal concerns.	___	___
12. Female speakers are more animated in their conversational style than are male speakers.	___	___
13. Women use less personal space than men.	___	___
14. When a male speaks, he is listened to more carefully than a female speaker, even when she makes the identical presentation.	___	___
15. In general, women speak in a more tentative style than do men.	___	___
16. Women are more likely to answer questions that are not addressed to them.	___	___
17. There is widespread sex segregation in schools, and it hinders effective classroom communication.	___	___
18. Female managers are seen by both male and female subordinates as better communicators than male managers.	___	___
19. In classroom communications, teachers are more likely to give verbal praise to female than to male students.	___	___
20. In general, men smile more often than women.	___	___

ANSWERS: 1. T; 2. T; 3. F; 4. T; 5. T; 6–9. F; 10–15. T; 16. F; 17. T; 18. T; 19. F; 20. F

Source: "How Wide Is Your Communication Gender Gap?" by Hazel R. Rozema, Ph.D., Milliken University, and John W. Gray, Ph.D., University of Arkansas at Little Rock. Reprinted by permission.

Culture influences many aspects of communication, including such nonverbal elements as eye contact, facial expression, physical proximity, and touching. These Latino men find it natural to greet each other on the street with a hug. Many northern Europeans would be more comfortable with a handshake.

Cultural Differences in Communication Style

The uses and interpretations of both verbal and nonverbal communication vary widely from culture to culture. In England, for example, nonverbal gestures are considered brash and undesirable. But in Italy, France, and the Polynesian islands of the southwest Pacific, among other places, nonverbal gestures are common.

Cultural differences can affect not only how well a message is understood but also the way in which the messenger is perceived as an individual. A graduate student from India related the following incident, which occurred when he first arrived in the United States. The student was fairly fluent in English, but he was totally unfamiliar with American customs. One day he was walking down the street with a fellow student he had recently befriended. Without giving it much thought, he reached toward his friend and began holding hands with him as they walked down the street. Having assumed his friend was heterosexual, the American student was somewhat startled and asked his friend why he wanted to hold hands. The Indian graduate student became confused and said it was customary in India for two close friends to hold hands to show their friendship.

Clearly, actions may be interpreted quite differently in different cultures. The nature and scope of our nonverbal communication are largely determined by our cultural heritage, as well. For example, studies have documented the different ways in which men react to beautiful women around the world: The American male lifts his eyebrows, the Italian presses his forefinger into his cheek and rotates it, the Greek strokes his cheek, the Brazilian puts an imaginary telescope to his eye, the Frenchman kisses his fingertips, and the Egyptian grasps his beard (Axtell, 1993).

Westerners consider direct eye contact important, but many cultures see it as a personal affront, conveying a lack of respect. In Japan, for example, when shaking hands, bowing, and especially when talking, it is important to glance only occasionally into the other person's face. One's gaze should instead focus on fingertips, desk tops, and carpets. In the words of one American electronics representative, "Always keep your shoes shined in Tokyo. You can bet a lot of Japanese you meet will have their eyes on them" (Parker Pen Co., 1985, p. 40).

In most Latin countries, from Venezuela to Italy, the *abrazo* (hug) is as common as a handshake. Men hug men; women hug women; men hug women. In Slavic countries, this greeting is better described as a bear hug. In France, the double cheek-to-cheek greeting is common among both men and women. A traditional bow from the waist is the standard greeting for the Japanese, who are averse to casual touching. Many Americans, however, feel uncomfortable with bowing, but to the Japanese, it means "I respect your experience and wisdom."

Using Communication to Develop Intimacy

Good, positive communication is a hallmark of successful close relationships. A man might say, "We're best friends. We talk about everything. I don't know what I'd do if she weren't around to listen to my problems. She lets me know, very clearly, when she's upset about something. But I don't feel attacked. It's like, we both just sit down and work out a solution." Poor communication, on the other hand, often minimizes the possibility of establishing a close relationship. People may say, "We don't communicate." "He never talks." "She always nags." "He doesn't understand me."

Communication is important at every stage of a close relationship. The seeds of marital failure are often sown early in a relationship—sometimes even before marriage. Poor communication before marriage is likely to continue after marriage. One study of premarital couples assessed individuals' feelings and attitudes toward communication in their relationships. The assessment focused on the level of comfort each partner felt in sharing feelings and in understanding each other. Couples who scored low on communication were more likely to be dissatisfied in their marriage or divorced 3 years later (Larsen & Olson, 1989).

Communication is also important for families across the family life cycle. When children arrive, the complexities of family life increase, and positive communication becomes even more important. One of the challenges for families is parent-adolescent communication. Often adolescents have more-negative perceptions than their parents of how well things are going in the family. A study of 540 families with adolescents found that families with open communication patterns and positive communication tended to be stronger. *Open communication* is the ability to share feelings and ideas with one another; *positive communication* is the extent to

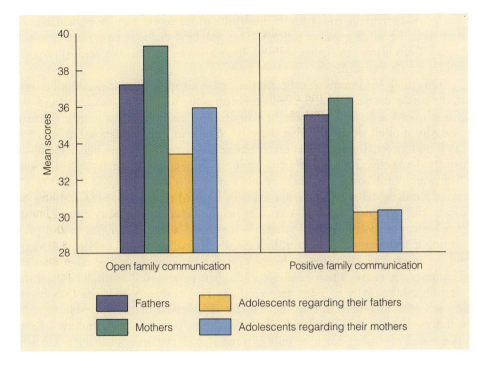

Figure 9.1 Parent-Adolescent Communication. *Source: Families: What Makes Them Work* (2nd ed.) (p. 233) by D. H. Olson, H. I. McCubbin, H. Barnes, A. Larsen, M. Muxen, M. Wilson, 1989, Los Angeles: Sage. Copyright © 1989 by Sage Publications. Used by permission of the publisher.

which communication lacks conflict and difficulties. Figure 9.1 shows that both mothers and fathers tended to rate the quality of communication between themselves and their teenagers higher than the teens rated the communication (Olson, McCubbin, et al., 1989).

Communication is a complex process, but understanding certain principles can help individuals improve their interactions with others. For example, it is useful to know that people send subtle verbal and nonverbal messages to each other no matter what they say or do, even when they aren't consciously trying to say or do anything. Therefore, one important principle of communication is that "you cannot *not* communicate." Noncommunication is also a form of communication.

Communication as a Cooperative Endeavor

Communication depends on both the skillful sending and the skillful receiving of messages. Believing that you sent a clear message is no guarantee that it was decoded (understood) in the way you intended. The only way to know whether the message you sent is what was received is to ask the other person what he or she heard. Having the receiver restate what was said tells the sender whether the message was understood.

When disagreement and conflicts arise, there is a natural tendency to blame the other person and deny or minimize personal responsibility for creating and maintaining the conflict. For example, a couple has an argument over the husband's refusal to discuss issues in the relationship that are important to the wife. The more she pushes him, the more the husband withdraws. He says to her, in effect, "I wouldn't withdraw so much if you stopped nagging me." To which the wife retorts, "I wouldn't nag you if you would discuss these important things with me."

The discussion finally ends with the husband's withdrawing even more, which only reinforces the wife's negative feelings. This potential dialogue ends in two monologues: Each blames the other for what has happened and neither accepts responsibility for the outcome.

One model of interpersonal communication assumes a linear cause and effect. In the battle just described, the husband blames the wife because she nags and the wife blames the husband because he withdraws. This is an example of the **linear causality model,** which says that there is a direct, or linear, relationship between cause and effect. Interpersonal communication that reflects this linear model is usually destructive rather than productive. Both people end up saying, in effect, "If it weren't for you, I wouldn't act this way."

A family systems model better explains both what has happened and how to escape this type of situation. According to the **circular causality model,** both people deny responsibility for what has happened and for changing it and preventing it from happening again. In a circular causality model, one person sends out a message, which causes a change in and a response from the other person. That response causes a new response in the first person, and so on. The communication cycle usually escalates into conflict. The husband's and wife's responses to each other's comments trap them in a vicious circle of causality: He says, "I withdraw because you nag," and she says, "I nag because you withdraw." Each spouse sees his or her behavior only as a reaction to the other's behavior, not as a determining factor in the other's response. In essence, they are both escalating the conflict.

It is best to avoid the "blame game" and to focus on working together to find solutions that are acceptable to everyone involved. Whereas blaming is a competitive endeavor in which one side tries to beat the other, genuine communication is a cooperative endeavor in which the participants focus on agreement. (See Chapter 10 for a detailed discussion of various approaches to conflict resolution.)

Content and Relationship Messages

When people communicate with each other, they send out two kinds of information. The most obvious component of communication is content—that is, the facts, opinions, and experiences people relate to one another. This is also called the *report* component of communication. The report component is usually relatively straightforward and for the most part is given verbally. The other component of communication is the message—that is, what the individual conveys about the relationship at hand—for example, whether it is a friendly relationship. This is called the *relationship*, or *command*, component of communication. More subtle than the report component, the relationship component is often conveyed nonverbally. Although the content of the message being communicated may be straightforward, it is always interpreted in light of the accompanying message about the relationship between the people involved in the communication.

Nonverbal Communication

In communicating with other people, it is important to pay close attention to nonverbal messages. In fact, some researchers estimate that nearly 65% of all face-to-face communication is nonverbal. It is ironic, then, that we select our words so

People send some of their most powerful messages nonverbally. With her head pushed forward aggressively, the corners of her mouth turned down, and her eyes set in a fixed stare, the woman on the right conveys an intense and intimidating presence. Her conversational partner responds by pulling her head back, smiling tentatively, and clasping her hands together. We don't know the content of their conversation, but we can guess something about their relationship.

carefully when they comprise only 35% of the communicated message and that we pay such little attention to the nonverbal messages we convey.

Verbal communication includes both spoken and written words. Spoken communication has various nonverbal aspects to it: tone of voice, volume, pitch, speed of speech, and rhythm of speech. Written communication also has nonverbal aspects: the style of writing (handwritten, printed, typed, sloppy, neat) and the medium (personal stationery, a card, a napkin; Argyle, 1988).

Nonverbal communication takes a wide variety of forms (Argyle, 1988). It includes facial expressions, eye contact, gestures and other body movements, spatial behavior (e.g., how far apart two people stand or sit from each other), body contact, nonverbal vocalizations (e.g., sighs, grunts), and posture. Nonverbal communication is just as difficult to interpret as verbal communication. Is that yawn boredom, or is it a reflexive action?

The relationship component of communication has a central influence on the accurate transmission and interpretation of nonverbal messages. For example, if you saw two people hugging at the airport, you would assume they have a close relationship. In other words, people make guesses about a relationship based on nonverbal behavior and the context in which they observe the behavior.

In a classic study, Daniel Sternberg and Ernest Beier (1977) examined nonverbal communication in married couples. Through the use of observational measures and written measures designed to assess each couple's level of couple harmony, the researchers were able to correlate characteristic nonverbal behaviors with certain types of marital relationships. They found that couples who had little disagreement during topical discussions tended to sit more closely together, touch each other more frequently, and engage in more eye contact than couples who experienced a great deal of disagreement during these discussions. Moreover, they found that when both the husband and the wife were described as high complainers (a label assigned by the researchers to those couples who complained and cast blame on each other), the couple sat farther apart, established minimal eye contact, and talked more than any other type of couple tested. Conversely, couples described as low complainers displayed the greatest amount of nonverbal affection and caring, including touching each other, assuming open-arm and open-leg postures, and maintaining eye contact.

Mixed Messages and Double Binds

People often send **mixed messages**—messages in which there is a discrepancy between the verbal and the nonverbal components. The receiver hears one thing but simultaneously feels something else. When the verbal and the nonverbal messages conflict, people tend to rely more on the nonverbal information. For example, a person collapses into his or her favorite chair to watch a favorite television show and says to another person, "Is there anything you want me to help you with now?" Although the verbal message conveys a willingness to help, the nonverbal actions express just the opposite. The person sending the message is hoping that the listener notices the discrepancy and responds to the nonverbal cues, enabling the speaker to watch the program while at the same time giving the impression of being willing to help out.

We all send mixed messages for a variety of reasons every day, but they often stem from an unwillingness to be direct and honest in our communication. Mixed messages can become a barrier to real understanding. Directness in communication minimizes misunderstanding and confusion.

Whereas a mixed message is a conflict between the verbal and the nonverbal components of a communication, a **double bind** occurs when the verbal and nonverbal messages (*interaction* component) relay information that causes some question or conflict about the relationship between the speaker and the receiver (the relationship component). The receiver is in a double bind when the speaker creates a situation—legitimate or not—that calls into question the type of relationship the receiver has with the speaker.

An example of a double bind is when one person tells a friend a secret and later learns from other people that the friend told them the secret. Because the supposed friend told a secret that was not to be shared, the speaker questions not only the trustworthiness of the friend but also the existence of the friendship. When one questions the relationship, one is caught in a double-bind situation.

Although a double bind can occur in any relationship, the probability of its occurring is greater if the relationship component is unclear. When the relationship between the two parties is established and clearly defined, the relationship component plays a less significant part in the interpretation of the message, and, consequently, the content can be more accurately understood. For example, if you said to someone, "You really are feebleminded," that message could be interpreted in a variety of ways, depending on the relationship you had with that person. If the person was a close friend, she or he would probably realize that you were just joking and might respond in a similar fashion. If, however, the other person was someone you just met, he or she might not only *not* know how to interpret what you said but also question whether she or he would want a relationship with you at all.

Furthermore, the potential for a double-bind message hinges on the quality and mood of a relationship. If a husband brings his wife flowers, for example, the way she interpret this behavior will depend on the mood of their current relationship. If she is feeling good about the relationship, she will likely interpret the flowers as a sign of affection. Depending on recent events, however, she might also see them as a bribe, an apology, or preparation for something to come. She might worry about what this act means, an indication that she is unsure or distrustful of her husband's behavior. Again, the interpretation depends on the quality and current mood of their relationship and on past experiences related to this event.

In summary, when the relationship between the two parties is established and clearly defined, the relationship component plays a less significant part in the interpretation of the message, and, consequently, the content is more accurately understood.

Metacommunication: Clarifying Your Communication

The original description of double-bind communications by Gregory Bateson (Bateson, Jackson, Haley, & Weakland, 1956) described a situation in which a mother visited her schizophrenic son in the hospital. When the man tried to embrace his mother, she stiffened, pulled away from him, and asked, "Don't you love me anymore?" On the verbal level she was implying love, but nonverbally she was rejecting him. Because of his dependent relationship with her, he was unable to respond verbally to the double-bind situation she had created.

The primary way of preventing or unbinding a double bind is known as **metacommunication**—simply, communicating about communicating. It is sometimes easier for children to pick up and respond to conflicting messages than it is for adults, as illustrated in this exchange: A man was talking with a 5-year-old boy he liked very much. The boy was describing how much he disliked girls. The man commented that he really liked girls but disliked boys. After a moment of perplexity, the boy responded, "You're teasing!"—and they both laughed. In spite of the conflicting message about their relationship, the child was able to understand and to point out the incongruence. Because the man acknowledged the discrepancy, they were both able to see the humor in the situation. It did not turn into a double bind.

It is often more difficult to respond to a double-bind message that occurs within a close and dependent relationship. Because of the significance of the relationship, the possibility exists that metacommunicating might create more problems. Paradoxically, the more dependent the relationship in which the double-bind messages occur, the greater the resistance to clarifying these messages. The dilemma is this: In order to improve a relationship, one must be willing to risk losing it. Consequently, the more one has invested in a relationship, the less willing one is to discuss or change it, even though change is often necessary if the relationship is to remain vital or to grow. Because many individuals are not willing to take this "existential risk," their relationships become increasingly predictable and routine.

When a couple wants to really connect with each other, they have to use all their communication skills—speaking honestly, listening attentively, requesting clarification, giving constructive feedback. Such efforts pay off in high-quality moments like the one this couple is enjoying.

Although double binds are usually seen as detrimental to a relationship, they can also prove beneficial. They can, first of all, create a situation in which one person feels the need for a clearer definition of the relationship. This can be accomplished by discussing the nature of the relationship directly, to clarify and possibly to renegotiate its nature.

Using Communication to Maintain Intimacy

Developing and maintaining communication skills are lifelong processes. Being good at communicating takes time, practice, and attention to detail. In this section we will focus on specific speaking and listening skills. Box 9.3 lists some key

Improving Your Communication Skills

1. *The foundation of all communication is effective listening.* There are a number of ways to enhance one's listening skills:

   a. Face your partner and maintain eye contact if at all possible.

   b. Provide appropriate nonverbal feedback—nod, smile, frown, and so forth.

   c. Don't interrupt; wait for the person to complete her or his message; avoid unsolicited advice, comments, and criticism.

   d. Use the "two-question" approach: Ask a question; listen to the answer; ask a second question in response to the answer. Following up on what the person is saying shows that you are interested.

   e. Use "how," "what," "where," and "when" questions instead of concentrating on "whys."

   f. The goal of questions is to better understand the other person's point of view, not to interrogate the person so blame can be affixed.

   g. Make sure your biases don't interfere with your listening skills.

2. *Take responsibility for your messages by using "I" statements and avoiding statements beginning with "you."*

3. *Make constructive requests which seek to change the way you interact with the other person.* Requests should: (a) begin with "I would like . . ." statements; (b) call for positive actions; (c) be respectful by using words like "please"; (d) be couched in the language of wants rather than needs.

4. *Consistently praise your partner for fulfilling your requests, and be sure to respond to your partner's requests.*

5. *Offer each other ongoing, positive feedback.* Negative feedback is likely to make things worse, but positive information will probably help keep the relationship open to positive change.

6. *Clarify your understanding of what your partner is saying by restating what you have heard or seen in your own words; ask your partner to confirm if you are understanding correctly.*

Source: Helping Couples Change (p. 97) by R. B. Stuart, 1980, New York: Guilford Press. Copyright 1980 by R. B. Stuart. Reprinted by permission of the publisher.

suggestions from psychologist Richard B. Stuart for improving your communication skills.

Speaking: The Art of Self-Disclosure

It is very important that as a speaker you speak for yourself, not for others. Communication problems often occur when a person tries to speak for another person, especially in a close relationship. Another way to avoid unnecessary friction is to stay away from *you should*s and *we*s. Again, the issue is one of power and control.

Self-disclosure occurs when an individual reveals to one or more people some personal information or feelings that they could not otherwise learn. We acquire information about an individual in many ways—from mutual acquaintances, from the person's behavior, and even from the clothes she or he wears. Self-disclosure differs from these other ways in that the individual willingly and with some forethought discloses the information. (Self-disclosure does sometimes also occur inadvertently.)

Self-disclosure requires both an awareness of information (reactions, goals, feelings, etc.) about oneself and a predisposition to disclose that information. For example, an adolescent may want to discuss her vocational goals with her parents, goals that do not include college. Her parents, however, are set on her going to a particular college. The daughter complies with her parents' wishes to avoid conflict and never discloses her true feelings about going to college. Thus, although she is aware of her feelings, her predisposition to disclose does not overcome her desire to avoid conflict.

Self-Disclosure and Intimacy   Patterns of self-disclosure vary with each type of relationship, but relationship type is not the sole determinant of self-disclosure. High and low levels of disclosure occur between strangers, friends, and intimates. But factors such as motivation for and frequency of disclosure are likely to be related to relationship type. Let's look at three different relationships—between strangers, between friends, and between intimates—and compare the patterns of self-disclosure among them.

If you were to ask your average city bus rider why he or she never reveals personal information to the bus driver, the answer you'd probably get is "that wouldn't seem right." What this means is that disclosure does not seem appropriate between people who don't really know each other. Personal disclosure to strangers seems inappropriate because there is no relationship history to serve as a foundation for the disclosure. There are, of course, exceptions to the general rule. When one stranger discloses to another, it may be because the discloser knows that he or she will never see the other person again and therefore feels there is little risk.

"I was on a plane trip from Texas to Chicago," related Lydia, a young art student. "I found myself seated next to a young man who, like myself, was a student. We talked casually for a few minutes, mentioning where we had spent our vacations. However, by the time the plane had reached cruising altitude, he began asking me questions about my relationship with my boyfriend, future plans for marriage, motivations for marrying, and a host of other pointed and personal questions.

"I was rather surprised to be asked to reveal such personal information, but I was even more surprised to find myself answering his questions. At first I was wriggling with discomfort at disclosing to a complete stranger. But although the questions were startling, his manner was not at all offensive. In fact, he seemed rather likable. As he also revealed some information about himself, I revealed more personal information and feelings to him. I guess I felt I had nothing to lose because I would never see him again."

Strangers also engage in self-disclosure in structured support groups such as Weight Watchers, Alcoholics Anonymous, or group psychotherapy. Here, self-disclosure is encouraged so that the group may help the person work through feelings related to a specific goal or task. Because the groups's purpose is to help the group member deal with problems that he or she might feel uncomfortable ex-

SALLY FORTH   BY GREG HOWARD

© 1997 Greg Howard. Reprinted with special permission of King Features Syndicate.

pressing in another situation, there is less concern about the appropriateness of self-disclosure.

Self-Disclosure in Friendships and Intimate Relationships Although self-disclosure is not expected between strangers, it is expected and desired between good friends. The discloser is usually aware of how the receiver will react to a disclosure, based on what has gone on previously in the relationship. Although self-disclosure between friends may be quite selective, it may also become quite intimate and personal as the friends increase their mutual trust and exclusivity. In a relationship between friends, self-disclosure increases the listener's obligations because the listener also feels compelled to self-disclose. Mutual disclosure helps the friendship develop more equally on both sides. Their close relationship and previous knowledge about each other allow friends to move quickly from impersonal to personal communication: One moment they may be talking about a mutual friend's wedding and the next about their personal feelings about their own marriages.

In some intimate relationships, including marriages and parent-child relationships, there is unfortunately less self-disclosure than in close friendships. Among married couples, partners often assume they know each other. Some even finish each other's sentences. But this assumption can be problematic, inhibiting communication. Also, couples often allow themselves only "leftover" time to share. At the end of the day, they may exchange pleasantries, review the day's activities, and talk about friends and the children, but they rarely take the time to talk with each other about their relationship, their hopes, and their dreams. Most married couples take their intimacy for granted. Consequently, they stop exploring new aspects of each other's personality and feelings. Some husbands and wives think that

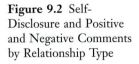

Figure 9.2 Self-Disclosure and Positive and Negative Comments by Relationship Type

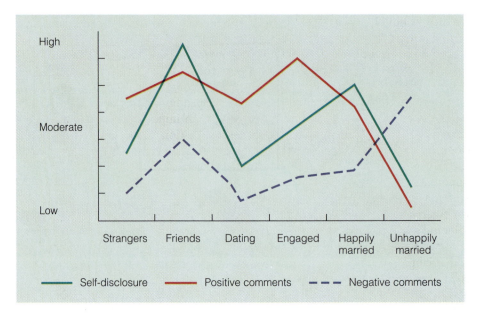

love alone will make the spouse understand all their needs and desires: "*If* she (he) loved me, she (he) would know what I want." However, spouses cannot guess their partner's inner feelings. Two people must *tell* each other what they need and want. Revealing new information allows the other partner to share in one's changes and increases the intimacy of the relationship. Failure to reveal changes can result in partners' "growing apart" from each other.

Figure 9.2 summarizes some research on self-disclosure, positive comments, and negative comments in various types of relationships. (The positive and negative comments were about the partner and sometimes about the relationship.) Interactions with strangers tend to involve low to moderate self-disclosure and many more positive than negative comments. The greatest degree of self-disclosure and a high level of positive comments are seen in close friendships, which are also characterized by a moderate amount of negative comments. Dating relationships tend to have a higher level of expression of positive feelings and lower levels of both self-disclosure and negative comments. As couples move toward engagement, positive comments are at their highest, and both self-disclosure and negative comments increase. Happily married couples tend to be moderate to high on both positive and negative comments, as well as on self-disclosure. In contrast, unhappily married couples are very low on positive comments, very low on self-disclosure, and very high on negative comments.

Listening: A Difficult Skill

We hear only half of what is said to us, understand only half of that, believe only half of that, and remember only half of that.

—Mignon McLaughlin, *journalist*

Comedian Lily Tomlin urges us to "listen with the same intensity reserved only for talking." If one communication skill could be considered a foundation for intimacy, it would be listening. A very perceptive person once said, "Listening is really a lot more fun. When I'm talking, I'm not learning a thing."

People have a tendency to judge one another, listening to what others say and then deciding whether they are "right" or "wrong." "Being right" usually means that we agree with the other person, and "being wrong," that we disagree with the other person. Good listening skills require suspending judgment and spending more energy trying to understand other people. An important listening skill is to restate the speaker's ideas and feelings for verification. Although this approach slows down communication, it minimizes misunderstanding and conflict. When the goal of communication is to control other people, listening skills are of little importance. If the goal is to connect with other people and to develop genuine emotional intimacy, however, listening is essential.

Sherod Miller and his colleagues consider listening to be the process of developing a full understanding of another person's "story" (situation, concern, point of view). Effective listeners are aware of and make choices about how much they will attempt to direct or influence the speaker's telling of the story. Miller and his colleagues noted that the listener's motives are paramount and identified three basic motives, or goals, among listeners: (1) to lead by persuading, (2) to clarify by directing, and (3) to discover by attending (Miller & Miller, 1997).

The distinguishing factor of each of these three listening motives is the degree of control, or power, the listener desires over the situation. Does the listener follow the leader, allowing the speaker to relate the story in her or his own way? Or does the listener become the leader—getting the speaker to tell the story in the way the listener wants to hear it? Either approach affects the quality and integrity of the information that is exchanged.

Persuasive listening is hardly listening at all; the "listener" is really looking for an opening to jump in and control the direction of the conversation. Sometimes the persuader resembles a television reporter trying hard to get that 10-to-15-second sound bite for the evening news.

Directive listening involves less control than persuasive listening, but it does attempt to channel, or direct, the conversation. Studies indicate that excellent salespeople (those most likely to make the sale) ask four times as many questions as the average salesperson asks (Miller & Miller, 1997). The questions control the direction of the conversation, steering it where the directive listener wants it to go. Directive listening has certain advantages. It quickly focuses a conversation, and if the speaker cooperates, it allows the directive questioner to take charge of the dialogue. The major disadvantage of directive listening, however, is that in the interest of efficiency, crucial elements of the story may be lost. Directive listeners who use the approach in a very curt manner often fail to really understand what they are being told. By controlling the direction of the conversation, the directive listener may also lead the speaker down a blind alley into a trap.

Attentive listening is a mode in which the listener simply lets the speaker tell the story spontaneously and without interruption, encouraging rather than directing the teller. Busy people sometimes feel that attentive listening is too time-consuming. In fact, it is more efficient than the other approaches because it lets the speaker get to the *real* point, avoiding misunderstanding and confusion. It is clearly the must effective listening mode for building rapport and trust.

Attentive listening is a rare skill worth cultivating. It not only builds trust and intimacy in a relationship but also most efficiently allows a speaker to get her point across—without interruption or distraction.

"I hope I don't sound immodest," said Francis, a retired newspaper editor in Charlotte, North Carolina, "but I think the main reason people have always liked me over the years is because I'm a good listener. I really enjoy hearing what other people have to say. I don't have any desire to sit in judgment of them, or to feel superior, or to give out a lot of advice. I simply like to listen and try to understand how their world works. It's always very interesting.

"People take this as a supreme compliment. They smile when they see me coming, and they're always coming up to me to tell me the latest story about their lives because they know I'll appreciate it if it's funny or sympathize with them if it's sad. It's really kind of fun. I always know what's happening, more than anyone else I know. My ability to listen served me well all those years in the newspaper business, too."

Assertive, Passive, and Aggressive Communication

Researchers have identified three styles of responses in interpersonal communication: passive, aggressive, and assertive (Alberti & Emmons, 1990). Each response style has effects on both the respondent and the partner. Assertive statements were consistently found to be the most accurate, expressive, self-enhancing, and productive in terms of achieving a goal.

Assertive communication involves the expression of thoughts, feelings, and desires as one's right as an individual. Because it is self-expressive, assertive com-

CATHY   BY CATHY GUISEWITE

munication frequently uses the personal pronouns *I* and *me.* Assertiveness is associated with feelings of self-esteem, self-confidence, and determination to express opinions or feelings. Assertiveness, in sum, is giving yourself the right to be who you are without infringing on the rights of your partner to be who he or she is. Assertiveness enables people to feel good about themselves and increases the likelihood of achieving personal goals. Because assertiveness encourages expressiveness rather than defensiveness, it facilitates intimacy between partners.

Passive communication is characterized by an unwillingness to say what one thinks, feels, or wants. Passive behavior is frequently associated with feelings of anxiety about others' opinions, overconcern about the feelings of others ("I just didn't want to hurt her"), and fears about saying or doing anything that can be criticized ("I was afraid of saying the 'wrong' thing"). Passive responses reinforce feelings of low self-esteem, limit expressiveness, leave a well of hurt and anxious feelings, and make achievement of personal goals unlikely. Receivers of passive responses often feel anger at and lack of respect for the sender, realizing that their goals have been achieved at the sender's expense. Passive behavior does little to enhance either person's feelings about oneself or the other and creates distance rather than intimacy.

Aggressive communication aims to hurt or put down another person and to protect the self-esteem of the aggressor. Aggressive statements are characterized by blame and accusation ("You always . . . ," "You never . . ."). Aggressive behavior is associated with intense, angry feelings and thoughts of getting even. When people act in an aggressive manner with their partners, it reinforces the notion that the partner is to blame for the aggressor's frustration, that it is the partner's responsibility to make things "right." Aggressiveness is expressive behavior, but it is all too often self-enhancing at the other's expense. Goals may be achieved, but

Table 9.3 Communication Patterns and Intimacy

COMMUNICATION PATTERN		RELATIONSHIP	WHO WINS	LEVEL OF INTIMACY
Person A	**Person B**			
Passive	Passive	Devitalized/boring	Both lose	Low
Passive	Aggressive	Dominated	I win, you lose	Low
Aggressive	Aggressive	Conflicted	Both lose	Low
Assertive	Assertive	Vital/growing	Both win	High

only by hurting and humiliating the other. The partner may also retaliate in kind. Because aggressive behavior focuses on the negative aspects of people rather than the negative aspects of the "situation," it generally escalates in negative spirals, leaving both partners feeling hurt and frustrated and creating distance in the relationship.

Assertiveness, passiveness, and aggressiveness are not personality traits; they are types of responses or behaviors. In most cases, it is inappropriate to label oneself or another an assertive, passive, or aggressive person. Some people use certain types of behaviors in specific situations or with certain people. For example, some women report that they have difficulty expressing their feelings or desires assertively in sexual relationships.

Because passive and aggressive responses affect intimacy negatively, becoming aware of the kinds of situations that elicit these nonintimate behaviors can enable individuals to practice more assertive responses. Table 9.3 illustrates how various communication patterns affect intimacy. For example, if both Person A and Person B have a passive style of communication, the relationship is likely to be devitalized and boring. In a conflict, both tend to lose because neither makes an effort to say what he or she thinks or wants. And in the end, the level of intimacy in the relationship is low, and the relationship is unsatisfying to both. Intimacy has the best chance of growing when both persons are assertive, because this combination of response styles creates a win-win situation. (Box 9.4 offers some excellent suggestions for improving intimacy through communication.)

Positive and Negative Communication Cycles

A recent study of over 15,000 married couples revealed that a positive communication cycle involves assertiveness and self-confidence and that a negative communication cycle is characterized by avoidance and partner dominance (Olson, 1997). The definition of assertiveness, self-confidence, avoidance, and partner dominance are as follows:

Assertiveness is a person's ability to express his or her feelings and desires to a partner.

Self-confidence is a measure of how a person feels about herself or himself and the ability to control things in her or his life.

B O X   9 . 4

Using Communication to Increase Intimacy

- Look for the good in your partner, and give him or her compliments.

- Praise your partner as much as possible.

- Take time to listen, listen, listen.

- Listen to understand, not to judge.

- After listening carefully, summarize your partner's comments before you share your reactions or feelings.

- Share your feelings by using "I" statements (i.e., "I feel" or "I think").

- When issues arise, avoid blaming each other, and talk directly about how to deal with the issue differently.

- If issues persist, focus on creating as many new solutions as you can, and then try them one at a time.

- If problems still persist, seek counseling early, when it's easier to find solutions.

- Give your relationship the priority and attention you did when you were dating.

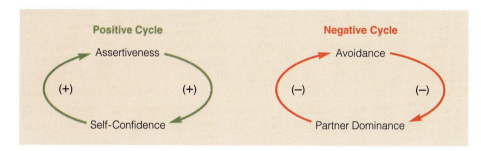

Figure 9.3 Positive and Negative Communication Cycles

Avoidance is a person's tendency to minimize issues and a reluctance to deal with issues directly.

Partner dominance is the degree to which a person feels his or her partner tries to be controlling and dominant in their relationship.

In a positive communication cycle, as people become more assertive with their partner, they also tend to become more self-confident. This occurs, in part, because assertiveness often enables people to get more of what they want from others. Getting more of what they want tends to make them feel more self-confident. And as they gain more self-confidence, they tend to be more willing to be assertive. This positive cycle illustrates how communication skills can help people develop more positive feelings about each other (Figure 9.3).

In a negative communication cycle, as one person avoids making decisions, the other partner will take over and become more dominant, and as one partner becomes more dominant, the other partner may further withdraw (i.e., become avoidant). The combination of avoidance and partner dominance creates the negative communication cycle.

Research has found that couples in which both partners are assertive and self-confident tend to have very happy marriages. Conversely, couples in which one partner is dominant and the other is avoidant tend to have unhappy marriages.

Table 9.4 People High in Assertiveness
• Low in avoidance ($r = -.72$)
• Low in partner dominance ($r = -.50$)
• Like personality of partner ($r = .49$)
• Feel good about communication with partner ($r = .77$)
• Feel good about conflict resolution with partner ($r = .68$)

The Positive Influence of Assertiveness

Assertive communication involves the expression of thoughts, feelings, and desires as one's right. It is self-focused and, therefore, favors "I" statements rather than "you" statements. An assertive person is able to ask for what she or he wants without demanding it or infringing on the rights of others. Assertive people tend to feel better about themselves because they are able to express themselves.

One goal in helping a couple improve their relationship is to try to help both people become more assertive with each other. Increasing assertiveness tends to increase each person's self-confidence and decrease avoidance and perceived partner dominance. Assertiveness generally has a positive impact on the person and on a couple's relationship.

Research has found a correlation (r) between assertiveness and the following personal and relational benefits (Table 9.4). As people became more assertive with their partner, they tended to be lower in avoidance ($r = -.72$) and lower in partner dominance ($r = -.50$). They also tended to like the personality of their partner more ($r = .49$) and to feel good about their communication with their partner ($r = .77$) and about how they resolved conflict with their partner ($r = .68$; Olson, 1997).

In general, assertive individuals feel better about their partner and their relationship than nonassertive individuals. When both persons are assertive with each other, the level of intimacy increases because both partners are able to ask for what they want and, thereby, increase the probability that they will get what they want.

The Negative Influence of Avoidance

Avoidance, or a person's unwillingness or inability to deal with problematic issues, tends to be highest in people who are passive or nonassertive. Conversely, people who are very assertive tend to be low on avoidance.

Increasing evidence suggests avoidance creates problems in close relationships. John Gottman (1994), a prominent researcher on marriage, describes the *avoidant style* in his book *Why Marriages Succeed or Fail*. According to Gottman, avoidant couples often minimize conflict by *agreeing to disagree*. Another common technique that avoidant couples use is *stonewalling*—shutting out the other person and not responding to them.

In a couple skills program called PREP (Prevention and Relationship Enhancement Program), developed by Howard Markman and Scott Stanley (1994), counselors discovered that avoidance was very problematic for couples. In their book *Fighting for Your Marriage* (1996), Markman and Stanley describe the process of avoidance. They define avoidance as the reluctance to have any discussion that would raise problematic issues. When couples regularly avoid talking about risky

Table 9.5 People High in Avoidance
• Low in assertiveness ($r = -.72$)
• High in partner dominance ($r = .62$)
• Dislike personality of partner ($r= -.59$)
• Dislike communication with partner ($r = -.66$)
• Dislike conflict resolution with partner ($r = -.71$)

issues, this is a sign that avoidance is becoming a more common style that will lead to problems in the long run.

Researchers have found a positive correlation between avoidance and partner dominance ($r = .62$); this means that the more a person uses avoidance, the more they perceive their partner as dominant (Table 9.5). People who are high on avoidance also tend to perceive their relationship with their partner in more negative terms. One study found that people high in avoidance tended to dislike the personality of their partner ($r = -.59$) and did not feel good about the way they communicated ($r = -.66$) or resolved conflict ($r = -.71$) with their partner (Olson, 1997).

In summary, it appears that assertiveness has a very positive impact on a couple's relationship, whereas avoidance has a negative influence. Learning assertiveness tends to help people overcome the more negative style of avoidance, so the more both people in a relationship can help each other become assertive with each other, the greater chance they will have in building each other's self-confidence and decreasing their feeling of being dominated by their partner. Couples in which both partners are high in assertiveness and self-confidence will feel better about their communication, how they resolve conflict, and, ultimately, how happy they are with their relationship.

Summary

- Communication, the process of sharing messages, is an integral part of intimacy.

- In a national survey of couple communication strengths, happy couples agreed more often than unhappy couples that they were satisfied with how they talked to each other as partners, had no trouble believing each other, felt their partner did not make comments that put them down, were not afraid to ask their partner for what they wanted, and felt free to express their true feelings to their partner.

- The top five communication issues identified by couples in a national survey were the following: they felt their partner did not understand them; they wished their partner would share his or her feelings; they were afraid to share negative feelings for fear their partner would become angered; they felt their partner gave them the silent treatment; and they felt their partner made comments that put them down.

- Men and women tend to have different communication styles as a result of culturally established gender roles. Although communication styles can vary greatly from one individual to another, in general, men tend to be more competitive in their communication and women tend to be more focused on connecting emotionally with others.

- Basic principles of communication include the following: one cannot *not* communicate; the message sent is often not the message received; when communication fails, both people are to blame; all messages convey both content information and relationship information; nonverbal communication carries about 65% of the meaning in an interpersonal exchange; incongruent verbal and nonverbal communication can cause misunderstanding; and metacommunication (talking about talking) is useful for unbinding double binds.

- Self-disclosure—individual revelations of personal information or feelings—is a key to the development of intimacy.

- Listening is the process of developing a full understanding of another person's "story" (situation, concern, point of view). Persuasive listeners and directive listeners try to control the conversation. Attentive listeners aim at fully understanding the other person's point of view, an approach that encourages the development of genuine intimacy.

- Assertive communication assumes that expressing thoughts, feelings, and desires is the right of the individual. Passive communication is characterized by an unwillingness to say what one thinks, feels, or wants. Aggressive communication aims at hurting or putting down the other person.

- Assertiveness and self-confidence are key elements of a positive communication cycle. A negative communication cycle is characterized by avoidance and partner dominance.

- The more assertive, and less avoidant partners are, the more satisfying their relationship will be.

Key Terms

communication	metacommunication	passive communication
linear causality model	self-disclosure	aggressive communication
circular causality model	persuasive listening	
nonverbal communication	directive listening	assertiveness
	attentive listening	self-confidence
mixed message	assertive communication	avoidance
double bind		partner dominance

Activities

1. Study Jane Tear's chart, "Conversational Style and Gender," in Box 9.1. In small groups, discuss the hypothesis that men tend to use conversation in a competitive way in an effort to "win," whereas women tend to use conversation to build relationships. Is this true, or is it a stereotype? What are the values and limitations of each style?

2. Because males and females are socialized differently, adult male culture differs somewhat from adult female culture. What can parents do for their children in the early years to minimize confusion and misunderstanding between the sexes later on?

3. Use the Couple and Family Scales in Resource Section A to rate the communication in your family of origin now or at some time in the past. Identify the most positive and most negative aspects of that communication.

4. Use the Couple and Family Scales in Resource Section A to rate the communication at various stages of a current relationship (friendship, dating, cohabiting, marriage). How has the communication changed over time on each aspect of the scale?

5. Focus on assertive, passive, and aggressive behavior in this exercise. Form groups of four. Two people will role-play the following styles for 2 to 3 minutes while the other two people observe. After each segment, discuss what it felt like to play the assigned role or to observe the role-playing. When your group has role-played all three styles, compare and contrast the various styles.

   a. Assertive and assertive (both people are assertive)

   b. Passive and aggressive (one person acts passive; one acts aggressive)

   c. Assertive and passive (one acts assertive; one acts passive)

Suggested Readings

Alberti, R. E., & Emmons, M. L. (1990). *Your perfect right: A guide to assertive living.* San Luis Obispo, CA: Impact. Tips for learning to express oneself in direct, assertive ways, without being aggressive.

Cupach, W. R., & Spitzberg, B. H. (Eds.). (1994). *The dark side of interpersonal communication.* Hillsdale, NJ: Erlbaum. An exploration of family violence, distressed marital relationships, paradoxes, equivocation, conversational dilemmas, double binds, and so forth.

Lerner, H. G. (1993). *The dance of deception: Pretending and truth-telling in women's lives.* New York: HarperCollins. From sexual faking to family secrets, reveals how the struggle to tell the truth is at the center of women's deepest longing for intimacy, authenticity, and self-regard. The third volume in the author's trilogy, which includes *The Dance of Anger* and *The Dance of Intimacy.*

Miller, S., & Miller, P. A. (1997). *Core communication: Skills and processes.* Littleton, CO: Interpersonal Communication Programs. An excellent, practical, and readable guide to better communication and the development of intimacy.

Parker Pen Co. (1985). *Do's and taboos around the world.* Elmsford, NY: Benjamin. A fun collection of examples and anecdotes illustrating how communication and cultural practices around the world differ greatly; fosters understanding of and sensitivity to these differences.

Rugel, R. P. (1997). *Husband-focused marital therapy: An approach to dealing with marital distress.* Springfield, IL: Thomas. Focuses on how a marital therapist can help couples who have communication problems related to gender socialization, especially wives who are angry at their husbands for lack of emotional support and husbands who have been socialized to be emotionally inexpressive and autonomous and become defensive and unappreciative of their wife's relational orientation.

Tannen, D. (1990). *You just don't understand: Women and men in conversation.* New York: Morrow. Analysis by a communication specialist of the ways in which women and men talk differently and how these differences can lead to difficulty; useful couples reading.

Tannen, D. (1993). *Gender and conversational interaction.* New York: Oxford University Press. For readers who want a more academic approach to male/female differences in communication than Tannen's earlier work.

CHAPTER 10

Conflict and Conflict Resolution

Because people view the world from a wide variety of perspectives and have different goals, conflict is an inevitable part of intimate human relationships. In fact, the more intimate our relationships, the more chances there are for interpersonal conflict. Although conflict may be "normal" in a statistical sense, it does not have to escalate into verbal and physical violence. There are many constructive approaches to settling disagreements.

In this chapter we will begin with the results of a national survey (Olson et al., 1999) that identified the strengths of happily married couples versus unhappily married couples in how they resolve conflict. We will also review the five major conflict-resolution issues reported by couples in this survey. These data set the stage for the rest of the chapter, in which we will discuss conflict and anger and the relationship between intimacy and conflict. We will also explore sixteen rules for fair fighting and some basic approaches for constructive versus destructive conflict resolution.

Couple Strengths and Issues in Conflict Resolution

The results from a national survey of happy and unhappy married couples revealed the most common strengths for happy couples regarding conflict resolution (Olson et al., 1999). The most significant item distinguishing happy couples (69%) from unhappy couples (13%) was the ability to resolve differences. The survey also found that happy couples are also more than three times as likely (79%) as unhappy couples (25%) to feel understood by their partners when discussing problems. Happy couples reported more often (65%) than unhappy couples (19%) that they can tell their partner what is bothering them during an argument. Happy couples also agreed more often (58%) than unhappy couples (20%) on the best way to solve disagreements. Finally, happy couples were more than twice as likely (68%) as unhappy couples (33%) to agree that one partner does not end up feeling as though a problem is solely his or her fault (Table 10.1).

In terms of the most common conflict-resolution issues for couples, the national sample of 26,442 married couples revealed that a majority (73%) of married couples sometimes have serious disputes over unimportant issues (Olson et al., 1999; Table 10.2). Sixty-seven percent of the couples reported that their differences never seem to get resolved, and many couples (66%) differed on how to resolve their disagreements. Many couples (64%) said they cannot tell their partner what is bothering them when having a problem, and over half (58%) of the couples reported that they go out of their way to avoid conflict with their partner.

Conflict and Anger: An Overview

If conflict is not resolved, it continues to grow. In this section we will focus on the hierarchical process of conflict and discuss the value of early decision making in preventing problems and crises. We will explore some myths and taboos that limit our ability to express anger in a constructive manner and prevent us from establishing intimate relationships.

Table 10.1 Conflict-Resolution Strengths of Happy Versus Unhappy Married Couples

STRENGTH	PERCENTAGE OF COUPLES IN AGREEMENT	
	Happy Couples (*n* = 7,116)	Unhappy Couples (*n* =13,421)
Are usually able to resolve their differences.	69	13
Understand each other when discussing problems.	79	25
Feel free to express their concerns and feelings when having problems.	65	19
Have similar ideas about the best way to solve disagreements.	58	20
Share responsibility for problems.	68	33

Source: Adapted from Olson, Fye, & Olson, 1999.

Table 10.2 Top Five Conflict-Resolution Issues for Married Couples

ISSUE	PERCENTAGE OF COUPLES WITH PROBLEMS SURROUNDING ISSUE (*N* = 26,442)
Have serious disputes over unimportant issues.	73
Are unable to resolve differences.	67
Have differing ideas about the best way to solve disagreements.	66
Are unable to voice concerns or feelings when faced with a problem.	64
Have a tendency to go out of their way to avoid conflict with their partner.	58

Source: Adapted from Olson, Fye, & Olson, 1999.

The Hierarchy of Conflict

The hierarchy of conflict, illustrated in Figure 10.1, can be thought of as a continuum, ranging from discussions of daily events to crises. The lowest three levels in the conflict hierarchy represent common reasons for individuals to get together to have a discussion: to chat about daily events, to discuss ideas, and to express feelings. These discussions generally operate at a low level of tension and usually entail little or no pressure for making decisions. The next four levels in the hierarchy involve increasing tension and the need for a decision. An awareness of the need for a decision precedes decision making. If a decision that should be made is not made, this could lead to the development of a problem, which would then need to be solved. If the problem is not solved, it could lead to a crisis, which is more difficult to resolve.

Figure 10.1 The Hierarchy of Conflict

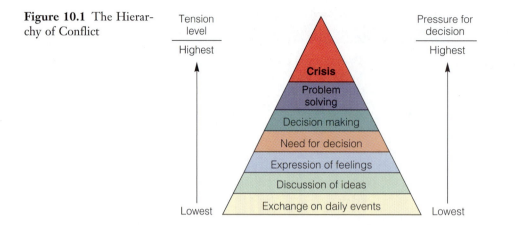

As an example of the hierarchical process of conflict, let's consider a couple, Joanne and Gary, who need to make a decision about birth control. The process involves three phases: the decision-making phase, the problem-solving phase, and the crisis-resolution phase.

Decision-Making Phase   If Joanne and Gary are aware that they need birth control, then they need to make a decision about the type of method(s) to use. If they are not aware, then they won't make a decision; this could lead to pregnancy (a potential problem), and an unwanted pregnancy could become a crisis. Even if they are aware of the need for a decision, however, they may not be willing or able to make a decision, which could also lead to crisis. In other words, deciding not to decide *is* in fact a decision, but it is one that often produces undesirable consequences. Even if they do make a decision, it may be either effective or ineffective. An effective decision might be to use the birth control pill, which would greatly minimize the chance of an unwanted pregnancy. An ineffective decision would be to choose, say, the rhythm method as their sole form of birth control.

Problem-Solving Phase   Problems can arise for Joanne and Gary if they made no decision or if the decision they made was ineffective. If Joanne becomes pregnant and neither Gary nor Joanne wants to have a baby, they have reached the problem level. In the problem-solving phase, Joanne could consider whether to have an abortion. If she does not want an abortion or fails to decide within 3 months, the problem becomes more serious.

Crisis-Resolution Phase   Not dealing with the unwanted pregnancy could lead Joanne and Gary into a crisis. A crisis has the highest level of tension and creates the most pressure for a decision. Both tension and pressure increase the difficulty of making an adequate decision. The failure to make a decision earlier (to decide, for example, on a type of birth control) or the failure to make an effective decision (deciding, for example, to use a lower-risk method of birth control) forces Joanne and Gary to make a more difficult decision (whether to have the child or an abortion, whether to get married, whether to relinquish the child for adoption).

If this couple is in a situation that requires a decision, they should deal with it as early as possible. When decisions are avoided, problems arise; when problems are ignored, crises develop.

One would expect Joanne and Gary to be aware of potential problems and to therefore make an early, effective decision to prevent problems and avert crisis. However, many individuals, couples, and families put off making easier, less complex preventive decisions. As a result, they are later faced with problems or crisis situations. This hierarchy of conflict model illustrates the sequential flow toward crisis and points up the importance of awareness and early decision making in preventing problems and crises.

Anger and Conflict Taboos

Most couples are afraid of negative emotions—anger, resentment, jealousy, bitterness, hurt, disgust, and hatred—and have a difficult time learning how to deal with them. A common tactic is to suppress negative emotions, hoping they will disappear with time. There are two predominant reasons for suppressing negative emotions (Crosby, 1991). One is sociological in nature; the other is psychological.

Our culture and many others have a taboo against the expression of anger. This message, transmitted verbally and nonverbally from generation to generation, says that nice and competent people do not show anger, that anger is wrong, and that anger indicates that something is terribly wrong in a relationship. This message requires individuals to deny their genuine feelings and keeps them from being in touch with their true emotions.

"I don't know what to do or think anymore," said Doris, married for 5 years to Edward. "I know he loves me . . . I guess. He's just got so many rules he lives by, and so many rules I'm supposed to live by and the kids are supposed to live by. Maybe it's easier for him to live by these rules. Maybe he doesn't really think about them. I don't know. I just can't live by them anymore. The tension in me is volcanic. I find myself crying uncontrollably sometimes. I never have been able to express my feelings. My body expresses them. And now my feelings have built up so I can't seem to keep from exploding."

The psychological reason for suppressing negative emotions has to do with human insecurity. Individuals think, "If I let other people know what I am really thinking and who I really am, they won't love me and I will be abandoned." In intimate relationships, partners struggle to find a delicate balance between dependence on each other and independence from each other. Some observers call that balance *interdependence*. In families, too, children and adolescents struggle to differentiate themselves from their parents and their siblings, to stake out territory and beliefs that are their own. People search for individuality while at the same time trying to maintain close relationships.

Some couples have been socialized to believe that all disagreements in a relationship are wrong. Some falsely assume that the essence of marriage is harmony at any price. Such beliefs can be devastating to a relationship in the long run.

> "When I was growing up, my parents gave me the impression that fighting was wrong in a happy family and that kids should be shielded from it," said Drew, a 30-year-old man from a Catholic background. "When they wanted to have a good argument, they would wait until we kids were out of the house or asleep. I grew up believing that my mom and dad never fought.
>
> "Estelle, my wife, is from an alcoholic family. Her father would get drunk and pull the telephone cord out of the wall, push her mom around, and hit the kids. The meeting of these two approaches to conflict in one marriage was quite perilous for a number of years. My wife sometimes pushed and pushed until I blew up. I would try to hold in my anger, but eventually I couldn't stand it any longer. One evening I got so mad I picked up a hamper full of clothes and was going to throw it at her."

Fortunately, Drew and Estelle were both intelligent, creative, and committed to the marriage. They stuck with each other long enough to find out how to face and deal with conflict in a positive and productive way.

People tend to have negative attitudes toward conflict due to the popular assumption that love is the opposite of hate. Love and hate are both intense feelings. Rather than being opposites, however, they are more like two sides of the same coin. The line between the two is a fine one, with feelings of love often preceding those of hate. Nevertheless, when negative feelings are stifled, positive feelings also die. People often say, "I don't feel anything toward my spouse anymore. Not love or hate. I'm just indifferent." Indifference—lack of feeling—is the opposite of anger and love and hate. In the words of one loving father about his children, "If I didn't give a damn, I wouldn't get mad." Anger and love are connected; we often are angriest with the ones we love.

Rollo May described the dynamic connection between love and hate when he said:

> A curious thing which never fails to surprise persons in therapy is that after admitting their anger, animosity, and even hatred for a spouse and berating him or her during the hour, they end up with feelings of love toward this partner. A patient may have come in smoldering with negative feelings but resolved, partly unconsciously, to keep these as a good gentleman does, to himself; but he finds that he represses the love for the partner at the same time as he suppresses his ag-

gression. . . . The positive cannot come out until the negative does also. . . . Hate and love are not polar opposites; they go together. (1969)

Myths, Theories, and Facts About Anger

In all matters of opinion, our adversaries are insane.
—MARK TWAIN

Bill Borcherdt (1989, 1993, 1996, 1998) offered an insightful perspective in his discussion of anger: "Of all the human emotions, anger has created the most harm and caused the greatest destruction within individuals, couples, families, and between social groups and nations" (1989, p. 53). Anger is a double-edged sword; just as it is directed at others, so it becomes internalized by the angry individual. As Borcherdt put it: "It is impossible to hate, despise, or resent somebody without suffering oneself." Although anger can sometimes make people feel good, it can also make them feel guilty and less positive about themselves.

Anger can also produce a feeling of strength and power. It deludes people into thinking that they are doing something constructive about the problems they face, when actually they are only making things worse. Anger lets people substitute feelings of superiority for those of hurt and rejection. It also allows them to think anything they want about another person without fear of retaliation.

Four common but false beliefs about anger are that it is externally caused, that it is best to express anger openly and directly, that it can be a helpful and beneficial emotion, and that it will prevent other people from taking advantage of you (Borcherdt, 1989). Let's take a closer look at these beliefs.

- *Anger is caused by others.* Many people believe that "somebody or something outside of you magically gets into your gut and makes you angry or gets you upset" (Borcherdt, 1989, p. 54). One's happiness or unhappiness, however, is not externally caused, Borcherdt points out. Anger, like any other human emotion, is self-created, usually when someone else does something we don't like.

- *The best way to deal with anger is to let it all out.* Although venting anger may make people feel better for the moment, it won't help them get any better. Letting it all out does not resolve the underlying issues. In fact, it tends to bring out those same feelings in others, increasing both people's anger.

- *Anger is a beneficial emotion.* Individuals may find in the short run that they get their way by getting angry, but in the long run they will push others away from them or provoke them to get even.

- *You're a wimp if you don't get angry.* Some people believe that if they don't get angry, others will take advantage of them or consider them weak and inferior. Borcherdt urges people to decide how they want to feel, rather than how someone else is going to make them feel. Firm and assertive statements, such as "I disagree" or "I don't like that," let us take more control of situations. We do not have to get angry; we choose to get angry—and we can therefore choose a different approach.

Other common myths and facts about anger appear in Box 10.1.

BOX 10.1

Anger: Myths and Facts

Facts

- Anger is a feeling, with psychological components.

- Anger is universal among human beings.

- The nonexpression of anger leads to an increased risk of coronary disease.

- The venting of anger— "catharsis"—is of value only when it sets the stage for resolution.

- Aggression leads to further aggression, not resolution.

- Most anger is directed toward those close to us, not toward strangers.

- Depression, shyness, and suicide are expressions of anger at oneself.

Myths

- Venting (by yelling or pounding pillows) "releases" anger and therefore "deals with" it.

- Women get less angry than men.

- Some people never get angry.

- Anger always results from frustration.

- Aggressive behavior is a sure sign of an "angry person."

- TV violence, active sports, and/or competitive work "releases" anger.

Source: Adapted from *Your Perfect Right: A Guide to Assertive Living* (6th ed.) (p. 107), © by Robert E. Alberti and Michael L. Emmons, 1990, San Luis Obispo, CA: Impact. Adapted by permission of Impact Publishers, Inc., P.O. Box 1094, San Luis Obispo, CA 94306.

Intimacy and Conflict

Someone once joked, "The major cause of divorce is marriage." Living together as a couple can be one of the most difficult challenges people face in life. In this section we will focus on how intimacy and conflict are bound together, the difficult balance between love and anger, the dance of anger that couples and families perform, and the sources of conflict in intimate relationships. We will also look at the significance of anger in all intimate relationships.

Intimacy Breeds Conflict

The more one knows about another person, the more possibilities there are for disagreement and dislike. If a relationship is to survive and thrive, each of these differences has to be worked through in some way. Folk wisdom tells us that "you always hurt the ones you love." Sociologists who have studied violence in America tell us that statistically, it is safer to be with strangers than with your spouse or lover. Police officers report that domestic calls are among the most dangerous calls they respond to.

George Bach and Peter Wyden (1969) argue in their book *The Intimate Enemy: How to Fight Fair in Love and Marriage* that verbal conflict is not only acceptable but highly desirable if it is constructive. According to Bach and Wyden, couples who fight together stay together, provided they know how to fight properly. Couples who don't fight and therefore don't resolve issues can become

FEIFFER®

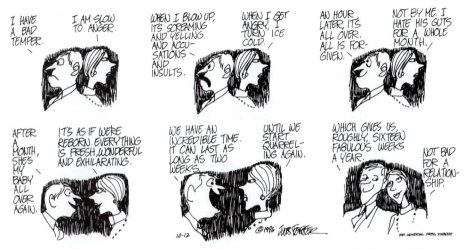

emotionally distanced from each other. Bach and Wyden's approach to conflict generated controversy when it first appeared; many felt the idea was too radical. However, the approach has helped many couples by encouraging them to discuss issues openly rather than denying them and assuming they would fade over time.

Love and Anger in Balance

In marriage counseling, couples commonly bring up the issue of balancing separateness and togetherness (the cohesion dimension on the Couple and Family Map. The challenge—or *growing edge* as family therapists call it—for couples is to preserve "a comfortable balance between the freedom of the individual partners to act independently and to develop their own individual patterns and abilities, while at the same time enjoying the rewards of a deeply shared life" (p. 113). With too much togetherness, marriage becomes a form of bondage. With too much separateness, the relationship dies from lack of attention.

Love and anger must also be kept in balance. "In every marriage the two dynamic forces are love, which seeks to draw the couple together, and anger, which tends to drive them apart" (Mace, 1982b, p. 115). Anger can be a healthy emotion if it helps a couple create an interdependent relationship.

Anger becomes an ally of the partners when they use it to attend to those areas in the relationship that need work. If the partners do not find a constructive way to use anger, however, they may gradually drift apart. The common divorce scenario is not one of fireworks but one of a gradual loss of closeness (Mace, 1982b, p. 116). In short, fear of anger can lead to disengagement, and disengagement can lead to emotional divorce, which often leads to legal divorce.

In a mature marriage, anger is seen not as an enemy but as a friend. Nevertheless, partners must use it carefully and at appropriate times. Experts suggest that couples make a contract never to attack each other when angry (Mace, 1982b,

p. 116). Feelings of anger signal that something is not right with the relationship. Rather than act on these feelings as they arise, partners should wait until they have calmed down and cooled off to calmly and rationally work things out. In other words, if they use anger as a barometer to signal an impending storm, partners can work together to prevent major damage to the relationship.

The Dance of Anger

It is our job to state our thoughts and feelings clearly and to make responsible decisions that are congruent with our values and beliefs. It is not our job to make another person think and feel the way we do or the way we want them to.

—Harriet Goldhor Lerner (1985)

In her book *The Dance of Anger,* Harriet Goldhor Lerner urges people to closely observe how they manage anger. She graphically describes her own style of managing anger when she is under stress:

> When stress mounts, I tend to underfunction with my family of origin (I forget birthdays, become incompetent, and end up with a headache, diarrhea, a cold, or all of the above); I overfunction at work (I have advice for everyone and I am convinced that my way is best); I distance from my husband (both emotionally and physically); and I assume an angry, blaming position with my kids. (1985, p. 190)

Lerner developed a guide to various styles of anger management and labeled these styles pursuer, distancer, overfunctioner, underfunctioner, and blamer. Lerner's styles can be categorized in terms of the Couple and Family Map based on the types of intimate relationships they tend to lead to.

Using the Couple and Family Map terminology, **pursuers** tend to want to create connected or enmeshed types of intimate relationships that are very high in cohesion. Lerner describes pursuers as people who react to their anxiety by seeking greater togetherness in a relationship. Pursuers place a high value on talking and expressing feelings, believe other people should do the same, and tend to criticize a partner who can't tolerate feelings of closeness. When the partner wants more emotional space, the pursuer feels rejected and pursues the partner more vigorously before coldly withdrawing.

Distancers tend to create disengaged or separated types of intimate relationships that are low in cohesion. Distancers want emotional space when stress is high. They are private, self-reliant people rather than help-seekers. They have difficulty showing neediness, vulnerability, and dependency. Partners tend to describe them as being emotionally unavailable, withholding, and unable to deal with feelings. Distancers often manage anxiety by retreating into their work and may terminate a relationship entirely when things become too intense. Distancers tend to open up the most when they are not pushed or pursued.

The **dance of anger** is Lerner's metaphor to describe how human beings relate to each other. Think about the dance of a pursuer and a distancer. As the pursuer moves closer, the distancer retreats. Then, as the pursuer unhappily backs off, the distancer's comfort level increases and the distancer moves toward the pursuer.

Different relationship styles often emerge when people are under stress. "Pursuers" tend to seek greater closeness as their anxiety increases; "distancers" tend to retreat to get more space. All couples need to find a comfortable balance between togetherness and separateness.

The pursuer warms up again and moves in on the distancer, who again begins to retreat. Back and forth, ebb and flow. Just as people have different tastes in food, clothing, and cars, so they have different needs and feelings about closeness. Using the vocabulary of the Couple and Family Map, pursuers and distancers have difficulty finding a comfortable balance between separateness and togetherness. Left to their own devices, family relationships would move back and forth between the extremes of being enmeshed or being disengaged.

Lerner describes **underfunctioners** as people who in many areas of life just can't seem to get organized. These people are too high in flexibility (chaotic). Underfunctioners tend to become less competent under stress, letting others take over or fill in. These people are described at work and in the family as "the fragile one," "the sick one," "the problem," "the irresponsible one." Underfunctioners have difficulty showing their strong and competent side to intimates.

Overfunctioners, on the other hand, know what is best not only for themselves but for everybody else as well. These people are low in flexibility (rigid or structured). In difficult times, overfunctioners move in quickly to advise, rescue, and take charge. They can't seem to stay out of the way and let other people solve their own problems. In this way they avoid thinking about their own problems. Overfunctioners are commonly characterized as "always reliable" and "always together" people; they have difficulty showing their vulnerable, underfunctioning side, especially to people who are having troubles.

Using Lerner's dance metaphor, how would a couple composed of an overfunctioner and an underfunctioner dance? The overfunctioner would hide feelings of inferiority and incompetence by swooping in to "save" the underfunctioner, making the underfunctioner's task more difficult in the long run by depriving her or him of the opportunity to develop personal strengths.

Although most people have an impulse to blame others when things go wrong, some people habitually avoid responsibility for their part in problems. "Blamers" such as this man tend to expend a great deal of energy trying to get others to change.

Some may think that a couple made up of an overfunctioner and an underfunctioner would be a complementary one; however, this type of relationship would be tenuous. The overfunctioner might eventually tire of saving the underfunctioner, or the underfunctioner might tire of looking and feeling so incompetent. For the relationship to endure and become strong, the partners would have to find that delicate balance between chaos and rigidity.

Lerner's fifth style, the **blamer,** is a person who has a short fuse and responds in times of stress with emotionally intense feelings. Blamers often fall in the rigidly enmeshed category, an unbalanced type of family system. Blamers spend a lot of energy trying to change other people. They involve themselves in repetitive cycles of fighting, which may relieve tension but which also perpetuate old patterns. Blamers hold others responsible for their feelings and see others, rather than themselves, as the problem.

Lerner notes that women in our society are encouraged to overfunction in the areas of housework, child care, and "feelings work." In all other areas of endeavor, however, women are socialized to be pursuers and underfunctioners. Men, on the other hand, are socialized to be distancers and overfunctioners. Both sexes are good at blaming other people, but Lerner believes that women today do it more conspicuously than men because most women still feel they have less power in our society and resent their subordinate status.

All five ways of managing anger can be useful at times, but problems occur when one style dominates. It is important to find a balance between pursuing and distancing, underfunctioning and overfunctioning, blaming and taking the blame. In Lerner's (1985) words, "You will have a problem . . . if you are in an extreme position in any one of these categories or if you are unable to observe and change your pattern when it is keeping you angry and stuck" (p. 193).

"I think dance of anger is a good metaphor for how we operated in the early years of our marriage," said Curt, a writer, over a cup of coffee at the Pike Place Market in Seattle. "It almost seemed choreographed, it was so predictable. Eileen would do her part of the dance, and then I would respond with my part of the dance, back and forth, back and forth, and then all hell would break loose. It could get really ugly. I was so mad at her once, I thought I could kill her.

"I think a big part of the problem was we were simply replaying old videotapes of the families we grew up in. Her family in Puyallup was a soap opera par excellence. They loved to fight and did it well all their lives. My dad was an attorney in Bellingham, and he could really pour on the B.S. as well. He'd filibuster over the dinner table in his melodramatic way for ages, and my mother would finally crack and become a bitch on wheels. It was pretty predictable. It made me sick to my stomach. I left home when I was 17.

"Fortunately, Eileen and I could see the pattern in our own marriage. We read some books and articles about more positive approaches to settling our differences. We experimented and finally found better ways to get along. Luck probably played a part in it all—as did the fact that we mellowed a bit with age and just simply didn't enjoy a good brawl anymore. For whatever reason, we don't dance and brawl as much. Nobody's thrown anything for a long time. We don't fall into the old habits. We simply sit down and work things out. Thank God."

Sources of Conflict in Couples

Although many assume that newlyweds rarely fight, studies reveal that they do; the top five issues generating conflict are money, family, communication style, household tasks, and personal tastes (Arond & Pauker, 1987). One survey found that nearly 40% of the 530 participating newlyweds had at least one "fight" a week, and that nearly 70% had at least one fight a month (Arond & Pauker, 1987). "Fights" lasted from minutes to days; almost two thirds (63%) of the newlyweds checked minutes, another third (33%) checked hours, and only 4% indicated that their fights lasted days. Conflicts-resolution styles for "big conflicts" varied considerably: The top three approaches were "discussing things calmly" (59%), "suffering silently" (41%), and "screaming" (47%).

Sources of conflict often change as time passes in a relationship. Edward Bader and his colleagues gathered data about couple conflict over a period of 5 years (Bader, Riddle, & Sinclair, 1981). The researchers interviewed couples just before marriage and then reinterviewed them 6 months, 1 year, and 5 years after marriage. Before marriage, the man's job and issues of time and attention tied for first place in terms of arousing the most conflict. Six months after marriage, household tasks rose to number one, and handling money was number two; time and attention issues had fallen to third place in the conflict sweepstakes. At the end of the first year of marriage, household tasks were still number one, time and attention issues were second, and handling money was third. At the end of 5 years, household tasks were tied with time and attention issues for first place, but sex had moved

BOX 10.2

Communication Patterns in Successful and Unsuccessful Relationships

Psychology professor John Gottmann and his colleagues have been conducting scientific experiments for 20 years on more than 2,000 couples, using video cameras, EKG monitors, and specially designed instruments for observing what happens when couples interact. These researchers observe how couples talk to each other, examining facial expressions, gestures, fidgeting behaviors, and so on, as well as physiological clues such as changes in heartbeat and respiration during conflict. They also note listening skills and expressions of sarcasm and contempt. The results are like a "CAT scan of a living relationship."

The common denominator of a stable marriage is, according to Gottmann, that the couples are "nicer to each other." The ratio of positive to negative moments in their relationship is 5 to 1. "Positive moments nurture the affection and joy that are crucial to weather the rough spots," Gottmann says.

And what about divorce-prone couples? If there is a negative interaction for every positive one, the couple is divorce-bound. Danger signs include *criticism* (at-tacking a spouse's personality or character), *contempt* (insulting and psychologically abusing a spouse), *defensiveness* (denying responsibility, making excuses, whining), and *stonewalling* (retreating from the conversation into stony silence). When these behaviors become routine, the marriage has serious problems.

To argue in a healthy manner, Gottmann offers these strategies:

- Call a time-out and cool off.

- Edit the argument, responding only to constructive criticisms and ignoring the nastiness.

- Stay focused rather than wandering around verbally.

- Put the fight into perspective, and be willing to see that most issues are not all that important.

- Be affectionate, understanding, empathetic, and validating.

- Use humor, and be able to laugh at yourself.

Source: Adapted from *Why Marriages Succeed or Fail*, copyright © 1994 by J. Gottmann Ph.D., with N. Silver, New York: Simon & Schuster. See also *What Predicts Divorce? The Relationship Between Marital Processes and Marital Outcomes*, copyright © 1994 by J. Gottmann Ph.D., Hillsdale, NJ: Lawrence Erlbaum Associates; and *The Seven Principles to Making Marriage Work*, copyright © 1999 by J. Gottmann Ph.D. and N. Silver, New York: Crown.

from a lowly thirteenth position to third. The researchers concluded that the basic tasks of living together (how to divide housework, how much time and attention to give to each other, how to handle money, and related issues) created the most conflict for couples.

Box 10.2 summarizes findings on communication in stable and unstable relationships.

Approaches to Conflict Resolution

Grant me the serenity to accept what can't be changed,
The courage to change things that can be changed,
And the wisdom to know the difference.
    —Reinhold Niebuhr (1951/1988, p. 600)

If anger is a normal part of intimate relationships, then fights and disagreements are likely to occur. The issue is how to fight fairly and constructively. In this section we will look at some suggestions for resolving conflicts in ways that preserve and enhance relationships.

Fighting Fair

The terms *fight* and *fighting* are commonly used in our society to describe verbal disagreements between people. They are also used to describe boxing matches and other physically violent encounters. When family therapists talk about rules for *fair fighting*, they are referring to rules that govern verbal exchanges. Calling verbal conflict a fight is useful. It draws attention to the fact that verbal disagreements are serious business and should be treated with caution and good sense (Crosby, 1991). Tension and anger build up during these exchanges, and verbal conflict can turn into physical conflict.

People should observe certain conventions when arguing with each other; they will feel safer voicing disagreement if they know that it will not get out of hand. Crosby argues that "if we can trust—really believe—that our partner will not abandon us or take advantage of our vulnerability, we can then learn to interact in an aboveboard, straightforward manner" (p. 170). Without this basic trust, people become defensive when they are accused or hide their defensiveness with a strong counterattack. The 16 ground rules for fair fighting (Crosby, 1991) are listed in Box 10.3 and explained below.

Negotiate From the Adult Position Using terminology from transactional analysis, Crosby argues that each partner should make a firm commitment to negotiate from the *Adult* position, rather than from the *Child* or the *Parent* position. Transactional analysis theorizes that people often replay old "tapes" in their minds and, under stress, are likely to act as they did when they were a child or as a parent acted toward them. Negotiating from the Child position, a person acts vulnerable and often feels hurt or threatened. Negotiating from the Parent position, a person rigidly repeats arguments and views held by her or his parents rather than interacting in new ways in this new situation. Negotiating from the Adult position, however, the person can listen carefully to the other, respond assertively and rationally, and work with the other person to find a solution acceptable to both.

Avoid Ultimatums An ultimatum is a nonnegotiable demand—"You do this or else"—and is a hallmark of dirty fighting. Fair fighting emphasizes negotiation, allowing each person room to bargain. Ultimatums generally lead to counterultimatums, leaving little room for genuine negotiation. An ultimatum puts the receiver in the Child position and the sender in the Parent position. Neither person gets a chance to negotiate from the Adult position.

If One Loses, Both Lose American society emphasizes competition in the marketplace, but in families competition can be problematic. Sometimes one partner is especially good at debating and may "win" most of the arguments. The other person may accuse the partner of using big words or sophisticated logic and become unhappy with the situation.

The better debater may win arguments, but he or she will lose just as surely as the partner does. The relationship will become less open and cooperative. The

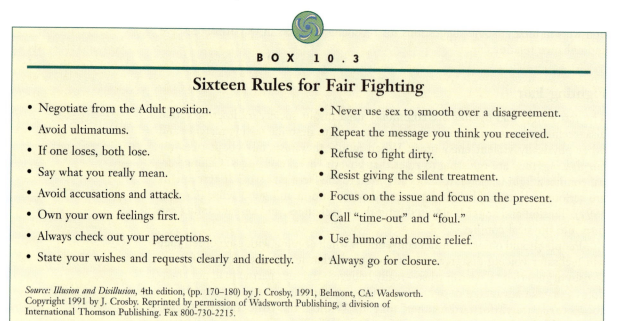

B O X   1 0 . 3

Sixteen Rules for Fair Fighting

- Negotiate from the Adult position.
- Avoid ultimatums.
- If one loses, both lose.
- Say what you really mean.
- Avoid accusations and attack.
- Own your own feelings first.
- Always check out your perceptions.
- State your wishes and requests clearly and directly.

- Never use sex to smooth over a disagreement.
- Repeat the message you think you received.
- Refuse to fight dirty.
- Resist giving the silent treatment.
- Focus on the issue and focus on the present.
- Call "time-out" and "foul."
- Use humor and comic relief.
- Always go for closure.

goal of fighting fair in a family is not to win or lose the argument but to work together to find solutions that are acceptable to everyone.

Say What You Really Mean   As conflict increases, people often fail to say what they really mean. They may give in on issues when they don't really want to in order to protect the other person's feelings, but they are also protecting themselves from pain or embarrassment. The more people get in touch with and share their feelings, the earlier a solution can be found.

Take, for example, the issue of cohabitation. Two partners consider whether to move in together or to wait until marriage to live together. One person might feel positive about cohabiting; the other person might feel ambivalent, seeing both the positive and the negative consequences. Because cohabitation is a complex issue, the ambivalent partner should write down the pros and cons: "I love him"; "Mom and Dad will be mad"; "I'm afraid he will take advantage of me and I'll end up doing all the housework"; "I'm afraid I'll have to support him financially, and I can't even support myself now." The ambivalent partner can then see more clearly why she or he is feeling undecided and share these feelings with the other partner.

Avoid Accusations and Attack   When people are accused, they tend to react either by accusing the other person in turn or by withdrawing. "You" statements are implicit or explicit signals of attack: "You make me mad," "You always do that," or "It's all your fault." Most people become defensive and angry in response to statements of this sort.

Own Your Own Feelings First   Instead of attacking with "you" statements, use "I" statements: "I feel hurt," "I feel rejected," or "I feel disappointed." Although the difference between saying "I" and saying "you" may seem small, it is significant. By using "I" statements, the speaker is clearly pointing out that something

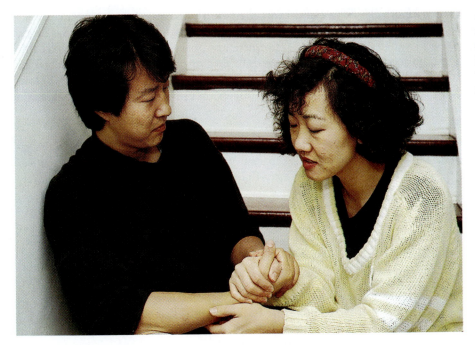

A key to positive communication is taking responsibility for one's own feelings. "I" statements set the tone for constructive interaction.

is wrong in the relationship and is simply putting the issue on the table for discussion. The "I" statement indicates the other person is innocent until proven guilty, rather than vice versa.

Always Check out Your Perceptions   Miscommunication is often the catalyst for disagreements. Don't assume that you know what is really going on until you have talked with the other person. Also, don't try to guess what the other person is thinking or feeling. It is your responsibility to ask.

State Your Wishes and Requests Clearly and Directly   Dogs and cats often do a better job of communicating their needs than humans do. Because they are afraid of being turned down or rejected, people often do not say directly what they want. One common approach is to ask a leading question, one that hints at the desired result without directly asking for it. For example, someone who wanted to go out to the movies might ask, "Wouldn't you like to see a movie tonight?" The indirect approach might work sometimes, but it is not a reliable way for people to get what they want.

Never Use Sex to Smooth Over a Disagreement   People sometimes use sex as a tool or a weapon in an argument. When people use sexual persuasion to get their mate to agree with them, the underlying issue or conflict often remains unresolved, or if the disagreement is about some immediate problem, it is likely that no decision will be made. Also, the partner who feels pressured into a decision might later resent the other partner.

Repeat the Message You Think You Received   Active listeners let their partner know that they correctly heard what the partner was saying. Crosby calls this process "football": "You can't throw the ball (the message) back to your partner until you prove to your partner that you caught the ball (the message) he or she threw to you" (1991, p. 176). Active listeners don't repeat the message verbatim but simply restate it in their own words to show their partner that they understand it. Active listening does three valuable things: it forces people to listen; it slows down reaction time, which keeps the discussion calmer and more rational; and it aids in understanding the message.

Refuse to Fight Dirty Dirty fighters lose the battle before they begin the attack. They prove their inability to deal positively and fairly with the situation. Crosby (1991) lists a variety of dirty-fighting techniques:

- *Gunnysacking.* **Gunnysacking** is an alienating tactic in which participants stuff their true feelings into a deep sack, thus preventing the other person from knowing what they are really feeling. The problem is that the gunnysack can hold only so much. When the sack overflows, gunnysackers may verbally or physically attack the other person.

- *Passive-aggressive behavior.* Like gunnysackers, people who engage in **passive-aggressive behavior** feign agreement or act like everything is okay when in fact they really disagree with what is happening. Over time, these people often become hostile and aggressive.

- *Rapid-fire questioning.* Rapid-fire questioning is an adversarial technique often used by police and lawyers to confuse a suspect or a witness. Some partners might try the same approach during arguments, but such techniques do not build intimate relationships or resolve conflicts.

- *Verbal abuse.* Name-calling, yelling, pouting, and sulking all belong in the category of dirty-fighting techniques. None of them are helpful in resolving conflict.

Resist Giving the Silent Treatment Refusing to talk—the silent treatment—is an attempt to get even with or to manipulate a partner. Shutting out another person emotionally in the hope that she or he will give in is a form of psychological torture and an approach that rarely resolves conflict. Disagreements don't go away by themselves; they may lie dormant for a while, but they eventually resurface, often in a less manageable form than before. The shut-out partner's anger and frustration might also increase, even though that might not have been the intent of the "silent" partner.

Focus on the Issue and Focus on the Present Constructive arguments focus on the here and now and stay on the topic. Arguments that leap from one issue to another accomplish very little. Bringing up the past usually is a ploy for placing blame. In a fair fight, the relevant question is not "Where have we been?" but "Where are we going from here?"

Call "Time-out" and "Foul" When verbal interchanges get too intense, a time-out can be useful. The length of the time-out depends on how emotionally overwrought the participants are. Sometimes an hour is sufficient; sometimes a day is needed. Time-outs shouldn't last too long, however, because one or both partners may refuse to deal with the issue again.

Another helpful tool is calling a "foul" when fair-fighting rules are broken. If one person brings up the past or uses a dirty-fighting technique, the other partner should call a "foul." This gives both partners a chance to calm down and think things through before trying again to resolve the disagreement.

Use Humor and Comic Relief   Sometimes laughing is just as beneficial as crying to relieve tension, but laughing is *always* better than yelling. Arguing people usually look and sound pretty foolish to an objective third party. In a conflict, people need to step back, look at the situation from a new perspective, and laugh at themselves if possible. (Note, however, that sarcasm or laughing at a partner rarely helps resolve disputes.)

A useful form of humor is **incongruity humor,** which focuses on seeing the incongruous things in life—the things that don't fit together logically—rather than on blaming others or putting them down. Take, for example, a divorce court judge who had to listen for 3 hours to attorneys and the divorcing couple argue over who was to have possession of a 9-foot-long metal pipe. The judge tried to help the couple see the humor in the situation as a way of reducing tension.

Always Go for Closure   **Closure** is the resolution of an issue. Arguing couples should strive for closure as soon as possible or practical. Letting the argument drag on increases the likelihood of gunnysacking, passive-aggressive behavior, or the silent treatment. The sooner people reach genuine agreement, the better. Resolution lets the feelings of bonding and respect return to the relationship.

Constructive and Destructive Approaches

Peace cannot be kept by force. It can only be achieved by understanding.
—ALBERT EINSTEIN (1931/1993, p. 690)

In destructive approaches to conflict resolution, partners bring up old issues, express only negative feelings, reveal selective information, focus on people rather than on issues, and emphasize differences—all with the goal of minimizing change. There is often a winner and a loser, which decreases intimacy. Conversely, in constructive conflict resolution, partners focus on current rather than past issues, share both positive and negative feelings, provide information in an open manner, accept mutual blame, and search for similarities. Both partners win, and as a result intimacy increases and trust grows in the relationship. Table 10.3 compares constructive and destructive ways of resolving conflict.

Styles of Conflict Resolution

Learning how to deal effectively with conflict is one of the most important steps in creating strong relationships. Because conflict resolution is so critical, many therapists focus their efforts on understanding and describing useful approaches and identifying counterproductive ones.

Table 10.3 Constructive and Destructive Approaches to Conflict Resolution

AREA OF CONCERN	CONSTRUCTIVE APPROACH	DESTRUCTIVE APPROACH
Issues	Raises and clarifies issues	Brings up old issues
Feelings	Expresses both positive and negative feelings	Expresses only negative feelings
Information	Complete and honest information	Selective information
Focus	Conflict focuses on issue rather than person	Conflict focuses on person rather than issue
Blame	Accepts mutual blame	Blames other person(s) for the problem
Perception	Focuses on similarities	Focuses on differences
Change	Facilitates change to prevent stagnation	Minimizes change, increasing conflict
Outcome	Both win	One wins and one loses, or both lose
Intimacy	Resolving conflict increases intimacy	Escalating conflict decreases intimacy
Attitude	Trust	Suspicion

Figure 10.2 illustrates a useful model for comparing conflict-resolution styles. The model is based on the belief that each style of conflict is composed of two partially competing goals: concern for oneself and concern for the other person. Concern for oneself is measured by how aggressive one is, and concern for the other focuses on the level of cooperation. This model of conflict resolution identifies five styles: the competitive style, the collaborative style, the compromise style, the avoidance style, and the accommodating style (Kilmann & Thomas, 1975). There are advantages and disadvantages to all five styles.

Competitive style. People who use a **competitive style** of conflict resolution tend to be aggressive and uncooperative, pursuing personal concerns at the expense of the other. Those with a competitive style gain power by direct confrontation and try to "win" without adjusting their goals and desires in light of the other person's goals and desires. Life is a battleground for people with this type of style. They tend to identify with the following statements: "Once I get wound up in a heated discussion, I find it difficult to stop," and "I like the excitement of engaging in verbal fights" (Wilmot & Hocker, 1985, p. 41). A competitive style is usually not conducive to developing intimacy.

Collaborative style. People who use a **collaborative style** of conflict resolution are highly assertive in regard to reaching their goals but have a great deal of concern for the other person. Collaborators would identify with the following statements: "When I get into a conflict with someone, I try to work creatively with them to find new options," or "I like to assert myself,

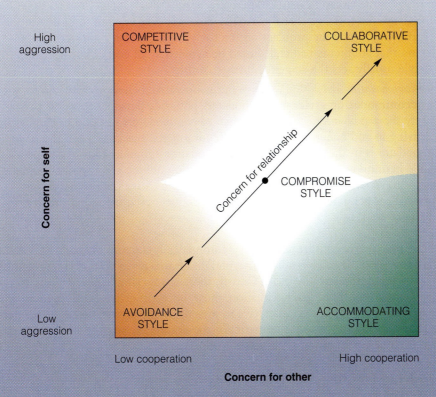

Figure 10.2 Styles of Conflict Resolution. *Source:* "Interpersonal Conflict: Handling Behavior as Reflections of Jungian Personality Dimensions" by R. Kilmann and K. Thomas, 1975, *Psychological Reports, 37,* pp. 971–980. Copyright © 1975 *Psychological Reports.* With permission from the publisher and the author.

and I also like to cooperate with others" (Wilmot & Hocker, 1998). Collaborators tend to burn out on relationships because they invest so much energy into resolving conflict. Another problem with the collaborative style is that good collaborators are powerful and sometimes use their strength to manipulate others.

Compromise style. People who use the **compromise style** (which is intermediate on both the aggression and cooperation axes, as shown in Figure 10.2) would identify with these statements: "You have to be satisfied with part of the pie," or "When disagreements occur, you each have to give a little" (Wilmot & Hocker, 1998). The compromise style is more direct than the avoidance style, but it does not push the issues as much as the collaborative style. Compromise is less time-consuming than collaboration, but it also reinforces the notion that the relationship is one between equals. The downside of the compromise style is that it favors an easy "formula" for conflict resolution, which may not be the best solution for all involved.

Avoidance style. Nonassertive and passive behaviors characterize the **avoidance style** of conflict resolution. Avoiders pursue neither their own concerns nor the concerns of the other person. They sidestep the issue by changing the subject or withdrawing from the conflict. The avoidance style has certain advantages: It gives the avoider time to think about whether any good will come from continuing the fight and about whether others could manage the situation better. There are several disadvantages of this style: It conveys the message that the avoider does not care enough to deal with the problem; it puts the problem on the back burner; and it reinforces the notion that conflict is bad and should be avoided at all cost. The avoidance style usually sets the stage for further conflict.

Accommodating style. Nonassertive but cooperative behavior characterizes the **accommodating style.** Accommodaters put aside personal concerns to satisfy the wants and needs of the other. Accommodaters respond to conflict by giving in and being reasonable—both advantages, but only when the accommodater is in the wrong. Also, accommodation minimizes losses and possible harmful consequences in a losing situation. There are also disadvantages to this style: Accommodation tends to reduce creative options because it sacrifices genuine dialogue; it may also produce resentment and the desire to get even.

No one style of conflict resolution is automatically superior to another (Wilmot & Hocker, 1998). Each has advantages and disadvantages in certain circumstances and between different individuals. Clearly, there are no simple or easy ways to resolve human conflicts. Each situation must be approached with caution and thoughtfulness. People in conflict have to consider many factors, including the personalities of those involved, the merits of the argument, and the level of investment each has in continuing the relationship.

Resolving Conflict: Six Basic Steps

Let us begin anew, remembering on both sides that civility is not a sign of weakness, that sincerity is always subject to proof. Let us never negotiate out of fear, but let us never fear to negotiate.

—John F. Kennedy (1961/1990, p. 101)

Family therapists assume that most tension and fights between couples signal the need for conflict resolution. In this section we will examine the basic strategies authorities generally agree are useful for successful negotiation within intimate relationships. The steps are clarifying the issue, finding out what each person wants, identifying various alternatives, deciding how to negotiate, solidifying agreements, and reviewing and renegotiating. We will look at each of these strategies and pay particular attention to the communication skills necessary for effective conflict resolution. It is during periods of conflict that good communication skills take on additional importance.

Clarifying the Issue   Conflicts and fights are probably caused as frequently by misunderstanding as they are by genuine differences. Often people argue over something they don't really disagree on but only thought they did. Clarifying the issue helps; sometimes true differences get pushed aside or covered over by side issues. These types of misunderstandings can be minimized by using the following techniques:

- Both partners should spend some time alone to think through what is bothering them. During this time, they should ask themselves questions that focus on the issue and on their thoughts, feelings, and desires about the issue: "What situation(s) triggered how I'm feeling?" "What was going on that made me feel uncomfortable?" "How would I like things to be different?" "What are some things I want for myself?"

- Both partners should try to understand fully what the other partner is saying. Using good listening skills, the listener should repeat back to the speaker what is being "heard"—both its content and its feeling—until the speaker is satisfied that the listener has understood the message. In addition, the listener can ask questions to clarify or to elicit more information from the speaker. By focusing questions directly on what the speaker is sharing, the listener facilitates identification of the conflict.

- Each partner is responsible for keeping the discussion focused. This can be done by agreeing to talk at another time about side issues that may arise or by using reminders such as "Let's refocus" or "Now, where were we?" to keep the discussion from drifting.

- Each partner should sum up what the other has said after each person has had an opportunity to talk. Clearly identifying and echoing the problem ensures that both partners agree on what the issue is.

Finding out What Each Person Wants   After both people are clear about what the issue is, the discussion should shift to identifying what each person wants. Omitting this part of the process often leads to unsatisfactory negotiations and repetitive fights. This step is important because it helps to minimize hurtful exchanges between frustrated couples; each partner has to identify what he or she wants rather than recounting "how bad things have been." Identifying needs can be a difficult process for some couples, but it can be facilitated if both partners genuinely ask each other to express their desires. If one partner says, "I don't know what I want, but I just know I don't want things to be the way they have been," this is a straightforward signal that this part of the process has not been completed.

Identifying Various Alternatives   During this step, partners look at the various options of achieving resolution. This step often leads to new insights. **Brainstorming** ideas can be a fun and creative process because both partners are working together to find ways to deal with an issue. Research indicates that brainstorming increases people's skill at identifying useful alternatives (Warmbrod, 1982).

Deciding How to Negotiate   After the various alternatives have been identified, it's time to try to work out some agreements, or plans, for change. There are several strategies couples can use to negotiate differences. Each has advantages and disadvantages.

- *Quid pro quo.* A Latin term meaning "this for that," **quid pro quo** is a negotiating strategy by which parties agree that "I'll do this if you'll do that." For example, the Smiths have been bickering over the weekly household chores. Each feels that he or she is doing more than the other. After discussing the alternatives for dividing the tasks more equally, they

Brainstorming—thinking of as many solutions to a problem as possible—is a creative way to address conflicts in a relationship. Generating alternatives highlights the fact that many possibilities exist, even when partners think they're at an impasse.

readily move into a quid pro quo bargain. Jack agrees to do a certain number of the tasks, and Marlene agrees to do the rest. This strategy is effective because it clarifies what each person is going to do. The major disadvantage of this strategy is that it can easily break down if one person fails to keep her or his agreement. Another disadvantage is the difficulty of finding relatively equivalent divisions.

- *Quid pro quid.* A Latin term meaning "this for this," **quid pro quid** is an agreement to do something the other person asks you to do in exchange for being able to do something you want to do. For example, Brent's wife, Nancy, wants him to accept more responsibility for taking care of the children. He agrees to be fully responsible for the children for two nights in exchange for a night out with his friends. This bargaining strategy has advantages over the quid pro quo method in that the consequences for not living up to the bargain are clear and are not based on what the other partner does. This strategy works especially well when one partner is asking the other to change because it enables the partner who agrees to the change to give himself or herself something he or she wants as well. This helps avoid power struggles in which one partner feels she or he has to change simply because the other demands that things be different. The disadvantage of this strategy is that many couples have difficulty reaching any type of mutually acceptable agreement.

- *Agreeing to disagree.* After exploring all the alternatives, a mutually agreeable solution is not always possible; the negotiating strategy then is **agreeing to disagree.** For example, Len wanted to invest the couple's savings in some lakefront property, and Lesley wanted to take a trip to Europe. After long hours of discussion, both felt even more strongly about what they wanted. Because they couldn't agree on either course of action, they agreed to disagree—and left the money in the account. When the issue is not critical to the maintenance of the relationship, agreeing to disagree leaves open the possibility of finding a solution later. When the differences are more basic, however (for example one partner wants children and the other does not), agreeing to disagree will only work in the short run.

Solidifying Agreements   Partners may need to try several negotiation strategies before reaching agreement. But when an agreement is reached, it's important that both people are clear about what has been agreed to and that both do indeed agree. Partners must be careful to avoid bulldozing the other into an agreement. Too often, in their haste to "get things wrapped up," people make agreements they know they can't stick to. Couples should take the time to fully explore what the agreement means for each person before giving it the final stamp of approval. They should be sensitive to each other's reservations. It's a good idea to avoid making agreements while either partner is upset. Pressure tactics, such as implied threats, often win the battle but lose the war. When both partners are in agreement, they should make a contract by writing down everything they've agreed to in simple, clear language. Couples should post the agreement as a reminder of what each is to do. They should also agree to review the situation within a short period of time.

Reviewing and Renegotiating   Once an agreement has been negotiated, it is easy to assume that "that's settled once and for all." Unfortunately, this is rarely the case. Carrying out an agreement often brings other issues to light. It is not unusual to discover that the agreement does not really resolve the problem. A timely review ensures that bad feelings about the agreement do not go on too long.

When agreements break down, partners distrust or are disillusioned about each other's genuine interest in working together. Broken agreements should be reviewed as soon as possible. Couples often discover that one or the other simply "forgot" to do what was agreed upon. It is important for people to remind themselves that change is rarely smooth and that it is also rare for any person to live up to any agreement completely. But if both partners are invested in each other's personal well-being and want their relationship to grow, couples can positively resolve just about any conflict.

Summary

- According to a national survey of married couples, happy couples are more able than unhappy couples to resolve their differences, to understand each other when discussing problems, to feel at ease expressing their feelings to each other, to reach consensus on ways to resolve their differences, and to share responsibility for their problems.

- According to the same national survey, the major conflict-resolution issues that married couples experience are the following: serious disputes over unimportant issues, an inability to resolve differences, disagreement on the best way to resolve issues, an inability to voice concerns or feelings about problems, and a tendency to avoid conflict with their partner.

- Conflict is inevitable in any intimate relationship. It can be thought of as a process that moves from decision making to problem solving to crisis resolution; making decisions when they are called for helps prevent crises.

- Most couples are afraid of negative emotions and have a difficult time learning how to deal with them. A common tendency is to suppress anger for fear of damaging the relationship. Because love and hate are so closely tied, however, the suppression of anger can lead to loss of affection in a relationship.

- Popular myths about anger include the belief that anger is caused by others, that the best way to deal with anger is to let it all out, that anger is a beneficial emotion, and that you're a wimp if you don't get angry.

- Intimacy and conflict are inextricably tied together. Anger keeps people from developing unhealthy dependencies on each other. Interdependence, a balance between dependency and independence, seems to work best.

- People manage stress and anger in a number of ways: Pursuers seek greater togetherness in a relationship; distancers want emotional space when stress is high; underfunctioners become less competent under stress; overfunctioners tend to take charge in tough times; and blamers believe everyone else is responsible for their problems.

- The top five issues that generate conflict between newlyweds are money, family, communication style, household tasks, and personal tastes.

- People should observe certain conventions, or "rules for fair fighting," when they are arguing; these rules make the argument safer and more likely to lead to a satisfactory conclusion.

- Some styles of conflict resolution are the competitive style, pursuing personal concerns at the expense of others; the collaborative style, being highly assertive in regard to reaching one's goals while also showing great concern for the other person; the compromise style, an intermediate style between aggressiveness and cooperation; the avoidance style, avoiding conflict by changing the subject or withdrawing; and the accommodating style, which involves nonassertive and cooperative behaviors.

- Family therapists and other authorities generally agree on six steps for resolving conflict: clarify the issue, find out what each person wants, identify various alternatives, decide how to negotiate, solidify agreements, and review and renegotiate.

Key Terms

pursuer	passive-aggressive behavior	avoidance style
distancer		accommodating style
dance of anger	incongruity humor	brainstorming
underfunctioner	closure	quid pro quo
overfunctioner	competitive style	quid pro quid
blamer	collaborative style	agreeing to disagree
gunnysacking	compromise style	

Activities

1. Using Harriet Lerner's ideas about the various styles of managing anger, focus on someone with whom you have an important relationship. Does one of you tend to be a pursuer or a distancer? an overfunctioner or an underfunctioner? a blamer or a blame-taker? Rate each of you on a scale from 1 (low) to 10 (high) on each of the dimensions. Are you performing any dance based on these style differences? If so, how might you create a healthier dance?

2. Use John Crosby's 16 rules for fair fighting as the basis for a small-group discussion. Group members should first rate themselves on each of the rules. Then members should discuss some practical things they can do to become fairer fighters.

3. Think of an ongoing disagreement you have had with someone in an important relationship, one that has been difficult for you both to resolve. Agree to discuss the issue. See if you can work out the disagreement using the six basic conflict-resolution steps discussed at the end of this chapter.

Suggested Readings

Borcherdt, B. (1993). *You can control your feelings: 24 guides to emotional self-control*. Sarasota, FL: Professional Resource Press. Sound advice for dealing with frustration in one's life and anger in one's soul.

Crosby, J. F. (1991). *Illusion and disillusion: The self in love and marriage*. Belmont, CA: Wadsworth. A guide to positive communication and the development of intimacy; helps readers see through the illusions they create about their loved ones and explains how to overcome the disillusion that inevitably follows to create a sound relationship.

Gottmann, J., & Silver, N. (1994). *Why marriages succeed or fail*. New York: Simon & Schuster. An excellent in-depth analysis of couple interaction patterns that are predictive of successful versus divorcing couples.

Gottmann, J., & Silver, N. (1999). *The seven principles to making marriage work*. New York: Crown. Psychologist Gottmann's latest work for a general audience.

Lerner, H. G. (1985). *The dance of anger*. New York: Harper & Row. An excellent exploration of the very predictable, almost choreographed ways in which people deal with anger in intimate relationships, along with suggestions from a clinical psychologist for dealing positively with that anger.

Lerner, H. G. (1996). *Life preservers: Staying afloat in love and life*. New York: HarperCollins. Recent thoughts from Lerner, a psychologist at the Menninger Clinic in Topeka, Kansas.

Markman, H. J., Stanley, S., & Blumberg, S. L. (1994). *Fighting for your marriage*. San Francisco: Jossey-Bass. Provides an overview of the authors' PREP communication program for couples; contains very useful suggestions for resolving couple conflict.

CHAPTER 11

Managing Economic Resources

Financial issues are the most common stressors for couples and families across the life cycle, regardless of how much money they make (Bowen, Pittman, Pleck, Haas, & Voydanoff, 1995; Voydanoff, 1991). In addition, many couples planning to marry are unwilling or unable to simply talk about financial issues. On a more positive note, however, research has consistently demonstrated that couples who handle their money and finances well also tend to be more happily married (Olson, McCubbin, et al., 1989).

Money, of course, cannot buy family happiness. As one observer noted, "The best things in life are not things." There are countless examples of financially secure people who have not figured out how to have a fulfilling relationship with their partner, their parents, or their children. The media remind us of this almost daily with stories of rich but unhappy politicians, business people, royalty, movie stars, and so forth. On the other hand, there seems to be little truth to the "poor but happy" scenario, either. Economic hardship and problems in couple and family relationships are often related. Researchers have found that divorce, marital separation, domestic violence, and the abuse of alcohol and other drugs are more likely among the poor than in any other socioeconomic group (Bowen et al., 1995; Voydanoff, 1991). Earning an adequate income and managing money efficiently and effectively are important for a couple's and a family's well-being. If they have enough money to meet their basic needs, couples and families can turn their attention to enhancing the quality of their lives and their relationships.

In this chapter we will focus on financial issues, particularly as they relate to intimate relationships and to families across the life cycle. Money problems are often related to an inability to develop an open and well-organized couple or family system. These financial problems then lead to more stress and conflict in the marriage or family. We will explore the field of financial resource management, whose aim is to achieve economic goals and harmony in intimate relationships. Finally, we will take a close look at the advantages and disadvantages of buying on credit and how to avoid the related financial pitfalls.

We will begin this chapter, as we have several others, with a look at a national survey that examined couple strengths and issues for married couples (Olson et al., 1999). In the following section, we will focus on couple strengths in terms of financial management, comparing happy couples with unhappy couples. We will also review the findings of this survey regarding the five most common financial-management issues married couples experience.

Couple Strengths and Issues in Terms of Personal Finances

Based on a national sample of 7,116 happy married couples and 13,421 unhappy married couples (Olson et al., 1999), the financial-management item that most distinguishes happy couples from unhappy couples is a lack of difficulty in deciding how to handle finances (happy couples 69%, unhappy couples 26%; Table 11.1). Three quarters (75%) of happy couples reported having no concerns about how money is handled in their marriage, as compared to only 35% of unhappy couples. Happy couples were significantly less likely (67%) to have major debts than unhappy couples (30%). Happy couples were also more satisfied (56%) than unhappy couples (21%) with their decisions about saving money. Furthermore, happy

Table 11.1 Financial-Management Strengths of Happy Versus Unhappy Married Couples

STRENGTH	PERCENTAGE OF COUPLES IN AGREEMENT	
	Happy Couples (*n* = 7,116)	Unhappy Couples (*n* = 13,421)
Have no difficulty making financial decisions.	69	26
Have no concerns about how money is handled in their marriage.	75	35
Have no problems with major debts.	67	30
Are satisfied with their decisions about saving.	56	21
Agree on how to spend money.	52	21

Source: Adapted from Olson, Fye, & Olson (1999).

Table 11.2 Top Five Financial-Management Issues for Married Couples

ISSUE	PERCENTAGE OF COUPLES WITH PROBLEMS SURROUNDING ISSUE (*N* = 26,442)
Wish their partner were more careful spending money.	65
Disagree on how to spend money.	64
Are unable to budget or keep records of money spent.	51
Have problems with credit cards or charge accounts.	47
Have difficulty deciding how to handle finances.	46

Source: Adapted from Olson, Fye, & Olson (1999).

couples were more likely (52%) to agree on how to spend their money than were unhappy couples (21%).

The major financial issues for a national sample of 26,442 married couples, surveyed by Olson and colleagues (1999), are presented in Table 11.2. The two most common financial-management issues voiced by couples were wishing the spouse were more careful spending money (65%) and disagreeing on how to spend money (64%). Over half (51%) of married couples reported problems with budgeting and keeping records of money spent. About half (47%) of couples also said they have problems with the use of credit cards or charge accounts. Finally, many couples (46%) indicated they have difficulty deciding how to handle their finances.

The Stresses of Family Finances

To some people, money means power; to others, love. For some the topic is boorish, in bad taste. For others, it's more private than sex. Add family dynamics to the mix, and for many you have the subject from hell.

—KAREN S. PETERSON (1992a)

Although Americans make more money per capita than residents of many other countries, financial issues tend to dominate our lives. A national poll found that only 62% of the people in a random sample of U.S. households were satisfied with their current standard of living (M. Levinson, 1991). An enduring paradox about money is that no matter how much families have, they always seem to need more.

> "When our first daughter was a toddler 20 years ago, my take-home pay was about $3,100 a year," related Paul, a contractor and writer of children's books. "Adjusted for inflation today, that might be about $10,000. Things were tight, but we lived pretty well in many respects. We traveled a lot—cheaply, of course—and we enjoyed life. We were, for the most part, happy. Today, we have three teenagers and our family income is approaching $80,000 a year. Frankly, money causes me just as much anxiety today as it did way back then. And I really can't say we're any happier."

Most people, no matter what their income, would likely say that if they only had $5,000, $10,000, or $25,000 more a year, things would be better. Family economist Karen Craig (personal communication, 1991) put it this way, "Wants are insatiable. The more you make, the more creative you are in spending." There never seems to be enough money, whether one's income is $10,000 or $100,000; couples and families often find themselves with some debt each month. Many people assume that material things will bring them happiness but find instead that their possessions have a certain power over them: The house and car must be repaired, the clothes cleaned, the swimming pool maintained, any extra money invested wisely. As one observer said, "Everything you own owns you."

Clearly, *money* is a powerful word. It evokes a variety of emotions: envy, fear, anger, hope, scorn, lust, disgust. Pollsters consistently find that money matters are the most common source of disagreement in U.S. couples and families. For example, a survey of 2,555 randomly sampled American adults found that *money* was the biggest fighting word in their families (Goodman, 1986). Thirty-seven percent of the respondents said money was the major problem, followed by children and childrearing issues (29%), household chores (26%), and diets and health (21%). Family therapists point out, however, that many of these arguments are not really about money. They are actually battles over power and control in a marriage or family, over competing hopes and dreams, over different visions of the good life and how to live it.

Finances: A Family Problem

For most Americans, money is a source of anxiety and discomfort that continues across the life span. Olson, McCubbin, and colleagues (1989) found in their study of 1,000 families that money is the most commonly reported source of stress and strain that families face. Many families at each stage of the family life cycle felt finances were problematic. The most difficult periods of the family life cycle financially were the childbearing stage, the adolescent stage, the launching stage, and the retirement stage. About half of the families in the childbearing stage reported stress and strain related to finances. During the adolescent stage, money-related problems apparently peaked; 60% of the families reported feeling stress in this area. This dropped to 40% at both the launching and the retirement stages.

What specific stressors cause problems for families across the life cycle? Olson, McCubbin, and colleagues (1989) found the most common stressful issue for 45% of the respondents was increased strain on the family's money for food, clothing, energy, and home care as the family grew. A close second in the list of the top ten financial stressors across the family life cycle was the purchase of a car or another major item. Third, and closely related to number two, was stress due to taking out or refinancing a loan to cover increased expenses. Number four was tuition for the child(ren)'s education, and number five was a change in conditions (economic, political, weather) that hurt family investments and/or income (Olson, McCubbin, et al., 1989). Table 11.3 summarizes these and other stressors across the life cycle.

Money problems often have a negative effect on individual well-being and family relationships (Bowen et al., 1995; Voydanoff, 1991). Family members simply don't get along as well with each other when they are suffering from economic distress. Employment instability—job loss or uncertainty over the future of a job—can be a major stressor. Those who are unemployed have an increased likelihood of suffering from depression, anxiety, and psychophysiological distress (stress-related physical problems). If a man is unemployed, his wife is also likely to experience psychological distress from trying to deal with the situation. Low income is also related to several types of psychological distress (Bowen et al., 1995; Voydanoff, 1991).

Finances and Couple Conflict

It's not surprising that conflict over money is common among couples because becoming a couple means exchanging financial independence for financial interdependence. Among other financial issues, partners have to decide together how much they can afford to spend on rent or a mortgage. It is probable that the two will have different ideas about how to spend money. Working out a successful compromise can take a good deal of negotiation. "Partners who feel they have equal control over how money is spent have a more tranquil relationship," according to Blumstein and Schwartz (1983, p. 89).

Why do couples fight over money? In a survey of 400 physicians, mostly psychiatrists, nearly half (49%) believed that quarrels over money occur in marriage primarily because one spouse uses money as a way of dominating and controlling the other (Mace, 1982a). Thirty-four percent of the physicians believed that money quarrels were primarily due to the differences in spouses' spending priorities, and 14% of the physicians saw differences in spouses' thriftiness as the primary source of conflict.

Another study focused on how a sample of newly married couples handled finances and made family decisions over the first 10 years of their marriage (Schaninger & Buss, 1986). The investigators were especially interested in differences between those couples who divorced and those who remained happily married. They found that happily married couples practiced role specialization. Furthermore, the wife was more influential and the husband less dominant in the handling of family finances. There was also greater joint decision making about

Table 11.3 The Top 10 Financial Stressors for Families Across the Life Cycle

	Average Across Stages	Stage 1 Couples n: (207)	Stage 2 Childbearing (269)	Stage 3 School-age (232)	Stage 4 Adolescents (494)	Stage 5 Launching (352)	Stage 6 Empty Nest (230)	Stage 7 Retirement (234)
1. Money for food, clothing, and energy	45%	50%	57%	46%	62%	54%	30%	15%
2. Purchase of a car or other major item	43	50	49	49	43	51	32	23
3. Taking out a loan	31	38	33	29	33	35	17	*
4. Child(ren)'s education	29		13	21	30	51	*	*
5. Problems with family income	26	24	32	26	34	24	27	13
6. Medical/dental expenses	23	20	31	29	31	23	13	17
7. Purchase or construction of a home	16	24	21	10	*	*	11	*
8. Bad investments	16	12	18	12	18	18	18	14
9. Overuse of credit cards	15	17	11	15	16	14	*	*
10. Starting a business	10	10	*	11	*	*	10	*

*Less than 10%.

Source: Adapted from *Families: What Makes Them Work* (2nd ed.) (pp. 285–288) by D. H. Olson, H. I. McCubbin, H. Barnes, A. Larsen, M. Muxen, M. Wilson, 1989, Los Angeles: Sage. Copyright © 1989 by Sage Publications. Used by permission of the publisher.

Money—the lack of it or different ideas about how to spend it—is the most common source of family conflict. Although having expenses that exceed income will always cause stress, money causes fewer conflicts for couples who have learned to compromise and to share financial decision making.

family issues and more influence by the wife in family decision making. Equality at an early stage was important for the vitality of the marriage.

Coping With Financial Stressors

Why do some couples and families survive economic hard times whereas others are torn apart? Researchers have focused on coping resources and coping behaviors in trying to answer this question (Bowen et al., 1995; Voydanoff, 1991). Coping resources can come from oneself and from the family. Foremost among **personal coping resources** are self-esteem and mastery. To survive economic hard times, individuals need to feel good about themselves, to feel as if they are capable of standing up to the onslaught. They need a sense of mastery, the confidence in their ability to learn new skills and techniques to meet changing situations.

Family coping resources include cohesion, adaptability, and a willingness to adopt nontraditional family roles in the face of changing economic circumstances—all characteristics of a healthy family system. Consider, for example, the following family: the mother has never worked outside the home, and her husband has lost his job at a manufacturing plant. He has been out of work for 6 months, and the family has used up its savings. To keep the family afloat, the wife finds a job as a clerk at a convenience store. In this crisis situation, the family coping resources include cohesion (the ability to stick together in tough times and to empathize with each other's plight) and adaptability (the ability to change to deal with the crisis).

Social support, or help from other people, can be critically important in times of economic distress. Major types of social support include instrumental aid (such as money, goods, and services), emotional support, and information (such as advice and feedback). Social support can come from a variety of people, including a spouse or an immediate family member, extended family, co-workers, neighbors, self-help groups, and human-service professionals. When social support is available and is used by an individual in financial crisis, it generally provides increased psychological well-being and improved quality of family life (Bowen et al., 1995; Kessler, Turner, & House, 1988; Voydanoff, Donelly, & Fine, 1988).

When the major wage earner of a family loses his or her job, there are several options:

- Other family members can go to work outside the home.

- The family can increase its participation in the so-called informal economy, exchanging goods and services for cash or by barter.

- The family can decide together how to cut back expenditures dramatically.

Cutting the budget is not easy, and families have reported depression, low marital satisfaction, and high tension when forced to do so. Nonetheless, there are certain approaches that have been found to make things worse in times of economic distress. Denying that there is a problem; keeping feelings to oneself; and eating, drinking, or smoking to relieve tension tend to increase marital stress (Wilhelm & Ridley, 1988).

"I was out of work for 26 months over a period of 40 months, but who was counting? It was probably the most devastating experience in my life," Stan, a middle-aged man living in Boston, said. "I applied for 205 jobs before I finally found one that worked out. People say, 'All you have to do is get off your butt and you can find work.' I used to believe that myself. But it's not that easy. With a master's degree in education, I was happy at one point to find work delivering newspapers on Sunday morning at 3 A.M.

"My self-esteem was so low I felt I wanted to die. One morning I was so depressed that I was lying on the living room floor, just feeling broken. My daughter stepped over me as she went out the front door to high school. My son stepped over me on his way out the door to college. My wife stepped over me on her way out the door to her job. At the time, it felt like I had died and they didn't even notice. They simply stepped over the body and went about their business.

"Now I know that they really were upset about my unemployment. My wife, Sally, was probably as upset about it as I was. But there was nothing any of them could do at the time but go on with their own lives. They tried to comfort me, but many times I was beyond comforting. Fortunately, I found a good job that I enjoy. It doesn't pay all that well, but I love having it. Being without work was terrifying. Even talking about it still upsets me today, 10 years later."

CATHY®   BY CATHY GUISEWITE

Why Do Finances Cause Problems?

There are several reasons finances cause problems for families:

- Money is a taboo topic in many families.
- Couples tend to have unrealistic expectations about finances.
- Many couples do not create and stick to a budget.
- Some families overspend and rely too heavily on credit.
- Partners have different styles of spending and saving.
- One partner uses money as a tool to gain power and control over the other partner.
- Partners have different ideas about the meaning of money.

Money: A Taboo Topic

In the dating phase, couples are more likely to talk about any topic other than their financial situations; it's not very romantic to talk about potential income, the use of credit cards, and views on savings. In contrast, among married couples, money matters are the most common source of arguments (Blumstein & Schwartz, 1983).

"I thought we talked about everything before marriage," said Marcia, a 42-year-old computer technician. "But we never seemed to get around to money—what it means to each of us and how it should be spent. Because I saw money as a symbol of security, I wanted to scrimp and save. I wanted to build a house, a nest, and feel safe inside. Because he saw money as a tool to achieve freedom and independence, he wanted to use it for adventure. We were doomed from the beginning to fight over money."

The discussion of money between parents and children, however, is often nonexistent. Nonetheless, many financial advisors and counselors argue that it is essential to break the family pattern of financial silence. If parents refuse to help their children learn how to manage money, it "creates people who depend on us," according to psychologist Jane Nelsen. "When we don't teach kids responsibility, their self-esteem suffers. They feel inadequate. That teaches them to manipulate us to get what they want. They don't develop their own capabilities" (cited in Peterson, 1992b). By setting a budget for adolescent spending, parents can prevent many emotional struggles with their teenagers.

Common Financial Pitfalls

Before marriage, many young couples have unrealistic expectations about how much money they can expect to earn and how much things will cost (Arond & Pauker, 1987). Most couples also do not invest time or effort in the careful construction of a budget. Although budgeting requires some attention to detail and record keeping, a budget can keep couples out of financial trouble and alleviate emotional struggles between partners.

Overspending is another common financial problem, one closely associated with buying on credit. Credit paves the way to many family financial crises. And the high interest rates on credit-card balances (often double the rate on bank loans) can make it difficult for many to pay back more than the interest on their debt. It can be very difficult for many couples and families to get out of debt without a realistic budget.

When it comes to spending and saving styles, individuals vary greatly; these differences in style can generate considerable conflict between partners and in families. Ideally, it is a good idea for couples to talk about their spending patterns before marriage; however, most couples do not find out until after marriage how different their spending/saving styles are. The greater the difference in styles, the greater the possibility of conflicts over money. Two very common—and conflicting—types are spenders and savers. **Savers** compulsively save money, often keeping very little free for essentials. They may buy only the cheapest items, even if they are of poor quality and not cost-effective in the long run. **Spenders** love to purchase items both for themselves and for others.

Although most people do not exhibit the extremes of either style, many have a tendency toward one of the two styles. It is often easier to identify another person's style than to describe our own. Nevertheless, it is wise for potential partners to discuss their spending and saving styles with each other honestly.

Money can also be a means of gaining and maintaining power over a partner or other family members. Power struggles complicate financial issues. Couples can minimize conflict by setting up clear rules about handling money. If both partners have an income, they may each retain power over their separate earnings. If they do so, they will also need to pool part of those earnings to pay for joint expenses (rent, food, and so forth) or to make large purchases or investments. This takes mutual trust, openness, and solidarity on financial issues. If one partner makes most or all of the money in the family, she or he can use this as a powerful weapon in times of disagreement. Although the "higer-earning" partner may not admit it, the other partner often senses the attitude "I earned it, I'll spend it my way."

Money is not just the paper, coin, or plastic used to buy things. It can also be a source of status, security, enjoyment, or control. If partners have incompatible attitudes about money, extravagant purchases are likely to cause conflicts between them.

The Meaning of Money

Arond and Pauker (1987) have identified four common orientations toward money: A questionnaire for assessing your money orientation is provided in Box 11.1.

- *Money as status.* A person with a status orientation is interested in money as power—as a means of keeping ahead of one's peers.

- *Money as security.* A person with a security orientation is conservative in spending and focuses on saving.

- *Money as enjoyment.* A person with an enjoyment orientation gets satisfaction from spending, both on others and on himself or herself.

- *Money as control.* A person with a control orientation sees money as a way of maintaining control over her or his life and independence from a partner or other family members.

BOX 11.1

Money—What Does It Mean to You?

Use the following scale to respond to each of the items below:

1 = Strongly disagree; 2 = Disagree; 3 = Uncertain; 4 = Agree; 5 = Strongly agree

_____ 1. It is important to me to maintain a lifestyle similar to or better than that of my peers.

_____ 2. In making a major purchase, an important consideration is what others will think of my choice.

_____ 3. Since money equals power, I am willing to work hard for money in order to have more power.

_____ 4. I really enjoy shopping and having nice things.

_____ 5. Saving money for a rainy day is an important principle to live by.

_____ 6. If I had a moderate amount of money to invest, I would be more likely to put it into multiple resources that are relatively safe than into one fairly risky source that has the potential to make a lot of money.

_____ 7. Being "flat broke" is one of the worst things that could happen to me.

_____ 8. Saving for retirement is an important financial goal for me.

_____ 9. If I suddenly came into a windfall of $1,000, I would use the money for something I have always wanted to do or have.

_____10. Since "You can't take it with you," you might as well spend it.

_____11. Money can't buy happiness, but it sure helps.

_____12. Few things in life give me greater pleasure than making a great buy.

_____13. I like/would like having my own business because I can/could control my financial destiny.

_____14. I like being able to make decisions about how to spend the money I earn.

_____15. It bothers me to be dependent on someone else for money.

_____16. I feel uncomfortable if someone offers to "pick up the tab" at a meal we have shared because I feel indebted to them.

Scoring and Interpretation After taking the quiz, add up your answers to the four questions for each category and record your scores below. Scores for each category can range from 4 to 20, with a high score indicating more agreement with that approach. It is possible to have high or low scores in more than one category. General guidelines for interpreting your scores appear in the box below. Record the interpretation for your score in each category on the scoring chart.

Category	Items	Your Score	Interpretation of Score		Score	Interpretation
Money as Status	1–4	_____	_____		17–20	Very High
Money as Security	5–8	_____	_____		13–16	High
Money as Enjoyment	9–12	_____	_____		9–12	Moderate
Money as Control over life	13–16	_____	_____		4–8	Low

It is possible for a person to have more than one orientation but not two conflicting approaches—for example, enjoyment *and* security.

Family Income and Expenses

In this section we will focus on the average income of U.S. families and on income variations among different ethnic and cultural groups and between men and women. We will also explore typical family expenses and differences in family net worth. Finally, we will examine the financial feasibility for both spouses to work outside the home, especially if they have children.

What does *living in poverty* mean? It means that people might not have adequate food or a decent place to sleep. (In the case of the homeless, it could mean living in a refrigerator box in an alley or under a bridge.) It means people cannot afford to see a physician when they are ill or to purchase medicine when they need it. Being poor may mean having no telephone, no radio, no television, no means of transportation. It often means that children attend substandard schools or that their parents move so often looking for work that the children do not attend school at all. Poverty is a very stressful state of affairs.

Lower-middle-income families, although not officially "poor" by government standards, also find it quite difficult to make ends meet. In both two-parent and single-parent lower-middle-income families, about three quarters of all family expenditures can go for housing, food, and transportation. This leaves little money for anything else.

Many people have argued that excessive wealth, like poverty, can be burdensome. "Growing up rich is not an unmixed blessing," according to Frank S. Pittman, a psychiatrist who has worked with both poor and rich families. He states, "Great wealth has undoubted benefits, but it is not good for children. It distorts their functional relationship with the world, it belittles their own accomplishments, and it grotesquely amplifies their sense of what is good enough. It is addictive" (Pittman, 1985, p. 464). The problems of the rich, however, are qualitatively different from those of the poor. Writer James A. Michener, who was both rich and poor in his long life, concluded, "For anyone to claim, as some do, that the damage from having too much is comparable to that from having too little is nonsense, pure and simple nonsense" (1991, p. 249).

Family Income

More than half the families in the United States are considered middle-income families. The U.S. Bureau of the Census currently defines the middle-income range as between $15,000 and $75,000 per year. Lower-income families make less than $15,000 per year, and upper-income families make more than $75,000. Figure 11.1 breaks the lower- and middle-income categories down into various subcategories. It also illustrates that although most U.S. families (67%) are middle income, a disproportionate share of the money in this country goes to affluent families: Roughly 46.5% of family income goes to only 18.6% of America's families. By contrast, lower-income families comprise 14% of U.S. families but make only 4% of the money. The rich have gotten richer since the mid-1980s, and both middle-income and lower-income families have lost ground.

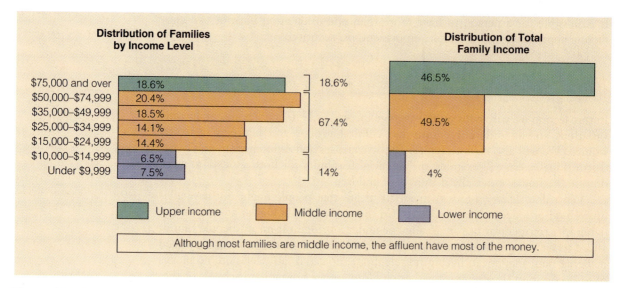

Figure 11.1 Income Levels of U.S. Families, 1996. *Source:* U.S. Bureau of the Census, 1997.

Table 11.4 Income Levels by Ethnic Group and Family Structure

ETHNIC GROUP/TYPE OF FAMILY	MEDIAN INCOME
All groups	
All families	$41,224
Married couples	47,129
Female householder, no husband present	21,348
White	
All families	$43,265
Married couples	47,608
Female householder, no husband present	24,431
Black	
All families	$26,838
Married couples	41,362
Female householder, no husband present	15,589
Hispanic	
All families	$25,491
Married couples	30,195
Female householder, no husband present	14,755

Source: U.S. Bureau of the Census (1997, p. 720).

Ethnic Income Differences   There are considerable income differences across ethnic groups in the United States (Table 11.4). For example, among all types of family households, the median income for White families is $43,265; for Black families, $26,838; and for Hispanic families, $25,491. Table 11.4 also indicates that for these three ethnic groups, married couples earn substantially more income than the average in their group and single parents make significantly less.

A medical degree costs at least 8 years of college tuition, but the expense is small in comparison to a lifetime of high earnings, which the degree virtually guarantees. Nevertheless, women graduates often earn less than their male counterparts because they are more likely to interrupt or curtail their careers in order to have and care for their children.

Gender Income Differences   There is a large difference in the average income of males and females at all educational levels, with men making more than women at each level (U.S. Bureau of the Census, 1997). The average American man working full-time earns $40,367 per year, whereas the average American woman working full-time earns $26,547. The discrepancy between the incomes of males and females in Black and Hispanic families is smaller than that in White families.

Education pays off financially; income rises dramatically as one's level of education increases. Individuals with 8 or fewer years of formal education in this country earn on average $20,550. Those with a high school diploma average $23,330. People with a college degree earn an average of $67,529 (U.S. Bureau of the Census, 1997). The financial benefit of education for White males is greater than it is for females and other minority groups. Women with 4 years of college earn less than men with only a high school diploma.

Economists and other social observers cite a number of reasons for these income differences. Women often drop out of the labor force to have children and then stay at home to care for them for a few years. Meanwhile, men gain seniority in the labor force and get more job-related experience. Although it is illegal to pay women less for doing the same job, women have little legal recourse when they are paid lower wages for jobs that may require essentially similar skills. Also, salaries in fields traditionally dominated by women tend to be lower than those in fields traditionally dominated by men. Many people attribute these tendencies to discrimination and sexism.

The "equal pay for comparable work" approach takes a fresh look at "men's" and "women's" work. Proponents argue that pay should be based not on traditional gender-role assumptions but on the comparative difficulty of the job. How much should a secretary be paid in comparison with a plumber? a child-care worker in comparison with a computer service technician? Some states have developed

As more women have joined the workforce and more families need two incomes to meet their expenses, debates have increased about the differences in salaries paid to men and women for similar kinds of work. If a female secretary and a male computer technician, for example, have the same amount of education, experience, and job responsibility, why is the secretary apt to be paid less?

elaborate formulas. A job's worth, in terms of salary, is calculated on the basis of the number of years of education, training, and experience it demands and the difficulty or risk it involves.

Why do Whites tend to make more than African Americans and Hispanics, even when their educational levels are similar? Many observers argue that racism is still active in the United States and that the difference in income can be traced to discrimination. Some believe, however, that a number of other factors also play a part. The first is urban residence. Many jobs sought by minorities have moved from the cities, where most people of color live, to the suburbs, where there are fewer African Americans and Hispanics. The second factor is the type of employment; minorities are more likely than Whites to work in service industries, where salaries are lower. The third factor is tenure; many college-educated minorities are relative newcomers to the labor market and have had less time than Whites to earn promotions and higher pay.

The controversy over the income gap between White males, females, and minorities in our country is not likely to end soon. The disparity in income between

ITEMS		AMOUNT
Housing, total		**$10,466**
Shelter	$5,932	
Fuels, utilities, and public services	2,193	
Household operations and furnishings	1,911	
Housekeeping supplies	430	
Transportation, total		**5,661**
Vehicles	2,639	
Gasoline and motor oil	1,006	
Other vehicles and public transportation	2,016	
Food, total		**4,505**
a. Food at home, total	2,803	
b. Food away from home	1,702	
Tobacco products and smoking supplies		**269**
Health care		**1,732**
Pensions and Social Security		**2,967**
Life and personal insurance		**374**
Apparel and services		**1,704**
Alcoholic beverages		**277**
Other expenditures		**4,198**
Total		**$32,507**

Table 11.5 Average Annual Expenditures, by Category, for All Urban U.S. Households

Source: U.S. Bureau of the Census (1997, p. 461).

the haves and the have-nots is a problematic issue in a society where millions of people are living at or near the poverty level.

Annual Household Expenses

How couples and families allocate their income for various expenditures depends on their income level. For example, poor people spend a higher percentage of their income on food and housing than rich people do. After meeting their basic needs, the rich can afford many luxuries that are out of reach for most people. Table 11.5 presents U.S. Census Bureau figures for all urban households in this country. (Urban households are those located in cities and surrounding suburbs that have a population of more than 100,000.) The largest expenditure is for housing, followed by transportation and then food. The amount dedicated to various categories varies widely among families, however, according to personal taste, philosophy of life, and decisions to skimp in one area and spend freely in another. Expenses that vary widely include food, housing, vehicles, and clothing.

Family Net Worth

Using Census Bureau data, researchers reported that the median net worth for all households in 1996 was $56,000; for White households, $63,400; for Hispanic households, $7,650; and for African American households, $8,900 (Garman & Forgue, 1997). As measured by their median net worth, most White families have some cushion against financial hard times. Hispanic and African American families, on the average, live much closer to the financial edge. This can be a source of stress.

As expected, net worth and education are closely related. In 1996, households headed by college graduates had a median net worth of $104,000; those headed by high school graduates had a net worth of $50,000; and those headed by individuals with no high school degree had a net worth of $26,300.

Households headed by a married couple in 1996 had a median net worth of $76,200; the figure dropped to $24,300 for households headed by an unmarried male and to $14,400 for those headed by an unmarried female. The researchers concluded that two people can earn, save, invest, and create significantly more net worth than a single person (Garman & Forgue, 1997).

Does It Pay to Work Outside the Home?

Financially and emotionally, there are both advantages and disadvantages for two parents of young children to both work outside the home. By the year 2000, an estimated 68% of all women in the United States will be working outside the home, up from 57.5% in 1990 and 43.3% in 1970 (U.S. Bureau of the Census, 1997). This means that there will be more two-income families at all age levels.

One of the sobering facts of life for two-income families is that the second income often seems to disappear when the expenses associated with earning it are paid. A hypothetical example: Assume the second income in the family is a reasonably good one—$28,000 a year, or $2,333 a month. Each month, federal, state, and Social Security taxes could conceivably take about $942. Child care for two children under school age could easily take another $550 a month. Working outside the home also entails increases in clothing expenditures, say, $110 extra a month; personal-care and dry-cleaning bills may also go up an extra $45 a month. Lunch costs may rise about $110 monthly, and transportation to work could add at least $55 a month. After all is said and done, the $2,333 monthly salary is reduced to $521—about $3.25 an hour—in real income.

One woman who quit her $7-an-hour job in a family decision to rely solely on the husband's income said, "I had the feeling that all my money was going for clothes, lunch, and day care for my daughter." It is important to emphasize, however, that there are many reasons beyond financial ones for working outside the home, including personal and professional development, networking with others, and getting a break from child care at home.

Financial Resource Management

Family resource management is a field that studies the processes of planning and using human resources toward the optimal development of both the individual and the family. It focuses on relationships and activities within the home as well as outside it (Rettig & Hogan, 1993). Resource management is an important aspect of family living because it involves the mobilization of resources toward important values and central life purposes, helping family members meet changing goals and concerns across the life span. Family resource management looks at the family as a problem-solving group and views management as a means of achieving some of the most prized qualities of life (Rettig & Hogan, 1993).

The decision-making process in family resource management can be broken down into the following specific actions (Rettig, 1986):

- Perceiving desired or necessary changes
- Facing the problem
- Agreeing to solve the problem
- Discussing the meaning and definition of the problem
- Identifying personal needs
- Negotiating and mediating the issues
- Imagining and creating desirable alternative outcomes
- Agreeing on value priorities, goals, and policies
- Planning the mobilization of resources for high-priority goals
- Implementing policies and plans
- Controlling and adjusting plans
- Evaluating and assessing results
- Planning for the future

The Process: Stages and Steps

Building on a management model developed by Bea Paolucci and her colleagues, Bauer and Wollen (1990) have illustrated the value of a systematic approach to managing resources. The two basic stages are (1) organizing and planning and (2) implementing decisions.

Organizing and Planning The organizing-and-planning stage of family resource management includes three steps: value clarification, goal setting, and resource allocation.

VALUE CLARIFICATION **Values** are ideas we have about what we consider desirable in life—what we believe is right, what we hold dear, and what we feel committed to. Values are personal and deeply ingrained, and we use them to organize the world around us and to direct our plans and activities. Although we may not realize it, values influence all our choices (Bauer & Wollen, 1990).

One reason arguments over money can become so heated is that decisions about money stem from values. When someone else questions or attacks our financial decisions, we often feel personally attacked. In family money management, it is important that individuals clarify their personal values and then find a way to work together so that each individual's values can be expressed. Compromise may be necessary to maintain the well-being of the family unit.

GOAL SETTING   When they have clarified their values and have found a way to preserve individuality, family members can begin to set goals together. **Goals** are objectives, or purposes, an individual or a family wants to achieve; and economic, human, and environmental resources are the tools for attaining them. Because the basic purpose of any kind of management is achieving goals, family members must discuss, clarify, and prioritize their goals as part of the financial management process (Bauer & Wollen, 1990).

Goals must be attainable and realistic, and they also must be stated in specific and measurable terms. A well-conceived goal indicates exactly what needs to be done and when it needs to be done. Goals can be set for both the short term and the long term. We organize our daily lives around short-term goals: "Today I'm going to fill out the forms at the credit union to make sure money is deducted each month from my paycheck." But these short-term goals generally relate to long-term objectives: "Eventually, I will have saved enough money for a down payment on a house."

RESOURCE ALLOCATION   Successful family resource management at all stages of the family life cycle depends on a realistic assessment of individual and family resources. **Resources** are the tools, talents, and possessions we use to create a lifestyle, solve everyday problems, and reach goals. A complete assessment of family resources includes an examination of economic, environmental, and human resources.

Economic resources can be divided into four types: income, fringe benefits, credit, and wealth. *Environmental resources* include the physical environment (land, plants, and water), political and community resources (schools, police, and social service agencies), and social resources (religious bodies, community groups, and service organizations) available to the family. *Human resources* include the mental, emotional, and physical qualities individuals possess: physical skills (such as woodworking, typing, gardening), social skills, and mental skills (such as problem solving, planning, decision making); interests (a desire or willingness to be involved in a particular activity); attitudes (a willingness to adapt, self-confidence, friendliness); human energy (an individual's capacity for mental, physical, and emotional activity); and time (Bauer & Wollen, 1990). This list illustrates just how many different resources we have at our disposal. The process of resource allocation means using the best resource to do the job effectively and efficiently.

Implementing Decisions   The implementation of decisions is the second stage of family resource management; it involves three steps: facilitating, checking, and adjusting.

FACILITATING   This stage begins with the facilitation of the decisions agreed upon in the organizing-and-planning stage. Family members facilitate the implementation of their decisions by drawing upon all the resources they command. Human resources are probably a family's greatest resource. Enthusiasm for the task at hand makes the work go more smoothly. Good judgment, initiative, and skill in communication all make the implementation process easier.

CHECKING   During the implementation stage, it is essential to monitor the situation regularly and to carefully evaluate whether the plan is working. For example, did we really make as much money at work this month as we had hoped? Were expenses as low as we predicted? Can we handle the 17% increase in health insurance this year?

ADJUSTING   Often, families find that their initial assessment of the financial picture was less than perfect. Minor (and sometimes major) adjustments to plans are usually necessary. Say, for example, that you didn't know much about roofing when you bought your old house, and now winter rains are turning your king-sized mattress in the upstairs bedroom into a water bed. A new roof will cost $8,000. Finding the money for the roof may require numerous adjustments to your financial plans. No matter what the stage of the family life cycle, unexpected expenses are bound to arise.

Budgeting Guidelines

Budgeting is the regular, systematic balancing of income and expenses. It is a personal system for making sure there is enough money to cover the essentials and, one hopes, a few extras.

To construct a workable budget, individuals need to examine their personal values about saving and spending; they must also have a good idea of what things really cost. To begin with, couples need to establish how much income they can count on. They should then outline their expenses by category: shelter, transportation, food, clothing, and so forth. After developing categories that reflect their particular circumstances, they must estimate how much money they will need to pay for each category.

Most people don't take the time to create a budget. An accurate budget requires that a couple or family record their expenses on a regular basis so they know how much they are spending in each category. At the end of the month, the couple can look at the recorded expenditures and develop a budget for the next month. Individuals usually find budgeting easier than families do because they don't need to negotiate decisions and work out priorities that are appropriate for the entire family.

Budgeting is a continuous process of assessment and adjustment. A good budget is simple, realistic, and clear. A good budget builds in some personal control for each family member. It also distinguishes between wants and needs, with needs given priority but a few wants satisfied if possible. A good budget treats credit as debt, not income. Charging something or deciding to pay for it "on time" creates a fixed expense that adds to a family's debt.

A sample budget for a married couple who both work outside the home is shown in Table 11.6. In looking at the budget, remember that every budget is unique; no one is "average" or "typical." This two-income couple had only a $60 surplus at the end of the month. Unfortunately, too many couples go deeper into debt each month, rather than accrue savings. Careful planning and use of resources is the difference between comfort and crisis. In Box 11.2, sociologist Carlfred Broderick, who teaches marriage and family courses at the University of Southern California, discusses the hard realities of budgeting.

Table 11.6 A Monthly Budget for a Two-Income Couple

Income (after taxes, Social Security, retirement, and health insurance)	
Husband's take-home pay	$ 1,430
Wife's take-home pay	1,010
Interest earned on savings	30
Total income	**$2,470**
Fixed expenses	
Rent	$ 485
Bank loan (automobile)	150
Utilities	110
Telephone	45
Insurance	95
Furniture payments	170
Savings	260
Day-to-day and discretionary expenses	
Food	$ 280
Clothing	175
Entertainment	130
Personal care	80
Gas, oil, insurance, and car maintenance	140
Miscellaneous	290
Total expenses	**$2,460**
Surplus	**$ 60**

Source: Adapted from *Financial Management Extension Consultant Program: Young Singles and Young Couples* (MI-3891) (p. 28) by J. W. Bauer and B. J. Wollen, 1990. Copyright © Minnesota Extension Service, University of Minnesota. Reproduced with permission of the publisher. Copies available from Distribution Center, 20 Coffey Hall, 1420 Eckles Ave., St. Paul, MN 55108-6064.

Pooling Money: Pros and Cons

Should two-income couples pool their money? This is a difficult question that partners have to answer together and one they should discuss before marriage. One study found that couples who favored pooling money were neither more nor less satisfied with money management issues in their relationship than those couples who insisted on keeping money separate. Each group of couples believed their system was the right way to handle money (Blumstein & Schwartz, 1983, p. 108).

Many newly married couples feel obligated to pool their money, believing that a refusal to do so might be interpreted as a lack of commitment. Married couples tend to favor pooling more than cohabiting couples, but those who remarry after divorce are more likely to maintain separate funds, perhaps because they worry about the permanence of the new relationship or because they bring financial assets or liabilities to the new relationship (Blumstein & Schwartz, 1983).

Pooling is simpler because there are fewer accounts to balance. But because each spouse must keep the other informed about financial transactions, pooling entails some loss of independence. If one partner forgets to record a check written on the joint account and causes an overdraft, a conflict is inevitable.

BOX 11.2

A Lesson in Budgeting

It is always an instructive experience to watch a class of unmarried undergraduate students draw up a budget for the first year of marriage. Inevitably the students assume two substantial incomes. One or possibly both are expected to bring a car with them into the marriage. They are scandalized to learn how much of their paychecks they will never see due to deductions for various federal and state taxes. They are not aware that some companies also deduct substantial amounts for pension or retirement funds, insurance, or parking privileges. Even so, the diminished total is still substantial, and they plunge into the list of monthly expenditures with some zest. They allot so much for a decent apartment and utilities, so much for food, so much for eating out, for entertainment or hobbies, for clothes, for insurance, for transportation, for medical and dental expenses, for personal allowances, for laundry, for subscriptions to newspapers and magazines, for church or charity, for gifts.

The married students in the class sit shaking their heads as the numbers are put on the board. Inevitably there is an overrun on the first approximation, so the class painfully and reluctantly cuts back a few dollars here and there. Finally they come up with a balanced budget and a feeling of relief that it is really not so bad after all. Then someone says, "But what if the woman gets pregnant and they lose her income?" A grim silence settles over the class. Someone else says, "She just can't. They can't afford a baby, even on both incomes." "What? Not ever?" "Well, I don't see how—not on that budget." Yet it is clear that couples do it all the time.

Eventually a married student will confess that he or she and spouse live on a fraction of the money listed. How? Well, they almost never eat out, they drive only one car, and they don't have much furniture because they can't afford it. Not infrequently students accuse me of having set up this situation to discourage them from ever getting married. That is not true. But it is true that some of the toughest issues to face in the transition from romantic courtship to the realities of marriage are in the area of money.

Source: *Marriage and the Family* (4th ed.) (pp. 231–232) by C. Broderick, 1992, Englewood Cliffs, NJ: Prentice-Hall. Copyright 1992 by C. Broderick. Reprinted by permission of the publisher.

"We had a very organized system all worked out when we got married," explained Janice, a middle-aged Kansas City woman who was talking about her second marriage. "We were older. Frank was 49 at the time. I was 35. We were very logical. We kept separate accounts, not wanting to pool our income. He had his business expenses to cover, and I had my business expenses. I had the three kids, from my first marriage. It seemed logical for him to pay for his things and for me to pay for my things. Keep it separate, keep it orderly.

"Our logical system worked for about 3 months, and then he got cancer and was out of work for 11 months. No income. I had to pay for everything out of my income. It was tight, but we made it financially. And Frank recovered from the cancer and has a good prognosis.

"Then not long after the cancer episode, almost as if to even things up a bit, my first husband came roaring back and took us into court in an extended custody battle over the children. He charged that I was a rotten mother and that he should be awarded the kids. His charges were complete nonsense, but the fight lasted 2 1/2 years and cost $35,000 before we finally won. There was no way I could pay for all that, so Frank dipped into his savings and helped me out.

"He said he did it because it was only fair: I had saved him in his time of crisis, the cancer, and he loves the children and feels like a father to them and wanted me to be happy. Now we share all our money and feel more like a couple.

(Continued. . .)

> *(...Continued)*
> "Actually, I'm glad we did. We have created a really good marriage by not keeping the books so precisely. We don't worry so much about money anymore."

Savings

Thrift used to be a basic American virtue. Now the American virtue is to spend money.

—David Brinkley

Most poverty-level and lower-income families are incapable of saving much money. They spend a high percentage of their income to meet basic needs such as food, clothing, shelter, and utilities. However, middle- and upper-income families are in a good position to save something each month, and there are very good reasons for them to do so.

Perhaps the best reason for saving is to prepare for the possibility of a financial crisis. Accidents, illness, pregnancy, job loss, divorce, and many other crises are all too common—and they all have financial consequences. At least 6 months' salary should be saved for emergencies. By following a few simple guidelines, couples and families can save 10% to 20% of their income per year. Thomas Garman and Raymond Forgue (1997), experts in financial management, offer six guidelines for those who want to save money:

- *Don't buy on impulse.* Know what you're shopping for, and don't buy anything you don't really need.

- *Avoid buying on credit.* The high interest rates credit cards charge can double the cost of an item.

- *Buy at the right time.* Avoid peak-demand, and therefore peak-price, periods. Watch for sales, but don't buy something just because it's cheap. Look for quality.

- *Don't pay extra for a brand name.* Generic items are often as good as and are usually cheaper than brand-name goods. Again, look for quality.

- *Recognize that convenience costs money.* The local store may be handy, but a once-a-week trip to the discount center may yield savings.

- *Question the need to go first-class.* Do you really need the "best"? Can you really afford the most expensive version of a given product or service?

Perhaps the most important fact of the financial world is that interest on savings compounds. Money invested in a safe place at a good rate of return grows at a steady rate. Albert Einstein is reported to have called compound interest "the greatest mathematical discovery of all time." By saving a few hundred dollars a month over 30 or 40 years, a person can become a millionaire. It takes some planning and careful budgeting, but the result is relative financial gain and security. Table 11.7 shows the result of saving $100 a month and investing it at 6% and 12% rates of growth over various periods.

YEARS	AMOUNT INVESTED	INTEREST RATE 6%	12%	DIFFERENCE
Table 11.7 The Results of Saving $100 a Month at Different Interest Rates				
10	$12,000	$ 16,766	$ 23,586	$ 6,820
20	24,000	46,791	96,838	50,047
30	36,000	100,562	324,351	223,789
40	48,000	196,857	1,030,970	834,113

Credit: Uses and Abuses

There are both advantages and disadvantages to using credit. Buying on credit is easy, but it is important not to overdo it. Excessive debt can result in bankruptcy. Financial counseling can help those who have gotten into problems with credit.

Advantages and Disadvantages of Credit

Buying on credit is very popular for a number of reasons (Bauer & Wollen, 1990). It is convenient, and it also allows people to enjoy something while paying for it, to take advantage of sales, and to have something in case of an emergency. The disadvantages of credit include the generally high interest charges and the potential for overuse. Credit should be used with caution. Unfortunately, it is a very seductive luxury.

Purchasing a Home

The family dwelling has psychological significance in virtually all cultures. It provides the family's space and binds them together as a unit. It can be a haven, a place of rest and enjoyment, somewhere to kick off one's shoes and escape the pretenses of polite society.

A home is usually the most expensive item Americans buy. Careful deliberation should go into its purchase. One rule of thumb is that whether renting or buying, a family should spend no more than one week's take-home pay per month for housing expenses. Housing expenses are either rent or the total of all house-payment expenses (mortgage payment, insurance, and real estate taxes). Families who can find adequate shelter for 20% to 25% of their take-home pay are likely to be in relatively good financial health. Unfortunately, many lower-income families find themselves paying 50% of their income or more for housing.

Renting Versus Buying Generally speaking, it is wiser to buy a home than to rent. Rent money is gone forever, whereas each mortgage payment gradually increases one's equity in the home while inflation increases the net worth of the dwelling. There are, however, many exceptions to this generalization, and families must carefully analyze their unique financial situation to decide if buying a home is the right choice for them.

There are numerous advantages to both renting and buying (Garman & Forgue, 1997). The advantages of renting include mobility, perhaps some

Credit is a very seductive luxury that should be used with caution.

amenities (pool, tennis courts, party rooms, laundry facilities), and a lifestyle that involves fewer responsibilities. No large down payment is needed (only a security deposit), and the relatively fixed housing expenditure (rent) makes budgeting easier.

The advantages of buying include pride of ownership, a better credit rating, and a monthly payment that remains constant for many years (that is, with a fixed-rate mortgage). The federal income tax deductions for mortgage interest and real estate property taxes are a major advantage, as is the potential for the home to increase in value over time. Owning a house forces one to save; each payment represents an asset that is growing in value. A homeowner can also borrow against equity as the value of the home increases. Furthermore, owners can make home improvements and alterations, which can increase the value of the home and/or add to the enjoyment of the dwelling.

The disadvantages of renting are that it offers no tax deductions and no potential gain from the rising value of the property. Furthermore, rents rise with inflation, and many rental units have restrictions on noise level, pet ownership, and children. One disadvantage of buying is the substantial down payment that is needed; this can reduce available funds for other things. Also, the cost of maintenance and repairs can be high. A home is a big commitment in time, emotion, and money.

Table 11.8 illustrates the financial benefits of buying versus renting. The example is based on renting a home for $600 a month or buying a similar home for a slightly lower mortgage payment of $545.48 a month. Careful study of the table shows that renting in this particular situation costs more than buying by about $2,155 a year.

Table 11.8 Should You Buy or Rent?		
	CALCULATING THE COST TO:	
	Rent	**Buy**
Cash-flow Considerations		
Annual rent ($600/month) or mortgage payments ($545.48/month)	$7,200	$6,546
Property and liability insurance	270	425
Real estate taxes	NA	2,000
Maintenance	NA	320
Less interest on funds not used for down payment (at 5%)	−750	0
Cash-flow cost for the year	**$6,720**	**$9,291**
Tax and appreciation considerations		
Less principal repaid on the mortgage loan	NA	−725
Plus tax on interest from funds not used for down payment (28% tax bracket)	210	NA
Less tax savings due to deductibility of mortage interest (28% tax bracket)	NA	−1,630
Less tax savings due to deductibility of real estate property tax (28% tax bracket)	NA	−560
Less appreciation on the dwelling (2% rate)	NA	−1,600
Net cost for the year	**$6,930**	**$4,776**

Source: Personal Finance (5th ed.) (p. 292) by E. T. Garman and R. E. Forgue, 1997, Boston: Houghton Mifflin. Copyright © 1997 Houghton Mifflin Co. Reprinted by permission of the publisher.

The Cost of Home Loans   Family resource management specialists advise people to shop carefully for a loan when purchasing a home. The difference in the monthly payment between a 9% and a 10% home loan might not be much, but over the life of the loan—which usually lasts anywhere from 15 to 30 years—the savings on interest payments can be substantial. A very modest 25-year mortgage loan of $60,000 will cost the borrower more than $151,000 at 9% interest but more than $157,000 at 10% interest. One percentage point makes a $6,000 difference over the 25-year life of the loan. These figures also show that a $65,000 or $75,000 home (assuming a $5,000 or $15,000 down payment plus a $60,000 loan) really costs more than double its price when the interest on the mortgage is considered.

Credit Overextension

Out of debt, out of danger.—from a Chinese fortune cookie

Credit overextension, a situation in which excessive debts make repayment difficult, is a serious problem that can cause considerable stress on families. The following danger signs suggest credit overextension (Bauer & Wollen, 1990; Garman & Forgue, 1997):

- *Debt exceeds normal limits.* People who spend more than 15% to 20% of their disposable income to repay debts (excluding mortgage loans) are likely to be in trouble. If the percentage increases each month, the situation becomes even more serious.

- *Monthly expenses exceed income.* When too much income goes to debt repayment, people may use credit cards to purchase things they would normally buy with cash. They may also use high-interest-rate cash advances from their credit cards. Both actions increase the overall debt load.

- *Using savings to pay for everyday expenses.*

- *Paying the minimum payment only.* Rather than paying each month's bills in full, people begin to pay only what they must, increasing their debt from month to month.

- *Reaching or exceeding credit limits.* People who are at or near the limits of their various lines of credit or those who are requesting increases in their credit limits may be in trouble.

- *Picking which creditors to pay.* As monthly bills mount and sources of additional credit are exhausted, people begin to pick and choose among creditors, paying a few one month and others the next.

- *Borrowing from one source to pay another:* People who use a cash advance from one credit card to pay the monthly bill on another credit card are likely to be in trouble.

- *Total debt is unknown.* People who cannot quickly estimate how much they owe often have multiple creditors to whom they owe large amounts.

- *Loss of a job would mean immediate financial disaster:* When a wage earner loses a job, it is a serious financial crisis for most families. But the full effects may not be felt immediately by families who have a savings cushion. Those who are already overextended in terms of credit have no resources with which to weather any loss of income.

Debt and Bankruptcy

Bankruptcy is a legal term indicating that a person is financially insolvent and unable to pay her or his debts. More than 1 million people declare personal bankruptcy in the United States each year (U.S. Bureau of the Census, 1997). Although bankruptcy offers some protection from creditors, it is not a solution to financial problems because bankruptcy blemishes one's financial record for many years, making many financial matters more difficult. In our society bankruptcy signifies an individual's inability to handle money wisely, and society exacts various punishments on those who declare bankruptcy.

To stay out of debt and avoid bankruptcy, it is helpful to know why some people assume too much debt. It is interesting that level of income is not clearly related to debt. Debt-free families and debt-ridden families alike come from all socioeconomic levels.

Excessive debt may be due to any or all of the following reasons: credit spending, crisis spending, careless or impulsive spending, and compulsive spending.

Unwise *credit spending* can lead to overextension. *Crisis spending*—resulting from unexpected events in life such as unemployment, uninsured illness, and business income decline or failure—can throw personal finances into turmoil. *Careless or impulsive spending* includes overpaying for items that could be purchased for less, purchasing inferior merchandise that does not last, and buying things one does not really need. *Compulsive spending* occurs because some people simply can't say no to salespeople or because they have an uncontrollable impulse to acquire material things.

The healthiest of families can become financially overextended. Excessive debt is not necessarily a sign of stupidity or a personality defect, nor is it an indicator of immorality. A miscalculation can lead to financial problems. Ignorance in a highly technical area or a financial downturn beyond one's control in a global industry can precipitate trouble. Fortunately, there are a number of time-tested strategies for families who have become overextended. Although these solutions are not easy, they are far better than the alternative of bankruptcy:

- Develop and stick to a balanced budget.

- Avoid making any new financial commitments. Do not incur any new debt.

- Destroy all credit cards or lock them up so that they can't be used.

- Develop a plan for repaying all debts. If the budget cannot handle the repayment schedule, try to negotiate lower payments and lower payback periods.

- Pay off debts with the highest interest rates first.

- Work to reduce the total number of debts.

- Make a plan to pay at least a small amount on each debt each month.

- Avoid debt-consolidation loans. These can set the stage for new borrowing, especially on credit cards.

Financial Counseling

If they have made no progress in 3 to 6 months, people who are overextended should seek financial counseling. Many large employers have budget counselors available through the human resources department or an employee assistance program. When financial difficulties are a symptom of a deeper marital or personal problem (alcohol or other drug abuse, depression, violence), a therapist may be the best way to approach the crisis.

For example, a single parent continues to support her 25-year-old son, even though his cocaine addiction is dragging her down financially. The son deals cocaine to come up with some of the $3,000 or $4,000 a month he needs to support his drug habit. He regularly borrows money from his mother and even steals and pawns her possessions. Consumed by guilt, she covers up for him, pays the bills, and lends him money, denying his drug habit. This mother needs not only a competent financial advisor to help her deal with the mountain of debts she has accumulated but also a personal therapist to help her come to grips with her son's drug problem, for which he must take responsibility.

People seeking financial counseling should avoid "credit clinics," which charge fees of $250 to $2,000 or more for their services. Some of these businesses advertise that they will negotiate new repayment schedules with creditors, but people in financial trouble can work directly with their creditors or can find help from nonprofit personal counseling organizations (Bauer & Wollen, 1990; Garman & Forgue, 1997). The human-services section of most local telephone books lists resources. Another possible resource is the network of more than 1,000 Consumer Credit Counseling Service (CCCS) agencies across the United States. Each year about a million people seek credit and budget counseling advice from CCCS.

"We were near bankruptcy when we finally decided to go to a family therapist who specialized in financial issues," said Vera, a 35-year-old woman from Birmingham, Alabama. "It was the best thing we could have done. She helped us see that we both looked at money differently, and she helped us reconcile our differences. We had to cut up a lot of credit cards and go on a strict financial diet.

"But it worked, and today we are in good shape financially. More important, we understand each other much better and know how to avoid ugly arguments while still maintaining genuine communication."

Summary

- According to a national survey of married couples, happy couples—as compared to unhappy couples—have less difficulty making financial decisions, have fewer concerns about how money is handled in their marriage, have fewer major debts, are more satisfied with their decisions about saving, and agree more often on how to spend money.

- Married couples fight over finances more than any other topic. The top five financial-management issues that married couples identified in a national survey were the following: they wish their partner were more careful about spending money; they disagree on how to spend money; they are unable to budget and keep a record of money spent; they have problems with credit cards or charge accounts; and they have difficulty deciding how to handle their finances.

- Financial issues are the most common stressor for U.S. families across the family life cycle, regardless of their income level. The most financially trying periods are the childbearing, adolescent, launching, and retirement stages.

- Money problems are often related to a couple's or a family's inability to develop specific spending and saving plans. Some arguments are not really about money, however, but about power and control in the relationship.

- Personal and family coping behaviors that help people through difficult economic times include self-esteem, cohesion, and adaptability. Social support from family members and others and the use of family service agencies are also important resources. Coping strategies that make things worse include denying the problem and failing to disclose feelings.

- Finances cause problems for couples and families because people (1) consider the topic of money taboo, (2) have unrealistic expectations about finances, (3) do not create and stick to a budget, (4) overspend and rely too heavily on credit, (5) differ in their spending and saving styles, (6) use money as a tool to gain power and control over their partner, and (7) have different ideas about the meaning of money.

- More than half the families in the United States are considered middle-income families, defined by the U.S. Bureau of the Census as earning between $15,000 and $75,000 per year. However, a disproportionate share of the money in this country goes to affluent families, with 18.6% of families receiving roughly 46.5% of the personal income. About 14% of U.S. families are lower-income families, but they make only 4% of all personal income.

- White families in the United States make more money, on average, than Hispanic and African American families. The median income for White families is $43,265 and is considerably higher than that of African American ($26,838) or Hispanic ($25,491) families. Males make more money than females, and there is a clear relationship between educational level and income.

- The two major stages in the process of family resource management are (1) organizing and planning, which involves value clarification, goal setting, and resource allocation, and (2) implementing decisions, which involves facilitating, checking, and adjusting financial plans.

- Budgeting is the regular, systematic balancing of income and expenses. To budget successfully, individuals need to examine their personal values about saving and spending and to monitor their plan monthly.

- Couples who pool their money are neither more nor less satisfied with money management issues in the relationship than couples who have separate accounts.

- Most poverty-level and lower-income families are incapable of saving much money because they must spend most of their income to meet basic needs. Middle- and upper-income families should put aside at least 6 months' income in savings for financial emergencies.

- Monthly housing expenses should consume no more than one week's take-home pay. Generally, buying a home is a better investment than renting.

- Credit spending, crisis spending, careless or impulsive spending, and compulsive spending are four reasons people go into excessive debt. Families who cannot reduce their debt over a period of 3 to 6 months should seek financial and perhaps personal counseling.

Key Terms

personal coping resources	spender	resources
family coping resources	values	budgeting
saver	goals	bankruptcy

Activities

1. Write a few paragraphs describing how money was handled in your family of origin and how you handle money today. Then form groups of five or six for discussion. After having read the essays out loud, identify similarities and differences that emerge. Have someone record these observations and report them to the class. Identify the common themes among all the group reports.

2. Are you a spender or a saver? How about your partner? Consider the similarities and differences between your style and your partner's style.

3. Pair off into "couples" and discuss the following questions (Dyer & Dyer, 1990) as if you were planning to marry. Then report your discussions to the class.

   a. Do you believe that all your assets belong to both of you and that all your debts are your joint responsibility?

   b. Do you expect to share equally in financial decisions? If not, how do you plan to make financial decisions?

   c. Do you plan to use a budget? Why or why not?

   d. How do you feel about each partner's having a personal allowance for which he or she is not accountable to the other?

   e. How do you feel about buying small items on credit? large items?

   f. What will you do about the debts each of you brings into the marriage?

   g. Who will be the treasurer? the checkwriter? the bookkeeper? the investor?

4. Figure out your own personal budget, using the Personal Budgeting Form on page 357. Fill in each blank, estimating how much you spend in each area. How much can you put into savings? How much surplus will you have at the end of each month?

Suggested Readings

Anderson, E. A., & Koblinsky, S. A. (1995). Homeless policy: The need to speak to families. *Family Relations, 44,* 13–18. A summary of current research on the characteristics of homeless families, with an overview of government policy.

Bauer, J. W., & Wollen, B. J. (1990). *Financial Management Extension Consultant Program: Young singles and young couples.* St. Paul, MN: Minnesota Extension Service. A useful tool that helps young people manage money successfully.

Poduska, B. E. (1993). *For love and money: A guide to finances and relationships.* Pacific Grove, CA: Brooks/Cole Publishing. A practical guide to handling finances in a way that enhances a relationship.

Rubin, L. B. (1992). *Worlds of pain: Life in the working-class family* (2nd ed.). New York: Basic Books. The current edition of the 1976 classic qualitative study of working-class couples, providing "flesh and blood" insights.

Rubin, L. B. (1994). *Families on the fault line: America's working class speaks about the family, the economy, race, and ethnicity.* New York: HarperCollins. A study based on 162 interviews with working-class and lower-middle-class families in various U.S. cities.

VanderStaay, S. (1992). *Street lives: An oral history of homeless Americans.* Philadelphia: New Society. Sensitizes the reader to the human dimensions of extreme poverty in the United States.

Personal Budgeting Form

Monthly Income	$_____

Expenses

Food, total $_____
   Meals and snacks at home
   Food away from home
   Alcoholic beverages
   Other_____

Housing, total $_____
   Rent or mortgage
   Fuels, utilities, and public services
   Household operations and furnishings
   Housekeeping supplies
   Other_____

Apparel and services $_____

Transportation, total $_____
   Vehicles
   Gasoline, maintenance, insurance
   Public transportation

Health care $_____

Life and other personal insurance $_____

Pensions and Social Security $_____

Other expenditures $_____

Savings $_____

Monthly Expenses	$_____
Surplus (if any)	$_____

PART IV

Stages of Marriage and Family Life

BOX 12.1

Facts About Marriage

- Approximately 1.8 million couples marry each year.

- Approximately 1.0 million couples divorce each year.

- In about half (47%) of all marriages, one of both people have been married at least once before.

- In 1997, the bridegroom's average age was 27; the bride's average age was 25.5. In 1960, the average age was 22.8 for the bridegroom and 20.3 for the bride.

- Engagements last an average of 9 months.

- The average U.S. wedding costs about $15,000.

- The average age at divorce is 36 for males and 33 for females.

- Approximately half of all marriages end in divorce.

- The average length of a marriage is 7 years.

- Over 1 million couples with children divorce each year.

Source: U.S. Bureau of the Census (1997).

to remarry and instead either stay single or choose cohabitation over marriage. Marriage has been on the decline for the last two decades, and it appears that increasingly fewer people will choose to get married or to remarry in future years.

The Benefits of Marriage

Society has a large stake in strengthening marriages. Children should be our central concern and, in general, they are better when raised by two parents. Marriage also typically improves the health and economic wellbeing of adults, stabilizes community life and benefits civic society.

—THEODORA OOMS (1998b, p. 4)

Because the media so often focuses on the negative aspects of marriage (marital violence, divorce), many people often fail to see the positive effects of marriage, which are numerous. Linda Waite reviewed various studies that examined the positive effects of marriage on individuals (Waite & Gallagher, 1999; Waite 1995, 1998). These benefits are as follow:

- *Married people lead a healthier lifestyle.* People who are married tend to avoid more harmful behaviors than do single, divorced, or widowed persons. For example, married people have much lower levels of problem drinking, which is associated with accidents, interpersonal conflict, and depression in women. In general, married people lead a healthier lifestyle in terms of eating, exercise, and avoiding harmful behaviors.

- *Married people live longer.* At every age level, married people live several years longer than do single, divorced, or widowed persons. This is often because they have emotional support in their partner, and the availability of more economic resources.

- *Married people have a satisfying sexual relationship.* Married couples have sex about 6 to 7 times per month, as compared to an average of 7 times for cohabiting couples and only 3 to 4 times for singles. In terms of sexual satisfaction, over half (54%) of the married males and 43% of married females are extremely satisfied with their sexual relationship. For cohabiting couples, about 44% of the males and 35% of the females are extremely satisfied.

- *Married people have more wealth and economic assets.* Because a married couple can pool their economic resources, they tend to be more wealthy. In fact, the median household wealth for a married couple is $132,000, as compared to $35,000 for singles, $42,275 for widowed individuals, $33,670 for divorced individuals, and $7,600 for separated individuals. Married couples have greater wealth in part because two can live for the price of $1\frac{1}{2}$ persons by sharing the cost of housing, household appliances, furniture, utilities, and so on.

- *Children generally do better raised in a two-parent home.* Children from two-parent homes tend to do better emotionally and academically. They are half as likely to drop out of school; they have higher grades; and they are less likely to get pregnant. Children from two-parent homes also get more parental attention (such as parental supervision, help with schoolwork, and quality time with each child) than do children from single-parent homes. Also, children from single-parent homes have a much higher probability of growing up in poverty and experiencing a lower quality of life.

In summary, being married has a very positive impact on an individual's emotional and physical health. Some have suggested that the question isn't whether marriage has a positive effect on individuals but whether more healthy and happy people choose to marry rather than remain single. Nonetheless, an extensive analysis from a variety of studies demonstrates that selective factors in who marries do not explain the positive benefits of marriage (Waite, 1995, 1998). It is, in fact, the synergy of pooling a variety of resources that makes marriage beneficial to individuals.

A Formula for a Successful Marriage

A loving relationship can bring two people enormous benefits; it can help them grow as friends and lovers, and it can even heal wounds. Most counselors agree that the chances of marital success are greater if both partners enter marriage as friends; but the chances of achieving a successful intimate relationship are slim for a couple in which one plays the role of therapist and the other the role of patient. A careful review of research and clinical experience reported by many professionals indicates that a marriage has a better chance for success if potential partners meet the following conditions:

- *Both individuals are independent and mature.* The more mature and independent two people are, the easier it is for them to develop an interdependent relationship that can facilitate intimacy. Independence and maturity often increase with age, a good reason for waiting to marry. In fact,

Independent and mature people are likely to have acquired the self-knowledge and self-confidence necessary for an intimate relationship and a successful marriage. Because they can express their needs honestly and assertively and respond unselfishly to each other's needs, such couples are more likely to be friends as well as lovers.

the single best predictor of a successful marriage is the age of the couple. This is partly because older people are typically more stable and know what they want in marriage.

- *Both individuals love not only each other but themselves.* Self-esteem is very important in an intimate relationship. It is difficult to truly love another person without also loving oneself. People need to feel secure and self-confident before they can be truly giving and loving to another.

- *Both individuals enjoy being alone as well as together.* To balance the separateness and togetherness that an intimate relationship requires, partners need to enjoy separate activities and time apart. Time apart reminds partners of the value of the relationship and increases the importance and value of time together. Too much togetherness can lead to such negative behaviors as attempting to control one's partner and failing to appreciate the partner.

- *Both individuals are established in their work or occupation.* A stable and satisfying occupation or job fosters both financial and emotional security.

When people's jobs are going well, they are able to devote more time and energy to their relationships. Conversely, the greater the stress at work, the less positive energy there is for a relationship.

- *Both individuals know themselves.* An intimate relationship requires openness and honesty between partners. They must be able to evaluate their personal strengths and failings objectively and not blame their problems on other people. They must also know what they want from and can give to their partner.

- *Both individuals can express themselves assertively.* One key to developing intimacy is assertiveness—expressing oneself in a direct and generally positive manner. People who are not assertive in their communication often adopt a passive-aggressive approach. The more clearly partners can ask for what they want from each other, the better the chances for compliance. (See Chapter 9 for a detailed discussion on assertive communication.)

- *Both individuals are friends as well as lovers.* When people focus on their lover's needs, they find that the loved one tends to focus on their needs. This has been called the *law of enlightened self-interest.* Developed by social exchange theorists to describe successful relationships, the principle holds that being less selfish is in a person's best interest because it helps to build cooperative and intimate relationships that benefit everyone. Nonpossessive caring encourages the partner to grow and to reach his or her potential. Both partners generally benefit.

Reasons for Marrying

Most couples are able to list many positive reasons for getting married, but they often have difficulty identifying reasons not to marry. In this section we will explore a variety of both positive reasons and negative reasons for getting married.

Positive Reasons

There are many good reasons to get married, and marriages based on positive motives have a higher chance of success.

Companionship   Sharing one's life with another person is one common reason for marriage. Companionship enables partners to share the journey of life. However, although some people assume that marriage will end loneliness, it seldom does unless both partners feel good about themselves.

Love and Intimacy   The need for love and intimacy is related to the need for companionship. A good marriage can be a precious gift. Take, for example, actor Bill Cosby and his wife, Camille. The couple met on a blind date. They have four daughters, and friends view their relationship as a kind of "marital miracle." Cosby has been described as a very strong and purposeful individual, but he is said to melt in Camille's presence. "I've seen Bill walk into a crowded room, suddenly spot her, and start crawling toward her across the floor," one colleague reported. "Every time he looks at her, it's as if he's seeing her for the first time. It's like they're still on a high-school date." One reporter noted that when the subject of Camille came up, Cosby's eyes misted over and his voice quavered as he said, "It's hard to describe a relationship with so much growth in it. It goes past just missing her when she's not here. I'm just very, very fortunate that the person I trust the most trusts me and the person I love the most loves me. I love her so much" (Waters, 1985). Unfortunately, it is difficult to maintain such intensity in a long-term relationship; most couples report that passion decreases over the years.

Supportive Partnership   Marriage provides the opportunity for growth as a human being and for nurturing the growth of one's partner. A marriage cannot survive if the partners think only of their own development, career needs, or needs for recognition and accomplishment. But sharing each other's successes and genuinely supporting each other in the quest for betterment and achievement enhance and stabilize a relationship. To achieve this, both people must be willing and able to give of themselves. A mutual-admiration marriage has an excellent chance of success.

Sexual Partnership   Marriage has long been considered a stable source of sexual satisfaction for both partners. Although the "sexual revolution" of the 1960s and 1970s prompted many people to conclude that sex and marriage did not necessarily have to go together, the AIDS epidemic has caused a countershift in sexual attitudes to some degree. Marriage is often seen as a way to legitimize one's sexual feelings and behavior. Nonetheless, if sex is the major reason for marrying, the marriage will not have a very good chance of surviving.

Sharing Parenthood   Another traditional reason for marrying is to have children, but parenthood can be a mixed blessing. Most parents find rearing children to be a challenging, frustrating, and, at the same time, very satisfying task. When the children are grown up and independent, most parents say that they have had enough parenting for one lifetime, but they also say that if they had it to do all over again, they would again decide to have children. Parenthood clearly is not for everyone, and it can unite or divide a couple. Parents who successfully raise children forge important bonds between them. Approached realistically, parenthood remains a very sound reason for marriage.

Negative Reasons

There are also a number of poor reasons for getting married. Unless these issues are dealt with before marriage, they can create considerable challenges for a couple.

Premarital Pregnancy   "Having to get married" because of a premarital pregnancy is not a good way to go into marriage. Although the partners have shared sex, they may have not yet developed other aspects of true intimacy and may lack a real understanding of who they are marrying. Sex partners are not necessarily friends.

Almost one out of three children (30%) are born out of wedlock (U.S. Bureau of the Census, 1997). The rate of children born out of wedlock varies considerably by ethnic background: for African Americans the rate is 68%; for Native Americans, 55%; for Hispanics, 45%; for Caucasians, 23%; and for Asian Americans, 10%. These rates have increased dramatically in the past decade, and there are indications that they will not decrease unless interventions are developed to address this growing problem.

Rebellion Against Parents   Although many people are uncomfortable admitting it, they use conflict with parents as a reason for marrying. Marriage as rebellion against repressive parents or a dysfunctional family of origin may seem a rational option for a young person. People who have suffered in the cross fire of long-term conflicts between their parents or have been the victims of parental alcohol or drug abuse or of physical, emotional, or sexual abuse all have legitimate reasons to flee from their families. But a legitimate reason for leaving one's family of origin is not necessarily a legitimate reason for getting married. It is better to develop one's independence and to come to terms with one's family of origin before thinking about marriage.

Seeking Independence   Closely related to the need to escape or rebel is the need to be independent. Young adults have a drive to succeed on their own. But becoming independent from one's family of origin is something that only an individual can do. People cannot rely on their partner to do it for them.

Rebounding From Another Relationship   The rebound syndrome—another negative reason for getting married—seems to be easier to detect in other people than in ourselves. We might respond to a friend's warning, "Oh, no! I understand what you're saying, but this relationship is *different*." People tend to frame new relationships in positive terms, focusing on the joys and ignoring the fact that they may be reacting against their previous relationship. People on the rebound may "need" the new partner for emotional support, but a marriage works better when two people "want" rather than "need" each other. A rebound relationship is in danger from the start because the object of affection is seen not only as a friend or lover but also as a therapist or healer of the wounds of the old relationship.

Family or Social Pressure   Many families put subtle and not-so-subtle pressure on people to marry when they are relatively young. Both males and females may be pressured, but women often feel more pressure as they reach their late 20s. Many students who go to college find that the classmates they left behind in their hometown are soon married and pregnant. People who choose for many good reasons not to marry young or who choose not to marry at all should not succumb to this pressure. Marrying against one's own desires is unlikely to produce a happy relationship.

Economic Security   Although economic security has been a traditional reason for marrying, it has dubious merits today. With half of today's marriages likely to end in divorce, young women simply cannot afford to be dependent financially on their husbands. Add widowhood to this equation, and it becomes quite clear that all women need to know how to support themselves financially.

There is the genuine possibility of unemployment for one or both spouses over the course of a marriage. Many people experience the trauma of being out of

BOX 12.2

Warning Signs of a Problem Marriage

Monica McGoldrick, an eminent family therapist, has compiled the following list of warning signs of a problem marriage. The more characteristics that ring true, the higher the potential for marital problems.

1. The couple meets or marries shortly after a significant loss.

2. The wish to distance from one's family of origin is a factor in the marriage.

3. The family backgrounds of each spouse are significantly different (religion, education, social class, ethnicity, age of the partners).

4. The spouses come from incompatible sibling constellations.

5. The couple resides either extremely close to or at a great distance from either family of origin.

6. The couple is dependent on either extended family financially, physically, or emotionally.

7. The couple marries before age 20.

8. The couple marries after an acquaintanceship of less than 6 months or after more than 3 years of engagement.

9. The wedding occurs without family or friends present.

10. The wife becomes pregnant before marriage or within the first year of marriage.

11. Either spouse considers her or his childhood or adolescence an unhappy time.

12. Either spouse has a poor relationship with siblings or parents.

13. Marital patterns in either extended family were unstable.

Source: Adapted from "The Joining of Families Through Marriage: The New Couple" (p. 231) by M. McGoldrick. In *The Changing Family Life Cycle: A Framework for Family Therapy* (2nd ed.) by B. Carter and M. McGoldrick, 1989, New York: Gardner Press. Copyright © 1989 by Allyn & Bacon. Reprinted by permission.

work for an extended period. Marriage does not automatically produce economic security, but couples continue to search for the elusive goal. Financial problems are the most common marital problem Americans cite in national polls.

In summary, there are many positive and negative reasons for marrying, and people in love are often not objective when it comes to analyzing their motives and actions. Being rational and realistic about one's reasons for marrying is not easy; nevertheless, people who marry mainly for positive reasons are likely to have sounder marital relationships. For warning signs of potential marriage problems, see Box 12.2.

Parental Perspective and Influence on Marriage

A marriage is influenced by the parents of both partners. Folk wisdom tells us that when you get married, you marry a whole family, not just one person. This observation becomes increasingly clear as a couple moves toward marriage.

To examine the influence of parents on the premarital relationship, Stewart and Olson (1990) studied 5,128 premarital couples. Although all these couples were

Figure 12.1 Parents' Marital Status and Couples' Premarital Satisfaction. *Source:* From *Predicting Premarital Satisfaction on PREPARE Using Background Factors* by K. L. Stewart and D. H. Olson (1990), unpublished manuscript, Prepare/Enrich, Inc. Minneapolis, MN. Copyright © 1990 Prepare/Enrich. Used by permission of the publisher.

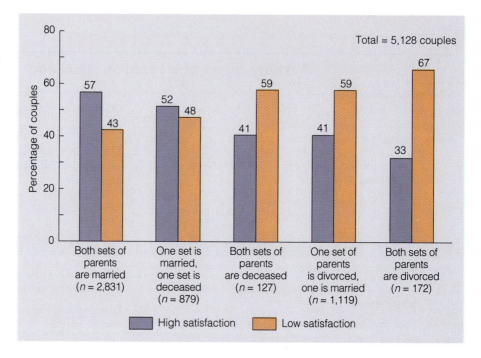

planning on marriage, not all were satisfied with their premarital relationship. People get married for many reasons, as discussed earlier. For a marriage to be strong and to last, the relationship must be healthy. Unfortunately, some premarital couples do not get along well even before marriage. Of all the premarital couples, two groups were studied: those who were very satisfied with their premarital relationship (the upper third of the total group) and those who were the least satisfied with their premarital relationship (the lower third of the total group). The middle third of the total group was not included in this analysis.

Stewart and Olson asked each of the engaged couples if their parents were positive or negative about the upcoming marriage. They found that of the engaged couples in which both sets of parents were negative about the upcoming marriage, 88% had low premarital satisfaction. Of the engaged couples in which only one set of parents was negative about the upcoming marriage, 73% said they had low premarital satisfaction. Looking at the data from the positive side, if both sets of parents were positive about the upcoming marriage, 58% of the engaged couples reported that they had a positive premarital relationship. This study demonstrates that parents are very accurate in their perception of a premarital couple's relationship, particularly if the couple is having problems. This is because "outsiders" such as parents are often more realistic and less idealistic than a couple in love. It is, therefore, important for a premarital couple to pay attention to outside feedback, particularly if others express serious concerns.

Another important determinant of a couple's premarital satisfaction is the parents' marital status. As presented in Figure 12.1, when both sets of parents were married, 57% of the premarital couples reported being highly satisfied with their relationship. When both sets of parents were divorced, however, 67% of the engaged couples reported low premarital satisfaction.

Will a couple with divorced parents also divorce? And will a couple with happily married parents have a good marriage relationship like that of their parents? Although there clearly is a strong tendency in the direction of the parental pattern, the premarital couple with divorced parents might simply need to work harder to overcome the issues and problems they have experienced in their families of origin.

"Divorce was no fun in our family," said Shelley as she sat on her living-room couch in her home in Omaha. "I was 12 at the time and I thought my family was the only awful family in the world. Dad was running around with his girlfriend, and Mom cried all the time. I can't think of many good things to say about divorce.

"But there is one: It made me very, very careful about getting married. I just didn't jump into it like some friends I know. Maybe I was even a bit too picky. I turned down two guys—one, I was even engaged to.

"Finally, though, after I had been going with Dave for 2 years, he broke down my barriers. I was 27 at the time and never married. He had been married for 3 years in his early 20s. I was really hesitant about getting involved with a guy who had been divorced. But he passed all my tests and put up with my gun-shy attitude toward marriage.

"We've been married 8 years now and I think it's going to work. But I still don't count on anything, because of what happened to Mom and Dad. We're careful to take good care of our marriage. Every day."

Preparing for Marriage

The dignity of a vocation is always to be measured by the seriousness of the preparation made for it. How then do we appraise marriage?
—R. Herbert Newton

Couples who marry for the first time often spend months of preparation and thousands of dollars on their wedding, a ceremony and celebration that last only a few hours, but most invest little time or money preparing for their marriage, which is intended to last a lifetime. The wedding is a time-honored American tradition; preparing for marriage is not. Although divorce probably causes as much or more pain in America than do automobile accidents each year, there is no "behind-the-wheel" test for couples planning to marry. But failing to prepare is like preparing to fail. Many couples in which one or both partners were married before agree; they see marital preparation as essential to making the new marriage work.

Can Couples Prepare for Marriage?

Before the wedding, couples spend hours talking about the wedding flowers, the size of the diamond and the design of its mounting, the color of the groomsmen's ties, and so on, but they rarely discuss such topics as finances, in-laws, and role relationships. Partners may fear that such challenging, serious topics would threaten the other partner or provoke a battle that could endanger the wedding.

Without instruction and preparation, people are no more expert at developing intimate relationships than they are at parenting. Writing about his own family-building experiences, Norbert Wiener, one of the original developers of the modern computer, said, "One has only one life to live and there is not time enough in which to master the art of being a parent" (Wiener, 1956, p. 224).

Only a small percentage of couples take advantage of courses on marriage and family life. A higher percentage spend an hour or two before the wedding with a minister, rabbi, or priest discussing marital issues. Still, one or two hours seems a meager investment in a relationship expected to last a lifetime.

Premarital programs can help couples learn to be realistic about marriage. Couples need to know that marriage takes a tremendous investment of time, effort, and energy and that they must work at their relationship throughout their life together. Premarital preparation can get the marriage off to a good start.

Good educational programs for premarital couples should be more available (Olson, 1992). Even after the wedding, couples would be well-advised to continue their studies on marriage by reading and discussing books on marriage or by attending marriage enrichment seminars or workshops as preventive maintenance.

If it weren't for concerned clergy who insist that couples meet with them at least once before marriage, many couples would have no premarital preparation. In fact, about 35% of all couples (usually those who are not married in a church or synagogue) receive no premarital services or programs. About 25% of couples meet once or twice with their clergy to discuss marriage issues. About 20% of couples attend church-sponsored small-group couples workshops or retreats where they discuss marriage. Because many clergy feel inadequately trained to work with couples, an increasing number are using premarital inventories to help them assess couple's relationships. About 15% of couples both consult with clergy and complete a premarital inventory. However, only about 5% of premarital couples obtain the most intensive and effective type of premarriage counseling, which incorporates structured programs to build both communication and problem-solving skills (Olson, 1992).

How Effective Are Premarital Programs?

Some approaches to premarital counseling are clearly more effective than others. Lectures are intended to produce changes in negative attitudes and to reinforce positive attitudes about family topics, but large lecture courses are not an effective way of helping individual premarital couples prepare for marriage. Rosalie Norem and her colleagues (Norem, Schaefer, Springer, & Olson, 1980) evaluated five different premarital education programs involving the large-group lecture format. The programs, which ran anywhere from 6 to 8 weeks, were judged by professionals to be well conceived and creatively presented, yet they produced no attitude change among participants. The researchers concluded it was much like pouring water over a duck's back. Another negative outcome of the large-group lecture format was that it discouraged most couples from considering future marriage enrichment programs. It also decreased couples' willingness to go to a marriage counselor if marriage problems occurred in their relationship. In general, the lectures disappointed rather than excited the couples.

Another study evaluating premarital counseling found that using a premarital inventory with couples was clearly superior to traditional discussion sessions with clergy and to the large-group lecture format (Druckman, Fournier, Olson, & Robinson, 1981). The researchers used a premarital inventory called **PREPARE**

BOX 12.3

The PREPARE Premarital Program

Goals

- To help a couple explore their relationship strengths and growth areas.
- To help a couple increase their communication skills (i.e., their ability to share feelings and to listen attentively).
- To help a couple learn how to resolve conflict using the 10-step conflict model.
- To help a couple discuss their families of origin and current relationship style.
- To help a couple develop a workable budget and financial plan.
- To help a couple develop their personal, couple, and family goals.

The 14 Relationship Areas Assessed

Communication styles	Financial management	Family and friends
Conflict resolution	Personality issues	Religious beliefs
Equalitarian roles	Sexual relationship	Cohesion in family of origin
Idealistic distortion	Children and parenting issues	Flexibility in family of origin
Realistic expectations	Leisure activities and interests	

Source: Adapted from Olson (1996)

(an acronym for *P*marital *P*ersonal *A*nd *R*elationship *E*valuation), which assesses 14 content areas of the engaged couple's relationship (Box 12.3). The inventory was administered to the couples by counselors and clergy; the couples' answer sheets were scored; and a 15-page computer report was sent to the counselor or clergy, who then interpreted the results for the couple and worked with them for one or two sessions. The premarital inventory has an advantage over the large-group lecture format because it encourages the couple to look at each other and at the relationship more realistically.

Bernard Guerney and his colleagues also found their Relationship Enhancement Program for both married and premarital couples to be effective (Guerney & Maxson, 1991). This program is aimed at increasing the premarital couple's empathy and self-disclosure skills as well as their positive feelings about their relationship. The researchers studied couples 6 months after the program ended and found that the skills they learned persisted, although they had dropped considerably from the level achieved immediately after the program ended.

Bader, Microys, Sinclair, Willett, and Conway (1980) developed a pioneering program for premarital couples designed to improve their conflict-resolution skills. The researchers concluded that these kinds of skills can be taught to couples. Not only were the skills still present when the couples were retested a year later, researchers found that the skills of couples who had taken the course had actually improved as time passed (as compared to a control group who had not taken the course and showed no change in conflict-resolution skills a year later).

A study by Norman Wright (1980) also indicated that marriage preparation can be useful. He surveyed 1,000 couples after marriage and found that those who had had at least six premarital sessions felt they had benefited from the experience and had a lower rate of divorce than those who had not participated.

"I think the lectures were very helpful and the readings were good," said Jean. "We would discuss some of the articles they assigned us on our dates. It helped." Jean and her husband, Jeff, are a middle-class couple living in Minneapolis. She is an accountant, and he runs a small advertising firm.

"But really, what I liked the best were the discussions with other couples," Jeff added. "The leader got us going, and we really took off. It was great to hear other couples talk about what was happening in their relationships. I thought Jean was pretty cranky when she would complain about my buddies from the basketball team and how we would always go out drinking together.

"When I saw similar situations from other women's perspectives, though, it made more sense. I kind of scaled back on my go-go attitude," he concluded.

"It's lucky you did," Jean smiled. "I was pretty mad at you at the time."

What Constitutes an Effective Premarital Program?

It is evident from the research that there are at least three essential components to an effective premarital program:

- *The couple should take some type of premarital inventory and should receive feedback on the results.* A premarital inventory increases the couple's awareness of the strengths and potential problem areas in their relationship. It also helps them discuss their relationship. In addition, the process establishes a relationship with a clergy member, a counselor, or a married couple with whom the couple can consult should they need intensive counseling for serious problems. Finally, it prepares them for later marriage enrichment.

- *The couple should receive training in communication and problem-solving skills.* These skills help the couple deal with various relationship issues by teaching them empathy as well as techniques for self-disclosure, resolving conflict, and problem solving.

- *The couple should participate in a small discussion group in which couples share their feelings.* This increases a couple's ability and willingness to share with other couples, lets the couple see how other couples relate and deal with issues, and may foster friendships with other couples.

A good premarital program should start 6 to 12 months before marriage and last 6 to 8 weeks. Unfortunately, most premarital couples do not begin marriage preparation until 2 or 3 months before their wedding. When a couple cannot complete a comprehensive program before marriage, they should enroll in some sort of program after marriage.

Predicting a Successful Marriage

Love is not enough to make a successful marriage. The truth of this can be seen in divorce statistics: Most people who marry are in love, but roughly half of those who marry eventually divorce. If love at the time of marriage is a poor predictor of marital happiness, what characteristics *do* predict a happy marriage? Studies demonstrate that the type of relationship a couple has before marriage is very predictive of whether they will have a successful and happy marriage.

To identify factors that predict marital satisfaction, researchers conducted two long-term studies of couples. Engaged couples were questioned 3 to 4 months before their marriage and then followed to a point 3 to 4 years after their marriage. The first study was done by Blaine Fowers and David Olson (1986); the replication study was done by Andrea Larsen and David Olson (1989). Both studies found that 80% to 85% of the time it was possible to predict, on the basis of their PREPARE inventory scores *before* marriage, whether a couple would later be happily married or divorced.

As mentioned earlier, PREPARE is a premarital inventory of questions that couples answer to identify the strengths in their relationship and also the areas where growth is needed. Feedback on their responses helps couples learn how to communicate and resolve conflicts; it also helps motivate couples to invest the time and energy needed to improve their marriage. PREPARE, developed in 1980 by David Olson, David Fournier, and Joan Druckman (1989), contains 125 questions grouped into 14 different categories (see Box 12.3).

Fowers and Olson (1986) wanted to see if problems up to 3 or 4 years *after* marriage could be predicted 3 or 4 months *before* marriage. They found that couples who were happily married after 3 years had had significantly higher scores *before* marriage in 11 of the 14 categories in the PREPARE inventory than did couples who had divorced. The characteristics that best predicted a happy marriage were relationship characteristics: realistic attitudes about their relationship, satisfaction with the personality of their partner, enjoyment communicating with their partner, satisfaction with their methods of resolving conflicts together, and agreement on their religious/ethical values.

The replication study (Larsen & Olson, 1989) found very similar results. This study found that the happily married and divorced/separated groups differed significantly on 13 of the 14 PREPARE categories before marriage. Only on questions in the area of children and parenting were the two groups similar before marriage.

As Figure 12.2 shows, the couples who were happily married after 3 years scored significantly higher in every category except children and parenting. One new finding in the replication study was that having more equalitarian role relationships and a good balance of individual versus joint leisure activities also were important predictors of a happy marriage. In other ways, the results of the replication study were very similar to those of the initial study.

Another interesting finding from both studies involved couples who took the PREPARE inventory and then decided not to marry. Generally, 10% to 15% of the couples who take PREPARE and receive feedback make that choice. In comparing the couples who canceled their upcoming marriage with those who were

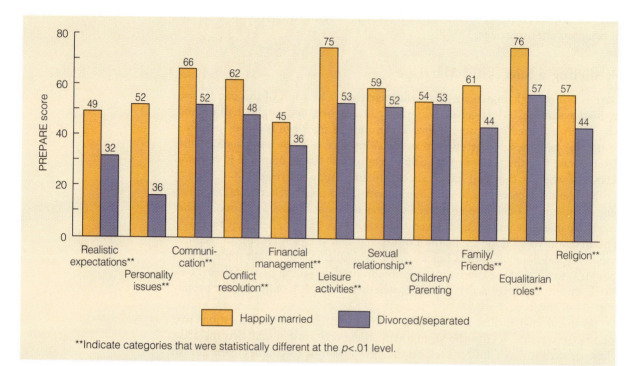

Figure 12.2 Scores of Happily Married Versus Divorced/Separated Couples. *Source:* "Predicting Marital Satisfaction Using PREPARE: A Replication Study" by A. S. Larsen and D. H. Olson, 1989, *Journal of Marital and Family Therapy, 15,* p. 318. Copyright 1989 by *Journal of Marital and Family Therapy.* Reprinted by permission of the American Association for Marriage and Family Therapy; reproduced by permission of the publisher via Copyright Clearance Center, Inc.

happily married or divorced/separated after 3 years, the researchers found that the couples who canceled were almost identical to the group who later divorced or separated. The researchers concluded that the couples made a good decision in not marrying because they had few relationship strengths and therefore a high probability of getting divorced.

PREPARE is not, however, a test to be passed or failed. It is a questionnaire that can help couples discuss more fully their strengths and areas in which they need to grow. It is important for couples with many unresolved relationship issues to try to resolve these differences before marriage. Researchers have consistently demonstrated that problems in premarital relationships do not magically disappear after marriage. Rather, these problems often intensify.

More than 1 million premarital couples have taken the PREPARE Program, and more than 30,000 counselors and members of the clergy have been trained nationally to administer the questionnaire and to use the results in premarital counseling. Couples interested in taking PREPARE should ask their clergy or a counselor or visit the Web site which describes the PREPARE Program in more detail (www.lifeinnovation.com).

Marriage problems and divorce cause tremendous pain for millions of people in the United States. Research with PREPARE has found that couples whose marriages are happy tend to have a successful premarital relationship. In summary, happy premarital couples—who generally become happily married couples—are those who:

- Are realistic about the challenges of marriage.

- Communicate well.

- Resolve conflicts well.
- Feel good about the personality of their partner.
- Agree on religious and ethical values.
- Have equalitarian role relationships.
- Have a good balance of individual and joint leisure activities.

Awareness of these research findings and accurate assessment of the strengths and problem areas of a relationship *before* marriage can avert a great deal of heartbreak later in marriage.

Families of Origin and Premarital Counseling

When a couple gets married, each partner is also joining the other partner's family. As such, the Couple and Family Map can be useful for helping partners discuss and compare their **families of origin**—the families in which they were raised during childhood—before they marry. The case study that follows involves Kathy and Jim, a couple whose family backgrounds are quite different. They explored these differences in premarital counseling.

A Structurally Enmeshed Family of Origin

Kathy grew up in a *structurally enmeshed* family (Figure 12.3). She is the third oldest of six children, who at the time of counseling range in age from 18 to 27. Kathy's parents have been married for 28 years. All of the children except Kathy live and work in the town in which they grew up. Kathy's family is structured on the flexibility dimension of the Couple and Family Map for the following reasons: While growing up, the children knew what was expected of them. The parents were firm yet fair with discipline and enforcement of family rules. The mother was strong and a thorough organizer, and the father was equally strong and even stubborn at times. The father acted as the head of the household but respected his wife's education, contributions, and ability. The mother was comfortable playing a somewhat traditional role and worked hard at keeping the family organized.

Kathy's family is enmeshed on the cohesion dimension. They are a close-knit Catholic family from a small town. Except for 18-year-old John, all of the children have left home, and all except Kathy have settled in the local community. The children drop by the family home several times a week. On weeknights, they play cards or just sit around and talk. The whole family gets together at least every other Sunday for dinner. The mother is heavily involved in each of her children's lives. She feels excited when they are excited and guilty when they are down, and she is always trying to help them. The father is less involved in the lives of his children but expects them to visit often, especially on weekends.

A Flexibly Disengaged Family of Origin

Jim grew up in a *flexibly disengaged* family (see Figure 12.3). He is the older of two children; his brother is four years younger. His parents have been married for 27

Figure 12.3 Family of
Origin and Ideal Type of
Marriage

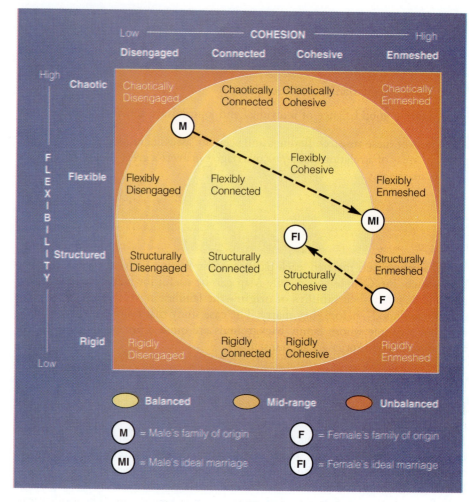

years but are now separated. After several years of frustration, the mother decided
that she had had enough and asked her husband for a separation; he moved out
several months ago. He has been asking for a reconciliation, claiming he's changed,
but she is suspicious of these "instant" changes and has decided to "wait and see"
if they are permanent.

Jim's family is currently flexible in terms of how it functions, but over the past
several years, it has undergone certain changes. For many years, it was closer to a
structured family: The mother and father had traditional male and female roles;
father handed down the rules, and mother backed him up. After 15 years as a homemaker, however, Jim's mother went back to school and got a 2-year certificate in
bookkeeping. Her self-esteem improved, and she became more confident and assertive in her relationship with her husband. The family system became more flexible. Jim's father began helping out around the house. He became more lenient
with the boys when he saw that they were fairly responsible and willing to pitch
in around the house.

In terms of cohesion, the family is currently disengaged. When they were
young, the boys were very involved in school activities, and the parents each had

separate interests. The father hunted and fished, and the mother had her church activities. The father took the boys hunting and fishing when they got old enough, and they went on several canoe trips together. But these outings were the only times they were together. Most of the time, family members went their own ways and did their own thing. Each person in the family had his or her own friends, and these friends were sometimes more important to each person than family members were.

Goals for the Relationship

Kathy and Jim disagree somewhat on how cohesive (close) they want to be in their marriage, in part due to their families of origin. These two diverse family systems present some problems for this couple. Kathy would like a *cohesive* type of marriage but one in which she would have more emotional space and greater autonomy than in her enmeshed family of origin. Jim would like an *enmeshed* marriage, in reaction to his disengaged family of origin (see Figure 12.3). He has experienced a lot of pain and disappointment due to the breakup of his parents' marriage and has vowed not to make the mistakes they did. He doesn't want to be in another disengaged system in which people go their own way and do not connect emotionally.

This couple is struggling to negotiate just how much closeness they want from the relationship. Because it's hard for Jim to say what he is really feeling and to share his need for closeness in a direct way with Kathy, she sometimes interprets his desire for closeness as an attempt to control her. But Kathy wants to avoid the overcontrolling atmosphere of enmeshment that existed in her family. So she sometimes backs away from Jim when he is needy and wants closeness. Jim isn't always aware of how he tries to control Kathy or even why he wants to. He is more aware of the outcome of his efforts—her withdrawal.

What both Jim and Kathy have in common is the desire for a *structured* type of marriage. Although Jim sympathizes with his mother, he emotionally leans toward his father's value of a more structured type of system, with more stable male-female roles and predictable family rules and patterns. This is the level of flexibility with which he is most comfortable. Kathy would also like a structured marriage with fairly stable roles but with a distribution of responsibilities. She likes the predictability of a structured system but does not want it to become rigid like her family of origin. The desire for a structured system is a goal they both share and one they can work together to achieve.

The Wedding and Newlywed Years

In this section we will look at some guidelines for planning a wedding and at the difficult process of adjustment newlyweds face during the first few years of marriage.

The Wedding

Despite the great expense it often entails, a wedding is not a marriage. Today, the average wedding costs about $15,000. This figure includes the wedding ceremony, sit-down meals, reception, entertainment, gifts, honeymoon, and so forth. The average engaged couple spends about $4,000 of their own money on their wedding and honeymoon.

Whether a wedding is simple or extravagant, it is a milestone in the lives of two families, not just two people. Decisions about the date, the place, the kind of ceremony, the size of the wedding party, the guest list, and the reception often require negotiation among the couple and their relatives so that everyone will feel that their preferences have been considered.

Although the wedding ceremony is an important celebration that also bonds friends and families, it can also create some problems. Decisions about the guest list and the kind of reception can create intense struggles between family members and the bride and groom.

Arond and Pauker (1987) have developed some useful guidelines for couples planning their wedding:

- Begin planning at least 1 year in advance.
- Try to consider the feelings of others, particularly family members.
- Consider what is important to you and what your budget is.
- Be assertive—it's *your* wedding.
- Use the preparations as a time to share and make decisions as a couple.
- Try to keep it simple so that you can enjoy it.

As the wedding approaches, many couples become anxious about the ramifications of this critical decision—marriage. In a survey of couples who were soon to be married, the researchers found that 67% of the individuals questioned whether they were making the right decision; 51% were concerned about having enough money to get married; 48% were concerned about getting along with in-laws; and 42% wondered whether they would "goof up" the ceremony (Arond & Pauker, 1987).

Newlyweds: The Difficult Adjustment

There is hardly any activity, any enterprise, which is started with such tremendous hopes and expectations and which fails so regularly as love.

—ERICH FROMM

The first year or two of marriage are for many couples the most difficult, even if they lived together before the marriage and feel they have a good relationship. Marriage is a more difficult transition than most couples anticipate, often because

380

He likes to make a quick circuit of the store, picking up whatever appeals to him. She likes to make a list of what they'll need for the week and shop for bargains. Newlyweds discover differences in their habits and preferences every day and must find ways to accommodate these differences if their marriage is to succeed.

couples expect marriage to be easy and to be similar to what they have experienced with each other previously.

In a comprehensive study of newlyweds, Arond and Pauker (1987) surveyed 455 newlyweds and also asked 75 couples who had been married for a few years to look back on their first year of marriage. The newlywed stage is a difficult transition because the partners must leave their families of origin, give up their independence, and begin to function as a couple. This study found that about half the couples doubted their marriage would last and felt they had significant marital problems during this first year. About 40% found marriage harder than they had expected and also felt that their partner had became more critical after marriage. Sixty-three percent had marital problems related to money; 25% had sexual problems, even though 85% had engaged in sex before marriage; and 35% said relationships with single friends worsened after marriage.

Many of the couples studied had gone into marriage with a wealth of experience together (Arond & Pauker, 1987). Sixty-three percent had vacationed together before marriage; 48% had shared household expenses before marriage; 22% had bought a house or a car together before marriage; and 85% had had a sexual relationship before marriage. But the study found no statistical relationship between living together before marriage and happiness with the sexual relationship or the total relationship after marriage. In fact, the researchers found that couples who had lived together before marriage had significantly lower marital satisfaction scores than those who had not cohabited before the wedding.

One of the major reasons newlywed couples find the adjustment to marriage so difficult is that they are typically idealistic. Premarital relationships are often filled with fantasies and myths, especially the notion that the partner will change undesirable traits after the couple is married. Unfortunately, marriage neither changes people nor makes it easier for others to change them. In fact, marriage often magnifies undesirable traits. A person who is sloppy before marriage will be

BOX 12.4

Premarital Fantasies and Marital Realities

She married him because he was such an assertive male; she divorced him because he was such a domineering husband.

He married her because she was so gentle and petite; he divorced her because she was so weak and helpless.

She married him because he could provide a good income; she divorced him because all he did was work.

He married her because she was so attractive all the time; he divorced her because she spent too much time in front of the mirror.

She married him because he was so romantic and sociable; she divorced him because he was a fun-loving playboy.

He married her because she was so quiet and dependent; he divorced her because she was so boring and clinging.

She married him because he was the life of the party; she divorced him because he was such a dud at home.

He married her because she was so sociable and talkative; he divorced her because she could only discuss trivia.

She married him because he was such a good athlete; she divorced him because he was always playing or watching sports.

He married her because she was so neat and organized; he divorced her because she was too compulsive and controlling.

sloppy after marriage—but the sloppiness will become more apparent in the closeness of marriage.

One young woman reported that her fiancé was kind and gentle with her until the night before the wedding. Then, he became angry and shoved her in an argument over the cost of the ceremony. She thought he did this because he was tense about the upcoming ceremony, so she went through with the wedding. In the first 6 months of marriage, she was physically abused on eight separate occasions, with the severity of the abuse increasing as the months passed. She divorced her groom after 1 year of marriage. Box 12.4 shows how some premarital fantasies look as marital realities.

Arond and Pauker (1987) offer five recommendations to newlywed couples for making their adjustment to marriage easier in the early years:

- *Acknowledge and handle hostility.* Anger and aggressiveness are natural in an intimate relationship. They must be acknowledged and the feelings expressed in constructive ways.

- *Tolerate imperfections and differences.* Differences between two people are natural and should be seen as a strength, an important aspect of individuality. Couples need to learn how to agree and how to agree to disagree.

- *Separate from your families of origin.* Although families of origin are important, couples must invest in their marriage and not let parents interfere with it. Partners should also avoid using parents as leverage against each other.

- *Be committed.* A marriage cannot be taken for granted. Partners need to remind each other of their ongoing commitment.

Happy couples learn to weather the stresses of life. They are, above all, best friends and enjoy spending time together. In fact, they are likely to find each other more interesting as the years go by.

- *Realize that marriage has its ups and downs.* Married couples have many good times. But they also have their share of struggles, challenges, and differences, which often provide opportunities for growth, both personally and in the relationship.

The Early Years of Marriage

Five Types of Marriage

Using a national sample of 6,267 married couples, Olson and Fowers (1993) identified five significantly different types of married couples: vitalized, harmonious, traditional, conflicted, and devitalized. The marital typology was based on a couple's scores from the ENRICH couple inventory. The couple's Positive Couple Agreement (PCA) scores measured the couple's agreement in describing their relationship in positive terms. The inventory evaluated 10 relationship domains: personality issues, communication, conflict resolution, financial management, leisure activities, sexual relations, children and parenting, family and friends, equalitarian roles, and religious orientation (Olson, 1996).

William Allen (1996) identified the same five types of couples in a sample of 415 African American couples. His findings demonstrate the similarity of these types across ethnic groups.

In the Olson and Fowers study (1993), **vitalized couples** had the highest levels of satisfaction across all of the aspects of their marriage. Their PCA scores were particularly high on marital interaction scales such as communication and conflict resolution. The couples in this group tended to be older and more educated, had higher-status jobs, and had been married longer. The majority (86%) of vitalized couples had never considered divorce (see Figure 12.4).

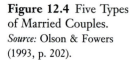

Figure 12.4 Five Types of Married Couples. *Source:* Olson & Fowers (1993, p. 202).

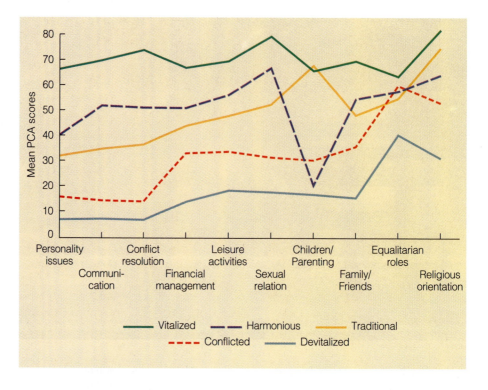

Harmonious couples were the second most satisfied type of couple, with moderately high PCA scores on the scales assessing marital satisfaction. Like vitalized couples, harmonious couples tended to be more educated and have higher-status jobs. Harmonious couples had the fewest number of children, yet they reported significant dissatisfaction with their parenting.

Traditional couples had high PCA scores in the traditional areas of children and parenting, equalitarian roles, and religion. These couples agreed that religion is an important aspect of their marriage. They had lower scores in the relationship skills areas of communication and conflict resolution, and they tended to dislike the personality of their partner. Most (92%) of traditional couples were either in their first marriage or had been married longer; they were also more educated. Fewer women in traditional couples were employed full-time as compared to the women in other marital groups. Traditional couples also tended to marry younger, have more children, and have similar religious backgrounds. The most distinctive finding for traditional couples was that they tended to stay married even when they were dissatisfied with their marriage.

Conflicted couples had moderately low PCA scores overall, yet they had higher PCA scores in the areas of equalitarian roles and religious orientation. Furthermore, these couples had problems with communicating and solving problems. Conflicted couples tended to be younger, had been married fewer years, were less educated, and had lower job status. In 46% of conflicted couples, both spouses were dissatisfied, and in 42%, both spouses had considered divorce.

Devitalized couples had the lowest scores on all of the ENRICH scales. Couples in this group were characterized by pervasive unhappiness in almost all areas of their marriage and were 10 times more likely to be separated than the other

Table 12.1 Four Types of Premarital Couples and Marital Satisfaction and Status After 3 Years of Marriage

FOUR PREMARITAL TYPES	VERY HAPPILY MARRIED	LESS HAPPILY MARRIED	SEPARATED/ DIVORCED	TOTAL COUPLES
Vitalized	60%	23%	17%	100%
Harmonious	46	29	25	100
Traditional	34	50	16	100
Conflicted	16	30	54	100

couple types. In 88% of devitalized couples, one or both of the spouses had considered divorce.

Interestingly, when the same analysis was done with premarital couples, four types of premarital couples were identified (Fowers & Olson, 1992). The devitalized type was missing, which makes sense because premarital couples are typically optimistic and happy with their relationship. The total sample consisted of 5,030 couples; there were roughly 25% to 30% of couples in each of the four types. Researchers subsequently conducted an outcome study to examine the relationship between the four premarital types (vitalized, harmonious, traditional, and conflicted) and the marital relationship three years after marriage (Fowers, Montel, & Olson, 1996).

Vitalized couples had the highest level of marital satisfaction, followed by harmonious, traditional, and conflicted couples, in that order (Table 12.1). More specifically, three years after marriage, 60% of vitalized couples were very happily married, and only 17% were divorced or separated. Conversely, 16% of conflicted couples were very happily married, and 54% were separated or divorced. Traditional couples were the least likely to divorce or separate, even though half of these couples were less happily married. These results clearly demonstrate that marital stability and satisfaction can be predicted based on premarital relationship quality.

Issues and Strengths

As already noted, couples face many challenges during the early years of marriage. Their resources as individuals and as a couple are tested, sometimes severely. Some couples find that these challenges strengthen their relationship; for other couples, the challenges signal the beginning of the end of the marriage. A national survey of marriage across the life cycle focused on the stressors at each major stage (Olson, McCubbin, et al., 1989). For married young couples who did not have children, the major stressors were work and family issues, financial issues, intrafamily issues, and issues related to illness (Figure 12.5).

Among *work and family issues*, 40% to 54% of the couples had had to deal with problems related to a promotion or job change, a decrease in job satisfaction, or difficulty with people at work. About one in four had lost or quit a job. Whether positive or negative, all of these changes are stressful. *Financial issues* were also a major concern among the young couples, with half feeling they needed more money. Over half had purchased a car or another major item, and more than a third had taken out a major loan. One in four had purchased or built a home, and

Figure 12.5 Stressors and Coping Resources of Young Couples. *Source: Families: What Makes Them Work?* (2nd ed.) (p. 209) by D. H. Olson, H. I. McCubbin, H. Barnes, A. Larsen, M. Muxen, and M. Wilson, 1989, Los Angeles, CA: Sage. Copyright © 1989 by Sage Publications. Used by permission of the publisher.

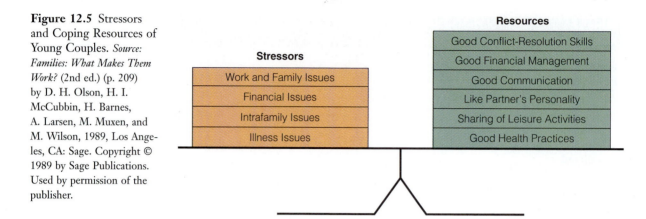

one in five was faced with increased medical/dental costs. Among *intrafamily issues*, more than one third reported that chores were not getting done. Nearly a third complained that the husband was away from home too much, and about 20% noted that the wife was away from home too much. One in five couples felt that disagreements and problematic issues were not getting resolved. Finally, *illness issues*, including the death of parents and close relatives, caused stress in as many as 30% of the relationships.

This survey also studied why some couples were able to cope with these stressors more effectively than others. The couples who coped most successfully had good conflict-resolution and communication skills, were able to manage their money effectively, liked each other's personalities, shared leisure activities together, and had good health-maintenance practices. In other words, couples who coped well drew on personal and relationship strengths to overcome the stressors.

Numerous studies have focused on the qualities of a happy marriage. Jeanette Lauer and Robert Lauer (1985) studied 351 couples, most of them happily married. They asked the couples to identify the major characteristics that kept their marriages strong and vital. The Lauers found that in marriages that survive, the spouses saw each other as best friends and as someone they liked to spend time with. The couples also felt that marriage required a long-term commitment and that it was sacred. They felt that they agreed on life goals and noted that they found their spouses more interesting over time. In addition, they enjoyed fun times together and they liked their sexual relationship. In sum, these happy couples valued their relationship and gave it the priority it required to be mutually satisfying. Box 12.5 shows the average rankings from this study of the characteristics that keep a marriage alive; note the high level of similarity in ranking between husbands and wives.

Changes in Marital Satisfaction Over Time

Researchers have consistently found that marriage satisfaction tends to decrease over time. In a longitudinal study of newlywed couples, Lawrence Kurdek (1998) found that over the first four years of marriage, the marital satisfaction for both males and females dropped each year and at a similar rate. As marital satisfaction dropped, there was an increase in the severity of depression, especially among women.

BOX 12.5

What Keeps a Marriage Going?

	Priority	
	Husbands	**Wives**
My spouse is my best friend.	1	1
I like my spouse as a person.	2	2
Marriage is a long-term commitment.	3	3
Marriage is sacred.	4	4
We agree on aims and goals.	5	5
My spouse has grown more interesting.	6	6
I want the relationship to succeed.	7	7
An endearing marriage is important to social stability.	8	10
We laugh together.	9	8
I am proud of my spouse's achievements.	10	15
We agree on a philosophy of life.	11	9
We agree about our sex life.	12	14
We agree on how and how often to show affection.	13	10

Source: Marriage and the Family: The Quest for Intimacy by Robert Lauer and Jeanette C. Lauer. Copyright © 1991 Times Mirror Higher Education Group, Inc., Dubuque, Iowa. All rights reserved. Reprinted by permission of the McGraw-Hill Companies.

Another important study focused on change in marital satisfaction for couples who had firstborn sons; this study followed couples for five years (Belsky & Hsieh, 1998). Using the *love scores* from fathers and the *conflict scores* from wives, Jay Belsky and Kuang-Hua Hsieh (1998) found three distinct patterns of change. One group of couples, called the *stays good* group, maintained a good relationship over four years. In this group, the fathers' love level stayed high and the wives' conflict level stayed low. In another group, the *good gets worse* group, the fathers' love level was initially high and then dropped and the wives' conflict level was initially low and then became high. In the third group, the *bad to worse* group, the fathers' love level was initially low and went lower and the wives' conflict level was initially high and stayed high. This typology of couples is very useful because it more clearly demonstrates the dynamics of change than can an instrument that records average scores across all couples, which is the typical approach to measuring change. What this study reveals is that some couples can maintain a healthy marriage in spite of having a child, whereas other couples' marriages become less loving and more conflicted.

Another type of marriage study examined how marriage changes before and after having a child. Audrey Bryan (1998) assessed married couples as they began a class on childbirth and then reassessed them after their child was born. She administered the ENRICH inventory at the beginning of the class and identified five types of married couples from most happy to least happy: vitalized couples (22%), harmonious couples (27%), traditional couples (8%), conflicted couples (23%), and devitalized couples (20%).

The percentage of couples who showed no change over time varied greatly by marital type. Over two thirds (70%) of the vitalized couples stayed the same, and about one quarter (26%) became traditional couples. For the harmonious couples, about one quarter (27%) became happier, vitalized couples; another quarter (23%) became traditional couples; and one third (35%) became less happy, conflicted couples. About half (55%) of the traditional couples stayed traditional, whereas 18% became vitalized and 18% became conflicted. For the conflicted couples, over one third (37%) stayed conflicted and another third (37%) became less happy, devitalized couples. About 70% of the devitalized couples stayed devitalized; 20% became conflicted; and 10% became traditional.

So, in general, most of the marriages changed as a result of having children. The least change was seen in the best marriages (vitalized) and the worst marriages (devitalized). The other three types experienced changes for better and worse.

Changes in Policy and State Laws to Strengthen Marriage

Due to a growing concern over the rate of divorce (about 50%) in the United States, legislators are pushing for changes in the laws to impose more requirements on couples planning to marry. Florida was the first state to pass a comprehensive package of legislation designed to strengthen marriage and reduce divorce. Passed in the Florida State Legislature in 1998, the Marriage Preparation and Reservation Act became effective in January 1999. The bill had four key components:

- High school students are required to take a course in marriage and relationship skill-based education.

- Engaged couples are encouraged to take a premarital preparation course of at least four hours. Those who do so qualify for a reduction in their marriage license fee. Each courthouse is to keep a roster of religious and secular approved courses.

- Each couple applying for a marriage license will be given a handbook prepared by the Florida Bar Association informing them of their legal rights and responsibilities as married partners to each other and to their children, both during marriage and in the event of marital dissolution.

- Couples with children who file for divorce must take a parent-education and family-stabilization course. (Ooms, 1998b, p. 33).

Organizing Communities to Work Toward Improving Marriage

Another movement to improve marriage is called the Community Marriage Policy, which has been adopted by over 100 communities throughout the United States (McManus & McManus, 1998). This idea was created and nationally promoted by Mike McManus in the early 1990s as part of his Marriage Savers program, which originated with the publication of his book *Marriage Savers* (1995). The Community Marriage Policy is designed to bring clergy members, judges, marital therapists, and others together to support a variety of premarital and marital enrichment programs to help improve marriages. One part of the initiative encourages premarital couples to enroll in a program that employs a premarital inventory; provides feedback on the inventory results through a therapist, clergy member, or mentor couple; and incorporates a group couple skill-based program. Following marriage, couples are encouraged to participate in a marriage enrichment programs to help them continue to build and strengthen their relationship.

Some Recommendations for a Happy Marriage

Reviewing the research and clinical observations discussed throughout this chapter, here are a number of recommendations for developing a meaningful and vital marriage relationship:

- Individuals should not be pressured to marry early; they should mature emotionally and establish themselves in their chosen profession before making a marriage commitment.

- Marriage is not for everyone. Family members and friends should recognize this and not pressure anyone who has chosen the single life into getting married.

- Couples should be encouraged to relate openly and honestly rather than to play traditional dating/mating games.

- Couples should spend 1 year in premarital counseling before they marry, and they should not marry until they have established a meaningful relationship and resolved major difficulties.

- The decision of parenthood should be made jointly, and it is best if it follows the decision to marry. Couples should establish a strong and viable marriage relationship before they have children.

- Couples should be creative and flexible in their roles and mutual responsibilities, not only during the initial phase of marriage but throughout the life cycle.

Summary

- Three trends point to the changing role of marriage in the United States today. First, a decline in the popularity of marriage is indicated by a decrease in the number of marriages to an all-time low. Second, fewer couples who get divorced choose to remarry. And third, the number of couples living together has increased from 500,000 couples in 1970 to over 4 million couples at present.

- Marriage offers a number of benefits. As compared to single or divorced individuals, married couples lead a healthier lifestyle, live longer, have a more satisfying sexual relationship, have more wealth and economic assets, and generally do a better job raising children.

- Couples have a better chance for a happy marriage when both individuals are mature, love each other and themselves, enjoy being alone and together, are established in their work, are assertive with each other, and are friends as well as lovers.

- Positive reasons for marriage include companionship, love and intimacy, a supportive partnership, sexual satisfaction, and parenthood. Negative reasons for getting married include a premarital pregnancy, rebellion against or escape from parents, independence, replacing a lost love (rebound relationships), family or social pressure, and economic security.

- Couples spend too little time preparing for marriage. They often fear that exposing their differences will end the relationship. Resolving differences before marriage, however, provides a better chance for marital happiness.

- A very low percentage of couples in the United States enroll in a comprehensive marriage preparation program. The most useful programs include (1) a premarital inventory to assess strengths and areas of potential growth and a discussion of the assessment results with a trained counselor, (2) a small discussion group in which couples share feelings and concerns with each other, and (3) training in communication and problem-solving skills.

- Researchers have developed an inventory that couples can take before marriage to assess the strengths in their relationship. The inventory can predict a couple's chances of marital success or failure with 80% to 85% accuracy.

- Love is not enough to make a successful marriage. Researchers have identified the following relationship characteristics to be predictive of marital happiness: realism about the relationship, acceptance of the partner's personality, good communication, good conflict-resolution skills, agreement on religious/ethical values, equalitarian role relationships, and a balance of individual and joint leisure activities.

- The first year or two of marriage are, for many couples, the most difficult. Some strategies for adjusting to marriage in the early years include acknowledging and handling anger and aggressiveness openly, tolerating imperfections and differences, separating from families of origin, being committed to the marriage, and realizing that there are ups and downs in marriage.

- A national survey identified five types of marriage: from most to least happy they are *vitalized, harmonious, traditional, conflicted,* and *devitalized.* Studies suggest that these types exist across ethnic groups.

- Major stressors for newlywed couples include work and family issues, financial issues, intrafamily issues, and illness. Couples who cope well tend to have good conflict-resolution and communication skills, manage their money effectively, like each other's personalities, share leisure activities, and practice good health-maintenance habits.

- Numerous studies have found that marriage satisfaction tends to decrease over time for most couples. Another study identified three distinct patterns of change in marriage: *stays good, good gets worse,* and *bad to worse.*

- Due to a growing concern over the high rate of divorce in our country, legislators are pushing for laws to stengthen marriage, such as offering incentives for engaged couples to attend premarital preparation courses and requiring high school students to take courses on marriage and relationship skills. Communities are also getting involved in developing a variety of premarital and marital enrichment programs.

Key Terms

PREPARE

family of origin

vitalized couple

harmonious couple

traditional couple

conflicted couple

devitalized couple

Activities

1. List what you feel are positive and negative reasons for getting married. Share the list with a partner or with others in a small discussion group.

2. How do you know if you are ready for marriage? Discuss this issue with a small group, and formulate some guidelines to help people decide whether they are ready to marry.

3. *For dating or engaged couples:* Both partners should write down five things they like about their partner and five things that sometimes bother them. Then both partners should discuss the items on the lists very carefully and listen to each other so that the exchange is positive and constructive.

4. For those dating or engaged couples interested in taking the PREPARE inventory, first contact a counselor or a member of the clergy in your area. If you cannot locate someone trained in PREPARE, send a stamped, self-addressed envelope to Life Innovations (P.O. Box 190, Minneapolis, MN 55440-0190) for a list of trained counselors in your community.

Suggested Readings

Arond, M., & Pauker, S. L. (1987). *The first year of marriage.* New York: Warner.

Gottman, J. M. (1995). *Why marriages succeed or fail.* New York: Simon & Schuster.

McManus, M. J. (1995). *Marriage savers: Helping your friends and family avoid divorce.* Grand Rapids, MI: Zondervan.

Ooms, T. (1998b). *Toward more perfect unions: Putting marriage on the public agenda.* Washington, DC: Family Impact Seminar.

Waite, L., & Gallagher, M. (1999). *The case for marriage.* Cambridge, MA: Harvard University Press.

CHAPTER 13

Parenthood: Choices and Challenges

Parenthood is the process of raising our children from infants to the adults who will provide continuity within the family for years to come. There is no greater responsibility or challenge, and for many people who do the job well, there is no greater satisfaction than seeing one's children grow, learn, and enjoy life. Parenthood has been called the world's most difficult job—offering no pay, no fringe benefits, no vacation, and precious little thanks. Counselor Jennifer James wryly remarked that "the first half of our lives is spoiled by our parents, and the last half by our children" (1984). But as one observer noted, and many would agree, "Children fill a space in your life you never knew was empty."

A parent's job is to give a child both "roots and wings" (Orr & Van Zandt, 1987, p. 87). This is no easy task. Rearing children may indeed be life's greatest mixed blessing. It is full of good times and bad times, frustrating challenges and elating successes. A baby's first stumbling steps and first words, a teenager's first love, a grown child's first baby—all are important transitions that parents remember. At the same time, children bring heavy responsibilities and drain parents of energy, finances, and time.

There is no book on rearing children that answers all the questions and no clear path to family happiness. The road is difficult, and there are no guarantees. In the words of Governor Christine Todd Whitman of New Jersey, in a commencement address at Wheaton College, "I don't mind saying that I have the most important and fulfilling job in the world. It demands responsibility, knowledge of finance, being on call 24 hours a day, combining firm leadership with careful negotiations, and keeping one's promise. That job is being a parent" (1995).

In this chapter we will examine the challenge of parenthood and take a look at some of the conventional wisdom that surrounds it. Among the challenges are the effects of parenthood on marriage, the decision whether to have children, and the financial burdens of raising children. We will discuss various parenting styles and how they relate to the family styles of the Couple and Family Map. We will also explore issues in parenting and some practical approaches to raising children, including coparenting. We will touch on the benefits of parent education and family therapy and conclude with a summary of the many satisfactions of parenting.

First, however, let's take a final look at the national survey that examined couple strengths and issues for married couples (Olson et al., 1999). We will begin with the results of the survey regarding the parenting strengths of happy couples versus unhappy couples. Next, we will review the five most common parenting issues as reported by 19,196 married couples.

Couple Strengths and Issues in Parenting

In a national survey of married couples, Olson and colleagues (1999) identified the following parenting strengths. As Table 13.1 shows, happy couples were more than three times as likely (54%) as unhappy couples (17%) to agree on how to share the responsibilities of raising their children. Happy couples were also more than three times as likely (73%) as unhappy couples (23%) to be satisfied with the amount of attention they focus on their marriage versus the amount of attention they focus on their children. Three times as many happy couples (69%) reported agreeing on how to discipline their children than did unhappy couples (21%). Sixty-one percent of happy couples believed that having children brought them closer

Table 13.1 Parenting Strengths of Happy Versus Unhappy Married Couples

STRENGTH	PERCENTAGE OF COUPLES IN AGREEMENT	
	Happy Couples (*n* = 4,363)	Unhappy Couples (*n* = 10,613)
Agree on how childrearing responsibilities are shared.	54	17
Are satisfied with the amount of attention they focus on their marriage as opposed to on their children.	73	23
Agree on how to discipline their children.	69	21
Agree that having children has brought them closer.	61	20
Agree that the father spends enough time with their children.	53	22

Source: Adapted from Olson, Fye, & Olson (1999).

Table 13.2 Top Five Parenting Issues for Married Couples

ISSUE	PERCENTAGE OF COUPLES WITH PROBLEMS SURROUNDING ISSUE (*N* = 19,196)
Feel the father does not spend enough time with children.	46
Are dissatisfied with how childrearing responsibilities are shared.	42
Are dissatisfied with the amount of attention they focus on their marriage as opposed to on their children.	42
Disagree on how to discipline their children.	40
Feel more dissatisfied with their marriage since having children.	38

Source: Adapted from Olson, Fye, & Olson (1999).

as a couple, only 20% of unhappy couples shared this view. Finally, happy couples were more than twice as likely (53%) as unhappy couples (22%) to agree that the father spends enough time with the children.

Table 13.2 identifies the top five parenting issues for a national sample of 19,196 married couples. The most frequently reported parenting issue (46%) was that the father does not spend enough time with the children. Forty-two percent of married couples were dissatisfied with how childrearing responsibilities were shared, and almost half (42%) were dissatisfied with the amount of attention they focused on their marriage as opposed to on their children. Forty percent of married couples with children disagreed on how to discipline their children, and 38% reported feeling more dissatisfied in their marriage since having children.

The Challenge of Parenthood

Many authorities have noted that parenthood is the last bastion of amateurism in our society. Plumbers, bookkeepers, computer analysts—all need some kind of formal training, certificate, or license. About the only job that doesn't require some special kind of education is nurturing the young to adulthood.

Our society tends to shy away from "intruding" into family matters, and rearing children is certainly a family matter. But some have gone so far as to argue that education and even something like an internship should be mandatory before people can become parents—that is, that a license should be required for parenthood—although such a proposal has little chance of becoming law. Nevertheless, its proponents underscore the importance of parenting: Society benefits from parents' successes but also suffers from their mistakes.

Adults with problems often had problems as children, and many times they pass their problems on to the next generation. For example, one therapist described a counseling session with an abused woman who had fled from her husband after repeated beatings; the woman's 18-month-old son accompanied her. During the session, the toddler became angered over some minor issue and ran at his mother. In his frustration, he put his hands around her neck and tried to strangle her. He was imitating almost precisely what he had seen his father do a few days earlier. With counseling, this pattern could be changed so that the boy would not repeat his father's behavior.

Conventional Wisdom About Parenting

All societies have folk beliefs that are widely accepted and rarely examined. They may be commonplace, but they are not necessarily common sense. For the purposes of our discussion, we will call these common beliefs *conventional wisdom*. Although conventional wisdom often seems commonsensical, it occasionally gets us into trouble. As one observer has noted, we do not need common sense at all; what we need is *uncommon sense*. Conventional wisdom on parenthood often sugarcoats the subject, romanticizing a task that is too important for people to undertake with rose-colored glasses. What follows is a list of commonly held folk beliefs in our society, along with some comments that offer a more balanced and realistic view:

- *Rearing children is nothing but fun.* Although childrearing can be fun, it is also a thankless and very demanding job. Parents have to *make* childrearing fun if they are to enjoy it.

- *Children will turn out well if they have "good" parents.* Parents are an important factor in a child's development, but they are only one influence among many, including siblings, school, the mass media, and the child's peer group. The goal of parenting must be to instill values and model positive behaviors that children will internalize and use in their lives. But there are no guarantees. Some good parents work hard at parenting only to see their children get into great difficulty in life.

- *Children are always sweet and cute.* Although children can be adorable, they can also be selfish and destructive, as well as extremely active. In fact, they possess the full range of human qualities—positive and negative—

A first haircut is one of the many milestones that mark a child's growing up. Although this toddler may not remember the experience, his mother will likely remember this event in his transition from baby to little boy.

that adults must deal with in each other. Parents who have no break from watching over children can easily become exhausted. Box 13.1 reports the results of a research project that explored one young child's high level of activity.

- *Children improve a marriage.* Rearing children is a team effort. The bond between partners can intensify as they raise their children together. But children also put tremendous pressure on an intimate relationship.

- *Good parents can manage any child, no matter what the child's nature.* This myth is based on the notion that a human being is born a *tabula rasa*, a blank slate upon which the environment writes its script. But research on infants indicates that to some degree temperament is present at birth: Some babies are calm and content; others are cranky. Although the family environment parents construct for their young is tremendously important, it is not, as mentioned earlier, the only influence or the sole determinant of a child's developmental outcome. It is important to note that children also strongly shape their parents' behavior.

- *Today's parents are not as good as yesterday's.* Standards for raising children have gotten higher, making the challenge for today's parents even greater. Society now expects parents to be more democratic in their approach, to take the child's feelings into account when decisions are made, and to involve older children in the decision-making process.

- *Couples without children are frustrated and unhappy.* Many singles and couples without children are very happy and content. Many of them do, however, have close relationships with children of extended-family members or of friends.

BOX 13.1

How Active Are Young Children?

When young parents first hear the term *hyperactive*, it seems to describe their own child almost perfectly. And, indeed, every young child is hyperactive at times, although only a small percentage are hyperactive in a clinical or dysfunctional sense. John DeFrain and Patricia Welker wanted a better understanding of just how active a young child is, so Welker followed 18-month-old Alyssa DeFrain around for a "typical" day in the child's life. During this 24-hour period, Alyssa was asleep for 12 hours.

Welker recorded everything the toddler was doing at 15-second intervals on long sheets of paper in tiny handwriting. In sum, Alyssa performed 4,652 separate and recognizable activities. She never appeared frantic in her work or play, but she rarely did nothing. In fact, much of the time she was doing two or three things at once: looking at her big sister, drawing a picture, and curling circles in the rug with her toes.

Alyssa's 4,652 actions were divided into 221 different behavioral categories, including the following: watches/looks at something (643), manipulates/experiments with an object (96), gives something to someone (46), takes something from someone when offered it (48), lies down (26), listens (172), talks (529), grunts incoherently (78), cries (62), fusses (25), screams (17), sings (22), dances (16), falls down (9), resists (11), points (85), hits something (16), picks up a book (24), walks (299), picks up something other than a book (210), changes body position during 58-minute nap (41), laughs/giggles (34). It's not surprising that a parent who has to supervise all these activities, run interference for the busy child, and keep the youngster out of trouble sinks into bed exhausted at the end of the day.

- *One child is too few.* Although many believe that only-children are spoiled and selfish, that is not necessarily the case. Studies have found that there are both advantages and disadvantages to having only one child. One child is less expensive to raise, is less demanding on the parents, places fewer limits on the parents' freedom, and receives more parental attention. On the downside, parents of only-children sometimes focus too much attention on or overprotect the child, thus limiting the child's exposure to peer companions and possibly even causing him or her to feel lonely.

- *There are no bad children, only bad parents.* Most parents want the best for their children and do what they can to achieve that. Nevertheless, some fail at parenting because of ignorance, lack of support, or their own unhealthy family background.

- *All parents are adults.* As reflected in our nation's teenage pregnancy rates, many adolescents are unfortunately becoming parents. The most recent statistics indicate that 13.1% of all birth mothers are teenagers (U.S. Bureau of the Census, 1997). Childrearing is difficult for adults, but it is particularly challenging for teenage parents.

- *Children appreciate the sacrifices their parents make and the advantages they provide.* Most parents want to be appreciated for the sacrifices they make for their children. Unfortunately, children often do not realize their parents' importance until they themselves become parents. Parents need to learn to enjoy the everyday pleasures and satisfactions of raising their children and to appreciate any small thanks they may receive along the way.

- *Parenthood receives top priority in our society.* Making money—not parenthood—receives top priority in our society. Parents are pressured to put their jobs first if they seek promotions—and sometimes even if they simply want to hold onto their jobs.

- *Love is enough to guarantee good parental performance.* Love certainly helps parents put up with the many difficulties of childrearing, but success at parenting also requires hard work and good parenting skills.

- *Single-parent families are problematic.* Although rearing children is hard enough for two-parent families and can be more difficult for a single parent, a stable one-parent family is superior to an unstable two-parent family (DeFrain, Fricke, & Elmen, 1987; White, 1991).

- *Parenting gets easier as children get older.* Although most parents hope that parenting will get easier as their children mature, they typically find that their parenting issues change and become more difficult. Adolescence is the most challenging stage for a majority of parents because adolescents are seeking greater autonomy and freedom from parental control.

- *Parenting ends when the children leave home.* For most parents, parenting does not end when a child leaves home. Adult children often return home to live after a divorce, a job loss, or some other life crisis. Furthermore, parents are often called on to help with the care of their children's children; grandparenting brings joy, but it can also be exhausting.

- *The empty-nest syndrome leaves many parents lonely and depressed.* One observer has noted, "After the kids leave home, some parents suffer from the empty-nest syndrome; others change the locks." Many parents enjoy the freedom that comes with not having adolescents at home. The middle-aged parent may get a job or change jobs, travel, or take up a new avocation. After they leave home, adult children are often surprised to watch their parents blossom and enjoy life in a variety of new ways.

- *Parents alone should rear the young.* Parents are ultimately responsible for raising their children, but society has a stake in children's development into adulthood and needs to support parents in this challenging process.

The Transition to Parenthood

Parenthood isn't something that happens gradually; the 9 months of a normal pregnancy should give prospective parents time to think about parenthood and to plan for the arrival of the baby. But many parents are unprepared for the challenges that will confront them when the infant arrives. They may take classes to prepare for childbirth, but few prepare for the responsibilities of parenting itself.

Parenthood as Crisis: Effects on Marriage   When the baby is born, parenting begins. For some it is a crisis. E. E. LeMasters gained prominence in the 1950s with his report in the *New York Times* of a study entitled "Parenthood as Crisis."

LeMasters argued that due to romantic notions about parenthood, people go through a process of disenchantment when they have children. LeMasters was flooded with letters from parents, most of whom agreed with his findings. In his research, LeMasters had interviewed 46 couples and found that 83% defined the coming of a child as a "crisis" for their marriage (LeMasters, 1957). Other researchers have debated these findings ever since; the definition of the term *crisis* remains controversial (Belsky, 1991; Belsky & Kelly, 1994).

Becoming a parent is definitely stressful for most couples, and most find it harder than they anticipated. A major review of studies on the transition to becoming a family (Cowan, Cowan, Heming, & Miller, 1991) found that couples having their first child faced many issues in their marriage. The transition increased couples' stress level, increased the number of differences between partners, and lowered their marital satisfaction. In general, the decrease in marital satisfaction was twice as large for women as for men and it was often attributed to the women's feeling that their partner was not as involved as they were in dealing with child care and household tasks.

Parenthood means that a married couple will have less time for each other. Before the baby, the couple could focus attention on their relationship and had time to enjoy each other's company. "Free" time markedly diminishes with the birth of a child, and a couple's focus shifts to nurturing the baby. Parents often find themselves exhausted after many nights awake with a hungry, crying, or sick infant. Few parents know much about caring for an infant until they have one of their own.

As a child grows older, the parents' job does not get any easier. Change only creates new challenges. The colic may end, but the child is soon toddling around, sticking fingers in wall sockets, emptying houseplant soil on the living-room rug, or spreading Vaseline from the medicine cabinet all over the bathroom. Fortunately, most parents have a sense of humor and patience—and also realize the importance of covering sockets, locking cupboards, and putting many things out of the reach of a toddler.

The playfulness and pleasure of preparenting days disappear for some couples, and life becomes more serious. The couple's sexual relationship is often affected by the demands of raising a child. Most couples find that their sexual activity decreases because they are exhausted. Spontaneity in social patterns can also diminish. For example, parents of infants don't just drop in on friends when "dropping in" means packing baby bottles, diapers, plastic pants, and a change of clothes. (See Box 13.2 for a humorous look at some common challenges of parenting.)

Financial Issues and Children

One of the surprises for most parents is how much children cost, not just in terms of time and energy but also money. Raising children is a very expensive venture, no matter what a family's income. An analysis of the expense of raising a child, based on data from the Family Economics Research Group at the U.S. Department of Agriculture, was summarized by Larry Kellman (1997). The data were broken down into six major categories: housing, food, transportation, clothing, health care, and education. As expected, the amount of money spent on a child varied with the income level of the family. For lower-income families, earning an average of $21,600 a year, the cost of raising each child from birth to age 17 was

BOX 13.2

Mother Murphy's Laws for Raising Children

1. Parenthood is much easier to get into than out of.

2. If your spouse hasn't already driven you nuts, your kids will.

3. Nobody really wants your job, but everyone thinks they can do it better.

4. Those who think they can do it better messed up when they had the chance.

5. Bad traits are inherited from your spouse's side of the family.

6. Good traits are inherited from your side of the family.

7. By the time you've finally learned something about raising children, you're a grandparent.

8. Your mother knows best. About everything. And she'll never let you forget it.

9. You don't have to be a Supermom to succeed in both your career and childrearing. All you need is a $100,000 job and live-in help.

10. The day after you get a raise at work, your day-care center will inform you that tuition is being increased.

11. The increase in tuition will exceed your raise.

12. Taking care of your baby is easy, as long as you don't have anything else to do.

13. The more experts you consult, the more solutions you'll find for any parenting problem.

14. Psychologists know best. About writing books.

15. When you're pregnant, everyone gives you advice.

16. After you've had your baby, everyone gives you advice.

17. When your baby becomes a teenager, everyone gives you advice—especially your teenager.

18. When your teenager "leaves the nest," everyone gives you advice.

19. When you become a grandparent, you get to pass on all that good advice to your children.

20. By the time you can afford to start a family, you're too old to do it. (And you know enough not to.)

Source: Adapted from *Mother Murphy's Law* by B. Lansky, 1986, New York: Meadowbrook/Simon & Schuster. Copyright 1986 by Bruce Lansky. Adapted by permission of the publisher, Meadowbrook Press.

"When the last of our three children finally left home this summer," said Dick, the CEO of a software company in Phoenix, "I calculated that my wife and I would have more than $1,000 a month extra to spend. But it doesn't really matter. We'll have more money, and the house will be a lot quieter, but I can't say we'll be any happier. We'll probably pay off a few bills with the extra money and buy some new furniture and a living-room rug as soon as we don't have adolescents clomping about, spilling food everywhere." He paused, then added wistfully, "But I'm not sure the money will bring us happiness. That big old, empty house will be kind of hard to rattle around in at night."

$110,040. For middle-income families, earning an average of $46,100 a year, the cost of raising each child was $149,820. And for upper-income families, earning an average of $87,300 a year, the cost increased to $218,400 (Figure 13.1).

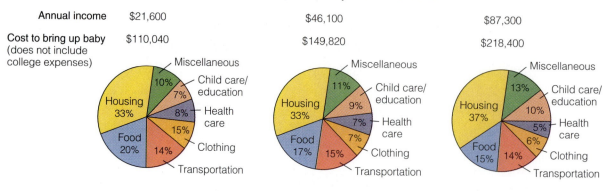

Figure 13.1 Cost of Raising a Child. *Source: Kellman, 1997.*

An important aspect of socializing children is helping them learn to understand and manage finances. Sharon Danes (1992) did a systematic study of 182 parents to learn when they thought it was appropriate to introduce their children to a variety of financial activities. About 70% of parents felt that children 8 years or younger were mature enough to receive an allowance, and 64% felt that they could open their own savings account. Almost half the parents surveyed felt that 12- to 14-year-olds could be responsible for their own clothing budget, and 29% believed that they were mature enough to be told the family's income. About half the parents felt that 15- to 17-year-olds should know about car insurance and have their own checking account. More than half the parents believed that by age 18 to 20, adult children should have and be responsible for their own credit card and be able to apply for and make the payments on a loan.

Adoption

By most estimates, 4% of Americans are adopted. This is not a high percentage, but it has been estimated that 6 in 10 Americans have some kind of experience with adoption: A family member or close friend was adopted, or the individual had adopted a child or placed a child for adoption. Many other Americans consider adopting a child at one point in their life and spend a good deal of time discussing the issue with friends and relatives. Concern about adoption in this country, then, is relatively high (Elshtain, 1998).

Since the mid-1970s, adoption practices in the United States have changed dramatically (Grotevant, 1997). In the past, confidentiality in adoption was the norm; today, trend is toward "openness" in adoption, which means that there is increasing contact between adoptive families and birth parents. The contact may be either direct or mediated (e.g., through an adoption agency). Some adoption professionals argue that fully open adoption should be standard practice and that the secrecy of confidential adoptions has been harmful to all those involved.

Others argue that openness is experimental and may prove to be harmful: Confidential adoption has worked well, so why change it?

To understand the issue of openness in adoption, Harold Grotevant and Ruth McRoy recruited a nationwide sample of adoptive families and birth mothers with a "target" adopted child between the ages of 4 and 12 when the first interview occurred between 1987 and 1992. The sample included 720 individuals: both adoptive parents in 190 adoptive families, at least one adopted child in 171 of the families, and 169 birth mothers. Families were sampled across the full range of openness in adoption: *confidential* (no information shared between birth parents and adoptive parents); *mediated* (information shared, with the adoption agency as the go-between); and *fully disclosed* (ongoing direct contact between birth parents and adoptive family members). Adoptive families were interviewed in their homes.

As predicted, when compared with parents in confidential adoptions, parents in fully disclosed adoptions reported higher levels of acknowledgment of the adoption, more empathy toward the birth parents and child, a stronger sense of permanence in their projected relationship with their child, and less fear that the birth mother might try to reclaim the child (Grotevant, McRoy, Elde, & Fravel, 1994).

Researchers have found, however, that many adoptive parents fail to involve the child in mediated and open adoptions (Wrobel, Ayers-Lopez, Grotevant, McRoy, & Friedrick, 1996). In one sample, almost half the children in mediated adoptions did not participate in the contact their adoptive parents were having with their birth mother, but most of these children were not aware they were being excluded. However, most of the children in fully disclosed adoptions were included in meetings with birth parents.

It appears that couples who have greater openness in the adoption process also have better family communication (Mendenhall, Grotevant, & McRoy, 1996). In one study, adoptive couples' interviews were coded for communication skills using Olson's Couple and Family Map Scale. Couples who had greater openness in adoption showed significantly higher levels of self-disclosure, listening skills, empathy, tracking, and respect.

Relationships between the adoptive family and the birth mother are also being examined through the lens of *boundary ambiguity* (Boss, 1988). Boundary ambiguity occurs when a family member is physically absent but psychologically present, or vice versa. Fravel (1995) examined the psychological presence of the birth mother in the adoptive family system. It appears that boundary ambiguity is almost inevitable in adoptive families. In many adoptive families, boundary ambiguity can exacerbate family stress because of an inability to determine who is inside or outside the family system. Adoptive families who have a higher level of tolerance for ambiguity, however, seem to handle open adoption more effectively. (For more on boundary ambiguity, see Chapter 15.)

The Child-Free Alternative

There are various terms applied to the choice not to have children, including *nonparenthood, voluntary childlessness,* and the **child-free alternative.** Although the number of couples choosing not to have children is on the rise, many wonder whether a person or couple can be happy and fulfilled in life without having

Parenthood is not for everyone, and couples who have decided not to have children can find happiness and fulfillment with each other, with their careers and avocational interests, and with friends and family.

children. Government figures indicate that 9.3% of American women between the age of 18 and 34 do not have children (U.S. Bureau of the Census, 1997). More couples are considering not having children because they know how difficult parenting is, and they want more freedom and more time for their marriage. A review by Jean Veevers (1980) of 22 studies of child-free marriages revealed some interesting answers to common questions about childlessness:

- *What long-term effects does voluntary childlessness have?* Two studies on this aspect of childlessness found that although adult children are often very important to their parents in old age, older people without children also do quite well. (Aging parents may even find themselves rejected or neglected by their adult children.) Those without children often prepare for their later years by developing a network of friends and relatives to help meet their needs. They also learn how to cope with isolation if necessary (Rempel, 1985).

- *Is there something wrong with people who don't wish to have children?* Veevers found that the majority of studies on this topic concluded that nonparents exhibit no more psychopathology or deviance than a control group of randomly sampled parents. It has been argued that African Americans, Native Americans, and Mexican Americans tend to be more family oriented than Whites and consider children an important part of marital life (Mindel, Habenstein, & Wright, 1988).

- *Do people without children do better in their careers?* Apparently, many people without children do very well. Voluntary childlessness leaves people with time and energy that can be focused on career goals. A disproportionate number of high-ranking businesswomen and professionals are childless.

- *Is the quality of a child-free marriage as good as that of a marriage with children?* Recent studies have found more vital and happy relationships among child-free couples than among those with children (Olson, Mc-Cubbin, et al., 1989; Somers, 1993). This is, in part, because child-free couples can devote more time to their marriages and because they are more likely to divorce if they do not have a good relationship than would be a couple with children.

Styles of Parenting

Two key aspects of parenting behavior that researchers often study are parental support and parental control (Amato & Booth, 1997). **Parental support** is defined as the amount of caring, closeness, and affection that a parent exhibits or gives to a child. **Parental control** is defined as the degree of flexibility that a parent uses in enforcing rules and disciplining a child. The level of support and control that parents exercise has a social, psychological, and academic impact on the child. Increasingly higher levels of parental support are related to a variety of positive outcomes for children, including better academic achievement, higher self-esteem, more social competence, and better psychological adjustment (Amato & Booth, 1997).

Whereas there is a linear relationship between greater support and positive outcomes for children, there is a curvilinear relationship between parental control and positive outcomes in children. Amato and Booth (1997) found that if parenting is either too lenient (chaotic) or too strict (rigid), there are more problems with the overall psychological adjustment of the adolescent. Findings from their study and a variety of studies have also found that a more moderate (balanced) level of parental control is related to positive outcomes for children. Children from balanced-parenting families tend to have a higher level of self-esteem, more friends, greater affection for their parents, and more satisfaction.

Sons and daughters often have different experiences growing up in the same family because they are treated differently by each parent. Although it appears that mothers do not function that differently with sons than with daughters, fathers tend to pay more attention to sons. As a result, daughters often feel closer to their mother than to their father. Both parents have a tendency to punish sons more than daughters, and many still tend to assign tasks based on gender—more boys mow the lawn, and more daughters clean the house. In general, parenting style has about the same impact on both the sons and the daughters (Amato & Booth, 1997).

Diana Baumrind (1991, 1995) has identified four parenting styles and has done considerable work using those styles. Baumrind's four styles are the democratic (authoritative), the authoritarian, the permissive, and the rejecting styles of parenting. To these four styles we have added the uninvolved style, which we identified using the Couple and Family Map. Baumrind also labeled three styles of behavior in preschool children—energetic-friendly, conflicted-irritable, and impulsive-aggressive—and correlated those behaviors with her parenting styles (Table 13.3).

Table 13.3 Parenting Style and Children's Behavior

PARENTING STYLE	CHILDREN'S BEHAVIOR
Democratic style	Self-reliant, cheerful, achievement oriented
Authoritarian style	Conflicted, irritable, unhappy, unstable
Permissive style	Impulsive, rebellious, underachieving
Rejecting style	Immature, psychologically challenged
Uninvolved style	Solitary, withdrawn, underachieving

Democratic Style

In **democratic parenting,** parents establish clear rules and expectations and discuss them with the child. Although they acknowledge the child's perpective, they use both reason and power to enforce their standards. The democratic style is similar to the balanced type of system in the Couple and Family Map (Figure 13.2); these families tend to be *connected* to *cohesive* on the cohesion dimension and structured to flexible on the flexibility dimension. Considerable research on parenting has demonstrated that balanced family systems tend to have children that are emotionally healthier and happier and are more successful in school and life (Olson, 1996). Children of democratic-style parents exhibit what Baumrind describes as energetic-friendly behavior. These children are very self-reliant and cheerful. They cope well with stress and are achievement oriented. Many other observers concur with Baumrind (Rueter & Conger, 1995; Steinberg, Lamborn, Darling, Mounts, & Dornbusch, 1994).

Authoritarian Style

In **authoritarian parenting,** parents establish rigid rules and expectations and strictly enforce them. These parents expect and demand obedience from their child. The authoritarian style is located in the lower right quadrant of the Couple and Family Map; these families tend to be *structured* to *rigid* on the flexibility dimension and *cohesive* to *enmeshed* on the cohesion dimension. As the authoritarian style becomes more intense, the family moves toward the *rigidly enmeshed* style. This type of family system is particularly difficult for adolescents, who tend to rebel against authoritarian parenting. In Baumrind's observations, children of authoritarian-style parents are often conflicted-irritable in behavior: moody, unhappy, vulnerable to stress, and unfriendly.

Permissive Style

In **permissive parenting,** parents let the child's preferences take priority over their ideals and rarely force the child to conform to their standards. The permissive style is located in the upper right quadrant of the Couple and Family Map; these fam-

Democratic parents are actively involved with their children. They set standards and discuss them with the child. Children of these parents tend to be self-reliant and achievement oriented, and they cope well with stress.

ilies tend to be *flexible* to *chaotic* on the flexibility dimension and *cohesive* to *enmeshed* on the cohesion dimension. As the permissive style becomes more extreme, the family moves toward the *chaotically enmeshed* style, a style characterized by constant change and forced togetherness, which is not healthy for children. Baumrind observed that children of permissive-style parents generally exhibit impulsive-aggressive behavior. These children are often rebellious, domineering, and underachieving.

Rejecting Style

In **rejecting parenting,** parents do not pay much attention to their child's needs and seldom have expectations regarding how the child should behave. The rejecting style is located in the lower left quadrant of the Couple and Family Map; these families tend to be *structured* to *rigid* on the flexibility dimension and *connected* to *disengaged* on the cohesion dimension. As the rejecting style becomes more extreme, the family moves toward the *rigidly disengaged* style, which leaves children feeling uncared for even though they are expected to behave and have many rules to follow. As a result, children from these homes are often immature and have psychological problems.

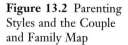

Figure 13.2 Parenting Styles and the Couple and Family Map

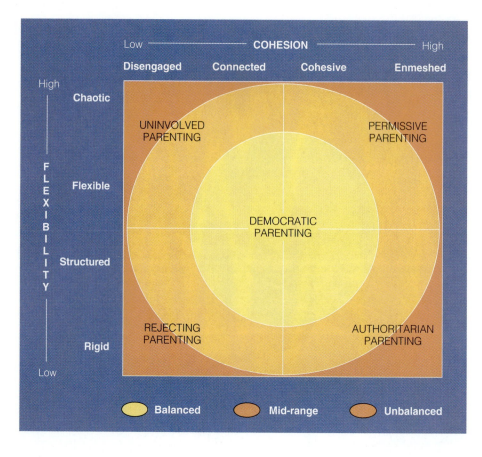

Uninvolved Style

In **uninvolved parenting,** parents often ignore the child, letting the child's preferences prevail as long as those preferences do not interfere with the parent's activities. The uninvolved style of parenting is located in the upper left quadrant of the Couple and Family Map; these families tend to be *connected* to *disengaged* on the cohesion dimension and *flexible* to *chaotic* on the flexibility dimension. As the uninvolved style becomes more extreme, it moves toward the *chaotically disengaged* pattern, in which children are left on their own without emotional support and a lack of consistent rules and expectations. The uninvolved style of parenting is not often discussed in published research, but it is in many instances combined with the rejecting style. Children of uninvolved parents are often solitary, withdrawn, and underachieving.

In a major study of parenting that surveyed 11,669 high school students, the democratic (authoritative) style of parenting had the most positive impact on an adolescent's development (Avenevoli, Sessa, & Steinberg, 1999). Democratic parenting was significantly related to lower psychological distress, higher self-esteem, a higher grade point average, lower levels of drug use, and less-delinquent behavior. The importance of democratic parenting held up across ethnic groups and various levels of income.

In contrast to the positive outcomes of democratic parenting, authoritarian parenting was related to greater psychological distress, lower self-esteem, a lower grade point average, and—interestingly—lower substance abuse (Avenevoli et al., 1999). Permissive parenting, considered the opposite of authoritarian parenting, was related to higher self-esteem, lower psychological distress, and lower substance abuse but also a lower grade point average and some delinquency. Neglectful parenting was the most problematic parenting style. It was related to greater adolescent distress, lower self-esteem, a lower grade point average, and greater drug use and delinquency compared to the other styles.

Avenevoli and colleagues (1999) also investigated the importance of parenting style versus family structure (single- versus two-parent) and socioeconomic level. Although they found that two-parent (intact) families from a variety of ethnic groups and socioeconomic levels were more democratic and less neglectful in their parenting style than were single-parent families, the differences between the two types of families were quite small and practically insignificant. The researchers concluded that the most important finding was "that family structure does not meaningfully moderate the relation between parenting and adjustment across a wide variety of socioeconomic and ethnic groups" (p. 87). The parenting style was the most critical variable in determining adolescent development and adjustment (Aveneoli et al., 1999). Thus, regardless of ethnic background, socioeconomic level, or family structure, children of democratic-style parents have the best psychological and educational outcomes.

Issues in Parenting

Parenting is a complex process that raises many questions: How shall we raise the children? How strict should we be, and how will we discipline our children? How soon should we begin toilet training? Will day care meet all our children's needs if both of us work outside the home? How can we share household and parenting responsibilities so that neither one of us feels overburdened or resentful? Before we tackle the issues surrounding these and other questions, let's take a look at some interrelated and complementary theoretical approaches to parenting.

Theoretical Approaches to Childrearing

Much of the parenting research has been done by child-development professionals, who are increasingly adopting a more *systemic approach* to parent-child relationships. Although much of the earlier work focused on the influence of the parent on the child, child-development professionals began to recognize how much the child also influences the parent. A now-classic book by Richard Bell, *Child Effects on Adults* (1977), demonstrated the importance of focusing on the child's influence on the parent. Even at the time of the book's publication, the idea was not new to proponents of family systems theory, but it was a breakthrough for traditional child-development researchers. In the 1980s, a strong consensus developed about the need to study **bidirectional effects**—both the effects of the child on the parent and those of the parent on the child—in order to understand parent-child dynamics. A systemic perspective takes this one step further, viewing the parent-child relationship as an interactive cycle, a circular process of mutual influence.

Several theories of child development have had an impact on approaches to raising children. Freud and his followers focused on the importance of childhood,

Teaching a child appropriate behavior does not necessarily mean punishment for bad behavior. A more effective technique is reinforcing good behavior with praise and a hug.

when the foundation for later life is laid down. Freudians and other proponents of the **psychodynamic theory** have emphasized the importance of providing a positive emotional environment for the child, who needs to believe that the world is a safe and good place and that parents can be trusted to be kind and consistent. Although individuals who have suffered enormously in childhood can make dramatic, positive changes later in life, it is best if we can help children succeed from the very beginning.

Jean Piaget and proponents of **organismic theory** were interested in cognitive development, the development of the mind. Piaget held that the mind develops through various stages over the course of childhood and adolescence. He observed that children think very differently than adults do. Child-thought is primitive and mystical; young children have only the beginnings of logical reasoning. Thought processes develop slowly toward higher forms into adulthood. This theory encourages parents to select toys and activities that are developmentally appropriate for their children and not to expect more than their children are capable of at any given stage.

The **behaviorists,** operating from **learning theories,** have developed some practical, positive approaches for dealing with children's behavior. Rather than focusing on punishment, behaviorists encourage "accentuating the positive," known as **reinforcement.** When a child does something positive, reward the child. Picking the appropriate reinforcer is not easy; "different strokes for different folks" often applies. Most children respond quite well to money, but praise and a hug are usually equally or even more effective. (Adults, too, appreciate praise from a boss for giving that extra effort.) A parent's job is to be creative in developing new reinforcers.

Perhaps the greatest positive reinforcement is simply enjoying each other's company. For example, when invited to speak about our research on strong families at a conference, your authors often go on a "journey of happy memories" with the audience. We ask people to recall the "best time" they can remember as a child: "Close your eyes. Think back to when you were a kid. Picture the best time you can remember with your family. Go right back to the scene as if you were there once again. What are you doing with your family? What's happening? Who's there? Get into it. Feel it. . . ." Then, we ask them to open their eyes, and we call for volunteers to describe what they just saw in their mind's eye:

> "I'm in the living room. It's Thanksgiving. The whole family is gathered together, standing and sitting around the piano. We're all singing songs. Us kids are giggling and squirreling around, too. It's wonderful."
>
> "We're on vacation. We're at the lake 2 hours north of our hometown. We're camping out. We're telling ghost stories around the campfire."
>
> "I remember how we'd play games every Friday night. Just lie on the floor in the living room and play simple board games and laugh together."
>
> "When I was 12, my job was to scrub the kitchen floor with Mom every Saturday morning. We'd be on our hands and knees—just the two of us—scrubbing and laughing and flicking water at each other. It was great!"

We have gone on this journey of happy memories with literally thousands of people over the past 20 years, and the most remarkable thing we have found is that adults rarely recall something that cost a lot of money. On only a handful of occasions has anyone recalled an expensive event: a costly vacation to a theme park, a big meal in a fancy hotel. The vast majority of our happiest memories from childhood come from experiences that cost almost nothing. The key element is this: People who love one another are together, enjoying each other's company, being kind to one another.

It's very clear: Simple things can be tremendously reinforcing to a good relationship. These good times not only enhance the bond between parents and children, they also foster cooperation in children.

Discipline

For many years there has been an ongoing controversy in this country over the issue of how to discipline children. The endless debates in the media seem to focus on two questions: Who is to wield power and control in the family, parents or children? and—if the answer is the parents—Is physical punishment an acceptable means to establish authority over children?

On one side of the debate are those who question the logic of making a child feel *bad* in order to make a child *good.* For example, Murray Straus, a sociologist at the University of New Hampshire, argues in his book *Beating the Devil out of Them: Corporal Punishment in American Families* that corporal punishment increases

Facts About Corporal Punishment

- More than 90% of American children have been hit by their parents.

- At least 84% of Americans believe that spanking is sometimes a necessary type of discipline.

- Corporal punishment is legal in every state in America.

- Studies show that children who were hit are more likely as adults to be depressed, abuse their own children and spouses, and have impaired learning and delinquency.

Source: Straus, M.A. (1994) *Beating the devil out of them:* Corporal Punishment in American Families, N.Y., Lexington Books. With permission from the author.

antisocial behavior in children rather than decreasing it (Straus, 1994; Box 13.3 lists some of Straus's findings from his research on corporal punishment in the United States). Dubbing spanking "virtuous violence," Straus believes that all forms of physical punishment have long-term harmful consequences, not only for children and parents specifically but for society as a whole. By teaching the young that big people have the right to hurt smaller people, spanking contributes to some degree to the relatively high level of violence in American society. On the other side of the debate are those who argue that spanking is not violence but a tool for teaching children the difference between right and wrong.

Diana Baumrind (1996) has entered the debate, arguing for a middle ground between two sides that she thinks have demonized each other. Although punishment can get out of hand and turn dangerous, if used within "a responsive and supportive parent-child relationship, prudent use of punishment is a necessary tool in the disciplinary encounter," she argues. Baumrind advocates a balance between the two extremes—permissiveness and authoritarianism. Behavioral compliance is a necessary part of child socialization but not the complete goal of childrearing.

Because one very important aspect of parenting is the development of a positive bond with one's child, an overemphasis on punishment seems counterproductive. Rather than argue over whether spanking "works" or not, we should draw on the experiences of the many parents in this country who do not physically punish their children and yet have children who are calm, thoughtful, loving, and well behaved. How do these parents raise children without spanking? A number of strategies are apparent: spending a good deal of positive, fun time with the child so that a strong bond develops; reasoning with the child, rather than just giving orders; redirecting the child to other activities if the child is too young to be reasoned with; and using time-out procedures if the child is old enough to understand them, which give both parent and child a bit of breathing space in tense situations. These and many other techniques help create a harmonious atmosphere in the home.

"Teach children, don't hit them" could well be the motto of these parents who have found more positive approaches to maintaining control in the household. This approach is not easy, of course, and takes a good deal of wisdom, time, and patience. No parent is perfect, and almost all parents behave toward their children

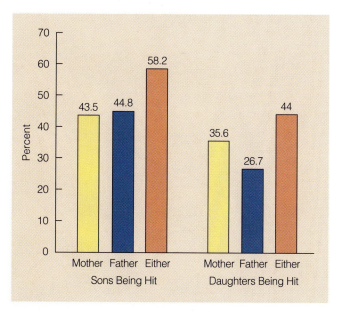

Figure 13.3 Frequency of Adolescent Sons and Daughters Being Hit by a Parent. *Source:* Straus (1994).

in ways they later regret. But parents who try to use positive methods believe that harmony in parent-child relationships is a considerable reward for the effort expended.

Corporal Punishment and Its Consequences

Corporal punishment is the use of physical force as punishment, correction, or behavior control. Corporal punishment usually refers to spanking or slapping but can also include grabbing, shoving, or hitting with an object. Corporal punishment is typically thought of as a means to discipline and punish young children, but it often continues into the teen years. In his research, Straus (1994) found that more men (58.2%) than women (44%) recall being hit as adolescents. Furthermore, adolescent sons are equally as likely to be hit by their fathers as by their mothers, whereas adolescent daughters are about a third more likely to be hit by their mothers (Figure 13.3).

Several studies have found a direct linear relationship between corporal punishment received as a teenager and levels of adult depression in a sample of over 6,000 adults (Straus, 1994). Even when statistical analysis was controlled for other variables, such as poverty and witnessing violence between parents, it was found that the more corporal punishment teenagers experienced, the more depressive symptoms they had as adults. This relationship was stronger for women than it was for men (Figure 13.4). Also, adults whose parents hit them a lot as adolescents were more likely to have suicidal thoughts than adults who were not hit as adolescents.

In 1979 Sweden passed a law making it illegal for parents to spank their children. (Norway, Finland, Denmark, and Austria followed by forbidding corporal punishment as well.) The no-spanking law is not a criminal code; there are no criminal penalties for punishing parents who do spank their children. The law was designed instead to support, educate, and help parents rather than to label parents who use corporal punishment as "bad." After the law was passed, the Swedish

Figure 13.4 Relationship Between Corporal Punishment Received as a Teenager and Adult Depression. *Source:* Straus (1994).

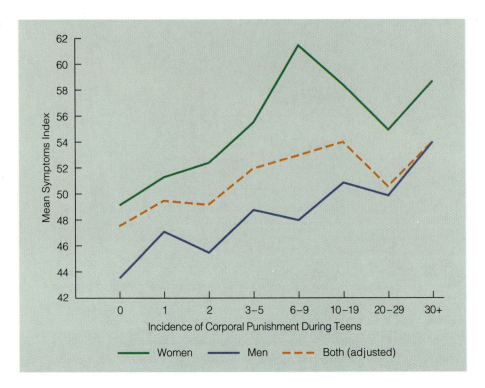

government distributed to parents with young children booklets that listed alternative forms of discipline.

In American society, punishment of children by hitting and spanking has been an almost ubiquitous aspect of childhood. In fact, at least 90% of American children have been hit by a parent (Straus, 1994). The sheer prevalence of corporal punishment alone demonstrates that social norms exist to legitimize it. But sometimes changes in public opinion are brought about by changes in social policy. As in the case of Sweden at the time the no-spanking law was introduced, many Swedes objected to and ridiculed the law. Today, most Swedes (71%) favor managing children without corporal punishment; the dramatic decline in support for corporal punishment began almost immediately after the law went into effect (Straus, 1994).

There is some evidence that the use of and support for corporal punishment in the United States is decreasing. Based on data merged from seven national surveys, the percentage of Americans who approve of corporal punishment declined from 94% in 1968 to 68% in 1994 (Straus & Mathus, 1996). Research findings also indicate differences in support of corporal punishment across sociocultural groups: Approval of corporal punishment is more common among African Americans, men, people who are less educated, older age groups, and individuals living in the southern United States.

Straus argues that corporal punishment is a culturally permissible act of violence, and may actually increase the chances of misbehavior and crime. In fact, several classic studies have demonstrated a link between corporal punishment and aggression. Preliminary analyses from a long-term follow-up study conducted by Straus and colleagues shows that corporal punishment does increase behavior problems (Straus, 1994).

The Increasing Use of Day Care

As more mothers work outside the home, the demand for day-care facilities increases (U.S. Bureau of the Census, 1997). In 1991, 23% of parents used organized day care; in 1995, the number had grown to 39% for children under the age of 6. Dependence on grandparents and other relatives for day care decreased somewhat between 1991 and 1995, from 53% to 48%. As such, the reliance on nonrelatives to care for preschool children is expected to increase as more mothers return to the workplace.

One research team has argued that employed mothers turn to relatives for child care not only for cost-saving reasons but also because they prefer care from extended family members (Kulthau & Mason, 1996). These researchers suggest that public policies that encourage the use of relatives for child care might actually increase parental satisfaction and the quality of child care. Another research team found that parents who value developmental characteristics of child-care programs tended to choose center care and that parents for whom hours, location, and cost of care were important chose care in a home. Additionally, parents who think it is important that the child know the caregiver were more likely to choose family care (Johansen, Leibowitz, & Waite, 1996).

The critical question is how day care affects children, both positively and negatively. An ambitious National Institute of Child Health and Human Development study offered some answers to this question. Researchers at 14 universities worked in nine states and followed 1,364 children from birth to age 3—the largest and most diverse group ever studied. More than 20% of the children received full-time care from their mothers; and the rest were in day-care centers or the homes of paid caregivers. Almost half of the children spent 30 hours or more a week in these settings.

The researchers reported two significant findings. First, they found that high-quality day care—defined as settings in which adults speak with children a great deal and in a responsive way—had a slight advantage over day-care settings in which the adults were less attentive: Children's language and learning abilities were somewhat enhanced in the high-quality settings. The second and most noteworthy conclusion of the researchers was that day care itself had far less impact on the emotional and mental development of the children than did the character of their family life (Lacayo, 1997).

Although the interest and need for day care continues to rise, the United States is one of the few countries that does not have national day-care policies or standards. Day-care workers, who typically earn only minimum wage, often have little direct training. It is a sad commentary on our society that we fail to train and reward the people who are responsible for caring, teaching, and nurturing so many of our children.

Coparenting

A growing number of parents have adopted a cooperative approach to parenting, known as **coparenting**. Traditional family roles—in which dad was the provider and mom the nurturer; dad was "tough" and was mom "tender"—are changing. More mothers are working outside the home, and more men are sharing in parenting tasks. An increasing number of mothers are providing income for their families and enjoying their connection to the world outside the home. At the same time, an increasing number of fathers are experiencing the joy of watching their children grow and learn.

Some couples share the responsibilities equally: Mother and father each do half the child care, half the housework, and half the work outside the home. But most couples do not divide up the tasks exactly equally. One young father explained, "I'm a better cook, so I tend to do more of that. She likes to see a neat, clean house, so she concentrates on that. We both like taking care of the girls, but I do baths and bedtimes because she's so tired at the end of a day of nursing." Flexibility is the key.

Researchers have found a number of advantages to the coparenting model. Parents report greater satisfaction with their marriage and family life than they had before they adopted the coparenting approach. They also report improved relationships with their children. Some partners even considered divorce before they changed their attitudes about childrearing. Coparenting frees men to spend more time relating to, caring for, and relaxing with their children and frees women to pursue outside interests. Both parents have much to gain from active involvement in their children's growth. Parenthood is much too important and much too time consuming to be left to one person (DeFrain, 1979; Risman & Johnson-Sumerford, 1998; Schwartz, 1995).

Another important benefit of coparenting is that it brings fathers into the family on an emotional level. Some observers have concluded that fathers often "draw on their life at home to take care of their emotional needs, but . . . distance themselves from the emotional needs of other family members" (Larson & Richards, 1994). Some fathers enjoy being nurtured at home but don't want to nurture others in the home or don't have the capacity to do so. The experience of coparenting can help men learn how to attend to the emotional needs of others. This is a skill that has often been neglected because in our culture we tend to socialize men for competition, not cooperation.

A problem with coparenting is that sometimes the marriage gets lost in the shuffle. The mother is working outside the home, caring for the children, doing housework; the father is doing the same. Two outside full-time jobs and the job of maintaining a family and household add up to at least three full-time jobs for only two people. Often the marriage is neglected while the spouses concentrate on their employment responsibilities and their family and household tasks. The couple might be doing great at the office and great with the kids but still end up getting divorced because they forgot to focus on their relationship with each other. They need to remember that the foundation for the whole operation is a strong marriage.

Fatherhood Today

Coparenting may be gaining popularity as an ideal, but the reality in many cases is quite different (Kouneski, 1996). Although the images of father as breadwinner and mother as nurturer are slowly breaking down, new images—especially for fathers—have not yet taken hold. More than half of American mothers with children under 18 are now in the workforce, but many fathers have not become proportionately involved in nurturing tasks. The value of fatherhood has not increased.

Some scholars have gone so far as to ask, Is the father even a part of the family? David Blankenhorn (1995) has found that nearly 40% of children live in homes where the biological father is not present. Wade Horn (1995) estimates that 6 out of 10 children born in the 1990s will be "fatherless" before reaching adulthood. What forces are responsible for these trends? And what can be done about them?

The Absent Father   Two major threats to a father's presence in a child's life are divorce and nonmarital childbearing, both of which are increasing. Marriages are continuing to fail at a high rate, and a growing number of families are starting out without a father (U.S. Bureau of the Census, 1997). One-third of births are to single women. Virtually all children born outside of marriage live with their mothers, and in two thirds of these cases, the father never establishes paternity.

In 90% of divorce cases, the children reside with their mothers. Many fathers, no longer living with their children, struggle to stay involved with them. But research has shown a pattern of gradual withdrawal by nonresidential fathers and growing alienation between fathers and children. One large national study found that about two thirds of children of divorce had a poor relationship with their fathers; among children whose parents were not divorced, less than a third (29%) had a poor relationship with their fathers (Zill, Morrison, & Coiro, 1993). Conflict between the former spouses also affects the quality of the father-child relationship by creating strains on the child that may offset any advantages of having the father actively involved.

When fathers remain in frequent contact and when conflict between the parents is low, fathers are more likely to make regular child support payments (Seltzer, 1991). There is a strong association between a divorced father's economic support and the well-being of his children. So frequent contact, low parental conflict, and economic support have a positive effect on the child's well-being. Nevertheless, many fathers would like to have the opportunity to contribute to their children's lives in deeper and more meaningful ways.

The Father as Nurturer   Research in child development has shown that fathers are just as capable as mothers in performing nurturing tasks (assuming the fathers are living with their children). Children can establish attachment relationships with fathers as they do with mothers. Fathers respond to the needs of their infants, picking up on their cues, just as mothers do. When mothers are present, however, fathers tend to back off and defer to them.

Fathers are more likely to be involved in the care of children if the parents are dual earners, but only when the mother works different hours than the father. When parents work the same hours, mothers tend to come home to a "second shift" of family work (DeLuccie, 1995).

Some studies report that women want men to be nurturing in their families, whereas other studies have shown that many mothers do not want increased father involvement (Hogan, 1993). The home is said to be a place of power and control for women, whereas the workplace is where men have traditionally dominated. Some women do not want to share their power or their role as the "more important parent." Men's involvement as fathers can be shaped, positively or negatively, by the mothers' expectations and support.

In sum, it seems that fathers are fully capable of nurturing and caring for their children, but other factors—social, cultural, and interpersonal—tend to discourage them from doing so wholeheartedly. This is particularly unfortunate in light of the belief, put forth by some feminist scholars, that as more men become

DOONESBURY   BY GARRY TRUDEAU

Doonesbury © 1986 G. B. Trudeau. Reprinted with permission of Universal Press Syndicate. All rights reserved.

involved in nurturing tasks, inequalities in the workplace and the family will be reduced (Silverstein, 1995).

Responsible Fatherhood   What is the appropriate role for a father? It must first be acknowledged that every society constructs and defines roles for men and women; the role of father is no exception. In our society today, there is no single definition or description of this role. If a father is living at home with his children, he may be married and coparenting or single and parenting alone. Living apart from his children, he may be young and unwed, with or without paternity established. If divorced, he may have joint physical or legal custody or just visitation rights (Doherty, Kouneski, & Erickson, 1998).

Although single fathers and divorced fathers with custody have nurturing roles thrust upon them, it appears that many other fathers in our society are given quite a wide latitude in how involved they want to be in the family. Unlike mothering, fathering appears to be a choice that men make in the face of contextual pressures. They can be very involved—or they can walk away.

To develop new roles, fathers need the support of mothers. They also need the support of society in general—in the workplace, in the courts, and in the social service agencies that serve families. This support may be forthcoming. Recognizing the holistic nature of family health, family service programs now attempt to involve fathers when they work with families. Additionally, new community-based programs have emerged to support fathers in their efforts to be responsibly involved in their families. Jim Levine and Ed Pitt (1995), discussing their experience as practitioners who work with families, advance this definition of paternal responsibility: A responsible father waits to have children until he is prepared to support the child, financially and emotionally; he establishes legal paternity; and he actively provides physical and emotional care for the child, as well as financial support, in cooperation with the mother.

Given the pressures of living in our society, it may be that mothers and fathers will never achieve equal coparenting. Perhaps it is more important that they nurture a loving, cooperative marriage relationship. In a 1996 report prepared for the federal Health and Human Services Department, William J. Doherty, Edward

F. Kouneski, and Martha F. Erickson recommend that fathering programs involve mothers and focus on the well-being of the mother-father partnership. They believe that new programs should be developed to promote caring, committed, and collaborative marriages. The future of fathering, it seems, is intricately linked with healthy relationships between men and women who have formed equal partnerships meant to last.

> *The best gift a father*
> *Can give his children*
> *Is to love*
> *Their mother.*
> —ANONYMOUS

Good Fathering Makes a Real Difference in Children Kristin A. Moore (1998) of Child Trends, a private organization that monitors research and policies related to children and parenting, conducted a major review of research on fathering. She found that fathers can have a very positive impact on their children's development—whether or not the father lives with the child or is a noncustodial partner. The specific conclusions from this review are as follow:

- The more fathers are involved in the routine activities of their children, the more likely the children will have fewer behavior problems, be more sociable, and do better in school.

- Fathers often promote children's development more through physical play, whereas mothers do it through talking and teaching.

- Across different ethnic groups, fathers tend to assume the important role of economic provider, protector, and caregiver.

- Fathers who provide economically for their children also stay more involved with their children, even if they live apart.

- Fathers who pay child support tend to have children who behave better and do better in school.

Parent Education and Family Therapy

In meeting the challenges of raising children, parents often turn to professionals for guidance, either for education or for therapy. **Parent education** usually involves a presentation of information in a group setting followed by a group discussion of generic parenting problems, such as communication, discipline, imparting values to children, sibling rivalry, and choosing adequate day care. In **family therapy,** a therapist typically work with a single family with one or more specific problems, including sexual abuse, spouse abuse, child abuse or neglect, a runaway child, a child's attempted suicide, a child's coming out as a gay man or a lesbian, or the abuse of alcohol or other drugs.

Both parent education and family therapy take place in a variety of settings, and fees range widely. Services through public agencies are often less expensive than those offered by private practitioners. Parent education programs are usually much cheaper than therapy, and many are free or cost very little. One of the main advantages of parent education programs is their ability to show parents that they are not the only ones having trouble figuring out how to raise their kids; this can be tremendously comforting to troubled parents. In an effective parent education session, a professional might present ideas to the group for 15 to 30 minutes and then let parents break into small groups to discuss their own family's trials and tribulations. Parents soon learn that they are all "in the same boat." Breaking the tension and discussing common issues can be the foundation for positive change and growth in the family.

Researchers Martha Zaslow and Carolyn Eldred (1998) conducted an important study of the New Chance parenting program; the sample consisted of 290 teenage mothers who lived under difficult situations. Zaslow and Eldred found that although the program helped the mothers improve their parenting and nurturing skills, it had no effect on improving the cognitive and social development of their children. The study demonstrated the importance of the social context in the lives of the children. It suggests that ecological stressors such as poverty, unstable housing, and a mother's depression also had an impact on the children's development. The researchers recommended that to increase the effectiveness of the course, more training sessions should be added and that parents should receive instruction that would help them improve their income and overall quality of life.

The New Chance program is only one of many parent education programs that have been developed over the years (Anglin, 1985; Arcus, Schvaneveldt, & Moss, 1993a, 1993b). Any community of reasonable size offers a surprisingly rich variety of programs, including programs for abusive and neglectful parents, foster parents, adoptive parents, single parents, bereaved parents, and chemically dependent parents; programs for stepfamilies; childbirth education programs; family stress management programs; marriage and family enrichment programs; and sex-education and other programs for parents and teenagers.

Challenges and Pleasures of Parenthood

An enduring problem for parents is how to translate philosophy into action. One important goal is to provide children with a basic foundation upon which they can build, as illustrated by Kahlil Gibran's poem "On Children":

> *Your children are not your children.*
> *They are the sons and daughters of Life's longing for itself.*
> *They come through you but not from you,*
> *And though they are with you yet they belong not to you.*
> *You may give them your love but not your thoughts,*
> *For they have their own thoughts.*
> *You may house their bodies but not their souls,*
> *For their souls dwell in the house of tomorrow,*
> *which you cannot visit, not even in your dreams.*
> *You may strive to be like them, but seek not to make them like you.*
> *For life goes not backward nor tarries with yesterday.*
> *You are the bows from which your children as living arrows are sent forth.*
> *The archer sees the mark upon the path of the infinite,*
>   *and He bends you with His might that His*
>   *arrows may go swift and far.*

Let your bending in the archer's hand be for gladness;
For even as He loves the arrow that flies,
  so He loves also the bow that is stable.
(1923/1976, pp. 18–19)

Each day parents are confronted with difficult questions that have complex answers. To find these answers, parents must learn to relate their personal philosophy to what is actually occurring with their children:

- "I don't believe in spanking, but this kid is driving me crazy!"

- "I love to watch my children grow, but I also need a life of my own. How do I balance the two?"

- "He flunked his math test again. I told him I would help him study for it, but he didn't want to study. Should I let him suffer the consequences of failing?"

There are also myriad pleasures associated with being a parent. Bill Meredith, Nick Stinnett, and Benjamin Cacioppo (1985) surveyed 702 Midwestern parents, focusing on the satisfactions they experienced in their parental role. The study found that 76% of the sample were satisfied with parenthood; 16% were neither satisfied nor dissatisfied; and 8% were dissatisfied with the parenting role in general. Table 13.4 lists the specific satisfactions parents cited.

"I can't imagine a life without my children," said Karim, a 45-year-old businessman from Detroit. "Sure, I get mad at them. They bug me, and I yell at them once in a while. But I love them so much, and their journey through life is so much fun to watch. I keep wondering: 'What's the next chapter of the story going to be? What are they going to do next? What will they all become?'

"I suppose I could have concentrated on my career more if I hadn't had children, but love has always counted far more to me than money. You can't hold a $100 bill in your lap and read a story to it."

Summary

- A national survey of married couples revealed considerable differences in how happy couples versus unhappy couples handle parenting. Happy couples tend to agree more on how childrearing responsibilities are shared, to be more satisfied with the amount of attention they focus on their relationship as opposed to on their children, to agree on how to discipline their children, to agree that having children has brought them closer as a couple, and to feel that the father spends enough time with their children.

- According to a national survey, the top five parenting issues for married couples are the following: the father does not spend enough time with their children; partners are dissatisfied with how childrearing responsibilities are shared; partners are dissatisfied with the amount of attention they focus on their

Table 13.4 Common Satisfactions of Parenthood

SPECIFIC SATISFACTION	PERCENTAGE RECORDING THE RESPONSE
Watching children grow and develop	74
Love for children	65
Pride in children's achievement	62
Sharing	54
A growth experience	45
Passing on values	44
Fun to do things with	43
General enjoyment	41
Feeling of being part of a family	40
Self-fulfillment	39
Feel needed	39
Enjoying physical contact	37
Feeling closer to spouse	36
A purpose for living	32
Enjoying the simple aspects of life	31
Companionship	27
Hope for the future	26
New appreciation for my parents	25
Adds stability to life	25
Shared marital project	24

Source: "Parent Satisfactions: Implications for Strengthening Families" (p. 147) by W. H. Meredith, N. Stinnett, and B. F. Cacioppo. In *Family Strengths 6: Enhancement of Interaction,* edited by R. Williams, H. Lingren, G. Rowe, S. Van Zandt, P. Lee, and N. Stinnett, 1985, Lincoln, NE: Department of Human Development and the Family, Center for Family Strengths, University of Nebraska. Copyright 1985 by Center for Family Strengths. Reprinted by permission.

marriage as opposed to on their children; partners disagree on how to discipline their children; and partners feel their marriage is less satisfying since having children.

- Parenthood is both extremely challenging and, for most parents, very satisfying emotionally.

- Conventional wisdom on the subject of parenthood in our society is commonplace. Although many people might believe the conventional "truths," research on parenthood indicates that the picture is more complex.

- Parenthood changes a couple's world: They have less time for each other and for individual interests; they may have money problems; and many find it physically exhausting, especially mothers.

- A middle-income couple (earning an average annual income of $46,100) will spend about $149,820 to raise each child through the age of 17.

- Researchers have found that voluntarily childless individuals and couples can have just as satisfying a life as those who have children. Child-free people have more time for intimate relationships and for their careers, and in old age they often rely on friends and relatives for support.

- Parenting styles differ, and some are more effective than others. The democratic style is favored today because it appears to produce self-reliant children who cope well with stress. Other parenting styles are authoritarian, permissive, rejecting, and uninvolved.

- Many parenting styles can be related to the cohesion and flexibility dimensions of the Couple and Family Map. The democratic style falls into the balanced areas of the model because it exhibits dynamic balances on both the dimensions. Because other styles fall near the extremes of the model, they are less-effective approaches to rearing children.

- How to discipline children is a major issue for many parents, as well as a source of some debate in our society. Corporal punishment is widely used in the United States; statistics suggest that 90% of all children have been hit by their parents and that 84% of Americans believe that spanking is sometimes necessary.

- Research on punishment has found that children who are hit are more likely to hit their partners and children later in life, to be depressed, and to exhibit learning impairments and delinquent behavior.

- Families at all income levels are increasing their use of day care. The majority of day care is provided by centers rather than by family members such as grandparents and other relatives. In spite of the rising demand for day care, the United States is one of the few countries that does not have national day-care policies or standards.

- Positive approaches to childrearing include (1) reinforcing (rewarding) children's positive behavior rather than punishing negative behavior and (2) coparenting, a sharing of traditional male and female roles between parents.

- Numerous studies demonstrate the important role a father plays in a child's development—whether he lives with the child or is a noncustodial parent.

- In the United States, many parent education programs have been developed as a response to the challenges of raising children and the diversity of American families. Many trained professionals provide both information and one-on-one therapy.

- Although parenting poses many challenges, it is also very gratifying for parents. A study on parental satisfaction indicates that parents enjoy watching their children grow, are proud of their children's achievements, enjoy sharing fun times with their children, feel self-fulfilled and needed, feel closer to their partner, and derive from parenting a purpose for living.

Key Terms

child-free alternative	rejecting parenting	learning theories
parental support	uninvolved parenting	reinforcement
parental control	bidirectional effects	coparenting
democratic parenting	psychodynamic theory	parent education
authoritarian parenting	organismic theory	family therapy
permissive parenting	behaviorist	

Activities

1. Read Kahlil Gibran's poem "On Children" carefully and write a brief essay analyzing his philosophy of parenthood. On what points do you agree and disagree?

2. Set a time and place to interview your father and/or mother about their beliefs on rearing children and the challenges and joys they have experienced over the years as parents. A good interview takes careful planning: Write down 15 to 20 questions you want to be sure to ask. Then write up your interview in a short paper and share it with the class or a small group. You might like to audiotape or videotape the interview. (These tapes might even become family treasures.)

3. Parenthood can be a thankless task; children are often too busy and too overwhelmed by their own problems and concerns to think about their parents' feelings. Write a letter to your parents, thanking them for all the things they have done for you and for their unique human qualities.

4. Spend an afternoon with some children you know—your nieces and nephews, a neighbor's children, or a friend's kids. Write down your reactions to this brief "parenting" experience.

Suggested Readings

Arcus, M. E., Schvaneveldt, J. D., & Moss, J. J. (Eds.). (1993). *Handbook of family life education: Foundations of family life education* (Vol. 1) and *The practice of family life education* (Vol. 2). Newbury Park, CA: Sage. Excellent resources for parent educators.

Biller, H. B. (1994). *The father factor: What you need to know to make a difference.* New York: Pocket Books. By a researcher who has probably written more about the father's role in child development than any other author over the past 30 years.

Bozett, F. W., & Hanson, S. M. H. (Eds.). (1991). *Fatherhood and families in culture context.* New York: Springer. Chapters on historical and cross-cultural perspectives, social class and fatherhood, religion and fatherhood, rural and urban influences, the future of fatherhood, and more.

Dinkmeyer, D. C., & MacKay, G. D. (1996). *Raising a responsible child: How to prepare your child for today's complex world.* New York: Simon & Schuster. A revision and update of a very popular book for parents.

Elshtain, J. B. (1998, September 14 and 21). The chosen family: Adoption, or the triumph of love over biology. *The New Republic,* 45–48, 50–54. An excellent review of four recent books on adoption, its history, and the controversy that surrounds it.

Gilbert, L. A. (1993). *Two careers/one family.* Newbury Park, CA: Sage. Up-to-date information on families in which both parents work full-time.

Klagsbrun, F. (1992). *Mixed feelings: Love, hate, rivalry, and reconciliation among brothers and sisters.* New York: Bantam Books. A rather scholarly yet readable book that focuses on the complexity of our feelings about our siblings.

May, E. T. (1995). *Barren in the promised land: Childless Americans and the pursuit of happiness.* New York: Basic Books. Focuses on both voluntary and involuntary childlessness. Little has been written on voluntary childlessness in recent years. A strength of this book is that the author quotes individuals extensively, letting the childless speak for themselves.

Spock, B., & Parker, S. J. (1998). *Dr. Spock's baby and child care.* New York: Dutton. The seventh edition of the top-selling parenting book in the world.

Zigler, E. F. (1992). *Head Start: The inside story of America's most successful educational experiment.* New York: Basic Books. A look at this approach to early childhood education by a professor at Yale University who has been involved in the program from its early days.

CHAPTER 14

Midlife and Older Couples

As the life expectancy of the average American has increased dramatically over this century, researchers' interest in midlife and older couples has also grown. Understanding families in the middle and later years provides a perspective on life's journey. What happens to couples and their marriages in these years directly affects the lives of the younger generations. Middle age can be a time of personal and relationship growth, but it also offers many challenges. And aging has as much to do with psychological and social factors as it does with chronology and biology.

In this chapter we will focus on several key issues of middle age, beginning with a look at the effects of midlife on job satisfaction, sexuality, and the marriage relationship. We will explore reasons for divorce in middle age and offer suggestions for strengthening a marriage. We will also take a look at some contemporary phenomena—the "empty nest," the "cluttered nest," and the conflicting generational demands between which middle-aged individuals are often "sandwiched"—and discuss the topic of grandparenthood.

We will examine family life in the later years in an attempt to answer the question "How old is 'old'?" and also to debunk the conventional wisdom about old age. We will also touch on retirement and family dynamics among aging couples and conclude with a section on the death of a spouse.

Family Life in the Middle Years

What images does the term *middle age* conjure up? For most young college students their mom and dad are the first to come to mind. Middle age can be a relaxing time, a time of thankfulness that the challenges and fears of youth have been overcome. But middle age can bring new pressures, new challenges.

"Life begins at 40," an old saying goes. The kids may leave the nest. Family income may reach a peak. But *middlescence* can set in. In the middle years, some people mourn lost opportunities, the road not taken, and wonder what their lives would have been like if only they had been bolder, smarter, or luckier. Middlescents also often yearn for a taut young body and freedom from the grind.

In Erik Erikson's schema, middle age can be a time for generativity or stagnation (1950). The question of middle age is, "Can we remain productive despite boredom and malaise? (Can an old dog learn new tricks?)" Millions of people transform their lives in the middle years by starting new careers or falling in love. Those who are flexible, who can adapt to new circumstances and "roll with the punches," will be much more likely to succeed. The inflexible ones may survive but will probably not excel—and they will be less likely to enjoy the process of living than those who are flexible. (Box 14.1 presents a broad-ranging study of family stress in the middle years. It details both the types of stressors families face and their strategies for coping with stress.)

Defining Middle Age

A popular societal definition of **middle age** is the period of life between ages 35 and 65, but age alone does not tell the whole story, especially when applied to the middle years. The eminent gerontologist Bernice Neugarten notes philosophically that the middle years are the time when people begin to think about how many

Family Stress in the Middle Years

A team of university-based family researchers in nine states conducted the largest study ever undertaken of family stress and coping in the middle years. More than 1,900 families in Indiana, Iowa, Kansas, Kentucky, Louisiana, Michigan, Minnesota, Missouri, and Nebraska responded to a 27-page questionnaire about the stressors they faced and how they coped. The research focused on intact families, consisting of a middle-aged husband, a wife, and at least one child still living at home.

Types of Stressors

Families in the study were asked to rank various stressors. The top 10 stressors identified by both husbands and wives were the following:

1. A family member's involvement with the judicial system.

2. A major financial loss.

3. Serious emotional problems.

4. A serious illness or accident involving a child.

5. A serious illness or accident involving the primary wage earner.

6. Marital separation.

7. The death of an adult brother or sister.

8. Loss of the primary wage earner's job.

9. The death of either spouse's parent.

10. The illness of either spouse's aged parent.

This list represents an average of the rankings reported by both husbands and wives. Wives perceived family-related matters to be more stressful, in general, whereas husbands considered job-related and financial concerns to be more stressful.

The researchers found that stressors have an additive effect. The greater the number of stressors, the more likely a family is to experience emotional, relational, and health difficulties. In short, the more troubles we have, the more likely we are to become physically and emotionally ill, and the more likely our family relationships are to suffer.

Stress-Related Symptoms

Reported symptoms of stress, from most common to least common, were:

1. Irritability.

2. Weight problems.

3. Muscle tension or anxiety.

4. Use of prescription drugs.

5. Difficulty relaxing.

6. Use of tobacco.

7. Depression.

8. Headaches.

9. Frequent colds or flu.

10. Difficulty sleeping.

Parents generally reported more symptoms of stress than children. Wives reported more symptoms than husbands.

Coping With Stress

The families were asked how they coped with life's stressors. They ranked their stress-management techniques in descending order:

1. Attending church services.

2. Sharing concerns with friends.

3. Facing problems head-on and trying to find solutions.

4. Participating in church activities.

5. Sharing difficulties and doing things with relatives.

6. Seeking information and advice from their family doctor.

7. Seeking information and advice from people in other families who had faced similar problems.

8. Asking for and accepting help from neighbors.

9. Seeking help from community agencies and programs.

10. Seeking professional counseling.

If the signs appear in a family, the family needs to find help. First and foremost, the results support talking. The researchers found the most common coping skill to be talking—talking, to other family members, to relatives, to friends, to professionals. The researchers also stressed the importance of proper nutrition, adequate rest and sleep, plenty of exercise, and fun activities to add some spice to life.

Source: Adapted from "Stress, coping and adaptation in the middle years of the family life cycle," by the Cooperative Extension Service, Iowa State University, Ames, on research conducted by the North Central Regional Committee 164. Agriculture Research Service, U.S. Department of Agriculture, Washington, DC, 1989.

...s they have left rather than how many they've already lived (1968). One ...ddle-aged man described life as a rainbow: At the beginning are infancy, early ...hildhood, adolescence, and young adulthood; around the very highest point of the rainbow are the middle years; and nearing the end of the rainbow are the later years of life. When one reaches the crest of the rainbow, the middle years, one can clearly see the remainder of life for the first time. "When I reached middle age," the man explained, "I saw the rest of my life clearly. It looked like more of the same old stuff I had grown tired of over the past 10 years. Some people might call it a middle-aged crisis," he continued. "I thought of it as a middle-aged opportunity, and I've been changing steadily ever since."

Evelyn Duvall, a distinguished family sociologist, worked with Reuben Hill to develop the family life cycle stages and family development theory. From Duvall and Hill's perspective, middle age is that time that begins when the last child leaves home and continues through to retirement (Duvall & Miller, 1985). This, very roughly speaking, comprises the 15 years between ages 50 and 65. In this book we take a somewhat broader view of middle age by including families with teenagers, families launching young adults, middle-aged parents with an empty nest, and retirement. All four stages put together roughly span the ages 35 to 65, neatly coinciding with society's definition of the middle years.

The size of the 50 to 59 age group, often called the 50-something population, will increase about 50% by the year 2006 (U.S. Bureau of the Census, 1995). This group will gain 12.4 million people, growing from 25.3 million in the mid-1990s to 37.7 million people in 2006. Because of their numbers, these aging baby boomers will exert pressure on society to focus more attention on the retirement, health care, and empty-nest issues that will be important to them. Their buying power will also ensure that purveyors of health care and other consumer goods will design their services and products with them in mind.

Middle Age: A Crisis or Opportunity?

For many, **midlife crisis** is an apt term. During their 40s and 50s, many people will experience the death of a parent or family member, career changes, physical changes in appearance and health, and noticeable changes in relationships with a spouse and children. The realization that one's life is half over and that many goals have not been attained or that there is nothing now to look forward to can cause emotional upheaval.

Despite this common perception—and even the popularity of the term *midlife crisis*—evidence does not support the existence of a midlife crisis. Although people do experience crisis and stress at important transition points in life, including midlife, data show that midlife is not any more stressful than other life stages. In fact, midlife is often a time of stability, freedom, and control, as well as a time to redefine life and relationships.

Statistically, midlife does not bring about an increase in divorce, depression, suicide, or alcoholism. In fact, a recent survey found that people in their 40s find life more exciting than younger or older adults (National Opinion Research Center, 1996). With age comes greater work satisfaction and satisfaction with one's finances, a reduction in depression, and a rise in one's general happiness. Additionally, older people are less likely to divorce than younger people, and suicide

One of the biggest changes of middle age is the children's departure from home for college or a job. Parents who are flexible usually enjoy the freedom from daily responsibility for their children and are likely to develop new interests or even start a new career.

rates drop during middle age (National Opinion Research Center, 1996). In fact, the statistics in Figure 14.1 suggest that *early life* is more a time of crisis than midlife.

Three pioneers in research and thought on the middle years, Daniel Levinson, Roger Gould, and Gail Sheehy, offer their perspectives on midlife. Levinson (1978, 1994) observed that the middle years can bring on a tumultuous personal struggle. "Every aspect of their lives comes into question, and they are horrified by much that is revealed. They are full of recriminations against themselves and others. They cannot go on as before, but need time to choose a new path or modify the old one" (1978, p. 199).

In contrast, Gould (1975, 1979, 1993), looking at middle age from a developmental perspective, suggests that between ages 43 and 50, people come to terms with their life, develop a reasonable picture of themselves, and are comfortable with their strengths and limitations. After 50, people tend to mellow. They acknowledge their accomplishments, and their sense of urgency diminishes. At the same time, they recognize and accept not having achieved all their goals. Finally, Sheehy (1976, 1995), in her popular book *Predictable Crises of Adult Life*, argues that whether the middle years are a time of "transition" or a time of "crisis" or simply a time of "challenge" is essentially up to the individual.

The Middle-Aged Person and the Working World

Many people in their 20s and 30s bounce from job to job. Sooner or later, however, these people (especially members of the middle class) settle into a relatively comfortable position—one that provides a reasonably good income, requires expertise, and involves interaction with amiable co-workers. The job, in short,

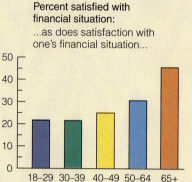

Percent who are very satisfied with their work: Work satisfaction seems to increase with age...

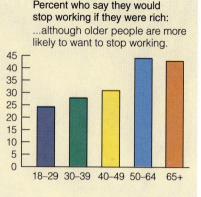

Percent who say they would stop working if they were rich: ...although older people are more likely to want to stop working.

Percent satisfied with financial situation: ...as does satisfaction with one's financial situation...

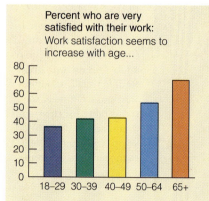

Percent who describe their marriage as very happy: Middle-aged people may be less happy about their marriages...

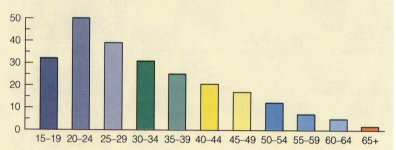

U.S. divorces per married 1,000 men in 1990: ...but they are less likely to get divorced than are younger people.

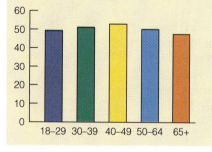

Percent who find life exciting: People in their 40s find life more exciting than younger or older adults.

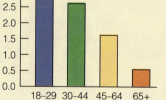

Percent suffering from depression in the past year: Depression seems to decrease with age...

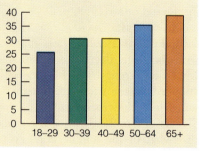

Percent who say they are very happy: ...and happiness seems to go up.

Figure 14.1 Personal Satisfaction of Adults by Age Group. *Source:* General Social Survey, National Opinion Research Center (1996), University of Chicago. Used with permission.

becomes as comfortable as an old shoe. After 10 or 15 years, though, job satisfaction may level off due to **routinization.** It might be years (or possibly never) before there's any chance for a lateral move or promotion.

Middle-aged people often feel trapped by their work. Making a career change in midlife, however, can be risky: The tradeoff for a new, more interesting job may be a pay cut. If a person cannot figure out how to make the old job fulfilling again, however, boredom, anxiety, or anger may reach the boiling point. Fights with bosses

Between the age of 43 and 50, people usually come to terms with life and are able to realistically assess their strengths and weaknesses.

and co-workers (and one's family) often have their roots in these common middlescent developments.

Women who return to college or to work outside the home when their children reach a more independent age find themselves at the onset of a second, distinct career in their life. Middle-aged women returning to the work marketplace after a long absence are at a certain disadvantage because they lack up-to-date on-the-job experience. Although they may have acquired tremendous insights and skills from their work in the home and in the community that would translate well on the job, they often experience discrimination. Employers sometimes demean these talents. Worse yet, women themselves often do not realize how competent they are and suffer from feelings of inferiority.

The good news about this two-career approach to life is that just when one career, parenthood, is running out of steam and may be becoming burdensome, a new career in the working world is waiting in the wings. Delighted with her new job teaching at a community college, one woman stated, "I've been recycled. I've been a mother of four children for 15 years. And now I'm a *person* again!" At age 42, to use a common expression, she was "born again."

Sexuality in Middle Age

As noted in Chapter 7, sexual activity often declines steadily over the years of a marriage, as stress and boredom take their toll. Fortunately, among couples who are creative and committed, sex can remain a source of intense pleasure throughout the middle years. Two issues of concern during this time are menopause and "male menopause."

Menopause   The most dramatic age-related change in female reproductive functioning, after puberty, is **menopause,** the end of monthly menstrual periods. Sheehy (1992) refers to menopause as the "silent passage" because it is so rarely discussed openly. Menopause occurs, on average, around the age of 50 but can begin as early as a woman's mid-30s or as late as her early 60s. Because of various hormonal changes, menopause signals the cessation of a woman's ability to have children. Reproductive organs shrink, and the amount of fatty tissue in the breasts and other parts of the body decreases. The vulva becomes thinner, losing its capacity to engorge with blood, and the vagina shrinks and loses some elasticity. Vaginal secretions that provide lubrication during intercourse diminish.

Many women experience distress—including irritability, insomnia, "hot flashes," headaches, and depression—during menopause. Some physicians recommend taking hormones orally, by injection, or by use of a transdermal patch to relieve these symptoms, which result from hormonal imbalances. Hormone-replacement therapy is a common approach to relieving some of the discomfort that menopause can bring. It can also minimize the loss of bone mass that can occur after menopause.

In general, most women perceive menopause as a transition period rather than a problem. Even though physical responses change, a woman's perception of pleasure and satisfaction during intercourse remain the same or may even increase. A number of factors may be involved, including freedom from fear of pregnancy and the fact that the couple may be rediscovering each other after losing contact during the challenging full-time parenting years (Boston Women's Health Book Collective, 1998; Hyde & DeLamater, 1997; Masters et al., 1995; Sheehy, 1992).

"Male Menopause"   Sexual changes related to age also occur in men. Production of the male hormone **androgen** declines slowly and steadily in most men until about age 60, when it levels off. For most men, this decline in hormone production does not cause the emotional and physical changes that some women experience during menopause. In other men, the symptoms are so similar to those experienced by menopausal women that physicians label the condition **male menopause,** a term that generates some controversy in the medical community.

As men get older, the amount of fluid ejaculated with orgasm tends to diminish, as does the strength of the ejaculation. The testicles become smaller and less firm; erections become less frequent and also less rigid. By age 50 the average male may require 8 to 24 hours after orgasm before he is capable of having another erection. Most men also require more time to reach orgasm, but this can be viewed as a benefit, as a lengthening of the period of pleasure for both the man and his partner (Hyde & DeLamater, 1997).

The Middle-Aged Marriage

Many marriages are happier before children arrive and after they leave home (Olson, McCubbin, et al., 1989). For many couples in the middle years, marital satisfaction may reach a low point and then increase as the adolescents leave home.

Divorce in the Middle Years   Maggie Hayes (1979) conducted one of the first studies of the phenomenon of divorce in the middle years, exploring why it occurs and what people can do to strengthen their ties to each other to prevent it. Hayes found that marriages that ended in divorce in the middle years had survived that long for two major reasons: children and money. The couples had generally gotten off to a good start in their marriages; two thirds felt that the early years of the relationship had been good but that marital satisfaction had deteriorated very gradually as time passed. Hayes was especially interested in the dynamics of this deterioration process and reported a number of important contributing factors:

- *Dominance of the husband.* Only 17% of the people in Hayes's study considered their marriages to be equal partnerships. The vast majority of both spouses viewed the husband as dominant, with many wives describing their position in the relationship as little more than that of an indentured servant. "He wouldn't let me" was a phrase Hayes heard repeatedly. The men appeared to fear their wives' personal growth or independence. They squelched the woman's efforts to get a job, go back to school, handle money, or even learn to drive a car—describing these desires as "overindependence." Both partners often referred to their marriage as "boring."

- *Failure to communicate and to share.* About 75% of the people interviewed considered their partner hard to talk with. Husbands were especially unable to share their feelings; wives often accused them of being too judgmental, too much of a know-it-all, or fearful of conflict. Most of the couples seldom talked with each other. One in five often quarreled, but almost half said they "seldom" quarreled, indicating little interest in the relationship. The vast majority of people said their partner contributed little or nothing to their self-esteem. Women tended to have lower self-esteem than men.

  Shared couple activities had decreased over time in most of these marriages. Work, children's activities, housework, and individual interests took precedence. When Hayes asked, "What did you do together that gave you the most pleasure?" many people could think of nothing to say. There was no reservoir of happy memories from which to draw. Couples failed to express love and concern verbally, and the desire for closeness, warmth, kissing, and touching had disappeared. Sex had become a bore, and innovative behavior was resisted by the spouse.

- *Career involvement.* The husband's career successes often had a negative effect on the marriage, drawing him away from a spouse whom he no longer considered interesting. A husband's lack of career success was also perceived as damaging to the relationship. Among couples who divorced

FOR BETTER OR FOR WORSE   BY LYNN JOHNSTON

For Better or For Worse © Lynn Johnston Prod., Inc. Dist. by United Feature Syndicate, Inc.

in middle age, 75% of the wives were working. The effects cut both ways: The positive effects of more income and personal growth for the wife were often offset by the husband's resentment of the time and attention the wife gave to her work.

- *Extramarital involvements.* Seventy-five percent of the men and 25% of the women whose marriages had ended in divorce said they had been sexually unfaithful. More of the men had been unfaithful earlier in the marriage without the wife's knowing it. Affairs in the middle years tended to become serious emotional involvements. Women who had had an affair often said that they viewed it as a way of affirming themselves as women after being ignored as wives. Both men and women viewed affairs as destructive to the marriage.

- *Midlife change.* The *male midlife crisis,* a term often used in the popular literature to describe certain changes during the middle years, was cited in many of these broken marriages. The most common story Hayes heard from wives was that the husband had developed an obsession with his appearance: buying a new wardrobe, exercising, losing weight, changing his hairstyle. This was followed by absences from home, irritability, absent-mindedness, and self-centeredness.

Strengthening Marriage in the Middle Years   Hayes observes that we can all learn a lot about marriage from divorced people. Based on the experiences of the people she interviewed, Hayes offers several recommendations for strengthening marriage during the middle years:

- Establish priorities early in marriage, with the spouse at the top of the list. Do not allow parenthood to overshadow the marriage.

- Be alert for warning signs of marital problems, which include nagging, sarcasm, possessiveness, criticism, and personal discontent.

Successful middle-aged couples tend to be those who have shared feelings and activities throughout their marriage, in spite of the competing demands of jobs and children. They continue to express love and concern both verbally and physically.

- Strive toward equality in all aspects of the marriage. Each partner should feel important and powerful.

- Seek a balance between togetherness and personal growth; either extreme can be harmful to a marriage.

- Good sex in a relationship in the middle years does not come naturally; it is a result of a positive daily life together.

- Develop a network of friendships with other couples who are concerned about maintaining a quality marriage.

- Evaluate the marriage from time to time, and attend a marriage enrichment workshop.

- Avoid boring or frustrating work situations; a midlife career change may be beneficial.

- Consider a lifestyle change rather than a partner change in middle age to add pizzazz to the marriage.

A happy marriage is the key to a content spouse. The best way to deal with infidelity is to prevent it from occurring.

Empty Nest, Spacious Nest, or Cluttered Nest?

The term **empty-nest syndrome** describes the feelings of malaise, emptiness, and lack of purpose that parents sometimes experience when their children leave home. Some parents do suffer from these feelings, and most go through a period of adjustment when their children leave the nest. But the empty nest is a boon for many parents, giving them more time and energy to invest in their marriage. To emphasize the positive aspects of this time, we prefer the term **spacious nest.** There is more room in the home for the parents' things—and more money and time in the marriage for each other.

The opposite of the spacious nest is the parental nest refilled with **boomerang kids**—adult children who return home as a result of divorce, job loss, or an inability to make it in the "real world" (Okimoto & Stegall, 1987). Bernice Neugarten and Dail Neugarten have noted, "The so-called 'empty nest' . . . is not itself stressful for most middle-aged parents. Instead, it is when the children do not leave home at the appropriate time that stress occurs in both the parent and the child" (1996, p. 35).

Today, middle-aged parents of young adults are less likely to find themselves with empty nests than were their counterparts 20 or 30 years ago. More young adults are postponing marriage or are marrying and divorcing. A phenomenon called the **cluttered nest** occurs when adult children return to the parental nest to live after college graduation while they get established professionally and financially and save enough money to move into their own apartments or homes (Schnaiberg & Goldenberg, 1989).

Data from the U.S. Bureau of the Census indicate that about one in four (27%) 18- to 34-year-olds are living with their parents, according to Andrew Cherlin (1993), a family demographer. Low wages and high unemployment contribute to young people's difficulty in making it on their own. Dividing this age group into two subgroups, the researchers found that in 1992, 54% of all 18- to 24-year-olds and 12% of all 25- to 34-year-olds were living with their parents. "Very, very few people will live with their parents when they get married, but if you aren't married, being at home can look like a reasonable alternative. Thirty years ago, it wasn't that acceptable to still be living at home after you were 20 years old. Now it's very common" (Cherlin, 1993).

Researchers offer some practical suggestions to help parents launch their adult children (Okimoto & Stegall, 1987). They suggest that parents should:

- Remind their children that they are living in the parents' home.
- Consider charging their children for room and board.
- Set house rules.
- Limit financial support.
- Support all signs of independence and encourage their children to seek employment, even in a less-than-desirable job.

However, the problems associated with boomerang kids and cluttered nests may be exaggerated. Parents generally understand the difficulties young people face in trying to make it on their own in the working world and are usually willing to help out. Most parents like their adult children and enjoy their company. Research on parents who have adult children living at home indicates that the majority are satisfied with the living arrangement and have mostly positive relationships with their adult children. (Aquilino, 1997; Aquilino & Supple, 1991).

> "What was I supposed to do?" one middle-aged mother in suburban Washington, D.C., asked rhetorically. "Slam the door in her face?" This woman was talking about her daughter, who returned home with two preschool-aged children after her divorce. "She had no money. Her husband's lawyer was threatening to take the kids away, and she was so depressed I thought she might overdose on pills. I had to help. I love my daughter and I love my grandchildren.
>
> "I knew they wouldn't be with us forever. I knew she would be getting back on her feet soon enough. I knew I could help. What are families for?"

Caught in the Middle: The Sandwich Generation

Besides struggling with adolescents, empty or cluttered nests, and boomerang kids, people in their middle years are also apt to have growing responsibilities for their aging parents. For this reason, middle-aged parents have been described as the **sandwich generation.**

Caring for an elderly family member can be a burden for the caregiver, but it can also increase intimacy between a parent and an adult child. One study of 133 pairs of adult caregiving daughters and their elderly mothers reported that about half the mothers and daughters saw their relationship as having been positively affected by the caregiving situation, whereas most of the rest reported no change in the quality of their relationships (Walker, Shin, & Bird, 1990). Caregiving also gives the younger generation the opportunity to return in some small way the many kindnesses bestowed upon them early in their life (Allen & Walker, 1992; Walker, Pratt, & Oppy, 1992). Caregiving is not a one-way street, however; even very troubled and frail older adults have many things to offer, including good advice, the wisdom and perspective that comes from a long life, financial aid, and friendship.

For some middle-aged parents, though, the stress of caring for their children—whether adolescents or young adults—and for frail aging parents can be too great. Exhaustion and anger can reach a boiling point and create intergenerational conflicts. These can also produce neglect or abuse of the elderly, which unfortunately are relatively common in the United States (Stull, Bowman, & Smerglia, 1994; Winston, 1994).

Grandparenthood

If I had known grandchildren would be this fun, I would have had them first.
—BUMPER STICKER

The most recent data available from a national survey of people age 65 or older reveal that 75% have living grandchildren. Many people become grandparents long

Because they do not have to bother with the daily chores of childrearing, grandparents are free to develop a more creative relationship with their grandchildren, sharing activities and interests with them. For most grandparents, one of the greatest satisfactions of grandparenthood is seeing a continuation of themselves through another generation.

before age 65; the first grandchild is often born when grandparents are in their early or mid-40s (Aldous, 1995; Troll, 1989, 1997).

For most people, grandparent-grandchild interaction is very enjoyable. Three fourths of all grandparents have contact with their grandchildren weekly (Troll, 1989). Although grandparents are not directly responsible for the well-being of their grandchildren, they do have a vested interest in their development.

In one study, 90 grandmothers were asked about the value to them of the grandparent-grandchild relationship to them (Timberlake, 1980). Eighty percent said they valued the intergenerational relationship because it provided a continuation of themselves through another generation. Such statements as "Oh, she certainly has Grandma's eyes!" or "He sure is stubborn—just like Grandpa was" reflect this attitude. Timberlake also found that three of five grandmothers said grandchildren filled a need for creativity, accomplishment, competence, and a reconfirmation of their own identity. Building a relationship with a grandchild is certainly a creative endeavor and gives the grandparent a sense of accomplishment. Further, nurturing such a relationship takes great skill and reinforces the grandparent's sense of self-worth and sense of importance to the family as a whole (Doress & Siegal, 1987; Doress-Worters, 1994).

Because grandparents usually do not have day-to-day responsibility for childrearing and do not have to discipline the child, they can often build a more stress-free relationship with the grandchild than the parents can. From the parents' perspective, grandparents often seem to "spoil" their grandchildren. From the grandparents' perspective, the so-called spoiling is simply a matter of accentuating the positive. One anonymous humorist explained that "the reason grandparents and grandchildren have such strong affection for each other is that they have a common enemy."

By and large, the grandparent role is mutually enjoyable for grandparents and grandchildren, and it gives the parents a welcome break. Although grandparenting can sometimes overwhelm and tire out grandparents, the role is generally one of joy. "I can enjoy these kids so much now . . . so much more than I really could my own kids. I don't have to worry about them. Their mom and dad can do the worrying."

Clarice Orr and Sally Van Zandt have written movingly about the importance of grandparents:

> Grandparents are significant family resources to enrich the lives of their grandchildren. Perhaps through more intergenerational contact, grandparents can "patch and mend" some of the "raveled ends" and "tattered seams" of the new extended family. They will realize that by their actions they can sprinkle stardust in the eyes of their grandchildren. Above all, elders need to learn there are but two lasting bequests they can give their children and grandchildren: one is roots and the other is wings. (1987, p. 87)

Family Life in the Later Years

The later years of life can be bittersweet. For those who were successful in raising a family and planning for retirement, the later years are easier than for those who have family or financial problems. Some older adults experience loneliness and isolation. Many must make do on limited funds. And elder abuse by younger family members occurs in some families.

Although many studies of older people have focused on the negative aspects of aging, a recent study demonstrated that many people become happier as they age. Daniel Mroczek and Christian Dolarz (1999) found that older men, especially those who are married, are happier than are younger men. Older men seem to regulate their emotions more effectively and are more able to maximize the positive and minimize the negative. In a sample of 2,727 men from ages 25 to 74, the older men reported having fewer negative emotions and, in general, were happier than younger men. Younger people reported feeling sad, nervous, hopeless, or worthless more often than did older participants. Thus, aging seems to have some positive aspects when it comes to emotions.

U.S. society is going through a "demographic revolution" as the life span of the population increases. Since 1900, the average life expectancy in the United States has increased from 47 years to 75 years (Brubaker, 1991). Average life expectancy differs somewhat between men and women: For men it is 72.0 years; for women, 78.8 years. Also, the longer individuals live, the longer they can be expected to live: When individuals reach age 45, their life expectancy increases to 78 years; when they reach age 65, their life expectancy rises to 82; and if they live to age 85, on average, they will live 6 years longer (Metropolitan Life Insurance Co., 1993).

Due to increased life expectancy, American society is growing older. Trends indicate that the population of older persons is increasing rapidly. In 1970 there were roughly 7.5 million people over the age of 75, and by 1995 that number had almost doubled to over 13 million (U.S. Bureau of the Census, 1997). Individuals over 85 years of age numbered about 1.4 million in 1970 and doubled to over 3 million by 1995.

Defining Old Age

Old age is often said to begin at 65, which in our society is the typical age of retirement. But any exact chronological starting point for old age is bound to be arbitrary. In some parts of the world where life expectancy is lower, a person might be old at 35 or 40. Even in our own society, we see enormous variation among older adults. We all know active 75-year-olds and feeble 50-year-olds.

Part of the reason for this variation is that "old age" spans a long period of time and encompasses many phases and changes. Duvall and Miller (1985) divide older adults into three distinct groups: (1) the young-old, those between 55 and 65, who are still working and at the peak of their social and vocational status; (2) the middle-old, those between 65 and 75, who tend to be retired and in good health and have abundant time to follow their interests; and (3) the old-old, those over age 75, who as a group tend to be the frailest, loneliest, and poorest of the old.

Aging is in part a psychological phenomenon. How an older person feels depends largely on her or his mental attitude toward both the accomplishments of the past and the possibilities of the future. For most purposes, a person who feels "young at heart" *is* still young. Of course, aging is also a biological reality, and some variations among older adults are a result of their different genetic heritages. Aging is also a social phenomenon. If society forces people into retirement at 65, it is in effect declaring them to be old. Such social definitions are powerful influences on how a person feels and acts. Finally, aging is part of the family process, one that occurs in the context of ongoing interpersonal relationships with spouses, parents, children, and other family members whose attitudes help us redefine ourselves as we grow older.

Despite the challenges of aging—the wrinkles, the lower energy levels, the failing eyesight or poor hearing—many people adapt to these changes and continue to live fruitful lives. How we as individuals, and as members of families and communities, define the later years powerfully influences our well-being during this time.

Conventional Wisdom About Old Age

Grow old along with me! The best is yet to be, The last of life, for which the first was made.

—Robert Browning (1864/1970, p. 811)

Many people in our society accept the conventional wisdom about old age, most of which is negative. It is important, though, that we set the record straight about these false beliefs, which foster a form of prejudice known as **ageism,** prejudging an older person negatively solely on the basis of age. In the following section, we hope to deconstruct some of the most common myths about old age.

At 65, You're "Over the Hill"   Attitude has a good deal to do with how "old" one is. People whose attitudes toward life remain positive generally lead happier and more fulfilling lives in their later years. Many symptoms popularly associated with old age—cognitive impairment, falling, dizziness, loss of bladder control, and loss of appetite—are symptoms of disease, not of normal aging.

Older couples often have more time to enjoy leisure activities together. They may also return to hobbies or activities they previously did not have time to enjoy while working.

Most Older Adults Are Poor Median annual income decreases after people reach about age 55. For example, households with adult members ages 45 to 54 have the highest median income before taxes: $55,029. In households with adult members ages 55 to 64, median income before taxes is $45,264; for the 65-and-older age group, median income falls to $28,301 (U.S. Bureau of the Census, 1997). Keep in mind, though, that almost 80% of those over age 65 own their own home free and clear, and their household expenses are generally lower because their children no longer live with them.

A Harris poll found that 68% of all the people in the United States under age 65 thought that money was a problem for older people but that only 17% of those 65 or older considered money a problem (Hunt, 1982). Older adults have relatively lower incomes than younger people, but most do not perceive this to be troublesome.

Older Adults Lose Their Sex Drive Young people have a hard time imagining that their parents make love, let alone their grandparents and great-grandparents. Nonetheless, most older people enjoy sex, but they have sexual intercourse less often than when they were younger (Cross, 1993; Hodson & Skeen, 1994; Mayo Foundation for Medical Education and Research, 1993). In one study of 202 healthy retirement-home residents ages 80 to 102, the researchers found that 88% of the men and 72% of the women fantasized about being intimate with a partner (Bretschneider & McCoy, 1988). Sexual feelings and sexual behaviors can continue across the life span. Notable exceptions are people who have some kind of physical disability and those who believe they shouldn't enjoy sex at their age.

Table 14.1 Sexual Activity Among Older Adults						
FREQUENCY OF	**39–50**		**51–64**		**65+**	
SEXUAL INTERCOURSE	**M**	**F**	**M**	**F**	**M**	**F**
A few times a week	54%	39%	63%	32%	53%	41%
Weekly	29	29	18	33	16	33
Monthly	9	11	11	8	20	4
Rarely	8	21	8	27	11	22

Source: The Janus Report on Sexual Behavior (p. 25) by S. S. Janus and C. L. Janus, 1993, New York: Wiley. Copyright 1993 by S. S. Janus and C. L. Janus. Reprinted by permission.

The *Janus Report*, a national survey of sexual behavior, reported that sexual activity was higher in men than in women. There was some decrease in frequency as people became older, but the rate did not decrease as dramatically as many assumed (Table 14.1).

Older Adults Are Usually Sick   People over 65 have about half as many *acute* illnesses as those between 17 and 44. It is true, of course, that *chronic* conditions tend to accumulate over time, and older adults commonly suffer from sensory losses—hearing, vision, and taste. But as the American Association of Retired Persons points out, these problems do not keep most older adults from enjoying an active, healthy life. People who have adapted to change throughout life will likely find ways to cope with most of the changes that aging brings.

Older Adults Become Senile   The term *senility* is not often used by gerontologists today because it has little specific meaning. Although brain damage can be caused by a series of small strokes, most progressive organic brain impairment is caused by disease, such as Alzheimer's disease. Assuming that memory loss or change in behavior in older adults is a function of age can cause one to overlook a disease that might be successfully treated. All too often, people attribute an older person's anger or depression to old age, when in fact it may be due to a life occurrence that would cause similar symptoms in a younger individual (see Blieszner & Shifflett, 1990; Rybash, Roodin, & Santrock, 1991).

Most Older Adults End up in Nursing Homes   Eighty percent of older adults who are sick and need long-term care are cared for by their family. Less than 5% of the people in the United States over age 65 are in a nursing home, and most of those people are over age 85. African American families are less likely to institutionalize their elderly family members than are White families (J. Burr, 1990). Few families abandon their loved ones in their later years, and few families wantonly "warehouse" older members in a nursing home. It is also important to note that the vast majority of nursing homes have dedicated staffs and try very hard to meet the needs of infirm older people.

Most Older Adults Are Lonely   The conventional wisdom about the lonely elderly brings to mind a picture of a frail old man sadly rocking in his chair on the front porch of a public home for the aged. No one comes to visit him, and he babbles to himself of times gone by. There are certainly cases like this, but older adults as a group are not necessarily lonely. John Woodward (1988) has studied loneliness across the life span for more than 25 years and has found that older adults have, on average, the lowest loneliness scores. His findings argue against the stereotype that the later years are a time of emptiness and endless reminiscence.

Woodward cautions, however, that his research does not indicate that older adults are *not* lonely, only that of all the groups he and his colleagues have studied, they are the *least* lonely. "Loneliness is a central and inevitable theme in human existence," Woodward contends. "Everyone gets lonely. Some elderly are abjectly lonely, and some adolescents are rarely lonely."

Older Adults Are Isolated From Younger Family Members   A national study (Troll, 1989, 1994) found that more than half of all people over age 65 who have children live either in the same household with an adult child or in the same neighborhood as their child. Contact with other family members, especially adult children, is rather frequent. Most older adults enjoy their privacy, preferring not to live in the same house as their adult children and their grandchildren. Of older people who have adult children but live alone, however, half live within 10 minutes from a child. On the day they were interviewed for this study, half of the older people with children reported that they had seen one of their adult children the day they were interviewed, and about three quarters reported having seen at least one of their adult children during the week preceding the interview. This study also revealed that even in those cases where the geographical distance between them is considerable, older and younger family members tend to stay in contact.

What about the quality of these contacts—a much more difficult characteristic to measure. One way to measure quality is to assess the amount of help family members give each other. In a national study, 7 out of every 10 older adults with children said they helped their children, and 7 out of every 10 older adults said they helped their grandchildren. Five out of every 10 said they even helped their great-grandchildren. Seven out of 10 older people also said they received help from their children. This help included home repairs and housework, care during an illness, and different kinds of gifts. In addition, older people reported that they helped their adult children by caring for grandchildren. In short, it appears that older people are not isolated from younger family members and that these contacts are generally happy ones (Mancini & Blieszner, 1991).

Retirement

The stereotypical view of retirement is a dreary, downhill period of life in which people lose their self-esteem and immerse themselves in memories of better days; they stop being productive working citizens and slowly waste away. To the contrary, research shows that retired people are no more likely to be sick or depressed than people of the same age who are still on the job. In fact, most people adapt satisfactorily to retirement, with few long-term changes in their health, psychological well-being, or family relationships (Fletcher & Hansson, 1991).

There are, of course, examples of people who find retirement difficult and depressing. A woman said of her recently retired husband, "He used to be a powerful executive with 200 employees under him. He would work long, hard hours and then come home to relax and enjoy his hobbies. He retired 5 years ago, and ever since he's been terribly depressed."

Most older people adjust well to voluntary retirement, especially those who get involved in new activities.

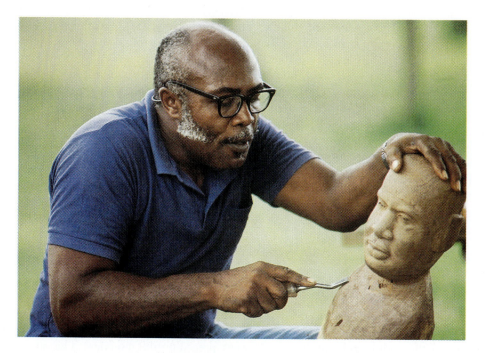

Fortunately, positive retirement stories are the general rule. Most men and women report they adjust quite well to voluntary retirement, and studies consistently find that satisfaction with life remains fairly high for the majority of retired people. Those who have difficulty with retirement are often people who have had difficulty making major transitions in life, people who are shy or lonely, and people with few instrumental (task-oriented or proactive) and communal (social) abilities (Fletcher & Hansson, 1991).

Retirement from the working world has traditionally not been as difficult a task for women as for men because women usually have household responsibilities that make the transition smoother. But Carolyn Kitchings Johnson and Sharon Price-Bonham (1980) point out that employment is not a secondary role for *all* women. Some women find retirement quite difficult, and the proportion of women in this category will presumably increase as the percentage of women in the workforce grows.

As with any major life transition, retirement takes some adjustment. Retired people report a number of problems associated with this transition, including sleeplessness, aimlessness, and sadness over not seeing work friends and colleagues regularly. But other retirees are quick to point out that they have gotten involved in so many new activities that they have less free time than they did when they were working and would like to slow down a bit.

Retirement affects marriage in different ways. For couples who place a high value on intimacy and family relationships, retirement can bring more freedom to enjoy each other and the family. Some wives—especially those who always assumed traditional roles and traditional divisions of labor—are pessimistic about the husband's impending retirement, perhaps fearing the retiree will intrude on their domestic territory.

Family Dynamics and the Aging Couple

A number of family researchers have studied long-term marriages. From their findings, George Rowe and Marcia Lasswell were able to divide **longevis marriages**—marriages that last 50 years or more—into three categories: (1) couples who are very happy and blissfully in love, (2) couples who are very unhappy but who continue the marriage out of habit or fear, and (3) couples in between, who are neither very happy nor very unhappy and accept the situation (cited in Sweeney, 1982). Lasswell estimated the "very happy" number at roughly 20% of the total and the "very unhappy" number at 20%. Both researchers also found a negative relationship between the number of children couples had and marital happiness: Couples with larger families tended to have less happy marriages. "We can't explain that, except the study indicated that a dip in marital happiness is almost always concurrent with the time the children are a heavy responsibility for parents," Rowe said (p. 23). He theorized that the more children a couple has, the longer this period of responsibility lasts and the more the relationship is drained by parenting responsibilities.

Timothy Brubaker (1985) reviewed 25 studies of older couples' relationships and identified three common patterns in the studies:

- Some couples experience a decline in marital quality during the middle years of the marriage, and then the marriage improves in the later years.

- For some couples, the marriage declines gradually in quality as the years go by, with the trend line from the newlywed days to later life moving steadily downward.

- For some couples, the trend line remains stable in the middle years and into the later years. Those who were happy when the children were at home will remain happy when the children leave home and when they retire. Those who were unhappy as a couple when the kids were at home will continue to be unhappy when the nest empties and they retire.

In general, the quality of the marital relationship shows continuity over the years. Couples who did not get along well in their early years together are likely not to get along well in the later years of their marriage. "In the later years, those who have vital, rewarding relationships will most generally experience continued positive interactions within the marriage, while those who have difficult, unsatisfying relationships will most likely experience continued negative marital interactions" (Brubaker, 1991, p. 229).

Losing a Spouse

The death of a spouse is a difficult life transition for most, and for some it is a devastating personal crisis (Van Zandt, Mou, & Abbott, 1989). Brubaker (1990) outlined three characteristic stages of the grieving process:

1. **Crisis-loss stage of grief.** In the first few days and weeks after the loss, the survivor is in a chaotic state of shock. Common reactions are "I can't believe this is happening to me." "I'll do anything to bring her back." "What am I going to do now?"

Spouses who got along well in their early years are likely to get along well in their later years, too. For some couples, in fact, marriage gets better with age.

2. **Transition stage of grief.** In the transition period, the survivor begins trying to create a new life. Grief lessens in its intensity, and the bereaved person sees the possibility of a life ahead.

3. **New-life stage of grief.** The survivor changes her or his lifestyle and proves to the world and to herself or himself that it is possible to live satisfactorily as a single person. The widow or widower develops an identity without the partner.

Grief lasts longer than was long believed to be the case—up to 2 years, according to research on widows. A widow's grief can include a range of feelings, from sadness and anger to fear and anxiety. The prevalence of anxiety in the first 3 years after a husband's death led one researcher to see its role in mourning as crucial (Sable, 1989, 1992). Other researchers see depression as a significant risk among bereaved spouses (Farberow, Gallagher-Thompson, Gilewski, & Thompson, 1992; Gilewski, Farberow, Gallagher, & Thompson, 1991).

"We were married for 54 years," an older woman in Fort Myers, Florida, explained. "It wasn't all perfect, but we were pretty good friends. He's been gone now for 7 months and I'm still adjusting. I'm doing okay, but not great. I'm trying to get involved in some church groups, and in a senior aerobics class.

"I'll make it through this, but I don't like it. The hardest part is the evenings. It's just so quiet without him around. This is going to take a while. We were together for 54 years, and now all of a sudden he's gone. This is going to take some time.

"When you lose someone who's been so much a part of your life for so long, you're never going to be the same. Think about it: How could you be?"

In the United States, 11 out of every 12 people who have lost a spouse are women. This is because women live about 7 years longer on average than men and because they tend to marry men older than themselves. Three out of 4 wives can expect to become widows. Widowhood involves a number of challenges: the shaping of a new identity (from a partner in a couple to a single individual), financial problems (which may force many back into the job market), and health problems. Important factors in successfully coping with the loss of a spouse include maintaining a sense of autonomy and involving oneself in social relationships and community affairs (A. T. Day, 1991).

Summary

- Middle age roughly spans ages 35 to 65, a period during which many couples are (1) still raising teenagers, (2) launching young adults and then coping with their absence from or return to the home, and (3) entering retirement.

- For many, the challenges of middle age include coping with routinization in the job, developing a new or second career outside the home (especially for women), coping with the transition of menopause and "male menopause," maintaining the emotional and sexual health of the marriage, dealing with the empty or the cluttered nest, and managing the demands of aging parents.

- Marriages fail in the middle years for five main reasons: dominance of one partner (usually the husband) in the relationship; failure to communicate and to share; career involvement; extramarital involvements; and midlife changes.

- Recommendations for strengthening a marriage in the middle years include making one's spouse the number one priority, being alert to warning signs of marital trouble, establishing an equal partnership, helping the spouse feel important and powerful, balancing togetherness and personal growth, working to keep the sexual relationship exciting, networking with other committed couples, evaluating the marriage and attending marriage enrichment workshops, changing frustrating job situations, and changing one's lifestyle rather than one's partner to revitalize the marriage.

- One of four 18- to 34-year-olds in the United States is living with his or her middle-aged parents—a phenomenon that has been called the cluttered nest. Suggestions for launching or relaunching adult children include charging for room and board, setting house rules, limiting financial support, and encouraging all signs of independence and employment-seeking.

- People in their middle years are often "sandwiched" between two or more competing responsibilities: caring for adolescents, dealing with boomerang kids (adult children returning to the parental nest), and caring for their own aging parents. The results can be both positive (a closer relationship between the caregiver and the aging parent) and negative (too much stress).

- Grandparenting reinforces continuity of the generations and brings pleasure to most grandparents. Of those 65 or older, 75% have living grandchildren.

- U.S. society is undergoing a "demographic revolution" due to the increasing life span of its population. Today, average life expectancy is 75.

- Aging involves psychological, biological, social, and family factors. How individuals feel about their lives and how others view them have a lot to do with how "old" they feel.

- Conventional wisdom about old age includes the following inaccurate beliefs: at 65, you're "over the hill"; most older adults are poor; older adults lose their sex drive; older adults are usually sick; older adults become senile; most older adults end up in nursing homes; most older adults are lonely; and older adults are isolated from younger family members.

- Contrary to stereotypes, retirement is not a negative period of life. Approximately 75% of those who retire voluntarily adapt satisfactorily to retirement, with few long-term effects on their health, psychological well-being, or family relationships.

- Not all marriages of long duration are happy. People stay married out of habit, out of fear, or (in about 20% of these marriages), simply because they are happy. The fewer the number of children, the happier the marriage seems to be.

- The death of a spouse is a difficult life transition for most and a devastating personal crisis for some. More women than men will lose a spouse. Important factors in successfully coping with the loss of a spouse include maintaining a sense of autonomy (a belief in one's ability to direct one's own life) and being involved in social relationships and community affairs.

Key Terms

middle age	empty-nest syndrome	ageism
midlife crisis	spacious nest	longevis marriage
routinization	boomerang kids	crisis-loss stage of grief
menopause	cluttered nest	transition stage of grief
androgen	sandwich generation	new-life stage of grief
male menopause	old age	

Activities

1. Discuss career issues with a middle-aged man or woman. Ask the individual to trace her or his career development. What conclusions can you come to?

2. Interview your parents (if they are middle-aged) or other middle-aged individuals about the stresses of midlife and their means of coping with them.

3. Interview a middle-aged person who is "sandwiched" between trying to support adolescent or young-adult children and caring for an elderly family member. Prepare 10 or 15 questions for the interview, and record 5 or 6 general conclusions. Share your ideas with other class members who have done the same thing.

4. After reading the section on grandparenthood, prepare some questions and interview a grandparent. This can be an easy and rewarding exercise because grandparents and young adults often have an automatic bond.

5. Interview an older couple. Ask them to tell you the story of their family, including information about their parents and grandparents. Focus part of the interview on intergenerational relationships.

6. Write down your feelings about death and share them in a small-group discussion. Record the similarities and differences in the group's observations.

Suggested Readings

Boston Women's Health Book Collective. (1998). *Ourselves, growing older.* New York: Simon & Schuster/Touchstone. An excellent book on the biological changes and social and psychological needs of older women.

Brubaker, T. H. (1991). Families in later life: A burgeoning research area. In A. Booth (Ed.), *Contemporary families: Looking forward, looking back* (pp. 226–248). Minneapolis: National Council on Family Relations. An excellent review of research in this area by a noted student of aging.

Conrad, R. T. (1993). *"What should we do about mom?" A new look at growing old.* Bradenton, FL: Human Services Institute. A loving approach to the challenge families face when older members need a great deal of specialized care.

Kübler-Ross, E. (1991). *On death and dying.* New York: Macmillan. Discusses the psychological aspects of coping with one's own eventual death or the death of a loved one.

Kübler-Ross, E. (1993). *On children and death.* New York: Collier Books/Macmillan. Focuses on terminally ill children.

Mancini, J. A., & Blieszner, R. (1991). Aging parents and adult children: Research themes in intergenerational relations. In A. Booth (Ed.), *Contemporary families: Looking forward, looking back* (pp. 249–264). Minneapolis: National Council on Family Relations. An excellent overview.

Neugarten, B. L., & Neugarten, D. A. (Ed.). (1996). *The meanings of age: Selected papers of Bernice L. Neugarten.* Chicago: University of Chicago Press. Brings together 40 years of work by Neugarten, a renowned authority on aging.

Ring, K., & Valarino, E. E. (1998). *Lessons from the light: What we can learn from the near-death experience.* New York: Insight Books. Case studies of near-death experiences.

Sheehy, G. (1992). *The silent passage: Menopause.* New York: Random House. A useful reference for those approaching menopause.

Sheehy, G. (1995). *New passages: Mapping your life across time.* New York: Random House. The latest work by Sheehy on predictable crises in the middle years of life.

Turner, B. F., & Troll, L. E. (1994). *Women growing older: Psychological perspectives.* Thousand Oaks, CA: Sage. Adds to the limited literature exploring how one's sex affects the aging process.

PART V

Challenges and Opportunities

CHAPTER 15

Family Stress and Coping

Problems within families, and the stress related to those problems, are growing. More than half of all couples currently planning to marry will end up divorcing. Violence between spouses and family members occurs in 30% of all families. Sixty percent of all siblings experience at least one violent episode in their dealings with each other. One in five murder victims is killed by a family member. Roughly 4 million children are abused, and approximately 5,000 are killed by adults each year in the United States. And caseworkers estimate that for every physically abused child, 5 to 10 others may be neglected (U.S. Bureau of the Census, 1995). Untold numbers are emotionally battered by their parents. Alcohol-related issues plague roughly one in three U.S. families, and problems from the use and abuse of other drugs are widespread. Stress-related maladies—including heart attacks, ulcers, migraine headaches, hypertension, back troubles, and possibly even cancer—are increasing.

Stress is a fact of life for individuals and families. The important question is how to manage it. Stressful events and issues can bring families closer together—or they can divide and shatter them.

In this chapter we will look at stress from various perspectives, exploring whether stress can be beneficial, how much stress is too much, the connection between stress and physical health, and why the ability to deal with stressors varies from family to family. Researchers have found both that families experience certain common types of stressors and that some of these are more prevalent at certain stages of the family life cycle than at others. We will explore these subjects, and discuss the characteristics of families who deal with stress successfully.

Cross-Cultural Perspective on Family Stress

Following are some of the aspects of family stress that are common across cultural groups:

- *Families from all cultural groups experience family stress.* Although the causes of family stress and the types of issues that are most stressful may vary by cultural group, all families seem to experience and understand the concept of family stress.

- *All stressors either begin or end up in the family.* No matter what the origin of a stressor, it eventually affects the family system and its members.

- *All families must find resources (internal and/or external) to help them cope with or manage the stress in their lives.* Families from various cultural groups probably differ in the specific resources they use to manage family stress. Although research on understanding successful coping strategies in various cultures is underway, little work focuses on identifying the range and variety of coping resources used by different cultural groups. This type of information could greatly enhance our cross-cultural understanding of stress and coping.

- *All families have some internal strengths for managing stress in their family system.* Many studies of various ethnic groups have assumed a deficit model of family functioning—that is, a model based on the premise that something is wrong or missing. More often than not, this model is Eurocentric as well, assuming that the features of Western families are essential in all families. Cross-cultural studies of families have seldom sought to identify family strengths within a cultural group; instead, they have focused on the problems in families from different cultures. By building on a family strengths model, it is possible we will more clearly identify useful coping strategies across cultures.

- *To manage their stress, families tend to first use internal resources (those inside the family system) before seeking external resources (those outside the family system).* Across cultural groups, most families rely on their internal resources first, seeking external help only after internal resources have proven to be inadequate.

> "When the tractor rolled and Dad was killed, we were stunned," Joanne said. "We were in a state of shock for several days. It was like walking through a terrible dream world. I was 17 at the time. After the funeral and after all the food that people had brought over ran out, we kind of had to start picking up the pieces of our lives. We clearly had no choice. The cows needed milking. Life was going on without us.
>
> "We relied on ourselves, first and foremost. I took on a lot of Mom's responsibilities, and Mom took on much of what Dad had been doing. Tommy, who was 15 at the time, became a big part of Dad, too.
>
> "But we couldn't do it alone, without Dad, so Uncle Harley and Uncle Bud jumped right in. I love them for it. They each gave us a couple hours a day for several months till we could get adjusted, and countless hours at planting time and harvest. The neighbors all jumped in, too. Fortunately, in a small farming community people look out for each other. The work they put in was helpful, but I still think the most helpful thing was we didn't feel so all alone out there on the 640 acres. That could get to you, terribly quick."

In addition to seeking commonalties, it is also important to be open to differences, which increase our appreciation of diversity and our opportunities to learn from each other. The definition of the family system used here is broad and includes both the nuclear and extended family systems. In many cultures, the extended family system often plays a more significant role as a resource for managing family stress than the nuclear family system.

The Curvilinear Nature of Stress

Hans Selye, the pioneer of stress research, defined stress as "the nonspecific response of the body to any demand made upon it" (1974, p. 14). It is immaterial whether the demand is positive or negative; both create the same physiological response. **Stress** is the body's reaction to the demands of life. **Stressors** are external events that cause an emotional and/or a physical reaction. Although people often think of stress as negative, its impact depends on how it is viewed by each individual. Stress is a very personal issue.

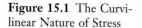

Figure 15.1 The Curvilinear Nature of Stress

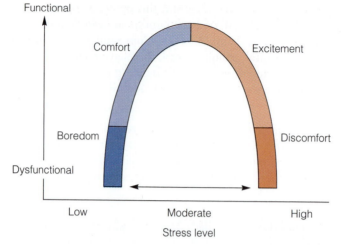

A paradoxical aspect of stress is that both too much and too little stress are problematic for individual and family functioning, but moderate levels of stress are usually positive. In other words, there is a curvilinear relationship between stress and functioning (Figure 15.1). Thor Dahl (1980) described four reactions to different levels of stress: boredom, comfort, excitement, and discomfort. Too little stress is unhealthy and is associated with boredom and lack of motivation. Too much stress is also unhealthy and leads to feelings of discomfort, or **distress.** Low-to-moderate levels of stress are healthy and can feel comfortable. Moderate-to-high levels of stress can also be healthy, creating excitement and energy. This motivating, positive kind of stress is called **eustress.**

Another paradoxical aspect of stress is that individuals continually need to seek an appropriate balance between too much and too little stress. This dynamic balance can often be difficult to achieve; most people feel pushed toward higher levels of stress. A major goal of life is to cope with stressors effectively. Happiness is not so much the absence of stress as it is the ability to manage stress effectively.

Stress and Life Events

The work of T. H. Holmes and R. H. Rahe (1967) has greatly influenced much of the current research on the relationship between life changes and signs of emotional and physiological stress in individuals. These researchers developed a scale of 43 "life events" that require some type of change of behavior, or readjustment. The scale is called the Holmes and Rahe Social Readjustment Rating Scale, but it is often referred to as the Holmes and Rahe Stress Test. These life events include personal, family, financial, and occupational stressors. Table 15.1 lists the top 14 stressors identified by Holmes and Rahe. It is noteworthy that 11 of the top 14 stressors are marriage and family issues. In fact, the scale could legitimately be called a Marriage and Family Stress Test.

Holmes and Rahe found a relationship between life changes and health. Of those people who scored between 0 and 150 points on the scale, more than 30% experienced a serious negative health change in the 2 years that followed. (A serious negative health change might be the development of an ulcer, enduring de-

Table 15.1 Holmes and Rahe Social Readjustment Rating Scale	
EVENT	**IMPACT (POINTS)**
* 1. Death of spouse	100
* 2. Divorce	73
* 3. Marital separation	65
4. Jail term	63
* 5. Death of close family member	63
6. Personal injury or loss	53
* 7. Marriage	50
8. Fired at work/lost job	47
* 9. Marital reconciliation	45
*10. Retirement	45
*11. Change in health of family member	44
*12. Pregnancy	40
*13. Sex difficulties	39
*14. Gain of new family member	39

Note: Impact points indicate the severity of the impact of the stressor on individuals, couples, or families.
*Stressors related to couples and families.

Source: "The Social Readjustment Rating Scale" by T. H. Holmes and R. H. Rahe, *Journal of Psychosomatic Research, 11,* p. 213. Copyright 1967 by Elsevier Science Inc. Reprinted by permission of the publisher.

pression, cancer, the onset of alcoholism, or a heart attack.) Of those who scored between 151 and 300 points, about 50% experienced a serious negative health change in the 2 years that followed. And of those who scored more than 300 points, almost 90% experienced a serious negative health change in the 2 years following the rating.

Holmes and Rahe theorized that physical and emotional problems are likely to occur when individuals experience a cluster of major and minor changes in life. It is noteworthy that the life events on the scale are not necessarily negative. Having a baby is usually seen as a positive occurrence, for example, but it is also stressful and requires readjustment.

One middle-aged woman scored above 700 on the Holmes and Rahe Stress Test. She received her divorce in January and remarried in August; her new husband moved out 3 months later; and by late November she had a new live-in companion. Her mother died during the year, and the woman started and lost two jobs. She had a sprinkling of other life changes during the year, including two car accidents and many bills. As might be predicted, she became very depressed and considered suicide.

Stress Pileup

An important concept is **stress pileup:** the occurrence and after-effects of several stresses within a short period of time. For example, stress in a couple's relationship is often taken by each person to their job, and stress at work is often brought home. In a study of stress in 400 people, Kenneth Stewart (1988) asked questions

Homeless families experience a pileup of stressors: no income, no place to live, difficulty in obtaining health care, disruption in the children's schooling, and isolation from relatives and friends. Only the most resilient families are able to survive against these odds.

about stress in each area of the person's life. He found that stresses in the various areas of life were interrelated. For example, family stress was highly related to personal stress, and couple stress and family stress were also very related, as were couple stress and personal stress (Figure 15.2). This study clearly demonstrated that focusing on stress in only one area of life gives at best a partial picture of the total stress in a person's life.

Stressors for Families

Researchers have provided answers to many questions about family stress. We will explore some of their work in this section.

Common Types of Family Stressors

Pauline Boss has done extensive research on family stress theory and has summarized many of her ideas in the book *Family Stress Management* (1988). Boss has identified 12 different types of family stressors, grouped into 6 pairs: internal and external, normative and nonnormative, ambiguous and nonambiguous, volitional and nonvolitional, chronic and acute, and cumulative and isolated. She has defined these types of stressors as follows:

Internal: Events that are initiated by someone inside the family, such as drunkenness, suicide, or violence.

External: Events that are initiated by someone or something outside the family, such as earthquakes, terrorism, the inflation rate, or cultural attitudes toward women and minorities.

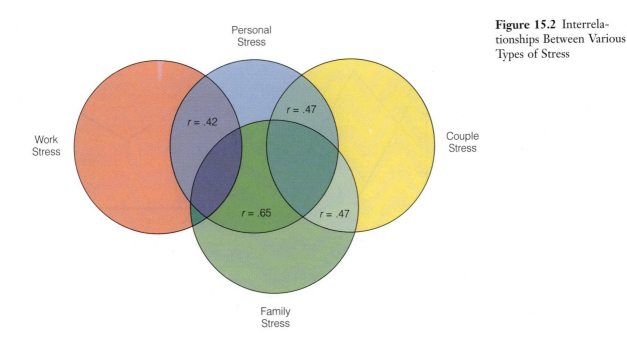

Figure 15.2 Interrelationships Between Various Types of Stress

Normative: Events that are expected over the family life cycle, such as marriage, birth, launching an adolescent, aging, or death.

Ambiguous: The facts surrounding the event are unclear. You may not even be sure that it's happening to you and your family. For example, your employer announces that it plans to lay off 20% of the workforce but doesn't say who.

Volitional: Desired, sought-after events, such as a freely chosen job change, college entrance, or a wanted pregnancy.

Chronic: A situation of long duration, such as diabetes, chemical addiction, or ethnic discrimination.

Cumulative: Events that pile up, one after the other, so that there is no time for resolution between them. In most cases, such a situation is dangerous.

Nonnormative: Events that are unexpected, such as winning a lottery, getting a divorce, dying young, or being taken hostage. Such events are often, but not always, disastrous.

Nonambiguous: The facts surrounding the event are clear, including what is happening, when, how, how long, and to whom—for example, a severe thunderstorm moving into the area over the next 2 to 3 hours.

Nonvolitional: Events that are not sought out but that just happen, such as being laid off or the sudden loss of a loved one.

Acute: An event that lasts a short time but is severe, such as breaking a limb, losing a job, or flunking a test.

Isolated: An event that occurs alone and that can be pinpointed easily.

Boss's well-organized description of various types of stressors has helped clarify why people perceive and react differently to stress and how their reactions depend on the type and severity of the stressor.

Figure 15.3 The Occurrence of Stressors Across the Family Life Cycle. *Source:* Adapted from *Families: What Makes Them Work* (2nd ed.) (p. 123) by D. H. Olson, H. I. McCubbin, H. Barnes, A. Larson, M. Muxen, M. Wilson, Sage Publications. Copyright © 1989 Sage Publications. Used with permission of the publisher.

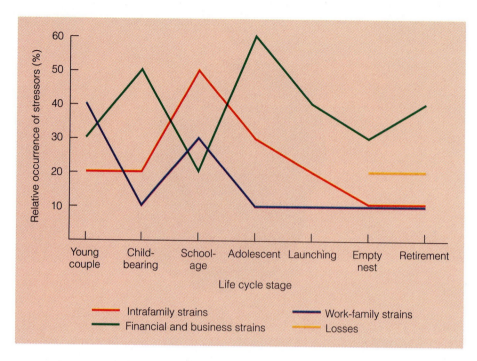

Stressors Across the Family Life Cycle

A study of 1,000 intact families looked in a systematic way at the stressors families face at each stage of the family life cycle (Olson, McCubbin, et al., 1989). The researchers asked husbands and wives in each life cycle stage to identify the stressors and strains that their family had experienced over the past year. The percentages of couples reporting the four most prominent stressors and strains at each of the seven life cycle stages are shown in Figure 15.3.

Stage 1: Young Couples Without Children   Young couples indicated the most stress and strain in four areas of life: work-family strains, financial and business strains, intrafamily strains, and illness and family "care" strains. In this period, many young couples faced changes in job/work situations and other problems at work, including increasing workload, dissatisfaction with the job, and conflict with the boss and other employees. Couples struggled with debts and increased expenses, as well as with the husband's absences for work-related concerns and uncompleted home tasks. Young couples also suffered from personal illnesses and were affected by illnesses involving parents and relatives.

Stage 2: Childbearing Stage   Families at the childbearing stage reported struggles primarily with financial and business strains but also with intrafamily strains, pregnancy and childbearing strains, work-family strains, and illness in the family. Financial strains increased in this period. Especially noteworthy were the strains caused by taking out or refinancing a loan; the purchase of a car; medical expenses; or a change in economic, political, or weather conditions that adversely affected the family's income. Stressors that occurred during the childbearing stage included greater involvement in outside activities, decrease in satisfaction with the job, and illness of a relative or friend.

Stage 3: Families With School-Age Children   Although financial strains (the pressure of paying off a loan or two, and increased expenses) continued to stress some families, the majority of stressful life events associated with Stage 3 fell into the categories of intrafamily stressors and strains and work-family problems. Families with school-age children faced an increase in family-related demands, such as children's outside activities, chores that did not get done, sibling rivalry and conflicts, and child management problems. Also, father/husband absence was a concern for many families. Decreased job satisfaction was felt by some; work responsibilities were increasing for many; and others were changing jobs or careers.

Stage 4: Families With Adolescents   Researchers found that financial strains concerned most of these families; intrafamily strains concerned some; and work-family strains concerned a few. More than two thirds experienced an increase in outside activities related to adolescent children; almost half felt tasks and chores were not getting done; and about a third were having difficulty managing their teenagers. But money was the greatest concern at this stage, especially as it related to the costs associated with having teenage children. Providing food and clothing, paying the utilities, and maintaining the home were a strain on the majority of families. Some also faced payments on major loans, and changing economic conditions were hazardous for others. With adolescents nearing college age, the cost of children's education was seen as a stressor.

Stage 5: Launching Families   Over half of the parents complained about increased expenses for food, clothing, energy, and home care; children's education continued to be a major source of stress in the family; and loans or refinanced loans were burdensome for more than a third. Families in this stage struggled with transitions (young adult members leaving home), with nearly half of the adolescents beginning college. Families in the launching stage also experienced intrafamily strains, including an increase in children's activities and an increase in uncompleted tasks or chores.

Stage 6: Empty-Nest Families   Financial strains still ranked highest, followed by illness, losses, intrafamily strains, work-family strains, and marital strains. Some families struggled with uncompleted chores. And about one in five couples reported increased difficulty with their sexual relationship. Financial hardships caused by a change in economic, political, or weather conditions were reported by more than a quarter of the couples. Other problems included the stresses of major purchases; food, clothing, energy, and home care costs; a decrease in job/career satisfaction; serious illness of a relative or friend; and death of a spouse's parent, close relative, or close friend.

Stage 7: Families in Retirement   For families in retirement, the major stressor continued to be financial, followed by serious illness or death of a parent, spouse, relative, or close friend. Work-family and intrafamily stresses were also present. Financial strains continued to be a major source of stress for 40%. A few couples were faced by threats to family investments or income. Major purchases were

Figure 15.4 Family Stress and Family Satisfaction. *Source:* From *Families: What Makes Them Work* (2nd ed.) (pp. 122, 181) by D. H. Olson, H. I. McCubbin, H. Barnes, A. Larson, M. Muxen, M. Wilson, Sage Publications. Copyright © 1989 by Sage Publications. Reprinted by permission of the publisher.

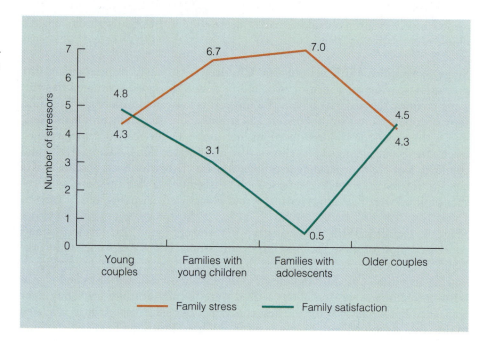

troublesome for some; increased expenses for medical and dental care were troublesome for others; and food, clothing, energy, and home care costs were also stressful.

Conclusions   Following are some general conclusions that can be drawn from this study about stressors and strains across the family life cycle:

- Stressors and strains are common at all stages of the family life cycle.

- Financial strains are reported across all stages, ranking first in five of the seven stages. Intrafamily and work-family strains are also present across the stages.

- A major pileup of stressors and strains occurs at the adolescent and launching stages, at which couples also report the lowest level of family satisfaction (Figure 15.4).

- A dramatic drop in stress and an increase in family satisfaction are seen in older couples whose children have left home.

- Husbands and wives generally agree in their assessments of the number of demands upon them. However, wives report slightly more demands at four stages (childbearing, school-age, launching, and empty-nest) than husbands.

Perhaps people who have a high tolerance for messiness and lateness come from families who have difficulty completing tasks. This difficulty is common not only among families with young children, when clutter and unfinished chores are to be expected, but during every stage of the family life cycle among almost half of all families.

Common Life and Family Events at All Stages of the Life Cycle

Olson, McCubbin, and their colleagues (1989) identified the following common life and family events that affected at least 10% of the families at all seven life cycle stages:

- *Uncompleted tasks.* The myth is that the "normal" intact American family is well-functioning, efficient, and effective. Uncompleted tasks are a problem in every stage of the life cycle for almost half of all families.

- *Emotional difficulties in family life.* At every stage of the family life cycle, an average of 15% to 20% of families reported experiencing emotional problems, with the highest rates at the adolescent (19%) and launching (28%) stages.

- *Sexual difficulties between husband and wife.* An average of about 20% of couples at all stages reported sexual problems, with more problems occurring during the adolescent and launching stages.

- *Unstable economic conditions.* Because this study was conducted during a period of some economic uncertainty, it is not surprising that 25% to 30% of families in all stages of the life cycle reported problems associated with hard economic times. High unemployment, crop failures due to weather, political turmoil leading to cuts in government budgets, and other conditions kept many families on edge.

- *Major economic investments and purchases.* Homes, children's educations, and business investments were other major financial expenses that caused worry for families across all stages, especially for those at the launching stage. Nearly half of all families had purchased a car or another major item for which they had taken out a loan.

- *Medical and dental expenses.* Rising interest rates, the higher cost of living, and increases in health care costs made it difficult for some families at every stage to adequately cover medical and dental bills, with 25% to 30% of families identifying these expenses as concerns. Health care expenses were especially troublesome during the childbearing and childrearing stages. Low-income families tended to sacrifice quality of care and preventive health care to reduce medical and dental expenses.

- *Money for the basics of family living.* Almost half of the families in every stage reported stress caused by the struggle to provide food and clothing, pay utilities, and cover housing costs. Families with adolescents were the most heavily burdened, with 62% reporting this concern.

- *Changing jobs or careers.* The challenges of the working world put a good deal of stress on families at all stages of the life cycle but especially at the young couple stage, where nearly half (46%) experienced this issue as they sought to establish themselves in a career. This challenge was also particularly stressful for one third of the families at the launching stage; wives often were reentering the workforce after rearing children, and husbands were growing dissatisfied with the career they had been in for 10 or 20 years.

- *Losing, quitting, or retiring from a job.* When a family member left a job—by choice or by the employer's decision—many families experienced a good deal of stress. Although this situation could occur in any stage of the family life cycle, it was particularly common in the young couple and launching stages.

- *Illness and death in the family.* The serious illness of a close relative or family member affected roughly one third of families at all stages but was especially prominent in the launching and empty-nest stages. Death affected about one fifth of families throughout the life cycle, but it was most prevalent in the launching, empty-nest, and retirement stages.

Boundary Ambiguity and Family Stress

In a recent book called *Ambiguous Loss* (1990) Pauline Boss vividly describes the effects of ambiguous loss on individuals and families. Another valuable contribution to family stress research is Boss's (1988) definition of **family coping** as "the management of a stressful event or situation by the family as a unit with no detrimental effects on any individual in that family" (p. 60). The family system uses cognitive, affective, and behavioral processes to manage the stress.

On *Día de los Muertos,* according to custom, the dead are permitted to visit living relatives and friends. Mexican families decorate family graves and picnic in the cemetery. This tradition, which juxtaposes the joys of life with an unsentimental acceptance of death, allows people to explicitly acknowledge the physical and psychological absence of family members who have died.

An understanding of stress is enhanced by Boss's (1999) use of the term **boundary ambiguity,** a lack of clarity about whether a person is in or out of the family system. The two related variables in boundary ambiguity are physical and psychological presence or absence. Boss also linked this concept to the level of stress that a given situation creates (Figure 15.5). Low ambiguity (congruence between physical and psychological presence or absence) is related to low stress. When there is both physical and psychological absence, as in the death of a family member or an amicable divorce, it is possible for the family to grieve and then to move on with their lives. Likewise, situations in which there is both physical and psychological presence, as in a happy family or marriage, are also low in stress.

At high levels of boundary ambiguity, family stress is highest and most difficult to manage. Physical absence and psychological presence keep the grieving process from occurring because the whereabouts and condition of the person are not known. This situation occurs when a child is kidnapped; it is also seen in noncustodial parents who are concerned for their absent children. Physical presence and psychological absence, as occurs when a family member suffers from alcoholism or has Alzheimer's disease, is also very stressful. Because the member is not emotionally available, family members cannot adequately resolve issues.

Family Stress Theory

Family stress research started with the early work of Reuben Hill (1949), who began studying American families separated during World War II and reunited when the men came home. He was interested in the fact that families faced with the same event—separation—varied so widely in their ability to adjust or adapt to the

Figure 15.5 Boundary Ambiguity and Family Stress. *Source: Family Stress Management* (p. 75) by P. Boss, 1988, Newbury Park, CA: Sage Publications. Copyright © 1988 by Sage Publications. Reprinted by permission of Sage Publications.

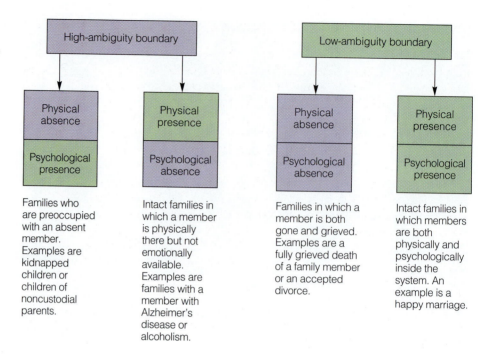

event. Some families who were separated by the war adapted rather well to the situation and reunited with relative ease. Others did not weather the separation well and were quick to divorce upon the soldier's return (see Boss, 1999).

The ABC-X Model of Family Stress

Hill's explanation of this phenomenon became known as the **ABC-X Family Crisis Model** (1958). The components of the model are the following:

A = the stressor

B = the family's crisis-meeting resources

C = the definition the family gives to the stressor

X = the crisis

Hill defined a **stressful life event** as "an event that creates a change in the family system" and a **crisis** as "any sharp or decisive change for which old patterns are inadequate." One dictionary defines crisis as simply "a turning point in life." A turning point, however, can lead in either a negative or a positive direction; therefore, contrary to popular view, a crisis does not have to be negative.

One could use the ABC-X Model to describe, for example, the outcome of an adolescent's running away from home. The event (A), the adolescent's running away, will turn into a crisis (X) if family members do not use their interpersonal skills as a resource (B) and if they do not (C) define the event in a way that takes into account the seriousness of the adolescent's behavior.

The Double ABC-X Family Stress Model

Hill's colleagues, H. I. McCubbin and J. Patterson (1982), developed what they called a **Double ABC-X Family Stress Model,** which they believed more accurately described family adjustment and adaptation to stressors or crises. The Double ABC-X Model builds on Hill's ABC-X Model of family stress, but whereas Hill's model focuses on a single stressor event, McCubbin and Patterson's model looks at the cumulative effects of stress. The Double ABC-X Model relabels Hill's *A* factor (the stressor) *Aa,* or *family pileup* of events. *Aa* includes family hardships and prior strains that continue to adversely affect the family, along with the stressor.

In the Double ABC-X Model, a stressor is seen as a life event (either expected or unexpected) that affects the family unit at a particular time. This event produces change in the family system. **Family hardships** are defined as demands on the family that accompany the stressor event. For example, the stressor event of losing one's job leads to the family hardship of reduced income. **Prior strains** are lingering residual effects of family tensions and prior stressor events that may still trouble the family.

In the Double ABC-X Model, McCubbin and Patterson take into account Holmes and Rahe's finding that stress pileup is a factor in how people cope with crisis. Pileup of stress can help explain why one event can be the "straw that breaks the family's back." For example, parents who abuse their children are often found to have high scores on the Holmes and Rahe Stress Test (Holmes & Rahe, 1967). They may be lonely and isolated; be stuck in a terrible marriage; have little money, education, and earning potential; and live in substandard housing, with no car or telephone for contact with the outside world. A normal child growing up with a parent in this type of situation is at risk for abuse because any action on the child's part can be the "last straw" for the vulnerable parent.

When the family unit encounters a new stressor event, prior strains often worsen as the pressure builds. Consider, for example, a married couple who are in intense conflict over money. The wife's career sets the stage for major conflict when the couple finds out that their daughter has a serious and chronic illness. The daughter's illness raises questions about whether the wife, who is just beginning to advance in her career, should now stay home and care for her daughter, cut back on the hours she works, hire outside help to care for the child, or ask the father to help more with the daughter's care. This "last straw" may create so much stress for the couple that they end up getting a divorce. Hill's ABC-X Model has proved fruitful for researchers trying to understand families in crisis; McCubbin and Patterson's refinement, the Double ABC-X Model, has made the theory even more useful.

A Roller Coaster Course of Adjustment

Hill (1958) described the course of family adjustment to a crisis as a "roller coaster course of adjustment." According to Hill, family adjustment involves: (1) a period of disorganization, (2) an angle of recovery, and (3) a new level of organization.

As an example, consider how a stillbirth affects most families. Such an event is, of course, terribly painful for the parents, surviving siblings, and other family members; all of them initially experience loneliness and despair (DeFrain, Martens, Stork, & Stork, 1986). The course of adjustment for the average parent of a stillbirth is charted in Figure 15.6.

Figure 15.6 Family Recovery Process Following a Stillbirth (couple scores). *Source:* Reprinted and adapted with permission from *Stillborn: The Invisible Death* by J. DeFrain, L. Martens, J. Stork, & W. Stork. Copyright © 1986 University Press of America. First published by Lexington Books. All rights reserved.

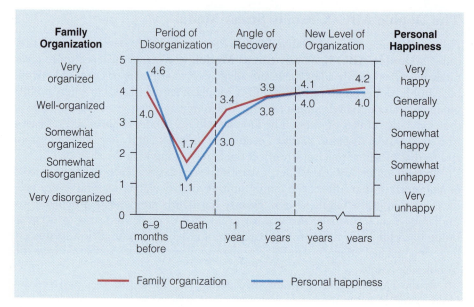

The process of recovering from such a crisis takes a long time. Two to three years seems to be about the average for parents, but five years of grief is not uncommon. The recovery process lasts longer for families who believe it is not healthy to talk about death; this conspiracy of silence probably makes a couple's pain much greater than it might otherwise be. Couples who grieve openly, talking and crying with loved ones and friends, recover more quickly. It also appears that recovery takes about the same amount of time for men and women. A common myth is that men are "stronger" than women, that they can stand up better against pain. Men who act tough and do not have the courage to reach out for the help they need take longer to heal than those who are not afraid to admit their hurt.

"It was very difficult for me after the baby died," Joseph said. "Allison was in the hospital for a week after the stillbirth with complications from the delivery. She was very, very ill. Somehow I had to keep on going. I went to work every morning because my boss is about as understanding as a rock. I snuck out to the hospital during lunch break every day.

"Right after work ended at 4:30, I'd run over to our child care provider's, get the kids, take them home, and feed them. Then I'd jump in the car with them again and go get my mom, and she'd come over and watch them while I went to the hospital for a couple of hours with Allison. Then home, crash, sleep a second, and start all over the next morning at 5:30. On and on and on. I thought I would lose my mind, but I just couldn't because Allison was so ill.

"She recovered slowly from it all, and I had to be terribly, terribly strong. I had to go into a kind of trance to get through it. After a couple of months, though, she was getting a little better, and one Saturday I just cracked. I was looking out the back window at our neighbor holding her new baby, and I threw a cookie jar at the wall. Man! Peanut butter cookies flying everywhere.

(Continued. . .)

(. . .*Continued*)

"Allison knew right away what was happening. She took me in her arms, and we sat down on the couch and I cried and cried. It was finally my turn to grieve for baby Jamie. I had never had time before that."

Family System Changes in Response to a Major Stressor

An important aspect of family systems is the ability to change in response to major stressors. Consider, for example, a family in which the husband, Peter, experienced a major heart attack at the age of 56. He had been a successful businessman, and his wife, Martha, had worked part-time since their oldest son, Dan, was a freshman in college and their daughter, Rachel, was a junior in high school.

The family system before and the changes in the family system after the husband's heart attack are illustrated using the Couple and Family Map (Figure 15.7). Before the heart attack (point A), the family was *flexibly connected*, which is appropriate for their stage of the life cycle. Immediately after the heart attack (point B), the family system became *chaotically enmeshed* because the family did not know if the father was going to live. The family, along with close relatives and friends, gathered at the hospital and huddled together in a mutually supportive way. This high level of closeness and bonding created enmeshment, and the fact that the family had to change all of its daily routines and roles created a chaotic system.

During the first and second week after the heart attack, the family became a little less enmeshed, but they developed a more rigid style of operating, creating a *rigidly enmeshed* system (point C). This rigidity was an attempt to bring some stability to the chaos by reorganizing some of the family routines. From about the third to the sixth week, the family changed again, becoming a *structurally cohesive* system (point D). Some of the rigidity was no longer needed and some of the enmeshed closeness decreased, but the family remained closer than they were before the crisis.

This example illustrates one family's ability to adapt to a crisis. The family changed system types several times over the 6-week period following the crisis, and these changes were beneficial in helping the family deal with this major stressor.

After studying the impact of stress on over several hundred couples and families by plotting the changes on the Couple and Family Map, the following general principles of change related to stress were developed (Olson, 1996). First, under stress couples and families often move in the direction of becoming more extreme on both flexibility (a move toward a more chaotic system) and cohesion (a move toward a more enmeshed system). Second, communication almost always increases during a stressful event. Third, once the stress has abated, couples and families usually return to a similar—but rarely to the same—type of system they had before the stress. Fourth, couples and families often require a minimum of six months to a year to adjust to a major stress. Fifth, balanced couple and family systems tend to become unbalanced during the stress and then return to another balanced system about a year later.

Figure 15.7 A Family System Before and Changes After a Husband's Heart Attack

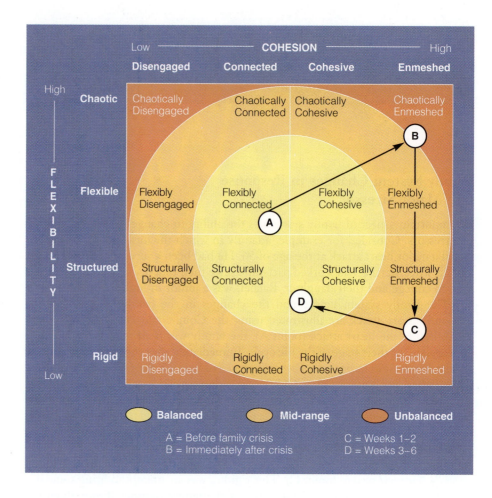

Families Who Manage Stress Successfully

To learn why some families cope well with stress whereas others fail, Olson, McCubbin, and their colleagues (1989) focused on specific family resources and also evaluated the type of family system around which families were organized. Two conclusions were very evident from the study: (1) balanced families coped better with stress than unbalanced families, and (2) balanced families had better communication and a larger behavioral repertoire.

Balanced families cope more effectively with stress because they have more personal and relationship resources, including better communication and problem-solving skills. Families who cope well also have the ability to see problems as challenges to be confronted or dealt with head-on rather than avoided or denied.

At the adolescent and launching stages of the life cycle, when family stress is the highest and family satisfaction the lowest, these researchers studied why some families with adolescents coped more effectively with stress than others did. The most significant finding was that families who coped well were headed by couples with a strong marriage relationship. Although the strength of the relationship was important across the family life cycle, the marriage became more important when adolescents were challenging authority and seeking their own independence.

Families who cope successfully with stress communicate well, have good problem-solving skills, and are usually headed by a couple who are happy with their marriage and quality of life.

The study identified the specific stressors (demands) at the adolescent and launching stages and the specific resources of the couples and families who coped well. The stressors included financial strains, intrafamily struggles, work-family issues, and family transitions. The resources of the parents in families who coped well included good financial management, satisfaction with the partner's personality, and a good network of families and friends on which they relied for support. In addition, the couple had a good sexual relationship and were very happily married. Last, they felt good about their overall quality of life, regardless of how much money they made.

Family Coping Strategies

The Chinese pictograph or symbol, for the word *crisis* is a composite of two other pictographs: the symbols for *danger* and *opportunity* (Figure 15.8). For thousands of years, the Chinese have understood that a crisis can be a dangerous time but also a time to look for new opportunities. Strong families tend to agree with that idea. In one study, fully 77% of the strong families reported that in the midst of the hurt and despair of a serious crisis, there were also positive outcomes (Stinnett et al., 1981). Eighteen percent of the families were uncertain whether anything "good" had developed out of the crisis, and only 5% were convinced that the crisis was all "bad."

What good could possibly come out of a disaster? Many families say that after they have weathered a crisis together, their relationships with each other are stronger, more positive, and more loving. People who have gone through a crisis often relate how they became stronger as individuals as well as closer to their partners and families. They grow to appreciate their families more and become more willing to share with them.

Theoretical Perspectives

Boss (1988) clarified the difference between coping as a family resource and coping as a process. She also explained why the concept of **managing stress** is a more

473

Figure 15.8 The Chinese Pictograph for *Crisis*

Danger   **Opportunity**

accurate description of how families handle stressors than is *coping with stress:* A family's coping resources are considered strengths, but simply having these strengths available is no guarantee the family will use them to *manage* the stress. Boss (1992) also noted that resources are derived from all aspects of life: psychological, economic, and physical.

S. E. Hobfoll and C. D. Spielberger (1992) completed an excellent overview of family stress models and research, observing the commonalties and differences among family stress theories and identifying the important family resources across a variety of models. The major resources and strengths were cohesion rather than separateness, flexibility/adaptability rather than rigidity, communication rather than privacy, boundary clarity rather than boundary ambiguity, and order and mastery rather than chaos and helplessness.

W. R. Burr and S. R. Klein (1994) have provided a systemic model of family stress that is considered less linear and deterministic than the ABC-X Model. Focusing on nine dimensions of family life (cohesion, marital satisfaction, communication, daily routines, contention, family development, leadership, family rituals, and emotional climate), the researchers interviewed 46 families who had experienced one of the following six stressors: bankruptcy, troubled teens, displaced homemaker, child with a handicap, child with muscular dystrophy, or infertility. They assessed how the family's response to the stressor influenced the functioning of the family system (roller coaster, increased functioning, no change, mixed, or decreased functioning). Their descriptive analysis demonstrated the diversity of resources that families used to manage stress.

Burr and Klein (1994) also provided an excellent summary evaluation of past studies of the most useful coping strategies for families. They identified six general coping strategies that encompass numerous specific strategies. The six general family coping strategies are cognitive, emotional, relationships, community, spiritual, and individual development (Table 15.2).

A Case Study

Let's look closely at a family experiencing the crisis of unemployment, using the general concepts from the Burr and Klein model (see Table 15.2). The Newman family has five members: Natalie, the mother, who has been at home caring for

Table 15.2 Major Family Coping Strategies	
GENERAL	**SPECIFIC**
Cognitive	Gain knowledge
	Reframe situation
Emotional	Express feelings
	Resolve negative feelings
	Be sensitive to others' emotional needs
Relationships	Increase cohesion
	Increase adaptability
	Increase trust and cooperation
Community	Seek help and support
Spiritual	Be involved in religious activities
	Maintain faith
Individual development	Develop autonomy, independence

Source: Adapted from *Reexamining Family Stress* (p. 133) by W. R. Burr and S. R. Klein, 1994, Thousand Oaks, CA: Sage. Copyright © 1994 by Sage Publications. Reprinted by permission of Sage Publications.

three daughters for the past 12 years; Albert, the father, an aeronautical engineer who specializes in electrical system design for a large airplane manufacturing company; and the girls, Sylvia, 12, Natasha, 9, and Alexis, 5. The Newmans have been accustomed to a good income for the past 10 years as Albert quickly moved up through the ranks of his company to middle management. But now the bottom has fallen out of the airplane industry for the forseeable future, and Albert is one of hundreds who have been laid off.

The family listens in shock as Albert explains what has happened, and in the days and weeks and months that follow, the family creates and recreates a series of plans to reorganize itself in the face of this severe crisis. For this family, the crisis becomes a jigsaw puzzle that they work on together to solve. Each day, solutions take form as new pieces are connected.

Being a strong family, the parents and children are good at using many coping strategies. First, at a family meeting at the dinner table a few days after the initial shock fades, they agree that it's a bad situation but that it's nobody's fault, and they all resolve to help find solutions (a cognitive strategy and a relationships strategy). Albert notes that over the years they have accumulated enough savings to be able to hold out for at least a year if they can all work together to reduce their spending (a cognitive strategy and a relationships strategy).

Natalie redefines the situation, noting that it is not only a crisis but an opportunity for growth: "I had been thinking about finding a part-time job now that the girls have gotten older, and this will give me the chance to get back and polish up my accounting skills" (a cognitive strategy). Five-year-old Alexis sees the distressed look on her father's face and crawls up on his lap. "You'll be okay, Daddy. I'll take care of you," she promises, bringing tears to her father's eyes (an emotional strategy). Albert takes a deep breath and acknowledges that Natalie's finding a part-time job would be a great idea. "What I'd really like," he notes, "is to get out of the business world altogether. You know, I haven't been very happy for a long time. I'd like to find a part-time job for a while also and see if I could go back to school. I'm not too old to go in a new direction, and if I could get my master's degree or even aim toward a doctorate, maybe I could get a job teaching in a high school or college. I like young people" (a cognitive strategy).

"You're great with kids!" chimes in 12-year-old Sylvia (an emotional strategy). Natasha and Alexis add that they'll be sure to help Mom more around the house now that she's going to be working outside the home (a relationships strategy). "You won't have to pick up so much around the house because of me," Natasha adds. "I can give myself a bath now, Mom," Alexis volunteers (individual development strategies). Natalie makes a suggestion: "We should tell all our friends at church about the layoff. You don't have to feel ashamed, Albert. They know how bad the industry's business has been. Someone at church might be able to find some part-time work for both of us" (a community strategy).

"I think we can get through this!" Albert concludes. "We're good people. We have each other. We will do it, and we'll be better as a family because of this" (spiritual and cognitive strategies).

> "For a period in our marriage, we made the mistake of focusing totally on the kids and our jobs and we forgot about our own personal health and our marriage," Jack said. "Something jolted us back into reality. It was when our friends Sarah and Michael divorced. It was such a shock to us. They seemed to be in such good shape together.
>
> "But when it was all over, Sarah told Mary how life had gotten to going so fast and she and Michael had just drifted further and further apart. One day, it had seemed to her like 'poof . . . it's gone.' She had asked Michael quietly to leave, and he quietly left.
>
> "We talked and talked about them, and we grieved for them and for ourselves because we could see the same thing happening with us. And we changed things for the better: We focused on our marriage, deciding it was the foundation for the whole operation.
>
> "It's really good with us now."

A Cross-Cultural Analysis

In an important study, Mary Hanline and Steven Daley (1992) observed the coping strategies used by African American, Hispanic, and Caucasian families with a disabled child and similar families without a disabled child. Each family member completed the F-COPES and the Family Strengths scales. The F-COPES scale measures family coping resources, including social support, spiritual beliefs, reframing, and passive appraisal. The Family Strengths scale measures family pride and family accord. To avoid reinforcing stereotypes, the researchers emphasized the strengths of each family rather than directly comparing families from the different ethnic groups.

The strongest families used more social support from family and friends and had stronger spiritual beliefs. Another common strategy was **reframing,** redefining the stressor as a challenge rather than denying the problem; this approach helps family members to deal with the problem directly and helps build pride. In contrast, some families, with and without a disabled child, tended more often to use passive appraisal, the denial of problems, which in turn leads to more family conflict.

Social Support

Support from one's social network is often very important in the face of problems. This **social support network** includes kin, friends, neighbors, social service institutions, and special self-help groups. Americans historically have placed tremendous emphasis on self-reliance. Most people are taught to take care of themselves, and they try to keep their problems close to home. This "tough-it-out" approach, however, is not very helpful in many situations. When individualistic spirit is carried to extremes, people suffer in isolation. An important element of healthy or strong families is their ability to reach outside the family to the community for help. All families need to draw on outside resources for help, and they also need to support other families in exchange for the aid they receive. Families should strive neither to be totally independent of nor to be overly dependent on one another. Rather, families should establish interdependence.

A study by Carolyn Attneave (1982) illustrated the importance of interdependence for families dealing with a crisis. A medical clinic wanted to know who would be the best risk for a new type of kidney dialysis machine that could be taken home and run by patients with a little help from their family. The investigators found that families who had a large support network (15 people or more) were more likely to be successful in helping the dialysis patient than were those with a small support network (less than 15 people). Who makes up this life-saving support network? Simply put, it is an interdependent network of friends and acquaintances who share good times and bad times and who trust that they will get what they need from each other.

Families need a social support network, especially in times of trouble. Contrary to the notion that strength means facing a problem without any help, research indicates that the strength to cope with problems comes from close connections with friends, neighbors, and relatives. This African American church provides support in countless ways to its members.

The Biopsychosocial Approach and Family Problems

An increasing number of studies show that the family is an important resource in dealing with people's psychological and physical problems. There is also growing evidence about the interrelationships among a person's physical symptoms, psychological issues, and social context (family and environment).

The **biopsychosocial approach** to stress management and health care integrates biomedical and psychosocial approaches. The idea and term originated with George Engel (Doherty & Campbell, 1988). The biopsychosocial approach contrasts with the biomedical approach, which assumes a separation between the mind and the body and does not make a connection between physical problems and a person's emotional and social context.

Within a biopsychosocial framework, an individual's physical and emotional problems are also the family's problems. Both the individual and the other family members are actors and reactors to each other. For example, a child who has a serious asthma attack and needs to go to the emergency room creates a major stressor for the family. The asthma affects the family, and the family's reaction influences the care the asthmatic child will get. Asthma, then, becomes part of the family system—and thereby becomes a family problem.

A wealth of clinical research indicates that a family system can increase a patient's compliance with treatment plans and help bring about a variety of health–improving changes, such as losing weight, quitting smoking, and breaking a chemical dependence (Becker, 1989; Campbell, 1995).

The biopsychosocial approach also assumes that family stress is a good predictor of serious physical symptoms and poor mental health in an individual. In a major study, G. R. Parkerson, E. Broadhead, and C. J. Tse (1995) used the Duke Social Support and Stress Scale, developed by Parkerson, to investigate the relationship between family stress and physical symptoms. They found that family stress scores were better predictors than social stressors or social support variables of severe illness, more hospitalizations, and higher medical expenses.

Medical Care and the Family

Theodor Litman (1974) states: "The family constitutes perhaps the most important social context within which illness occurs and is resolved. It consequently serves as a primary unit in health and medical care" (p. 497). Effectively implementing a biopsychosocial approach requires moving toward a more family-focused approach to medical care. As already discussed, the family provides a primary social context for dealing with stress and with physical symptoms. In their classic 1983 book *Family Therapy and Family Medicine*, William Doherty and Mac Baird identified several links between the family and medical care:

- Family members transmit diseases to one another.

- Health behaviors (such as food preferences and exercise) are learned and maintained in the family system.

- Individual and family stress affects health and recovery from illness.

- The family helps define health and illness in its members.

- The family often decides when and where to go for health care.

- The family is the social group most immediately affected by an individual's illness and medical treatment.

- Family support facilitates recovery from illness.

As a result of the growing importance of the biopsychosocial approach to stress management and health care, more professionals are working with families as a way to help treat physical symptoms. Susan McDaniel, Jeri Hepworth, and William Doherty's 1992 book *Medical Family Therapy: A Biopsychosocial Approach to Families with Health Problems* discusses the values and techniques that are important for helping families help themselves. The most basic assumption is that "all human problems are biopsychosocial systems problems: there are no psychosocial problems without biological features and no biomedical problems without psychosocial factors" (p. 26).

Another outcome of the biopsychosocial approach is a new professional career called **medical family therapy.** McDaniel, Hepworth, and Doherty (1992) define the field as *medical* because it focuses on a variety of health problems, including chronic illness and health behaviors. It is called *family therapy* to identify the foundation for the work as family systems theory. This approach emphasizes collaboration; the patient, the family, and health care providers all work together in the best interest of the patient and family.

The Family's Influence on Health Behaviors

As suggested by the biopsychosocial approach, families can help their members cope with illness as well as help them stay healthy. A Gallup poll of 1,011 adults focused on why people take steps (such as quitting smoking, cutting down on alcohol, exercising more, losing weight, and eating a healthier diet) to improve their health habits.

Married people live longer than single people. Although death, heart disease, cancer, stroke, and accidents affect married people, statistically speaking, singles—especially those who are widowed or divorced—are more likely to suffer from these problems. The Gallup survey tried to discover why this is so and concluded that healthy families have the power to help their members deal constructively with stress. Healthy, supportive families also help members change their health behaviors. They are more likely than others to help their loved ones quit smoking, change their dietary habits, and establish and maintain an exercise program.

Of the adults sampled by the Gallup organization, 87% had made a behavior change to try to improve their health over the previous few years. Of those, 15% had quit smoking, 39% had reduced their alcohol consumption, 44% had learned ways of controlling job stress, 45% had started exercising more, 46% had lost weight, and 60% had become more careful about their nutritional intake.

Married men were twice as likely (22%) to have quit smoking as single men (11%), and they were more likely (42%) to have lost weight than were single men (31%). Who helped these men make these difficult health-behavior changes? According to the researchers, the data were quite clear on this point: "Family and

SALLY FORTH   BY GREG HOWARD

loved ones shape our health habits more than doctors do." Medical doctors were influential, especially in regard to smoking and diet and among those over 50 and those who were divorced, widowed, or separated. But in general, more people were helped by family and loved ones than by doctors.

Before family members can be helpful, however, individuals must be open to being helped. The Gallup study identified profound differences among women, single men, and married men in their ability to accept help or encouragement from other people. Single men were found to be the "real rugged individuals," the ones most likely to insist that they didn't need help from anyone in changing their behavior. Married men were much more open to help and also tended to rely on their wives for help. Many husbands credited their wives with helping them to change, but few wives felt their husbands had been of much help to them. Even though gender roles in this country are slowly evolving, women still appear to be the caretakers of the family's health.

Doherty and Thomas Campbell (1988) have written extensively about the relationship between the family and health behaviors. They have found, for example, that research clearly demonstrates that smokers tend to be married to other smokers and that married smokers often smoke about the same amount as their partner. Adolescents are more likely to smoke if the same-gender parent smokes. Smokers find it easier to quit if their partner quits at the same time. Positive reinforcement from the smoker's partner helps to prevent a relapse; nagging tends to increase the relapse rate. In other words, smoking is related to family dynamics.

Doherty and D. Whitehead (1986) studied family dynamics and cigarette smoking in more detail using the Family FIRO Model, a model with three dimensions: inclusion (being together or alone), control (who is in charge), and intimacy (personal closeness). They found that a person's ability to quit smoking was related to these family dynamics and that these dynamics could either encourage or hinder relapse.

"I was so stubborn about my smoking addiction," said Bill, a 34-year-old electrician living in Indianapolis. "Jan would nag and nag at me, and I'd just hunker down more and more. Get more stubborn. Finally, I think she just gave up."

"Yes," Jan explained, "I became totally convinced I was going to have a dead husband. His coughing in the morning was getting worse, and I figured he had irritated his lungs so totally that he would develop lung cancer. I wasn't angry with him anymore because I saw he was completely convinced he couldn't stop and was deep-down ashamed he was hooked. I finally just got depressed and stopped talking about it."

"Several months later," Bill continued, "I was still puffing away, and one morning I walked into the bathroom and our 5-year-old son Joey had cut out a little red construction-paper heart and taped it on the bathroom mirror. It said in his little scrawl: 'Daddy, I don't want you to die.'

"I never smoked another cigarette."

Summary

- Families in all cultures experience stress, even though the types of issues that cause the stress vary by cultural group. All stressors, regardless of their origin, eventually affect family members. All families have some internal resources for managing stress, which they tend to use before turning to resources outside the family.

- The relationship between stress and functioning is curvilinear. Too little stress creates boredom; too much stress creates discomfort and frustration. Eustress, a low-to-moderate or a moderate-to-high level of stress, is positive, motivating, and exciting.

- Much of the early research on stress focused on life events (e.g., divorce, personal injury, pregnancy) and how those events caused stress. Holmes and Rahe developed one of the most popular stress scales, which assigns impact points for various stressful events experienced over a year. This scale assumes that stress pileup, the accumulation of stressful life events, is what is most problematic for people.

- Boss identified six pairs of family stressors: internal/external events, normative/nonnormative events, ambiguous/nonambiguous events, volitional/nonvolitional events, chronic/acute events, and cumulative/isolated events.

- New stressors appear at each stage of the family life cycle; others are common across all stages. Financial issues concern families at all stages and all income levels. Intrafamily and work-family strains and the death of a family member or relative are also seen at all stages of the family life cycle.

- Stress is highest and family satisfaction is lowest among families with adolescents. Young and older couples without children in the home tend to have the least stress and highest couple satisfaction.

- Common life and family events at all stages of the cycle are uncompleted tasks, emotional difficulties, sexual difficulties between spouses, unstable economic conditions, major economic investments and purchases, medical and dental expenses, money for the basics of family living, changes in jobs or careers (including losing, leaving, or retiring from a job), and illness or death in the family.

- In Boss's concept of boundary ambiguity, the variables of physical and psychological presence or absence describe both the existence of ambiguity and the level of stress associated with it. Stress is high when ambiguity is high: when a person is psychologically absent but physically present or is physically absent but psychologically present. Concurrence of the variables reduces stress.

- Hill's ABC-X Model and McCubbin and Patterson's expanded Double ABC-X Model seek to describe why families react as they do during times of stress or crisis. Hill's variables include the stressor, the family's crisis-meeting resources, and the definition the family gives the event; the Double ABC-X Model recognizes the additive effect of family hardships that accompany the stressor and prior strains, the sum of which may cause a stress pileup.

- The roller coaster course of adjustment to stressors, described by Hill, involves a period of disorganization, an angle of recovery, and a new level of organization.

- An important aspect of family systems is the ability to change in response to major stressors. Balanced families are more capable of adapting to a crisis and dealing with stress effectively than are unbalanced families.

- In families who cope successfully with stress, the parents possess these resources: good financial management skills, appreciation for the personality of the partner, a strong social support network of families and friends, a good sexual relationship, a happy marriage, and satisfaction with the quality of their life.

- Families draw on a variety of resources and related coping strategies to deal with stressful issues: cognitive resources (reframing the situation), emotional resources (expressing feelings), relationship resources (increasing cohesion), community resources (seeking help and support from outside the family), spiritual resources (praying; seeking help from a pastor, priest, or rabbi), and individual resources (developing autonomy).

- The biopsychosocial approach to stress management and health care assumes that people's physical condition, psychological issues, and social context are interconnected. This systemic model focuses on the way physical symptoms relate to a person's emotional health and takes a comprehensive approach to a person's overall well-being.

Key Terms

stress

stressor

distress

eustress

stress pileup

family coping

boundary ambiguity

ABC-X Family Crisis Model

stressful life event

crisis

Double ABC-X Family Stress Model

family hardship

prior strain

managing stress

reframing

social support network

biopsychosocial approach

medical family therapy

Activities

1. Identify a major stressor experienced by you and your family, and plot how your family changed over time to deal with this major stressor on the Couple and Family Rating Form, Table A.2 in Resource Section A. Identify your family's position at four points in time: before the event, during the event, 1 to 2 months after the event, and 6 months after the event. (Review Figure 15.7 if necessary.)

2. List the family stressors and strains you recognize at the launching stage of the family life cycle. Then discuss family stressors and strains at the launching stage with your parents. Have each parent describe what the stressors are (or were) for her or him. Look at those areas in which your mother's response differs from your father's. Also compare their descriptions with yours.

3. Select a major stressor in your family and describe how your family reacted as a group. It can be the same stressor as the one you identified in Activity 1, or it can be a different one. Indicate what your family did that was helpful and not helpful in dealing with the stressor. What resources did you and your family find most useful for managing your stress?

Suggested Readings

Boss, P. (1999). *Ambiguous loss: learning to live with unresolved grief.* Cambridge MA: Harvard University Press.

Boss, P. (1988). *Family stress management.* Newbury Park, CA: Sage. A very comprehensive and useful book by a professor of family social science at the University of Minnesota, St. Paul, who has invested more than two decades in studying how families cope with stress and crisis.

McCubbin, H. I., Thompson, E. A., Thompson, A. I., & Fromer, J. E. (Eds.). (1994). *Sense of coherence and resiliency: Stress, coping, and health.* Madison: University of Wisconsin. Ways to assess how well families are functioning, developed over many years by a team led by Hamilton McCubbin, dean of the School of Family Resources and Consumer Sciences at the University of Wisconsin.

Ross, C. E., Mirowsky, J., & Goldsteen, K. (1991). The impact of the family on health: The decade in review. In A. Booth (Ed.) *Contemporary families: Looking forward, looking back* (pp. 341-360). Minneapolis: National Council on Family Relations. An excellent review of research supporting the thesis that an individual's physical health is related to the emotional well-being of his or her family.

CHAPTER 16

Divorce and Family Problems

In general, people don't marry with the expectation that they will divorce, but nearly one in two marriages ends in divorce. Because of its prevalence, divorce is viewed by many as a sign of the breakdown of the American family. But divorce can have a positive outcome, by freeing individuals from painful or difficult marriages that cannot be changed. Family life is a source of stress for many. At the extreme, family life can be shattered by domestic violence, neglect, emotional cruelty, incest, or the abuse of alcohol and other drugs.

In this chapter, we will examine the complicated process of marital dissolution, separation, and divorce. We will begin with a look at some trends in divorce in the United States: statistical trends, historical trends, and legal trends. We will then explore different ways of looking at divorce to better understand the reasons people divorce, and we will discuss the various processes of adjusting to divorce.

In the second half of this chapter, we will focus on the dark side of family life, looking first at the physical and sexual abuse of children. We will then turn the spotlight on spouse abuse and on sibling and child-to-parent abuse. Finally, we will take a close look at alcoholism and problem drinking and their relationship to domestic violence.

Trends in Divorce

Divorcees are people who have not achieved a good marriage—they are also people who would not settle for a bad one.

—Paul Bohannan (1970, p. 54)

Marriage continues to be popular in our society; unfortunately, the likelihood of a marriage being successful, as discussed throughout this book, is less than 50%. Some researchers argue that this figure may be too conservative, and they predict that two thirds of all marriages in the United States today will end in divorce (Martin & Bumpass, 1989). The projection for divorce in second marriages is closer to 60%. But marriage is so popular that about 75% of younger people who divorce are likely to remarry—three out of four divorced women and five out of six divorced men (U.S. Bureau of the Census, 1997). Figure 16.1 illustrates the divorce-remarriage patterns that can be expected with a 50% divorce rate.

Statistical Trends

In 1996, there were approximately 1.9 million marriages and 1 million divorces in the United States (U.S. Bureau of the Census, 1997). Divorce is part of a lengthy series of relationship processes, including dating, perhaps cohabitation, marriage, marital dissolution, marital separation, divorce, singlehood, dating, usually cohabitation, and remarriage. After a comprehensive review of research on divorce, Lynn White (1991) found that divorce is higher among lower-income couples, higher among Blacks than Whites, higher among people who marry at a younger age, and higher among religiously mixed marriages. The highest rate of divorce, 60% to 80%, is among women who marry in their teens, are of lower socioeconomic status, drop out of high school, and are pregnant when they marry.

The average age at divorce is 36 for men and 33 for women. The average length of first marriages that end in divorce is about 7 years. So, of the half of all

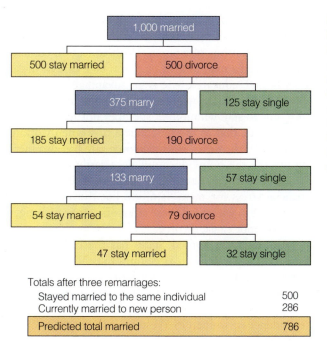

Figure 16.1 Estimated Divorce and Remarriage Rates for 1,000 Individuals Married in 1990.
Source: Family Science (p. 445) by W. R. Burr, R. D. Day, and K. S. Bahr. Copyright © 1993 Wesley Burr. Randal Day, Kathleen Bahr. Reprinted by permission of the authors.

first marriages that end in divorce, half of those end within the first 7 years (U.S. Bureau of the Census, 1997).

In terms of first marriages, divorce most often occurs during the first year or two. By the end of 5 years of marriage, 19% of couples are divorced; by the end of 10 years, 14% more are divorced. Another 7% divorce before 15 years of marriage; 7% more divorce before their 25th anniversary; and 3% more divorce before their 50th anniversary (L. K. White, 1991).

Historical Trends

The current U.S. divorce rate has dropped to under 10 (19.8) divorces per 1,000 for people 15 years of age and older for the first time since 1970. Thus, it appears the divorce rate is stabilizing (Whitehead, 1997). In the two decades before World War II (1920–1940), there were roughly 5 to 8 divorces per 1,000 people each year in the United States. By the end of World War II (1946), this rate had skyrocketed to more than 17 per 1,000 per year. The rate dropped dramatically in the 1950s to 9 to 10 per 1,000, but in the late 1960s it began a steep climb to a peak of more than 22 per 1,000 at the close of the 1970s and in the early 1980s. In the remainder of the 1980s and in the early 1990s, the divorce rate averaged about 21 per 1,000 people (U.S. Bureau of the Census, 1997).

Many explanations have been offered for the dramatic increase in divorces that began in the 1960s. Some claim that changes in divorce laws in the 1970s influenced the divorce rate, but others contest this explanation. Some of a conservative orientation argue that "women's liberation" was the cause. Others look at a whole complex of social factors, including economic conditions, level of education of women, and increasingly tolerant attitudes toward divorce.

Although educated women still face discrimination in the working world today, their chances for economic survival on their own are better than were those of past generations of women. With education comes the freeing knowledge that "I don't need a man to lean on. I can take care of myself." For most families, having a skilled, educated wife is an advantage in terms of family stability. But if an educated and skilled woman is not happy in her marriage, economics do not require her to stay with a man she does not love.

It is true that as the percentage of women working outside the home has increased over the years, so the divorce rate has also increased. But a woman's working outside the home does not necessarily cause divorce; many happy marriages involve two wage earners. A wife's working outside the home helps alleviate financial stress for many families, but the workplace adds other stressors. Some marriages can withstand these stressors; other marriages cannot. Stress alone, however, does not cause divorce.

Although the United States has the highest divorce rate of all the Western industrialized nations, divorce rates in other nations are catching up to ours. Economic prosperity brings with it more autonomy in mate selection for young people. In rural agrarian societies where parents choose marriage partners for the young, divorce rates are relatively low. Free choice and the relative economic independence of women in Western cultures are two important contributors to the higher divorce rate.

Additionally the marriage bond has lost some of its religious significance and has become more of a personal commitment between two people. Some churches and synagogues have not welcomed those who are divorced, but others have encouraged their participation. Discussion and support groups for divorced people now operate under the umbrella of more churches. Marriage is increasingly being regarded as a voluntary commitment between two people, one which they continue to keep as long as the relationship is mutually satisfying. This definition is far different from the traditional notion that marriage is for life.

Legal Trends

Since 1970, when the state of California introduced no-fault divorce, major changes have occurred in divorce laws across the United States. These changes came about as a direct response to the rising number of divorces and to the changing roles of women in this country. Today all 50 states have laws similar to California's (Parkman, 1992).

No-fault divorce abolished fault ("guilt" of one party) as the basis for dissolving a marriage. Under no-fault law, one party's assertion that "irreconcilable differences have caused the irremediable breakdown of the marriage" is sufficient for the granting of a divorce.

Traditional Divorce Law   Lenore Weitzman and Ruth Dixon have identified the four major elements of traditional divorce law that were transformed by the no-fault system of divorce (Weitzman & Dixon, 1980; Weitzman, 1985):

- *Gender-based divisions of role responsibilities.* Traditional family law assumed that the husband would provide financial support in a lifelong marriage. If the marriage ended and if the wife had been virtuous, she was granted

alimony—continued financial support. This gender-based division of labor was also recognized in regard to children. The husband remained responsible for their economic support after the divorce, and the wife was the preferred custodial parent.

- *Grounds for divorce.* Traditionally, fault—legal blame for the end of a marriage—had to be assigned, and only serious offenses were considered sufficient grounds for divorce. Evidence for misbehavior varied from state to state, but husbands charged with cruelty were often alleged to have caused bodily harm to their wives. Wives were more likely to be charged with neglecting their husbands or their homes.

  In practice, many couples wishing to divorce simply agreed privately to an **uncontested divorce**—one in which one party, often the wife, would charge the other party, generally the husband, with mental cruelty and the "accused" would agree not to challenge the "accuser" in court. Even though the parties colluded in the matter and often perjured themselves in court, the courts considered the grounds "appropriate violations" of the marriage contract.

- *Adversarial proceedings.* In the traditional system, lawyers "did battle" for their clients and divorces had to be "won." One partner was "guilty" and the other was "innocent."

- *Linkage of the financial settlement to determination of fault.* A finding of "guilty" or "innocent" had important financial consequences. Alimony could be awarded only to an innocent spouse: A wife found guilty of adultery, for example, could not receive alimony. Property awards were also linked to the determination of fault. This linkage produced heated accusations and counteraccusations.

No-Fault Divorce Law   Weitzman and Dixon (1980) have also explained how no-fault divorce law altered the four elements of traditional divorce law just listed:

- *Redefinition of the traditional duties of husbands and wives and establishment of equality between the genders as a norm.* Under no-fault laws, the husband is no longer considered by law to be the head of the family. Both spouses are presumed to be equal partners, with equal obligations for financial support and care of their children. Spouses are treated equally in respect to child custody, as well as finances and property.

  The so-called **tender years doctrine,** which presumed that young children would do better with their mother than with their father, has been replaced by the notion of joint custody as being in the "best interests of the child." Fathers are at least theoretically equal to mothers in questions of custody. In a small number of cases, fathers are winning not only custody but also child support.

- *Elimination of fault-based grounds for divorce.* Under no-fault laws, one spouse does not have to prove the other's adultery, cruelty, or desertion. The concept of *irreconcilable differences* recognizes the irrelevancy of discussing the reasons for the marital dissolution.

Because divorce can be traumatic for both adults and children, lawyers should not act as adversaries doing battle for their clients but rather should try to facilitate responsible communication. The lawyer's most important task is to help the divorcing parents restructure the family and minimize the emotional damage to both themselves and their children.

- *Elimination of the adversarial process.* Proponents of divorce reform argued that the adversarial nature of traditional divorce proceedings was harmful to all parties involved, especially to the children. Under no-fault, by facilitating accurate and responsible communication rather than doing battle, lawyers can help divorcing parents restructure the family and prepare to fulfill their postdivorce parenting responsibilities. Many spouses neither love nor hate each other at the end of a marriage; they are capable of an *amicable divorce* and are good candidates for joint custody of their children.

- *Basing of financial decisions on equity, equality, and economic need rather than on fault or gender-based role assignments.* In a no-fault system, each spouse's economic circumstances are assessed under the principle of equality between the sexes. No-fault laws adhere to the notion that divorced women should be self-supporting but that if that is not possible, they should receive fair compensation. Under the newer no-fault divorce laws, older homemakers are more likely to receive alimony than are younger homemakers. In some cases, a woman might receive support while she goes back to school for retraining. Recently, attorneys have been forcefully arguing that women who previously put their husbands through professional school are entitled to a share of their earnings for a period of time after the divorce.

Reformers of traditional divorce law argued that with an increasing number of women entering the labor force, alimony was rapidly becoming an anachronism. This, however, ignored the fact that female workers earn on average only about 60% of what male workers earn. There has been a backlash to the financial aspects of no-fault divorce (Parkman, 1992). Many see these reforms as antiwomen measures that punish women financially for divorce. Divorced women and their children suffer an immediate drop of 27% in their standard of living, whereas their ex-husbands experience an increase of 10% in their standard of living (Parkman, 1992).

No-fault divorce laws are based on the theory that equality results in a more positive outcome for all involved. How the theory works in practice depends on the decisions of individual judges who must adjudicate the 1 million divorces in the United States each year.

Effects of the Change   In evaluating the results of the no-fault system, researchers report a mixture of expected and unexpected findings. Although Weitzman and Dixon (1980; Weitzman, 1985) observed that no-fault divorce had no discernible effect on the divorce rate, more recent research reports that it did increase the divorce rate across the 50 states (Nakonezny, Shull, & Rodgers, 1995). The mandatory counseling feature of the system apparently did not bring about many reconciliations; it proved to be too little, too late for most marriages.

Indeed, no-fault has eliminated the hypocrisy of the old system, which forced spouses into pointing the finger whether they wished to or not, and it seems to have somewhat reduced the bitterness of the battles. The number of hearings before a final decree of divorce has declined markedly, and it was at these hearings when many of the most bitter battles were fought. Property settlements and spousal and child support appear to be fairer under the new guidelines. However, no-fault did eliminate one benefit of traditional divorce law for those who have a valid grievance: Because men can no longer be faulted for obvious wrongdoing, women, in particular, have lost a bargaining advantage in negotiating property settlements and alimony (Weitzman & Dixon, 1980; Weitzman, 1985).

Judges wryly comment that divorce court service is like a sentence in Siberia. Despite changes in divorce laws, divorce court remains "the saddest room in America." But no-fault laws have alleviated some of the tremendous pain of divorce and have facilitated greater cooperation in coparenting after the divorce.

Understanding Divorce

No emptiness on earth can compare with the loss of love.
        —Paul Theroux (1996, p. 425)

Both partners in a divorce often spend considerable time trying to unravel the reasons why their marriage ended. Although the task is difficult, it is essential to the postdivorce recovery process. The search for the "causes" of a divorce must take into consideration a number of factors and many points of view. In this section we will look at several important issues to understand why people divorce.

The Culture of Divorce

Divorce culture, a term Barbara Whitehead (1997) so poignantly describes in her book of the same name, is the notion that divorce has now become so accepted that it is almost the expected outcome of marriage. Before the 1950s, divorce was rare, and there was considerable social pressure to stay married, even if it was a

Table 16.1 Couples' Problems as Reported to Marital Therapists

TYPE OF PROBLEM	FREQUENCY OF PROBLEM	RANK OF PROBLEM	DIFFICULTY TREATING	DAMAGING IMPACT	COMPOSITE RANKING
Communication	87%	1	7	6	4.7
Power struggle	62	2	4	7	4.3
Unrealistic expectations	50	3	8	8	6.3
Sex	47	4	17	17	12.7
Decision making	47	5	14	14	11
Demonstrating affection	45	6	13	13	10.7
Money management	43	7	15	16	12.7
Lack of loving feelings	40	8	1	4	4.3
Children	38	9	18	18.5	15.2
Individual problems	38	10	5	9	8
Value conflicts	35	11	12	11	11.3
Role conflicts	32	12	16	15	14.3
Extramarital affairs	28	13	3	2	6

Source: Adapted from Whisman, Dixon, & Johnson (1997, tab. 1, p. 364). *Journal of Family Psychology*, 11, 361–366. Copyright © 1997 by the American Psychological Association. Adapted with permission.

bad and abusive marriage. But now divorce is linked with the pursuit of individual satisfaction, and there is less social pressure to stay married. Even the presence of children is not a deterrent to getting divorced as it was in the past. The challenges of divorce are even fodder for comedy, as in the popular movie *Mrs. Doubtfire*, in which a mother unknowingly hires the separated father as a nanny to care for their children.

Why Couples Divorce

"Marriage causes divorce!" is the facetious reply to the question "What causes divorce?" The stresses and strains of living together are simply too difficult for many couples. But the picture is more complicated. What are some of the interwoven factors that cause divorce? Why do some people divorce while others in apparently more troubled relationships stay married? Family researchers and family therapists have spent considerable time exploring what causes divorce.

In a national study of marital therapists who work with couples, Whisman, Dixon, and Johnson (1997) identified the most prominent problems reported by couples (Table 16.1). The results of their study demonstrate that poor communication, power struggles, unrealistic expectations about marriage, sexual relationship problems, and difficulties in decision making were the five issues reported by couples.

The study also provided an overall ranking based on the frequency, difficulty of treating, and damaging impact of each problem. Based on the overall ranking, the top five issues were power struggles, lack of loving feelings, communication, extramarital affairs, and unrealistic expectations. The most difficult problems for therapists to treat were lack of loving feelings, alcoholism, and extramarital affairs. The issues with the most damaging impact on the marriage were physical abuse, extramarital affairs, and alcoholism.

Taking time to understand each other and deal with difficult issues is essential for maintaining intimacy. When one or both partners hide unhappiness rather than discussing it, feelings for each other may gradually disappear, leaving only disinterest.

Unhappy Versus Happy Couples

To learn more about the characteristics of happily married versus unhappily married couples, Fowers and Olson (1989) studied a national sample of 5,039 married couples. There were 2,375 unhappy couples in the study, most of whom were in marriage counseling. The other 2,664 were happily married couples who had attended a marriage enrichment program. To confirm how satisfied the couples were, spouses were asked whether they had considered getting divorced. As expected, among the happy couples, 95% of the spouses said they had not considered divorce, whereas among the unhappy couples, 95% of the spouses had considered divorce.

In terms of background characteristics, the mean age was 33 for males and 32 for females. The couples had been married an average of 9.7 years; they had an average of 2.9 children; and the majority of the spouses had some college education. The surprising thing about the background characteristics was the similarity in age, years married, and number of children among the couples, whether happy or unhappy.

All the couples took the ENRICH marital inventory developed by Olson, Fournier, and Druckman (1989). Discriminate analysis (a statistical approach that determines how well a set of scales can discriminate between two specific groups) was used to see how well the ENRICH scales of couple agreement could discriminate between the happily and the unhappily married couples. The analysis showed that the scales could discriminate with about 90% accuracy between happily and unhappily married couples. Five of the scales were the most predictive: sexual relations, communication, conflict resolution, children and parenting, and leisure activities. However, scores of happy and unhappy couples differed significantly on almost all the scales, with happily married couples getting significantly

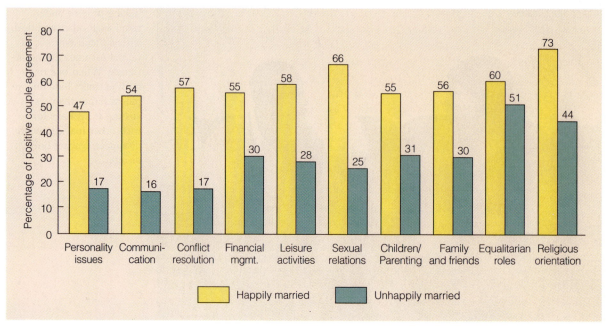

Figure 16.2 Agreement on Important Issues in Happily Married and Unhappily Married Couples. *Note:* Based on ENRICH couple agreement scores (*n* = 5,039 couples). *Source:* "ENRICH Marital Inventory: A Discriminant Validity and Cross-validation Assessment" (p. 71) by B. J. Fowers and D. H. Olson, 1989, *Journal of Marital and Family Therapy, 15* (1), 65–79. Copyright © 1989 by American Association of Marital and Family Therapy. Reprinted by permission.

higher positive couple scores on all of the scales except financial management and equalitarian roles. The three scales on which the two groups showed the most significant differences were communication, conflict resolution, and sexual relations. Figure 16.2 illustrates the average scores for the happily and the unhappily married couples.

Communication and Conflict Resolution Some authorities might say that communication problems are the central reason for divorce. Most divorcing people relate how communication, including the ability to resolve conflict and deal with problems, broke down in their marriage. Communication and conflict resolution are interrelated. Both are necessary skills in a happy marriage, as demonstrated by the Fowers and Olson (1989) study.

Sexual Relations An unsatisfying sex life is often associated with divorce. Some divorcing people contend that sex is only the battleground not the cause of the war. But an unsatisfactory sex life can be a significant source of stress in a marriage, and divorcing people often talk about their failed sexual relationship. Spanier and Thompson (1984) asked separated and divorced individuals to compare sexual satisfaction early in the marriage with sexual satisfaction just before they separated. The researchers found a dramatic decrease in sexual satisfaction.

The Impact of Divorce on Children

A significant question that parents face when considering divorce is what impact the divorce will have on their children. In many child custody cases, children often become the pawns of divorcing parents who want to get back at each other, thus forcing the courts to enter and decide what is in the children's best interests.

Judith Wallerstein and Sandra Blakeslee (1996) conducted an important longitudinal study of children of divorce. They found that divorce has a long-term impact on children. Even 5 years after a divorce, more than one third of the children they studied showed signs of moderate to severe depression. After 10 years some of the adult children were underachieving and having emotional problems, and after 15 years some adult children were having problems in their love relationships. Although this study had a small and biased sample and no control group, it did follow the same people over time and provides a useful perspective on divorce.

In contrast to the findings of Wallerstein and Blakeslee (1996), a research study by Buchanan, Maccoby, and Dornbusch (1996) found children from divorced families to be functioning rather well as adolescents. These researchers interviewed 522 adolescents from 365 northern California families and concluded that the adolescents were well adjusted and had good relationships with their parents. Those living with their mothers did better than those living with their fathers. Adolescents whose parents remarried were better adjusted than those adolescents whose parents were dating or cohabiting. Furthermore, adolescents of parents who shared feelings with their children seemed to do better, as long as the parents' openness did not cause the children to worry about their parents. Most of the adolescents continued to stay in touch with the noncustodial parent, but contact tended to drop off over time.

Amato and Booth (1996, 1997) conducted one of the best longitudinal studies on divorce, which they reported on in their book *A Generation at Risk*. In this study, these researchers interviewed parents and their children before and after divorce; the national sample consisted of 471 parents who had a 7-year-old child in 1980. When the child was 19, the researchers interviewed the adult children along with their parents, bringing the total sample to 942 adults.

One significant and consistent finding was that parents' marital quality in 1980 was related to the adult childrens' dating and marriage relationship quality 12 years later. The adult children had more problems with dating and, if married, had less happy marriages. Amato and Booth (1997) stated that "parents' marital unhappiness and discord have a broad negative impact on virtually every dimension of offspring well-being" (p. 219). They found that problems in the parent-child relationship often occurred prior to the divorce and that the divorce increased the problems in parenting. They also found that divorce had a negative impact on the father's affection for their children but not the mother's (Amato & Booth, 1996).

A surprising finding was that low-conflict marriages that ended in divorce (about two thirds of the marriages) had a more negative impact on the adult children's development than did high-conflict marriages that ended in divorce. Low-conflict couples do have some conflict and quarrels, but at a much lower level than high conflict couples. The findings suggest that in the case of high-conflict marriages, the divorce was good for the children in terms of their mental health. However, offspring of divorced couples who had low levels of marital conflict showed increased levels of psychological distress, fewer ties with kin and friends, less happy marriages, and a greater probability of divorcing themselves (Amato & Booth, 1997).

These findings have fueled the debate about whether parents with low levels of marital conflict should divorce. One study found support for divorce in high-conflict marriages but not in low-conflict marriages (McLanahan & Sandefur,

1994). Researchers concluded that children living in homes with high-conflict marriages (persistent and severe abuse) were better off if the parents divorced. They maintained, however, that children from low-conflict marriages would be better off if the parents remained together.

A study by Chase-Landsdale, Cherlin, and Kierman (1995) found that divorce seems to have a more negative impact on children who have fewer, rather than greater, emotional problems. This longitudinal study of over 17,000 children was done in Great Britain. This study and those by Amato and Booth (1996, 1997) and McLanahan and Sandefur (1994) seem to support the idea that divorce is more detrimental to children who are doing well in general as compared to those who are already having more serious emotional and behavior problems.

Amato and Booth (1997) also studied the consequences of divorce on income level and educational attainment in adult children of divorced parents. Their findings clearly demonstrate that higher levels of education in the parents had a positive impact on the children. Children of parents with higher levels of education were more socially active, had more friends, were happier, and had higher levels of self-esteem. Higher levels of education in the parents were also directly linked to the level of education achieved by their adult children, which subsequently had an impact on other quality-of-life outcomes for the adult children, including income level.

Amato and Booth's research (1997) also revealed that adult children of divorce had higher rates of cohabitation than did children from stable marriages and unstable marriages (Amato & Booth, 1997). At each age level from 20 to 26 years, adult children from divorced parents had the highest rate of cohabitation, followed by adult children from unstable marriages; adult children from stable marriages had the lowest rate of cohabitation. With adult children of divorce, the rate of cohabitation was 30% at age 20, 40% at age 23, and 48% at age 26; these rates were significantly lower for the other groups.

Adjusting to Divorce

The divorce process is stressful and even traumatic for many. As shown in Table 16.2, each phase—prior to, during, and after divorce—and outcome of divorce is experienced differently. As the figures in this table show, the most difficult time is the period leading up to the decision to divorce. After the divorce, most generally feel good about the property settlement, and they generally feel that their life is better overall than it was during the marriage. After divorce, some people withdraw for a while but gradually become involved with others again.

Paul Bohannan (1970) has described the divorce process as an intense journey that encompasses "six stations." These stations, or experiences, often overlap, occur in different sequences, and vary in intensity for each individual. The six experiences are:

- **Emotional divorce.** The deterioration of the marriage and the breakdown of bonding and communication, which are replaced by feelings of alienation.

- **Legal divorce.** The dissolution of the marriage by the legal system and the courts.

Table 16.2 Female and Male Reactions to Divorce

	COMBINED SAMPLE	FEMALE	MALE	SPOUSE FOR WHOM SITUATION IS BETTER OR WORSE
Characterization of Divorce Experience				More stressful for wife
Traumatic, a nightmare	23%	27%	16%	
Stressful, but bearable	40	40	40	
Unsettling, but easier than expected	20	19	24	
Relatively painless	17	13	20	
Most Difficult Period				Both rate predivorce as worse
Before decision to divorce	55%	58%	50%	
After decision, but before final decree	22	20	25	
Just after the divorce	21	19	23	
Now	3	3	3	
Best Time for Oneself and Children				Wife better now
Before decision to divorce	13%	8%	22%	
After decision, but before final decree	6	6	5	
Just after the divorce	14	15	12	
Now	67	71	62	
Feeling About Property Settlement				Wife more satisfied
Good or very good	70%	73%	68%	
Frustrated, unhappy	26	22	32	
Just glad to get out	4	6	1	
Postdivorce Income				Wife's income much lower
Much lower	31%	48%	7%	
Somewhat lower	16	18	12	
About the same	39	27	57	
Somewhat higher	11	6	17	
Much higher	3	1	7	
Change in Contact With Relatives				Wife has more contact now
More contact	32%	37%	25%	
No change	55	52	60	
Less contact	12	10	15	

Source: Adapted from "Reactions and Adjustments to Divorce" by S. L. Albrecht, 1980, *Family Relations, 29* (1), pp. 61, 63. Copyright 1980 by National Council on Family Relations. Adapted by permission.

- **Economic divorce.** The division of money and property and the establishment of two separate economic units.

- **Coparental divorce.** Decisions about child custody, single parenting, and visitation rights.

- **Community divorce.** Changes in relationships with friends and community members.

- **Psychological divorce.** The regaining of individual autonomy.

Emotional Divorce

When two people decide to marry, they feel so good because of the love they share. Divorce feels so awful because that love has been lost. Divorce involves a vast spectrum of emotions, and no two individuals react to it the same way. There are, however, some common patterns that appear in most divorces.

Anger and violence are very common with divorced couples. Many people who feel anger over the loss of a mate try to escape this pain or rage through chemicals. Even individuals who are not prone to abusing drugs can find no other way to cope. "I just needed to turn my brain off for a while," one husband said. "It hurt too much to think, and I couldn't stop thinking painful thoughts any other way."

Other people may fall into total emotional disrepair and depression, finding it impossible to function. They may sleep a lot and possibly think about suicide. One woman who lost her husband to her best friend put it this way, "I was so depressed I wanted to kill myself, but for three days I couldn't find the energy to get out of bed to get the pills in the bathroom to do it." Many physicians argue that the misery of a dissolving marriage can also weaken the body's resistance to disease. As noted in Chapter 15, colds, pneumonia, headaches, ulcers, and even cancer have been found to be related to marital stresses. One physician has even called marital conflict the "number one killer."

The crisis of divorce, like many other crises in life, often adds to the common human feeling of loneliness. In the words of one divorced mother of two young children, "This weekend is pretty lonely. All my weekday friends have weekend husbands. I've painted Billy's room, baked 10 dozen oatmeal cookies (Elizabeth's request), and got two weeks of shopping done and it is still only Saturday. Maybe I got married because weekends are so long."

In the midst of divorce, many people think, "No one can understand how terrible I feel now. No one has ever gone through this before." John Woodward, who has done a great deal of research on loneliness, argues that to feel lonely is a universal human condition. The crisis of divorce exacerbates these feelings of loneliness (Woodward, 1988). In the words of Robert Weiss, "Of all the negative feelings of the newly separated, none is more common or more important than loneliness. Only a minority fail to suffer from it, and even those who most keenly desired the end of the marriage often find the initial loneliness excruciating" (1973, p. 83).

The decision to divorce is rarely reached easily or quickly, and it may be fraught with ambivalence. Even when a spouse has moved out of the home, there is still a chance that he or she will return. Emotions run deep. Hate may exist in tandem with love. One minute a spouse thinks, "There's no way that I can survive this marriage"; and the next, "Oh, I miss her so much."

Legal Divorce

When Bohannan first conceived his six stations of divorce, he identified the traditional adversarial legal process as a significant challenge. No-fault laws have eliminated the element of blame, or fault, to some degree, but they have not removed all conflict from the proceedings. As Norman Krivosha (1983), former chief justice of the Nebraska Supreme Court, has noted, "If people don't want to live together, then let them divorce. By moving to no-fault divorce, we have shifted the fight from blame to property and custody." Competing attorneys do battle for their clients, and these "hired guns" try to get the most they can for whoever is paying the fee.

The adversarial approach may work reasonably well for resolving disputes between businesses or strangers, but families with children thrive on trust and cooperation. Divorcing parents have to deal with each other because they remain connected by their children. Rather than helping to mend the wounds of a broken family, the legal system often makes things worse. One judge commented, "Criminal court is easier, and a lot more fun."

In recent years, a nationwide movement toward the mediation of divorces has gained ground in the United States. A network of professional and volunteer mediators is growing, with the intent of keeping family disputes out of the legal system to minimize the emotional damage to ongoing family relationships. Rather than partners' each hiring legal representation, families can go to a trained mediator, who tries to work out the dispute in the best interest of everyone involved. The mediator works to find a win-win solution, as opposed to the win-lose approach of the courtroom.

Economic Divorce

Some spouses simply don't want to argue about the money, the house, the cars, the furniture. The pain of divorce seems too much to bear, and the financial details exceed their coping abilities. But the economic realities must be faced and resolved. Lawyers are useful for sorting out all the complications—and to represent divorcing partners' interests when they don't have the energy to do so themselves. Many people are so relieved to get out of an unhappy marriage that they don't want to think about the details. "Let him have anything he wants," many a lawyer has heard. "I just want to forget the whole thing."

Divorce can have a crippling financial legacy. Drastic downward mobility, a sort of reverse American dream, is one major consequence of divorce for many. A. Stroup and G. E. Pollock (1994) found, for example, that the incomes of divorced people are lower than the incomes of married people, by 30% for women and by 10% for men. Because children still usually remain with their mother after a divorce, it's especially important for women to get a fair income and property settlement.

After a divorce, many women are forced into the job market, some for the first time. They may have little job experience because they've been home caring for children. Their self-esteem may be low as a result of the breakup of the marriage, and they may have little confidence in their ability to find and hold a good job in a tight job market.

The term **feminization of poverty** refers to the statistical fact that the percentage of female single parents in the total percentage of people who are poor in this country is increasing. This increase of women in poverty is primarily due to the increasing divorce rate and the severe reduction in divorced women's income. The divorced woman, especially the mother with young children, is in a difficult fix. Her marriage proved unworkable and ending it was probably a good idea, but life after divorce often proves to be financially punishing.

Many newly divorced mothers with young children face the double challenge of finding affordable child care and a job that pays a livable wage but does not require specialized skills or extensive experience.

Coparental Divorce

Children play a role in making a satisfactory marriage relationship more difficult to achieve in some respects, but they are also a bond between parents, even in divorce and after it. About 60% of divorces involve children (Kitson & Morgan, 1991; L. K. White, 1991). Spouses may divorce each other, but parents cannot divorce their children. The most difficult dilemma facing many divorcing partners is the question of what will happen to the children. The coparental divorce experience reflects the reality that parents must work out how they will coparent even though they will no longer be married or live together.

It has been estimated that 80% of the children in divorced families live with their mothers, 6% live with their fathers, and 14% live with other relatives (Kitson & Morgan, 1991; L. K. White, 1991). Traditionally, women have taken the lion's share of the responsibility for the children in a divorce. Fathers have often found themselves with minimal visitation rights and little control. Such an outcome does not foster coparenting.

The majority of children wish to have continued contact with both parents after divorce (Kitson & Morgan, 1991; L. K. White, 1991). The youngsters, in essence, continue to love both parents even though the parents don't love each other. Ensuring that both parents have ongoing contact with their children is a difficult goal to achieve. If hostilities continue between the parents and the mother has been granted custody of the children, the father often finds himself in an uncomfortable situation. Although he may want to see his children, the visits can be punishing emotionally both for him and for the children. Many fathers simply fade out of the picture in this type of arrangement. They find that going to the zoo or on a picnic with their kids a few days a month is too bittersweet an experience. The father in this type of situation often charges that the mother has poisoned his

Most children want to maintain contact with both parents after a divorce. For the good of the children, the parents need to control any hostility they may feel toward each other. If the custodial parent makes visits too unpleasant for the noncustodial parent, the noncustodial parent may find it easier to simply fade out of the picture.

relationship with his children. The mother often maintains that the father showed no interest in the children before the divorce and that this pattern continued after the divorce. She may say that the children want to be with their friends on the weekend rather than with their father.

Objectively judging who is to blame in these circumstances is difficult, but the end result is generally quite clear. The father often drifts away from his children emotionally and feels little inclination to pay child support because he doesn't feel connected to them any more. If he marries again, he is likely to marry a woman with children of her own and may feel pressure from his new wife to be involved with "their" children. "I've got two sets of kids to support now," one father said. "One set isn't even really mine, and my own set, I can only see every other weekend."

As we discussed earlier, numerous studies have looked at the effects of divorce on children (Amato & Booth, 1996; Wallerstein & Blakeslee, 1996). These studies reveal three conclusions. First, divorce is a very difficult crisis in the lives of the vast majority of children who experience it. Most children grieve over the divorce and wish it were not happening. This is especially true in the case of marriage devitalization or burnout, in which the divorce may have come as a complete surprise to the children.

Second, many children are angry at their parents, and many are angry at themselves.

> "My best friend's parents got a divorce, and I felt so sorry for her," 11-year-old Jenna said. "I imagined once what it would be like if my parents got a divorce. I did this so I could understand what my friend was going through. Then when my parents got a divorce, I felt so guilty. I thought they got a divorce because I had imagined they got one."

When parents break up, children often feel responsible. It takes sensitive parents to help guide the children through their grief. Some parents, overburdened with their own anger and sadness, are of little help to their children.

Third, although divorce is difficult for almost all children, subjection to long-term marital hostilities is even worse. Amato and Booth (1997) found that a high-conflict home can have negative consequences for all family members. Children, in particular, respond to this type of environment with depression, anger, troubles in school, and various physiological symptoms.

Community Divorce

Divorce comes as a shock not only for members of the nuclear family, but for relatives, friends, neighbors, and colleagues at work. Many people are unsure of how to respond to divorcing friends and relatives. The best approach is to listen when they want to share and to be caring and supportive. Friends, parents, sisters, and brothers are often the most supportive. Conversely, most in-laws become out-laws; they tend to support and defend their relative, regardless of the reasons for the divorce. Parents are particularly stressed when their adult children divorce. As one research team described it, "The effects of divorce spread outward like the vibration rings caused by dropping a stone in a quiet pond. Our attention is drawn to the point where the stone hits the water, and less interest is given the larger area which is also disturbed by the impact" (Bader, DeFrain, & Parkhurst, 1982, p. 93).

Divorce research has tended to focus on the impacts on the divorcing couple and on their children but not on the effects on others, such as grandparents (Spitze, Logan, Deane, & Zerger, 1994). When Bader interviewed middle-aged parents of divorcing individuals, she found that although some were glad their child was getting a divorce, the overwhelming emotion most of them felt was sorrow. In the words of one mother, "At first it was like a death in the family to think that our son-in-law would not be a part of the family any longer."

Couple friends also have difficulty responding to a divorcing couple. Which of the partners should the couple friends continue to have contact with? It would be difficult to keep both ex-partners as friends, and it would seem awkward to invite just one person to a social occasion. The divorcing couple often feel bitter about losing their couple friends. However, couples who were primarily connected to only one of the partners often offer valuable support after a divorce.

Psychological Divorce

Many people getting divorced find it useful to talk with a marriage and family therapist or another professional skilled in working with personal and relationship problems. Counselors can provide insights and suggestions for adjusting to the single life. Many people also join support groups. Parents Without Partners and similar groups across the country can provide help to divorcing people seeking to grow through their crisis. These support groups bring together people with similar problems who can be mutually supportive and caring. Groups of divorced people also set up educational programs and social activities (dances, potlucks, camping trips). The main thing is to become actively involved with other people again.

When they are ready, many divorced people look forward to dating again. Friends are often a valuable source for identifying potential dating partners, as are

Dating after a divorce can be both scary and enjoyable. However, newly divorced people should not rush the emotional process of divorce, which can take anywhere from several months to a few years. They should ease into dating slowly, and they definitely should not rush into another marriage on the rebound.

commercial dating services (see Chapter 6). It is important, however, that divorced individuals begin dating gradually rather than rushing the process. The worst thing a newly divorced person can do is to marry again quickly, "on the rebound."

How Long Does It Take to Adjust?

How long does the divorce journey take? The answer is different for each person. The emotional process of divorce may last from several months to a few years after the divorce. The legal process may take only 6 months, but if children are involved and a custody fight occurs, the struggle could last several years. One father, who had been fighting for custody of his youngsters for 6 years, had incurred legal costs of close to $35,000.

The economic process of divorce may also last a long time. For example, if the ex-wife goes back to school after the divorce, she may be in school for 3 or 4 years. Both spouses suffer financially, but usually the wife is the primary financial loser.

The coparental divorce process can last from several months to years. If the couple is on friendly terms, they may work out a joint-custody arrangement that functions well in a few months. If not, battles over custody and child visitation may last a long time. The psychological divorce may also take a long time: Some people take several years to shift to a more independent lifestyle; others make the transition in a few months. As mentioned, these stations of divorce usually run concurrently and often overlap.

Divorce is often less problematic for people who can talk openly about it. When individuals accept the divorce as an important part of their life, they can then move on as independent and happy single people. Divorce is something that most people do not willingly choose, but it can often be a very valuable learning experience. As one man said, "Going through a divorce was an important part of my life that I wouldn't let anyone take away from me for a million dollars. And it was something I wouldn't want to go through again for a million dollars!"

Family Problems and the Family Systems Theory

For most people, the family is a shelter from the storms of the outside world, a secure base from which to cope with stressful times. But for a significant number, family life is a source of stress. Do families create problems for their individual members, or do individuals create problem families? For example, is schizophrenia in a family member "caused" by other family dynamics, or does a schizophrenic family member "cause" problems for and within the family? Is hyperactivity in children caused by inadequate parenting, or is the inadequate parenting a response to the difficulty of dealing with a hyperactive child?

According to the family systems theory, these questions are difficult if not impossible to answer. Because family members are tied together in an intricate web of relationships, what one member does automatically affects the other members and the family system itself. Rather than trying to identify "causes," family therapists focus on helping families acknowledge and deal with their unresolved issues. They ask families to ask themselves, Where do we go from here?

Studies of family problems bear out the premises of the family systems theory. These studies have looked at chemical abuse, physical abuse, sexual abuse, and psychological abuse. Overall, they show that a family with one troubled individual is often a family that is not functioning well as a whole.

The Family and Mental Illness

What are the families of troubled individuals, those with mental or emotional disorders, like? Researchers have used the family systems theory to study the families of individuals with schizophrenia and with anxiety neurosis. According to the *Diagnostic and Statistical Manual of Mental Disorders*, 4th ed. (American Psychiatric Association, 1994), **schizophrenia** is a mental disorder characterized by bizarre or grandiose delusions (such as delusions of being controlled or persecuted or of being God); auditory hallucinations (hearing voices); incoherent, illogical thinking; and very grossly disorganized behavior. **Anxiety disorders** are mental disorders characterized by panic attacks not caused by life-threatening situations or extreme physical exertion. Symptoms of panic attacks include heart palpitations, chest pain or discomfort, choking or smothering sensations, dizziness, feelings of unreality, tingling hands or feet, hot and cold flashes, sweating, faintness, trembling or shaking, fear of dying, and fear of losing control.

To test the hypothesis that balanced family types are more functional than unbalanced family types, researchers have conducted a number of studies. One of the earliest was done by John Clarke (1984), who found strong support for this hypothesis (Figure 16.3). Clarke studied four groups of families: families with a schizophrenic member, families with a member with an anxiety disorder, families who had completed therapy in the past, and healthy families (the control group). Clarke

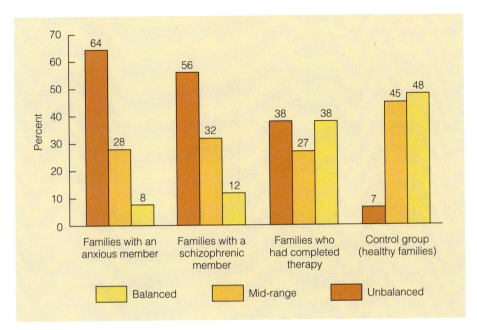

Figure 16.3 Problem Families and Their Family Types. *Source:* Adapted from *The Family Types of Schizophrenics, Neurotics, and "Normals"* by J. Clarke, 1984, unpublished doctoral dissertation, Department of Family Social Science, University of Minnesota, St. Paul.

found that a high percentage of families with anxious and schizophrenic members were unbalanced family types (64% and 56%, respectively), as compared to the healthy families (7%). Conversely, a high percentage of the healthy families were balanced family types (48%), as compared to the families with an anxious member (8%) and the families with a schizophrenic member (12%). Basically, what Clarke found is that individuals with problems are likely to live in families with problems. A person with an anxiety disorder or a person with schizophrenia is commonly found in a family having difficulty establishing a healthy sense of togetherness and having difficulty coping with stress and crisis in life.

The Family and Alcohol Abuse

One study found that families who had a chemically dependent family member were significantly different from families who did not have a chemically dependent member (healthy families; Killorin & Olson, 1984). This study focused on alcoholism and found that 20% of the families of alcoholics were unbalanced family types but that only 4% of the healthy families were unbalanced types. Furthermore, 65% of the healthy families were balanced, but only about one third (32%) of the families with an alcohol-dependent member were balanced. In other words, families of alcoholics tended to lack cohesiveness and the ability to adapt successfully to change.

Figure 16.4 illustrates the findings of this study. The "identified patient" is the alcoholic himself or herself. "Codependent spouse" refers to the partner of the alcoholic. The family systems theory uses the term **codependent** to describe a person, such as a spouse, whose actions enable the alcoholic to continue the drug dependence. **Enabler** is another term for someone with this behavior pattern. Both terms acknowledge that the codependent, or enabler, often unknowingly helps the alcoholic partner continue to drink.

Figure 16.4 Family Types of Families With and Without an Alcoholic Member. *Source:* from *Alcoholic Families and the Circumplex Model*, p. 26, by D. H. Olson, 1989, unpublished manuscript, Department of Family Social Science, University of Minnesota, St. Paul.

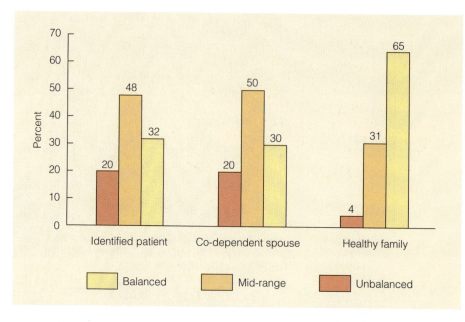

"Rather than forcing the issue and demanding that Emily go into treatment, I kept making excuses for her: to her boss, to her parents, to her friends. I'd say she was ill and wouldn't be in to work today, or that I'd forgotten to tell her about her brother's birthday party, or whatever." The speaker was Conrad, age 45, a businessman living in Petersburg, Virginia.

"In the short run, this worked. In the long run, it was a disaster. Emily didn't get the professional help she needed because I was so ashamed of what was happening to her and to our family. I was afraid it would hurt my business and our status in the church and the community. It ended up destroying our family, which was the greatest loss of all."

Physical Abuse and Neglect of Children

In a statistical sense, the American family is the most violent social institution in our society.

—MURRAY STRAUS AND RICHARD GELLES (1986, p. 466)

Child abuse is the physical or mental injury, sexual abuse, or negligent treatment of a child under the age of 18 by a person who is responsible for the child's welfare. Child abuse includes not only physical assault but also malnourishment, abandonment, neglect, emotional abuse, and sexual abuse (Gelles, 1997). The U.S. Advisory Board on Child Abuse and Neglect (1990) stated, "Beating children, chronically belittling them, using them for sexual gratification, and depriving them of the basic necessities of life are repellent acts and cannot be permitted in a civilized society."

Professionals who work in the area of child abuse point out that abuse and neglect occur in families from all social classes and at all income levels. Being a child

Words hit as hard as a fist.

Emotional abuse of a child is a dramatic and destructive sign that a family is not functioning well. To treat this problem, family systems therapists seek to help the family work through unresolved issues rather than to eliminate the "cause" of the abuse.

"You're pathetic. You can't do anything right!"
"You disgust me! Just shut up!"
"Hey stupid! Don't you know how to listen."
"Get outta here! I'm sick of looking at your face."
"You're more trouble than you're worth."

"Why don't you go find some other place to live!"
"I wish you were never born."
Children believe what their parents tell them. Next time, stop and listen to what you're saying. You might not believe your ears.

Take time out. Don't take it out on your kid.

Write: National Committee for Prevention of Child Abuse
Box 2866E, Chicago, Illinois 60690

of rich, well-educated parents does not necessarily guarantee safety, but research does indicate that abuse is seven times more likely among families with a yearly income of less than $15,000 (Straus, 1994)—perhaps a reflection of the stress such families experience.

Incidence

More than 1 million children are abused each year in the United States (U.S. Bureau of the Census, 1997, tab. 352, p. 218). Child neglect, the most commonly reported type of abuse, accounts for an estimated 49% of the cases reported in this country each year. *Physical abuse* (major and minor physical injuries) accounts for about 24% of reported cases, and *sexual abuse* accounts for 13% of all reported cases. *Emotional abuse* (psychological mistreatment or mental cruelty), although prevalent in our society, accounts for only 5% of the reported cases of child abuse each year (U.S. Bureau of the Census, 1997). *Sibling abuse* is probably the most common form

Running away from home is the way many children cope with abuse by a family member. For these youngsters, the bleak and often frightening experience of life on the streets is preferable to violence at the hands of someone who is supposed to care for them.

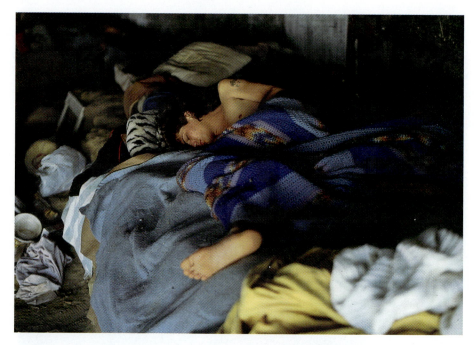

of physical abuse of children. In a study of 733 families, 82% of the children ages 3 to 18 reported sibling violence in their family in the preceding year.

American society tends to condone violent rather than nonviolent approaches to the discipline of children. Research indicates that most American parents approve of spanking and slapping their children, and almost two out of three parents do so in a given year (Straus, 1994). Even though spanking and slapping are clearly violent behaviors, they are not generally viewed as child abuse in our society. But why does our society consider it relatively acceptable to hit a child, a brother, or a spouse but unacceptable to hit an employee, a co-worker, or a salesperson?

In a national survey of parents, Straus and Gelles (1986) found that 10.7% admitted to using severe forms of punishment, including kicking, biting, punching, beating, hitting with a hand or an object, or wielding a gun or knife against them. Mothers are apparently slightly more likely than fathers to be violent or severely violent toward their children (Gelles & Straus, 1988), perhaps because they spend more time with them. Boys are more likely than girls to have violence inflicted upon them by their parents (Gelles & Cornell, 1985).

The Impact on Children

Abused babies tend to be extremely difficult to nurture and to rear because of what they have experienced. Abuse between a parent and a child, is a vicious cycle in which a negative act by the parent produces a negative response from the child, which in turn produces another negative response from the parent, and so on.

Researchers have found that abuse can compromise children's intellectual and social development in a variety of ways. Abused children tend to have lower IQ scores, learning problems, lower grades, and poorer school performance than do children who are not abused. Many abused children are aggressive, oppositional, and extremely wary. Other problems related to abuse include bedwetting; tantrums;

BOX 16.1

The Impact of Violence on Children

Murray Straus and Richard Gelles have been studying family violence for more than two decades. In one study, the research team interviewed 3,206 parents of children under 17 years of age who were living at home. The interviewers asked parents about problems their children had experienced and about their use of violence toward their children in the previous year.

The list of difficulties the parents talked about included difficulty making friends, temper tantrums, failing grades in school, disciplinary problems, misbehavior and disobedience at home, physical fights with other children, physical fights with adults, deliberately damaging or destroying property, stealing money or other items, drinking, using drugs, and getting arrested.

The risk of these problems for a child growing up in a violent home was nearly double the risk of these problems for a child whose home was free of violence. More than 40% of the children from violent homes had some problems in school, were aggressive, and/or had problems with drugs or alcohol. Only 23% of the children growing up in nonviolent homes experienced these same troubles. Children living in violent homes were also three to four times more likely to break the law and be arrested. A child growing up in a violent home often becomes part of a cycle of violence.

Source: Adapted from "The National Family Violence Surveys" (pp. 3–16) by M. A. Straus. In *Physical Violence in American Families* edited by M. A. Straus and R. J. Gelles, 1990, New Brunswick, NJ: Transaction Books.

inability to trust other people; difficulty relating to both peers and adults; generalized unhappiness; poor self-image; and the tendency to engage in juvenile delinquency, join a gang, run away from home, be truant from school, and become involved in violent crime (Gelles & Straus, 1988). Box 16.1 presents the results of a study on the effects of violence in the home on children and adolescents.

Transcending Abuse

Many abusive parents were themselves abused as children, but being abused as a child does not necessarily doom a person to pass the misery along to the next generation. Some abused children grow up to be happy and healthy adults, although transcending the pain of a violent childhood is very difficult. Since the early 1980s, researchers and clinicians have begun to focus on these "resilient" or "invulnerable" individuals. What they have found is that a nurturing relative, adult friend, or teacher often helped the troubled individual find a more positive approach to living.

Edward Zigler and his colleagues (1988) have estimated that the rate of "cross-generational transmission" of child abuse is about 25% to 35%. This means that about one quarter to one third of those who are physically or sexually abused or neglected as children will subject their own children to similar abuse. However, the majority (65% to 75%) of people abused as children "will care for their offspring as well as the general population." According to the researchers, "many adults abused as children remember the agony they once suffered and have sworn to give their own children a better start." The research team did make it clear, however, that individuals with a history of abuse are still about six times more likely to abuse their own children than is the average person, who has about a 5% likelihood of doing so (Zigler, Rubin, & Kaufman, 1988).

A man named Robert, who survived and transcended childhood trauma, recounted his experience of years of physical and emotional abuse in his family. When he was a teenager, Robert intervened one afternoon when his father was beating his mother. His father stormed into the basement after him, warning that he was going to kill him. Robert grabbed a hunting rifle and shot his father, who died soon after. When a police officer came to pick him up a few hours later, Robert recalled that the officer understood that the shooting was in self-defense. "He told me that I was a good boy, and that it wasn't my fault. I felt like it was the first time anyone had ever said anything kind to me in my whole life." Robert healed from his childhood trauma and went on to become a police officer himself, working with troubled young people. "I dedicated my life to the memory of that officer who made such a difference in my view of myself."

Clearly, the experience of childhood abuse does not predetermine that an abused child will grow up to abuse others later in life.

Families at Risk

A number of factors are related to the incidence of child abuse in a family.

- *Economic distress.* Unemployment, low income, illness in the family, and inability to pay for adequate medical care are stressors in the lives of many abusive parents.

- *Inadequate parenting skills.* Abusive parents often have unrealistic expectations of their children, have little knowledge of child development, and demonstrate an inability to bond with infants (Azar & Rohrbeck, 1986).

- *Parental personality problems.* Abusive parents often have low self-esteem and are likely to be more immature, less empathetic, and more self-centered than nonabusive parents. They also tend to be rigid, domineering, self-righteous, moralistic, and prone to anger. (Dubowitz & Egan, 1988).

- *Chemical abuse as a means of coping with stress.* Abusive parents often have high stress in their lives but have a difficult time dealing with that stress in a proactive, rational manner. Many turn to alcohol and other drugs to forget their troubles (Hamilton, Stiles, Melowsky, & Beal, 1987).

- *Social isolation.* Abusive families tend to be isolated from their community, with few friends or sources of outside support (Gelles & Cornell, 1985).

- *A special child.* Children with a chronic illness, an emotional disturbance, hyperactivity, mental retardation, or a physical handicap are at higher risk for abuse (Hawkins & Duncan, 1985). Children who were unplanned and are unwanted are also more likely to be abused, as are children whose birth was difficult.

- *Family size.* Researchers have found that the likelihood of child abuse tends to increase with family size. Parents of two children are 50% more

The likelihood of child abuse is greater when the parents are under stress because of unemployment, low income, or illness, especially if they are immature and know little about the development of children. During times of stress, parents need friends and other sources of support to help them cope with frustrations and relate to their children in a positive way.

likely to abuse their children than are parents of a single child. The rate of child abuse has been found to peak at five children and to decline in larger families (Gelles & Cornell, 1985).

- *Domestic violence in the family of origin.* Many abusive parents witnessed domestic violence between their own parents and were likely to have been physically punished themselves as children (Gelles & Cornell, 1985).

- *A violent subculture.* Some cultures and subcultures appear to be more tolerant of violent behavior toward children. For example, children who live in an unsafe neighborhood characterized by high levels of violence are at greater risk of being abused than are children growing up in a more peaceful neighborhood.

- *A violent marriage.* Parents who abuse their spouse are more likely to abuse their children than are parents whose marriage is peaceful.

- *Single parent.* Children who live with a single parent are more likely to suffer abuse than are those who live with two parents, perhaps due to the stresses often associated with single parenthood.

- *Stepparent.* A child living with a stepparent is more likely to be abused than is a child living with both natural parents, perhaps because the stepparent's lack of a biological tie with the child fosters intolerance. One study of preschoolers found the likelihood for abuse to be 40 times greater for stepchildren.

Treatment and Prevention

A growing body of professional literature demonstrates that Americans can do something about child abuse (Gelles, 1997). Parents can learn how to deal more positively and effectively with their children. Education is the key to preventing abuse; education and therapy are needed to help abusive families.

Professionals see child abuse as a family and societal problem. Treating the problem involves three interrelated strategies: (1) increasing the parent's self-esteem, (2) increasing the parent's knowledge of children and positive childrearing techniques, and (3) devising community support networks for families under stress.

Parents who mistreat children are commonly viewed as people who need more positive ways of coping with their many problems. Counselors working with abusive parents are often quite successful in facilitating positive behavioral changes. By focusing on these parents' strengths, a therapist can enhance the development of the parent's self-esteem and parenting skills. A counselor can also provide referrals to other community services: financial aid for families in economic distress, food stamps, aid in finding better housing, family planning and adoption services, and day care.

Many programs for troubled parents entail a parent-discussion-and-support-group component. Groups of parents, often facilitated by a professional, get together to share stories about life's ups and downs and to offer advice and support. Child abuse hotlines are also available to parents around the clock for help in dealing with difficult childrearing situations.

There are a number of things we as a society can do to prevent the abuse of children (Baumrind, 1994). They include working to reduce sources of social stress, such as poverty, racism, inequality, unemployment, and inadequate health care; eliminating sexism in the workplace and the home; providing adequate child care; promoting educational and employment opportunities for both men and women; supporting sex education and family planning programs in an effort to reduce unplanned and unwanted pregnancies; and working to end the social isolation of families in our culture.

Sexual Abuse of Children

Sexual abuse of children is a growing problem but one that is still underreported. There were about 125,000 allegations of child sexual abuse in the United States during 1995. By age 18, an estimated 27% of girls and 16% of boys will have been sexually abused (Darnton, Springen, Wright, & Keene-Osborn, 1991). There are two basic forms of child sexual abuse: incestuous abuse (intrafamilial abuse), which occurs between family members, and nonincestuous abuse (extrafamilial abuse), which occurs between nonfamily members (Finkelhor, 1984).

Incest is sexual activity of any kind between members of the same family, including grandparents, adopted children, stepparents, and in-laws. Incest is forbidden today in virtually every society. **Incestuous abuse** is the sexual exploitation of a child under the age of 18 by a relative. It is far more frequent between brothers and sisters, fathers and daughters, stepfathers and stepdaughters, and uncles and nieces than between mothers and sons (Peters, Wyatt, & Finkelhor, 1986; Russell, 1986). It is often an intensely damaging psychological experience, contributing to persistent, long-term sexual and social difficulties.

During the past decade the definition of incest has broadened. In addition to sexual intercourse, incest is now considered to include fondling, rubbing one's genitals against a child, and excessive or suggestive washing of a child's pubic area. It does not matter if the child is perceived by the adult as freely engaging in the sexual activity or even enjoying it. A child cannot give informed consent to the activity. Incest, thus, is an abuse of power and authority (Gorman, 1991).

Dynamics of Incestuous Families

Clinicians and researchers have invested a great deal of energy in understanding the causes of incest and the dynamics of incestuous families. C. A. Courtois (1988) cites four general dynamics that need to be examined to better comprehend an incestuous family: (1) the psychodynamic, which centers on the personalities and backgrounds of the family members; (2) the sociological or sociocultural dynamic, which focuses on social and cultural factors; (3) the family system dynamic, which examines the family as a unit; and (4) the feminist dynamic, which analyzes family gender roles and patterns.

Focusing on the family system dynamic, clinicians and researchers often find that incestuous families tend to be isolated and withdrawn from the outside world. Family members suffer from social, psychological, and physical isolation and try to meet most of their individual needs within the nuclear family. Appropriate boundaries do not exist between family members across generational lines. Individuation and independence are discouraged and even punished. Role reversal between parents and children is common. Emotional and physical deprivation predominate. Affection is most commonly expressed sexually (Courtois, 1988).

There are apparently two broad family system types in which incest occurs: the chaotic-style family and the normal-appearing family. The **chaotic-style family** is the stereotypical incestuous family. These families often have a multitude of problems reaching back through the generations. They tend to be of low socioeconomic status, and many individuals in the family are only marginally functional, with limited educational and vocational achievements. Substance abuse and trouble with the law are common. Abusers in a chaotic-style family are more likely to be punished for incest than are abusers in a normal-appearing family—and their punishment tends to be more severe (Courtois, 1988).

The **normal-appearing family** is seemingly healthy and functional to outsiders. The family is socially and financially stable and is usually well integrated into the community. The parents' marriage has lasted a long time. The family is often a traditional one, with the husband as head of the household. From the inside, however, the normal-appearing family is in trouble. Family members lack emotional energy and are unable to nurture one another. The parents are emotionally needy; abuse of alcohol or other drugs is likely. The children must not only care for themselves but are often caretakers for the parents. When a child discloses incest, denial and disbelief are the responses. In the case of a trial, the family's financial resources are used to defend the perpetrator and attack the child's credibility. The perpetrator, often the father, is rarely found guilty (Courtois, 1988).

Sex offenders generally live in and come from family types that are unbalanced on the Couple and Family Map, families that lack genuine emotional closeness, have poor communication skills, and have limited skill in dealing successfully with everyday stresses and major crises. Patrick Carnes (1989) found that 66% of sex

Figure 16.5 Sex Offenders and Their Family Types. *Source:* "Sexually Addicted Families: Clinical Use of the Circumplex Model" (p. 127) by P. J. Carnes. In *Circumplex Model* edited by D. H. Olson, C. S. Russell, and D. H. Sprenkle, 1989, New York: Haworth Press. Copyright 1989 by Haworth Press. Reprinted by permission.

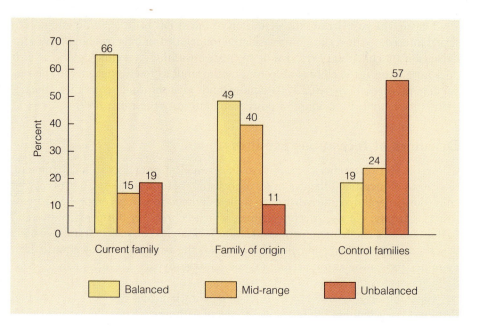

offenders were living in unbalanced types of families and that 49% had grown up in unbalanced families. In contrast, most families in the control group (no sex offender in the family) were balanced or mid-range types of families (Figure 16.5).

Effects of Sexual Abuse and Incest

The effects of sexual abuse seem to depend on who is doing the abusing, the manner of the abuse, and how long the abuse goes on (Gelles, 1997). The effects of forceful, hurtful, exploitive sexual relationships can last for a long time. The abused person may carry a burden of guilt, shame, fear, bitterness, anger, lowered self-esteem, and depression for years and may suffer from sleep disturbances and/or eating disorders (including anorexia and bulimia). Suicidal thoughts and self-destructive behaviors are common. Revictimization, increased vulnerability to rape and to marital violence, is common. Individuals may also have other sexual problems, such as difficulty trusting one's partner, an inability to relax and enjoy lovemaking, avoidance of sex, inhibited sexual desire, and an inability to achieve orgasm (Browne & Finkelhor, 1986).

Sexually abused children may have difficulties in school, including low grades and truancy. Many children who run away from home are incest victims, and many adolescent pregnancies and early marriages are associated with sexual abuse in the family (Browne & Finkelhor, 1986). One study by the Illinois Department of Children and Family Services found that more than half of the 445 teenage mothers questioned had been sexually abused as children or had been forced to have sex. The average age for the first incident was 11.5 years ("Teen Moms," 1987).

In general, the effects of incest have been likened to those of **posttraumatic stress disorder (PTSD).** Individuals regularly reexperience the trauma through recurrent invasive thoughts and uncontrollable emotions. They often feel detached from the external world and may feel compelled to avoid situations that remind them of the original trauma (Edwards, 1989).

Because very young children do not know the words to describe an act of sexual abuse, therapists have them use anatomically correct dolls to show what happened. A demonstration with dolls is more reliable than direct questions because small children often attempt to guess what answer the interviewer wants even though they do not understand the question.

Treatment and Prevention

In the case of father-daughter incest, the traditional solution was to protect the victim by removing the father from the home and imprisoning him. This left the victim and her family to fend for themselves in the wake of a great emotional trauma. Today the judicial system and the community family support network often work in concert to evaluate the family situation and recommend an approach appropriate for the family's circumstances. The goal might not necessarily be to incarcerate the perpetrator. In some situations he might be moved out of the home into a treatment setting while the remaining members of the family are helped in a variety of ways to come to terms with the trauma. Therapists might work on developing family members' self-esteem and improving family relationships. Referral might be made to an alcohol or other drug treatment program. Self-help groups for victims, perpetrators, and other family members operate in a number of cities. One goal is for family members to learn how the incest has affected each of them (Nadelson & Sauzier, 1986).

The conspiracy of silence surrounding incest is beginning to crumble in American society. A number of prominent people—among them, Roseanne, Oprah Winfrey, former Miss America Marilyn Van Derbur, and La Toya Jackson—have come forward to describe the abuse they experienced as children (Gorman, 1991). These very public disclosures often encourage less well known people to tell their stories and begin the long process of healing. Support groups for incest survivors provide safe places for sharing painful secrets with trustworthy individuals.

In an effort to prevent sexual abuse, many organizations and schools in this country have educational programs for children on "good touch and bad touch." Children are taught how to avoid potentially abusive situations, how to react when approached, how to say no so that people know they mean it, and how to persist in telling adults they trust what has happened until someone believes them.

Education can also help adults protect children from sexual abuse. Parents, teachers, physicians, mental health professionals, and police officers are key figures in the child protection team. Parents must overcome their reluctance to talk about these issues with their children. Finally, as a society we need to abandon some of our stereotypic sexual games. Sexuality should not be a commodity for exploitation but a positive gift for bonding and the expression of affection.

Spouse Abuse

The home is actually a more dangerous place for American women than the city streets.

—Dr. Antonia C. Novello, *former U.S. surgeon general*
("Family Violence," 1991, p. 3)

Although the family is usually considered to be a loving and supportive social institution, it is, in fact, more violent than the military, except in times of war (Gelles & Harrop, 1989). More than a third of the women who are murdered in this country die at the hands of their husbands or boyfriends. Domestic violence is the single greatest cause of injury to women, ranking higher than automobile accidents, muggings, and rapes combined ("Family Violence," 1991; Straus, 1989). A Johns Hopkins University study found that one in three U.S. women has been the victim of domestic abuse and that half of those have been assaulted before the age of 18 ("Study: 1 of 3 women," 1995). About 20% of all police officers killed each year in this country die while intervening in a family dispute (U.S. Department of Justice, 1989).

As shown in Figure 16.6, attackers in violent crimes vary according to the type of violent crime—rape, physical assault, or robbery. Most robberies are committed by strangers (84%), as compared to those committed by friends or family members (16%). Although the majority of rapes and assaults are committed by strangers (54% and 64%, respectively), friends and family members are involved in a larger percentage of rapes and assaults than in robberies. Almost half (46%) of the 100,000 rapes each year and a little over one third (36%) of all assaults are committed by a friend or family member (U.S. Bureau of the Census, 1997). Thus, it appears that friends and family members tend to be involved more in more intimate crimes, such as rape.

Incidence

Researchers estimate that approximately 3 million people, mostly women, are severely assaulted each year by their spouses (Gelles, 1997; Straus & Gelles, 1986). Most cases are not reported, for a variety of reasons. Victims often do not recognize the violence as abuse because in some ethnic and cultural groups violence toward women is the norm. Society's traditional respect for family privacy also inhibits reporting. Victims may feel guilt or shame for being abused or may fear their partner will retaliate if they report the incident.

Husband abuse occurs as well, but because men are generally bigger and stronger than women, husbands have higher rates of inflicting the most dangerous and injurious forms of violence on wives. Much violence by wives appears to be in self-defense (Straus & Gelles, 1986).

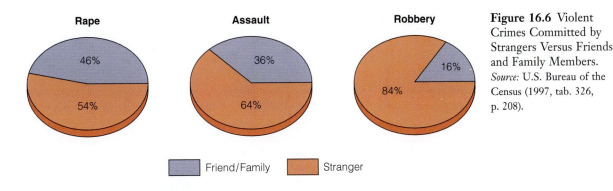

Figure 16.6 Violent Crimes Committed by Strangers Versus Friends and Family Members. *Source:* U.S. Bureau of the Census (1997, tab. 326, p. 208).

Although the number of cases reported to authorities has risen dramatically over the years, the actual rate of spouse abuse declined slightly according to a national survey conducted in 1975 and repeated in 1985 (Straus & Gelles, 1986). In 1975, 12.1% of the husbands admitted that they were violent toward their wives, and 3.8% said they were severely violent (15.9% total). In 1985, 11.3% of the husbands reported being violent toward their wives, and 3.0% reported being severely violent (14.3% total).

In 1975, 11.6% of the women reported being violent toward their husbands, and 4.6% said they were severely violent (16.2% total). In 1985, 12.1% of the wives reported being violent toward their husbands, and 4.4% said they were severely violent (16.5% total). The actual rate of violence was probably higher than reported because people are reluctant to admit to being violent. An unexpected finding was that the rate of wife-to-husband violence was somewhat higher than that of husband-to-wife violence (Straus & Gelles, 1986).

Straus and Gelles (1986) speculate that the small decline in husband-to-wife violence between 1975 and 1985 can be traced to an increase in the average age of marriage (younger couples tend to be more violent than older couples), a more prosperous economy in 1985 (violence has been linked to financial stress), and increasing public awareness that violence toward women is unacceptable.

A dating relationship is apparently more likely to be violent than a marital relationship. The National Family Violence Survey of 5,768 couples found that 20% of the dating couples had experienced a physical assault during the previous year, compared with 15% of the married couples (Stets & Straus, 1989). Courtship is a training ground for marriage and also, apparently, a training ground for spouse abuse. (See Chapter 6 for a detailed discussion on violence in dating relationships.)

"In the beginning I thought Jerry was abusive because he was drunk, but then it happened when he wasn't drunk, too." Norina, a 20-year-old college woman, continued, "I ignored it at first. I guess I thought it would quit. I also loved him so much I tried to cover it up.

"He became very demeaning toward me, and there was a lot of mental abuse. I wanted to quit seeing him, but he wouldn't accept it. I needed to get away, but he followed me wherever I went and watched every move I made. I didn't realize how bad the situation had become until one night at a party. He had followed me there but didn't speak to me most of the

(Continued. . .)

(. . .Continued)

night. He left—or so I thought. Because I was upset, I started to talk with a male friend of mine. Out of the blue my boyfriend returned, picked me up, and carried me outside behind a building. I was scared and started crying. I was so upset I couldn't listen to him. He kept slapping me and telling me to shut up and listen. A few of my friends were watching. They confronted my boyfriend, and he started fighting with them.

"The best thing I did was to go to a counselor. She taught me how to deal with my feelings. She made me realize that there was nothing more I could do in the relationship except get out. She also made me aware that there was nothing I could do about my boyfriend until he recognized that what he was doing was wrong and would go for help himself."

Spouse or partner abuse can be physical, sexual, or emotional. Spouse abuse and child abuse are closely linked. Seventy percent of the men who batter their partners also batter their children (Bowker, Arbitell, & McFerron, 1988; Jouriles & Norwood, 1995).

Relationship of Physical Abuse and Psychological Abuse

Marital violence has been found to be more common among young couples; among couples with low occupational status and income and job dissatisfaction; and among couples who are socially isolated, who have a greater number of dependent children in the home, and who experienced violence in their family of origin. Violent couple relationships are associated with poor conflict-resolution and communication skills and unequal decision-making responsibilities (which tend to be held solely by the husband; Arias & Page, 1999). Physical abuse almost always is accompanied by psychological abuse, but psychological abuse is often present in relationships in which there is no physical violence (Arias, 1999). However, abuse has been conceptualized as a developmental process in which psychological abuse occurs first and eventually may progress into physical aggression (Stets, 1990).

Although a woman who is psychologically abused will not have bruises or visible signs of injury, she will experience damage to her physical and psychological health. Psychologically abused women have an increased chance of serious or chronic illness, lower levels of relationship satisfaction, and lower levels of perceived power and control. These women experience psychological distress including fear, low self-esteem, depression, an inability to trust others, nightmares, guilt, feelings of inferiority, pessimism, low ego strength, introversion, and helplessness. They also may experience psychophysiological symptoms such as fatigue, backache, headache, general restlessness, and insomnia. Psychological abuse also compromises mothering skills and thus puts children at risk. Psychological abuse has been found not only to be a major predictor of a mother's depression but also of her children's depression and low self-esteem (Arias, 1999). In fact, data suggest that the psychological and behavioral dysfunction of children exposed to interparental psychological abuse is similar to that found in children exposed to interparental physical abuse.

Many symptoms experienced and reported by battered women mirror symptoms of PTSD (posttraumatic stress disorder). An investigation by Arias and Pape

(1999) found psychological abuse to be a significant predictor of women's PTSD symptomatology and intentions to end an abusive relationship. Psychologically abused women with low-PTSD symptomatology were associated highly with intentions to terminate the abusive relationship, but there was no significant association for women in the high-PTSD symptomatology group. Arias and Pape suggest that because psychological abuse targets cognitions and is incorporated into self-concept, higher levels of abuse-related distress may decrease a woman's ability to leave the abusive relationship. Based on these findings, Arias and Pape argue that shelters need to increase the duration of stay for women to ensure affective and cognitive improvements and to increase the probability that these women will find the support and strength to leave the perpetrator.

Factors Contributing to Spouse Abuse

Researchers and clinicians have hypothesized that a number of factors contribute to the likelihood of spouse abuse in a family. These factors are quite similar to those related to child abuse.

Violence in the Family of Origin   The family systems theory attributes a tendency toward domestic violence as an adult to growing up in a violent home, where the child learns to be a victim as well as a potential **victimizer.** Abused male children typically learn to be victimizers. They often develop a sort of "pecking order" attitude toward violence: You get beaten up when you're small; then when you're big, you repeat what you learned. Female children typically learn to be victims in their family of origin and are likely to become victims again in their marriage (Gelles & Cornell, 1985; Kruttschnitt, Heath, & Ward, 1986; Lincoln Family Service Association, 1991; Simons, Johnson, Beaman, & Conger, 1993; Steinmetz, 1987). As with child abuse, however, growing up in a home where spouse abuse occurs does not guarantee that one will become a victim or a victimizer as an adult (Gelles & Cornell, 1985; Stark & Flitcraft, 1985). People can and do make positive, life-affirming choices.

Theorists with a psychodynamically oriented approach might see some abusers as having a personality disorder that is facilitated by a "willing" victim. The abuser's sadism is reinforced by the victim's masochism. In a similar vein, **learned helplessness theory** postulates that battered women often have learned from childhood that they cannot afford to appear competent around competitive men who like to win. These women give power away to men, and this ingrained passivity leads to a lack of options in life. When abused, they feel they have no way out: nowhere to go, no job skills or career opportunities, no choice except to continue to take their punishment.

Low Self-Esteem   Low self-esteem is a factor in domestic violence. The abusive spouse may feel inadequate and may use violence to gain control. The abused spouse may passively accept the violence, feeling that she or he deserves nothing better.

Youth   Age and spouse abuse are statistically related. Marital violence is twice as likely among couples who are under age 30 than among those over age 30 (Gelles & Cornell, 1985).

Most women who are physically abused by their husbands or partners are reluctant to report the abuse and even more reluctant to end the relationship. One theory for this masochistic behavior is that these women were abused as children and know only the role of victim. Another theory is that throughout their lives they have been conditioned to act passively and as a consequence have few skills and little self-esteem and see no alternative to a brutal relationship.

Economic Stress   Although spouse abuse occurs in families at all income levels, economic stress increases the likelihood of wife battering. Spouse abuse is more likely in low-income families, and unemployed men are twice as likely to batter their wives as employed men are (Gelles & Cornell, 1985; Steinmetz, 1987).

Isolation   Social isolation is also a factor in abuse. Abusers often feel isolated and alone. They have fewer contacts with friends, neighbors, and relatives and engage in fewer social activities than nonabusers do. In stressful times they have no social support network upon which to call (Gelles & Cornell, 1985).

Alcohol   Alcohol is implicated in a high percentage of domestic violence incidents. Many men who assault their wives are found to have been drinking (Gelles & Cornell, 1985). Does drinking cause violence? Some observers argue that alcohol facilitates violence by helping to break down the abuser's inhibitions. But alcohol is never the sole cause of a violent episode. Drinking is no more an excuse for assaulting another human being than it is for killing someone in a car accident.

Male Dominance   Professionals and clinicians studying abuse from a feminist perspective have identified clues as to why men batter women. They note that many in our culture believe that males have the right to control or try to control their partners. Men have also been socialized to believe that aggression is an acceptable, normal response to stress and anger. A patriarchal family system influences males to assume the head-of-the-household role and women to accept subordinate status. Equalitarian decision making is associated with nonviolence in families. Research shows that levels of wife-beating and husband-beating are higher among husband-dominant couples than among democratic couples (Straus, Gelles, & Steinmetz, 1980).

Other Cultural Factors   Some observers are especially critical of sports in this country, saying that hypercompetitiveness and a win-at-any-cost attitude can lead to brutality in the home. Social philosopher Myriam Miedzian believes that boys today are being raised in a culture that discourages nurturing behavior and leads many to grow up to be men who denigrate and beat women. Miedzian cites studies that have found that boys who are involved in competitive sports demonstrate a lower degree of sportsmanship and fair play than boys who have not been involved in competitive sports. Miedzian concludes that "if you combine the emphasis on winning at any cost with the negative attitude toward women, it is not at all surprising that approximately one-third of the sexual assaults on college campuses are by athletes" (cited in Levy, 1991, p. 17).

In our culture the depersonalization and objectification of women are reinforced by pornography and by advertising that uses sexy women to sell products. Victim blaming is common, as rape trials often reveal. We live in a society with a high tolerance for overt coercion and the use of physical force to gain control over others (Pence, Duprey, Paymar, & McDonnell, 1989). All of these social factors are viewed as contributing to the epidemic of domestic violence in this country.

Patterns of Spouse Abuse

Clinicians commonly see a three-phase, cyclical pattern to wife battering: (1) a tension-building phase; (2) an explosion phase, in which the actual beating occurs; and (3) a loving or honeymoon phase, in which the battered woman is rewarded for staying in the relationship (L. Walker, 1979). The third phase can be very pleasant. Many women stay with their spouses or boyfriends because of the promises and gifts that often follow a violent incident.

A common belief in our culture is that venting anger verbally can prevent physical violence. This theory of **catharsis conflict,** as it has been called, is simply not true. Verbal aggression is not a substitute for physical aggression but actually goes hand in hand with physical aggression. The more verbally aggressive a couple is, the more likely they are to be physically aggressive with each other (Gelles, 1997).

Treatment and Prevention

Many clinicians and professionals who work in women's shelters are skeptical that batterers can alter their behavior without professional help and without the genuine desire to change. Some argue that battering men "have a good thing going," with a terrified wife and children who jump every time the batterer says jump.

Counselors commonly advise battered women to leave their husbands and go to a relative's or a friend's home or to a shelter for battered women. But this is easier said than done. Some men panic when women leave because they feel they are losing control. Panic can lead to even more violent behavior. "It's extremely rare that you read about a man who has beaten a woman to death while she's living with him," according to Ellen Pence, who works with battered women. "It's when she leaves him that he kills" (Simpson, 1989).

Fortunately, there have been many advances in treatment services for spouse abuse over the past two decades. The first shelter for battered women opened in 1974; today there are several thousand shelters across the country. Shelters provide safety for the abused spouse and children; temporary housing, food, and clothing; counseling to build a stronger self-concept; and practical guidance such as finding employment and legal assistance (Straus, 1989).

Responding to pressure from the women's movement, police departments are now more likely to make arrests in cases of domestic violence. Assault against a spouse is seen as a serious offense (Straus, 1989). After studying research findings indicating that men who had spent time behind bars were less likely to assault their partners again, the Duluth, Minnesota, police department was the first in the United States to make arrest mandatory for suspected batterers. The Duluth program requires batterers to attend at least 6 months of counseling and classes. If a man misses two meetings, he risks serving up to 10 days in jail. Studies done 2 years after the program was initiated found that 80% of the women whose partners had completed the program were no longer being battered (Simpson, 1989; Knudsen & Miller, 1992).

As a society, our ultimate goal should be the prevention of domestic violence. To do this we need not only to treat those families in which violence has occurred but also to address the causes of violence. We still live in a society that devalues women and children and glorifies power, the use of force, and the domineering behavior associated with alcohol abuse.

To help prevent the next generation from falling into the sexism/violence trap, Myriam Miedzian suggests encouraging schools to teach positive approaches to conflict resolution in the classroom and on the playground, to show children there are alternatives to violent behavior. Television should be prosocial and nonviolent rather than sexist and violent. We need to restrict violent pornography, which both demeans women and glorifies killing. Also, boys should be encouraged from a young age to be empathetic rather than aggressive (cited in Levy, 1991).

Sibling and Child-to-Parent Abuse

Domestic violence is not initiated only by adults, nor is it directed only at children and partners. Siblings also engage in violence, and children sometimes attack their parents.

Sibling Abuse

One of the most common forms of family violence is **sibling abuse.** Seventy-five percent of siblings experience at least one violent episode a year. Fifty percent of siblings are punched, kicked, or bitten each year, and 16% beat each other up. Guns or knives are used or their use is threatened in less than 1% of these incidents (Gelles & Cornell, 1985).

Siblings often learn physical violence in the home, usually from their parents. One study found that of the children who were repeatedly abused by their parents, 76% severely assaulted a sibling; only 15% of children whose parents used no physical punishment or other violence over the course of a year assaulted a sibling (Gelles & Cornell, 1985).

To prevent sibling violence, parents can do the following things: (1) not be violent toward each other, (2) be supportive of and nurturing toward their children, (3) give their children a strong, clear message that violence is not acceptable, (4) monitor their children's behavior and be watchful, and (5) avoid coercive discipline, which is associated with higher rates of fighting between siblings (Loeber & Dishion, 1984).

In sum, parents need to take the time to teach their children nonviolent ways of relating to each other. Older children, in particular, can be instructed to sit down together and come up with a nonviolent solution to their conflict. Their efforts at conflict resolution can be surprisingly creative.

Child-to-Parent Abuse

Although some authorities in our culture believe that it is acceptable for parents to hit children, few believe it is all right for children to hit parents. Because parents are usually physically and socially more powerful than their children, we assume that parents are immune to abuse by their children. But **child-to-parent abuse** occurs in many families.

In a nationwide survey of family violence, nearly 10% of the parents reported that they had been hit, bitten, or kicked at least once by their children. Three percent of the parents reported that they had been the victim at least once of severely violent behavior on the part of a child 11 years old or older. The researchers concluded that "children are capable of violent behavior that is as devastating as violence inflicted by adults" (Gelles & Straus, 1988). The research team heard stories of children pushing parents down stairs, setting the house on fire with the parents in it, and attacking parents with guns or knives in an effort to seriously injure or kill them. The majority of children who attack their parents are between the ages of 13 and 24.

Mothers are abused more often than fathers, probably because women usually are not as physically strong as men and because women are commonly viewed as acceptable targets for aggression. Mothers who have been abused by their husbands are more likely to be abused by their children (Gelles & Cornell, 1985). Teenagers who were once victims of parental violence often grow up to fight back.

Finally, family caseworkers report many situations in which an adult child physically or emotionally abuses her or his elderly parents. The stress of caring for an aging parent can be great, and abusive adult children sometimes argue that they are paying their parents back for abuse they suffered as children: "He did it to me. Now I have my chance to get even." Fortunately, many treatment programs are available to help people find positive and satisfying ways to relate to one another across the generations.

Alcohol Problems in Families

A family with a drinking problem is always a family in trouble.
　　　—Marcia Lasswell and Thomas Lasswell (1991, p. 256)

Alcohol is a drug that acts as a depressant to the central nervous system. It is the mood-altering ingredient in wine, beer, and hard liquor. Alcohol is absorbed into the bloodstream and travels to virtually every part of the body. When ingested in large amounts or over a long period of time, alcohol can kill. It can damage the liver, heart, and pancreas; other consequences include malnutrition, stomach irritation, lowered resistance to disease, and irreversible brain or nervous system damage (National Council on Alcoholism, 1989). **Alcohol abuse** is a generic term that encompasses both **alcoholism,** addiction to alcohol characterized by compulsive drinking, and **problem drinking,** alcohol consumption that results in a functional disability.

An estimated 12 million men, women, and children suffer from alcoholism in the United States; 16 to 19 million adults are problem drinkers. About 100,000 people die prematurely each year as a result of alcohol misuse (National Council on Alcoholism, 1989). Alcohol use is the leading cause of death in people between the ages of 16 and 24. Alcohol is a factor in almost half the murders, suicides, and accidental deaths in this country. Drunk drivers are involved in half of all fatal motor vehicle crashes, and 65 of every 100 people in the United States will be involved in an alcohol-related motor vehicle crash sometime in their life (R. H. Lauer, 1989; Lord, 1987; Taylor, 1988). To see if you have a problem with alcohol, review the warning signs in Box 16.2.

Alcohol as a "Cause" of Family Violence

A federal survey by the National Center for Health Statistics found that 4 in 10 adult Americans have been exposed to alcoholism in their families ("Alcohol Impacts," 1991). Alcohol is commonly associated with marital disruption, domestic violence, and many other family problems (Roosa, Tein, Groppenbacher, Michaels, & Dumka, 1993). Countless thousands of children are born each year with fetal alcohol syndrome—a constellation of birth defects, including mental deficiencies and low birthweight—which has been associated with heavy drinking during pregnancy.

Alcohol abuse is far more common among men than among women, although alcohol abuse by women is growing. Most literature has focused on the husband as the alcohol abuser and the wife and children as victims, but statistics show that alcohol-dependence problems among wives is on the rise.

Alcohol abuse and family violence are statistically related. A national sample of more than 2,000 couples found in general that the more often a spouse was drunk, the greater likelihood there was of physical violence in the marital relationship. The exception to this finding was when the alcohol abuse was extreme. In this case, when the spouse was "almost always" drunk, the level of physical violence dropped to a lower level (Straus, 1990).

Abused wives often see drinking as the "cause" of their husband's violent behavior. Richard Gelles concluded that "most of the wives subscribe to the 'conventional wisdom' that alcohol affects people in such a way as to release pent-up violence. The wives feel that if their husbands did not drink, they would not become violent" (Gelles, 1972, p. 113). Husbands involved in violent incidents in which alcohol played a part often concurred that drinking was the problem. "He would say, 'Look, this isn't me. It's the drink that is making me act this way'" (Dobash & Dobash, 1979, p. 118). A study of convicted child molesters found that those men who had been drinking at the time of the crime said that the drinking caused the offense: "I was intoxicated and I couldn't account for myself." "If I were sober, it never would have happened." "Drinking is the reason" (McCaghy, 1968,

BOX 16.2

Warning Signs for Alcohol Abuse

Following are some common warning signs of alcohol abuse. The more warning signs that apply, the greater the severity of the problem with alcohol use.

1. Drinking alone or secretively.

2. Using alcohol deliberately and repeatedly to perform or to get through difficult situations.

3. Feeling uncomfortable on occasions when alcohol is not available.

4. Escalating alcohol consumption beyond an already established drinking pattern.

5. Consuming alcohol heavily in risky situations (for example, before driving).

6. Getting drunk regularly or more frequently than in the past.

7. Drinking in the morning or at other unusual times.

Source: Core Concepts in Health (7th ed.—1996 Update) (p. 260) by P. M. Insel and W. T. Roth, 1996, Mountain View, CA: Mayfield. Copyright 1996 by Mayfield Publishing Company. Reprinted by permission.

p. 48). The trouble with these interpretations on the part of both the victim and the abuser, however, is that drinking is used to excuse the violent behavior and to lessen the drinker's responsibility for it, thus the perpetrator has no reason to change the violent behavior.

Even if there is no violence in the family of an alcoholic, there is likely to be a high degree of marital dissatisfaction and a large number of disagreements. Tension and verbal conflict are likely to be frequent (O'Farrell & Birchler, 1987). Researchers have estimated that half the divorces and half the juvenile arrests for delinquency in the United States occur in families with at least one alcohol-abusing member.

Spouses and children of alcohol abusers are at risk for developing serious physical and emotional problems. Although the majority of children reared in alcoholic homes are no more prone to suffer some kind of pathology, they are more likely to exhibit a variety of behavioral and emotional problems than are children from families without an alcoholic member. These problems include conduct disorders or delinquency, alcohol abuse, hyperactivity, difficulties with school work, anxiety, depression, or other health problems (West & Prinz, 1987). Box 16.3 relates a story about the results of alcohol and domestic violence.

The Family's Reaction to Alcohol Abuse

In a classic article, Joan K. Jackson (1954) was the first to describe how families attempt to live with an alcohol-abusing father. Jackson studied a sample of families of Alcoholics Anonymous members and outlined a seven-stage process. It is widely recognized today that there are many families with alcohol-abusing mothers or other members, and Jackson's insights are useful for understanding these families. These stages are also applicable to other chemical-dependence problems.

Stage 1: The family attempts to deny the problem. The problem drinker, when confronted by the sober adult about the drinking behavior, denies there is a

BOX 16.3

The Voice of a Survivor

"I'm a survivor of domestic violence; my Mom was a victim. My real father left when I was three years old. Prior to my thirteenth birthday, my Mom remarried. They were only married six months before the abuse started. He was only violent when he was drinking, and he never physically abused us three kids. He was abusing our Mom, the only person in our lives who ever loved and protected us. The abuse lasted less than three years.

On March 26, 1958, my Mom was killed by her batterer. He was drinking that Easter Sunday and insisted Mom accompany him for a car ride (she knew better than to refuse). They left the house around 4 p.m. This was to be the last time any of Mom's children saw her alive. My Mom was declared a fatality in a car accident, but that is not the real cause of Mom's death. My Mom died a victim of domestic violence.

Sixteen years after my Mom's death, through counseling, I was encouraged to go back and settle the destruction my Mom's death caused. To forgive my Mom was easy, probably the easiest thing I have ever done. But to forgive the abuser was altogether a different matter. My Mom never got out of the violence, but I did, and I've put the past in its proper place. I work with victims of violence, in the hope that victims become survivors. I sense my Mom agrees."

Source: Adapted from "Voices of Survivors," 1990, *Nebraska Domestic Violence Sexual Assault Coalition* (Spring), p. 6.

problem. The family accepts this statement and tolerates or rationalizes the abuser's drinking episodes.

Stage 2: The family tries to eliminate the problem. When the drinking can no longer be ignored, the sober spouse tries to control the problem drinker with threats, bribes, and/or by hiding the alcohol. Marital conflict increases, and family members isolate themselves from friends and neighbors in a futile effort to conceal the drinker's problem.

Stage 3: The family becomes disorganized. The sober spouse realizes that the problem cannot be rationalized away or concealed from the children or the drinker's employer and co-workers. The sober spouse also recognizes that it is futile to try to curtail the drinker's alcohol consumption. Conflict increases, with the children often caught between arguing parents.

Stage 4: The family makes a first attempt at reorganization. The sober spouse recognizes that the drinker cannot function adequately in the family—a recognition often precipitated by the drinker's mismanagement of family funds or by the drinker's violence toward the sober spouse or the children—and takes action. The sober spouse may assume the alcohol abuser's role in the family or may decide to leave the alcohol abuser. The sober spouse may seek assistance from various public agencies, counselors, and self-help groups such as Al-Anon. This network of support helps the sober partner gradually regain self-esteem and find the strength to go on. During this stage, the problem drinker is likely to bargain with the family, hoping to regain the lost family role and stature. If the family accepts the drinker's bargain but the drinker continues or resumes drinking, the destructive cycle begins again.

Stage 5: The family attempts to escape the problem. The sober spouse seeks a legal separation or divorce. The alcohol abuser often gives up drinking for a while, but the sober spouse has already shifted from inaction to action.

Stage 6: The family makes a second attempt at reorganization. After legal separation or divorce, the sober spouse assumes the roles formerly held by the problem drinker, and family life without the problem drinker is generally much better for all family members. The sober spouse may feel guilty for having left the troubled partner. The problem drinker may attempt to reenter the family or may try to "get even" with the family.

Stage 7: The family reorganizes, with the substance abuser seeking help. If the alcohol-abusing member seeks help and learns to control the drinking, the family may be able to reunite successfully. The process can be difficult; family roles will have to be reassigned once again, and family members will need to reassess their feelings toward the alcohol abuser.

Later researchers built on Jackson's work and outlined a number of coping strategies women commonly use when dealing with alcohol-abusing husbands. These include emotional withdrawal from the marriage; infantilizing the husband; threatening separation or divorce or locking the spouse out of the house; trying to avoid family conflict; assuming control over family finances; and acting out themselves by drinking, threatening suicide, or becoming involved with other men.

Treatment and Prevention of Alcoholism

In a classic model for treating alcoholism, Johnson (1973) outlined a five-stage process. First, alcoholics need to be confronted about their condition by people they trust and in a form they can receive. Even in the most advanced cases, alcoholics can recognize and accept some reality. Second, when the alcoholic has indicated a willingness to receive treatment, a carefully phased detoxification is begun. Medical treatment is necessary to deal with the acute symptoms. Third, it is essential to educate the alcoholic about the facts of alcoholism. Fourth, in individual and group therapy the alcoholic learns to identify defense mechanisms and break them down. The person gains a realistic insight into who he or she has become and begins to rebuild feelings of self-worth. Fifth, professionals and volunteer lay therapists help the alcoholic become established in the community again by helping the individual find a job, repair strained or broken family and personal relationships, and gain society's acceptance.

Self-help groups such as **Alcoholics Anonymous (AA)** (for alcoholics) and **Al-Anon** (for families of alcoholics) have chapters in most U.S. cities and towns. In some metropolitan areas, many different AA meetings are held at a variety of locations each week. These groups offer advice and support for troubled individuals and families. **Alateen,** founded on the AA model, is a support group for young people with alcoholic parents. In weekly meetings, members discuss their problems and learn from others in similar situations.

Some family therapists have been critical of programs that treat the alcoholic outside the context of the family, whereas some alcoholism treatment therapists have criticized family therapists for assuming that alcoholism can be cured simply by eliminating dysfunctional family patterns (Fenell & Weinhold, 1989). It is probably safe to say that problems in families can contribute to alcohol abuse in individual members and that the alcohol abuse then contributes to problems for that family. Those who work with alcohol abusers are becoming increasingly aware that family therapy is an important tool in the treatment of alcoholics and their family system (O'Farrell, 1992).

Alcoholics need to be confronted about their condition by people they trust and in a form they can receive. Even in the most advanced phases, alcoholics can recognize and accept some reality.

The National Council on Alcoholism and Drug Dependence (NCADD, 1995) in New York City argues that the disease can be stopped, citing the fact that 1.5 million Americans are in recovery. Some of NCADD's recommendations for people dealing with an alcoholic follow:

- *Recognize that alcoholism is a disease.* It is not a moral failure or a simple lack of willpower.

- *Learn as much as possible about alcoholism.* Most libraries have many books and articles on alcoholism and other addictions.

- *Do not become an enabler.* Do not support someone's drinking by pretending there is no problem (denial) or by protecting or lying for the alcoholic.

- *Avoid home treatments.* Do not try to solve the loved one's problem by preaching, complaining, acting like a martyr, or trying to reason with the drinker. Alcoholics need expert help from organizations such as Alcoholics Anonymous.

- *Get help for yourself.* The illness of alcoholism affects everyone close to the alcoholic. Many organizations help not only the alcoholic but family members and friends as well.

Acknowledging the Dangers of Legal Drugs

Our national fervor to stamp out addiction to illegal drugs has overshadowed the serious harm legal drugs cause in our society. Alcohol and tobacco cause many times the number of deaths attributable to illegal drugs—and the associated costs, in terms of lost time from work and medical bills, are much greater. NCADD (1995) estimates that about 180,000 to 200,000 Americans die each year from alcohol abuse (including alcohol-related medical problems, motor vehicle crashes, homicides, suicides, and other unintentional injuries).

Elizabeth Whelan, president of the American Council on Science and Health, reports that 500,000 smoking and nonsmoking Americans die each year from diseases related to legal cigarette smoking, as compared to an estimated 30,000 who die from illegal drugs (Whelan, 1995). Environmental tobacco smoke is one of the most widespread and harmful indoor air pollutants, according to the U.S. Environmental Protection Agency (Schepers, 1991). An estimated 30,000 to 53,000 nonsmoking Americans die each year from breathing other people's smoke (B. C. Coleman, 1995). And chewing tobacco and snuff, especially popular among adolescent males, have been linked to mouth cancer and throat cancer (Newman, 1990).

Medically, alcohol and cigarette addictions are the most difficult habits to break, according to Dr. William Brostoff. It is easier to withdraw or undergo detoxification from cocaine or even heroin than from alcohol or cigarettes ("Nation's Legal Drugs," 1986). It has been found that actively involving the spouse in the smoking cessation program increases the program's success (Doherty & Whitehead, 1986).

Almost all adult smokers begin to smoke before age 20, researchers have found. Recent studies indicate that family functioning is related to adolescent cigarette smoking. For example, William J. Doherty and William Allen (1994) found that families who were low in family cohesion (togetherness) and had a parent who smoked were the most likely to have a young adolescent who smoked. Similarly, Janet N. Melby and her colleagues found that harsh and inconsistent parenting was related to adolescent tobacco use and that nurturant and involved parenting was not (Melby, Conger, Conger, & Lorenz, 1993).

The family clearly is a major influence in our lives, either as a foundation for health and happiness or as an unhappy battleground. Emotional, physical, and sexual abuse does occur in families, and many families are plagued by alcoholism and addiction to other legal and illegal drugs. But these problems can be treated effectively. Fortunately, most families find ways to create relatively supportive and satisfying relationships among their members, which helps prevent family problems of all sorts.

Summary

- Statistics indicate that the average length for first marriages that end in divorce is 7 years. But marriage is so popular that about 75% of younger divorced individuals are likely to remarry—three out of four divorced women and five out of six divorced men.

- In the late 1960s, the U.S. divorce rate began to climb, leveling off from the late 1980s to the late 1990s. Some explanations for the increase include the effect of no-fault divorce laws, the women's liberation movement, economic conditions, the higher level of educational attainment among women, and increasingly tolerant attitudes toward divorce.

- No-fault divorce laws eliminated (1) fault as grounds for divorce, (2) gender-based division of responsibilities, (3) the adversarial nature of divorce, and (4) linkage of the financial settlement to the determination of fault. Some argue, however, that no-fault's principle of equity between the sexes penalizes women financially in divorce.

- The most prominent problems reported by couples seeking marital therapy are poor communication, power struggles, unrealistic expectations about marriage, sexual-relationship problems, and difficulties in decision making. For marital therapists, the most difficult problems to treat are lack of loving feelings, alcoholism, and extramarital affairs.

- Research on the effects of marital discord and divorce on children suggests that divorce is a crisis in the lives of most children who experience it. In addition to sadness and regret, many children experience anger at their parents and at themselves.

- Divorce has a broad, long-term negative impact on most aspects of a child's well-being. Research shows that children of divorce have higher rates of cohabitation and more unstable marriages than do children from stable marriages.

- A surprising research finding suggests that low-conflict marriages that end in divorce have a more negative impact on children than do high-conflict marriages that end in divorce.

- Bohannan identified six different but overlapping "stations" of the divorce process: emotional divorce, legal divorce, economic divorce, coparental divorce, community divorce, and psychological divorce.

- The duration and experience of the entire process of divorce varies with each individual. It appears, however, that when people can talk openly about divorce and accept it as an important part of their life, they can move on as happy single individuals.

- According to the family systems theory, family members' behaviors are all interrelated; each member's actions affects the other members and their actions. As such, the family systems approach focuses on helping families resolve issues rather than on identifying "causes" of family problems.

- Child abuse encompasses not only physical assault resulting in injury but also abandonment, neglect, emotional abuse, and sexual abuse. More than 1 million American children are abused each year. Abuse and neglect occur across all socioeconomic levels, although they are far more prevalent among low-income families.

- Children exhibit two extreme behavioral adaptations to abuse: aggressive, acting-out behavior or passive acceptance. Many abusive parents were themselves abused as children, but only about one quarter to one third of all children who are abused grow up to abuse their own offspring.

- Parental and family risk factors for child abuse include economic distress, inadequate parenting skills, parental personality problems, chemical abuse, social isolation, a special child, family size, domestic violence in the abuser's family of origin, a violent subculture or marriage, and single parenthood or stepparenthood.

- Treatment of child abusers involves three strategies: increasing the parent's self-esteem, educating the parent about children and childrearing techniques, and helping the parent develop a support network.

- Sexual abuse of children is categorized as intrafamilial (incestuous) or extrafamilial (nonincestuous). Incestuous abuse is the sexual exploitation of a child under the age of 18 by a relative. Child sexual abuse is seen in chaotic-style families (those with multiple problems over many generations) and in normal-appearing families (especially those in which roles are traditionally structured but parental nurturing skills are lacking).

- The effects of sexual abuse on the victim include difficulties in school, guilt or shame, anger, lowered self-esteem, depression, sleep and eating disorders, self-destructive thoughts and behaviors, increased vulnerability to rape or marital violence as an adult, and sexual difficulties. Support groups can help incest survivors resolve the effects of sexual abuse.

- Domestic violence is the single greatest cause of injury to women. An estimated 3 million people, most of them women, are severely assaulted each year in the United States by their spouses. Most incidents are not reported.

- Many of the risk factors for spouse abuse in a family are similar to those for child abuse: victimization as a child, low self-esteem, youth, economic stress, social isolation, alcohol abuse, and a male-dominated relationship. Cultural factors that implicitly support the objectification and denigration of women may also play a part.

- Counselors generally advise battered women to leave their husbands. Shelters for abused women and their children offer emotional support and counseling as well as practical help. Police arrest of perpetrators of domestic violence is more common today, and research indicates that men who spend time behind bars are less likely to assault their partners again.

- Sibling abuse and child-to-parent abuse are more common than might be expected. An estimated 75% of siblings are involved in a violent episode each year, and 10% of parents are victims of their children's violent behavior.

- An estimated 12 million men, women, and children in this country are alcoholics and 16 to 19 million adults are problem drinkers. Alcohol abuse and family violence or marital discord are related. It is estimated that half of the divorces and half of the juvenile arrests for delinquency in the United States occur in families with an alcohol-abusing member.

- In dealing with an alcohol-abusing member, families commonly go through seven stages. The family (1) attempts to deny the problem; (2) attempts to eliminate the problem; (3) becomes disorganized; (4) makes a first attempt at reorganization, when the sober spouse takes action; (5) attempts to escape the problem through separation or divorce; (6) makes a second attempt at reorganization; and (7) reorganizes, with the alcohol-abusing member seeking help.

- Successful treatment for chronic alcoholism involves five stages: (1) confrontation by trusted people in a form the alcoholic can receive; (2) detoxification under medical supervision; (3) education about the facts of the disease; (4) individual and group therapy to help the alcoholic identify and break down defense mechanisms; and (5) reestablishment in the family and community.

- Legal drugs cause more deaths than illegal ones. An estimated 180,000 to 200,000 Americans die each year from alcohol abuse, and about 500,000 Americans die from diseases linked to smoking. The highest estimate of deaths attributable to illegal drugs is 30,000 per year.

Key Terms

no-fault divorce	schizophrenia	learned helplessness theory
alimony	anxiety disorder	catharsis conflict
uncontested divorce	codependent	sibling abuse
tender years doctrine	enabler	child-to-parent abuse
divorce culture	child abuse	alcohol abuse
emotional divorce	incest	alcoholism
legal divorce	incestuous abuse	problem drinking
economic divorce	chaotic-style family	Alcoholics Anonymous (AA)
coparental divorce	normal-appearing family	Al-Anon
community divorce	posttraumatic stress disorder (PTSD)	Alateen
psychological divorce	victimizer	
feminization of poverty		

Activities

1. Interview someone who is divorced. Ask them to recount their experiences throughout the entire divorce process. Use Bohannan's six stations of divorce as a guide for your questions. Compare and contrast the results of your interview with others' in a small-group discussion.

2. Interview a young adult whose parents have gone through a divorce. Discuss your observations from the interview with others in a small group.

3. Describe in one or two paragraphs the most violent incident you have witnessed in your family. Note who was involved, what the dispute was about, and what happened. Read and discuss your description with a small group. How do you plan to avoid such violence in your family in the future?

4. Conduct a class survey, focusing on class members' perceptions of alcohol-related and other drug-related problems in their families. If appropriate, discuss the relationship of these problems to any violence that has occurred in their families.

5. In small groups, discuss the extent of alcohol and other drug abuse on campus. Also discuss any violent incidents, such as date rape, related to chemical abuse.

Suggested Readings

Ahrons, C. (1994). *The good divorce: Raising your family together when your marriage comes apart.* New York: Harper-Collins.

Ardell, T. (1995). *Men and divorce.* Thousand Oaks, CA: Sage.

Jacob, T. (1993). Family studies of alcoholism. *Journal of Family Psychology, 5* (March/June), 319–338. A useful review of research on the family and alcohol addiction.

Kaplan, L., & Girard, J. L. (1994). *Strengthening high-risk families: A handbook for practitioners.* New York: Lexington Books. Offers guidance for those interested in becoming part of the revolution in social services, focusing on home-based family treatment.

Kayser, K. (1993). *When love dies: The process of marital disaffection.* New York: Guilford. An interesting book with broad appeal.

Kirschner, S., Kirschner, D. A., & Rappaport, R. L. (1993). *Working with adult incest survivors: The healing journey.* New York: Brunner/Mazel. An integrated procedure for treating adults who have experienced abuse.

O'Farrell, T. J. (Ed.). (1993). *Treating alcohol problems: Marital and family interventions.* New York: Guilford. A systematic description and evaluation of family therapy techniques for each stage of alcoholism.

Parkman, A. M. (1992). *No-fault divorce: What went wrong?* Boulder, CO: Westview Press. Examines the financial consequences of no-fault divorce from an economist's perspective and proposes legal reforms to make divorces economically efficient and fair, as well as easier to obtain than before no-fault divorce laws were passed.

Simons, R. (1996). *Understanding differences between divorced and intact families.* Thousand Oaks, CA: Sage.

Stevenson, M. R., & Black, K. N. (1995). *How divorce affects offspring: A research approach.* Madison, WI: Brown and Benchmark. A review of the research literature.

Teyber, E. (1992). *Helping children cope with divorce.* New York: Lexington Books/Macmillan. Wisdom from a counselor with extensive experience.

Theroux, P. (1996). *My other life: A novel.* Boston: Houghton Mifflin.

Wallerstein, J. S., & Blakeslee, S. (1989). *Second chances: Men, women and children a decade after divorce.* New York: Ticknor & Fields. Insights from researchers who have been studying divorce for two decades.

Whisman, M. A., Dixon, A. E., & Johnson, B. (1998). Therapists' perspectives of couple problems and treatment issues in couple therapy. *Journal of Family Psychology, 11* (3), 361–366.

Wurtele, S. K., & Miller-Perrin, C. L. (Eds.). (1992). *Preventing child sexual abuse: Sharing the responsibility.* Lincoln: University of Nebraska Press. An excellent book for anyone interested in starting or improving a prevention program or simply wanting to learn more.

CHAPTER 17

Single-Parent Families and Stepfamilies

M ost divorces today involve children. Divorced single parents must deal with challenges that include loneliness and isolation, financial problems, and work overload. Despite these challenges, however, many divorced single parents develop healthy and functional families. Meanwhile, the noncustodial parent must also work to establish a new identity and to maintain a relationship with the children he or she has "lost" in the divorce.

Eventually, most divorced parents begin looking for a new mate, but they are generally much more skeptical about marriage than they were "the first time around." Even more difficult than finding a new partner is finding one who also cares about the children, and vice versa. Single parents who marry again then face the challenge of developing a stepfamily system that works.

In this chapter we will look at how people with children "pick up the pieces" after divorce and establish new family systems. We will compare these family systems with the nuclear family and also explore the stresses and strengths of both single-parent families and stepfamilies.

The Changing Picture of the Family

Some observers have suggested that single-parent families—also called one-parent, lone-parent, and solo-parent families—are problem families, but this generalization is inaccurate. Indeed, many divorced single parents do an excellent job of raising children who thrive at home and at school. So do many stepfamilies. This is not to say that single-parent families and stepfamilies are problem-free. Single-parent families and stepfamilies face many of the same challenges that other families face, yet they must also cope with additional, unique challenges.

The Increase in Single-Parent Families

Nearly one third of all American families were headed by a single parent in 1996; the number has increased rapidly over the past two decades. The proportion of single-parent families was about 11% in 1970 and rose to 20% in 1980. By 1990, the number had increased to 28%, and it reached 32% in 1996 (U.S. Bureau of the Census, 1997).

By far the majority of single-parent households are headed by females. There were almost 10 million single mothers heading households in 1996, compared with 1.8 million single fathers. Single fathers were twice as common in White families as in Black families.

Over the past several years, the number of single-parent households headed by females has increased most dramatically for families of color (Figure 17.1). In 1996, 26% of Caucasian households were headed by a single female parent; the rate was 37% for Mexican American households and 64% for African American households.

The rapid increase in the divorce rate since the late 1960s is seen by some observers as an accentuation of a long-term upward trend. The rate of remarriage went up during the 1960s but then declined steeply until the late 1970s, when it moderated. As noted in Chapter 16, an estimated 75% of younger men and women who divorce will eventually marry again (Glick & Lin, 1986). About two thirds of recent second or subsequent marriages were preceded by cohabitation (Bumpass & Sweet, 1989).

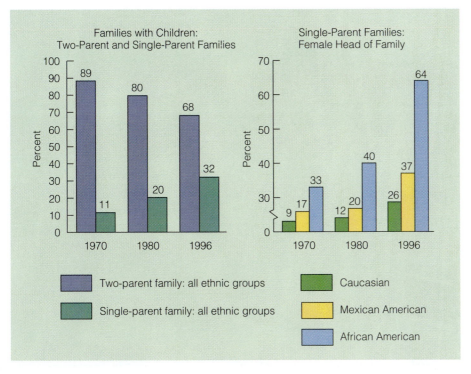

Figure 17.1 The Family in Transition. *Source:* U.S. Bureau of the Census (1997, p. 56).

On the average, first marriages that end in divorce last about 7 years. Those who marry a second time do so on the average in 2 to 3 years. Many second marriages also end in divorce, usually within 4 to 5 years. There are only minor differences among Caucasian, Mexican American, and African American families in these three sets of statistics (Norton & Mooran, 1987).

Authorities on marriage and divorce statistics on the national level believe that divorce rates and rates for subsequent marriages have probably peaked but are likely to remain high in the future (Glick & Lin, 1986; Norton & Mooran, 1987). Some people will marry only once, but the majority will divorce and marry again (Glick & Lin, 1986). It seems that these trends are the by-products of modern life.

Family Terminology

The changing nature of the family in our society has given rise to new terminology, which we will discuss and define in this section.

Binuclear Families Versus Single-Parent Families Constance Ahrons and Morton Perlmutter prefer the term *binuclear family* to *single-parent family* because it acknowledges the positive outcome that frequently results from divorce. Divorce is "a process that results in family reorganization rather than disintegration" (1982, p. 35). This reorganization of the nuclear family after divorce frequently results in the establishment of two households, the mother's and the father's. If one ex-spouse does not drop out of the family after the divorce and the two households continue to interrelate, then a **binuclear family** has been established.

In some binuclear families, children have a primary and a secondary home: One parent has **sole custody,** and the children live with that parent in the

After divorce, many families are not really single-parent families but binuclear families. Children whose parents have joint custody have two homes and usually move freely between the two. Binuclear families resulting from an amicable divorce may even come together for holidays and other celebrations.

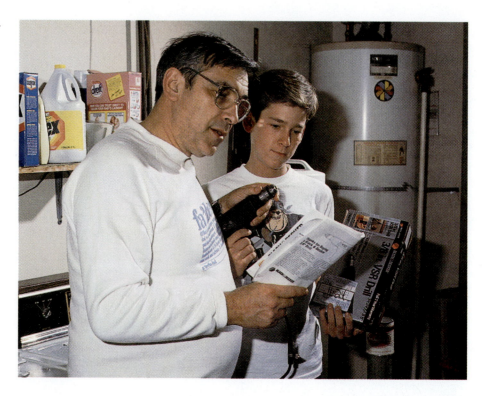

primary home; the other parent in the secondary home has rights of visitation with the children. In a smaller proportion of families, the homes of both divorced parents have equal importance—"one child, two homes." This arrangement has been termed **joint custody.** In an even smaller proportion of families, one parent has sole custody of one or more of the children, and the other parent has sole custody of the other child or children—an arrangement called **split custody** (DeFrain et al., 1987; Kaplan, Ade-Ridder, & Hennon, 1992; Kaplan, Hennon, & Ade-Ridder, 1993).

In binuclear families, relationships between the two households can vary greatly. Some ex-spouses continue the predivorce wars into the postdivorce years, whereas others get along wonderfully. A few binuclear families even share some holidays. The majority, however, rarely get together as a group. Ahrons and Roy Rodgers (Ahrons, 1994; Ahrons & Rodgers, 1987) have identified four types of relationships in binuclear families: *perfect pals, cooperative colleagues, angry associates,* and *fiery foes;* they also use the term *dissolved duo* to describe a relationship that is completely over.

Marriage Versus Remarriage A few words need to be said at this point about the term **remarriage.** The dictionary definition includes both marrying the same person again (a rare occurrence) and marrying a second (or subsequent) time after the death of or divorce from the first partner. In this text, *remarriage* refers exclusively to two spouses who have never been married to each other before.

Blended Families, Stepfamilies, and Reconstituted Families Emily Visher and John Visher (1992, 1996), well known for their research on stepfamilies, ob-

Many people who re-marry have children from a previous marriage, and the resulting combination can be a large stepfamily with complex dynamics. The children must estab-lish relationships with their stepparent and their stepsiblings, and the adults must learn new roles as stepparents.

ject to the term **blended family** for a variety of reasons. First and foremost, the label fosters unrealistic expectations that the new family will quickly and easily blend together into a harmonious family. Second, the term assumes a homoge-neous unit without a previous history or background. On the other hand, the terms **stepfamily** and **stepparent** have suffered from a number of stereotypes, often bringing to mind fairy-tale visions of "wicked stepmothers." In fact, most step-parent-stepchild relationships function relatively well. Other professionals prefer the term **reconstituted family** to *stepfamily* or *blended family*.

Growing Family Complexity

The joining together of two families in a second or subsequent marriage adds con-siderable complexity to a family system. A child of divorced parents who both re-marry will have two stepparents; a range of possible combinations of biological siblings, stepsiblings, and half-siblings; up to eight grandparents; and numerous extended relatives (aunts, uncles, cousins, etc.). Figure 17.2 illustrates one exam-ple of a binuclear family, with a child in the center. This figure is relatively com-plicated, and yet it shows only the relationships between the child and his or her parents, stepparents, stepsiblings, and half-siblings. If the child's relationships with the rest of the family—siblings, grandparents, and other relatives in the extended family—were added, the figure would become even more complicated. Of course, complexity in a family system is neither good nor bad in itself. Some binuclear families of enormous complexity function quite well. As one 7-year-old girl said, "I love my new family. I now have a whole lot more grandpas and grandmas, and they all give me presents!"

Figure 17.2 Sample Model of a Binuclear Family. *Source: Divorced Families: A Multidisciplinary View* (p. 155) by C. Ahrons and R. Rodgers, 1987, New York: Norton. Copyright 1987 Constance R. Ahrons and Roy H. Rodgers. Reprinted by permission of W. W. Norton and Company.

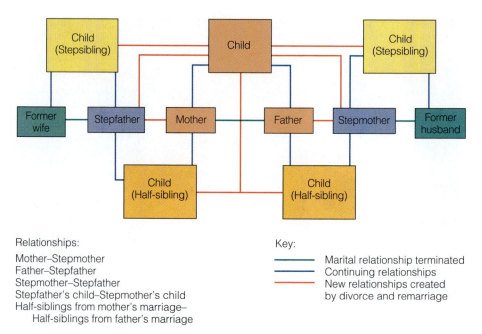

Relationships:
Mother–Stepmother
Father–Stepfather
Stepmother–Stepfather
Stepfather's child–Stepmother's child
Half-siblings from mother's marriage–
    Half-siblings from father's marriage

Key:
⎯⎯⎯ Marital relationship terminated
⎯⎯⎯ Continuing relationships
⎯⎯⎯ New relationships created
    by divorce and remarriage

As important new people are added to a family system, the number of potentially positive and negative human relationships increases geometrically. Take, for example, a man from a relatively small family who married a woman with a huge extended family. The fellow's mother-in-law has nine brothers and sisters and countless nieces and nephews. His father-in-law has four brothers and sisters, and these folks also have a massive number of progeny. "I have to have a program in hand when I go to a family picnic," the fellow chuckles. "Sometimes there will be more than 200 people at these gatherings. It's almost like going to a soccer game. They should all wear jerseys with numbers."

Differences Between Nuclear Families and Stepfamilies

Many stepfamilies falsely assume that they are like nuclear families. Table 17.1 highlights some of the salient differences between nuclear families and stepfamilies. First of all, there are usually two biological parents in a nuclear family, and the children are clearer about their biological heritage. In a stepfamily, one parent is not a biological parent, which can increase children's feelings of attachment to their biological parent. In a nuclear family the parents' marriage is ongoing and may have lasted many years, but in a stepfamily, one marriage partner has changed. The new couple have to balance their investment in the new marriage with the handling of parenting and stepparenting issues.

The bonds that children feel with their parents and vice versa are often stronger in nuclear families than in stepfamilies. There are often loyalty issues in stepfamilies, with children, particularly adolescents, feeling greater loyalty to their biological parents than to the stepparent. Many stepfamilies struggle with complex and sometimes conflictual dynamics. Issues regarding grandparents and step-grandparents add to the complexity. There can also be struggles between stepsib-

Table 17.1 Differences Between Nuclear Families and Stepfamilies

CHARACTERISTIC	NUCLEAR FAMILY	STEPFAMILY
Role as parent	Two parents Marital dyad are parents May be single parents	Two adults; one is a parent Marital dyad plus previous partner(s) are parents
Biological relationship	Biological family Biological relationship between both parents and children and between siblings Physical similarity often present	Nonbiological family Biological relationship between one parent and children Children of both parents might be included in family Lower level of physical similarity
Marriage history	Ongoing marriage Often first marriage Parents influence marriage	New marriage partner One or both previously married Parents and previous partner(s) influence marriage
Balancing marriage and parenting	Marriage came before child(ren) Maintaining marriage is goal Parenting often given priority over marriage	Marriage came after child(ren) Developing marriage is goal Marriage often given priority over parenting
Bonding	Bond is primarily to nuclear family and both parents Family rituals and celebrations increase bonding Extended families can support bonding	Bond often greater to one parent Stepparent bond takes time to develop Rituals must be developed and may create conflicts Extended families can create issues and decrease bonding
Loyalty issues	Roots are stable General sense of loyalty and belonging Loyalty to both parents more common	Roots are disrupted; can be rebuilt Loyalty and belonging more difficult to develop Initial loyalty to one parent is common
Parenting issues	Roles and responsibilities tend to develop gradually Child(ren) can play two parents off each other Parenting roles can be shared and can be conflictual Power hierarchy clear among siblings	Roles and responsibilities disrupted and often must be redefined Child(ren) can play two parents plus stepparents off against each other Parent and stepparent roles often create conflict Grandparents' and stepgrandparents' roles are unclear Power struggles to develop hierarchy among siblings and stepchildren
Financial issues	Parental income to own children No financial support expected from others Financial demands more predictable	Parents' and stepparents' income to own and/or stepchildren Child support payments can create issues More financial demands from new marriage and new family

Source: Adapted from *Treating the Remarried Family* (pp. 23–27), by C. J. Sager, H. S. Brown, H. Crohn, T. Engel, E. Rodstein, and L. Walker, 1983, New York: Brunner/Mazel. Copyright 1983 by Brunner/Mazel. Reprinted by permission of Taylor and Francis Inc.

Figure 17.3 Family Cohesion, Flexibility, and Communication in Nuclear Families and Stepfamilies. *Source:* Based on data from "Problem Areas in Stepfamilies: Cohesion, Adaptability, and the Step-father-Adolescent Relationship" by J. E. T. Pink and K. S. Wampler, 1985, *Family Relations, 34,* p. 331. Copyright 1985 by National Council on Family Relations.

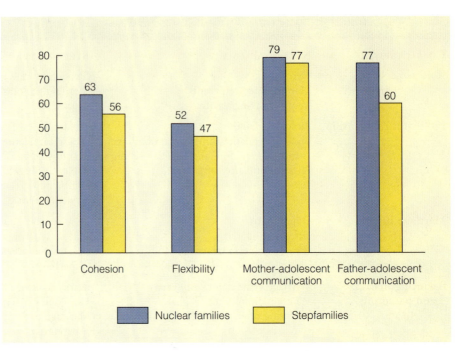

lings when both spouses bring children to the new family. Financial issues can also be complex. When both parents in a stepfamily have children, the financial resources available for child support payments and for meeting the financial demands of all the children can be limited.

One study compared 24 stepfamilies and 24 first-marriage families on the three dimensions of family cohesion, flexibility, and communication from the Couple and Family Map (Pink & Wampler, 1985). To measure cohesion and flexibility, data were collected using FACES (an acronym for Family Adaptability and Cohesion Evaluation Scales; Olson, Portner, & Bell, 1986). To assess family communication, data were collected using the Parent-Adolescent Communication Scale (Barnes & Olson, 1986). In each stepfamily, the mother, the stepfather, and one or more adolescents completed the questionnaires; in each first-marriage family, the two parents and the adolescents completed the questionnaires.

All stepfamily members indicated lower family cohesion and lower flexibility than did the members of first-marriage families (Figure 17.3). There was also poorer father-adolescent communication in the stepfamilies than in the first-marriage families as rated by the fathers from the two types of families. No differences were found, however, in the adolescents' communication ratings. There was no significant difference in mother-adolescent communication between the stepfamilies and the first-marriage families. The reason could be, in part, that the mother was almost always the biological parent in both types of families, whereas that was not the case with the fathers.

Family dynamics in stepfamilies are still unclear to researchers, however. Another team of investigators wanted to test the hypothesis that marital conflict is more frequent in stepfamilies than in biological families. They looked at nationally representative data on 2,655 Black and White married couples with children and compared the frequency of marital conflict. The researchers found, contrary to their expectations, that remarriage and stepchildren are not necessarily associated with more frequent marital conflict and that in some cases, they are associated with less frequent conflict (MacDonald & DeMaris, 1995). More research comparing the two family types is probably necessary, but some observers are skeptical of its usefulness, arguing that the comparison is like one between apples and oranges (K. Pasley, 1995, personal communication).

Single-Parent Families

Single-parent households, headed either by a mother or a father, are continuing to increase; they now constitute 32% of all households nationwide. In 1970, there were 2.9 million single-parent households headed by mothers in the United States; in 1996, the number was 9.8 million. There were 340,000 single-parent households headed by fathers in 1970; in 1996, there were 1.8 million (U.S. Bureau of the Census, 1997). The percentage of single-parent families headed by fathers increased from 10% of the total in 1970 to nearly 16% of the total in 1996 (U.S. Bureau of the Census, 1997).

Most of the literature on single-parent families since the 1960s has accentuated the negative (see Box 17.1). In this section, we will identify the stresses and strains unique to single parents as well as look at the positive aspects of growing up in a healthy single-parent family.

Divorced single-parent families can be put in four categories: (1) mothers with sole custody; (2) fathers with sole custody; (3) split-custody families, in which the father has sole custody of one or more children and the mother has sole custody of one or more children; and (4) joint-custody families, in which both the mother and the father share decision making. John DeFrain, Judy Fricke, and Julie Elmen analyzed these four types of single-parent families in their book *On Our Own* (1987). The authors studied 738 single parents in 45 states: 528 mothers with sole custody, 114 fathers with sole custody, 40 mothers and fathers with split custody, and 56 mothers and fathers with joint legal and physical custody. Their findings are summarized on the following pages.

Mothers With Custody

Divorced mothers who head single-parent families must cope with many stresses. Nonetheless, they also experience many joys.

Stresses One of the major problems for mothers with sole custody are limited finances, a situation often made worse by a father's failure to pay child support. In a study of 492 court records, K. D. Rettig, D. H. Christensen, and C. M. Dahl (1991) found that court-ordered awards met only 58% of the children's income needs when measured against poverty-level support. As expected, the parent with whom the children lived spent a much higher proportion of her (or his) income to support the children than did the parent with whom the children did not live. This serious problem in our country is made worse by the fact that only about half (48%) of noncustodial parents make full child support payments, 26% make partial payments, and 26% make no payments at all (Rettig et al., 1991).

Loneliness is also a common problem for most single parents. One mother commented, "The only real sorrow we feel about the arrangement [single parenthood] is that her father isn't with us to share in the daily goings on of family life."

BOX 17.1

Healthy Single-Parent Families

Since the late 1970s, researchers have become increasingly interested in the study of *successful* families and their strengths. (*Healthy*, *balanced*, *functional*, and *strong* are alternative terms researchers use to describe this type of family.) Today, although many family researchers continue to ask the question "Why do families fail?", other family researchers are focusing on the question "How do families succeed?"

Shirley M. Hanson (1986) used earlier family strengths research as a foundation for her pioneering efforts in the study of healthy single-parent families. She argues that single-parent families have gotten "bad press" from researchers over the years due to the types of families researchers have selected to study. Researchers, she noted, "have traditionally obtained their samples from clinical populations," thus focusing only on the dysfunctional aspects of some single-parent families.

Hanson, instead, recruited single parents for her study through newspaper advertisements and through appearances on radio and television talk shows. The families had to meet two criteria of health. First, family members themselves had to express the belief that

their family was healthy. Second, the descriptions members gave of their families had to reflect family strengths as identified by previous research.

Forty-two single-parent families participated in Hanson's research. Family members were interviewed in their homes and also filled out questionnaires. Hanson found that the single parents and their children exhibited fairly high levels of mental and physical health. She also noted that the mental and physical health of both parents and children was related to good communication, social support within and outside the family, socioeconomic status, religiousness, and problem-solving abilities.

Hanson's research is important because she found that "although single-parent families may experience many problems, they are not necessarily less able to manage than the other family configurations." Professionals who work with single-parent families need to know this so that they can help these families identify their strengths and accentuate the positive. This research should help counselors avoid the demoralizing trap of focusing only on problems.

The other parent is not there to kiss the child's scraped knee, to celebrate in the loss of the first tooth, or to join in the birthday parties—in short, the ups and downs of daily childrearing. "I bleed for my children when I see their loneliness in being away from Dad and former friends. I regret seeking more conversation and support from them in my own loneliness than they can give me," a mother said. Some mothers worry that the day may come when the children will no longer know their father. Some divorced mothers with custody also lament the loss of positive grandparent relationships. In many families, ties with grandparents are severed by the divorce.

For some single parents, battles with the ex-spouse continue for years. Many mothers with custody dread continued contact with the ex-partner. In the words of Ahrons and Rodgers (1987), these parents are not "perfect pals" or "cooperative colleagues" but rather "angry associates" and "fiery foes" who often square off against each other. In one mother's words, "Because their father sees them as often as he does, they're put in a heavy loyalty dilemma. Consequently, they return home feeling confused by guilt and wanting to blame or hate. This is all happening because their father is trying to get them to live with him. I will never have total peace as long as he's alive!"

Strengths   Strong single-parent families exhibit the same constellation of qualities as two-parent families exhibit: appreciation and affection for each of the family members; commitment to the family; open, honest, and straightforward

Healthy single-parent families share the same strengths that contribute to the well-being of strong two-parent families. This father genuinely enjoys spending leisure time with his children.

communication patterns; adequate amounts of time together; spiritual well-being; and the ability to cope creatively with stress and crisis. Besides facing many challenges, mothers with sole custody experience a number of specific joys, such as the freedom to make decisions about their own lives and the lives of their children without interference or harassment from hostile fathers. Also, in many families, divorce does not mean the end of meaningful relationships with grandparents. One single mother reported, "My ex-spouse's parents are extremely helpful. They take my preschool daughter some weekends, and the space is wonderful."

For some mothers with custody, the burden of almost total responsibility for the children is nearly unbearable, but others thrive on the responsibility. "The joy that is unique to being a single parent is the all-engulfing satisfaction when things are going well. You not only take all of the responsibility, but you receive all of the joy from the growth and new discovery that the child is experiencing."

Finally, some mothers with sole custody are thankful for fathers who stay involved with their children after the divorce. "The girls are always excited to see Dad. Dad is excited to see the girls. And I'm glad to be alone for a while." Former spouses sometimes remain friends, or at least neutral colleagues, in the challenge of rearing children after divorce. Their collaboration contributes to the health, happiness, and adjustment of the children. Sometimes both parents attend band concerts, Girl Scout meetings, open houses at school, and so forth.

Fathers With Custody

Family researchers have found that many fathers do a good job raising children after a divorce, just as many mothers who were formerly full-time homemakers successfully work outside the home after a divorce (Grief, 1995; Meyer & Garasky, 1993; Richards & Schmiege, 1993). For example, John DeFrain and Rod Eirick (1981) compared divorced single fathers and divorced single mothers on six major areas of adjustment to divorce: the process of divorce, the stresses of single parenthood, childrearing philosophies and behaviors, children's behaviors, relationships with the ex-spouse, and new social relationships. On most of the variables, the researchers found no significant statistical differences between the single-parent fathers and mothers. Most studies indicate that the answer to the question "Can fathers be good mothers?" is yes. It also appears that the sorrows and joys of solo parenting for fathers are very similar to those related by mothers with custody.

Stresses   Single-parent fathers often feel sorrow over the fact that the family unit has been broken up. Even though fathers see the new single-parent family as a family, it is not, in the eyes of many fathers, a complete family. "I feel sorry for my children because they don't have their mother anymore," one father said.

Many single fathers miss their ex-wives and find the loneliness nearly unbearable. Many also report that both time and money are limited. Single fathers with custody generally make more money than single mothers with custody, but time and money pressures are still common complaints among them. "I don't seem to have much time or money to do the things that I would like. It is difficult for me to meet women." Fathers often complain that they have no one with whom to share the joys of parenting. Also, many fathers report that the children miss their mother. "It is difficult when she asks, 'Why doesn't my mom call me or want to see me?'"

Strengths   But many single fathers report a considerable number of joys, such as being able to watch their children grow. "To see my son's mind develop" is a great joy. "He is quite intelligent, and his ambitions are much greater with me. The environment around his mother is extremely negative and shameful." Fathers also enjoy the love between themselves and their children. "Now there are only two in our family, and it's much harder on me but well worth it. We have more love and a stronger bond now." Having custody also means having control. Many single fathers, having been through lengthy and painful divorce and custody battles with their ex-wives, feel great relief.

For many fathers, single parenthood means getting closer to their children. One father proudly related how he had become closer to his children after adjusting his priorities in life by putting the children before his job and the housework. Fathers with custody have the opportunity to really enjoy their children in a more natural environment. "I get great pleasure from being with my son. This gives me a sense of accomplishment since I do have him and am making it work."

Although fewer men than women have sole custody of the children after a divorce, research shows that single fathers do just as good a job of childrearing as single mothers do and that they experience the same stresses of loneliness and limited time and money.

Some fathers do get along with their ex-spouse. One 54-year-old father who was caring for nine children said he was especially pleased that "my ex-wife and I get along. If there is a problem—and we do have some—I get on the phone, and we talk it out and resolve it. That's something we didn't do too well when we were married." Although the marriage is over, ex-spouses can sometimes build a solid partnership for the good of their children (Meyer & Garasky, 1993).

Split Custody

Split custody is a child custody arrangement that involves both divorced parents separately (DeFrain et al., 1987; Kaplan et al., 1992; Kaplan et al., 1993). Each parent has responsibility for at least one of their children and thus has all the stresses and strains of solo parenting.

Split custody is apparently the rarest of all parenting options after divorce, but it works quite well for many. Perhaps the most interesting question about split custody is why parents choose this arrangement. Many split-custody parents indicate that the child or children wanted it. A number of fathers said that their sons wanted to live with them, especially during adolescence.

"My oldest [14] told [my ex-wife] he'd rather live with me," related Edward, a 48-year-old contractor. "I told him it would be all right. She brought him to my house and asked me if I said he could stay. When I told her yes, she said, 'Good, you take him. I can't handle him anymore.' About 6 months later, she wanted him back, but he refused to go."

Mothers have told researchers of "losing" not only sons to their ex-husbands but daughters. Some "switching" of households may almost be inevitable after divorce; adolescents need to balance their fantasies with the realities of life in the other home with the other parent. They may find that the other home is no better than the home in which they currently live.

For many, split custody is a family decision, involving input from every family member. One parent commented, "Ever since the separation we have tried to do the right thing for the children and put aside our own differences. Therefore, the decision on custody was negotiated among the four of us, with no outsider involved."

Joint Custody

In their study of 738 families in 45 states, DeFrain and his colleagues (1987) found that no one particular custody arrangement is best for all families. Rather, each divorce is unique, and what is best for the children has to be decided on the basis of answers to numerous questions, including (1) Do the children and both parents feel it best that both parents continue contact with the children after the divorce? (2) Are both parents capable of maintaining an adequate home for the children? (3) Can the parents get along with each other well enough to manage a joint-custody arrangement after the divorce? If all members of the family can honestly answer yes to all three questions and can manage the innumerable details involved, then joint custody might be a feasible solution.

Joint-custody parents report less stress than single-custody parents. Joint-custody parents also have more time to pursue their own interests because the ex-spouse assumes a major share of the child-care responsibilities.

Studies indicate that joint-custody parents are more likely to come from a burned-out marriage; they are likely to neither love nor hate each other but are able to deal rationally with each other. Parents who fight for sole custody are more likely to dislike or hate their ex-spouse.

Coping Successfully as a Single Parent

Single parents have developed a number of successful strategies for coping with their unique station in life and offer the following suggestions for other single parents:

- Don't rush into a new relationship, particularly in an attempt to transfer your dependence onto another person. Let go of the past and move on. Realistically face what has happened. Learn from it; don't repeat it.

- Don't succumb to feelings of failure and worthlessness. Make the best of the situation, and don't blame yourself completely.

- Keep busy with constructive activities. Take up new (or old) activities you always wanted to find time to enjoy.

- Listen to others, but make your own decisions.

- Take one day at a time, setting small goals at first.

- Consider going back to school.

- Be flexible, adaptable, and independent.

Stepfamilies

Many divorced individuals with children are often cautious about entering into another marriage; many are skeptical about the institution of marriage. They tend to be more open to premarital and marital counseling because they recognize the merits of counseling as a process of learning. As one remarried man put it, "I take my car in for a tune-up every year, and I know our relationship could use some help at times."

Stages in the Formation of a Stepfamily

People go through three stages in the process of forming a new family through remarriage: (1) entering a new relationship, (2) planning the new marriage and family, and (3) remarrying and reconstituting the family (McGoldrick & Carter, 1989). These stages are summarized in Table 17.2.

Entering a New Relationship   Before beginning this stage, divorced individuals should feel that they have recovered from the loss of the first marriage. A full recovery from a crisis such as divorce can take a long time; many people marry again before they have completely recovered from their divorce. To successfully bond with the second partner, however, one must be divorced emotionally as well as legally from the first partner.

The major developmental issue during this stage of the process is a recommitment to the institution of marriage itself and to the idea of forming a new partnership and family. Before marrying again, individuals need to decide whether they want a new intimate relationship that requires closeness and personal commitment.

Planning the New Marriage and Family   In the second stage of this process, both spouses-to-be and their children must learn to accept their own fears about the new marriage and the formation of a stepfamily. This stage also requires acceptance of the fact that much time and patience are needed to adjust to the complexity and ambiguities of a new family.

One difficulty during this stage is dealing with multiple new roles: that of being a new spouse, a new stepparent, and a new member of a new extended family. The family will also need to make adjustments in terms of space, time, membership, and authority and to deal with affective issues, including feelings of guilt, loyalty conflicts, the desire for mutuality, and unresolvable past hurts. These feelings can come in a multitude of forms. For example, those planning to marry again often feel guilty because they must spend time and energy developing relationships with members of their soon-to-be family, often at the expense of time spent with the "old" family. One new stepfather acknowledged, "By spending so much time, money, and energy on my new spouse and stepchildren, I am neglecting my biological children."

During this second stage of planning the new marriage and family, a number of developmental issues or tasks must be addressed. All members of the new family need to work to build open, honest, straightforward communication patterns in order to avoid **pseudomutuality,** a false sense of togetherness. Other issues include building and planning to maintain cooperative coparenting relationships with ex-spouses, for the benefit of all parents and the children. It is also necessary to realign

Table 17.2 Stages in the Formation of a Stepfamily

STAGE	PREREQUISITE ATTITUDES	DEVELOPMENTAL ISSUES
1. Entering a new relationship	Achieving complete recovery from the loss of first marriage (adequate emotional divorce)	Recommiting to marriage and to forming a family, with a readiness to deal with the complexity and amount of effort required
2. Conceptualizing and planning the new marriage and family	Accepting one's own fears and those of the new spouse and children about remarriage and forming a stepfamily. Accepting the need for time and patience to adjust to the complexity and ambiguity of: a. Multiple new roles b. Boundaries: space, time, membership, and authority c. Affective issues: guilt, loyalty, conflicts, desire for mutuality, unresolvable past hurts	Working on openness in the new relationship to avoid pseudomutuality Planning for the maintenance of cooperative coparent relationships, with ex-spouses Planning to help the children deal with fears, loyalty conflicts, and membership in two systems Realigning relationships with the extended family to include the new spouse and children Planning the maintenance of connections for the children with the extended family of the ex-spouse(s)
3. Remarrying and reconstituting the family	Finally resolving one's attachment to the previous spouse and to the ideal of an "intact" family Accepting a different model of family with permeable boundaries	Restructuring family boundaries to allow for the inclusion of new spouse/stepparents Realigning relationships throughout subsystems to permit the interweaving of several systems Making room for relationships of all the children with biological (noncustodial) parents, grandparents, and other extended family Sharing memories and histories to enhance stepfamily integration

Source: Adapted from "Forming a Remarried Family" by B. Carter and M. McGoldrick. In *The Expanded Family Life Cycle: Individual, Family, and Social Perspectives,* Third Edition, edited by B. Carter and M. McGoldrick. Copyright © 1999 by Allyn & Bacon. Reprinted by permission.

relationships with both extended families so that there is a place for the new spouse. If family members can manage to do all these things relatively well, the remarriage will have a better chance of succeeding.

Remarrying and Reconstituting the Family   In the third stage of the process of forming a new family, the newly married partners need to strengthen their couple relationship so that they can function as coparents. Family members need to see that the new marriage is genuine and that the stepfamily that the couple has begun to build together is a good family.

There are a number of developmental issues or tasks during this third stage of the remarriage process. Family boundaries must be restructured to include the new spouse/stepparent. Relationships throughout the different subsystems of the "old" families may need to change to permit the interweaving of this new family system. In short, there must be room in the family for stepchildren, half-siblings, new sets of grandparents, and extended kin. It is also important to make room for relationships between all the children and their biological (noncustodial) parents, grandparents, and other extended family members. Sharing memories and histories from each side of the new stepfamily can enhance integration.

Guidelines for Stepfamilies

Emily Visher and John Visher developed an excellent set of helpful guidelines for both stepparents and stepfamilies. The **Stepping Ahead Program** (E. Visher, 1989), an eight-step program (described in more detail in Box 17.2), was designed to help stepfamilies avoid some common pitfalls and to get their new families off to a positive start. It involves:

1. Nurturing the couple relationship so that the new marriage will survive and thrive.

2. Finding personal space and time to relax and unwind from the challenges of a stepfamily.

3. Nourishing family relationships by spending time with each of the new family members.

4. Maintaining a close parent-child relationship.

5. Developing the stepparent-stepchild relationship.

6. Building family trust.

7. Strengthening stepfamily ties through a family discussion every week or two.

8. Working at keeping the bridges open to the children's other household so that coparenting can work smoothly.

"Blending" or "reconstituting" or "reorganizing" families with children after divorce and remarriage is very difficult. Stepparents face many challenges in dealing with the offspring of their new spouse (Ahrons, 1994; Ahrons & Rodgers, 1987; Visher & Visher, 1988, 1996). Stepparents must remember that they are taking on someone else's child and many of the childrearing responsibilities formerly held by a biological parent. Stepparents often find themselves either overidealized by their stepchildren early in the relationship or the victim of displaced hostility.

Not all members of a stepfamily are biologically related. This is an obvious enough fact and one that should, in theory, be relatively simple to deal with. But our culture considers biological family ties special. "Blood is thicker than water," the old saying goes. Biological family bonds are difficult to break. Many children of divorce keep hoping that Mom and Dad will reunite, and the new marriage of one of the parents dashes those hopes. When a stepparent enters the family, children truly know that their mother and father will never get back together. This can cause despair and bitterness toward the stepparent. The stepparent can

BOX 17.2

The Stepping Ahead Program

Step 1: Nurturing your couple relationship

Plan a weekly activity away from your household that you both enjoy doing together.

Arrange to have 20 minutes of relaxed time alone with each other every day.

Talk together about the running of your household for at least 30 minutes each week.

Step 2: Finding personal space and time

Take time to make a special "private" place for each of the adults and children in your household.

Each take 2 hours a week doing something for yourselves that you would like to do.

Step 3: Nourishing family relationships

Share with family members what you each appreciate about one another.

Step 4: Maintaining close parent-child relationships

Parent and child: Do something fun together for 15 to 20 minutes once or twice a month.

Step 5: Developing stepparent-stepchild relationships

Stepparent and stepchild: Do something fun together for 15 to 20 minutes once or twice a month.

Step 6: Building family trust

Schedule a family event once a month.

Step 7: Strengthening stepfamily ties

Hold a family discussion once every 2 weeks.

Step 8: Working with the children's other household

Give the adults in the children's other household positive feedback once a month.

Source: Adapted from "The Stepping Ahead Program" (pp. 58–89) by E. Visher. In *Stepfamilies Stepping Ahead*, edited by M. Burt, 1989, Lincoln, NE: Stepfamilies Press. Copyright 1989 by Stepfamily Association of America. Adapted by permission.

become the personification of evil in the child's mind: "If only *she* weren't around, Mom and Dad would get back together."

Even though the relationships between biological parent and child are well established, the couple in a stepfamily are newlyweds. It can be very difficult for the couple to balance marital needs and the children's needs. Family members loyalties are divided in new and complex ways when a new family member comes on the scene. If a stepparent does not recognize the stepchildren's long-standing bonds with the biological parent and move carefully, the stepparent can end up in a very difficult love triangle.

A common example is a single mother who lives alone with her children for a number of years before marrying again. The mother may have developed strong ties and a comfortable pattern of parenting with her children. If she has an adolescent son or daughter, the mother's relationship with the child may be more like that of a big sister than that of a parent. The adolescent may become very jealous of the new spouse. "She always used to want to talk to me after school. Now she spends all her time with him!"

In the case of single-parent families headed by a male, girls may develop an almost "wifelike" relationship with their father during the single-parent period, ac-

Remarried newlyweds can find it challenging to simultaneously build their relationship and to meet their children's needs. Biological parents need to forestall their children's jealousy toward the new stepparent, and stepparents must remember that their stepchildren's primary loyalty is to their biological parents.

cording to Geoffrey Grief (1995). Daughters often serve as confidante and household manager for their father, and many enjoy their new status. When the father marries again, the daughter may see the stepmother as a competitor for Dad's time and affection and an intruder on her wifelike roles.

Stepparents must avoid the tendency to try too hard; bonding takes a good deal of time. Newlyweds generally go out of their way to please each other, but the same approach taken with the stepchildren can create problems for the new stepparent. The stepparent knows that his or her new spouse's children are a major hurdle in establishing a successful marriage and feels that if she or he can only get along with the children, the chances for success in this new marriage are vastly improved. But children do not easily forsake the love of their birth parent for a stepparent. Adolescents, in particular, are often not very open to including an "outsider" in their family.

The stepparent needs to avoid the trap of trying to replace the former parent. In reality the stepparent is not so much a new parent in the family as a new adult in the family. The parent role has to develop slowly. The urge to build a solid new marriage can spur stepparents to play the "superstepmother" or "superstepfather" role, which is neither realistic nor beneficial.

Stepparents must also avoid favoritism in dealing simultaneously with their "real" children and their stepchildren. Children are not always pleasant to be around; they can at times be selfish, whiney, disobedient, and intrusive. Just as many parents have difficulty loving their own children when they are not acting lovable, so it is difficult for stepparents to love someone else's children at times. It is also important that stepparents not overcompensate for their tendency to favor their biological children by being more lenient with their stepchildren.

Stepparents also need to develop skills in dealing with complex financial realities in their new families. Although people who are marrying again are usually painfully aware of how challenging family money problems can be, few feel comfortable discussing money matters and financial planning before remarriage (Ihinger-Tallman & Pasley, 1987; Pasley & Ihinger-Tallman, 1994). Some even prefer to avoid talking about minor financial issues until they become more serious problems. Money problems are common in stepfamilies. For example, a father who remarries is sometimes in the difficult position of sending child support payments to his biological children, supporting his new family, and hoping that his new spouse's former husband will continue to provide financial support for the stepchildren.

Strengths of Stepfamilies

Research findings on stepfamilies are generally positive. In spite of the presumption that stepfamilies will fail to succeed because of the many unique challenges they face, most stepfamilies do relatively well (LeMasters & DeFrain, 1989). Research on stepfamilies (Coleman & Ganong, 1991; Ganong & Coleman, 1994) indicates that investigators have often failed to take into account the complexity of stepfamily relationships because of the number of people involved—extra parents, extra siblings, extra grandparents, extra sets of aunts and uncles, and so forth. Some stepfamily studies have also erred in using small samples of stepfamilies and nonrandom samples. Much of the data has been gathered through self-report questionnaires rather than through interviews or professional observations. And much of the data has come from only one family member, despite the fact that husbands, wives, children, and grandparents often have very different perceptions of what is going on in a family.

Coleman and Ganong (1991; Ganong & Coleman, 1994) concluded that there is little documented evidence that children in stepfamilies differ significantly from children in other family structures in terms of self-image, psychosomatic illness, or personality characteristics. Stepchildren are also comparable to children in nuclear families in regard to school grades, academic achievement scores, and IQ. Stepchildren have no more problems in the area of social behavior than children in nuclear families do. Finally, although emotional bonds between stepparents and stepchildren have been found, generally, to be less close than bonds between parents and children (Coleman & Ganong, 1991; Ganong & Coleman, 1994), most stepchildren say that they like their stepparents and get along well with them. Taking everything into account, there is no significant correlation between living in a stepfamily and problem behavior or negative attitudes in stepchildren. An increasing number of family researchers have called for a more objective approach to stepfamilies (Coleman & Ganong, 1991; Ganong & Coleman, 1994).

The goal of a study by Noel Schultz, Cynthia Schultz, and David Olson (1991) was to identify the major strengths of **simple stepfamilies,** which include children from only one parent, and compare them with those of **complex stepfamilies,** which include children from both parents. The researchers hypothesized and found that simple stepfamilies have more strengths than complex stepfamilies, reasoning that there is less complexity and conflict in simple stepfamilies than in complex stepfamilies. Figure 17.4 summarizes the data, which indicate that simple stepfamilies have more strengths than complex stepfamilies in the areas of personality issues, communication skills, ability to resolve conflict, parenting skills, and adjustment to the process of being a stepfamily.

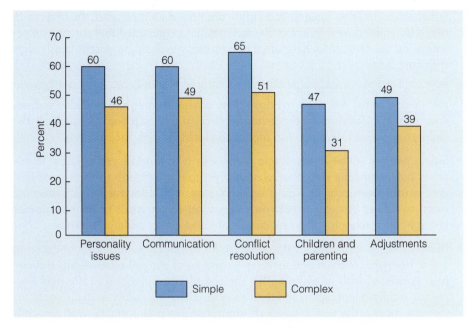

Figure 17.4 Strengths of Simple Versus Complex Stepfamilies (based on ENRICH). *Source:* Data from "Couple Strengths and Stressors in Complex and Simple Stepfamilies in Australia" by N. C. Shultz, C. L. Schultz, and D. H. Olson, 1991, *Journal of Marriage and the Family, 53,* p. 560. Copyright 1991 by the National Council on Family Relations.

One of the outcomes of the study by Schultz and his colleagues (1991) is a new premarital inventory called **PREPARE-MC** (Marriage with Children). This inventory was developed to better help couples prepare for a marriage that will create a stepfamily. PREPARE-MC contains 195 questions dealing with 14 important categories in a couple's relationship. The questions in PREPARE-MC were revised to focus specifically on issues relevant to stepfamilies. The couple inventory helps people deal with relationship issues before marriage. More people who have been married and divorced are open to preparing for a second marriage than are couples entering their first marriage.

Just because a first marriage ended in divorce does not mean a new marriage will also fail. In fact, the painful process of divorce can be a tremendous learning experience and can help provide the foundation for a successful new marriage and a strong stepfamily.

Summary

- In 1996, nearly one third of all U.S. families were headed by a single parent, most of whom were female.

- Differences between nuclear families and stepfamilies include biological parent-child ties, the nature and length of the couple's marriage, parent-child emotional bonds, loyalty issues, extended-family issues, power struggles between children, and the degree of demands on financial resources.

- There are four types of divorced single-parent families, or binuclear families: mothers with sole custody; fathers with sole custody; split-custody families (in which the father has custody of one or more children and the mother has custody of one or more children); and joint-custody families (in which mother and father share decision making and child-care responsibilities after the divorce in relatively equal time segments). Researchers have concluded that the type of relationship the ex-spouses have often determines which single-parent family style will work best.

- Divorced single parents face challenges that include loneliness and isolation, money problems, and work overload. Joys of single parenting include the freedom to make decisions without interference, the satisfaction of watching the children grow and develop, and increased closeness with the children.

- Single parents advise newly single parents to take time to get to know themselves before rushing into new relationships; to not succumb to feelings of failure, worthlessness, or self-pity; to keep busy with constructive activities; to listen to others but make their own decisions; to set small goals; to consider going back to school; and to remain flexible, adaptive, and independent.

- Many divorced individuals with children are extremely cautious about entering a new marriage. Remarriage involves letting go of the old relationship and any pain associated with it; planning for the complexities involved in the new couple and family relationship; and then reconstituting the family to make room for the new spouse, the new spouse's children, one's own children, and all the children's relationships with their biological parents and extended families.

- Stepparenting is challenging. Some of the pitfalls associated with stepparenting include trying too hard to establish a successful relationship with their stepchildren, provoking resentment or jealousy in their stepchildren, trying to replace the absent biological parent, and favoring their own children over their stepchildren.

- Steps in building a strong stepfamily include nurturing the couple, family, parent-child, and stepparent-stepchild relationships; building stepfamily trust and ties; keeping bridges open to the children's biological parents; and finding personal space and time for all family members.

- Research indicates that the majority of stepfamilies have strengths similar to those of other types of families. Stepchildren do not differ significantly from children in nuclear families in terms of self-image, academic achievement, or degree of problem social behavior.

Key Terms

binuclear family	blended family	Stepping Ahead Program
sole custody	stepfamily	
joint custody	stepparent	simple stepfamily
split custody	reconstituted family	complex stepfamily
remarriage	pseudomutuality	PREPARE-MC

Activities

1. Interview a member of a single-parent family. Ask not only about the stresses the family faces but also about the strengths in the family. How is the family dif-

ferent from a two-parent family? How is it similar? Discuss your findings with other students.

2. Interview a member of a stepfamily, focusing on both the strengths and the stresses in the family. Compare and contrast the family with a nuclear family. Share your findings with other students.

3. Review Table 17.1 and discuss the differences between a nuclear family and a stepfamily. What consequences do these differences have for the parents and the children in each type of family?

Suggested Readings

Ahrons, C. R. (1994). *The good divorce: Keeping your family together when your marriage comes apart.* New York: Harper/Collins. A useful, positive perspective on a difficult life event.

Burt, M. (Ed.). (1989). *Stepfamilies stepping ahead.* (3rd ed.). Lincoln, NE: Stepfamilies Press. A practical publication of the Stepfamily Association of America.

Clapp, G. (1992). *Divorce and new beginnings: An authoritative guide to recovery and growth, solo parenting, and stepfamilies.* New York: Wiley. Offers guidelines for navigating the difficult straits of loss, growth, and resolution.

DeFrain, J., Fricke, J., & Elmen, J. (1987). *On our own: A single parent's survival guide.* Lexington, MA: Lexington Books/Heath. How single parents survive and transcend a challenging situation; based on a study of 738 divorced mothers and fathers with sole custody, split custody, or joint custody of their children.

Folberg, J. (Ed.). (1991). *Joint custody and shared parenting* (2nd ed.). New York: Guilford Press. Positive outcomes for mothers, fathers, and children sharing parenting responsibilities after divorce.

Ganong, L., & Coleman, M. (1994). *Remarried family relationships.* Thousand Oaks, CA: Sage. Insights from researchers at the University of Missouri-Columbia who have devoted many years to furthering the understanding of stepfamilies.

Kelley, P. (1995). *Developing healthy stepfamilies: Twenty families tell their stories.* New York: Haworth. In one reviewer's words, "The most significant contribution of this book is a refreshing focus on health and strengths in stepfamilies instead of on seeing stepfamilies as an aberration of the norm."

Kissman, D., & Allen, J. A. (1993). *Single-parent families.* Newbury Park, CA: Sage. Contains current research and insights.

Pasley, K., & Ihinger-Tallman, M. (Eds). (1994). *Stepparenting: Issues in theory, research, and practice.* Westport, CT: Greenwood Press. Offers a broad selection of current and significant issues and findings.

Visher, E. B., & Visher, J. S. (1992). *How to win as a stepfamily* (2nd ed.). New York: Brunner/Mazel. Very practical advice from two pioneers in the study and understanding of stepfamilies.

Visher, E. B., & Visher, J. S. (1996). *Therapy with stepfamilies.* New York: Brunner/Mazel. The latest book by two of the foremost authorities on stepfamilies.

CHAPTER 18

Strengthening Marriages and Families

What does the future hold for you and your family? What does it hold for families across the United States? And what does it hold for families all over the world? If we extend the principles of the general systems theory, we can see that the futures of all families on earth are interconnected. The well-being of every individual and every family is intimately and inextricably linked to the well-being of others.

As emphasized throughout this book, families in this country are wonderfully diverse. The same is true for families around the world. This diversity adds zest to living. We do not all have to be the same to get along well together. In fact, by having different interests and capabilities, we offer strength to each other as individuals, family members, and citizens of our communities.

There is an apparent paradox here: As individuals and as families, we are all unique and different, yet deep down, as human beings, we are all quite similar. Our human commonalities have intrigued countless people from countless walks of life—novelists, poets, sociologists, anthropologists, singers and songwriters, economists, psychologists, educators (DeFrain, DeFrain, & Lepard, 1994). For example, novelist James A. Michener, a self-described "citizen of the world," dedicated a lifetime to understanding people around the world, living in an area for months or years and writing about what he saw and heard. He concluded that

> We are all brothers [and sisters]. We all face the same problems and find the same satisfactions. We are united in one great band. I am one with all of them, in all lands, in all climates, in all conditions. Since we brothers [and sisters] occupy the entire earth, the world is our home. (Michener, 1991, p. 249)

In the 1930s, cultural anthropologists assumed that every culture was unique. Then sociologist George Homans began amassing empirical observations that contradicted the notion of cultural uniqueness. Homans (1974) came to believe that certain societal institutions appear in every culture because of the universality of human nature.

Anthropologist Colin Turnbull devoted his life to studying the nature of human culture around the world and challenged age-old Western assumptions about the differences between so-called primitive societies and modern societies. In his book *The Human Cycle* (1983), Turnbull examined such disparate cultures as the Mbuti of Zaire, the Hindus of Banaras, and middle-class Western society. He described the human life cycle as it is experienced in each of these cultures and showed that from infancy to old age, the stages of life are identical in meaning in all these cultures. Turnbull believed that the experiences of love, work, loneliness, growing up, and growing old are universal; he also argued that these experiences may be handled far better by the so-called primitive societies. He concluded that behind all the different rites, customs, and religions, people in various cultures live in the same eternal, immutable human cycle, which is governed by the same laws.

Kenneth Boulding, an economist, philosopher, and general systems theorist, believes that human betterment is the end toward which we individually and collectively should strive. Betterment is a change in some system that is evaluated as "being for the better." It is an increase in the "ultimate good," that which is good in itself. Four great virtues make up this ultimate good:

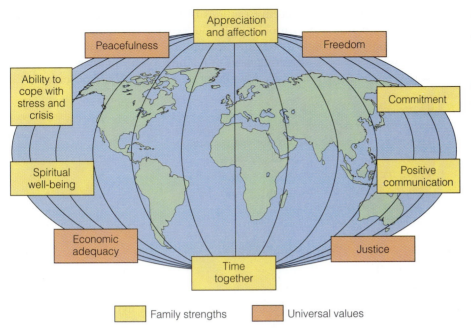

Figure 18.1 Family Strengths and Universal Values Around the World: A Proposed Model. *Source:* Adapted with permission from an illustration by Amie DeFrain.

- *Economic adequacy:* "riches," in contrast to poverty; nourishment, in contrast to starvation; adequate housing, clothing, health care, and other essentials of life.

- *Justice,* in contrast to injustice; equality, rather than inequality, in access to work, education, and health.

- *Freedom,* in contrast to coercion and confinement.

- *Peacefulness,* in contrast to war and strife.

Boulding (1985) believes these great virtues to be universal values.

Family life can be a deeply challenging yet fulfilling endeavor—a continuous quest for a sense of spiritual or emotional well-being in a tempestuous environment. Because all families and all family members must confront life's great challenges as they pass through the stages of human development, it is not surprising that strong, successful families around the world share similar qualities. These qualities, again, can be categorized as cohesion (a sense of togetherness and a commitment to one another, demonstrated by satisfying time spent together); flexibility (the ability to successfully meet the minor and major stressors of life, grounded in a shared set of goals, values, and beliefs that give family members a sense of spiritual well-being); and communication (the capacity to listen and talk effectively with one another and to express appreciation and affection for all family members; Figure 18.1). In other words, the basic foundation of successful families is remarkably similar from culture to culture. This is a wonderful notion because it gives us, as a family of humankind, something important to share, something we all can understand together.

The family strengths perspective cautions that if you look only for problems in families, you will find only problems. If you look for strengths, however, you will find strengths. A family's strengths become the foundation upon which its members build even more successful ways of relating to one another.

As folk singers Peter, Paul, and Mary sang in the song "River of Jordan":

We are only one river: We are only one sea.
And it flows through you, and it flows through me.
We are only one people. We are one and the same.
We are all one spirit. We are all one name.
We are the father, mother, daughter and son.
From the dawn of creation, we are one.
We are one. (Yarrow, 1972)

The Future of Families From a Global Perspective

Perhaps the ultimate general systems theory is the Gaia hypothesis, created by British scientist James E. Lovelock and several colleagues (Lovelock, 1979, 1987). These scientists were inspired by the first photographs of earth from space, which revealed the planet as a whole. They were stunned to see our planet in a new light: as a living and interconnected entity.

Lovelock argued that ecologists traditionally had been rooted in a very down-to-earth approach to natural history. They had focused on detailed studies of habitats and ecosystems without taking the whole picture into account. Charging that science had, in essence, missed the forest for the trees, Lovelock proposed the Gaia hypothesis, which considers earth to be a planet-sized entity, one with properties that cannot be predicted by simply summing its parts. Lovelock and his colleagues subsequently refined their vision, defining Gaia as

A complex entity involving the Earth's biosphere, atmosphere, oceans, and soil; the totality constituting a feedback or cybernetic system which seeks an optimal physical and chemical environment for life on this planet. The maintenance of relatively constant conditions by active control may be conveniently described by the term from systems theory of homeostasis. (Lovelock, 1987, p. 11)

What does all this have to do with strengthening families? From space, earth appears to be a single entity, a whole, without political boundaries or cultural divisions. From this vantage point, it is apparent that we all have to work together as a family of humankind to deal successfully with the major problems we face: among them, war, overpopulation, environmental degradation, and ethnic strife.

Family problems also know no boundaries from a global perspective: A tragedy for families in one region affects a whole country; a tragedy in one country affects the world. Individual families sometimes are crushed by events largely out of their control, and they simply are not capable of preventing or dealing successfully with catastrophe by themselves.

According to one popular bumper sticker, we should "think globally and act locally." Indeed, no individual is in a position to change the world single-handedly,

but by keeping attuned to global family concerns, we can act responsibly in our individual worlds. We can unite in groups to find solutions to large-scale problems that affect countless people.

Each morning a young man walked the beach,
picking up starfish that had washed up in the night.
Slowly, carefully, one by one, he threw them back
into the ocean, beyond the breakers.
One day an old man walked up to him and asked,
"Young man, why do you throw these starfish back,
day after day? There are thousands of them,
and you'll never make a difference."
The young man picked up a starfish, threw it back
into the ocean and said, "It makes a difference to this one."
—Author unknown

The Future of Your Family

The future of families in the United States and around the world begins with each of us as we create the future in our own family. We, the authors of your textbook, asked our students what the future would be like in their families. Following are some of their answers. (Their comments were tape-recorded with their consent. Names and identifying details have been changed to preserve anonymity.)

"I think we're a happier family than we were in the past because we laugh a lot," Marta, a 40-year-old divorced mother of three who was completing her college degree, responded. "The children think I'm really a liberated woman, and that's pretty exciting. I'd tell young people to hang in there with your parents and try and understand them, because they love you and they just want the very best for you."

* * * * *

"The future for my family?" 19-year-old Rachel replied. "I'm not sure. My parents have been divorced for about 15 years, and they're both re-married. My mom's happily remarried. My dad is not so happy. (I can't talk, this is so upsetting.) He always talks about my mom and what she's doing and what they'd be like if they were still together.

"My mom has done a really good job [tears, coughing] of showing us things are okay, even with stressful events. She has raised us very well, I believe. My father . . . he screwed up, and he's realizing it now. And he's telling it to me. . . . [tears] Sorry. And I just don't know what to say to him. Yeah, Dad, you blew it. And I think he's going to get divorced again. For myself, I have the biggest hopes. I know everyone does. But I feel that if I do get divorced, my mom showed me the way to do it right."

* * * * *

"As far as where we're going," 21-year-old Tanya noted, "I think we'll be okay because my partner, Darren, has a strong family. But I don't want my dysfunctional family to overshadow our life because that's something I want to overcome. . . . [tears] Why does everyone cry up here? [laughter] I want to overcome the statistics and have a strong marriage. But, if Darren turns out to be a problem like my dad [laughter], at least I know I can go on because my mom and dad are both very happy now without each other, so at least I know I have an out."

* * * * *

"Now, when it comes to my family, where's it going?" 31-year-old Nina, a graduate student, repeated the question thoughtfully. "I guess I hope that it grows stronger when we get back together, since we're apart now [he's in the military, serving overseas]. We'll be back together in June. Hopefully it will grow stronger, though we'll be a lot closer to our families and their problems. We've been a long way away in the past, and shielded from their problems. I think their problems will be more up front now, and that will either make or break our marriage. We'll either get sucked into the pit of misery they're in, or he'll just figure out that he can't take care of his family. They have to take care of themselves. You're responsible for your own destiny. You can either wallow in your pit, or

(Continued. . .)

(. . .Continued)

you can carry on in your life, in spite of your past, and be the best that you can be."

* * * * *

"Personally," responded 20-year-old David, "where's my family going in the future? I think we're doing okay. You always knock on wood, because you don't have complete control over your life, no matter how smart you think you are, or how long you've gone to school, or how much you've thought about it, or how many experts you've read, or who you've consulted. You get a real sense of humility, a feeling of humbleness, when you think how difficult life is and how little control you really have. We really don't live in a world where we have a huge amount of control."

* * * * *

"For the future," said 26-year-old Allan, "I want to raise my family differently than my parents did us. I want to be a closer family. There was so much communication that didn't happen in our family. We came home from school, laid our books down, and went into our rooms for the night. I think when I have a family some day I want it to be a very close-knit family, and I want to have open communication and to tell each other every day how much you love one another, because that's one thing our family missed."

* * * * *

"Our child Robbie's birth changed our life and the lives of our parents forever," Diana, a 28-year-old part-time student, responded. "Nothing anyone could have said to Paul or me would have prepared us for the reality of parenthood. Being parents is both the best and the hardest job in the world. It's very rewarding; it can also be very trying, especially when your wonderful 2-month-old son is hungry every 2 hours throughout the day and night and you, the mommy, are the only one in the world who can feed him . . . for obvious reasons.

"From the very beginning of my pregnancy, Paul was a very understanding and sensitive husband. He rubbed my back when it hurt, bought me saltine crackers when I was feeling nauseous, and told me to quit my job when I had swollen feet and could barely walk. Paul took great interest in me and what I was going through. He and I read many books together about babies, pregnancy, birth, and parenting. He went to all but one of my doctor's visits, carried our pillows to Lamaze class, and was a very supportive coach in labor. I believe my pregnancy with our son brought me and my husband closer together. There is something amazing about creating a life together. We had no idea about what we were getting ourselves into, but we were doing it together. I am thankful we have such a good marriage, because our strong foundation helped us to build our new family."

In summary, these students provided insights into their life experiences and their thoughts and dreams about their families in the future. Life inevitably brings challenges; the key to life in a strong family is to work together to meet these challenges.

Strengthening Your Marriage and Family Relationships

Fortunately, there are countless sources of support and strength for families in their quest to develop and maintain intimate, satisfying relationships. We will discuss several of them in this section.

Personal Strategies

In numerous studies, we have found that strong families successfully manage life's difficulties in a variety of ways (Stinnett, Stinnett, DeFrain, & DeFrain, 1999). These are some of their strategies:

- *Look for something positive in difficult situations.* No matter how difficult, most problems teach us something about ourselves and others that we can draw on in future situations.

- *Pull together.* Think of the problem not as one family member's difficulty but as a challenge for the family as a whole.

- *Get help outside the nuclear family.* Call on extended-family members, supportive friends, neighbors, colleagues, church or synagogue members, and community professionals. "It takes a whole village to resolve a crisis."

- *Create open channels of communication.* Challenges cannot be met when communication shuts down.

- *Keep things in perspective.* "These things, too, shall pass."

- *Adopt new roles in a flexible manner.* Crises often demand that individuals learn new approaches to life and take on different responsibilities.

- *Focus to minimize fragmentation.* Look at the big picture. Focusing on the details rather than the essentials can make people edgy, even hysterical.

- *Give up on worry, or put it in a box.* Worrying itself usually causes more misery than the problem at hand. Sometimes it's best to stuff the worry down or to resolve to worry 10 minutes a day and then forget about it. The mind simply has to rest.

- *Eat well, exercise, love each other, and get adequate sleep.* We often forget that we are biological beings. Like kindergartners, we need a good lunch and time to play. We need to have our hair stroked, we need a good hug, and we need a good nap.

- *Create a life full of meaning and purpose.* We all face severe crises in life. These challenges are simply unavoidable. Our aim should be to live a useful life of service to our community. Giving of ourselves brings a richness and dignity to our lives, in spite of the troubles we endure.

- *Actively meet challenges head-on.* Life's disasters do not go away when we look in another direction.

- *Go with the flow to some degree.* Sometimes we are relatively powerless in the face of a crisis. Simply saying to ourselves that things will get better with time can be useful.

- *Be prepared in advance for life's challenges.* Healthy family relationships are like an ample bank balance: If our relational accounts are in order, we will be able to weather life's most difficult storms—together.

Family Strategies

Most families operate in a reactive rather than a proactive manner and simply drift through life without a clear direction or meaning. But families can become more intentional, which means becoming more connected with each other and sharing meanings and experiences. William Doherty, a respected family therapist, wrote a useful book entitled *The Intentional Family: How to Build Family Ties in Our Modern World* (1997), to help families to become more intentional.

One very useful way to build an intentional family is to develop family rituals, which are repeated and coordinated activities that have significance for the family (Doherty, 1997). Three types of family rituals and the function they serve are described. *Connection rituals* facilitate bonding and include everyday activities like family meals and bedtime rituals. *Love rituals* increase intimacy in the couple and family and include celebration of special days like birthdays, Valentine's Day, Mother's Day and Father's Day. *Community rituals* help bond the family with the broader community of kin and friends and includes such activities as wedding, funerals, and graduations.

Programs for Couples and Families

Programs and services for couples and families range from informal networks to couple and family therapy. Table 18.1 lists program types in order of their therapeutic impact, from least to most intensive. As couple and family issues become more serious and chronic, a higher intensity of treatment is recommended. For example, it would be more appropriate for a couple who has been having marital problems for several years and has seriously considered divorce to see a couple therapist rather than to attend a self-help group. Although informal networks and self-help groups can be useful resources for some simple couple and family problems, neither usually has the expertise nor the techniques to treat serious problems.

Couple education programs can be very useful resources for couples without serious problems. These programs can help couples meet and learn from other couples. The skill-building programs often focus on communication and conflict-resolution skills, which couples can use to improve their relationships and resolve the differences that inevitably arise in any close relationship.

Couple therapy and family therapy are recommended when relationship problems between partners or among family members are chronic and intense. When problems involve the children, family therapy is called for. In families headed by two parents, the parents may also benefit from couple therapy, because parenting can put a great deal of stress on the couple relationship. Couple therapy and family therapy are most effective when begun before problems become severe and chronic.

Table 18.1 Programs for Couples and Families

	SERVICE	GOAL	PROVIDER
Informal networks	Personal advice	Advice and support	Family and friends
Self-help groups	Focus groups	Insight and support	Lay people concerned with similar issues
Education courses	Functional marriage and family courses	Awareness and knowledge	High school and college teachers
Couple enrichment	Marriage enrichment	Motivation	Lay couples
Couple education	Premarital and marital programs	Insight and skills in communication and conflict resolution	Clergy, counselors, social workers, and marital therapists
Couple and family therapy	Marital and family therapy	Insight and change in relationship dynamics	Marital and family therapists, psychologists

Premarital Counseling

Because of the risk of divorce and the importance of marital happiness, it seems logical that most couples would and should get premarital counseling. In fact, a growing number of couples do seek such counseling. Seeking premarital counseling is especially common for partners who have been married and divorced, presumably because they do not want this remarriage to fail.

There is increasing evidence that a good premarital program can help improve a couple's relationship and reduce their chances of divorce. As discussed in Chapter 12, an effective premarital program has at least three essential components: (1) a premarital inventory with individual feedback for each couple, (2) a skill-building component that focuses on communication and problem solving, and (3) small-group discussions in which couples can air their mutual issues. The program should last 6 to 8 weeks and should be started a year before the marriage so that the partners have time to develop their skills.

Premarital counseling is popular with most clergy. In a national study of 231 clergy from several Protestant denominations, 94% said they thought that all premarital couples should have counseling before marriage, and 100% said they provided premarital counseling to all couples before they would marry them (Jones & Stahmann, 1994). About 90% to 95% provided individual counseling to the partners, and about two thirds used some type of premarital inventory and gave the couple materials to read. Group lectures and group couple counseling were used by only about 5% of the clergy.

One of the most popular premarital programs in the United States is the PRE-PARE Program. As mentioned in Chapter 12, more than 1 million couples have participated in this program over the past 10 years. The specific goals of the program are to (1) help the couple explore their relationship strengths and growth areas, (2) help the couple learn to resolve conflict effectively using a 10-step conflict-resolution model, (3) help the couple discuss their family of origin and articulate the characteristics they would like to develop in their own marriage, and

Marriage enrichment experiences are increasingly popular, both as a means of helping couples deal with marital problems and as a way to deepen already strong relationships. These programs let couples explore issues and feelings in a supportive, relaxing environment, uninterrupted by the distractions of daily life.

(4) motivate the couple to invest time and energy in improving their relationship. The PREPARE program focuses on 14 important relationship areas, including communication, conflict resolution, financial management, and equalitarian roles. (For more information on the PREPARE program and to take a sample Couple Quiz, visit the website at www.lifeinnovation.com.)

Couple Programs

Interest in couple programs is on the rise (Hunt, Hof, & DeMaria, 1998). There are two types of couple programs. One type, referred to simply as a couple enrichment program, usually lasts 1 or 2 days and takes place on a weekend. The focus is on motivating the couple to increase the amount of personal information they share with each other. These relatively brief programs are helpful to some couples who already have a good marriage and want to improve it. However, for couples with more serious relationship issues, such programs can create problems (Doherty, Lester, & Leigh, 1986). One of the drawbacks of couple enrichment programs is that they can increase expectations without giving the couple the relationship skills to improve their marriage.

The second type of program, couple education, focuses on teaching communication and conflict-resolution skills. These programs are more effective than the 1- or 2-day couple enrichment programs. They usually last about 6 weeks and meet each week for about 2 hours. Skill-building programs that have demonstrated their effectiveness and value to couples include the Couples Communication Program by Sherod Miller, the PREP Program by Howard Markman, Scott Stanley, and Susan Blumberg (1994), the Relationship Enhancement Program by Bernard Guerney, and the PAIRS Program by Lori Gordon (Hunt et al., 1998).

A recent study compared three couple education programs (Hawley & Olson, 1995). The programs were Preston Dyer and Genie Dyer's Growing Together, Edward Bader's Learning to Live Together, and Don Dinkmeyer and Jon Carlson's Training for Marriage Enrichment (TIME). Seventy-one newlywed couples were assigned to the three programs, and 28 couples were assigned to a control group. All three programs were about 6 weeks long, and all focused on communication, conflict resolution, finances, role relationship, family of origin, and sexuality. Couples met in a small group with about 6 other couples and a trainer on a weekly basis for about 2 hours.

Ninety-eight percent of the couples in the couple programs said they would recommend the program to another couple, and 96% said they would repeat the experience. More than 85% felt the topics were very relevant, and 75% felt their group leader was helpful. There were significant improvements in the couples' scores on communication, conflict resolution, personality issues, financial management, dealing with family and friends, and marital satisfaction on some statistical tests, though not on others. The couples did, however, enjoy the experience and felt it was beneficial.

Marital and Family Therapy

If you did nothing more when you have a family together than to make it possible for them to really look at each other, really touch each other, you would have already swung the pendulum in the direction of a new start.

—Virginia Satir (1988)

Couples with persistent relationship problems should seek professional help as early as possible. Couples and families who receive help with problems before they become too severe have a much better chance of overcoming the difficulties and building a stronger relationship than do those who wait.

Choosing a Marital and Family Therapist   Specifically trained professionals who deal with relationship problems include marital and family therapists and some psychologists, psychiatrists, and social workers. Licensed marital and family therapists are certified by the American Association for Marriage and Family Therapy (AAMFT) and have received specialized training in relationship issues. Psychologists typically have a doctorate or a master's degree in psychology; some have training in working with couples and families, although their initial training tends to emphasize work with individuals. Psychiatrists are medical doctors who have additional training in the field of mental health. Some specialize in working with couples and families. Last, social workers receive some training in working with couples and families.

The most highly trained marital and family therapists are certified members of AAMFT or are licensed by the state in which they work. In most localities, the yellow pages of the telephone directory list marital and family therapists under "marital and family counseling." One can also consult a family service agency or the United Way for suggestions. Physicians or clergy may also be able to assist in the search for a qualified professional.

Following are some specific questions potential clients should ask a therapist *before* beginning therapy:

- What is your professional training and degree?

- How much specialized training and experience have you had in marital and family therapy?

- Do you usually see couples and families together or as individuals?

- What procedure will you use to evaluate our relationship?

- How much will you charge for that assessment?

- How frequently will we have sessions, and how long will they last?

- Can we establish a contract for a specific number of sessions?

- What will each session cost?

Couples who do not feel comfortable with the responses they receive to these questions should feel free to seek another therapist.

How Effective Is Marital and Family Therapy?   In the first national survey of the practice of marital and family therapists, 526 AAMFT therapists from 15 states commented on therapy with 1,422 clients (Doherty & Simmons, 1996). In addition, 492 clients rated their satisfaction with their marital and family therapy.

Marital and family therapists spent about half their time working with couples and families and half working with individuals. They spent about 20 hours a week seeing clients in therapy and carried a total caseload of about 24 clients. The common presenting problems were depression (44%), other psychological problems (35%), marital problems (30%), anxiety (21%), parent-child problems (13%), alcohol/drugs problems (8%), child behavior issues (8%), and family-of-origin issues (7%). The most frequent DSM-IV* diagnostic codes were adjustment disorder (25%), depression (23%), and anxiety disorders (14%).

Marital and family therapy is a relatively short process, as compared to traditional individual therapy provided by psychiatrists and some psychologists. The median number of sessions for the marital and family therapists was 12. The average length of therapy was 11 sessions for couples, 9 for families, and 13 for individuals. Most clients were seen biweekly. Based on the therapists' records, the average cost of therapy was $80 for each one-hour session, for a total of $780. Individual therapy was the most expensive ($845), couple therapy was next ($748), and family therapy was the least expensive ($585).

The outcome of the therapy was usually very successful from the perspective of both the client and the therapist. Overall, 83% of the clients felt the therapeutic goals had been achieved; 89% felt their emotional health had improved; 78% said their family relationships had gotten better; and 63% felt their relationship with their partner had also improved. In addition, most clients were very satisfied with their therapy: 98% rated the service as good to excellent; 97% said they got the kind of help they wanted; 98% said they were able to deal with their problems more effectively; 93% said their needs were met; 94% said they would return to the same therapist again; and 97% said they would recommend the therapist to a

---

*DSM-IV is the diagnostic manual for mental disorders.

"I GUESS THAT SETTLES IT."

Reprinted with permission from Harley Schwadron.

friend. In summary, it appears that marital and family therapy is a rather cost-effective and efficient approach to dealing with a range of emotional and relationship problems in individuals, couples, and families (Doherty & Simmons, 1996).

Key Characteristics of Family Resiliency   The goal of family therapists is to help families with problems develop skills that will help them become more resilient. Froma Walsh (1998) has identified the key characteristics of healthy families that are usually missing from problem families (Box 18.1). The *family organizational patterns* that are important are connectedness, flexibility, and social and economic resources. In terms of connectedness, healthy families are able to support each other emotionally and to collaborate with each other. Healthy families are also flexible; they are open to change and are able to adapt to challenges over time. Finally, healthy families often can rely on extended kin and a support network in times of need.

The *family communication processes* comprise clear communication, open expression of emotion, and collaborative problem solving. Healthy families exhibit skills in each of these areas, whereas families with problems tend to be lacking in these skills. As a result, family communication skills are often the focus of treatment with problem families.

The *family belief systems* that are important for family resiliency are making meaning of adversity, having a positive outlook, and having spiritual resources. Healthy families are able to face adversity directly and maintain a positive outlook. They are able to transcend their problems, often by drawing on their spiritual beliefs.

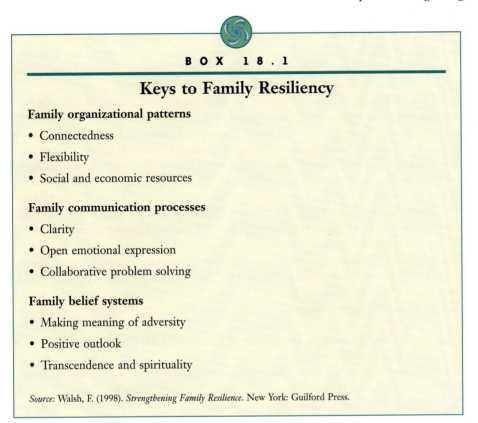

Source: Walsh, F. (1998). *Strengthening Family Resilience*. New York: Guilford Press.

Common Problems in Marital and Family Systems   Marital and family therapists working with families with problems often use the Couple and Family Map. Because it focuses on the key dimensions of connectedness, flexibility, and communication, the Couple and Family Map provides a useful framework for diagnosing and treating several common problems in marital and family systems.

One frequent problem couples seeking counseling describe is the feeling that they are at opposite extremes on the same dimension of the model. On the cohesion dimension, for example, one partner may want more togetherness, whereas the other partner may want more autonomy. Similarly, on the flexibility dimension, one partner may desire more flexibility in the family, whereas the other partner may want more rules (i.e., rigidity). When couples disagree on the balance of separateness (autonomy) and togetherness in their relationship, they can negotiate by jointly planning their schedules. When couples disagree on flexibility issues (rules or roles), they might try reversing roles at home for a week.

A second common problem for couples occurs when both partners are at the same extreme on one or both model dimensions. Both may be disengaged from the relationship because they are so heavily involved in career or outside interests that they have little time or energy for the marriage. Or both may be enmeshed, so invested in their partner that they have little room to develop personal interests and skills. When couples are disengaged, it is important for them to assess their commitment to the relationship. When couples are too enmeshed, one solution is for each of them to develop more separate interests and spend more time apart.

This all may sound quite simple, but difficulties arise because people see their relationships differently and have different expectations about them. For example, the wife and the husband often offer different family descriptions and goals. Add a teenage child, and another description will likely surface.

These differences in perception often increase when a couple or a family is in conflict. For example, a wife might describe her husband as a total monster who is drunk much of the time, has gone through numerous jobs in 5 years, and beats her and the young children regularly. Her husband might describe himself as a "social drinker" who happened to change jobs occasionally because of a string of bad luck with a few lousy bosses. Although his wife is a nag and has turned his young sons into a "bunch of sissies," he nobly has tried to discipline the children.

There is no avoiding this dilemma of differing family perceptions. By interviewing only one person in the family, either the husband or the wife, a counselor would get only a zoom snapshot rather than a panoramic view of the entire family and its complexity. The solution lies in getting everyone together, asking countless questions and dealing with the conflicting perspectives of all the family members. This approach produces a more valid—and also a more complex— picture of the family's dynamics.

Case Study: Diagnosis and Treatment of a Family With Problems   The Davis family has five members: Mary and Don, the parents; 18-year-old Ann; 16-year-old Julie; and 9-year-old Peter. Mary drank to relieve feelings of inadequacy in a family dominated by high achievers: Don and the oldest daughter, Ann. The middle daughter, Julie, also felt inadequate but tried to console her mother and was responsible enough to be a surrogate mother to Peter, the youngest child. The family came in for therapy shortly after Mary began treatment for her dependence on alcohol. Ann subsequently left home, angry at Mary for all the problems she had caused. Julie felt lost because her mother was being "taken care of" by other people and Julie's role as chief counselor had been usurped.

DIAGNOSIS   In terms of cohesion, the Davis family was *enmeshed.* They evidenced high emotional bonding as well as high mutual dependency. The mother and the two daughters competed intensely for approval from each other and from Dad. The family's external boundaries were closed. No one felt free to interact with people outside the family, partly because they were afraid Mary would be drunk and embarrass everyone. Friends and relatives were kept at a distance. The only time husband and wife made contact was when one of the children misbehaved. Then the two would team up as parents and support each other; otherwise, they did not interact much. The father-daughter coalitions, especially that between Don and Ann, were strong. In many ways, Don and Ann played the role of parents in the family, because Mary's drinking often made her incapable of parenting.

Individual activities were permitted but only within family-approved guidelines. Don and Ann spent a lot of time playing tennis together, but Julie's desire to spend the same amount of time away from the family "partying" with friends was not approved. Close friends, especially males, were not allowed. The family tried desperately to have fun at their cabin on the weekends. Everyone was required to go, and the implicit message was, "You *will* have fun!" The result was that nobody enjoyed the weekends at the cabin. Tending to Peter's needs kept Julie

Although the challenges can be formidable, families are capable of dramatic and positive change. Marital and family therapists can be helpful guides on the journey toward healing.

connected to the family after she became adrift when her mother entered the alcohol treatment program.

Much of the conflict in the family seemed to stem from its *rigidity*. The family system and each of its members could seldom think of new ways to solve problems. Also, no one in the family knew how to be appropriately assertive. Rather than making their point firmly but without malice or yelling, family members resorted to aggressive behaviors: screaming, throwing things, and occasionally striking each other.

Family roles were stereotypic and rigid. Mary saw herself as being in charge of the house, and she saw Don as the boss of the children, the rule enforcer. Mary made many threats but rarely carried them out. When things got out of hand, Don delivered punishment in a heavy-handed manner. When Mary felt upset about life, she tended to clean house or drink. She made life difficult for everyone by insisting that each be as compulsive about housekeeping standards as she was.

All in all, family leadership, rules, and roles were very rigid. As new situations developed in the family, the members did not have the flexibility to negotiate and create solutions that were reasonable. Ann and Julie could not discuss possible changes in a rational fashion with their parents. The Davises were locked in a dysfunctional family system that was rigidly enmeshed.

TREATMENT The family therapist sought to focus on those issues in the family on which some positive movement was already underway. On the dimension of cohesion, the goal was to increase the level of individual autonomy in the family—in short, to give each member more space. A related goal was to strengthen the marriage. In terms of flexibility, the family therapist taught family members how to negotiate and compromise with each other, rather than alternating between quiet passivity and conflict. Members were taught to see family rules as general guidelines to be discussed and interpreted as new situations arose in day-to-day living. This gave the children a chance to argue their points and even to change their parents' minds occasionally. When the family as a whole had improved on these dimensions, the focus shifted to the marriage.

Don and Mary continued in marital therapy as a couple. The therapist focused on ways the couple could learn to enjoy each other's company again. They were encouraged to go out on dates without the children and to do things they felt they hadn't had time to do together for many years. As the marriage improved, the number of disagreements with the children diminished. Why was this? As the marital coalition strengthened and Mary took back her rightful place on the parental team, it was less necessary for Julie and Ann to struggle for a position in coalition with Dad, and Julie no longer felt it necessary to try and fill the vacuum.

The family therapist got a good deal of help from Mary's alcohol counselors and from Alcoholics Anonymous. The chemical dependence specialists were adept at helping Mary maintain sobriety once she had attained it. Al-Anon, which focuses on the family of the alcoholic, gave Don and the children support and ideas in their struggle to live with an alcoholic. As Mary became more secure in her marriage with Don, she was able to be more supportive of Julie in her growth as an individual. The family became more adept at both separating from and connecting with each other.

Although family therapy may seem straightforward and common sensical to some, it is, in fact, a long and difficult process, requiring patience, self-discipline, and commitment. Families do change, however, and marital and family therapists can help families facilitate that change and deal with their problems.

2001: Recommendations for Strengthening Marriages and Families

The National Council on Family Relations (NCFR) is a nonprofit network of family professionals who work with couples and families through a variety of programs and services, including marriage and family courses, family life education, marriage enrichment, and marital and family therapy. Family professionals work in a variety of settings, including mental health centers, schools, churches, and health care facilities.

An NCFR presidential report, *2001: Preparing Families for the Future* (Olson & Kilmer Hanson, 1990), focuses on the future of families in the United States and around the world. Nineteen eminent family scholars contributed to the report, including 13 past presidents of NCFR. In this section we will look at several key points covered in the document.

"Families must be made a national priority if we are to effectively deal with the multitude of problems in our country today," according to David H. Olson, NCFR president from 1988 to 1989. "Most of the problems with individuals and society either begin or end up in the family" (Olson & Kilmer Hanson, 1990, p. 1). Families must cope with the problems that individual family members face. Yet as a nation we refuse to do much to support families, even though they represent a significant resource for dealing with the most serious problems our society confronts.

American families today are diverse in terms of ethnicity, family dynamics, and type of family structure. The traditional family pattern—of a husband, wife, and children in a nuclear family—has changed dramatically, and we see more single-parent families and stepfamilies across all cultural groups. Policies and programs must take family diversity into account, learn from it, and value the strengths it can provide. We must help families of all colors build on their unique strengths.

"In the 21st century, the United States will emerge as a nation with greater ethnic diversity, with a projected distribution of 33 percent of the population being people of color," according to Hamilton S. McCubbin, NCFR president from 1986 to 1987 (Olson & Kilmer Hanson, 1990, p. 37). McCubbin stresses the critical importance of social policies and programs to address the impact of cultural diversity on the nation as a whole.

According to Paul C. Glick, NCFR president from 1978 to 1979, "Marriage and childrearing patterns have become so complex that it is difficult to develop generalities that apply to every type of family. Earlier analyses of the family were made as if only couples in permanent first marriages existed. Because of the increase in divorce and remarriage, that scenario is now relevant to only a minority of married couples" (Olson & Kilmer Hanson, 1990, p. 2).

Patricia Voydanoff, director of the Center for the Study of Family Development at the University of Dayton, notes that the family characteristics of the labor force are changing as the number of two-earner families grows, especially among families with babies. Single-parent families are increasing, and the older-adult population in the United States is also growing. Thus, "Many working families are responsible for elder care and child care simultaneously" (Olson & Kilmer Hanson, 1990, p. 12). These changes increase the need for dependent-care programs.

M. Janice Hogan, NCFR president from 1989 to 1990, believes that "financial problems are pervasive family concerns. Most family members experience cycles of too many needs with two few resources" (Olson & Kilmer Hanson, 1990, p. 14). These economic challenges often lead to marital and parent-child conflict, home foreclosure, bankruptcy, and other negative consequences. Both internal family problems and external social forces contribute to problems in family economic management.

A big issue for families is health care. Catherine L. Gilliss, associate professor and director of the Family Nurse Practitioner Program at the University of California, San Francisco, notes that the cost of health problems in the United States is absolutely enormous but that education can play an important role in preventing disease: "Health problems represented in these astronomical costs are largely preventable through public health programs for promotion of health, reduction of risk, and services for the poor and underserved. The family's role in health protection and promotion has been overlooked by health planners and providers" (Olson & Kilmer Hanson, 1990, p. 32).

The AIDS epidemic threatens the health of millions of people around the world. Richard N. Needle, coordinator of AIDS research at the National Institute of Mental Health, believes that more effective research on AIDS prevention and on ways to help individuals and families deal with this epidemic is needed. He calls for "a formalized consortium of organizations planning to influence policy, set research agendas, or provide for continuing education of their members" (Olson & Kilmer Hanson, 1990, p. 34).

In a similar vein, James Maddock, past president of the American Association for Sex Education and Counseling, suggests that the term " 'family sexual health' should be a familiar and comfortable concept among policy makers concerned with family well-being." Currently, he sees the threat of AIDS and the prevalence of the sexual abuse of children as problems that leave parents "scared and confused" about how to successfully guide their children's sexual development (Olson & Kilmer Hanson, 1990, p. 22).

Alexis J. Walker, NCFR president from 1995 to 1996, argues that "the nature and experience of family life today varies considerably by gender." In essence, the man's world and the woman's world in the family are still quite different as a result of long-standing beliefs and practices in our culture legitimized by the laws, the courts, and individuals. "Although we are a long way from understanding why gender is related to violence and poverty, solutions can be sought. The goal of social policy should be to achieve a maximum quality of life for women, children, and men in families" (Olson & Kilmer Hanson, 1990, p. 16).

Bert Adams, NCFR president from 1983 to 1984, and Diane Adams, director of Community Coordinated Child Care (4-C) in Dane County, Wisconsin, write: "Child care is a way of life for millions of children and their families. Families still largely pay for child care on their own, without government support." They point out that the child-care infrastructure in this country is large and is growing in a relatively haphazard, unplanned manner. They caution, "Are we willing to take a risk that an unaccountable 'experiment' is taking place without planning and support for the kind of child care children receive?" (Olson & Kilmer Hanson, 1990, p. 18).

In the words of Elizabeth S. Force, NCFR president from 1968 to 1969, regarding older family members: "On my 70th birthday I said, 'In my old age I need three things: good health, loads of money, and somebody who gives a damn.' Seventeen years later, at 87, I stand by my list except I've changed the priorities: Somebody who cares has moved to first place." Force believes that the security blanket of caregivers for the elderly is threatened by several factors: diminishing family size, mobility, and the instability of families in America. "Other resources must respond to the need for emotional, financial, housing, and health support" (Olson & Kilmer Hanson, 1990, p. 20).

"Our society has a critical need to learn more about the dynamics underlying healthy family relationships," according to Graham Spanier, NCFR president from 1987 to 1988 and president of Pennsylvania State University (Olson & Kilmer Hanson, 1990, p. 4). Marriage and family strengths are the foundation on which individuals and families build a successful life together, and successful families are the foundation of a strong nation.

Some scholars claim that divorce is a sign that families are in a state of breakdown and decay; others see divorce as an opportunity for growth. Regardless of how one perceives divorce, Sharon J. Price, NCFR president from 1984 to 1985, argues that "we need to accept the reality of divorce as a viable family transition, to refocus on 'families' rather than a permanent 'family' and to examine both the positive and negative impacts of divorce" (Olson & Kilmer Hanson, 1990, p. 30).

"How can families be the most loving and supportive social institution and also the most violent?" asks Murray A. Straus, NCFR president from 1972 to 1973. "Over six million children and three million spouses are severely assaulted each

Happy and healthy families are an important foundation for raising children who are also happy and successful. Strong families also help their members cope with their personal problems and crises.

year. Physical abuse is a major threat to American families. Those who are not physically injured are often injured psychologically." Straus sees hope, though, arguing that "shelters and treatment programs have decreased the incidence of spouse and child abuse over the last decade. The trend is slow, and clear national policies and programs are needed" (Olson & Kilmer Hanson, 1990, p. 26).

The abuse of alcohol and other drugs is greatly affecting family life and the physical, emotional, and economic health of many Americans, according to Robert A. Lewis, professor of family studies at Purdue University. "The growing crime rate is also threatening society as we know it. There is a serious need for family and community involvement, for sweeping changes in attitudes toward the use of addictive substances. An all-out war against the abuse of drugs is necessary to curb the current drug and alcohol epidemic" (Olson & Kilmer Hanson, 1990, p. 28).

In the area of marriage and family enrichment, the late David Mace, NCFR president from 1961 to 1962 wrote: "I look to the day when we can guide couples continuously from the premarital period, through their first critical year together, right through the life cycle. With this kind of service a vast amount of human misery can be prevented" (Olson & Kilmer Hanson, 1990, p. 6).

"Family life education needs to help individuals develop and maintain mutually satisfying relationships. It also aims to promote skills in getting families to resolve the inevitable conflicts that arise from living with others," according to Richard Hey (NCFR president from 1969 to 1970) and Gerhard Neubeck (NCFR president from 1977 to 1978). "Family life education must affect students where they are, whether that is learning how to get along with parents, how to have a successful marriage, or how to enjoy and raise children" (Olson & Kilmer Hanson, 1990, p. 8).

Carlfred Broderick, NCFR president from 1975 to 1976, argues that "the future of marital and family therapy lies in the replacement of competing therapies with a tested set of broadly accepted principles of systemic intervention having specific components and therapeutic behaviors. This is the time for integration, evaluation, and digestion rather than for bold new paradigms" (Olson & Kilmer Hanson, 1990, p. 10).

"Children are the most valuable and vulnerable resource in our society, and many of them live in high-risk families. These families do not have healthy homes and are not rearing their children in responsible and effective ways," according to Wesley R. Burr, NCFR president from 1981 to 1982. "Ideally, our children should be reared in families where there is a safe, secure, and helpful environment." Burr believes that children are not just parents' responsibility but the whole society's responsibility: "We must find ways to adjust national, state, local, industrial, union, commercial, educational, residential, and religious policies and programs to provide a more healthy environment for these families" (Olson & Kilmer Hanson, 1990, p. 24).

With a nearly 50% divorce rate and with high rates of physical, emotional, and sexual abuse, we need to put more time and energy into prevention and education programs that can effectively prepare people to live together in cooperative and loving ways. These programs need to be more family based, beginning as early as the preschool and elementary-school years and continuing through middle school, high school, and college—literally, across all stages of the family life cycle. One way we can make families a national priority is to develop a family impact statement for every major piece of legislation at the local, state, and national level. This would help us focus on policies that are both more humane and more effective in serving individual and family needs.

Unless we make families a national priority now, as we enter the 21st century, there will be more crises that will drain our national resources. During the early years of the 21st century, one can hope that we will develop more creative family-based programs that will move us toward a more family-oriented society that takes into account diverse family structures and dynamics. Families are our greatest national resource. We must not continue to waste this resource.

Making Every Year the International Year of the Family

Families are the smallest democracy in any society. This idea echoes the theme of the 1994 United Nations International Year of the Family: "building the smallest democracy at the heart of society." UN conference documents extolled the family as

> The basic unit of society; appreciated for the important socioeconomic functions that it performs. Despite the many changes in society that have altered its role and functions, it continues to provide the natural framework for the emotional, financial, and material support essential to the growth and development of its members, particularly infants and children, and for the care of other dependents, including the elderly, disabled, and the infirm. The family remains a vital means of preserving and transmitting cultural values, and often educates, trains, motivates, and supports its individual members, thereby investing in their future growth and acting as a vital resource for development. (Czaplewski, 1995, p. i)

Figure 18.2 Symbol Adopted by 1994 United Nations International Year of the Family Conference, Malta

The 1994 International Year of the Family Conference was held in Malta. The symbol adopted by the conference is shown in Figure 18.2. The conference promoted the following seven principles (Czaplewski, 1995, p. i):

- The family constitutes the basic unit of society and therefore warrants special attention. The widest possible protection and assistance should be accorded to all families so that they may assume their responsibilities within the community.

- Families assume diverse forms and functions from one country to another, and within each national society. These forms and functions express the diversity of individual preferences and societal conditions. Consequently, the International Year of the Family encompasses and addresses the needs of all families.

- Activities for the International Year of the Family seek to promote the basic human rights and fundamental freedoms accorded to all individuals by the set of internationally agreed upon instruments formulated under the aegis of the United Nations.

- Policies aim to foster equality between women and men within families and to bring about a fuller sharing of domestic responsibilities and employment opportunities.

- Activities for the International Year should be undertaken at all levels— local, national, regional, and international—but the primary focus is local and national in scope.

- Programs should support families in carrying out their functions rather than provide substitutes for such functions. They should promote the inherent strengths of families, including their great capacity for self-reliance, and stimulate self-sustaining activities on their behalf. They should give an integrated perspective of families, their members, communities, and society.

- The International Year is intended to constitute an event within a continuing process that will extend far beyond the actual year.

Building on the seven principles, the conference developed six objectives for the International Year of the Family (Czaplewski, 1995, p. ii):

- Increase awareness of family issues among governments and the private sector.

- Encourage national institutions to formulate, implement, and monitor family policies.

- Stimulate responses to problems affecting and affected by the situations of families.

- Enhance the effectiveness of local, regional, and national programs for families by generating new activities and strengthening existing support.

- Improve the collaboration among national and international nongovernmental organizations in support of multisector activities.

- Build upon the results of international activities concerning women, children, youth, older adults, and those with disabilities and other major events of concern to the family and its individual members.

Your authors believe that every year should be the National and International Year of the Family. Families all around the world are tied together in an intimate web of life. If we continue to compete fiercely with one another as individuals and as nations, we will all no doubt continue to suffer the consequences: war, environmental degradation, racism, sexism, poverty, cynicism, and grief on a global scale. If, however, we learn to work together and share life's joys and sorrows, we—the people of Mother Earth—stand a reasonable chance of surviving and transcending our common human predicament. The challenges are clear. The question is whether we have the intelligence and the goodwill to act.

On a more personal note, resolve to keep building positive connections with your family and friends and to become genuinely involved in the life of your community and the family of humankind.

Summary

- Families in the United States and around the world are wonderfully different. Our diverse interests and capabilities give us the tools to build on each other's strengths to make a more vital society.

- Even though diversity is a fact of life and enhances living, our similarities as human beings and families are often overlooked and may be more important than our differences. Paradoxically, all human beings are unique and different, yet deep down we are all very similar.

- Families who are strong and successful around the world are likely to share the qualities of cohesion, flexibility, and communication.

- Perhaps the ultimate general systems theory is the Gaia hypothesis, which proposes that the earth is a living, interconnected entity with no political or cultural boundaries. From a global perspective, families, too, know no boundaries: We are all part of the human family.

- Couples and families with problems can find assistance from a broad range of educational and enrichment programs (such as self-help groups and skill-building programs), and from professional counselors. Unfortunately, most people don't seek help for problems until they are severe.

- Families must be made a national priority if we are to deal effectively with the multitude of problems in our country today. Most individual and social problems either begin or end up in the family. Families must cope with these problems, but we as a nation do little to support them.

- "Building the smallest democracy at the heart of society" was the theme of the 1994 United Nations International Year of the Family. Conference participants extolled the family as "the basic unit of society" and argued that because of this status, it warrants special attention.

- To become and remain a healthy individual and a member of a strong family, keep building connections with your family and friends and become genuinely involved in the life of your community and the family of humankind.

Activities

1. In small groups, discuss the Gaia hypothesis, which suggests that earth is a living entity. Consider ecological interconnections: how environmental issues affect large areas of our planet. Then consider human interconnections: how challenges that affect individuals and families in one region can affect individuals and families in other regions.

2. What will the future be like in *your* family? What can you do to make it brighter? Write a short essay on this topic, and share it with a small group.

3. What will the future be like for families in the United States and around the world? Discuss this issue in a small group.

4. What can we do as individuals to help other members of the human family? Discuss this issue in a small group.

5. What have you learned about families and about life in this class? Write a short essay on this topic, and share it with a small group.

6. For any or all of the preceding activities, share the findings of your small group with the class. What differences and common themes emerge from the class's overall findings.

Suggested Readings

Doherty, W. J. (1997) *The intentional family: How to build family ties in our modern world.* Reading, M.A.: Addison-Wesley Publishing. An excellent resource for how to develop and maintain important family rituals and how to become intentional.

Guerney, B., Jr., & Maxson, P. (1991). Marital and family enrichment research. In A. Booth (Ed.), *Contemporary families: Looking forward, looking back.* Minneapolis: National Council on Family Relations (pp. 457–465). Review of recent advances in marital enrichment techniques, by a team headed by a pioneer in the study of how to enrich relationships.

Hogan, M. J. (Ed.). (1995). *Initiatives for families: Research, policy, practice, education.* St. Paul, MN: National Council on Family Relations. NCFR's written contribution to the United Nations International Year of the Family.

Hunt, R. A., Hof, L., & DeMaria, R. (Eds.). (1998). *Marriage enrichment: Preparation, mentoring, and outreach.* Philadelphia: Brunner/Mazel. Provides an excellent overview of a variety of couple programs and recommendations for helping couples improve their relationship.

Lovelock, J. E. (1979, 1987). *Gaia: A new look at life on earth.* Oxford, England: Oxford University Press. Hypothesizes that the earth, through its atmosphere and oceans, functions effectively as one self-regulated organism.

Maddock, J. W., Hogan, J., Antonov, A. I., & Matskovsky, M. S. (Eds.). (1994). *Families before and after perestroika: Russian and U.S. perspectives.* New York: Guilford Press. Illustrates that major differences in political and social orientation do not necessarily go hand in hand with equally major differences in family issues.

McAdoo, H. P. (1993). *Family ethnicity: Strength in diversity.* Newbury Park, CA: Sage. A respectful celebration of ethnic and cultural diversity among families that can prompt discussion at home and in schools.

Menzel, P. (1995). *Material world: A global family portrait.* San Francisco: Sierra Club Books. Photographs of families around the world who have placed all their earthly possessions outside, in front of their home; remarkable contrasts among countries and cultures are fascinating.

Olson, D. H., DeFrain, J., & Olson, A. (1998). *Building relationships.* Roseville, MN: Life Innovations. A book for young adults in middle schools and high schools who are interested in creating satisfying friendships.

Olson, D. H., & Kilmer Hanson, M. (Eds.). (1990). NCFR presidential report—*2001: Preparing families for the future.* St. Paul, MN: National Council on Family Relations. Nineteen eminent family scholars make recommendations for improving the quality of family life.

Piercy, F. P., & Sprenkle, D. H. (1991). Marriage and family therapy. In A. Booth (Ed.), *Contemporary families: Looking forward, looking back.* Minneapolis: National Council on Family Relations (pp. 446–456). A comprehensive review of the field of marital and family therapy from 1980 to 1990, a decade in which the field grew considerably in popularity, in influence as a therapeutic approach, and in value in helping people with emotional issues.

Stinnett, N., Stinnett, N., DeFrain, J., & DeFrain, N. (1999). *Creating a strong family.* West Monroe, LA: Howard. Describes the qualities of strong families, with a special emphasis on spiritual well-being.

Weeks, G. R., & Treat, S. (1992). *Couples in treatment: Techniques and approaches for effective practice.* New York: Brunner/Mazel. A useful, eclectic book for beginning therapists.

Couple and Family Scales

The Couple and Family Map can be used to define the way in which a couple or a family interacts—that is, to describe the family system. The Couple and Family Scales are the tools an interviewer uses to place the couple or family in the Couple and Family Map. In this resource section we will outline the instructions for using these scales. The process consists of six steps:

1. Understanding the dimensions and concepts of the Couple and Family Map.

2. Interviewing the couple or family.

3. Completing the Coalition Rating Scale.

4. Assigning a scale value for each concept.

5. Assigning a global rating for each dimension.

6. Plotting the global ratings on the Couple and Family Map.

Step 1: Dimensions and Concepts

There are three primary dimensions in the Couple and Family Map: family cohesion, family flexibility, and family communication. Each dimension has several concepts that help define and describe it. Before doing an assessment of a couple or a family, the interviewer reviews all the concepts and their descriptions for each of the three dimensions. Table A.1 lists and describes the concepts for the three dimensions.

Step 2: Interview Questions

To assess a couple or a family, the interviewer, usually through a semistructured interview, evaluates the couple's or family's interactions in terms of each of the concepts for each dimension. Those experienced in using the Family and Couple Scales find it helpful to encourage the couple or family to discuss with each other the interview questions in Box A.1. The questions focus on the two dimensions of cohesion and flexibility but not on communication. To assess communication, the interviewer simply observes how the couple or family communicate while they are discussing the interview questions. The interviewer should encourage the couple or the family to talk directly to each other—*not* to the interviewer—so that the interviewer can observe how they interact with each other.

Step 3: The Coalition Rating Scale

After the interview, the interviewer first completes the Coalition Rating Scale (shown in Box A.2), if it applies. It is necessary to use this scale if one or more family members function differently from the rest of the family. For example, it is possible to have a *rigidly enmeshed* family with a *chaotically disengaged* husband. If there is a disengaged member or a coalition (see definitions given in Box A.2), these family members are rated separately from the rest of the family system. The interviewer completes the Coalition Rating Scale *first*, before completing the other scales.

Table A.1 Couple and Family Scales

Levels of Family Cohesion

COHESION							
DISENGAGED (UNBALANCED)		CONNECTED (BALANCED)		COHESIVE (BALANCED)		ENMESHED (UNBALANCED)	
SCORE 1	2	3	4	5	6	7	8
Separateness/ Togetherness High separateness		More separateness than togetherness		More togetherness than separateness		Very high togetherness	
I-We balance Primarily "I"		More "I" than "We"		More "We" than "I"		Primarily "We"	
Closeness Little closeness		Low to moderate closeness		Moderate to high closeness		Very high closeness	
Loyalty Lack of loyalty		Some loyalty		Considerable loyalty		High loyalty	
Activities Mainly separate		More separate than shared		More shared than shared		Mainly shared	
Dependence/ Independence High independence		More independence than dependence		More dependence than independence		High dependence	

Levels of Family Flexibility

FLEXIBILITY							
RIGID (UNBALANCED)		STRUCTURED (BALANCED)		FLEXIBLE (BALANCED)		CHAOTIC (UNBALANCED)	
SCORE 1	2	3	4	5	6	7	8
Leadership Authoritarian		Sometimes shared		Often shared		Lack of leadership	
Discipline Strict discipline		Somewhat democratic		Democratic		Erratic/inconsistent	
Negotiation Limited discussion		Organized discussion		Open discussion		Endless discussion	
Roles Roles very stable		Roles stable		Role-sharing		Dramatic role shifts	
Rules Unchanging rules		Few rule changes		Some rule changes		Frequent rule changes	
Change Very little change		Moderate change		Some change		Considerable change	

Levels of Family Flexibility

COMMUNICATION					
POOR		GOOD		VERY GOOD	
SCORE 1	2	3	4	5	6
Listening skills Poor listening skills		Appears to listen, but feedback is limited		Gives feedback, indicating good listening skills	
Speaking skills Often speaks for others		Speaks for oneself more than for others		Speaks mainly for oneself rather than for others	
Self-disclosure Low sharing of feelings		Moderate sharing of feelings		High sharing of feelings	
Clarity Inconsistent messages		Clear messages		Very clear messages	
Staying on topic Seldom stays on topic		Often stays on topic		Mainly stays on topic	
Respect and regard Low to moderate		Moderate to high		High	

BOX A.1

Interview Questions for Assessing Family Cohesion and Flexibility

Questions for Assessing Family Cohesion

1. *Separateness/Togetherness:* How much do family members go their own way versus spending time with the family?

2. *I-We balance:* Do family members have a good balance of time apart and together?

3. *Closeness:* Do people feel close to each other?

4. *Loyalty:* Is the family a top priority compared with work or friends?

5. *Activities:* Do people spend much time having fun together?

6. *Dependence/Independence:* Do family members stay in close contact?

Other Useful Questions to Assess Family Cohesion

1. How does your family celebrate birthdays and holidays?

2. Describe your typical dinnertime meal in terms of who is present, who prepares the meal, who cleans up, and the type of family interaction that occurs.

3. What is a typical weekend like in your family?

4. Do you have special times when you get together as a family?

Questions for Assessing Family Flexibility

1. *Leadership:* Is leadership shared between parents?

2. *Discipline:* Is (was) discipline strict?

3. *Negotiation:* How do you negotiate differences in your family?

4. *Roles:* Does each spouse do only certain tasks?

5. *Rules:* Do rules change in your family?

6. *Change:* Is change upsetting to your family?

Other Useful Questions to Assess Family Adaptability

1. How open is your family to change?

2. Is your family good at problem solving?

3. Does your family seem disorganized?

4. Who is in charge—the parent(s) or the child(ren)?

Step 4: Assigning Scale Values

After interviewing the couple or family, the interviewer rates them on each of the concepts that make up the three dimensions, using the scales in Table A.1. Before selecting a value, the interviewer carefully reads the descriptions for each concept and then selects a value from 1 to 8 that most closely represents the couple or family as a unit.

Step 5: Assigning Global Ratings

After assigning a rating for each concept in each of the three dimensions and recording those ratings on Table A.2, the interviewer makes a global rating for each of the three dimensions (cohesion, flexibility, and communication) and records the global ratings on Table A.2. The global rating for each dimension should be based on an overall evaluation rather than on a sum of the subscale (concept) ratings.

The Coalition Rating Scale

Instructions

The functioning of most families can be adequately described based on their assessment as a unit or group. However, some families include individuals or dyadic units (coalitions) whose functioning may be markedly different from that of the rest of the family as a group.

This Coalition Rating Scale provides a way of noting coalitions' or disengaged individuals' patterns in family systems. After observing the family's interactions, any coalitions or disengaged individuals should be identified by checking the relevant categories below.

Definitions

Coalition. A coalition is two or more people with a high degree of emotional closeness to one another. During family interaction, the members of a coalition are very connected to one another and may at times exclude other family members.

Disengaged Individual(s). A disengaged individual is emotionally separated from the rest of the family. Disengaged individuals often exhibit a low degree of involvement and interaction with other family members.

Coalitions	**Disengaged Individuals**
___ Mother-Son	___ Disengaged Mother
___ Mother-Daughter	___ Disengaged Father
___ Father-Son	___ Disengaged Child(ren)
___ Father-Daughter	___ Other
___ Son-Daughter	
___ Same-Sex Siblings	
___ Other	

(A husband-wife coalition is considered a positive dyad and is therefore not listed.)

Step 6: Plotting a Family System Type on the Couple and Family Map

Finally, the interviewer plots the couple's or the family's global ratings on cohesion and flexibility on the Couple and Family Map (Figure A.1). This determines the marital or family system type. If, for example, the interviewer assigns a family a global rating of 5 on the cohesion dimension and 4 on the flexibility dimension, the model will identify the family as *structurally cohesive,* one of the four balanced family types on the Couple and Family Map. If the family contains a coalition or a disengaged member, the interviewer also plots the coalition or member on the map.

Table A.2 Couple and Family Rating Form

COHESION								
	DISENGAGED		CONNECTED		COHESIVE		ENMESHED	
SCORE	1	2	3	4	5	6	7	8
Separateness/ Togetherness	☐	☐	☐	☐	☐	☐	☐	☐
I-We balance	☐	☐	☐	☐	☐	☐	☐	☐
Closeness	☐	☐	☐	☐	☐	☐	☐	☐
Loyalty	☐	☐	☐	☐	☐	☐	☐	☐
Activities	☐	☐	☐	☐	☐	☐	☐	☐
Dependence/ Independence	☐	☐	☐	☐	☐	☐	☐	☐
Global rating	☐	☐	☐	☐	☐	☐	☐	☐

FLEXIBILITY								
	RIGID		STRUCTURED		FLEXIBLE		CHAOTIC	
SCORE	1	2	3	4	5	6	7	8
Leadership	☐	☐	☐	☐	☐	☐	☐	☐
Discipline	☐	☐	☐	☐	☐	☐	☐	☐
Negotiation	☐	☐	☐	☐	☐	☐	☐	☐
Roles	☐	☐	☐	☐	☐	☐	☐	☐
Rules	☐	☐	☐	☐	☐	☐	☐	☐
Change	☐	☐	☐	☐	☐	☐	☐	☐
Global rating	☐	☐	☐	☐	☐	☐	☐	☐

COMMUNICATION						
	POOR		GOOD		VERY GOOD	
SCORE	1	2	3	4	5	6
Listening skills	☐	☐	☐	☐	☐	☐
Speaking skills	☐	☐	☐	☐	☐	☐
Self-disclosure	☐	☐	☐	☐	☐	☐
Clarity	☐	☐	☐	☐	☐	☐
Staying on topic	☐	☐	☐	☐	☐	☐
Respect and regard	☐	☐	☐	☐	☐	☐
Global rating	☐	☐	☐	☐	☐	☐

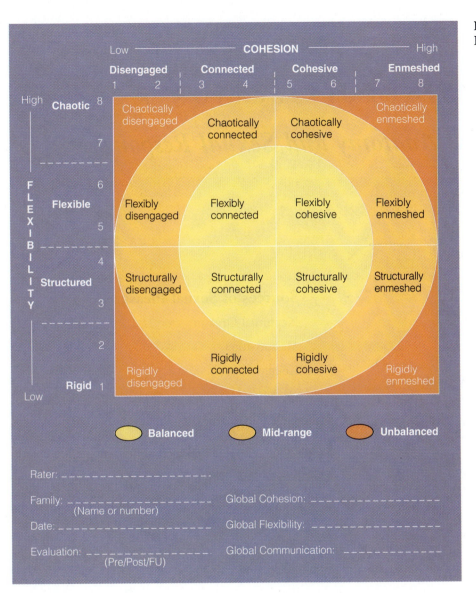

Figure A.1 Couple and Family Map

In this resource section we will briefly explore sexual anatomy—the structure of the male and the female sexual organs—as a basis for understanding human sexual response. We will discuss the mechanics of sexual arousal in both sexes and various sources of sexual pleasure. Finally, we will look at the influence of alcohol and other drugs on sexual response.

Sexual Anatomy

A baby's sex is determined at the moment of fertilization, but during the first few months of development inside the mother, boys and girls are virtually identical. A small bud develops between the fetus's legs that later becomes the boy's penis or the girl's clitoris. Two swellings emerge, one on either side of the bud. In boys, the swellings develop into a scrotum. In girls, a slit forms between the swellings and develops into a vagina. In the first few months of fetal development, the boy's primitive testicles and the girl's growing ovaries are located deep inside the abdominal cavity.

Although the mature sex organs of males and females differ in appearance, they developed from the same structures and perform similar functions. Each individual has a pair of **gonads:** Female gonads are called **ovaries,** and male gonads are called **testes** (or testicles). Gonads produce germ cells and sex hormones. The female **germ cells** are called **ova** (eggs) and the male germ cells are called **sperm.** Ova and sperm are the basic units of reproduction. Their joining can lead to the development of a new human being (Insel & Roth, 1998).

Female Sex Organs

The external sex organs, or **genitals,** of the female are called the **vulva** ("covering"). The *mons pubis* is a round body of fatty tissue covering the pubic bone, which becomes covered with hair during puberty. Below the mons pubis are two pairs of skin folds called *labia majora* (major lips) and *labia minora* (minor lips). The labia enclose (1) the clitoris, (2) the opening of the urethra, and (3) the opening of the vagina. The **clitoris** is covered by a *prepuce* (a fold of skin) called the *foreskin* or *clitoral hood* and has a shaft, a glans, and spongy tissue that fills with blood during sexual arousal; in this regard the clitoris and the penis are similar. Because the clitoris is highly sensitive to the touch, it plays an important role in female sexual arousal. The **urethra** is a tube connecting the urinary bladder to its opening, located in the female between the clitoris and the opening of the vagina. In the female, the urethra is independent of the genitals (Insel & Roth, 1998).

The **vagina,** the female organ for sexual intercourse, is a passage that leads to the internal reproductive organs. The opening to the vagina is partially covered by a membrane called the **hymen.** Although some people believe that an intact hymen is the sign of a virgin, this belief is a myth; the hymen can be stretched or torn during athletic activities, as well as by first sexual intercourse. The vagina is the birth canal during childbirth. It has soft, flexible walls that are normally in contact with each other. A cylinder of muscles surrounds the vagina; during sexual excitement, muscle tension increases, and the walls of the vagina swell with blood. The vagina leads to the **uterus** (or *womb*), a pear-shaped organ, slanting forward

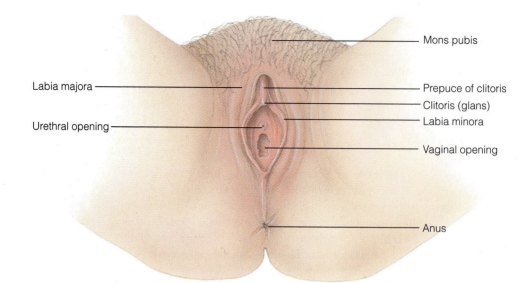

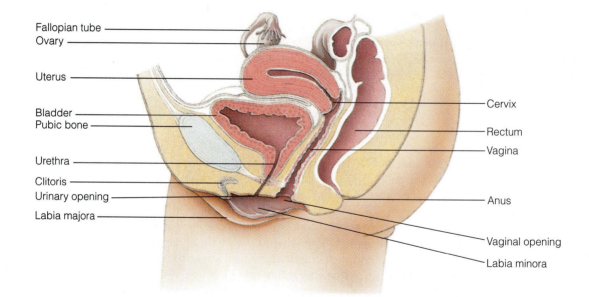

Figure B.1 Female Sex Organs. *Source: Core Concepts in Health* (8th ed. 1998 Update) (p. 105) by P. M. Insel and W. T. Roth, 1998, Mountain View, CA: Mayfield. Copyright 1998 by Mayfield Publishing Co. Reprinted by permission.

above the bladder, in which a fertilized egg implants itself and grows into an embryo, then a fetus. The neck of the uterus, called the **cervix,** projects into the upper part of the vagina. Two *oviducts* (or *fallopian tubes*) lead out from the top of the uterus. The fringed end of each tube surrounds an ovary. Approximately once a month, a mature ovum (egg) bursts from its follicle (sac or cavity) on the surface of one of the ovaries and passes down an oviduct into the uterus. The female sex organs are illustrated in Figure B.1.

Male Sex Organs

The external sex organs of the male are the penis and the scrotum. The **penis** is composed of spongy tissue, which engorges with blood during sexual arousal, causing the organ to enlarge and become erect. The **scrotum** is the pouch containing the man's two testes, in which sperm are produced. The process of sperm production is extremely heat sensitive, and the scrotum helps keep the testes cooler than the rest of the body. When the weather is hot, the scrotum muscles relax and the testes move away from the heat of the body; when it is cold, the scrotum muscles contract and the testes move upward toward the body. These reactions help to maintain the temperature differential necessary for sperm production. (It has been found, for example, that wearing tightly fitting undershorts in the summer can interfere with normal sperm production; Insel & Roth, 1998).

The most sensitive part of the penis and an important source of sexual arousal is the **glans,** the smooth, rounded tip. When a male is born, the **foreskin,** or prepuce, almost completely covers the glans. In 60% of males in the United States (and in an estimated 15% of males worldwide), this retractable fold of skin is surgically removed in a 5-minute procedure called **circumcision.** This surgery, usually performed in infancy, is done for religious and hygienic reasons.

Opponents of routine circumcision have called it "America's leading unnecessary surgery." In addition to being painful to infants, the process can cause irritation of the penis and poses the risk of surgical complications and errors. Proponents of circumcision argue that the procedure makes it easier to keep the penis clean and that circumcised males are less likely to develop cancer of the penis, a rare disease that occurs almost exclusively in uncircumcised men (Insel & Roth, 1998). The American Academy of Pediatrics (AAP) analyzed 40 years of available medical research on circumcision and said that "the benefits are not significant enough for the AAP to recommend circumcision as a routine procedure" (American Academy of Pediatrics, 1999). "The practice is not essential to the child's well-being at birth," the AAP argues, "even though it may have some potential medical benefits." The AAP further reported that although studies have found the risk for penile cancer to be three times greater for uncircumcised men than for circumcised men, only 9 to 10 cases of penile cancer are diagnosed per year per 1 million men. Thus, although the incidence of penile cancer is greater in uncircumcised men, the overall risk of developing this type of cancer is extremely low.

The male urethra runs the entire length of the penis and carries both urine and **semen** (a mixture of sperm and seminal fluid) to an opening at the tip of the glans. Although urine and semen travel through a common passageway, sphincter muscles control their entry into the urethra and prevent them from passing through at the same time (Insel & Roth, 1998). Sperm are produced in the testes in tightly packed seminiferous (sperm-bearing) tubules. These tubules empty into a maze of ducts that flow into a single storage tube, called the *epididymis*, on the surface of each testis. This tube then leads to the *vasa deferentia* (singular, *vas deferens*), two tubes rising into the abdominal cavity and connecting to the prostate gland.

Inside the prostate gland the vasa deferentia join the two seminal vesicles, whose secretions provide nutrients to the semen. The **prostate gland** produces some of the fluid in semen that nourishes and transports sperm. The seminal vesicles and the vasa deferentia lead on each side to the ejaculatory duct, which joins the urethra. *Cowper's glands*, on each side of the urethra, secrete clear, mucuslike

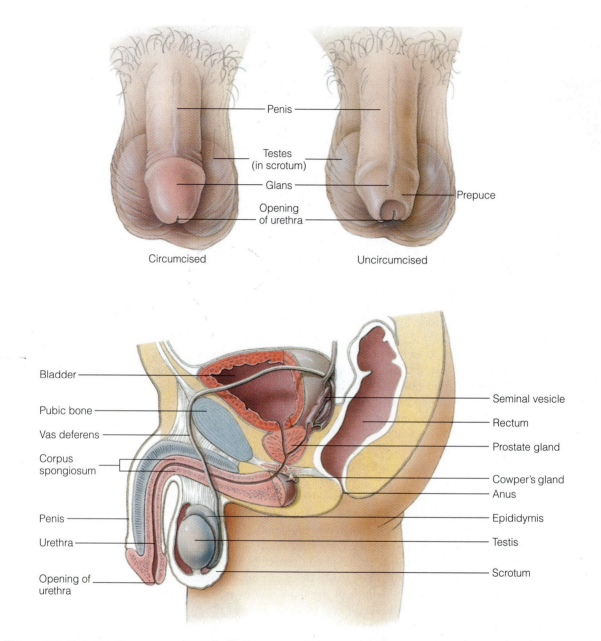

Penis

Testes
(in scrotum)

Glans

Opening
of urethra

Prepuce

Circumcised

Uncircumcised

Bladder

Pubic bone

Vas deferens

Corpus
spongiosum

Penis

Urethra

Opening of
urethra

Seminal vesicle

Rectum

Prostate gland

Cowper's gland

Anus

Epididymis

Testis

Scrotum

Figure B.2 Male Sex Organs. *Source: Core Concepts in Health* (8th ed. 1998 Update) (p. 106) by P. M. Insel and W. T. Roth, 1998, Mountain View, CA: Mayfield. Copyright 1998 by Mayfield Publishing Co. Reprinted by permission.

fluid during sexual arousal. This fluid appears at the tip of the penis. Although its purpose is not clearly understood, this fluid may contain a few sperm in some men. This is why withdrawal of the penis before ejaculation is not a reliable form of birth control. Figure B.2 shows the male sex organs.

Male and Female Arousal

Erotic stimulation leads to erotic arousal (excitement), and this can culminate for both females and males in **orgasm,** an intensely pleasurable experience. The sense of touch is at the center of the sexual experience. People touch each other with their hands, arms, legs, and faces. The senses of smell, hearing, vision, and taste are also important in sexual arousal. Perhaps just as important, sexual excitement is generated between people on a psychological level. People touch each other, figuratively speaking, with their eyes, their minds, their spirits. Arousal, clearly, is not simply the manipulation of sexual organs in a variety of ways. Sexual intimacy for many people is best when it is expressed as a matter of the heart. Thus, when the sexual aspect of a relationship dies, a couple may become distressed that it signals the death of feelings for each other in general (Cohen, 1987).

Researchers studying human sexual response speculate that there are neurological differences between men and women that may trigger a more complex and exciting orgasm in females. As recently as the early 1960s, the conventional wisdom was that men were basically more sexual than women. Sex researchers and therapists William H. Masters and Virginia E. Johnson shattered a number of myths about sexual intercourse, however, in their landmark study *Human Sexual Response* (1966). During a series of studies, subjects were fitted with electrodes to measure heart rate and breathing, sensors to gauge the strength of muscle contractions, and cameras to film the inside of the vagina. Nearly 700 participants were observed during intercourse and masturbation. The researchers tried to study a wide variety of people: For example, some of the participants were older, some were pregnant, some were homosexual.

To describe what they observed, the researchers developed a four-stage model: excitement, plateau, orgasm, and resolution (Figure B.3). These four stages of sexual response involve almost every part of the human body. The excitement phase is a period of gradual buildup—increasing muscle tension, vaginal lubrication, and the engorgement of blood vessels in the penis, the clitoris, and the nipples. Plateau is a sustained period of excitement: Heart rate and respiration increase, and the skin flushes. Orgasm is the discharge of the built-up tension, marked by muscle contractions throughout the body (particularly in the genital area), disgorgement of the collected blood, ejaculation in the male, and intense pleasure in both sexes. The resolution phase is a period of diminishing tension; the body returns rapidly through the plateau and excitement phases to an unstimulated state.

Masters and Johnson reported several striking similarities between men and women during sex: parallel sensitivities in the penis and the clitoris, flushing of the chest during the plateau phase, and identical rhythmic contractions of the anal sphincter during orgasm. They found at least one critical difference. In men the resolution phase was followed by a complete loss of sexual responsiveness, lasting anywhere from a few minutes in adolescents to a day or more in older men. Women, on the other hand, appeared capable of returning to another orgasmic experience at any point in the resolution phase. Some women experienced one orgasm after another in uninterrupted succession. It appeared that women were potentially more sexually responsive than men. Masters and Johnson's research overturned the Victorian notion of poorer female responsiveness and helped pave the way for a new sort of sexual liberation (Konner, 1988).

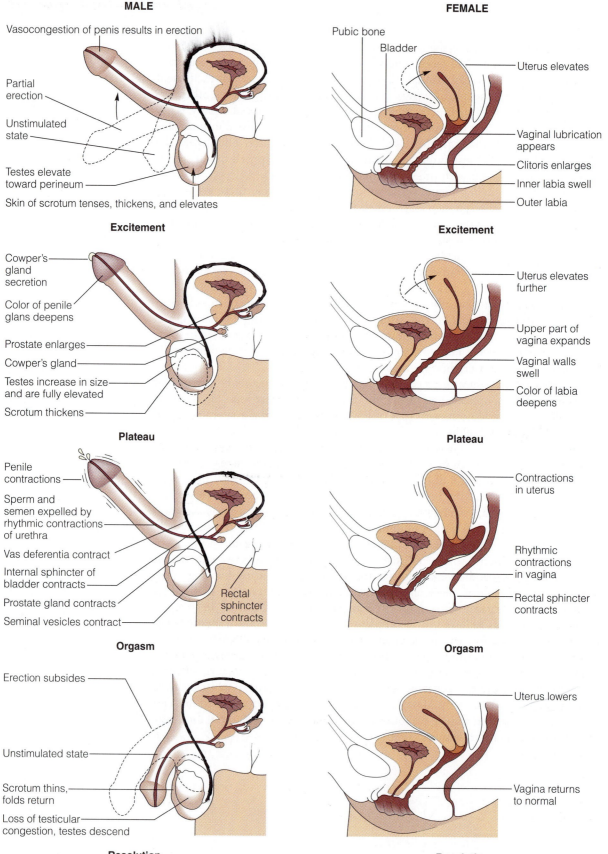

MALE

Vasocongestion of penis results in erection

Partial erection

Unstimulated state

Testes elevate toward perineum

Skin of scrotum tenses, thickens, and elevates

Excitement

Cowper's gland secretion

Color of penile glans deepens

Prostate enlarges

Cowper's gland

Testes increase in size and are fully elevated

Scrotum thickens

Plateau

Penile contractions

Sperm and semen expelled by rhythmic contractions of urethra

Vas deferentia contract

Internal sphincter of bladder contracts

Prostate gland contracts

Seminal vesicles contract

Rectal sphincter contracts

Orgasm

Erection subsides

Unstimulated state

Scrotum thins, folds return

Loss of testicular congestion, testes descend

Resolution

FEMALE

Pubic bone

Bladder

Uterus elevates

Vaginal lubrication appears

Clitoris enlarges

Inner labia swell

Outer labia

Excitement

Uterus elevates further

Upper part of vagina expands

Vaginal walls swell

Color of labia deepens

Plateau

Contractions in uterus

Rhythmic contractions in vagina

Rectal sphincter contracts

Orgasm

Uterus lowers

Vagina returns to normal

Resolution

Sources of Sexual Pleasure

In this section we will discuss various ways in which men and women achieve sexual satisfaction. We will also look at sexual preferences among members of both sexes.

Nocturnal Orgasm

Nocturnal orgasm is defined as sexual arousal and response that occurs during sleep. Both males and females experience these types of orgasms, which are often accompanied by erotic dreams. The popular term *wet dream* describes male ejaculation during sleep. From both scientific and psychological perspectives, nocturnal orgasms are generally considered enjoyable sexual experiences.

Masturbation

Masturbation, also called *autoeroticism* or *self-stimulation*, is one form of sexual expression. During a major survey of the sexual behavior of 2,765 people of various ages, Janus and Janus (1993) asked subjects about their masturbation habits. About 50% to 70% of those surveyed reported rarely or never masturbating. About 5% to 15% reported masturbating monthly, and 10% to 25% reported masturbating weekly. About 25% of the men reported masturbating several times a week; this was true for only about 5% to 10% of the women. In general, across all age groups, men masturbated more frequently than did women, and more women rarely or never masturbated than did men.

We will describe methods of masturbation in some detail here to help people understand what is stimulating to both women and men. This understanding can foster a more satisfactory sexual relationship.

Women most commonly masturbate by manipulating the clitoris and the inner lips. They may rub themselves up and down or in a circular motion, sometimes lightly or sometimes applying more pressure to the clitoris. Some women prefer rubbing the side of the clitoris, whereas others stimulate the glans of the clitoris directly. The inner lips may also be stroked or tugged. Some men imagine that women masturbate by inserting a finger or some similar-shaped object deep into the vagina. In fact, clitoral and labial manipulation is the most common form of female masturbation. Of those women in the Kinsey study who masturbated, 84% massaged the clitoris and labia, whereas only 20% inserted fingers or other objects into the vagina (Kinsey, Pomeroy, Martin, & Gebhard, 1953).

Almost all men reported masturbating by hand stimulation of the penis; it takes most men only 1 to 2 minutes to reach orgasm this way (Kinsey et al., 1948, p. 509). Most men encircle the shaft of the penis with their hand and move the hand up and down to stimulate the shaft and the glans. How tight the man grips the penis, how fast he moves his hand up and down, and how much he stimulates the glans varies from one man to another. Most men increase the speed of the up-and-down movements as they approach orgasm and slow or stop the stimulation at

Figure B.3 The Stages of Sexual Response. *Source: Core Concepts in Health* (8th ed.—1998 Update) (113) by P. M. Insel and W. T. Roth, 1998), Mountain View, CA: Mayfield. Copyright 1998 by Mayfield Publishing Co. Reprinted by permission.

orgasm because further motion is uncomfortable (Masters & Johnson, 1966). At the point of ejaculation, men often grip the shaft tightly. After ejaculation, the tip of the penis is hypersensitive, and men usually avoid further stimulation of the penis for a while.

From both scientific and mental health perspectives, there is little evidence to suggest that masturbation is a problem. Some people worry about "excessive" masturbation, but this is hard to define; however, masturbation that occurs so often that it precludes other important aspects of life could be termed excessive.

Couple Sex

Couples stimulate each other sexually in a wide variety of ways. Common approaches include mutual masturbation, oral sex, and a variety of coital positions. We will also discuss mutual orgasm in this section.

In terms of sexual pleasure and achieving an orgasm, both men (82%) and women (69%) favored sexual intercourse, according to the Janus survey of 2,765 individuals (Janus & Janus, 1993, p. 98). Surprisingly, 18% of women but only 10% of men preferred oral sex. Only 5% of men and 8% of women preferred masturbation as a way to achieve orgasm.

Mutual masturbation involves two partners who masturbate each other. It is a pleasurable practice, and the chance of pregnancy or the transmission of sexual diseases is lessened when it is done with care. Mutual masturbation is one of the major techniques gay-male and lesbian couples use during sexual intimacy (Allgeier & Allgeier, 1998).

Attitudes toward **oral sex**—using one's mouth to stimulate the partner's genitals—have become more and more accepting over the past few decades, especially among younger people and the more formally educated. Oral sex is a prelude to sexual intercourse for some couples; others enjoy it without intercourse. Partners can take turns satisfying each other or can simultaneously stimulate each other in the so-called 69 (head-to-foot) position. Couples interested in exploring oral sex should have a relatively positive image of their sexual organs, basic cleanliness, a willingness to try different positions and techniques, and open and honest communication about their likes and dislikes (Francoeur, 1982, 1997).

Human beings assume a wide variety of positions when engaging in **sexual intercourse.** Masters and Johnson (1966) found in their research that a woman's sexual response is likely to develop more rapidly and with greater intensity when she is on top of the man in the face-to-face position during sexual intercourse.

The typical coital position used in a culture often depends on the social status of females in that culture (Beigel, 1953). The woman-above position is most popular when sexual satisfaction is just as important for females as it is for men, as in several American Indian tribes and in cultures in the South Pacific. In contrast, Kinsey's research, conducted in the United States, concluded that "nearly all coitus in our English-American culture occurs with the partners lying face to face, with the male above the female. There may be as much as 70 percent of the population which has never attempted to use any other position in intercourse" (Kinsey et al., 1948, p. 578).

Today, this so-called **missionary position** remains popular among Americans, but couples likely experiment with many different positions. Feminism has changed many aspects of American culture, and its influence is clearly seen in the bedroom.

In the face-to-face, man-above position, a woman usually lies on her back, legs apart, knees slightly bent. An advantage of this face-to-face position is that partners can communicate feelings clearly through erotic kissing, eye contact, and facial expressions. Disadvantages of this position are that when the man's body is a great deal heavier than the woman's body, she is not as free to participate in sexual movements that are pleasurable to her; also, the man's hands are not as free to stimulate his partner's breasts in this position (Allgeier & Allgeier, 1998).

The advantage of the face-to-face, woman-above position for women is similar to one advantage of the man-above position for men: The woman is free to move in ways pleasurable to her. A further advantage of this position is that the man experiences less sexual intensity; if the woman is slower to respond sexually than the man, which is quite common, this position helps the man prolong the pleasure of his sexual arousal before ejaculation. In short, this position often increases the possibility that both partners will achieve simultaneous orgasm (Allgeier & Allgeier, 1998).

Side-by-side intercourse offers both partners the chance to control their own body movements simultaneously. In this position, penetration of the penis tends to be somewhat shallow, and movements are not quite as vigorous. But the position does allow for free movement of the hands (Allgeier & Allgeier, 1998). Rear entry, in which the man slides his penis into the female's vagina from behind, is the most common coital position among nonhuman species. Some people find it distasteful for this reason, but it has some advantages for couples. The rear-entry position can be quite restful, and it works well during the third trimester of pregnancy and during illnesses that do not permit exertion (Allgeier & Allgeier, 1998).

As mentioned earlier, when masturbating, most men slow down or stop manual stimulation of the penis during orgasm. Women masturbating generally prefer continued stimulation of the clitoris or mons during orgasm. During sexual intercourse, men tend to attempt deep vaginal penetration with little further thrusting during orgasm, whereas women prefer continued male thrusting during their orgasm. These differences in the typical sexual response styles of men and women make mutual, or simultaneous, orgasm difficult to achieve. Because women can continue coitus indefinitely after an orgasm whereas men tend to lose their erection after ejaculation, a "ladies first" approach to lovemaking often works well for couples. If, for example, the woman finds it easiest to achieve orgasm in the woman-above position or through oral sex, a couple can employ this approach until she reaches orgasm and then shift to the position the man considers most stimulating (Allgeier & Allgeier, 1998).

The Influence of Alcohol and Other Drugs on Sex

Sexual intercourse, in an important sense, is an act of relaxation. Sex therapist Terry Mason puts it this way, "In order to 'feel good,' you've got to relax and let some things happen. You can't be afraid or have a lot of anxiety and tension about someone experiencing a part of your body and you experiencing a part of theirs. You can't kiss all tensed up and you can't touch somebody in a very loving sort of way if you're tense or they're tense" (cited in Poinsett, 1988).

RESOURCE SECTION C

Pregnancy and Childbirth

In this resource section we will explain the reproductive process, infertility, and pregnancy. We will then look at the birth process and childbirth practices. Finally, we will discuss the changes a new baby brings to the family and the impact on the family of miscarriage, stillbirth, or infant death.

The Process of Reproduction

Conception is a complicated process. In this section we will discuss how conception occurs, the nature of infertility, and signs of pregnancy.

Conception

The average woman's menstrual cycle lasts 28 days. For as long as she is fertile (approximately 35 years, from about age 12 to about age 47), each cycle prepares her body for **conception** and childbearing. The most fertile period occurs about midway through the menstrual cycle, or 14 days before the next **menses** begins. This is the point at which **ovulation** occurs.

Estimates of women's fertility have ranged from 2 days in a menstrual cycle to 10 or more. Research published in the *New England Journal of Medicine* indicates there are 6 days in every menstrual month when a woman can get pregnant ("A Woman's Fertility Window," 1995). Dr. Arthur Wilcox, who teaches at the University of North Carolina, argues that conception is possible if a woman has intercourse on the 5 days before ovulation as well as on the day her ovaries release a new egg. Sex before the 6-day period almost certainly will not result in pregnancy, nor will intercourse just one day after ovulation. The researchers at the National Institute of Environmental Health Sciences in Research Triangle Park, North Carolina, also found that 94% of pregnancies resulted from sperm that had lingered less than 3 days. There were no pregnancies from sperm more than 5 days old.

There are approximately a half-million eggs in the female ovaries at birth. Only 400 to 500 of them will ripen and be released into the oviducts during a woman's lifetime. Unfertilized eggs live about 24 hours; then they disintegrate and are expelled along with the uterine lining during **menstruation.** Each egg—made up of 23 chromosomes, fat droplets, protein substances, and nutrient fluid—is about the size of a pinpoint (1/250 inch in diameter; Insel & Roth, 1998).

Sperm cells are even smaller than eggs (1/8,000 inch in diameter). One average male ejaculation contains approximately 300 million to 400 million sperm. Sperm contain 23 chromosomes and have a tail for mobility. When a male ejaculates during intercourse, the sperm are propelled into the woman's vagina. Unless a sperm reaches and fertilizes an egg, it will die within about 72 hours. Many sperm cells die in the acidic environment of the vagina. The survivors migrate to the cervix, or "neck" of the uterus, where secretions are more alkaline and hospitable to sperm. Once inside the uterus, many sperm fail to reach an oviduct or to enter the oviduct that contains the egg. If an egg is not present in the oviduct, the sperm swim erratically. If the sperm have found the oviduct with the egg, they swim directly toward it, apparently drawn by chemicals released by the egg. Those sperm that come in contact with the egg must penetrate the tough membrane that encases it.

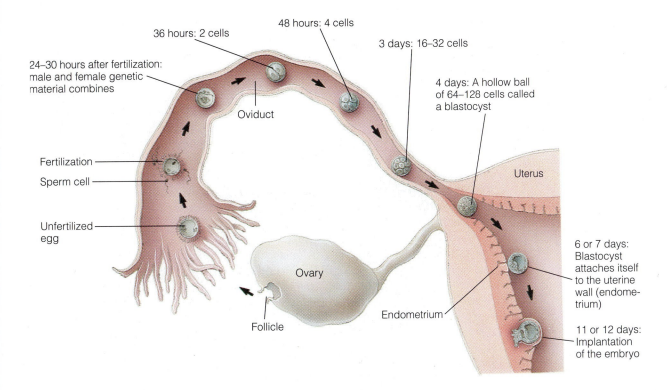

36 hours: 2 cells

48 hours: 4 cells

3 days: 16–32 cells

24–30 hours after fertilization: male and female genetic material combines

4 days: A hollow ball of 64–128 cells called a blastocyst

Oviduct

Fertilization

Sperm cell

Unfertilized egg

Uterus

Ovary

Endometrium

6 or 7 days: Blastocyst attaches itself to the uterine wall (endometrium)

Follicle

11 or 12 days: Implantation of the embryo

Figure C.1 Conception. *Source: Core Concepts in Health* (8th ed. 1998 Update) (p. 188) by P. M. Insel and W. T. Roth, 1998, Mountain View, CA: Mayfield. Copyright 1998 by Mayfield Publishing Co. Reprinted by permission.

Each sperm cell that makes contact with the egg deposits an enzyme that helps to dissolve this membrane. About 2,000 sperm manage to make it this far. The first sperm cell that meets a dissolved, bare spot on the egg cell can swim into the cell and merge with the nucleus of the egg. This union is called **fertilization.** The sperm's tail, which has served as a propeller during this journey, gets stuck in the outer membrane and drops off. The head of the sperm cell is implanted inside the egg, and no more sperm can enter, perhaps because on fertilization the egg releases a chemical making it impregnable (Insel & Roth, 1998). The fertilized egg travels for 3 to 4 days through an **oviduct** (fallopian tube) into the uterus (Figure C.1). The lining of the uterus has already become puffed out, which aids the implantation of the fertilized egg, the **zygote.**

The egg carries the hereditary characteristics of the mother and her ancestors; sperm cells carry the hereditary characteristics of the father and his ancestors. Each parent cell, the egg and the sperm, contains 23 chromosomes, and each chromosome has at least 1,000 genes. These genes are the genetic code, the chemical instructions for the design of every part of a new baby. These genes specify whether the new human being will be male or female, short or tall, blonde or brunette, and so on.

Environmental influences also affect the fetus's development a great deal during pregnancy. Health authorities urge a prospective mother to eat well; avoid alcohol, drugs, and smoking; get adequate rest and exercise; have medical checkups regularly; build intimate emotional relationships with a network of other people; and generally live a healthy lifestyle (Insel & Roth, 1998).

Infertility

Infertility is the inability to bear children. An estimated 1 in 13 American couples is unable to have children due to a variety of conditions that cause infertility (Insel & Roth, 1998).

There are several causes of infertility in women: failure to ovulate, menstrual cycle irregularities, endometriosis (abnormal tissue in the pelvic cavity, preventing conception), hormonal imbalances, scar tissue in the oviducts, physical abnormalities (an unusually shaped uterus), or an allergic response that kills the partner's sperm. Infertility in men is caused mainly by a low sperm count or by sperm with poor mobility. These problems can often be traced to an injury of the testicles, infection (mumps during adulthood is a common one), exposure to radiation, glandular disorders, birth defects, or exposure of the testicles to high temperatures (such as from taking hot baths).

Some types of infertility are subject to treatment; others are not. Surgery is sometimes helpful in repairing oviducts, clearing up endometriosis, and correcting anatomical problems. **Artificial insemination**—in which the man's sperm are collected, concentrated, and mechanically introduced into the woman's vagina or uterus—can sometimes aid conception in cases of male fertility problems. Some types of female infertility can be treated through **in vitro fertilization,** in which eggs are removed from the woman's ovary, fertilized in a laboratory dish with her partner's sperm, and implanted in her uterus. The most controversial approach to female infertility is **surrogate motherhood,** in which a fertile woman agrees—for a fee paid by the couple who cannot conceive—to be artificially inseminated by the husband's sperm, to carry the baby to term, and to give it to the couple at birth. Treatments for infertility are often expensive and emotionally draining, and chances for success are uncertain.

"Am I Pregnant?"

Common early indicators of pregnancy include the following:

- A missed menstrual period (although a woman can miss a period for many reasons, including stress, illness, and emotional upset).

- Nausea, usually but not always in the morning. **Morning sickness** tends to disappear by the 12th week of pregnancy.

- Changes in the shape, coloration, and sensitivity of the breasts. The breasts become fuller; the area around the nipples darkens; veins become more prominent; and the swelling causes tingling, throbbing, or minor pain.

- An increased need to urinate, resulting from pressure from the growing uterus on the bladder and hormonal changes.

- Fatigue and sleepiness caused by hormonal changes.

- An increase in vaginal secretions, either clear and nonirritating or slightly yellow and itchy.

- Retention of body fluids, including some swelling of the face, hands, and feet.

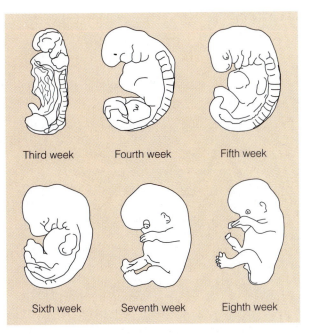

Figure C.2 The Fetal Development Process. *Source: Human Development: A Life-Span Approach*, NJ: Prentice-Hall. Copyright © 1998 by Prentice-Hall, Inc. Reprinted with permission of the publisher.

A woman who wants a highly reliable answer to the question "Am I pregnant?" can consult her physician, who can then perform a pregnancy test. The woman can also purchase a pregnancy test kit at a pharmacy. These home tests can determine pregnancy roughly 7 to 10 days after a missed menstrual period; they are reliable 95% to 99% of the time (Allgeier & Allgeier, 1998). Confirmation of the home test, as well as other information and services, can be obtained at a medical clinic.

Pregnancy and Preparation for Birth

Not more than 36 hours after fertilization, the egg has divided in half; by 48 hours, the egg has divided again into four. The process of division continues as the egg moves down the oviduct. Within 3 to 4 days the tiny fertilized mass, containing anywhere from 64 to 128 cells, reaches the uterus. The mass, called a **blastocyst,** is hollow at the center. The outer shell of cells (*trophoblast*) multiplies faster than the inner cells and eventually grows into the **placenta, umbilical cord,** and **amniotic sac.** The inner cells grow into three distinct layers: the innermost layer (*endoderm*) becomes the inner body parts; the middle layer (*mesoderm*) becomes muscle, bone, blood, kidneys, and sex glands; and the outermost layer (*ectoderm*) eventually grows into the skin, hair, and nervous tissue. Six or seven days after fertilization, the blastocyst begins implanting itself in the wall of the uterus, and its cells start to take nourishment from the uterine lining (Insel & Roth, 1998). Figure C.2 illustrates the stages of fetal development.

Pregnancy progresses over the course of three **trimesters,** periods of 13 weeks each. During each trimester, important prenatal milestones occur (Figure C.3). During the first trimester, the external appearance of the mother's body changes very little, although she may experience some or all of the common signs of

Figure C.3 Milestones of Prenatal Development.

Source: Understanding Children (2nd ed.) (p. 86) by J. A. Schickedanz, D. I. Schickedanz, K. Hansen, and P. D. Forsyth, 1997, Mountain View, CA: Mayfield. Copyright 1997 by Mayfield Publishing Co. Reprinted by permission.

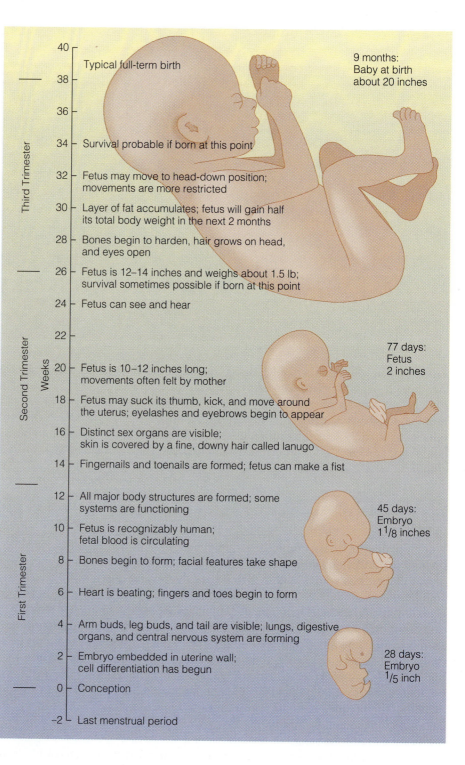

Third Trimester

- 38 Typical full-term birth
- 34 Survival probable if born at this point
- 32 Fetus may move to head-down position; movements are more restricted
- 30 Layer of fat accumulates; fetus will gain half its total body weight in the next 2 months
- 28 Bones begin to harden, hair grows on head, and eyes open
- 26 Fetus is 12–14 inches and weighs about 1.5 lb; survival sometimes possible if born at this point
- 24 Fetus can see and hear

9 months: Baby at birth about 20 inches

Second Trimester

Weeks

- 20 Fetus is 10–12 inches long; movements often felt by mother
- 18 Fetus may suck its thumb, kick, and move around the uterus; eyelashes and eyebrows begin to appear
- 16 Distinct sex organs are visible; skin is covered by a fine, downy hair called lanugo
- 14 Fingernails and toenails are formed; fetus can make a fist

77 days: Fetus 2 inches

First Trimester

- 12 All major body structures are formed; some systems are functioning
- 10 Fetus is recognizably human; fetal blood is circulating
- 8 Bones begin to form; facial features take shape
- 6 Heart is beating; fingers and toes begin to form

45 days: Embryo 1 1/8 inches

- 4 Arm buds, leg buds, and tail are visible; lungs, digestive organs, and central nervous system are forming
- 2 Embryo embedded in uterine wall; cell differentiation has begun
- 0 Conception
- –2 Last menstrual period

28 days: Embryo 1/5 inch

pregnancy listed earlier. In the second trimester, which some women consider the most peaceful part of a pregnancy, the mother gains weight, and it becomes clear to others that she is pregnant. Women who are happy about the upcoming birth often report a sense of well-being during the second trimester. The third trimester is often the most difficult part of the pregnancy. The increased demands the growing fetus places on the woman's body may make her lethargic and gradually intensify her impatience to give birth (Insel & Roth, 1998).

The pregnant woman has a great deal of responsibility, because everything that enters or comes in contact with her body can potentially affect the fetus (Insel & Roth, 1998). Her partner, family, and friends also have major responsibilities to support the mother in her efforts to maintain physical and mental health and, thus, aid in the baby's development. Prenatal care includes appropriate diet, exercise, rest, and the avoidance of alcohol and drugs not prescribed by a physician. There are many things to learn during pregnancy. Medical professionals and health educators specializing in pregnancy, labor, and delivery can be very helpful.

Although pregnancy and childbirth are clearly "natural" processes, numerous problems can arise, some of them life-threatening to the infant and the mother. Because of the potential for problems, women should receive regular medical evaluation and care during pregnancy.

Education for Childbirth

Education is extremely important during this period in a woman's and a couple's life. Expectant couples generally have many questions and sometimes fears that they can address with the help of resources such as books, films, and classes.

One positive development over the past 25 to 30 years has been the growth of childbirth classes. In most communities, the vast majority of pregnant women and their partners attend a series of educational sessions at a local hospital or clinic to help them prepare for the delivery. Sessions often involve presentations on prenatal development; nutrition and exercise during pregnancy; the role of fathers, grandparents, and other supporters; and many other issues. Question-and-answer sessions and practice drills of techniques that will be useful during labor and delivery are also common in these programs. The goal of these classes is to reduce fear and to manage discomfort and pain during this challenging time. Some people attend refresher sessions for subsequent pregnancies.

Fewer people take parenting classes after the baby is born, but these programs can be very helpful to new parents. Successful labor and delivery are only the first important steps in the journey of parenthood.

Nutrition and Exercise During Pregnancy

An adequate diet during pregnancy greatly improves a mother's chance of remaining healthy and of delivering a healthy baby. Inadequate diet has been associated with a variety of diseases mothers can develop during pregnancy. One goal of a healthy diet is to promote a full-term pregnancy: A normal-birthweight baby has a better chance of survival and of a healthy childhood than does a low-birthweight baby. Not only does a baby get all of its nutrients from its mother, but it competes for her nutrients when there are not enough to meet both of their needs (Insel & Roth, 1998).

Figure C.4 Weight Gain During Pregnancy. *Source: Sexual Interactions* (5th ed.) by A. R. Allgeier and E. R. Allgeier, 1998, Lexington, MA: Heath. Copyright 1998 by D. C. Heath & Co. Reprinted by permission.

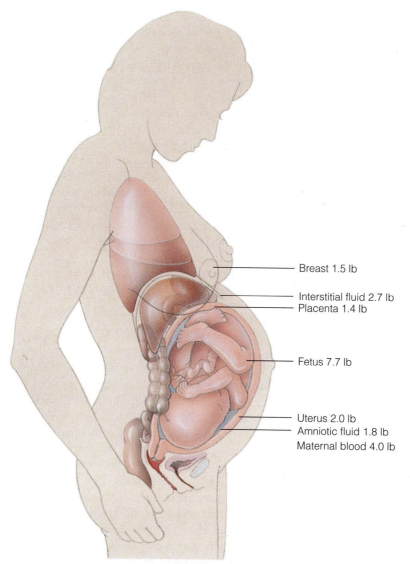

Breast 1.5 lb

Interstitial fluid 2.7 lb
Placenta 1.4 lb

Fetus 7.7 lb

Uterus 2.0 lb
Amniotic fluid 1.8 lb
Maternal blood 4.0 lb

A healthy weight gain for a mother during pregnancy is anywhere from 24 to 27 pounds (Figure C.4). The average gain is about 1.5 to 3 pounds a month for the first 3 months, and 1 pound every 9 days for the last 6 months. Approximately 80,000 calories are required during the course of a pregnancy. This may sound like a lot, but it is only 300 additional calories per day—the equivalent of one scoop of ice cream.

Medical authorities agree that moderate physical activity during pregnancy contributes to the mother's mental and physical well-being. Exercise keeps the muscles toned, which is helpful during delivery and in regaining a nonpregnant shape after childbirth. Unless their job is too stressful physically or emotionally, most women can continue working at their jobs into the final stages of pregnancy. A woman's need for rest and sleep increases during pregnancy, which puts great demands on her body (Insel & Roth, 1998).

Drug Use During Pregnancy

Although the placenta serves as a filter to protect the embryo from dangerous substances in the mother's blood, the so-called placental barrier is not foolproof. Many drugs pass easily through the placenta and can cause fetal damage. Alcohol is one of those drugs. **Fetal alcohol syndrome (FAS)** has been a subject of considerable concern recently. In fact, the Centers for Disease Control and Prevention have labeled it the leading cause of birth defects in the United States (Kelly, 1998). A small body, facial malformation, and poor mental capabilities are some of the ways FAS presents itself in children. Large-scale surveys indicate that babies of mothers who drink excessively are exposed to considerable risk of serious malformation during both the early, embryonic stage and the later phases of fetal development. In particular, alcohol easily damages eyes and vision (Masters et al., 1995). Pregnant women can eliminate the possibility of damage to the fetus by not drinking *any* alcohol during pregnancy.

Smoking is also dangerous to the developing fetus. Nicotine and carbon monoxide from smoking pass through the placental barrier into the fetal bloodstream. Babies born to women who smoked heavily during pregnancy almost always weigh less at birth than babies born to women who stopped smoking at the beginning of pregnancy. A smokeless working environment during pregnancy is also important for the mother's and baby's health.

Sex During Pregnancy

Pregnancy generates mixed emotions: joy, discomfort, wonder, fear, insecurity, curiosity, and enthusiastic expectation. Because this is an emotion-filled time, maintaining a healthy sexual relationship is important for pregnant women and their partners. With reasonable caution, couples can make love until the birth process begins. Most couples resume intercourse within 3 to 6 weeks after the birth of a child (Boston Women's Health Book Collective, 1998; Kelly, 1998).

Labor and Delivery

The first sign of impending birth is **labor,** contractions of the uterus that occur at regular intervals. During labor, the uterine muscles gradually stretch the cervical opening in preparation for birth, and those muscles also push the baby down into the vagina so that it can be born. Signs of the beginning of labor vary from individual to individual. In many mothers it is accompanied by a discharge of the bloody mucus that has plugged the cervix during pregnancy and prevented bacteria from entering the uterus. In some women, the amniotic sac ruptures ("the breaking of the waters") during early labor (Boston Women's Health Book Collective, 1998).

Three Stages of Labor

Medical tradition divides labor into three stages (Figure C.5).

Stage One   During the first stage of labor, the uterus contracts in rhythmic waves, and the cervical opening dilates (expands) to about 4 inches in diameter and

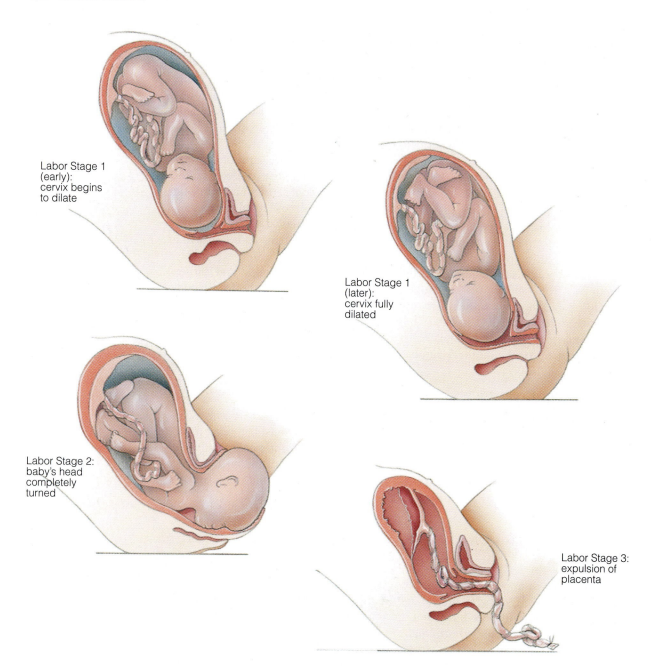

Labor Stage 1 (early): cervix begins to dilate

Labor Stage 1 (later): cervix fully dilated

Labor Stage 2: baby's head completely turned

Labor Stage 3: expulsion of placenta

Figure C.5 The Birth Process. *Source: Core Concepts in Health* (8th ed. 1998 Update) (p. 207) by P. M. Insel and W. T. Roth, 1998, Mountain View, CA: Mayfield. Copyright 1998 by Mayfield Publishing Co. Reprinted by permission.

effaces, or thins out. Early in stage one, contractions occur every 15 to 20 minutes and last approximately 1 minute. **Contractions**—tightenings of the uterine muscles—are followed by periods of relative relaxation. Later in stage one, the contractions increase in frequency and in length. By the time contractions are about 5 minutes apart, the woman should be in the hospital to begin preparation for the birth. (Later in this resource section we will take a look at some alternatives to the traditional hospital birth.) Most women spend all of stage one in a labor room at the hospital. Labor lasts 2 to 24 hours or more, and during long labors, labor pains may stop and start up again. During a first birth, labor averages about 10 hours. For subsequent babies, labor may average about 8 hours or less, often decreasing with each birth.

Stage Two   The second stage of labor—the **delivery,** or birth, itself—usually takes place in the delivery room and lasts a few minutes to an hour or more. Ninety-nine percent of all babies enter the world lengthwise, with 96% entering the cervix and traveling through the vagina headfirst. Three percent of babies are born buttocks first, called a *breech birth.* The remaining 1% of babies are in a transverse position, with the back near the cervix. In these cases, the medical team tries to rotate the baby lengthwise; if they do not succeed, a cesarean section must be performed.

When the baby's head reaches the entrance to the vagina, this is called *crowning.* The physician or nurse-midwife encourages the mother to "bear down," to help push the child out through the vagina (Boston Women's Health Book Collective, 1998).

The vagina can stretch a great deal to allow the baby to emerge, but the *perineum* (the tissue between the anus and the vagina) can stretch only so far before it tears. Physicians often prestretch the perineum early in labor to reduce the risk of tearing; extensive tearing makes infection more likely and slows recovery. Some physicians make a minor surgical incision in the perineum—an **episiotomy**—to prevent tearing. After the birth, the episiotomy is repaired with a few surgical stitches and usually heals in about 3 weeks. Although episiotomy has been a relatively routine medical practice in the United States for many years, some controversy surrounds the practice; pregnant women may want to learn more about the pros and cons of the procedure before delivery. Many feminists and childbirth groups consider episiotomies to be unnecessary in most deliveries (Boston Women's Health Book Collective, 1998).

As the baby's head passes through the birth canal, its body rotates somewhat so that the shoulders can exit. After the shoulders are delivered, the rest of the body slips out easily. Shortly after delivery, mucus is removed from the baby's mouth, and the baby begins breathing through its lungs, sometimes after a gentle slap from the physician. The umbilical cord is painlessly cut about 3 inches from the baby's body; the stub dries up and falls off in a few days. In many states, the newborn's eyes are treated against gonorrhea with silver nitrate or an antibiotic (Boston Women's Health Book Collective, 1998).

Stage Three   The third stage of labor is the expulsion of the **afterbirth,** or placenta and fetal membranes, by mild contractions from the uterus. To avoid infection, the physician or nurse examines the placenta carefully to ascertain that all of it has been expelled from the uterus. This third stage of labor may take only a few minutes or up to an hour. If an episiotomy was performed, it is repaired during this time.

After delivery, the baby is bathed, and in many hospitals the baby is then taken to the recovery room for a visit with the mother, father, and perhaps a few other very special people. Mothers are encouraged to be as active as reasonable soon after delivery—to walk around or use the bathroom, for example. (If the mother received anesthesia during delivery, she may not begin to walk around for 12 to 24 hours.) Some hospitals provide a "rooming-in" option for mothers who want their baby nearby all the time or at least when they are awake. Another option is to bring the baby to the mother every 3 to 4 hours to be breast- or bottle-fed. If all goes well, mother and baby go home in a few days (Allgeier & Allgeier, 1998). The first major challenge of parenthood has been met.

Cesarean Section

When normal vaginal birth is impossible or undesirable for some reason, a **cesarean section** (C-section), a surgical procedure, is performed to deliver the baby. C-sections are used in a variety of situations: if the baby is too large or the mother's pelvis is too small to allow the baby to move into the vagina; if labor has been very long and hard and the cervix has not dilated or if the mother is near exhaustion; if the umbilical cord has prolapsed (is preceding the baby through the cervix); if there is an Rh (blood factor) incompatibility; if there is excessive bleeding; or if the mother's or baby's condition takes a turn for the worse (Hyde & DeLamater, 1997).

C-sections are performed by making an incision through the mother's abdomen and then through the wall of the uterus. The baby is lifted out, and the uterine and abdominal walls are sewn up. Normal vaginal births are sometimes possible after a woman has delivered by cesarean; other women have two or three cesarean deliveries. The rate of complications related to C-sections is low, but recovery is somewhat longer than for vaginal birth, requiring 3 to 4 days in the hospital rather than 1 to 2 (Hyde & DeLamater, 1997).

The number of cesarean deliveries in the United States has risen dramatically in recent years. About 15% to 25% of U.S. births are C-sections, a considerably higher percentage than in some western European countries. This higher rate may reflect, among other things, the availability of sophisticated equipment for detecting fetal distress. A C-section may be performed if, for example, the fetal monitor shows that the baby is receiving inadequate oxygen during labor (Schickedanz, Schickedanz, Hansen, & Forsyth, 1997).

C-sections can be safer for both mother and baby when labor is prolonged and stressful, advocates say. They cite lower rates of maternal and neonatal mortality and of infant brain damage due to trauma during labor and delivery. Critics of C-sections argue that many cesareans are unnecessary, that they are simply more convenient for the physician in terms of anticipating and scheduling deliveries. The debate is likely to continue on a situation-by-situation basis.

Alternative Approaches to Birth

In the past and in many parts of the world today, childbirth has been seen as a natural phenomenon requiring little fanfare or special attention. In developed countries, however, beginning about 100 years ago, medical intervention became more and more common. Childbirth came to be viewed more as a medical condition or emergency. Reliance on drugs and anesthetics to reduce pain grew, as did the time for recovery from the birth experience. Labor and delivery became the sole province of physicians and nurses in hospitals. From a feminist perspective, women lost control to medical experts (Kelly, 1998).

Natural Childbirth   In 1932, British physician Grantly Dick-Read published *Childbirth Without Fear* (1932/1984), and women and their partners began to regain some of the control they had formerly held over the birth process. Dick-Read believed that medical intervention generated fear, and fear created more tension and pain. His approach, which he called *natural childbirth*, educated women about labor and delivery, and taught them relaxation techniques to reduce tension.

The Lamaze Method   The French obstetrician Fernand Lamaze introduced a similar method in the 1950s. The *Lamaze method* of "prepared childbirth" is widely popular today. In this method, the baby's father or a friend or relative serves as a coach for the mother. In prenatal classes the mother and her coach learn relaxation and breathing techniques for dealing with the intensity of labor. The woman remains active and alert during the birth of her baby (Kelly, 1998).

The Lamaze approach does not prohibit the use of painkillers during labor but usually reduces the need for them. Routine use of anesthesia during childbirth has been criticized, primarily because drugs can slow the progress of labor and affect the baby's well-being during the first several hours of life (Allgeier & Allgeier, 1998; Boston Women's Health Book Collective, 1998). One rational approach to the controversy over anesthesia and other painkillers is for a pregnant woman to participate in prepared childbirth classes and use the breathing and relaxation techniques of the Lamaze method during labor. If she discovers that she cannot control her pain and wishes an anesthetic, she can request it without guilt. The anesthetic should then be administered with great caution (Hyde & DeLamater, 1997).

Leboyer's "Gentle Birthing"   The French physician Frederick Leboyer (1975, 1995) advocated methods for reducing the shock of birth to the baby. Instead of a bright, noisy delivery area, Leboyer recommended a quiet, dimly lit, warm setting. In the Leboyer method, the baby lies on the mother's abdomen for a while before the umbilical cord is cut and then receives a gentle, warm bath.

Home Birth   Because medical complications occur in approximately 1 of 20 births, most professionals recommend delivery in a hospital, where there is access to advanced technology and professional assistance. Some couples choose to have their baby born at home, however. A trained and licensed **midwife** or certified nurse-midwife can assist in the process. It is also recommended that a cooperating physician be on call in case of an emergency (Allgeier & Allgeier, 1998; Kelly, 1998).

Birthing Rooms and Birthing Centers   In response to the desire that birth be a cooperative process between professionals and families and a balance of technology and tenderness, many hospitals have established birthing rooms and birthing centers. Birthing rooms are decorated more like bedrooms than like hospital rooms. Sometimes children and family members are allowed to be present for the birth, as is common in many societies. When a birthing room is used, the mother stays in the same room for labor and delivery. After delivery, the baby is checked for signs of distress, weighed and measured, and kept warm (Kelly, 1998).

Birthing centers humanize the birth process even further. Birthing centers are separate health-care facilities affiliated with hospitals. They have not only birthing rooms but kitchens and other rooms in which visitors and family members can stay. Birthing centers are usually staffed by nurses and nurse-midwives, although physicians are often in attendance for deliveries. They have emergency equipment and arrangements with a hospital if transfer for emergency care is necessary (Allgeier & Allgeier, 1998). Procedures and philosophy vary widely from institution to institution, and prospective parents are advised to consider their options carefully.

Physical and Psychological Changes After Birth

After the baby is born, the mother's body undergoes drastic physiological changes. Levels of the hormones estrogen and progesterone, having increased during pregnancy, drop sharply when the placenta is expelled and gradually return to normal over a few weeks to a few months. Other endocrinic changes include an increase in hormones associated with breast-feeding. As a result of the considerable stress a woman undergoes during labor and delivery, she may feel exhausted. Discomfort from delivery and from the episiotomy, if one was performed, is also common for the first few weeks after childbirth (Hyde & De LaMater, 1997).

For a day or two after birth, the mother often feels elated. Most highs in life, however, are often followed by lows. In terms of energy expended, mother and baby have indeed been through an ordeal. Within a few days after delivery, many women experience some depression and periods of crying.

Mood swings can range from mild to severe. The *maternity blues* or *baby blues* are the mildest form of depression, with sadness and tears lasting 24 to 48 hours. It is estimated that 50% to 80% of mothers experience mild baby blues after delivery. **Postpartum depression,** which affects 10% of mothers and lasts 6 to 8 weeks, is a bit more serious. It is characterized by a depressed mood, insomnia, tearfulness, feelings of inadequacy, an inability to cope, irritability, and fatigue (Berkow, 1997; Boston Women's Health Book Collective, 1998; Insel & Roth, 1998; Hopkins, Marcues, & Campbell, 1984).

A number of factors are thought to contribute to the depression women commonly feel after birth. Being in the hospital is stressful, and when the mother returns home, she faces a new set of stressors. Her energy level is low, yet she must care for a newborn, an exhausting task involving almost constant attentiveness. She may get up several times at night to attend to the baby, who may be hungry or sick, may need a diaper change, or may be crying for some unknown reason. Although pregnancy and childbirth are natural processes, the stresses of the associated physiological and physical changes disrupt a woman's life.

Over the years, however, many fathers have become actively involved in the challenging process of parenthood. During pregnancy, labor, and delivery, the father can be a friend, coach, and supporter. After the birth, fathers have a chance to share in the considerable stresses of parenthood. They can get up at night to feed the baby and can share in other caregiving tasks.

One very positive development over the past two decades has been the increase in support services for new parents. Many services were developed to help so-called at-risk families, those in which there is a potential for abuse or neglect of the baby. Among the risk factors commonly cited are high family stress, a parent who becomes angry easily, a very depressed parent, a parent with little extended-family support, a teenage mother, and alcohol or other drug abuse in the family.

There are also programs for parents who are not at risk for abuse or neglect of their infant but who are simply experiencing the everyday stresses and strains of parenthood. Childbirth and parenting classes are generally available and meet on a regular basis. Typically, a professional gives a short talk on a relevant topic, and a group discussion follows. Churches, synagogues, and other organizations also sponsor forums for parents to get together socially to share their insights and the challenges they are facing. These programs help parents realize that they are not alone and that they can find ways to cope during this difficult time.

Caring for an Infant

When the infant arrives, a new set of challenges faces the parents. They quickly learn that their baby is more in charge of their life than they are. During the early weeks, the important process of creating a new family begins.

Bonding With the Baby

For most women, the attachment process begins even before the baby is born. During pregnancy, most women develop a sense of the baby as a separate individual and form an emotional attachment to that individual (Leifer, 1980). Many parents-to-be give the fetus a name—some serious, some funny—and mothers and fathers occasionally talk to the baby in the womb, play music for it, massage it. Even before birth, the baby is part of the family. For most parents, bonding develops quickly after birth as they care for this dependent child.

Breast-Feeding

In the early part of the 20th century, **breast-feeding** declined in popularity; many viewed it as somehow "lower class." Bottled formula was considered antiseptic, scientific, sophisticated, and dignified. By the mid-1960s, only about 20% of women breast-fed their babies. A renewed interest in breast-feeding began soon after; by the mid-1980s the percentage had risen to 60%, but the current rate is about 50% (Insel & Roth, 1998).

One advantage breast-fed babies receive is a temporary immunity (so-called passive immunity) from antibodies in their mothers' milk; this protects them from a variety of diseases (including respiratory infections, colds, bronchitis, pneumonia, German measles, scarlet fever, and polio; Olds, London, & Ladewig, 1996). Most studies comparing the benefits of bottle-feeding and breast-feeding conclude that breastfeeding is usually better for the physical well-being of the baby. Human milk is more easily digested than is milk from other animals or from vegetable-based formulas (such as those made from soybeans). Although human milk contains less protein than cow's milk, human infants can utilize almost all of the protein in their mother's milk but only about half the protein in cow's milk. Breast-fed babies are less likely to have diarrhea or to be constipated than are bottle-fed babies; they also tend to have healthier teeth and are less likely to be obese or to get premature atherosclerosis. These apparent advantages led the American Pediatric Society to conclude that breast milk is superior to formula. For those women who simply cannot or prefer not to breast-feed their babies but wish the nutritional advantages of human milk, human milk banks now operate in many large metropolitan areas (Allgeier & Allgeier, 1998).

The average baby ingests about 1,000 calories a day from breast milk, and this can be a great help to a mother who gained more weight than she wished during pregnancy. Breast-feeding mothers generally can lose weight quite steadily without denying themselves food by nursing for 6 months or so (Allgeier & Allgeier, 1998). By about 6 months of age, however, breast milk alone cannot meet the growing baby's needs for calories and protein. It becomes necessary to supplement breast milk with solid food at that time or even earlier.

Although its advantages are many, breast-feeding causes stress and inconvenience for many women working outside the home. More important than the feeding choice is the quality of the relationship between a mother and her baby: A baby raised in a loving home can grow up to be a healthy, psychologically secure individual whether bottle-fed or breast-fed. Breast-feeding can be a happy experience for both mother and child, but the woman who nurses grudgingly may communicate feelings of resentment and unhappiness to her baby. The infant would be better off with a relaxed, loving, bottle-feeding mother.

Miscarriage, Stillbirth, and Infant Death

Less than 1% of infants born in the United States die in the first year after birth, and about 1% of all deliveries are stillbirths. Also, an estimated 10% to 14% of all known pregnancies end in miscarriage, and one third of all women experience a miscarriage at some time in their reproductive years (DeFrain, Ernst, & Nealer, 1997; Insel & Roth, 1998; Neugebauer et al., 1992; Rosenfeld, 1991; U.S. Bureau of the Census, 1997).

Miscarriage is defined as the termination of a pregnancy resulting from natural causes before the fetus is viable outside of the mother (that is, during the first or second trimester of pregnancy). Because women may not be aware that they are pregnant, the products of a miscarriage can be mistaken for a menstrual period. For this reason, some authorities have estimated that the true incidence of miscarried pregnancies may be as high as 15% to 20%. Studies of miscarried fetuses indicate that about 50% showed abnormalities, such as gross chromosomal abnormalities, that were incompatible with life. Psychological and physical trauma, contrary to popular belief, are not common causes of miscarriage. American society tends to define the loss of the fetus as "just a miscarriage," but to most women who experience a miscarriage, the loss is seen as a death—the death of a baby or the death of a dream (Day & Hooks, 1987; DeFrain et al., 1996; DeFrain et al., 1997).

Stillbirth is the death of a so-called viable fetus, a fetus that was mature enough developmentally to have lived outside the womb but for some reason or reasons was born dead. Stillbirths occur in the 7th–9th months of pregnancy (the third trimester). Before this time the event is called a miscarriage. Some causes of stillbirth are known. For example, some babies die of anoxia: The placenta sometimes compresses during delivery through the vagina, cutting off oxygen (Borg & Lasker,

1981). In nearly half of all stillbirths, however, studies indicate that there is no apparent reason for the death. The baby is perfectly formed but is born dead (Kirk, 1984).

The chances of infant mortality before the first birthday are about 1% in the United States. Some of these deaths are the result of **sudden infant death syndrome (SIDS),** for which the cause is unknown. A common scenario is that the parent or another caretaker puts the seemingly healthy infant in the crib for a nap and comes back a few minutes or hours later to find the baby has died. An autopsy reveals no apparent cause (DeFrain, Ernst, Jakub, & Taylor, 1991).

Although the chance of losing a baby to miscarriage, stillbirth, or SIDS is relatively small, the loss is a severe crisis in the lives of most families who experience it. When a baby dies, the family begins a long and difficult journey. Many parents and even some grandparents consider suicide after the loss of a baby; the pain and guilt can be overwhelming. Marriages are often strained by the loss, and parental relationships with surviving children sometimes suffer (DeFrain et al., 1996; DeFrain et al., 1997).

Research indicates that family members who have experienced the death of an infant are seriously at risk for major emotional and physical problems. Immediate and effective community support from relatives, friends, and professionals is essential. Most families recover from the death of an infant, but the road back to emotional well-being is long, difficult, and often very lonely. Three to five years of "recovery" is very common among bereaved parents, although as many point out, one never really recovers from such a tragedy (DeFrain et al., 1996; DeFrain et al., 1997).

Contraception

Methods of Contraception

Sterilization

Oral Contraceptives

Barrier Methods

Intrauterine Devices

Spermicides

Hormone Implants

Fertility-Awareness Methods

Ineffective Methods

Making Contraceptive Decisions

In the United States, there are 3.6 million births each year. It has been estimated that half the births result from unintentional pregnancies. Among the other 50%—the intentional conceptions—many are undertaken with little planning (Insel & Roth, 1998). Although parenthood is a challenge that lasts a lifetime, it appears that the majority of pregnancies occur by accident or with little forethought.

Why are unintentional pregnancies so common in our society? The answer, in short, is that effective contraception takes a good deal of planning and thought and sex, for most people, simply does not. Social psychologist Donn Byrne (1983) outlines five steps involved in effective contraception. Our commentary follows each of Byrne's steps:

1. *The individual must acquire and remember accurate information about contraception.* This is no small task.

2. *The individual must acknowledge the likelihood of engaging in sexual intercourse.* Many in our society—in particular, women—receive the message that nonmarital sex is wrong. Preparing for nonmarital sex thus seems doubly wrong.

3. *The individual must obtain the contraceptive.* This involves a visit to a physician, a drugstore, or a clinic. This also involves admitting both to oneself and to others that one is planning to have sex.

4. *The individual must communicate with her or his partner about contraception.* Partners who do not communicate cannot assume the other has taken preventive measures. Unfortunately, the likelihood of communication about contraception is relatively low.

5. *The individual must actually use the contraceptive method.* People sometimes resist using contraceptives because they consider some methods to be messy, interruptive, or unromantic.

Byrne's five steps make it clear that there are many barriers to the effective understanding and use of contraception. It is little wonder that so many pregnancies are unplanned.

The science of **contraception**—which focuses on the prevention of conception, or pregnancy—has from its very beginnings been an embattled research area. Pressure from conservative religious groups and politicians has impeded progress in this area in the United States.

The ideal contraceptive would be harmless, reliable, free of objectionable side effects, inexpensive, simple, reversible in effect, removed from the sexual act, and protective against sexually transmissible disease. Unfortunately, there is no such contraceptive.

Methods of Contraception

Birth control methods used by women and men in this country fall into six broad categories: sterilization, oral contraceptives, barrier methods, intrauterine devices (IUDs), spermicides, and hormone implants (Elmer-DeWitt, 1990; Hatcher et al., 1994, 1997; Hyde & DeLamater, 1997; Insel & Roth, 1998; Kelly, 1998). Fertility-awareness methods, which involve avoiding intercourse during the fertile phase of a woman's menstrual cycle, are also used by some.

Sterilization

Sterilization, or voluntary surgical contraception, is the contraceptive method of choice for 29% of U.S. women and for 11% of U.S. men. This method is used by men and women who do not wish to have children or who have had all the children they desire. The sterilization procedure for women, called **tubal ligation,** involves cutting or tying and sealing the woman's fallopian tubes to prevent passage of the ova into the uterus; the procedure is difficult to reverse. The male sterilization procedure, called **vasectomy,** involves surgically severing the vasa deferentia; it is also usually irreversible and should be considered permanent. Sterilization is a more complex procedure in women than in men. In actual practice, sterilization is typically 99.6% effective for women and 99.85% effective for men.

Oral Contraceptives

Oral contraceptives, or birth control pills, are favored by 28% of U.S. women. Oral contraceptives are 97% effective in preventing pregnancy. The *pill,* a combination oral contraceptive, contains the hormones **estrogen** and **progestin.** In addition to preventing pregnancy, the pill makes the menstrual cycle more regular, tends to reduce menstrual cramping, and is associated with lower incidences of breast and ovarian cysts and pelvic inflammatory disease (PID). Potential negative side effects of the pill include nausea, weight gain, fluid retention, breast tenderness, headaches, missed menstrual periods, acne, mood changes, depression, anxiety, fatigue, decreased sex drive, and circulatory diseases.

The *minipill* contains progestin only. Besides reliability, the minipill brings increased regularity to the menstrual cycle, tends to reduce menstrual cramping, and is associated with a lower incidence of breast and ovarian cysts and PID.

Barrier Methods

Barrier methods of contraception, favored by 20% of U.S. women, include condoms, diaphragms, and cervical caps. Failure rates are 12% to 18%.

Condom   Worn by the male over the penis during intercourse, a **condom,** made of latex rubber, catches semen and prevents it from entering the vagina. Condoms are available without a prescription and offer protection against sexually transmissible diseases (STDs). Although condom use is a contraceptive method a man can take responsibility for, one third of all condoms are purchased by women. Condoms can fail for a variety of reasons: breakage; not leaving a space at the tip of the condom to collect the semen; lubrication with petroleum jelly, which weakens latex; seepage of semen around the opening of the condom or if the condom slipps off in the vagina after coitus; storing the condom for more than 2 years or storing it at temperature extremes; and not placing the condom on the penis at the beginning of intercourse. Some people are allergic to rubber condoms. (Other "natural" kinds are also available.) Some men complain that condoms reduce sensation on the penis. The failure rate for condoms is about 12%.

Diaphragm   A **diaphragm** is a dome-shaped cup of thin rubber stretched over a collapsible metal ring. The diaphragm, which must be used with a spermicidal (sperm-killing) cream or jelly, is inserted into the vagina to cover the mouth of the cervix, blocking sperm from entering the uterus. Inexpensive and reusable, a diaphragm must be fitted by a physician. Common reasons for failure of a diaphragm to prevent pregnancy include improper fitting or insertion of the diaphragm, removal of the diaphragm too soon (sooner than 6 to 8 hours) after intercourse, insufficient use of spermicide with the diaphragm, damage to the diaphragm, leakage around the diaphragm, or dislodging of the diaphragm. Some people are allergic to the rubber in diaphragms (plastic diaphragms are also available), and some people are allergic to spermicides. Diaphragm users also have an increased risk of toxic shock syndrome, bladder infection, and vaginal soreness caused by pressure from the rim of the diaphragm. The failure rate for diaphragms is about 18%.

Cervical Cap   A thimble-shaped rubber or plastic cup, the **cervical cap** fits over the cervix and is held in place by suction. Like the diaphragm, it must be fitted by a clinician and is used with a spermicide; it can, however, be left in place for longer periods of time than the diaphragm. Potential problems that can result in pregnancy include improper fitting, insertion, or placement. Women using cervical caps also have a possible risk of toxic shock syndrome or of an allergic reaction to the rubber or the spermicide. Also, the cervical cap may abrade or irritate the vagina or cervix. The failure rate for cervical caps is about 18%.

Intrauterine Devices

Intrauterine devices (IUDs) are made of molded plastic and are inserted by a physician into a woman's uterus through the vagina. The IUD apparently works by causing an inflammatory reaction inside the uterus that attracts white blood cells. The white blood cells then produce substances that are poisonous to sperm and thus prevent fertilization of the egg. The inflammatory reaction can be halted by removing the IUD (Berkow, 1997).

Most U.S. manufacturers have stopped making IUDs because of the fear of costly lawsuits over their safety. Although they are still favored by 2% of women, IUDs have caused pelvic infections, some serious enough to have resulted in the death of about 21 women. Other negative side effects include uterine cramping, abnormal bleeding, and heavy menstrual flow. IUDs come in a variety of shapes. An IUD is inserted through the vagina and cervix into the uterus by a medical professional, where it remains until the woman wishes it to have it removed. So that the wearer can be sure the IUD has not been expelled by the uterus, a slender string attached to the IUD protrudes through the cervical opening just far enough into the vagina so that the woman can feel it with her finger. IUD failure rates are typically about 2%, mostly resulting from expulsion of the IUD without the woman's notice.

Spermicides

Favored by 3% of women, **spermicides** include foams, creams, jellies, and vaginal inserts (also called vaginal suppositories). They are available without a prescription. Spermicides must be inserted with an applicator into the vagina before intercourse and are only effective for a short time. Many couples dislike having to interrupt the sexual act to insert a spermicide. Failure rates are about 21%. Pregnancy can result when too little spermicide is used, if the spermicide is placed in the vagina too long before intercourse, if the woman douches within 6 to 8 hours after intercourse, or, in the case of suppositories, if the spermicide fails to melt or foam properly. Some people are allergic to the chemicals in spermicides. Some say they taste unpleasant during oral-genital sex.

Hormone Implants

Norplant is the trade name of an implant that is placed under the skin on the inside of a woman's upper arm and releases the hormone progestin. It provides 99.9% protection from pregnancy for up to 5 years. Approved by the U.S. Food and Drug Administration in December 1990, this type of implant is the newest, most effective contraceptive method to become available in the United States in many years. Women who cannot take birth control pills for various medical reasons are cautioned not to consider Norplant. Potential side effects include prolonged or irregular menstrual bleeding, severe headaches, vision loss, nervousness, depression, nausea, dizziness, skin rash, acne, anemia, changes in appetite, breast tenderness, weight gain, ovarian cysts, enlargement of the ovaries or fallopian tubes, and excessive growth of body and facial hair. Side effects may subside after the first year (Cohen, 1995; Goldberg, 1993).

Fertility-Awareness Methods

The various contraceptive methods known as **fertility awareness** are based on avoiding intercourse during the fertile phase of a woman's menstrual cycle. The methods differ in the way in which they identify the woman's fertile period.

The least effective fertility awareness approach—even for women who have regular menstrual cycles—is the *calendar method*. To use this method, a woman must carefully keep records of her cycles for 12 months. Then, to figure out when to abstain from intercourse, the woman subtracts 18 days from the shortest and 11 days from the longest of her previous 12 menstrual cycles. If, for example, her cycles last from 26 to 29 days, she needs to avoid intercourse from day 8 through day 18 of each cycle (Berkow, 1997).

The *temperature method* is based on the knowledge that a woman's body temperature drops slightly before ovulation and rises slightly after ovulation. After about 3 months of daily record keeping, a woman's temperature patterns usually become apparent. A third fertility awareness approach, the *mucus method*, is based on changes in cervical secretions throughout the menstrual cycle. Before ovulation, cervical mucus increases and is clear and slippery. During ovulation, some women can detect a slight change in the texture of the mucus, finding that it can be formed into an elastic thread that can be stretched between thumb and finger. After ovulation, cervical secretions become cloudy and sticky and decrease in quantity. One problem with this approach is the potential misreading of changes in the composition of the cervical mucus due to vaginal infections and vaginal products or medications.

Fertility-awareness methods of contraception are not recommended for women who have very irregular menstrual cycles (about 15% of all women) and for women for whom pregnancy would be a serious problem. Proponents of fertility awareness methods argue that they are about 90% effective. In practice, however, an estimated 20% of women using these methods become pregnant in any given year.

Ineffective Methods

Withdrawal of the penis before ejaculation is a highly unreliable way to prevent pregnancy. An estimated 19% of women whose partners use this approach will become pregnant in any given year.

Douching—flushing the vagina with vinegar or some other type of acidic liquid—is also an ineffective birth control method. Although it is true that some acidic solutions will kill sperm, it can take sperm only a minute to reach the cervical mucus; once there, they move freely into the uterus, where no douching solution can reach them. The douche itself, in fact, may even push some sperm into the uterus.

Making Contraceptive Decisions

In making rational choices about contraceptive methods, individuals and couples should take into account several considerations (Allgeier & Allgeier, 1998; Hyde & DeLamater, 1997; Kelly, 1998). First, people need to consider the health risks of each method in terms of personal and family medical history. IUDs are not recommended for young women without children, for example, because they increase the risk of pelvic infection and possible infertility. Oral contraceptives should be used only after an evaluation of a woman's medical history.

Individuals must ask themselves, How important is it to me to avoid pregnancy at this point in life? Oral contraceptives offer by far the best protection against pregnancy, but there are some risks associated with them. Condoms, diaphragms, and cervical caps have fewer related health problems than oral contraceptives, but the risk of pregnancy is greater with these methods. To maximize their effectiveness, they need to be used in combination with a spermicide and used every time a couple has intercourse.

The type of relationship one is involved in should also be considered. Barrier methods require more motivation than the pill because they generally must be used at or close to the time of intercourse. Both partners must have a well-developed sense of responsibility to ensure the success of these methods. Barrier methods often require cooperation between partners. If one has sexual intercourse only infrequently, barrier methods may make more sense than oral contraceptives.

Condom use, preferably with a spermicide, is critically important if there is any possibility of the presence of a sexually transmissible disease. Condoms are especially important for those who are not in an exclusive, long-term relationship. They are also useful for women taking oral contraceptives, because cervical changes that occur during hormone use can increase the likelihood of contracting certain disease.

Both partners should consider convenience and comfort. Oral contraceptives rank high in both regards, although, again, the possible negative side effects and health risks of the pill need to be factored into the equation. If a woman has difficulty remembering to take her pills, another method might be better.

The ease and cost of obtaining and continuing each method also need to be considered. Oral contraceptives require an annual pelvic exam and periodic medical checkups. Pills are also more expensive than barrier methods. Diaphragms and cervical caps require an initial examination and fitting. Norplant requires implantation by a physician.

Finally, religious and philosophical beliefs should be taken into consideration. Abstinence is the only acceptable approach for some individuals before marriage.

For those who wish to make responsible contraceptive choices, it is important to discuss the options with competent professionals. Both men and women should be knowledgeable in this very important subject area.

RESOURCE SECTION E

Abortion

In 1973 the U.S. Supreme Court overturned by a 7-to-2 vote laws that had made abortion in America a criminal act. Since that decision, approximately 21 million American women have chosen to have 35 million abortions, according to the Alan Guttmacher Institute. Researchers estimate that 48% of women in this country will have at least one unplanned pregnancy between the ages of 15 and 44 and that at current rates, 43% of American women will have had an abortion by age 45 (Goodman, 1998). There are close to 1.5 million abortions performed in the United States each year, representing about one third of all pregnancies (Kelly, 1998).

Strictly defined, **abortion** is the expulsion of a fetus from the uterus before the fetus has developed sufficiently to survive outside the mother (before viability). In common usage, abortion refers only to artificially induced expulsions, those caused by mechanical means or drugs. Spontaneous abortions, those that occur naturally and are not induced by mechanical means or drugs, are commonly called *miscarriages* (Insel & Roth, 1998).

Abortion Laws

For more than two centuries in early U.S. history (from the 1600s to the early 1900s), abortion was not a crime if it was performed before *quickening* (fetal movement, which begins at approximately 20 weeks). U.S. abortion laws followed English common law during this period. An antiabortion movement began in the early 1800s. It was led by physicians who argued against the validity of the concept of quickening and who opposed the performing of abortions by untrained people, who also threatened physician control of medical services. The controversy over abortion attracted minimal attention until the mid-1800s, when newspapers began advertising abortion preparations. Opponents of such medicines argued that women were using them as birth control measures and that women could also hide extramarital affairs through their use. The medicines were seen by some as evidence that immorality and corruption threatened America. By the early 1900s, virtually all states (at the urging of male politicians; women could not vote at the time) had passed antiabortion laws (Insel & Roth, 1998).

Social pressure for the legalization of abortion grew in the 1960s. Despite laws against abortion, many illegal abortions were being performed. Women sometimes died due to nonsterile or medically inadequate procedures (Cox, 1990). During this period, courts began to invalidate many of the state laws on the grounds of constitutional vagueness and a violation of the right to privacy (Francoeur, 1982, 1997; Insel & Roth, 1998).

In the 1973 landmark case *Roe* v. *Wade*, the U.S. Supreme Court made abortion legal by denying the states the right to regulate early abortions. The high court replaced the restrictions most states still imposed at that time with new standards governing abortion decisions. The court conceptualized pregnancy in three parts (trimesters) and gave pregnant women more options in regard to abortion in the first trimester (3 months) than in the second or third trimester. The court ruled that during the first trimester, the abortion decision must be left to the judgment of the woman and her physician. The court ruled that during the second trimester, the right to abortion remained but that a state could regulate certain factors in an effort to protect the health of the woman, such as the type of facility in which an abortion could be performed. The Supreme Court ruled that during the third trimester, the period of pregnancy in which the fetus is viable outside the uterus, a state could regulate and even ban all abortions except in situations in which they were necessary to preserve the mother's life or health (Francoeur, 1982, 1987; Hyde & DeLamater, 1997; Insel & Roth, 1998). In addition, in 1976 the Supreme Court decided in *Planned Parenthood* v. *Danforth* that neither the parents of a minor nor the husband of a woman had the right to veto a woman's decision to have an abortion (Francoeur, 1982, 1997).

Research indicates that babies born at or before 24 weeks rarely survive, that babies born at 25 to 26 weeks have a 50% chance of survival, and that a baby's chance of survival increases to 90% at 30 weeks ("Abortion Foes Vow," 1991).

After the Supreme Court's 1973 decision, the number of abortions performed each year rose steadily. The decision did not end the controversy over abortion; indeed, in many ways it seemed to intensify it (Francoeur, 1982, 1987; Insel & Roth, 1996, 1998).

Campaigns were begun on the national, state, and local levels by many groups hoping to overturn the decision and restore the ban on abortion. Some favored amending the U.S. Constitution; others worked to weaken the decision by chipping away at its edges in a variety of ways. The Supreme Court, hearing arguments against abortion nearly every year, continued to uphold its 1973 decision. In the original decision the court had voted 7 to 2 in favor of legalizing abortion; by the mid-1980s conservative appointments to the high court had cut the abortion rights majority on the court to an unpredictable 5-to-4 margin (Insel & Roth, 1996, 1998).

The controversy boiled over in July 1989, when the Supreme Court handed down its decision in the case of *Webster* v. *Reproductive Health Services*. Although the court did not overturn *Roe* v. *Wade*, it permitted several key abortion restrictions enacted by the Missouri state legislature in 1986 to stand. Two of the most significant restrictions upheld in *Webster* v. *Reproductive Health Services* were the prohibition of the use of all public facilities, resources, and employees for abortion services and the requirement for costly and time-consuming tests to determine fetal viability if a physician estimated the fetus to be 20 weeks or older.

In the 1989 decision, the majority of the Supreme Court justices also rejected *Roe*'s framework of trimesters, which had been an attempt by the justices in 1973 to balance women's rights and fetal rights. The 1989 decision did not, however, replace the trimester framework with any other standard for balancing these rights. The justices declined to address the preamble of the Missouri law, which stated that "the life of each human being begins at conception," arguing that this was only a "value judgment" and that this value judgment did not "regulate abortion" (Insel & Roth, 1996, 1998).

In 1992 tensions mounted again as the nation awaited a Supreme Court decision on *Planned Parenthood* v. *Casey*. Pro-choice activists feared the high court would overturn *Roe* v. *Wade* and make abortion an issue for state regulation. But in a narrow 5-to-4 decision in early July, the Supreme Court once more upheld the spirit of *Roe* v. *Wade* but once again restricted its reach. States were now free to restrict abortion as long as the restrictions did not place an "undue burden" on women. The Supreme Court held that the state of Pennsylvania could (1) impose a 24-hour waiting period before an abortion, (2) require doctors to tell women about other options beside abortion, (3) require women to sign an "informed consent" form before the procedure, (4) mandate parental notification for minors, and (5) make doctors provide statistical information about patients. However, the Court also held that the state of Pennsylvania could not force a woman to tell her husband that she was having an abortion (Clift, 1992).

Pro-choice forces expressed some relief after the inauguration of President Clinton in 1993, hoping that the retirement of conservative Supreme Court justices would give Clinton the opportunity to appoint more liberal justices who would vigorously defend abortion rights. Today, pro-life groups on the local, state, and national level continue to seek legislation that would make abortion a crime; at the same time, pro-choice groups work to ensure a woman's right to an abortion if she so chooses. Although the outcome of the abortion controversy cannot be predicted, it is unlikely that either side will give up the fight.

Twenty-five years after the Supreme Court's decision to legalize abortion, the American public still supports legalized abortion but says it should be harder to get and less readily chosen, according to a New York Times/CBS News Poll (Goldberg & Elder, 1998). Some observers call this a "permit-but-discourage" attitude, which indicates the general public's discomfort with abortion. Overall, 32% of the random sample of 1,101 Americans in the poll said abortion should be generally available and legal; 45% said it should be available but more difficult to obtain; and 22% said it should not be permitted.

Elizabeth Adell Cook, a professor of government at the University of Maryland commented on the poll results, arguing that they squared with President Clinton's view that abortions should be "safe, legal, and rare." She believes that there may be an emerging consensus in the U.S. regarding abortion, that "it should be allowed under some circumstances but it isn't to be taken too lightly. People think if there's a serious enough reason, it's okay, but if they don't think the reason is compelling enough, they think it's wrong" (Goldberg & Elder, 1998).

Abortion Procedures

About 90% of the abortions in the United States are performed within the first trimester (Kelly, 1998). The type of procedure used generally depends on how far along a woman is in her pregnancy. We will explain a variety of abortion procedures in this section, beginning with those used early in pregnancy and concluding with those employed later in pregnancy.

RU-486

Originally, **RU-486** was referred to as a morning-after pill, to be taken relatively soon after unprotected sexual relations—well before the potential implantation of a fertilized egg. In actuality, RU-486 can be taken by the 49th day following the last menstrual period and is thus an **abortifacient** (a measure used to induce abortion). RU-486 blocks uterine absorption of the hormone progesterone, causing the uterine lining and any fertilized egg to shed. Combined with another drug and under medical supervision, RU-486 has fewer health risks than surgical abortion and is effective 95% of the time. It is currently available by prescription in Europe. In the United States, its effectiveness and safety are being tested (Berkow, 1997; Insel & Roth, 1998; Kelly, 1998).

Both pro-choice activists and pro-life activists see RU-486 as a possible revolutionary development in the abortion controversy. If abortion could be induced simply, safely, effectively, and privately, the nature of the controversy surrounding abortion would change dramatically. Clinics that perform abortions are regularly picketed by antiabortion protesters, making the experience of obtaining a legal abortion difficult for many women. If RU-486 becomes a legal, widely available option for women in the United States, abortion will in essence have become an almost invisible, personal, and relatively private act—a potential gain for pro-choice activists but a looming stumbling block to abortion foes, who have marshalled their forces in an effort to counter the use of this drug.

Vacuum Aspiration

Also called *vacuum suction* or *vacuum curettage*, **vacuum aspiration** is a method of abortion that is performed during the first trimester of pregnancy, up to 12 weeks from the beginning of the last menstrual period. It is the most common abortion procedure used during the first trimester in the United States. Vacuum aspiration is performed on an outpatient basis and requires a local or a general anesthetic. It takes about 10 to 15 minutes, although the woman stays in the doctor's office, clinic, or hospital for a few hours afterward.

Medical professionals prepare the woman for the procedure in a manner similar to preparing for a pelvic examination. An instrument is then inserted into the vagina to dilate the opening of the cervix. The end of a nonflexible tube connected to a suction apparatus is inserted through the cervix into the uterus. The contents of the uterus, including fetal tissue, are then sucked out.

Vacuum aspiration is the most common method of early abortion in the United States for two reasons: it is simple, and complications are rare and usually minor. It does, however, pose a risk of uterine perforation; infection, with fever and chills; hemorrhaging; unsuccessful abortion, in which the fetus continues to grow; and failure to remove all the fetal material. Complications are most likely when the procedure is performed by an unqualified person who lacks professional training. Infection may occur if the woman fails to follow postprocedure instructions (Hyde & DeLamater, 1997; Kelly, 1998).

Dilation and Curettage

Dilation and curettage (D & C) is similar to vacuum aspiration but must be performed in a hospital under general anesthetic. It is performed between 8 and 20 weeks after the last menstrual period. By the beginning of the second trimester, the uterus has enlarged and its walls have become thinner. The contents of the uterus cannot be as easily removed by suction, and therefore the D & C procedure is used.

In a D & C, the cervix is dilated and a sharp metal loop attached to the end of a long handle (the curette) is inserted into the uterus and used to scrape out the uterine contents. D & Cs are also performed to treat infertility and menstrual problems.

Vacuum aspiration is preferable to a D & C because the former is done on an outpatient basis, eliminating the expense of hospitalization and often the risk involved in the use of general anesthetics. D & Cs also cause more discomfort than vacuum aspiration, and the risks of uterine perforation, infection, and hemorrhaging are greater.

Dilation and evacuation (D & E) is a related procedure used between 13 and 16 weeks after the last menstrual period. D & E is similar to both D & C and vacuum aspiration, but it is a bit more complicated, requiring the use of forceps and suction. It is performed in a hospital or at a clinic (Kelly, 1998).

Induced Labor

Induced labor is a method of abortion performed late in the second trimester, generally in a hospital. In *saline-induced abortion*, the most common type of induced labor, a fine tube is inserted through the abdomen into the amniotic sac, and some amniotic fluid is removed. An equal amount of saline solution is then injected through the tube, causing labor and miscarriage to occur within a few hours. In *prostaglandin-induced abortion*, hormonelike substances called prostaglandins are injected into the amniotic sac, injected intravenously, or inserted by means of a vaginal suppository with similar results.

Induced labor is the most common method of abortion for those pregnancies that have progressed late into the second trimester. Induced labor is both more costly and more hazardous than the methods explained earlier. Although serious complications are rare, they can occur. If the technique is done carelessly, saline solution can enter a blood vessel, inducing shock and possibly death. Also, a blood disorder is a possible, although rare, complication from induced labor.

Prostaglandin-induced abortion is preferable to saline-induced abortion because labor begins more quickly and is shorter. But saline-induced abortions do have advantages over prostaglandin-induced abortions: less risk of excessive bleeding, less risk of a retained placenta, less risk of a torn cervix as a result of too-rapid dilation, and less risk of the delivery of a live although nonviable fetus. Nausea, vomiting, and diarrhea are also more common with the prostaglandin method (Hyde & DeLamater, 1997).

Induced labor is physically more uncomfortable than the methods of abortion used earlier in pregnancy. It is also often more emotionally upsetting for the woman, because she experiences contractions for several hours and then expels a lifeless fetus (Kelly, 1998). Induced labor accounts for only 1% of abortions in the United States (Koonin, Kochanek, Smith, & Ramick, 1991).

Hysterotomy

A surgical method of abortion, **hysterotomy** is performed between 16 and 24 weeks after the last menstrual period. A cesarean section is performed, and the fetus is removed. Hysterotomies are relatively rare, but they are useful if the pregnancy has progressed to the late second trimester and the woman's health leads physicians to conclude that neither of the induction methods is appropriate (Hyde & DeLamater, 1997).

Methotrexate and Misoprostol

The number of obstetricians, gynecologists, and hospitals performing abortions has been dropping steadily, but that trend could change as doctors adopt a nonsurgical alternative that uses prescription drugs already marketed for other purposes (Brody, 1995; Raeburn, 1995). A study published in the *New England Journal of Medicine* reported that a two-drug combination, **methotrexate and misoprostol,** was effective in inducing abortions at home (Hausknecht, 1995). The researcher, Dr. Richard U. Hausknecht of the Mount Sinai School of Medicine in New York, worked with 178 healthy women seeking abortion within the first 63 days of pregnancy. The women received an injection of methotrexate; a week later, they followed up with either an oral tablet or a vaginal suppository of misoprostol. If an abortion did not occur after 7 days, the women were given another intravaginal dose of misoprostol. Overall, 171 of the 178 woman had successful abortions after the first or second dose of misoprostol. Seven women needed suction to complete the abortion. None of the women required a blood transfusion, although side effects included swelling of the mouth, brief diarrhea, and nausea. Most women rated their pain at less than 2 on a scale of 0 (low) to 4 (high). The women found this method preferable to surgical abortion.

Hausknecht said he believes many doctors have already started to prescribe the drugs and that others will do so in the future. Many observers predict this new method of abortion will stir further controversy because—like RU-486—it can be administered unobtrusively (Brody, 1995; Raeburn, 1995). Indeed confidentiality is one of its primary advantages, to both patients and their doctors. Hausknecht explained that because this method can be performed "very quietly," in a standard medical office setting, it is likely to lessen the threats and violence against abortion providers by some abortion foes (Raeburn, 1995).

Other Methods

There are several other methods of abortion, but they are not widely performed in the United States. In Japan, a variety of mechanical methods of stimulating the uterus to induce abortion are used. Although simple and inexpensive to perform, these methods are associated with a greater loss of blood and a higher risk of infection.

Early abortion, similar to vacuum aspiration, is performed as soon as a positive pregnancy test is received, up to 8 weeks after the last menstrual period. A flexible tube is inserted through the cervix without dilating it, and the contents of the uterus are sucked out. This procedure can be performed without an anesthetic (Hyde, 1990). **Menstrual regulation** (also called *endometrial aspiration*, *preemptive abortion*, and *menstruation extraction*) is similar to early abortion, but the contents of the uterus are sucked out before the woman's menstrual period is due, thus she does not know if she was pregnant or not. The procedure takes 2 to 10 minutes and is simple, inexpensive, and safe (Insel & Roth, 1998).

Physical and Emotional Aspects of Abortion

The chance of dying as a result of a legal abortion in the United States is far lower than the chance of dying during childbirth. Less than 1 in 100,000 abortions results in the death of a relatively healthy woman. In comparison, nearly 20 women die for each 100,000 pregnancies and births (Insel & Roth, 1996, 1998).

Infection is a possibility after an abortion, however. Women are advised to consult their physician if they have an elevated temperature, experience severe lower abdominal cramps or pain, experience heavy bleeding (heavier than their normal menstrual period), or if their menstrual period does not begin within 6 weeks after the abortion. Women are also advised to follow directions for prescriptions faithfully, to avoid strenuous physical activity, to rest as much as possible for several days, and to avoid sexual intercourse for 2 to 3 weeks following an abortion (Boston Women's Health Book Collective, 1998).

Some women experience feelings of guilt after an abortion; others feel great relief that they are no longer pregnant. Still other women are ambivalent: happy not to be pregnant but sad about the abortion. Some of the emotional highs and lows may be related to hormonal adjustments and may cease after the woman's hormone levels return to normal. The intensity of feelings associated with an abortion generally diminishes as time passes, but some women experience anger, frustration, and guilt for many years (Boston Women's Health Book Collective, 1998; Hyde & DeLamater, 1997; Kelly, 1998).

Those experiencing severe, negative psychological reactions to abortion are rare, according to a review of research findings by a panel commissioned by the American Psychological Association (Adler, David, Major, Roth, Russo, & Wyatt, 1992; Landers, 1989). The psychologists concluded that there is no such thing as "postabortion syndrome." They also noted that it is important to keep in mind that "the question is not simply whether abortion has some harmful psychological effects, but whether those effects are demonstrably worse than the psychological consequences of unwanted childbirth" (Landers, 1989). The investigators argued that abortion is not likely to be followed by severe psychological response but is best understood "within a framework of normal stress and coping rather than a model of psychopathology" (Adler et al., 1992, p. 1194). Many women find it helpful to talk about their experience with sympathetic family members, friends, and professional counselors.

An 8-year study of nearly 5,300 women confirmed what earlier researchers had found (Brody, 1998). Researchers at Arizona State University and Phoenix College found that abortion does not lead to lasting emotional trauma in young women who are psychologically healthy before they become pregnant; in contrast, women who are in poor emotional health after an abortion are likely to have been feeling bad about their lives before ending their pregnancies. The study was published in *Professional Psychology*, a journal of the American Psychological Association.

Decision Making and Unintended Pregnancy

When a woman suspects she is unintentionally pregnant, she should first confirm the pregnancy through a formal laboratory test. A physical examination by a physician will help to establish how long she has been pregnant. After pregnancy has been conclusively established, she can weigh her options carefully: carrying the child to term and keeping it, carrying the child to term and relinquishing it for adoption, or having an abortion. This is a decision that can greatly affect an individual's life. A woman facing this difficult decision should talk with several people she respects and trusts and who can remain calm and objective during the discussion (Kelly, 1998).

Married couples commonly choose to keep an unplanned baby, although abortion remains an option for many married women, especially those who feel they already have as many children as they can care for properly. Couples who are not married may choose to get married, although many authorities believe that pregnancy is not by itself a sufficient reason for marriage. Some young parents receive help rearing their babies from their own parents and other relatives while they complete their educations and become more capable of assuming parental responsibilities. However, grandparents are often less than excited about becoming "parents" once again.

Adoption agencies today have difficulty finding babies for all the couples who wish to adopt. The high rate of abortion has contributed to this situation, along with society's generally negative attitude toward relinquishing babies for adoption. Social attitudes are reflected in the expression "giving up the child for adoption." The majority of adolescent mothers who carry their babies to term thus choose to keep them, despite the difficulties young mothers face in this situation. Adoption is seen as a viable alternative by many people, however. Some agencies are making an effort to ease the pain young mothers may feel by allowing them to have continued contact with the child and its adoptive parents.

Many people have strong feelings about the dilemma of unintended pregnancy and are eager to influence the decision in one direction or another. The individual or couple experiencing the dilemma, however, carry the responsibility for the decision. Whatever the decision, an unintended pregnancy is often a very lonely and stressful time in a woman's life.

Preventing Abortion

The Planned Parenthood Federation of America argues that reducing the number of unintended pregnancies in this country will reduce the number of abortions. Using this line of thought, Planned Parenthood (1985) advocates the following ways to prevent abortion:

- *Make contraceptives more easily available.* Every public dollar spent on family planning saves at least two tax dollars in the next year alone in reduced health and welfare services associated with unintended births.

- *Provide young people with a better teacher than experience.* Support sex education programs instead of hoping that sex will disappear if no one talks about it.

- *Increase the involvement of men.* No woman ever made herself pregnant. Help men recognize equal responsibility in all aspects of sexuality, including obtaining and using contraception.

- *Develop new birth control methods that are temporary, safe, effective, easy to use, and without side effects.* Increase government support for research in this area.

- *Make America friendlier to children.* Research by the Alan Guttmacher Institute indicates that the United States is the only developed country in which teen pregnancy is increasing. Countries with lower rates were found to be more realistic about and accepting of sexuality and to have open access to family planning services.

Glossary

ABC-X Family Crisis Model A theoretical model of family crisis in which *A* denotes the stressor, *B* denotes the family's crisis-meeting resources, *C* denotes the family's definition of the stressor, and *X* denotes the crisis.

ability to cope with stress One of the six qualities (commonly found in emotionally healthy families) identified by researchers working within the family strengths framework.

abortifacient Anything used to induce abortion.

abortion Expulsion of a fetus from the uterus before it is sufficiently developed to survive on its own; commonly used to describe only artificially induced terminations of pregnancy.

accommodating style A style of conflict resolution characterized by nonassertive but cooperative behavior; accommodaters subjugate their own wants and needs to those of others.

acculturation The intermeshing of cultural traits and values with those of the dominant culture.

acquired immune deficiency syndrome (AIDS) A fatal condition caused by the human immunodeficiency virus (HIV), which suppresses the immune system; HIV is transmitted primarily through blood and semen.

afterbirth The placenta and fetal membranes, which are expelled from the uterus during the third stage of labor.

ageism A form of prejudice or discrimination in which one judges an older person negatively solely on the criterion of age.

aggressive communication A style of interpersonal communication that attempts to hurt or put down the receiver while protecting the aggressor's self-esteem.

agreeing to disagree A negotiating strategy in which two people are unable to agree on opposing courses of action and decide to take neither course of action.

AIDS *See* acquired immune deficiency syndrome.

Al-Anon A self-help group for families of alcoholics.

Alateen A support group for young people with alcoholic parents, based on the Alcoholics Anonymous model.

alcohol abuse A generic term that encompasses both alcoholism (addiction to alcohol characterized by compulsive drinking) and problem drinking (alcohol consumption that results in functional disability).

Alcoholics Anonymous (AA) A self-help group for alcoholics.

alcoholism Addiction to alcohol characterized by compulsive drinking.

alimony Court-ordered financial support to a spouse or former spouse following separation or divorce.

amniotic sac The membrane that encloses the fetus and holds the amniotic fluid, which insulates the fetus.

androgen Any of the hormones that develop and maintain male secondary sex characteristics.

androgyny A blending of traditionally masculine and traditionally feminine personality characteristics and role behaviors in one person; the absence of sex-typing with regard to roles.

anorgasmia A sexual dysfunction that prevents a woman from having an orgasm.

anxiety disorder A mental disorder characterized by attacks of panic that are not occasioned by life-threatening situations or extreme physical exertion.

appreciation and affection One of the six qualities (commonly found in emotionally healthy families) identified by researchers working within the family strengths framework.

arranged marriage *See* parent-arranged marriage.

artificial insemination The mechanical introduction of semen into the uterus in an attempt to cause pregnancy.

assertive communication A style of interpersonal communication that involves expressing one's self-interests and wishes without degrading or putting down the other person.

assertiveness A person's ability to express his or her feelings and desires.

assimilation Adopting the cultural traits and values of the dominant culture.

attentive listening A style of listening focused on fully understanding the speaker's point of view; characterized by encouragement of rather than direction of the speaker.

authoritarian parenting A parenting style characterized by the demand for absolute obedience to rigid rules and the use of punitive, forceful disciplinary measures.

autonomic power pattern A power pattern in a marriage in which both partners have about equal authority but in different areas of life; both make decisions in their particular domains independent of each other.

avoidance A person's tendency to minimize issues and a reluctance to deal with issues directly.

avoidance style A style of conflict resolution characterized by nonassertive and passive behavior; avoiders often withdraw from the conflict or change the subject.

balanced families Families who fit into the four central categories of the Couple and Family Map: families who are flexibly connected, flexibly cohesive, structurally connected, or structurally cohesive. *See also* unbalanced families; mid-range families.

bankruptcy The state of being financially insolvent or unable to pay one's bills.

barrier methods of contraception Devices that prevent pregnancy by physically blocking the sperm from entering the uterus, including condoms, diaphragms, and cervical caps.

behaviorist A clinician who, based on learning theories, has developed practical, positive ways of dealing with children's behavior; rather than focusing on punishment, behaviorists encourage "accentuating the positive." *See also* reinforcement.

belief system One of the four major components of the sociocultural context in which families live, centering on religious/spiritual/ethical beliefs and other ideas about how to live successfully and happily in the world. *See also* extended-family system; family system; social system.

bidirectional effects Both the influence of the child on the parent and the influence of the parent on the child; child development specialists and family scientists concur that studying these effects is important to an understanding of parent-child dynamics.

bilateral descent A method of tracing the lineage of children equally through ancestors of both mother and father.

binuclear family A postdivorce family in which both parents participate in the raising of their children despite living in separate households; the children generally reside with one of the parents.

biopsychosocial approach An approach to stress management and health care that assumes a connection among a person's physical symptoms, psychological issues, and social context.

bisexual Sexual orientation toward members of both sexes.

blamer A person whose style of anger management is characterized by a short temper, emotionally intense responses to stress, and the belief that others are responsible for her or his feelings and problems.

blastocyst An early stage of the fertilized egg, containing about 100 cells; implants itself in the uterine lining (endometrium).

blended family A term used to describe a stepfamily. Some researchers object to the term because it creates unrealistic expectations that the new family will quickly and easily "blend" together harmoniously and because it assumes a homogeneous unit, one without a previous history or background. *See also* stepfamily.

boomerang kids Adult children who come back to their parents' home to live as a result of divorce, job loss, or an inability to make it in the "real world."

boundaries The lines that both separate systems from and connect systems to each other. The notion of a boundary implies a hierarchy of interconnected systems, each larger than the one before it.

boundary ambiguity Lack of clarity about whether a person is either in or out of the family system; related to family stress levels. The concept includes two variables: physical and psychological presence or absence. High ambiguity (conflicting variables) produces high levels of stress.

brainstorming A conflict-resolution strategy that involves thinking of as many solutions to a problem as possible.

breast-feeding Feeding a baby from the mother's breast rather than from a bottle; usually better than bottle-feeding for the physical well-being of the baby.

budgeting The regular, systematic balancing of income and expenses.

Caring Cluster One of two groups of characteristics that distinguish romantic relationships from friendships; includes being an advocate for one's partner and giving the utmost. *See also* Passion Cluster.

case study A detailed description of a person or a family that illustrates a specific idea, concept, or principle of family science.

catharsis conflict The false belief that venting anger verbally prevents physical violence. Researchers who study family violence have found that verbal and physical violence are related.

centrifugal interaction Behavior that pushes system components away from one another, decreasing the system's connectedness.

centripetal interaction Behavior that pulls system components toward one another, resulting in the system's increasing connectedness.

cervical cap A thimble-shaped contraceptive device that fits snugly over the cervix; must be fitted by a physician and used with a spermicide.

cervix The narrow lower end of the uterus that adjoins the vagina.

cesarean section (C-section) Surgical delivery of the fetus by incising the mother's abdominal and uterine walls.

chaotic-style family One of two broad family system types in which incest occurs. These families often have a multitude of problems, many of which are heightened by socioeconomic, educational, and vocational conditions. Substance abuse and trouble with the law are common in these families. *See also* normal-appearing family.

child abuse The physical or mental injury, sexual abuse, or negligent treatment of a child under the age of 18 by a person who is responsible for the child's welfare.

child-free alternative The decision by married or co-habitating adults not to have children.

child-to-parent abuse Violence directed at a parent by a child.

chlamydia A sexually transmissible disease that causes inflammation of the urinary tract in men and vaginal inflammation in women.

circular causality model An interpersonal communication model that describes an interaction pattern in which both parties view their behavior as a reaction to the other's behavior rather than as something for which they are each responsible. The first person sends out a message that causes a change in and a response from the second person. That response causes a new response in the first person, whose response initiates another response from the second person, and so on. This type of communication cycle can escalate into conflict.

circumcision The surgical or ritualistic removal of the foreskin of the penis.

clitoris An erotically sensitive organ located at the upper end of the female's vulva above the urethral opening; becomes erect during sexual arousal; the counterpart of the male penis.

closed system A family system that has the capacity to maintain the status quo and avoids change; also called a *morphostatic system*.

closure The resolution of an issue.

cluttered nest The period during which young adults return to their parental home until they are established professionally and financially and can move into an apartment or home of their own.

coculture A distinct cultural or social group living within a dominant culture but also having membership in another culture, such as gay men and lesbians.

codependent A person, often a spouse, whose actions enable an alcoholic to continue to drink but who is often unaware of the ways in which her or his behavior "enables" the partner's drinking; also called an *enabler*.

cognitive development theory A model of child development that views growth as the mastery of specific ways of perceiving, thinking, and doing; growth occurs at discrete stages.

cohabitation Two unrelated adults sharing the same living quarters.

cohesion *See* family cohesion.

collaborative style A style of conflict resolution characterized by a high degree of assertiveness about reaching one's own goals coupled with a concern for the other person.

commitment Attachment to another. One of the six qualities (commonly found in emotionally healthy families) identified by researchers working within the family strengths framework; also, the cognitive component of Sternberg's three dimensions of love.

communication The way humans create and share meaning, both verbally and nonverbally; the foundation for developing and maintaining human relationships, especially intimate relationships. *See also* family communication; positive communication.

community divorce One of Bohannan's six different but overlapping experiences of divorce; involves changes in friendships and community relationships.

companionate love A type of love relationship characterized by commitment and intimacy but lacking intense passion; common between partners who have been together for many years.

competitive style A style of conflict resolution characterized by aggression, lack of cooperation, pursuit of personal concerns at the expense of the other, and the desire to "win" at all costs.

competitive symmetry A style of communication in which partners attempt to control the situation and the other by escalating the level of hostilities in a competitive manner.

complementary interaction A style of communication in which the partners adopt two different tactics: One is dominant and one is submissive. *See also* symmetrical interaction.

complementary needs theory The supposition that people are attracted to partners whose personalities differ from but complement their own. Family researchers have not found much support for this theory.

complex stepfamily A stepfamily that includes children from both parents. *See also* simple stepfamily.

compromise style A style of conflict resolution characterized by a willingness to give up something to resolve an issue.

conception The union of a sperm cell and the nucleus of an ovum (egg), which begins the development of the fetus; also called *fertilization*.

conceptual framework A set of interconnected ideas, concepts, and assumptions that helps organize thinking from a particular perspective. The field of family science includes a variety of major conceptual frameworks: family systems theory (or the family systems framework), the family strengths framework, the family development framework, the symbolic interaction framework, the social construction framework, and the feminist framework.

condom A rubber sheath placed over the penis before intercourse to prevent pregnancy and protect against sexually transmissible diseases.

conflicted couple A type of premarital and married couple characterized by few relationship strengths, low levels of relationship satisfaction, and a high risk of divorce.

conjugal family system A family consisting of a husband, a wife, and children; also called a *nuclear family*.

consanguineal family system A family system that emphasizes blood ties more than marital ties.

constructive intimacy games Games, or exercises, designed to increase intimacy in a relationship; people participate voluntarily, and they know the rules and goals of the game. *See also* destructive intimacy games.

consummate love A type of love relationship characterized by commitment, intimacy, and passion.

contraception A deliberate action (use of a device, drug, or technique) taken to prevent conception (pregnancy).

contractions Tightenings of the muscles, especially those of the uterus, during labor.

convenience A type of cohabiting relationship in which one partner takes and the other gives. A relationship of convenience is usually based on sexual, caretaking, economic, or social needs rather than on love.

coparental divorce One of Bohannan's six different but overlapping experiences of divorce; involves decisions about custody of the children, single-parenting, and visitation rights for the noncustodial parent.

coparenting A style of parenting in which both parents take on tasks and roles traditionally associated with only the mother or the father.

Couple and Family Map A graphic representation of dynamic relationships within families, comprising three central dimensions: cohesion (togetherness), flexibility (ability to change), and communication (a facilitating dimension that helps families move between the extremes on the cohesion and flexibility dimensions). Identifies 16 types of family relationship.

crisis A drastic change in the course of events; a turning point that affects the trend of future events; an unstable condition of affairs; a time of danger and a time of opportunity.

crisis-loss stage of grief A period of chaotic shock; the first of Brubaker's three stages of the grieving process. *See also* new-life stage of grief; transition stage of grief.

cross-cultural family study A research study focused on how cultural context influences family issues, among them, values and behaviors, courtship and marriage patterns, communication, roles, work and the family, childrearing patterns, and sexuality.

cross-validation A comparison of the results from one research method with those of another research method to see if the findings are similar or identical.

cultural identity A feeling of belonging that evolves from the shared beliefs, values, and attitudes of a group of people; the structure of the group's marital, sexual, and kinship relationships.

dance of anger Lerner's metaphor to describe styles of managing anger and ways in which these styles interact.

dating A form of courtship involving a series of appointed meetings for social interaction and activities during which an exclusive relationship may evolve between two people. Also called *individual-choice courtship*.

definition of the situation The concept that a situation is based on a person's subjective interpretation; hence, people can have different views of the same situation.

delivery The second stage of labor, lasting from the time the cervix is completely dilated until the fetus is expelled or removed by cesarean section.

democratic parenting A parenting style that establishes the parents' legitimate power to set rules while also recognizing the child's feelings, individuality, and need to develop autonomy; uses positive reinforcement, seldom punishment, to enforce standards. Also called *authoritative parenting*.

destructive intimacy games Games that reduce intimacy because people are often unaware of the game, do not voluntarily participate, and are often manipulated to behave in certain ways. *See also* constructive intimacy games.

devitalized couple The unhappiest type of married couple; characterized by few couple strengths and the highest risk for divorce.

diaphragm A cup-shaped rubber contraceptive device that is inserted in the vagina before intercourse to cover the cervical opening and block sperm from entering the uterus; must be fitted by a physician and used with a spermicide.

dilation and curettage (D & C) An abortion technique used in the second trimester of pregnancy; performed in a hospital under general anesthetic. After the cervix is dilated (opened), the embryo is removed from the uterus with a sharp instrument (curette).

dilation and evacuation (D & E) An abortion technique used in the second trimester of pregnancy. Suction and forceps are used to remove the embryo or fetus.

DINS dilemma Inhibited or hypoactive sexual desire in couples with many demands on their time. DINS stands for double income, no sex.

directive listening A style of listening in which the listener attempts to control the direction of the conversation through the use of questions.

distancer An individual who (1) wants emotional space when stress is high, (2) is self-reliant rather than a help-seeker, and (3) values privacy.

distress Feelings of discomfort caused by high levels of stress.

divorce culture The notion that divorce has become so accepted in the United States that it is almost expected as the outcome of marriage.

double ABC-X Model A descriptive model of family crisis that recognizes the impact of both hardships resulting from a crisis and unresolved prior crisis on the family's ability to cope; an outgrowth of Hill's ABC-X Family Crisis Model.

double bind A situation in which the message relayed by the speaker calls into question the type of relationship the receiver has with the speaker.

double standard Different standards of appropriate sexual and social behavior for the two sexes; the belief that premarital sex is more acceptable for males than for females.

douching An ineffective form of contraception in which a liquid containing vinegar or another acidic substance is squirted into the vagina following intercourse.

early abortion An abortion method similar to vacuum aspiration but performed as soon as a positive pregnancy test is received, up to 8 weeks after the last menstrual period. A flexible tube is inserted through the cervix without dilating it, and the contents of the uterus are sucked out.

ecology The study of how all the organisms in a system relate to one another.

economic divorce One of Bohannan's six different but overlapping experiences of divorce; involves the division of money and property and the establishment of two separate economic units.

ejaculatory incompetence A sexual dysfunction that prevents a man from ejaculating in his partner's vagina despite a firm erection and a high level of sexual arousal.

emancipation A type of cohabiting relationship based on the desire to break free of parental values and influence rather than on love.

emic perspective The analysis of a society from the inside. *See also* etic perspective.

emotional divorce One of Bohannan's six different but overlapping experiences of divorce; involves the deterioration of the marriage and the breakdown of bonding and communication, which are replaced by feelings of alienation.

empty love A type of love relationship involving commitment but no passion or intimacy.

empty-nest syndrome Feelings of malaise, emptiness, and lack of purpose that some parents experience when their last child leaves home. *See also* spacious nest.

enabler A person, often a spouse, whose actions permit an alcoholic to continue to drink; also called a *co-dependent.*

endogamy The practice of choosing a mate from within one's own ethnic, religious, socioeconomic, or general age group.

ENRICH A comprehensive marital inventory containing 125 questions in categories that are relevant to married couples and their satisfaction with their relationship. ENRICH is an acronym for **EN**riching **R**elationship **I**ssues, **C**ommunication, and **H**appiness.

epididymitis Inflammation of the testicles in men, often caused by untreated gonorrhea; can lead to sterility.

episiotomy A surgical incision from the vagina toward the anus, performed to prevent tearing of the perineum during childbirth.

equalitarian group Structured on the ideals of democracy, a group believing that the rights and perspectives of both sexes and of all generations ought to be respected. The societal norms of the United States are considered to be equalitarian.

equalitarian roles Social equality between the sexes; equal sharing of practical responsibilities and decision making by men and women. Also called *egalitarian roles.*

erectile dysfunction A sexual dysfunction in which a man has difficulty achieving or maintaining penile erection that is firm enough for intercourse.

estrogen Although often called the *female hormone,* any of a group of hormones, produced primarily by the ovaries, that are significant in controlling female physiological functions and directing the development of female secondary sex characteristics at puberty.

ethnic identity The geographic origin of a minority group within a country or culture; cultural identity transcends ethnic identity.

ethnocentrism The assumption that one's own culture is the standard by which to judge other cultures.

etic perspective The analysis of a society from the outside. *See also* emic perspective.

eustress A moderate-to-high level or a low-to-moderate level of stress that is energizing, motivating, positive, and healthy.

exogamy The practice of choosing a mate from outside one's own group.

expressive role According to Parson and Bales's model of the modern family, the wife-mother's role—caring for the emotional well-being of the family, providing nurturing and comfort. *See also* instrumental role.

extended family A nuclear family and those related to its members by blood, such as aunts, uncles, cousins, and grandparents.

extended-family system One of the four major components of the sociocultural context in which families live;

focuses on the degree of importance relatives outside the nuclear family have on the family's life.

family Two or more people who are committed to each other and who share intimacy, resources, decision-making responsibilities and values; people who love and care for each other.

family cohesion The togetherness or closeness of a family; one of the three dimensions of the Couple and Family Map.

family communication Interaction; sharing of thoughts and feelings; the facilitating dimension of the Couple and Family Map.

family coping A family's ability to manage stressful events or situations as a unit with minimal or no detrimental effects on any individual members.

family coping resources Resources of a healthy family system on which the family can draw in times of stress, including cohesion, adaptability, and a willingness to adopt nontraditional family roles in the face of changing economic circumstances. *See also* personal coping resources.

Family Database An integrated computerized database containing the data from all volumes of the *Inventory of Marriage and Family Literature*, which contains more than 100,000 research articles on families that have been published in English language journals since 1900.

family development framework A conceptual framework that focuses on how family members deal with roles and developmental tasks within the family unit as they move through the stages of the life cycle.

family flexibility A family's ability to change and adapt in the face of stress or crisis; one of the three dimensions of the Couple and Family Map.

family hardship A demand on a family that accompanies a stressor event. For example, the family hardship of reduced income accompanies the stressor event of losing one's job.

family of origin The family in which a person is raised during childhood.

family power The ability of one family member to change the behavior of the other family members.

family science An interdisciplinary field whose primary focus is to better understand families in order to enhance the quality of family life. Professionals whose main interest is the family tend to call themselves *family scientists;* those who develop educational programs for families sometimes call themselves *family life educators;* those who work clinically with troubled families are called *marriage* (or *marital*) *and family therapists.*

family strengths framework A conceptual framework proposing that if researchers study only family problems, they will find only problems in families, but that if they are interested in family strengths, they must study strong families; identifies six qualities that strong families com-

monly demonstrate: commitment, appreciation and affection, positive communication, time together, spiritual well-being, and the ability to cope with stress and crisis.

family system One of the four major components of the sociocultural context in which families live; focuses on the interconnectedness of family members. *See also* belief system, extended-family system, and social system.

family systems theory (or **family systems framework**) A conceptual framework that views everything that happens to any family member as having an impact on everyone else in the family, because family members are interconnected and operate as a group, or family system.

family therapy An approach to helping families; based on the belief that the roots of an individual's problems may be traced to troubled family dynamics.

fatuous love A type of love relationship in which commitment is based on passion but in which there has not yet been time to develop true intimacy.

femininity A gender-linked constellation of personality traits and behavioral patterns traditionally associated with females in a society.

feminist framework A conceptual framework that emphasizes the value of women's perspectives on society and the family, that recognizes women's subordination, and that promotes change in that status.

feminization of poverty The statistical fact that the percentage of female single parents in the total percentage of those who are poor in the United States is increasing.

fertility awareness A variety of contraceptive methods based on predicting a woman's fertile period and avoiding intercourse during that interval (or using an additional method of contraception during that time).

fertilization The union of a sperm cell and the nucleus of an ovum (egg); also known as *conception.*

fetal alcohol syndrome (FAS) Serious malformations (particularly of the facial features and the eyes) seen in children whose mothers drank excessively during their pregnancy.

flexibility *See* family flexibility.

foreskin In the female, the fold of skin that covers the clitoris (also called the *prepuce* or *clitoral hood*). In the male, the skin that covers the glans (tip) of the penis, removed in most male infants in the United States shortly after birth in the process of circumcision.

gender The learned characteristics and behaviors associated with biological sex in a particular culture. *See also* sex.

gender identity A person's internal sense of being female or male, which is expressed in personality and behavior.

gender polarization The organizing of social life according to male and female gender-role distinctions.

gender role The traits and behaviors assigned to males or females by a culture.

gender-role stereotype A rigid, simplistic belief about the distinctive psychological characteristics and behavioral patterns attributable to a man or woman based exclusively on sex.

general systems theory A set of principles and concepts that can be applied to all types of systems, living and non-living.

genital herpes A sexually transmissible disease caused by the herpes simplex virus; lesions similar to cold sores or fever blisters appear on the genitals.

genital warts A sexually transmissible disease caused by the human papillomavirus.

genitals The external sex or reproductive organs.

germ cells Reproductive cells produced by the gonads in both sexes. Female germ cells are called *ova* (eggs), and male germ cells are called *sperm*.

glans The extremity, or tip, of the male penis and the female clitoris; the most sensitive part of the organ and an important source of sexual arousal.

goals Specific, achievable objectives or purposes.

gonads Reproductive glands that secrete sex hormones and produce germ cells; the testes in men and the ovaries in women.

gonorrhea A sexually transmissible disease that usually remains localized in the genitals and is self-limiting, although if untreated, it can cause serious and permanent damage, including sterility. Symptoms are common in men, but gonorrhea is often asymptomatic and therefore difficult to detect in women.

gunnysacking An alienating ("dirty") fighting tactic in which a person saves up unresolved grievances until he or she explodes, resulting in a major confrontation.

harmonious couple A type of premarital and married couple characterized by many couple strengths, relationship satisfaction, and a low risk of divorce.

heterosexual Sexual orientation toward members of the other sex.

HIV *See* human immunodeficiency virus.

homogamy The tendency to marry someone of the same ethnic group, educational level, socioeconomic status, religion, and values.

homophobia Aversion to homosexuals and homosexuality.

homosexual Sexual orientation toward members of the same sex.

human immunodeficiency virus (HIV) The virus that causes AIDS.

husband-dominant power pattern A power pattern in a marriage in which the man is the boss.

hymen A thin membrane that may partially cover the female's vaginal opening before first intercourse.

hypothesis An assertion subject to verification or proof; a presumed relationship between variables.

hysterotomy A relatively rare surgical method of abortion, performed in the late second trimester of pregnancy, in which a cesarean section is performed to remove the fetus.

idiographic A theoretical approach that focuses on the study of individuals and individual differences. *See also* nomothetic.

incest Sexual activity of any kind between members of the same family.

incest taboo The nearly universal societal prohibition of intercourse between parents and children and between siblings.

incestuous abuse The sexual exploitation of a child under the age of 18 by a family member.

incongruity humor Humor that points out things in life that don't fit together logically; a tool for couples and families who want to "fight fair."

incubation period The time during which a disease-causing organism is multiplying in the body but does not cause any symptoms. HIV, the virus that causes AIDS, has a long incubation period.

induced labor A method of abortion performed in the late second trimester, generally in a hospital, in which a saline solution or prostaglandins are injected into the amniotic sac to cause the woman's body to expel the fetus.

infatuation A type of love relationship characterized by passion and lacking both intimacy and commitment.

infertility The inability to conceive a child.

insider perspective How people inside the family describe their relationships. *See also* outsider perspective.

instrumental role According to Parson and Bales's model of the modern family, the husband-father's role—being the breadwinner, the manager, and the leader of the family. *See also* expressive role.

intercultural marriage Marriage between people from two different cultural or ethnic groups.

interdependence of parts A characteristic of systems; the parts or elements of a system are interconnected in such a way that if one part is changed, other parts are automatically affected.

intimacy Sharing intellectually, physically, and/or emotionally with another person; the emotional component of Sternberg's three dimensions of love.

intimacy game The emotional manipulation of a partner or close friend into doing or giving something while concealing the desired outcome; undermines relationships by destroying closeness and sharing.

intimacy need fulfillment The satisfaction one receives from having personal needs fulfilled, which leads to greater intimacy; the fourth and final component in Reiss's wheel of love.

intimate experience   An experience in which one feels close to another or shares oneself in one area of life, such as intellectually, socially, emotionally, or sexually.

intimate relationship   A partnership involving an emotional bond between two people, with proven mutual commitment and trust, that provides personal and relationship security and rewards; a relationship in which one shares intimate experiences in several areas of life over time, with expectations that this sharing will continue.

intrauterine device (IUD)   A contraceptive device inserted by a physician into a woman's uterus to prevent conception from occurring.

in vitro fertilization   A method of treating female infertility. Eggs are removed from the woman's ovary, fertilized in a laboratory dish with her partner's sperm, and implanted in her uterus.

joint custody   A legal child custody arrangement following a divorce in which children divide their time between the homes of both parents, with both homes having equal importance: "one child, two homes."

Kaposi's sarcoma (KS)   A rare form of cancer that causes purple or brownish lesions resembling bruises on the skin and inside the mouth, nose, or rectum; the second most common cause of death in people with AIDS.

kinship   The relatedness of certain individuals within a group. Cultures have norms and expectations that structure and govern kin behavior.

labor   The stages of delivering a baby, consisting of contractions of the uterine muscles and dilation of the cervix, the birth itself, and the expulsion of the placenta.

learned helplessness theory   A theory that a learned passivity develops from giving power over oneself to another; that passivity increases helplessness, reduces problem-solving abilities, and limits options.

learning theories   Approaches to understanding human development that focus on how people learn to behave the way they do.

legal divorce   One of Bohannan's six different but overlapping experiences of divorce involves the dissolution of the marriage by the legal system and the courts.

liking   A type of love relationship characterized by intimacy but lacking passion and commitment.

lineage   Line of descent, influenced by cultural norms. Lineage determines membership in a kinship group, patterns of inheritance, and kinship obligations or responsibilities. *See also* matrilineal society; patrilineal society.

linear causality model   An interpersonal communication model that assumes a direct, or linear, relationship between cause and effect.

Linus blanket   A type of cohabiting relationship in which one of the partners is so dependent or insecure that he or she prefers a relationship with anyone to being alone.

longevis marriage   A long-term marriage that lasts 50 years or more.

looking-glass self   The idea that you learn about yourself based on the feedback you receive from others.

male menopause   Physical changes in men related to age, similar to those that occur in women during menopause.

managing stress   Pauline Boss's alternative to the phrase *coping with stress*; individual family members' use of their own resources to help their family deal with a stressor or work through a crisis.

marriage   An emotional and legal commitment between two people to share emotional and physical intimacy, various tasks, and economic resources.

masculinity   A gender-linked constellation of personality traits and behavioral patterns traditionally associated with males in a society.

masturbation   Self-stimulation of the genitals; also called *autoeroticism*.

mating gradient   The tendency of women to marry men who are better educated or more successful than they are.

matriarchal group   A group in which the mother or eldest female is recognized as the head of the family, kinship group, or tribe. Descent is traced through this woman.

matrilineal society   A society in which descent, or lineage, is traced through females.

matrilocal society   A society that encourages newly married couples to live with or near the wife's kin, especially her mother's kinship group.

medical family therapy   A therapeutic framework that uses family systems theory and the biopsychosocial approach in dealing with health problems in family members.

menopause   The cessation of ovulation, menstruation, and fertility in women as a result of aging.

menses   The menstrual flow in which the endometrial tissue is discharged.

menstrual regulation   A procedure in which the contents of the uterus are sucked out before the woman's menstrual period is due; as such, the woman never knows if she was pregnant. Also called *endometrial aspiration, preemptive abortion,* and *menstrual extraction.*

menstruation   The discharge from the uterus through the vagina of blood and the unfertilized ova; occurs about every 28 days in nonpregnant women between puberty and menopause.

metacommunication   Communicating about communicating.

methotrexate and misoprostol   Two prescription drugs that, in combination, function as an effective abortifacient.

middle age Generally speaking, the years between the ages of 35 and 65; from the standpoint of the family development conceptual framework, the middle years of the family life cycle are the launching period for young-adult children and the period before the parents' retirement.

midlife crisis A period of questioning one's worth, values, and contributions in life, usually beginning in a person's 40s or early 50s.

mid-range families Families who are extreme on one dimension of the Couple and Family Map but balanced on the other dimension. There are eight mid-range family types. For example, a family might be structurally enmeshed: extreme on cohesion (enmeshed) but balanced on flexibility (structured). *See also* balanced families; unbalanced families.

midwife A nonphysician who attends and facilitates a birth.

minority group A social group that differs from the rest of the population in some ways and that often experiences discrimination and prejudice.

miscarriage The termination of a pregnancy from natural causes before the fetus is viable outside of the mother (during the first or second trimester of pregnancy).

missionary position A coital position in which partners lie face to face, with the male above the female.

mixed message A message in which there is a discrepancy between the verbal and the nonverbal components: The receiver hears one thing but simultaneously feels something else.

monogamy A relationship in which a man or a woman has only one mate.

morning sickness Nausea experienced by many women during the first trimester of pregnancy, often but not exclusively in the morning.

morphogenic system A system that is open to growth and change; also called an *open system*.

morphostatic system A system that has the capacity to maintain the status quo, thus avoiding change; also called a *closed system*.

mutual dependency A relationship in which each person wants and needs the other person; the third component in Reiss's wheel of love.

mutual masturbation A sexual technique in which partners sexually stimulate each other to orgasm without having intercourse.

negative feedback Information or communication that is intended to minimize change in a system.

neolocal society A society that encourages newly married couples to establish their own separate, autonomous residence, independent of either partner's parental kinship group.

neutralized symmetry A style of communication in which partners respect each other, approach each other as equals, and avoid exerting control over each other.

new-life stage of grief The period during which the bereaved establishes a new lifestyle and exhibits to society and himself or herself that he or she can live satisfactorily as a single person; the last of Brubaker's three stages of the grieving process. *See also* crisis-loss stage of grief; transition stage of grief.

nocturnal orgasm Nonvoluntary ejaculation or orgasm occurring during sleep; in men, also called a *wet dream*.

no-fault divorce Divorce laws that do not place blame (fault) for the divorce on either spouse. One party's assertion that irreconcilable differences exist is sufficient grounds for dissolving the marriage.

nomothetic A theoretical approach that focuses on developing a theory that works for a great number of cases. Researchers using this approach believe it is possible to develop a general family theory. *See also* idiographic.

non-love A type of love relationship characterized by the absence of commitment, intimacy, and passion.

nonverbal communication The communication of emotions by means other than words, such as touch, body movement, facial expression, and eye contact.

normal-appearing family One of two broad family system types in which incest occurs. These families look healthy and functional to outsiders but have serious problems, including incest. The family structure is often traditional, but family members lack nurturing abilities. *See also* chaotic-style family.

Norplant The trade name of a contraceptive implant placed under the skin on the inside of a woman's upper arm; releases the hormone progestin.

nuclear family A kinship group in which a husband, a wife, and their children live together in one household; also called a *conjugal family system*.

old age Arbitrarily defined as beginning at age 65, which coincides for most people with retirement.

open system A family system that is open to growth and change; also called a *morphogenic system*.

oral contraceptives Birth control pills taken by mouth that contain hormones that suspend ovulation and thus prevent conception.

oral sex Stimulation of the partner's genitals with one's tongue or mouth.

organic sexual dysfunction Impairment of the ordinary physical responses of sexual excitement or orgasm as the result of physical or medical factors, such as illness, injury, or drugs.

organismic theory Developed by Jean Piaget and expanded by later theorists, a theory of child development emphasizing that children's minds develop through various stages and that children think very differently from adults; sees child-thought as primitive and mystical, with logical reasoning developing slowly into adulthood.

orgasm The climax of human sexual response, characterized by the release of physical and sexual tensions at the peak of sexual arousal.

outsider perspective How researchers or therapists perceive a family, in contrast with how family members perceive the family. *See also* insider perspective.

ovaries The female gonads (sex glands), which produce ova (eggs) and hormones.

overfunctioner An individual who knows what is best not only for herself or himself but for everybody else as well; they cannot let others solve their problems themselves.

oviduct In the female reproductive system, one of a pair of tubes through which ova (eggs) travel from an ovary to the uterus. Also called *fallopian tube*.

ovulation The regular monthly release in the female of one or more eggs from an ovary.

ovum (plural, **ova**) The female reproductive germ cell, or egg, produced by the ovaries.

painful intercourse A sexual dysfunction characterized by intense discomfort during sex; experienced by both women and men and often related to physical problems with the sex organs.

palimony "Equitable relief" (alimony) granted by a court to a cohabiting partner; legal precedent established in *Marvin* v. *Marvin* in 1979.

parent-arranged marriage A practice, common in nonindustrialized societies, in which the parents of the bride and groom select the future spouse and arrange the marriage ceremony. Based on the principle that the elders in a community have the wisdom to select an appropriate spouse, this type of marriage generally extends existing family units rather than creating new units.

parent education A lecture-and-discussion format for small or large groups of parents that is aimed at helping them learn how to raise children successfully.

parental control The degree of flexibility exhibited by a parent in terms of enforcing rules and disciplining her or his child(ren).

parental support The amount of caring, closeness, and affection a parent exhibits or gives to his or her child(ren).

partner dominance The degree to which a person feels his or her partner tries to be controlling and dominant in their relationship.

passion Intense physiological arousal; the motivational component of Sternberg's three dimensions of love.

Passion Cluster One of two groups of characteristics that distinguish romantic relationships from friendships;

includes fascination, sexual desire, and exclusiveness. *See also* Caring Cluster.

passive communication A style of interpersonal communication characterized by an unwillingness to say what one thinks, feels, or wants.

passive-aggressive behavior Feigning agreement or acting as if everything is okay but later becoming hostile or aggressive; an indirect way of expressing anger.

patriarchal group A group in which the father or eldest male is recognized as the head of the family, kinship group, or tribe. Descent is traced through this man.

patrilineal society A society in which descent, or lineage, is traced through males.

patrilocal society A society that encourages newly married couples to live with or near the husband's kin, especially his father's kinship group.

pelvic inflammatory disease (PID) A bacterial infection of the oviducts that can spread to the ovaries and uterus; often results from untreated sexually transmissible diseases such as gonorrhea and can lead to sterility.

penis The male organ of sexual intercourse.

permissive parenting A style of parenting in which the parents (1) permit the child's preferences to take over their ideals and (2) rarely force the child to conform to their standards.

permissiveness The extent to which couples are physically intimate before marriage.

personal coping resources Qualities that help people deal with stressors across the life cycle, such as an individual's self-esteem and mastery (confidence in personal abilities). *See also* family coping resources.

personification The belief that everything one's partner does is a reflection on oneself; leads to attempts to control the partner's behavior.

persuasive listening A style of listening in which the "listener" is looking only for an opportunity to take over and control the direction of the conversation.

placenta A vascular organ that joins the fetus with the mother's uterus and through which the fetus receives nutrients and discharges wastes; expelled in the final stage of labor, following the birth of the baby.

PLISSIT Model Annon's application of four levels of treatment in various sex therapies: permission (**P**), limited information (**LI**), specific suggestions (**SS**), and intensive therapy (**IT**).

plural marriage A marriage in which a man has more than one wife (polygyny) or a woman has more than one husband (polyandry).

pneumocystis carinii pneumonia (PCP) A life-threatening protozoan infection of the lungs; the major cause of death in AIDS patients.

polyandry A plural marriage in which a woman has more than one husband.

polygamy A marriage in which a man or a woman has more than one mate; a plural marriage.

polygyny A plural marriage in which a man has more than one wife.

positive communication One of the six qualities (commonly found in emotionally healthy families) identified by researchers working within the family strengths framework.

positive feedback Information or communication that is intended to create change in a system.

postmodernism A belief system that emphasizes multiple perspectives or "truths." Postmodernists are extremely skeptical in regard to questions of truth, meaning, and historical interpretation. No objective, universal truth can be seen, once and for all, and readily agreed upon. Instead, there is only a collection of subjective truths shaped by the particular subcultures in which we live. These multiple subjective truths are constantly competing for our attention and allegiance.

postpartum depression A feeling of depression after giving birth, characterized by irritability, crying, loss of appetite, and difficulty sleeping; thought to be a result of the many physiological changes that occur after delivery.

posttraumatic stress disorder (PTSD) A severe stress reaction characterized by the reexperiencing of past traumatic events.

power The ability of an individual in a social system to change the behavior of other members of the system through will, influence, or control.

prejudice Negative judgment or opinion having no or limited basis in fact; hostility to a person or a group based on physical characteristics.

premature ejaculation A sexual dysfunction in which a man is unable to control his ejaculation reflex voluntarily and reaches orgasm sooner than he or his partner wishes.

PREPARE A comprehensive premarital inventory that assesses a couple's relationship and determines how idealistic or realistic each person is in regard to marriage, how well the couple communicates, and how well the couple resolves conflicts and financial issues; acronym for **PRE**marital **P**ersonal **A**nd **R**elationship **E**valuation.

PREPARE-MC A premarital inventory for couples whose marriage will create a stepfamily. Like the PREPARE inventory, PREPARE-MC (**M**arriage with **C**hildren) contains questions dealing with important categories in the couple's relationship, but the questions focus on issues relevant to stepfamilies.

prior strain The residual effect of family tensions and prior stressor events that may still trouble a family at the time another stressor occurs.

problem drinking Alcohol consumption that results in functional disability.

progestin A hormone connected with pregnancy and contained in oral contraceptives.

propinquity Nearness in time or place; in mate selection, the tendency to choose someone who is geographically nearby.

prostate gland A gland located near the base of the male urethra that produces some of the fluid in semen that nourishes and transports sperm.

pseudo-kin-group A type of kinship group in which relationships resembling kinship ties develop among "unrelated" individuals.

pseudomutuality A false sense of togetherness.

psychodynamic theory Developed by Freud and his followers, a theory of human development that emphasizes the importance of providing a positive emotional environment during early childhood, when the foundation for later life is laid down.

psychological divorce One of Bohannan's six different but overlapping experiences of divorce; involves the regaining of individual autonomy.

psychosocial sexual dysfunction Impairment of the ordinary physical responses of sexual excitement or orgasm as a result of psychological, developmental, interpersonal, environmental, or cultural factors.

pursuer An individual who wants a very high degree of togetherness and expression of feelings in a relationship.

quid pro quid A strategy for negotiating differences in which one person gets to do what he or she wants in exchange for doing something another person requests; "this for this."

quid pro quo A strategy for negotiating differences in which one person agrees to do something in exchange for the other person's agreement to do something else of equal value or importance; "this for that."

race A group of people with similar and distinctive physical characteristics.

racism Discrimination or prejudice based on the belief that people's physical characteristics determine their human capacities and behaviors and that groups of people with certain characteristics are inferior to others.

rapid orgasm A sexual dysfunction in which a woman consistently reaches orgasm sooner than she or her partner wishes; the counterpart of premature ejaculation in the male.

rapport The process of communication in which two people develop understanding and a sense of closeness; the first component in Reiss's wheel of love.

reconstituted family A term used to describe stepfamily. *See also* blended family; stepfamily.

reframing An internal family coping strategy that involves redefining a stressful experience in a positive way so that it can be confronted directly and dealt with successfully.

reinforcement   Rewarding desired behavior to increase the likelihood that it will be repeated.

rejecting parenting   A style of parenting in which parents pay little attention to their children's needs and set few or no expectations for their children's behavior.

remarriage   A marriage in which one or both partners marry following divorce or the death of a spouse; in this book, remarriage refers to couples who have never been married to each other before.

representative sample   A random selection of individuals who accurately reflect the characteristics of a particular group.

research study   An investigation designed to test a specific hypothesis.

resource theory of family power   A theory that the balance of power in a marriage is related to the relative resources (especially money, level of education, and occupational prestige) each spouse has in the relationship.

resources   Assets that can be used to achieve goals; economic, human, and environmental tools.

retarded ejaculation   A sexual dysfunction in which prolonged and strenuous effort is needed to reach orgasm.

role   The expected behavior of a person or group in a given social category, such as husband, wife, supervisor, or teacher.

role making   The process of creating new roles or revising existing roles.

role taking   The process whereby people learn how to play roles correctly by practicing and getting feedback from others.

romantic love   A type of love relationship characterized by intimacy and passion but lacking commitment.

routinization   A situation, often encountered in middle age, in which one's job lacks the challenge it once offered and becomes boring.

RU-486   An oral antiprogesterone steroid that acts as an abortifacient if taken within the first 6 weeks of pregnancy. It is currently available by prescription in Europe, but its effectiveness and safety are still being tested in the United States.

sandwich generation   Parents, usually in their 50s and older, who are simultaneously responsible for childrearing and for caring for their own aging parents; individuals who are "caught in the middle" between two generations.

saver   A person whose money-handling style is characterized by compulsive saving, often to the point of having little money free for the essentials.

schizophrenia   A mental disorder characterized by bizarre or grandiose delusions; auditory hallucinations; in-

coherent, illogical thinking; and very grossly disorganized behavior.

scrotum   The pouch or sac of skin behind the penis that holds the testes, the two male gonads.

segregation   Isolation of an ethnic group within the dominant culture.

self-confidence   A measure of how a person feels about herself or himself and the ability to control things in her or his life.

self-disclosure   Revealing to another person personal information or feelings that that individual could not otherwise learn.

self-revelation   Self-disclosure; the second component in Reiss's wheel of love.

semen   The milky fluid made up of sperm and seminal fluid that is ejaculated from the penis at orgasm.

sex   Being biologically male or female; also, sexual activity or behavior. *See also* gender.

sex educator   A trained teacher who provides general information and principles about sex and sexuality, generally in a group setting.

sex ratio   The relationship between the number of men and the number of women of a given age.

sex therapist   A trained individual who teaches and counsels clients individually, in pairs, or in small groups about sex and sexuality.

sex therapy   A process of education and counseling designed to help people overcome sexual problems.

sexual dysfunction   A state in which one's sexual behavior or lack of it is a source of distress; any malfunction of the human sexual response that inhibits the achievement of orgasm, either alone or with a partner.

sexual intercourse   Coitus; the insertion of the male's penis into the female's vagina.

sexual orientation   A person's self-identification as a heterosexual, homosexual, bisexual, or transgender.

sexuality   The set of beliefs, values, and behaviors by which one defines oneself as a sexual being.

sexually transmissible disease (STD)   Any of several highly contagious diseases that may be passed from one individual to another through sexual contact. The seven major STDs are HIV infection (which leads to AIDS), syphilis, gonorrhea, chlamydia, genital herpes, genital warts, and viral hepatitis.

sibling abuse   Physical violence between siblings; probably the most common form of abuse of children.

SIDS   *See* sudden infant death syndrome.

simple stepfamily   A stepfamily that includes children from only one parent. *See also* complex stepfamily.

singlehood   The state of being unmarried, divorced, or unattached to another person.

social construction framework   A conceptual framework that proposes that human beings are profoundly immersed in the social world and that our understanding of this world and beliefs about this world are social products.

social environment All the factors, both positive and negative, in society that impact individuals and their relationships, such as mass media, the Internet, changing gender roles, and growing urban crowding.

social learning theory A psychological theory of development that focuses on learning through observation, imitation, and reinforcement.

social support network An interdependent group of family members, friends, and acquaintances that a person can draw on for support when facing problems.

social system One of the four major components of the sociocultural context in which families live; encompasses the influence of the community, laws, economic resources, educational opportunities, and other external factors on the family. *See also* belief system; extended-family system; family system.

sole custody A child custody arrangement following a divorce in which only one parent has legal and physical custody of the child or children; the other parent generally has visitation rights.

spacious nest A positive descriptive term for the time in a marriage when the children have left home. *See also* empty-nest syndrome.

spender A person whose money-handling style is characterized by a love of purchasing items for himself or herself as well as for others.

sperm The male reproductive cells produced by the testes.

spermicide A contraceptive substance (gel, cream, foam, or vaginal insert) that is toxic to sperm; usually used with a barrier device; may protect against certain sexually transmissible diseases.

spiritual well-being One of the six qualities (commonly found in emotionally healthy families) identified by researchers working within the family strengths framework.

split custody A legal child custody arrangement following a divorce in which each parent has sole custody of one or more of the children.

STD *See* sexually transmissible disease.

stepfamily The family created when one or both partners in a marriage have a child or children from a previous marriage. *See also* blended family; reconstituted family.

stepparent An adult who is married to one's biological parent but who is not one's birth parent.

Stepping Ahead Program An eight-step program designed to build strengths in stepfamilies.

stereotype A standardized, oversimplified, often foolish and mean-spirited view of someone or something.

sterilization Any procedure, but usually a surgical one, by which an individual is made incapable of reproduction.

stillbirth The birth of a dead baby that was developmentally mature enough to have lived outside the womb; occurs between the seventh and ninth months of pregnancy (the third trimester).

stress The nonspecific response of the body to any demand made upon it.

stress pileup As described by the Double ABC-X model, the occurrence and after-effects of several stresses within a short period of time, which can strain an individual's or a family's coping abilities.

stressful life event An event that creates a change in the family system.

stressor An external event that causes an emotional and/or a physical response and that can precipitate a crisis.

submissive symmetry A style of communication in which each participant tries to give control of the situation, and responsibility for it, to the other.

subsystem In the general systems theory, a small system that is part of a larger suprasystem.

sudden infant death syndrome (SIDS) The sudden, unexpected death of an infant, which cannot be explained by postmortem examination or tests.

suprasystem In the general systems theory, a large system that incorporates smaller subsystems.

surrogate motherhood A controversial approach to female infertility in which a fertile woman agrees—for a fee paid by a couple who cannot conceive—to be artificially inseminated by another person's husband's sperm, to carry the baby to term, and to give it to the infertile couple at birth.

symbolic interaction framework A conceptual framework that focuses on the internal perceptions of family members and examines how they learn roles and rules in society through interaction and shared meaning.

symmetrical interaction A style of communication in which partners send similar messages designed to control how the relationship is defined. *See also* complementary interaction.

syncratic power pattern A power pattern in a marriage in which both partners share authority equally and make decisions jointly.

syphilis A sexually transmissible disease that occurs when mucous membranes or broken skin come into contact with an infectious lesion.

system A set of interconnected components that form a whole; what happens to one component affects all the other components.

tender years doctrine The legal presumption under traditional divorce laws that young children would do better with their mother than with their father after a divorce.

testes The male gonads (sex glands), which produce testosterone and manufacture sperm; also called *testicles*.

testing A type of cohabiting relationship undertaken as a trial in a situation closely resembling marriage.

theory Systematically organized knowledge applicable in a wide variety of circumstances; especially, a system of assumptions, accepted principles, and rules of procedure devised to analyze, predict, or otherwise explain the nature or behavior of a specified set of phenomena.

time together One of the six qualities (commonly found in emotionally healthy families) identified by researchers working within the family strengths framework.

traditional couple A type of premarital and married couple characterized by some external strengths (such as religion and friends) but fewer internal strengths (such as communication and conflict-resolution skills).

transgender An individual who believes that he or she is a victim of a biologic accident that occurred before birth and has been imprisoned within a body incompatible with his or her real gender identity. A majority of transgender persons are biologic males who identify themselves as females, usually early in childhood.

transition stage of grief The period during which the bereaved's grief lessens and he or she begins to recognize that a new life is possible; the second of Brubaker's three stages of the grieving process. *See also* crisis-loss stage of grief; new-life stage of grief.

trimester One of three periods of about 3 months each into which pregnancy is divided.

tubal ligation A female sterilization procedure in which the oviducts (fallopian tubes) are cut or tied and sealed.

umbilical cord A flexible structure that connects the fetus to the placenta and through which nutrients pass to the fetus and waste products are discharged.

unbalanced families Families who fall at the extremes on both the flexibility and the cohesion dimensions of the Couple and Family Map: chaotically enmeshed, chaotically disengaged, rigidly enmeshed, or rigidly disengaged, families. *See also* balanced families; mid-range families.

uncontested divorce Under traditional divorce law, a divorce in which one party would charge the other party with an infraction that was considered by the court as grounds for granting a divorce and the accused party would agree not to challenge the accuser in court. In many cases parties were forced to collude and to perjure themselves in order to divorce.

underfunctioner An individual who is too highly flexible and disorganized and becomes less competent under stress.

uninvolved parenting A style of parenting in which parents ignore their children and let them do what they wish unless it interferes with the parent's activities.

urethra The tubular structure in men and women that carries urine from the bladder to an external opening. In men, semen passes through this duct before ejaculation.

uterus An organ within the female pelvic cavity in which the fertilized egg develops into the fetus. Also called the *womb*.

vacuum aspiration An abortion method, used during the first trimester of pregnancy, in which the uterine contents are removed by suction.

vagina The expandable passageway that leads from the uterus to the vulva in the female; acts as the birth canal during childbirth and receives the erect penis during sexual intercourse.

vaginismus A sexual dysfunction in which a woman's vaginal muscles involuntarily constrict, preventing intercourse.

validation The process of ensuring that a research instrument measures what it is intended to measure.

values Personal, lasting, deeply held basic beliefs about what is good, desirable, and important in life.

vasectomy A male sterilization procedure in which the vasa deferentia are severed and tied.

victimizer One who victimizes others. Children who grow up with violence often learn the potential for victimizing others as adults.

viral hepatitis A liver infection caused by any of three viruses: hepatitis A, B, and C. The B virus and the C virus are most likely transmitted sexually, because they are found in saliva, semen, vaginal secretions, and blood. Hepatitis A usually enters the body in food contaminated with fecal matter and is not considered to be a sexually transmitted disease.

vitalized couple A type of premarital and married couple characterized by many couple strengths, high marital satisfaction, and a low risk of divorce.

vulva The external female genital organs.

wholeness A characteristic of systems; general systems theorists believe that the whole is more than the sum of its parts.

wife-dominant power pattern A power pattern in a marriage in which the woman is the boss.

withdrawal Removal of the penis from the vagina before ejaculation; an unreliable method of contraception.

zero-sum game A game in which one side's margin of victory equals the other side's margin of defeat, producing a final sum of zero; what one person wins, the other loses.

zygote The fertilized ovum (egg).

References

Abbott, D. A., & Meredith, W. H. (1988). Characteristics of strong families: Perceptions of ethnic parents. *Home Economics Research Journal, 17* (2), 140–147.

Abortion foes vow to fight: Maryland's governor OKs abortion-rights law. (1991, February 19). *Lincoln* [NE] *Journal*, p. 2.

Adams, M. (1976). *Single blessedness: Observations on the single status in married society.* New York: Basic Books.

Adler, N. E., David, H. P., Major, B. N., Roth, S. H., Russo, N. F., & Wyatt, G. E. (1992). Psychological factors in abortion: A review. *American Psychologist, 47* (October), 1194–1204.

Agnew, R. (1984). The effect of appearance on personality and behavior: Are the beautiful really good? *Youth and Society, 15* (3), 285–303.

Ahrons, C. (1994). *The good divorce: Keeping your family together when your marriage comes apart.* New York: HarperCollins.

Ahrons, C., & Perlmutter, M. (1982). The relationship between former spouses: A fundamental subsystem in the remarriage family. In J. C. Hansen & L. Messinger (Eds.), *Therapy with remarriage families* (pp. 31–46). Rockville, MD: Aspen.

Ahrons, C., & Rodgers, R. H. (1987). *Divorced families: A multidisciplinary view.* New York: Norton.

Alberti, R. E., & Emmons, M. L. (1990). *Your perfect right: A guide to assertive living.* San Luis Obispo, CA: Impact.

Albrecht, S. L. (1979). Correlates of marital happiness among the remarried. *Journal of Marriage and the Family, 41,* 857–867.

Alcohol impacts four of ten adults. (1991, October 1). *Lincoln* [NE] *Star,* p. 3.

Aldous, J. (1995). New views of grandparents in intergenerational context. *Journal of Family Issues, 16* (1), 104–122.

Allen, K. R., & Walker, A. J. (1992). Attentive love: A feminist perspective on the care giving of adult daughters. *Family Relations, 41* (July), 284–289.

Allen, W. D. (1996). Five types of African-American marriages based on ENRICH. Unpublished doctoral dissertation, Department of Family Social Science, University of Minnesota, St. Paul.

Allen-Meares, P. (1989). Adolescent sexuality and premature parenthood: Role of the Black church in prevention. *Journal of Social Work and Human Sexuality, 8* (1), 133–142.

Allgeier, A. R., & Allgeier, E. R. (1995). *Sexual interactions* (4th ed.). Lexington, MA: Heath.

Allgeier, E. R., & Allgeier, A. R. (1998). *Sexual interactions: Basic understandings* (5th ed.). Boston: Houghton Mifflin.

Alpern, D. M. (1988, March 14). It scares the hell out of me. *Newsweek,* 44.

Altura, J. (1974). Poem. In J. Gillies, *My needs, your needs.* New York: Doubleday.

Amato, P. R. (1993). Children's adjustment to divorce: Theories, hypotheses, and empirical support. *Journal of Marriage and the Family, 55* (February), 23–83.

Amato, P. R., & Booth, A. (1996). A prospective study of divorce and parent-child relationships. *Journal of Marriage and the Family, 58,* 356–365.

Amato, P. R., & Booth, A. (1997). *A generation at risk: Growing up in an era of family upheaval.* Cambridge, MA: Harvard University Press.

American Academy of Pediatrics. (1994). *The pediatrician's role in helping children and families deal with separation and divorce.* New York: Author.

American Academy of Pediatrics. (1999, March 1). *American Academy of Pediatrics releases new circumcision policy* [On-line]. Available: http://www.eurekalert.org/releases/uncchaao022699.html.

American Psychiatric Association. (1994). *Diagnostic and statistical manual of mental disorders* (4th ed.). Washington, DC: Author.

Anglin, J. P. (1985). Parent education: Can an old tradition address new needs and new realities? In R. Williams, H. Lingren, G. Rowe, S. Van Zandt, P. Lee, & N. Stinnett (Eds.), *Family strengths 6: Enhancement of interaction* (pp. 203–225). Lincoln, NE: University of Nebraska, Department of Human Development and the Family, Center for Family Strengths.

Annon, J. S. (1976). *The behavioral treatment of sexual problems.* Hagerstown, MD: Harper & Row.

Annon, J. S. (1994). *The behavioral treatment of sexual problems:* Vol. 1, *Brief therapy;* Vol. 2: *Intensive therapy.* Honolulu: Enabling Systems. New York: Harper & Row.

Aquilino, W. S. (1997). From adolescent to young adult: A prospective study of parent-child relations during the transition to adulthood. *Journal of Marriage and the Family, 59* (August), 670–686.

Aquilino, W. S., & Supple, K. R. (1991). Parent-child relations and parents' satisfaction with living arrangements when adult children live at home. *Journal of Marriage and the Family, 53* (February), 13–27.

Arcus, M. E., Schvaneveldt, J. D., & Moss, J. J. (Eds.). (1993a). *Handbook of family life education: Vol. I. Foundations of family life education.* Newbury Park, CA: Sage.

Arcus, M. E., Schvaneveldt, J. D., & Moss, J. J. (Eds.). (1993b). *Handbook of family life education: Vol. 12. The practice of family life education.* Newbury Park, CA: Sage.

Argyle, M. (1988). *Bodily communication.* New York: Methuen.

Arias, I. (1999) Women's responses to physical and psychological abuse. In X. Arriaga & S. Oskamp (Eds.), *Violence in intimate relationships.* Newbury Park, CA: Sage.

Arias, I., & Pape, K. T. (1999). Psychological abuse: Implications for adjustment and commitment to leave violent partners. *Violence and Victims.*

Arond, M., & Pauker, S. L. (1987). *The first year of marriage.* New York: Warner Books.

Asai, S. (1996). *Gender roles and power allocation in Japanese society and families.* Unpublished manuscript, University of Minnesota, Family Social Science, St. Paul.

Attneave, C. (1982). The role of support systems in building family strengths. In N. Stinnett, J. DeFrain, K. King, H. Lingren, G. Rowe, S. Van Zandt, & R. Williams (Eds.), *Family strengths 4: Positive support systems* (pp. 309–314). Lincoln: University of Nebraska Press.

Avenovoli, S., Sessa, F. M., & Steinberg, L. (1999). Family structure, parenting practices, and adolescent adjustment. In E. M. Hetherington (Ed.), *Coping with divorce, single parenting and remarriage* (pp. 65–90). Mahwah, NJ: Erlbaum.

Axtell, R. E. (Ed.). (1993). *Do's and taboos around the world.* New York: Wiley.

Azar, S. T., & Rohrbeck, C. A. (1986). Child abuse and unrealistic expectations: Further validation of the parent opinion questionnaire. *Journal of Consulting and Clinical Psychology, 54* (6), 867–868.

Azubike, I. C. (1987). Building strengths within the Black family. In H. G. Lingren, L. Kimmons, P. Lee, G. Rowe, L. Rottmann, L. Schwab, & R. Williams (Eds.), *Family strengths 8–9: Pathways to well-being.* Lincoln: University of Nebraska, Department of Human Development and the Family, Center for Family Strengths.

Baca-Zinn, M. (1980). Chicano men and masculinity. *Journal of Ethnic Studies, 10* (2), 29–44.

Baca-Zinn, M. (1995). Social science theorizing for Latino families in the age of diversity. In R. E. Zambrana (Ed.), *Understanding Latino families: Scholarship, policy, and practice, Vol. 2* (pp. 177–189). Thousand Oaks, CA: Sage.

Bach, G., & Wyden, P. (1969). *The intimate enemy: How to fight fair in love and marriage.* New York: Morrow.

Bader, E., Microys, G., Sinclair, L., Willett, E., & Conway, B. (1980). Do marriage preparation programs really work? A Canadian experiment. *Journal of Marital and Family Therapy, 6,* 171–179.

Bader, E., Riddle, R., & Sinclair, C. (1981). *Family therapy news.* Washington, DC: American Association for Marital and Family Therapy.

Bader, L., DeFrain, J., & Parkhurst, A. (1982). What parents feel when their child divorces. Family Perspective (Spring), 93–100.

Baldwin, S. E., & Baranoski, M. V. (1990). Family interactions and sex education in the home. *Adolescence, 25* (Fall), 573–582.

Barkas, J. L. (1980). *Single in America.* New York: Atheneum.

Barnes, H., & Olson, D. H. (1986). Parent-adolescent communication. In D. H. Olson, H. I. McCubbin, H. Barnes, A. Larsen, M. Muxen, & M. Wilson (Eds.), *Family inventories* (pp. 51–57). St. Paul: University of Minnesota, Family Social Service.

Barnhill, L. R. (1979). Healthy family systems. *Family Coordinator, 28,* 94–100.

Barratt, M. S., Roach, M. A., Morgan, K. M., & Colbert, K. K. (1996). Adjustment to motherhood by single adolescents. *Family Relations, 45* (April), 209–215.

Bateson, G., Jackson, D. D., Haley, J., & Weakland, J. (1956). Toward a theory of schizophrenia. *Behavioral Science, 1,* 251–264.

Bauer, J. W., & Wollen, B. J. (1990). *Financial management extension consultant program: Young singles and young couples.* St. Paul: Minnesota Extension Service.

Baumrind, D. (1991). The influence of parenting style on adolescent competence and substance abuse. *Journal of Early Adolescence, 11* (1), 56–95.

Baumrind, D. (1994). The social context of child maltreatment. *Family Relations, 43,* 360–368.

Baumrind, D. (1995). *Child maltreatment and optimal caregiving in social contexts.* New York: Garland.

Baumrind, D. (1996). The discipline controversy revisited. *Family Relations, 45* (October), 405–414.

Beavers, W. R., & Hampson, R. B. (1990). *Successful families.* New York: Norton.

Becker, L. A. (1989). Family systems and compliance with medical regimen. In C. N. Ramsey (Ed.), *Family systems in medicine* (pp. 416–434). New York: Guilford Press.

Becvar, D. S., & Becvar, R. J. (1993). *Family therapy: A systemic integration* (2nd ed.). Boston: Allyn & Bacon.

Beigel, H. G. (1953). The meaning of coital postures. *International Journal of Sexology, 4,* 136–143.

Bell, R. Q. (1977). *Child effects on adults.* Hillsdale, NJ: Erlbaum.

Belsky, J. (1991). Parental and nonparental child care and children's socioemotional development: A decade in review. In A. Booth (Ed.), *Contemporary families: Looking forward, looking back* (pp. 122–140). Minneapolis: National Council on Family Relations.

Belsky, J., & Kelly, J. (1994). *The transition to parenthood: How a first child changes a marriage: Why some couples grow closer and others apart.* New York: Delacorte Press.

Belsky, J., & Kuang-Hua Hsieh (1998). Patterns of marital change during the early childhood years: Parent personality, coparenting and division-of-labor correlates. *Journal of Family Psychology, 12,* (4) 511–528.

Bem, S. L. (1993). *The lenses of gender: Transforming the debate on sexual inequality.* New Haven, CT: Yale University Press.

Bem, S. L. (1995). Dismantling gender polarization and compulsory heterosexuality: Should we turn the volume down or up? *Journal of Sex Research, 32* (4), 329–334.

Berger, C. R. (1980). Power and the family. In M. Roloff & G. Miller (Eds.), *Persuasion: New directions in theory and research* (pp. 197–224). Beverly Hills, CA: Sage.

Berger, P., & Luckmann, T. (1966). *The social construction of reality.* Garden City, NY: Doubleday.

Berkow, R. (Ed.). (1997). *The Merck manual of medical information: Home edition.* White House Station, NJ: Merck Research Laboratories.

Bernard, J. (1970). Women, marriage, and the future. *Futurist, 4,* 41–43.

Bernstein, B. E. (1977). Legal problems of cohabitation. *Family Coordinator* (October), 361–366.

Berscheid, E. (1982, January 11). America's obsession with beautiful people: Interview with Ellen Berscheid, psychologist. *U.S. News & World Report,* 60–61.

Berscheid, E., & Reis, H. T. (1998). Attraction and close relationships. In D. T. Gilbert, S. T. Fiske, & G. Lindzey (Eds.), *The handbook of social psychology* (4th edition), (pp. 193–281). New York: McGraw Hill.

Bierstedt, R. (1950). An analysis of social power. *American Sociological Review, 6,* 7–30.

Billingsley, A. (1986). *Black families in White America.* Englewood Cliffs, NJ: Prentice-Hall.

Blair, S. L., & Lichter, D. T. (1991). Measuring the division of household labor: Gender segregation of housework among American couples. *Journal of Family Issues, 12* (1), 91–113.

Blair, S. L., & Qian, Z. (1998). Family and Asian students' educational performance: A consideration of diversity. *Journal of Family Issues, 19* (4), 355–374.

Blankenhorn, D. (1990). American family dilemmas. In D. Blankenhorn, S. Bayne, & J. B. Elshtain (Eds.), *Rebuilding the nest.* Milwaukee: Family Service America.

Blankenhorn, D. (1995). *Fatherless America: Confronting our most urgent social problem.* New York: Basic.

Blieszner, R., & Shifflett, P. A. (1990). The effects of Alzheimer's disease on close relationships between patients and caregivers. *Family Relations, 39* (January), 57–62.

Blood, R. O., & Wolfe, D. M. (1960). *Husbands and wives.* Glencoe, IL: Free Press.

Blumstein, P. W., & Schwartz, P. (1983). *American couples.* New York: Morrow.

Blumstein, P. W., & Schwartz, P. (1990). Intimate relationships and the creation of sexuality. In D. P. McWhirter, S. A. Sanders, & J. M. Reinisch (Eds.), *Homosexuality/heterosexuality: Concepts of sexual orientation.* New York: Oxford University Press.

Blumstein, P. W., & Schwartz, P. (1991). Money and ideology: Their impact on power and the division of household labor. In R. L. Blumberg (Ed.), *Gender, family, and economy: The triple overlap.* Newbury Park, CA: Sage.

Bohannan, P. (1970). The six stations of divorce. In P. Bohannan (Ed.), *Divorce and after* (pp. 29–55). New York: Doubleday.

Borcherdt, B. (1993). *You can control your feelings: 24 guides to emotional self-control.* Sarasota, FL: Professional Resource Press.

Borcherdt, B. (1996). *Head over heart in love: 25 guides to rational passion.* Sarasota, FL: Professional Resource Press.

Borcherdt, B. (1998). *Feeling right when things go wrong.* Sarasota, FL: Professional Resource Press.

Borg, S., & Lasker, J. (1981). *When pregnancy fails: Families coping with miscarriage, stillbirth, and infant death.* Boston: Beacon Press.

Boss, P. (1999). *Ambiguous loss: Learning to live with unresolved grief.* Cambridge, MA: Harvard University Press.

Boss, P. (1988). *Family stress management.* Newbury Park, CA: Sage.

Boss, P. (1992). Primacy of perception in family stress theory and measurement. *Journal of Family Psychology, 6* (2), 113–119.

Boston Women's Health Book Collective. (1992). *The new our bodies, ourselves.* New York: Touchstone/Simon & Schuster.

Boston Women's Health Book Collective. (1998). *Our bodies, ourselves for the new century: A book by and for women.* New York: Touchstone/Simon & Schuster.

Boughner, S., Davis, A. Spencer, & Mims, G. A. (1998). Social construction: A family perspective for the 21st century. In J. D. West, D. L. Bubenzer, & J. R. Bitter (Eds.), *Social construction in couple and family counseling.* Alexandria, VA: American Counseling Association.

Boulding, K. (1985). *Human betterment.* Beverly Hills, CA: Sage.

Bowen, G. L., Pittman, J. F., Pleck, J. H., Haas, L., & Voydanoff, P. (Eds.). (1995). *The work and family interface: Toward a contextual effects perspective.* Minneapolis: National Council on Family Relations.

Bowker, L. H., Arbitell, M., & McFerron, J. R. (1988). On the relationship between wife beating and child abuse. In K. Yllo & M. Bograd (Eds.), *Feminist perspective on wife abuse* (pp. 158–175). Newbury Park, CA: Sage.

Boyd-Franklin, N. (1989). *Black families in therapy: A multisystems approach.* New York: Guilford.

Bozzi, V. (1985, August). Choose me. *Psychology Today,* 60–61.

Bretschneider, J. G., & McCoy, N. L. (1988). Sexual interest and behavior in healthy 80- to 102-year-olds. *Archives of Sexual Behaviors, 17,* 109–129.

Brick, P. (1989). Toward a positive approach to adolescent sexuality. *SIECUS Reports, 17* (5).

Broderick, C. (1984). *Marriage and the family* (2nd ed.). Englewood Cliffs, NJ: Prentice-Hall.

Brody, J. E. (1995, August 31). Abortion method using two drugs gains in a study. *New York Times,* p. A1.

Brody, J. E. (1998, February 12). Study questions abortion's mental health risks to women. *Lincoln* [NE] *Journal Star,* p. 2A.

Brown, E. M. (1991). *Patterns of infidelity and their treatment.* New York: Brunner/Mazel.

Browne, A., & Finkelhor, D. (1986). Initial and long-term effects: A review of the research. In D. Finkelhor (Ed.), *Sourcebook on child sexual abuse.* Beverly Hills, CA: Sage.

Browning, R. (1970). Grow old along with me! In I. Jack (Ed.), *Browning: Poetical works.* Oxford: Oxford University Press. (Original work published 1864.)

Brubaker, T. H. (1985). *Later life families.* Beverly Hills, CA: Sage.

Brubaker, T. H. (Ed.). (1990). *Family relationships in later life* (2nd ed.). Newbury Park, CA: Sage.

Brubaker, T. H. (1991). Families in later life: A burgeoning research area. In A. Booth (Ed.), *Contemporary families: Looking forward, looking back* (pp. 226–248). Minneapolis: National Council on Family Relations.

Bryan, A. A. (1998). *Facilitating couple relationships during the transition to parenthood.* Unpublished doctoral dissertation, Department of Family Health Nursing, University of Wisconsin, Eau Claire.

Brydon, S., & Scott, M. (1997). *Between one and many* (2nd ed.). Mountain View, CA: Mayfield.

Buchanan, C. M., Maccoby, E. E., & Dornbusch, S. M. (1996). *Adolescents after divorce.* Cambridge, MA: Harvard University Press.

Bulcroft, K., & O'Conner-Roden, M. (1986, June). Never too late. *Psychology Today,* 66–69.

Bumiller, E. (1985, December 20). Marriages still arranged but may be vetoed in India. *Washington Post,* p. 8.

Bumpass, L. (1999, March). (Interviewed by Nadya Labi.) A bad start: Living together may be the road to divorce. *Time,* 61.

Bumpass, L., & Lu, H. H. (1998). "Trends in cohabitation and implications for children's family contexts." Unpublished manuscript. Center for Demography, University of Wisconsin, Madison.

Burgess, B. J. (1980). Parenting in the Native American community. In M. D. Fantini & R. Cardinas (Eds.), *Parenting in a multicultural society* (pp. 63–73). New York: Longman.

Burgess, E. W., & Wallin, P. (1943). Homogamy in social characteristics. *American Journal of Sociology, 49* (2), 109–124.

Burr, J. (1990). Race/sex comparisons of elderly living arrangements. *Research on Aging, 12* (December), 507–530.

Burr, W. R., Day, R. D., & Bahr, K. S. (1993). *Family science.* Pacific Grove, CA: Brooks/Cole.

Burr, W. R., & Klein, S. R. (1994). *Reexamining family stress.* Thousand Oaks, CA: Sage.

Burt, M. (Ed.). (1989). *Stepfamilies stepping ahead* (3rd ed.). Lincoln, NE: Stepfamilies Press.

Burton, S. (1990, May 14). Straight talk on sex in China. *Time,* 82.

Byrne, D. (1983). Sex without contraception. In D. Byrne & W. A. Fisher (Eds.), *Adolescents, sex, and contraception.* Hillsdale, NJ: Erlbaum.

Calderone, M. S., & Johnson, E. W. (1989). *The family book about sexuality.* New York: Harper & Row.

Cameron, S. C., and Wycoff, S. M. (1998). The destructive nature of the term race: Growing beyond a false paradigm. *Journal of Counseling & Development, 76,* 277–285.

Campbell, T. L. (1995). *The effectiveness of family interventions in the treatment of physical illness.* Unpublished manuscript, University of Rochester, Department of Family Medicine, Rochester, NY.

Carnegie Task Force on Meeting the Needs of Young Children. (1994). *Starting points: Meeting the needs of our youngest children.* New York: Carnegie Corporation.

Carnes, P. (1989). *Counseling sexual abusers.* Minneapolis: CompCare.

Caron, S. L., Bertran, R. M., & McMullen, T. (1987). AIDS and the college student: The need for sex education. *SIECUS Report XV* (6, July/August), 6–7.

Carson, D. K., Dail, P. W., Greeley, S., & Kenote, T. (1990). Stresses and strengths of Native American reservation families in poverty. *Family Perspective, 24* (4), 383–400.

Carter, B., & McGoldrick, M. (1999). *The expanded family life cycle: Individual, family, and social perspectives.* Boston: Allyn and Bacon.

Cate, R. M., & Lloyd, S. A. (1991). *Courtship.* Newbury Park, CA: Sage.

Centers for Disease Control and Prevention. (1994, February). *HIV/AIDS surveillance report.* Atlanta, GA: Author.

Chase-Lansdale, P. L., & Brooks-Gunn, J. (Eds.). (1995). *Escape from poverty: What makes a difference for children?* New York: Cambridge University Press.

Chase-Lansdale, P. L., Cherlin, A. J., & Kiernan, K. E. (1995). The long-term effects of parental divorce on the mental health of young adults: A developmental perspective. *Child Development, 66,* 1614–1634.

Children's Defense Fund. (1988). *A children's defense budget: FY 1989.* Washington, DC: Author.

Christopher, F. S., & Roosa, M. W. (1990). An evaluation of an adolescent pregnancy prevention program: Is "just say no" enough? *Family Relations, 39,* 68–72.

Christopher, S. (1995). Adolescent sexuality: Trying to explain the magic and the mystery. In N. Vanzetti & S. Duck (Eds.), *A lifetime of relationships* (pp. 213–242). Pacific Grove, CA: Brooks/Cole.

Clarke, J. (1984). *The family types of schizophrenics, neurotics and "normals."* Unpublished doctoral dissertation, University of Minnesota, Department of Family Social Science, St. Paul.

Clift, E. (1992, July 13). Abortion angst: How the court's ruling will affect women, doctors and activists on both sides. *Newsweek,* 16–19.

Cohen, S. (1995, October 1). 50,000 women plan lawsuits over Norplant contraceptive. *Lincoln* [NE] *Journal Star,* p. 7A.

Cohen, S. S. (1987). *The magic of touch.* New York: Harper & Row.

Cohen, W., & Tharp, M. (1999, January 11). Fed-up cities turn to evicting the homeless: One urban problem with no good answer. *U.S. News & World Report,* 28.

Cole, W., Dickerson, J. F., & Smilgis, M. (1994, October 17). Now for the truth about Americans and sex: The first comprehensive survey since Kinsey smashes some of our most intimate myths. *Time,* 62–70.

Coleman, B. C. (1995, September 27). Secondhand smoke threatens workers, new study reveals. *Lincoln* [NE] *Journal Star,* p. 5A.

Coleman, J. C. (1988). *Intimate relationships, marriage, and family* (2nd ed.). New York: Macmillan.

Coleman, M., & Ganong, L. H. (1991). Remarriage and stepfamily research in the 1980s: Increased interest in an old family form. In A. Booth (Ed.), *Contemporary families: Looking forward, looking back* (pp. 192–207). Minneapolis: National Council on Family Relations.

Coley, R. L., & Chase-Lansdale, P. L. (1998). Adolescent pregnancy and parenthood: Recent evidence and future directions. *American Psychologist, 53* (2), 152–166.

College sex habits mostly unchanged. (1990, March 22). *Lincoln* [NE] *Journal,* p. 31.

Cook, E. P. (1985). *Psychological androgyny.* New York: Pergamon.

Cook, E. P. (1993). No woman is an island: Women and relationships. In E. P. Cook et al. (Eds.), *Women, relationships, and power: Implications for counseling* (pp. 15–47). Alexandria, VA: American Counseling Association.

Cook, E. P. (1995). Role salience and multiple roles: A gender perspective. *Career Development Quarterly, 43* (1), 85–95.

Cook, E. P. (1997). Gender discrimination in Jessica's career. *Career Development Quarterly, 46* (2), 148–154.

Corbett, T. (1993). Child poverty and welfare reform: Progress or paralysis? *Focus, 15* (1), 1–17.

Corrales, R. (1975). Power and satisfaction in early marriage. In R. E. Cromwell & D. H. Olson (Eds.), *Power in families* (pp. 197–216). New York: Halsted/Wiley.

Courtois, C. A. (1988). *Healing the incest wound.* New York: Norton.

Cowan, A. L. (1989, August 21). Women's gains on the job not without a heavy toll. *New York Times,* p. I1.

Cowan, C. P., Cowan, P. A., Heming, G., & Miller, N. B. (1991). Becoming a family: Marriage, parenting and child development. In P. A. Cowan & M. Hetherington (Eds.), *Family transitions* (pp. 79–109). Hillsdale, NJ: Erlbaum.

Cowley, G. (1989, March 13). How the mind was designed: Evolutionary theory is yielding rich new insights into everything from cognition to sexual desire. *Newsweek,* 56–58.

Cox, F. D. (1990). *Human intimacy: Marriage, the family and its meaning.* St. Paul, MN: West.

Cox News Service. (1990, September 22). Admitting cheating isn't easy, but some marriages survive. *Lincoln* [NE] *Sunday Journal and Star,* p. 1J.

Craddock, A. E. (1984). Correlations between marital role expectations and relationship satisfaction among engaged couples. *Australian Journal of Sex, Marriage and the Family, 4,* 33–46.

Crofoot, M. (1996). Cited in S. Bingham, *The last ranch: A Colorado community and the coming desert* (p. i). New York: Pantheon.

Crohan, S. E. (1996). Marital quality and conflict across the transition to parenthood in African American and white couples. *Journal of Marriage and the Family, 58* (November) 933–944.

Cromwell, R. E., & Olson, D. H. (Eds.). (1975). *Power in families.* Newbury Park, CA: Sage.

Cronin, M., & Leviton, J. (1989, January 30). The other dangers of close encounters. *Time,* 62.

Crosby, J. F. (1991). *Illusion and disillusion: The self in love and marriage.* Belmont, CA: Wadsworth.

Cross, R. J. (1993). What doctors and others need to know: Six facts on human sexuality and aging. *SIECUS Report, 21* (5), 7–9.

Cupach, W. R., & Spitzberg, B. H. (Eds.). (1994). *The dark side of interpersonal communication.* Hillsdale, NJ: Erlbaum.

Curran, D. (1983). *Traits of a healthy family.* Minneapolis: Winston Press.

Czaplewski, M. J. (1995). Preface. In M. J. Hogan (Ed.), *Initiatives for families: Research, policy, practice, education* (p. i). St. Paul, MN: National Council on Family Relations.

Dahl, T. (1980). *Model of stress.* Unpublished manuscript University of Minnesota, Minneapolis.

Daly, M., & Wilson, M. (1985). Child abuse and other risks of not living with both parents. *Ethology and Sociobiology, 6,* 197–210.

Danes, S. (1992). Parental perceptions of children's financial socialization. In R. Imas (Ed.), *Proceedings of the Association for Financial Counseling and Planning Education* (pp. 16–35). Charleston, SC: Association for Financial Counseling and Planning Education.

Darnton, N., Springen, K., Wright, L., & Keene-Osborn, S. (1991, October 7). The pain of the last taboo. *Newsweek,* 70–72.

Davis, K. E. (1985, February). Near and dear: Friendship and love compared. *Psychology Today, 19,* 22–30.

Davis, M., & Scott, R. (1988). *Lovers, doctors, and the law.* New York: Perennial/Harper & Row.

Day, A. T. (1991). *Remarkable survivors: Insights into successful aging among women.* Washington, DC: Urban Institute Press.

Day, R. D., Gilbert, K. R., Settles, B. H., & Burr, W. R. (1995). *Research and theory in family science.* Pacific Grove, CA: Brooks/Cole.

Day, R. D., & Hooks, D. (1987). Miscarriage: A special type of family crisis. *Family Relations, 36,* 305–310.

DeFrain, J. (1974, October 26). *A father's guide to parent guides: Review and assessment of the paternal role as conceived in the popular literature.* Paper presented at the annual meeting of the National Council on Family Relations/American Association of Marriage and Family Counselors, St. Louis.

DeFrain, J. (1975). *The nature and meaning of parenthood.* Unpublished doctoral dissertation, University of Wisconsin, Madison.

DeFrain, J. (1979). Androgynous parents outline their needs. *Family Coordinator* (April), 237–243.

DeFrain, J. (1991). Learning about grief from normal families: SIDS, stillbirth, and miscarriage. *Journal of Marital and Family Therapy* (July), 215–323.

DeFrain, J., DeFrain, N., & Lepard, N. (1994). Family strengths and challenges in the South Pacific: An exploratory study. *International Journal of the Sociology of the Family, 24* (2), 25–47.

DeFrain, J., & Eirick, R. (1981). Coping as divorced single parents: A comparative study of fathers and mothers. *Family Relations, 29,* 264–273.

DeFrain, J., Ernst, L., Jakub, D., & Taylor, J. (1991). *Sudden infant death: Enduring the loss.* New York: Lexington Books/Macmillan.

DeFrain, J., Ernst, L., & Nealer, J. (1997). The family counselor and loss. In J. R. Woods, Jr. (Ed.), *Loss in pregnancy or the neonatal period: Principles of care with clinical cases and analyses.* Pitman, NJ: Jannetti.

DeFrain, J., Fricke, J., & Elmen, J. (1987). *On our own: A single parent's survival guide.* Lexington, MA: Lexington Books/Heath.

DeFrain, J., Martens, L., Stork, J., & Stork, W. (1986). *Stillborn: The invisible death.* Lexington, MA: Lexington Books/Heath.

DeFrain, J., Millspaugh, E., & Xie, X. (1996). The psychosocial effects of miscarriage: Implications for health professionals. *Families, Systems, & Health: Journal of Collaborative Family Health Care, 14* (3), 331–347.

DeFrain, J., & Stinnett, N. (1992). Building on the inherent strengths of families: A positive approach for family psychologists and counselors. *Topics in Family Psychology and Counseling, 1* (1, January), 15–26.

Degler, C. N. (1980). *At odds.* New York: Oxford University Press.

DeLuccie, M. (1995). Mothers as gatekeepers: A model of maternal mediators of father involvement. *Journal of Genetic Psychology, 156* (1), 115–131.

DeMaris, A., & Rao, K. V. (1992). Premarital cohabitation and marital stability. *Journal of Marriage and the Family, 54* (February), 178–190.

Denneny, M. (1979). *Lovers: The story of two men.* New York: Avon.

Demo, D. H., & Acock, A. C. (1991). The impact of divorce on children. In A. Booth (Ed.), *Contemporary families: Looking forward, looking back* (pp. 162–191). Minneapolis: National Council on Family Relations.

Detzner, D. F. (1992). Life histories: Conflict in Southeast Asian refugee families. In J. F. Gilgun, K. Daly, &

G. Handel (Eds.), *Qualitative methods in family research* (pp. 85–102). Newbury Park, CA: Sage.

Dewit, D. J., Wister, A. V., & Burch, T. K. (1988). Physical distance and social contact between elders and their adult children. *Research on Aging, 10,* 56–80.

Dick-Read, G. (1984). *Childbirth without fear: The original approach to natural childbirth* (5th ed.). New York: Harper & Row. (Original work published 1932.)

Dobash, R. E., & Dobash, R. D. (1979). *Violence against wives.* New York: Free Press.

Dobson, J. (1983). *Love must be tough.* Waco, TX: Word Books.

Doherty, W. J. (1992, June). Private lives, public values. *Psychology Today, 25,* pp. 32–37.

Doherty, W. J., & Allen, W. (1994). Family functioning and parental smoking as predictors of adolescent cigarette use: A six-year prospective study. *Journal of Family Psychology, 8* (3), 347–353.

Doherty, W. J., & Baird, M. A. (1983). *Family therapy and family medicine.* New York: Guilford Press.

Doherty, W. J., & Campbell, T. L. (1988). *Families and health.* Newbury Park, CA: Sage.

Doherty, W. J. (1997). *The intentional family.* Reading, MA: Addison-Wesley Publishing.

Doherty, W. J., Kouneski, E. F., & Erickson, M. F. (1998). Responsible fathering: An overview and conceptual framework. *Journal of Marriage and the Family, 60* (May), 277–292.

Doherty, W. J., Lester, M. E., & Leigh, G. (1986). Marriage encounter weekends: Couples who win and couples who lose. *Journal of Marital and Family Therapy, 12,* 49–61.

Doherty, W. J., & Simmons, D. S. (1996). Clinical practice patterns of marriage and family therapists: A national survey of therapists and their clients. *Journal of Marital and Family Therapy, 22,* 9–25.

Doherty, W. J., & Whitehead, D. (1986). The social dynamics of cigarette smoking: A family system perspective. *Family Process, 25,* 453–460.

Doress, P. B., & Siegal, D. L. (1987). *Ourselves, growing older: Women aging with knowledge and power.* New York: Simon & Schuster/Touchstone.

Doress-Worters, P. B. (1994). Adding elder care to women's multiple roles: A critical review of the caregiver stress and multiple roles literatures. *Sex-roles, 31* (9–10), 597–616.

Druckman, J. M., Fournier, D. F., Olson, D. H., & Robinson, B. E. (1981). *Effectiveness of various premarital preparation programs.* Unpublished manuscript, University of Minnesota, Department of Family Social Science, St. Paul.

Dubowitz, H., & Egan, H. (1988). The maltreatment of infants. In M. B. Straus (Ed.), *Abuse and victimization across the life span* (pp. 32–53). Baltimore: Johns Hopkins University Press.

Duke, J. T. (1999, March 6). Mormon family life and cohabitation. Reported by Bob Mims, *Salt Lake Tribune.*

Duvall, E. M., & Miller, B. C. (1985). *Marriage and family development* (6th ed.). New York: Harper & Row.

Dyer, P., & Dyer, G. (1990). *Growing together.* Minneapolis: PREPARE/ENRICH.

Edwards, P. (1989). Assessment of symptoms in adult survivors of incest: A factor analytic study of the responses to childhood incest questionnaire. *Child Abuse and Neglect, 13,* 101–110.

Ehrlich, H. (1984, December 31). Double duty for moms: Keeping house and a job is a strain. *USA Today,* p. 1.

Einstein, A. (1988). Cosmic religion. In L. D. Eigen and J. P. Siegel (Eds.), *The Macmillan dictionary of political quotations.* New York: Macmillan. (Original work published 1931.)

Elias, M. (1985, February 7). Most singles are enjoying life to fullest. *USA Today,* p. D1.

Elmer-DeWitt, P. (1990, February 26). A bitter pill to swallow. *Time,* 44.

Elshtain, J. B. (1998, September 14, 21). The chosen family: Adoption, or the triumph of love over biology. *The New Republic,* 45–48, 50–54.

Emery, R. E., & Laumann-Billings, L. (1998). An overview of the nature, causes, and consequences of abusive family relationships. *American Psychologist, 53* (2), 121–135.

Epstein, N. B., Bishop, D. S., Ryan, C., Miller, I., & Keitner, G. (1993). The McMaster model of family functioning. In F. Walsh (Ed.), *Normal family processes* (pp. 138–160). New York: Guilford Press.

Erikson, E. H. (1950). *Childhood and society.* New York: Norton.

Erikson, E. H. (1968). Life cycle. In D. L. Sills (Ed.), *International encyclopedia of the social sciences* (p. 9). New York: Free Press/Macmillan.

Family violence top health issue. (1991, October 17). *Lincoln* [NE] *Star,* p. 3.

Farberow, N. L., Gallagher-Thompson, D. E., Gilewski, M. J., & Thompson, L. W. (1992). Changes in grief and mental health of bereaved spouses of older suicides. *Journals of Gerontology, 47* (6), 357–366.

Fay, R., Turner, C., Klassen, A., & Gagnon, J. (1989). Prevalence and patterns of same-gender sexual contact among men. *Science, 246,* 338–348.

Fenell, D. L., & Weinhold, B. K. (1989). *Counseling families: An introduction to marriage and family therapy.* Denver: Love.

Finkelhor, D. (1984). *Child sexual abuse: New theory and research.* New York: Free Press.

Finkelhor, D., & Araji, S. (1986). Explanations of pedophilia: A four-factor model. *Journal of Sex Research, 22,* 145–161.

Fitzpatrick, M. H. (1988). *Between husbands and wives: Communication in marriage.* Beverly Hills, CA: Sage.

Fletcher, W. L., & Hansson, R. O. (1991). Assessing the social components of retirement anxiety. *Psychology and Aging, 6* (March), 76–85.

Fowers, B. J., Montel, K. H., & Olson, D. H. (1996). Predicting marital success for premarital couple types based on PREPARE. *Journal of Marital and Family Therapy,* 103–119.

Fowers, B. J., & Olson, D. H. (1986). Predicting marital success with PREPARE: A predictive validity study. *Journal of Marital and Family Therapy, 12* (4), 403–413.

Fowers, B. J., & Olson, D. H. (1989). ENRICH marital inventory: A discriminant validity and cross-validation assessment. *Journal of Marital and Family Therapy, 15,* 65–79.

Fowers, B. J., & Olson, D. H. (1992). Four types of premarital couples: An empirical typology based on PREPARE. *Journal of Family Psychology, 6* (1), 10–21.

Fox, G. L. (1980). Love match and arranged marriage in a modernizing nation: Mate selection in Ankara, Turkey. *Journal of Marriage and the Family, 42* (4, November), 180–193.

Frahm, L. (1987, November 21). Growing beyond macho attitudes. *Lincoln* [NE] *Star,* p. 10.

Francis, D., Hadler, S. C., Prendergast, T. J., Peterson, E., Ginsberg, M. M., Lookabaugh, C., Holmes, J. R., & Maynard, J. E. (1984). Occurrences of hepatitis A, B, and non-A, non-B in the United States: CDC Sentinel County hepatitis study. *American Journal of Medicine, 76,* 69–74.

Francoeur, R. T. (1982). *Becoming a sexual person.* New York: Wiley.

Francoeur, R. T. (Ed.). (1997). *International encyclopedia of sexuality.* New York: Continuum.

Franklin, B. (1980). Poor Richard's almanac (May). In E. M. Beck (Ed.), *Familiar quotations: John Bartlett.* Boston: Little, Brown. (Original work published 1733.)

Franklin, C. W., II. (1989). The male sex drive. In L. Richardson & V. Taylor (Eds.), *Feminist frontiers II* (pp. 274–278). New York: Random House.

Fravel, D. L. (1995). *Boundary ambiguity perceptions of adoptive parents experiencing various levels of openness in adoption.* Unpublished doctoral dissertation, University of Minnesota, St. Paul.

Friedan, B. (1963). *The feminine mystique.* New York: Norton.

Friedan, B. (1985, November 3). How to get the women's movement moving again. *New York Times Magazine,* pp. 57–61.

Fromm, E. (1956). *The art of loving.* New York: Harper Bros.

Frost, J. J., & Forrest, J. D. (1995). Understanding the impact of effective teenage pregnancy prevention programs. *Family Planning Perspectives, 27,* 188–195.

Frost, R. (1946). *The poems of Robert Frost.* New York: Random House.

Furstenburg, F. F., Brooks-Gunn, J., & Morgan, S. P. (1988). *Adolescent mothers in later life.* New York: Cambridge University Press.

Gallup, Inc. (1989). *Love and marriage.* Princeton, NJ: Gallup Organization.

Gallup Poll. (1996). *Gender and society: Status and stereotypes.* Princeton, NJ: Gallup Organization.

Galvin, K. M., & Brommel, B. J. (1986). *Family communication: Cohesion and change* (2nd ed.). Glenview, IL: Scott, Foresman.

Ganong, L., & Coleman, M. (1994). *Remarried family relationships.* Thousand Oaks, CA: Sage.

Garbarino, J. (1995). Growing up in a socially toxic environment: Life for children and families in the 1990s. In G. B. Melton (Ed.), *Nebraska symposium on motivation: Vol. 42. The individual, the family, and the social good: Personal fulfillment in times of change* (pp. 1–20). Lincoln, NE: University of Nebraska Press.

Garbarino, J., Sebes, J., & Schellenbach, C. (1984). Families at risk for destructive parent-child relations in adolescence. *Child Development, 55,* 174–183.

Garman, E. T., & Forgue, R. E. (1991). *Personal finance* (3rd ed.). Boston: Houghton Mifflin.

Garman, E. T., & Forgue, R. E. (1997). *Personal finance* (5th ed.). Boston: Houghton Mifflin.

Gary, L. E., Beatty, L. A., & Berry, G. L. (1986). Strong Black families: Models of program development for Black families. In S. Van Zandt, H. Lingren, G. Rowe, P. Zeece, L. Kimmons, P. Lee, D. Shell, & N. Stinnett (Eds.), *Family strengths 7: Vital connections* (pp. 453–468). Lincoln: University of Nebraska, Department of Human Development and the Family, Center for Family Strengths.

Gay, P. (1984). *The bourgeois experience: Victoria to Freud.* New York: Oxford University Press.

Gelles, R. J. (1972). *The violent home.* Beverly Hills, CA: Sage.

Gelles, R. J. (1997). *Intimate violence in families* (3rd ed.). Thousand Oaks, CA: Sage.

Gelles, R. J., & Cornell, C. P. (1985). *Intimate violence in families.* Beverly Hills, CA: Sage.

Gelles, R. J., & Harrop, J. W. (1989). Violence, battering and psychological distress among women. *Journal of Interpersonal Violence, 4,* 400–420.

Gelles, R. J., & Straus, M. A. (1988). *Intimate violence.* New York: Simon & Schuster.

Gergen, K. J. (1982). *Toward transformation in social knowledge*. New York: Springer-Verlag.

Gergen, K. J. (1985). The social constructionist movement in modern psychology. *American Psychologist, 40,* 266–275.

Gergen, K. J. (1991). *The saturated self: Dilemmas of identity in contemporary life*. New York: Basic Books.

Gibran, K. (1976). *The Prophet*. New York: Knopf. (Original work published 1923.)

Gilewski, M., Farberow, N. L., Gallagher, D. E., & Thompson, L. (1991). Interaction of depression and bereavement on mental health in the elderly. *Psychology and Aging, 6* (1), 67–75.

Gilligan, S. G. (Ed.). (1993). *Therapeutic conversations*. New York: Norton.

Glenn, N. D. (1996). "Values, attitudes, and the state of marriage." In Popenoe, D., Elshtain, J. B., & Blankenhorn, D. (Eds.), *Promises to keep*. Lanham, MD: Rowman and Littlefield Publisher (pp. 15–33).

Glick, P. (1989). Remarried families, stepfamilies, and stepchildren: A brief demographic analysis. *Family Relations, 38,* 24–27.

Glick, P., & Lin, S.-L. (1986). More young adults are living with their parents: Who are they? *Journal of Marriage and the Family, 48* (February), 107–112.

Goldberg, C., & Elder, J. (1998, January 16). Poll finds support for legal, rare abortions. *Lincoln* [NE] *Journal Star,* p. 1.

Goldberg, M. S. (1993). Choosing a contraceptive. *FDA Consumer, 27* (7), pp. 18–25.

Goldenberg, I., & Goldenberg, H. (1991). *Family therapy: An overview*. Pacific Grove, CA: Brooks/Cole.

Goldstein, A. P., Keller, H., & Erne, D. (1985). *Changing the abusive parent*. Champaign, IL: Research Press.

Gomel, J. N., Tinsley, B. J., Parke, R. D., & Clark, K. M. (1998). The effects of economic hardship on family relationships among African American, Latino, and Euro-American families. *Journal of Family Issues, 19* (4), 436–476.

Goodman, E. (1998, January 22). 21 million already have decided. *Lincoln* [NE] *Journal Star,* p. 6B.

Goodman, M. (1986, November). Americans and their money: 1986. *Money,* 159.

Gorall, D. M. and Olson, D. H. (1995). Circumplex model of family systems: Integrating ethnic diversity and other social systems. In R. H. Mikesell, D. D. Lusterman, & S. H. McDaniel (Eds.), *Integrating family therapy: Handbook of family psychology* (pp. 217–233). Washington, DC: American Psychological Association.

Gordon, S., & Gordon, J. (1990). *Raising a child conservatively in a sexually permissive world*. New York: Fireside/Simon & Schuster.

Gordon, S., & Snyder, C. (1989). *Personal issues in human sexuality: A guidebook for better sexual health*. Boston: Allyn & Bacon.

Gorman, C. (1991, October 7). Incest comes out of the dark. *Time,* 46.

Gottman, J., & Silver, N. (1994). *Why Marriages Succeed or Fail*. New York: Simon and Schuster.

Gould, R. L. (1975, August). Adult life stages: Growth towards self-tolerance. *Psychology Today,* 74–78.

Gould, R. L. (1979). *Transformations: Growth and change in adult life*. New York: Simon and Schuster.

Gould, R. L. (1993). Transformational tasks in adulthood. In G. H. Pollock & S. I. Greenspan (Eds.), *The course of life: Vol. 6. Late adulthood* (rev. and exp. ed., pp. 23–68). Madison, CT: International Universities Press.

Graham, L. (1998, December 13). Where have all the small towns gone? *Parade,* pp. 6–9.

Gray, P. (1998, January 18). Paradise found. *Time,* 67.

Green, S. K., Buchanan, D. R., & Heuer, S. K. (1984). Winners, losers, and choosers: A field investigation of dating initiation. *Personality and Social Psychology Bulletin, 10* (4), 502–511.

Gregersen, E. (1983). *Sexual practices: The story of human sexuality*. New York: Franklin Watts.

Greven, P. (1991) *Spare the child: The religious roots of physical punishment and the psychological impact of physical abuse*. New York: Knopf.

Grief, G. L. (1995). Single fathers with custody following separation and divorce. *Marriage and Family Review, 20* (1/2), 213–232.

Grimes, D. (1994). Teens need doll's drastic lesson. *Sarasota* [FL] *Herald-Tribune Syndicate.*

Griswold, R. L. (1993). *Fatherhood in America*. New York: Basic.

Grotevant, H. D. (1997). Family processes, identity development, and behavioral outcomes for adopted adolescents. *Journal of Adolescent Research, 12* (1), 139–161.

Grotevant, H. D., McRoy, R. G., Elde, C., & Fravel, D. L. (1994). Adoptive family system dynamics: Variations by level of openness in the adoption. *Family Process, 33,* 125–146.

Guerney, B., Jr., & Maxson, P. (1991). Marital and family enrichment research. In A. Booth (Ed.), *Contemporary families: Looking forward, looking back* (pp. 457–465). Minneapolis: National Council on Family Relations.

Gurin, J. (1985). From "me" to "we": The us generation. *American Health* (October), 40–41.

Hall, D. R., & Zhao, J. Z. (1995). Cohabitation and divorce in Canada: Testing the selectivity hypothesis. *Journal of Marriage and the Family, 57,* 421–427.

Hamilton, A., Stiles, W. B., Melowsky, F., & Beal, D. G. (1987). A multilevel comparison of child abusers with nonabusers. *Journal of Family Violence, 2,* 215–225.

Hanline, M. F., & Daley, S. E. (1992). Family coping strategies and strengths in Hispanic, African-American, and Caucasian families of young children. *Topics in Early Childhood Special Education, 12* (3), 351–366.

Hanson, S. M. H. (1986). Healthy single-parent families. *Family Relations, 35,* 125–132.

Harmon, A. (1998, August 30). Researchers say cyberspace sad, lonely: People who spend time online are more depressed. *Lincoln* [NE] *Journal Star,* p. 5A.

Harris, J. (1997). *I kissed dating goodbye.* Sisters, OR: Multnomah.

Hatcher, R. A., Trussell, J., Stewart, F., Stewart, G. K., Kowal, D., Guest, F., Cates, W., & Policar, M. S. (1994). *Contraceptive technology 1992–1994* (16th rev. ed.). New York: Irvington.

Hatcher, R. A., et al. (1997). *The essentials of contraceptive technology.* Baltimore, MD: Population Information Program, Center for Communication Programs, Johns Hopkins School of Public Health.

Hausknecht, R. U. (1995). Methotrexate and misoprostol to terminate early pregnancy. *New England Journal of Medicine, 333* (9), 537.

Havel, V. (1994). In T. Lasley (Ed.), *Teaching peace: Toward cultural selflessness* (p. 3). Westport, CT: Bergin & Gravey.

Hawkins, W. E., & Duncan, D. F. (1985). Children's illnesses as risk factors for child abuse. *Psychological Reports, 56,* 638.

Hawley, D. R., & Olson, D. H. (1995). Enriching newlyweds: An evaluation of three enrichment programs. *American Journal of Family Therapy, 23,* 129–147.

Hayes, M. P. (1979). Strengthening marriage in the middle years. In N. Stinnett, B. Chesser, & J. DeFrain (Eds.), *Building family strengths: Blueprints for action* (pp. 387–398). Lincoln: University of Nebraska Press.

Hayes, M. P., Stinnett, N., & DeFrain, J. (1980). Learning about marriage from the divorced. *Journal of Divorce, 4* (Fall), 23–30.

Hellmich, N. (1990, April 4). Marriage is no. 1 with men. *USA Today,* p. 1D.

Henshaw, S. (1987). Characteristics of U.S. women having abortions, 1982–1983. *Family Planning Perspectives, 19* (1), 5–9.

Henshaw, S. (1990). Major decline in availability of abortion. *Contemporary Sexuality, 24* (8), 6.

Henton, J., Cate, R., Koval, J., Lloyd, S., & Christopher, S. (1981). Romance and violence in dating relationships. *Journal of Family Issues, 4* (3, September), 467–482.

Herbert, B. (1994, March 2). Op-ed column from the *New York Times.* Cited by J. A. Michener, *This noble land: My vision for America* (p. 176). New York: Random House.

Herbst, P. G. (1952). The measurement of family relationships. *Human Relations, 5,* 3–35.

Hernandez, D. J. (1997). Child development and the social demography of childhood. *Child Development, 68* (1), 149–169.

Higginson, J. G. (1998). Competitive parenting: The culture of teen mothers. *Journal of Marriage and the Family, 60* (February), 135–149.

Hill, R. (1949). *Families under stress.* New York: Harper.

Hill, R. (1958). Generic features of families under stress. *Social Casework, 49,* 139–150.

Hobfoll, S. E., & Spielberger, C. D. (1992). Family stress: Integrating theory and measurement. *Journal of Family Psychology, 6* (2), 99–112.

Hochschild, A. (1989). *The second shift.* New York: Viking.

Hochschild, A. R. (1997). *The time bind: When work becomes home and home becomes work.* New York: Metropolitan Books.

Hocker, J. L., & Wilmot, W. W. (1985). *Interpersonal conflict.* Dubuque, IA: Brown.

Hodson, D. S., & Skeen, P. (1994). Sexuality and aging: The hammerlock of myths. *Journal of Applied Gerontology, 13* (3), 219–235.

Hofferth, S. (1996). Child care in the United States today. *The Future of Children, 6* (2), 41–61.

Hogan, M. J. (1993). Family futures: Possibilities, preferences and probabilities. *Marriage and Family Review, 18,* 255–262.

Holmes, T. H., & Rahe, R. H. (1967). The social readjustment rating scale. *Journal of Psychosomatic Research, 11,* 213–218.

Homans, G. G. (1974). *Social behavior: Its elementary forms* (rev. ed.). New York: Harcourt.

Hopkins, J., Marcues, M., & Campbell, S. B. (1984). Postpartum depression: A critical review. *Psychological Bulletin, 95,* 498–515.

Horn, W. F. (1995). *Father facts.* Lancaster, PA: The National Fatherhood Initiative.

Houseknecht, S. K. and Sastry, J. (1996). Family decline and child well-being: A comparative analysis. *Journal of Marriage and the Family, 58,* 726–739.

Hunt, B. (1982, June). Six myths about old age. *Reader's Digest,* 113–116.

Hunt, R. A., Hof, L. & DeMaria, R. (Eds.). (1998). *Marriage enrichment: Preparation, mentoring and outreach.* Philadelphia: Brunner/Mazel.

Hunter, A. G. (1997). Counting on grandmothers: Black mothers' and fathers' reliance on grandmothers for parenting support. *Journal of Family Issues, 18* (3), 251–269.

Hyde, J. S. (1990). *Understanding human sexuality* (4th ed.). New York: McGraw-Hill.

Hyde, J. S., & DeLamater, J. D. (1997). *Understanding human sexuality* (6th ed.). Boston: McGraw Hill.

Ihinger-Tallman, M., & Pasley, K. (1987). *Remarriage.* Newbury Park, CA: Sage.

Insel, P. M., & Roth, W. T. (1996). *Core concepts in health* (7th ed.—1996 update). Mountain View, CA: Mayfield.

Insel, P. M., & Roth, W. T. (1998). *Core concepts in health* (8th ed.). Mountain View, CA: Mayfield.

Jaccard, J., Dittus, P. J., & Gordon, V. V. (1998). Parent-adolescent congruency in reports of adolescent sexual behavior and in communications about sexual behavior. *Child Development, 69* (1), 247–261.

Jackson, J. K. (1954). The adjustments of the family to the crisis of alcoholism. *Quarterly Journal of Studies on Alcohol, 15,* 562–586.

Jackson, J. K. (1992). *Wellness: AIDS, STD, and other communicable diseases.* Guilford, CT: Dushkin.

Jacob, B. (1986, August 8). Romance flowers in friendship's warmth. *USA Today,* p. 5D.

James, J. (1984, September 23). You. *Seattle Times/Post-Intelligencer,* p. F4.

Janus, S. S., & Janus, C. L. (1993). *The Janus report on sexual behavior.* New York: Wiley.

Johansen, A. S., Leibowitz, A., & Waite, L. J. (1996). The importance of child-care characteristics to choice of care. *Journal of Marriage and the Family, 58* (August), 759–772.

Johnson, C. K., & Price-Bonham, S. (1980). Women and retirement: A study and implications. *Family Relations, 29* (July), 380–385.

Johnson, P. (1998). Performance of household tasks by Vietnamese and Laotian refugees: Tradition and change. *Journal of Family Issues, 19* (3), 245–273.

Johnson, V. E. (1973). *I'll quit tomorrow.* New York: Harper & Row.

Jones, E. F., & Stahmann, R. F. (1994). Clergy beliefs, preparation, and practice in premarital counseling. *Journal of Pastoral Care, 48,* 181–186.

Jouriles, E. N., & Norwood, W. D. (1995). Physical aggression toward boys and girls in families characterized by the battering of women. *Journal of Family Psychology, 9,* 69–78.

Kagan, J. (1964). *The nature of the child.* New York: Basic Books.

Kantor, D., & Lehr, W. (1974). *Inside the family.* San Francisco: Jossey-Bass.

Kaplan, L., Ade-Ridder, L., & Hennon, C. B. (1992). Issues of split custody: Siblings separated by divorce. *Journal of Divorce and Remarriage, 16* (3–4), 253–274.

Kaplan, L., Hennon, C. B., & Ade-Ridder, L. (1993). Splitting custody of children between parents: Impact on the sibling system. *Families in Society, 74* (3), 131–144.

Keillor, G. (1994, October 17). It's good old monogamy that's really sexy. *Time,* 71.

Kellman, L. (1997, December 25). Price of a baby grows and grows: From birth to 17: $149,820. *Lincoln* [NE] *Journal Star,* p. 1A.

Kelly, G. F. (1994). *Sexuality today: The human perspective* (4th ed.). Guilford, CT: Dushkin.

Kelly, G. F. (1998). *Sexuality today: The human perspective* (6th ed.). Boston: McGraw-Hill.

Kennedy, J. F. (1990). Inaugural address. In D. B. Baker (Ed.), *Political quotations.* Detroit: Gale Research. (Original work published 1961.)

Kerckhoff, A. C., & Davis, K. E. (1962). Value consensus and need complementarity in mate selection. *American Sociological Review, 27,* 295–303.

Kessler, R. C., Turner, J. B., & House, J. S. (1988). Effects of unemployment on health in a community survey. *Journal of Social Issues, 44,* 69–85.

Killorin, E., & Olson, D. H. (1984). The chaotic flippers in treatment. In E. Kaufman (Ed.), *Power to change: Alcoholism.* New York: Gardner Press.

Kilmann, R., & Thomas, K. (1975). Interpersonal conflict: Handling behavior as reflections of Jungian personality dimensions. *Psychological Reports, 37,* 971–980.

Kilpatrick, A. C. (1986). Some correlates of women's childhood sexual experiences: A retrospective study. *Journal of Sex Research, 22,* 221–242.

King, B. M., Camp, J., & Downey, A. M. (1991). *Human sexuality today.* Englewood Cliffs, NJ: Prentice Hall.

King, M. L., Jr. (1999, January 17). Cited by President Bill Clinton in his weekly radio address. *CNN Headline News.*

Kinsey, A., Pomeroy, W., & Martin, C. (1948). *Sexual behavior in the human male.* Philadelphia: Saunders.

Kinsey, A., Pomeroy, W., Martin, C., & Gebhard, P. (1953). *Sexual behavior in the human female.* Philadelphia: Saunders.

Kirk, E. P. (1984). Psychological effects and management of prenatal loss. *American Journal of Obstetrics and Gynecology, 149,* 46–50.

Kitson, G. C., & Morgan, L. A. (1991). The multiple consequences of divorce: A decade review. In A. Booth (Ed.), *Contemporary families: Looking forward, looking back* (pp. 150–161). Minneapolis: National Council on Family Relations.

Klein, M., & Gordon, S. (1992). Sex education. In C. E. Walker & M. C. Roberts (Eds.), *Handbook of clinical child psychology* (2nd ed., pp. 933–949). New York: Wiley.

Knudsen, D., & Miller, J. L. (Eds.). (1992). *Abused and battered: Social and legal responses to family violence.* New York: Aldine & deGruyter.

Kohlberg, L. (1966). Cognitive stages and preschool education. *Human Development, 9,* 5–17.

Kolb, T. M., & Straus, M. A. (1974). Marital power and marital happiness in relation to problem-solving ability. *Journal of Marriage and the Family, 36,* 756–766.

Kolbe, L. (1992, April 10). Quoted in "Most teens have had sex by 16," says CDC study. *Chicago Tribune,* p. C5.

Konner, M. (1988). Is orgasm essential? *The Sciences* (March/April), 4–7.

Koonin, L. M., Kochanek, K. D., Smith, J. C., & Ramick, M. (1991). Abortion surveillance, United States, 1988. *Morbidity and Mortality Weekly Report, 40* (No. SS-1), 15–42. Washington, DC: National Office of Vital Statistics.

Koop, C. E. (1988). *Understanding AIDS: A message from the surgeon general* (Health and Human Services Publication No. [CDC] HHS-88-8404). Washington, DC: U.S. Government Printing Office.

Kottak, C. P. (1989). *Anthropology: The exploration of human diversity* (4th ed.). New York: Random House.

Kouneski, E. F. (1996). *Fatherhood today.* Unpublished article, University of Minnesota, Family Social Science, St. Paul.

Kouri, K. M., & Lasswell, M. (1993). Black-White marriages: Social change and intergenerational mobility. *Marriage and Family Review, 19,* 241–255.

Krivosha, N. (1983). Transcription of tape-recorded interview with Nebraska Supreme Court Chief Justice Krivosha, conducted by graduate students of the Department of Human Development and the Family, University of Nebraska-Lincoln.

Kroll, J. (1991, June 10). Spiking a fever. *Newsweek,* 44–47.

Krugman, R. D., Lenherr, M., Betz, L., & Fryer, G. E. (1986). The relationship between unemployment and physical abuse of children. *Child Abuse and Neglect, 10,* 415–418.

Kruttschnitt, C., Heath, L., & Ward, D. A. (1986). Family violence, television viewing habits, and other adolescent experiences related to violent criminal behavior. *Criminology, 24* (2), 235–267.

Krysan, M., Moore, K. A., & Zill, N. (1990). *Identifying successful families: An overview of constructs and selected measures.* Washington, DC: Child Trends, Inc. [2100 M St., NW, Suite 610] and the U.S. Department of Health & Human Services, Office of the Assistant Secretary for Planning and Evaluation.

Kulthau, K., & Mason, K. O. (1996). Market child care versus care by relatives: Choices made by employed and nonemployed mothers. *Journal of Family Issues, 17* (4), 561–578.

Kurdek, L. A. (1998). The nature and predictors of the trajectory of change in marital quality over the first 4 years of marriage for first-married husbands and wives. *Journal of Family Psychology, 12* (4), 594–510.

Lacayo, R. (1997, April 14). The kids are all right: Day care — a new study says it's mostly harmless, sometimes helpful and less important than home. *Time,* 76.

Lambert, B. (1990, July 17). Ten years later, hepatitis study still yields critical data on AIDS. *New York Times,* p. C3.

Landers, A. (1989, January 22). Survey says sex lives fizzle after marriage. *Lincoln* [NE] *Sunday Journal Star,* p. 4D.

Landers, S. (1989). Koop will not release abortion effects report. *American Psychological Association Monitor* (March), 1.

LaRossa, R., & Reitzes, D. C. (1993). Symbolic interaction and family studies. In P. G. Boss, W. J. Doherty, R. LaRossa, W. R. Schumm, & S. K. Steinmetz (Eds.), *Sourcebook of family theories and methods* (pp. 135–162). New York: Plenum.

Larsen, A. S., & Olson, D. H. (1989). Predicting marital satisfaction using PREPARE: A replication study. *Journal of Marital and Family Therapy, 15,* 311–322.

Larson, R., & Richards, M. H. (1994). *Divergent realities: The emotional lives of mothers, fathers, and adolescents.* New York: Basic Books.

Lasswell, M., & Lasswell, T. (1991). *Marriage and the family* (3rd ed.). Belmont, CA: Wadsworth.

Lauer, J., & Lauer, R. (1985, June). Marriages made to last. *Psychology Today, 19,* pp. 22–26.

Lauer, R. H. (1989). *Social problems and the quality of life* (4th ed.). Dubuque, IA: Brown.

Laumann, E. O., Gagnon, J. H., Michael, R. T., & Michaels, S. (1994). *The social organization of sexuality: Sexual practices in the United States.* Chicago: University of Chicago Press.

Laumann, E. O., Gagnon, J. H., Michael, R. T., Michaels, S., & Kolata, G. (1995). *Sex in America: A definitive survey.* Boston: Little, Brown.

Lavee, Y., Sharlin, S., & Katz, R. (1996). The effect of parenting stress on marital quality: An integrated mother-father model. *Journal of Family Issues, 17* (1), 114–135.

LeBoyer, F. (1975). *Birth without violence.* New York: Knopf.

LeBoyer, F. (1995). *Birth without violence: The book that revolutionized the way we bring our children into the world.* Rochester, VT: Healing Arts Press.

Lee, G. R., Peek, C. W., & Coward, R. T. (1998). Race differences in filial responsibility expectations among older parents. *Journal of Marriage and the Family, 60* (May), 404–412.

Lee, G. R., & Stone, L. H. (1980). Mate selection systems and criteria: Variation according to family structure. *Journal of Marriage and the Family, 42* (2, May), 319–326.

Lee, S. M., & Yamanaka, K. (1990). Patterns of Asian American intermarriage and marital assimilation. *Journal of Comparative Family Studies, 21,* 287–304.

Leifer, M. (1980). *Psychological effects of motherhood: A study of first pregnancy.* New York: Praeger.

LeMasters, E. E. (1957). Parenthood as crisis. *Marriage and Family Living, 19,* 325–355.

LeMasters, E. E., & DeFrain, J. (1989). *Parents in contemporary America: A sympathetic view.* Belmont, CA: Wadsworth.

Leo, J. (1986, November 24). Sex and schools: AIDS and the surgeon general add a new urgency to an old debate. *Time*, 54–60, 63.

Lerner, H. G. (1985). *The dance of anger.* New York: Harper & Row.

Leslie, L. A., Anderson, E. A., & Branson, M. P. (1991). Responsibility for children: The role of gender and employment. *Journal of Family Issues, 12* (2, June), 197–210.

Levine, J. A., & Pitt, E. W. (1995). *New expectations: Community strategies for responsible fatherhood.* New York: Families and Work Institute.

Levinson, D. (1978). *The seasons of a man's life.* New York: Knopf.

Levinson, D. J. (1994). *The seasons of a woman's life.* New York: Knopf.

Levinson, M. (1991, November 4). Living on the edge. *Newsweek*, 20.

Levy, D. S. (1991, September 16). Why Johnny might grow up violent and sexist. *Time*, 16–19.

Lewis, J. M. (1989). *How's your family?* New York: Brunner/Mazel.

Lewis, R. (1981). Patterns of strengths of American Indian families. In J. R. Red Horse, A. Shattuck, & F. Hoffman (Eds.), *The American Indian family: Stresses and strengths* (pp. 101–106). [Proceedings of the Conference on Research Issues, Phoenix, Arizona, April 1980.] Isleta, NM: American Indian Social Research and Development Associates.

Lewis, R. A., Kozac, E. B., Milardo, R. M., & Grosnick, W. A. (1981). Commitment in same-sex love relationships. *Alternative Lifestyles, 4* (1), 22–42.

Lewis, R. A., Spanier, G., Atkinson, V. L. S., & Lehecka, C. F. (1977). Commitment in married and unmarried cohabitation. *Sociological Focus, 10* (4), 367–374.

Lincoln Family Service Association. (1991). *Violence workshop resources.* Lincoln, NE: Family Service Association.

Lino, M. (1991a). Expenditures on a child by single-parent families. *Family Economics Review, 4* (1), 2–24.

Lino, M. (1991b). Expenditures on a child by two-parent families. *Family Economics Review, 4* (1), 25–38.

Litman, T. J. (1974). The family as a basic unit in health and medical care: A social-behavioral overview. *Social Science and Medicine, 8*, 495–519.

Loeber, R., & Dishion, T. J. (1984). Boys who fight at home and school: Family conditions influencing cross-setting consistency. *Journal of Consulting and Clinical Psychology, 52* (5), 759–768.

LoPiccolo, J., & Stock, W. E. (1986). Treatment of sexual dysfunction. *Journal of Counseling and Clinical Psychology, 54* (2), 158–167.

Lord, L. (1987, November 30). Coming to grips with alcoholism. *U.S. News & World Report*, 56–62.

Lore, R. K., & Schultz, L. A. (1993). Control of human aggression: A comparative perspective. *American Psychologist, 48* (January), 16–25.

Lovelock, J. E. (1979, 1987). *Gaia: A new look at life on earth.* Oxford, England: Oxford University Press.

Lung, C. T., & Daro, D. (1996). *Current trends in child abuse reporting and fatalities: The results of the 1995 annual fifty state survey.* Chicago: National Committee to Prevent Child Abuse.

MacDonald, W. L., & DeMaris, A. (1995). Remarriage, stepchildren, and marital conflict. Challenges to the incomplete institutionalization hypothesis. *Journal of Marriage and the Family, 57* (May), 387–398.

Mace, D. (1982a). Current thinking on marriage and money. *Medical Aspects of Human Sexuality, 16*, 109–118.

Mace, D. (1982b). *Love and anger in marriage.* Grand Rapids, MI: Zondevan.

Mace, D., & Mace, V. (1980). Enriching marriages: The foundation stone of family strength. In N. Stinnett, B. Chesser, J. DeFrain, & P. Knaub (Eds.), *Family strengths: Positive models for family life.* Lincoln: University of Nebraska Press.

Macklin, E. D. (1980). Nontraditional family forms: A decade of research. *Journal of Marriage and the Family, 42* (November), 905–922.

Madden, M. E. (1987). Perceived control and power in marriage: A study of marital decision making and task performance. *Personality and Social Psychology Bulletin, 13*, 73–82.

Malinowski, B. (1929). *The sexual life of savages.* New York: Harcourt.

Mancini, J. A., & Blieszner, R. (1991). Aging parents and adult children: Research themes in intergenerational relations. In A. Booth (Ed.), *Contemporary families: Looking forward, looking back* (pp. 249–264). Minneapolis: National Council on Family Relations.

Margolin, L., & White, L. (1987). The continuing role of physical attraction in marriage. *Journal of Marriage and the Family, 49*, 21–27.

Markman, H., & Stanley, S. (1996). *Fighting for your marriage: Positive steps for preventing divorce and preserving a lasting love.* San Francisco: Jossey-Bass.

Marsella, A. J. (1998). Toward a "global-community psychology." *American Psychologist, 53* (2), 1282–1291.

Martin, T. C., & Bumpass, L. L. (1989). Recent trends in marital disruption. *Demography, 26*, 37–51.

Masters, W. H., & Johnson, V. (1966). *Human sexual response.* Boston: Little, Brown.

Masters, W. H., Johnson, V., & Kolodny, R. C. (1988). *Masters & Johnson on sex and human loving.* Boston: Little, Brown.

Masters, W. H., Johnson, V., & Kolodny, R. C. (1992). *Human sexuality.* (4th ed.). New York: HarperCollins.

Masters, W. H., Johnson, V. E., & Kolodny, R. C. (1993). *Biological foundations of human sexuality.* New York: HarperCollins.

Masters, W. H., Johnson, V. E., & Kolodny, R. C. (1995). *Human sexuality* (5th ed.). New York: HarperCollins.

May, R. (1969). *Love and will.* New York: Norton

Mayo Foundation for Medical Education and Research. (1993). Sexuality and aging: What it means to be sixty or seventy or eighty in the '90s. *Mayo Clinic Health Letter* (February), 1–8.

McAdoo, H. P. (1993). *Family ethnicity: Strength in diversity.* Thousand Oaks, CA: Sage.

McAdoo, H. P. (Ed.). (1997). *Black families* (3rd ed.). Thousand Oaks, CA: Sage

McCaghy, C. (1968). Drinking and deviance disavowal: The case of child molesters. *Social Problems, 16,* 43–49.

McCubbin, H. I., & Patterson, J. (1982). Family adaptation to crises. In H. I. McCubbin, A. Cauble, & J. Patterson (Eds.), *Family stress, coping and social support.* Springfield, IL: Thomas.

McDaniel, S. H., Hepworth, J., & Doherty, W. J. (1992). *Medical family therapy: A biopsychosocial approach to families with health problems.* New York: Basic Books.

McGoldrick, M., & Carter, S. (1989). Forming a remarried family. In S. Carter & M. McGoldrick (Eds.), *The family life cycle: A framework for family therapy* (pp. 265–294). New York: Allyn & Bacon.

McGoldrick, M., Giordano, J. & Pearce, J. K. (1996). *Ethnicity and family therapy* (2nd ed.). New York: Guilford.

McGoldrick, M., & Preto, N. G. (1984). Ethnic intermarriage: Implications for therapy. *Family Process, 23,* 347–364.

McGowan, J. (1991). *Postmodernism and its critics.* Ithaca, NY: Cornell University Press.

McIntosh, J. (1991). Middle-age suicide: A literature review and epidemiological study. *Death Studies, 15* (1), 21–38.

McLanahan, S., & Sandefur, G. (1994). *Growing up with a single parent: What hurts, what helps.* Cambridge, MA: Harvard University Press.

McLeod, B. (1986, July). The oriental express. *Psychology Today,* 48–52.

McLeod, J. (1997). *Narrative and psychotherapy.* London: Sage.

McLuhan, M. (1968). *War and peace in the global village.* New York: McGraw-Hill.

McLuhan, M. (1989). *The global village: Transformation in world life and media in the 21st century.* New York: Oxford Press.

McManus, M., (1995). *Marriage savers: Helping your friends and family avoid divorce.* Grand Rapids, MI: Zondervan.

McManus, M., & McManus, H. (1998). Marriage savers and community marriage policy. In T. Ooms (Ed.),

Strategies to strengthen marriage (pp. 81–96). Washington, DC: Family Impact Seminar.

McRoy, R. G., Grotevant, H. D., & Ayers-Lopez, S. (1994). *Changing practices in adoption.* Austin, TX: Hogg Foundation for Mental Health.

Mead, M. (1935). *Sex and temperament in three primitive societies.* New York: Morrow/Quill.

Medicine, B. (1981). American Indian family: Cultural change and adaptive strategies. *Journal of Ethnic Studies, 8* (4), 12–13.

Meier, P. (1991, January 6). War of words: Women talk about how men and women talk. *Minneapolis Star Tribune [First Sunday],* p. 8.

Melby, J. N., Conger, R. D., Conger, K. J., & Lorenz, F. O. (1993). Effects of parental behavior on tobacco use by young male adolescents. *Journal of Marriage and the Family, 55* (May), 439–454.

Mendenhall, T. J., Grotevant, H. D., & McRoy, R. G. (1996). Adoptive couples: Communication and changes made in openness levels. *Family Relations, 45,* 223–229.

Meredith, W. H., Stinnett, N., & Cacioppo, B. F. (1985). Parent satisfactions: Implications for strengthening families. In R. Williams, H. Lingren, G. Rowe, S. Van Zandt, P. Lee, & N. Stinnett (Eds.), *Family strengths 6: Enhancement of interaction* (p. 147). Lincoln: University of Nebraska, Department of Human Development and the Family, Center for Family Strengths.

Metropolitan Life Insurance Co. (1993). Life expectancy in U.S. at selected ages (1991 estimates). In *World Almanac and Book of Facts* (p. 940). New York: World Almanac.

Meyer, D. R., & Garasky, S. (1993). Custodial fathers: Myths, realities, and child support policy. *Journal of Marriage and the Family, 55* (February), 73–89.

Michener, J. A. (1991). *The world is my home.* New York: Random House.

Michener, J. A. (1996). *This noble land: My vision for America.* New York: Random House.

Miller, B. C., McCoy, J. K., Olson, T. D., & Wallace, C. M. (1986). Parental discipline and control attempts in relation to adolescent sexual attitudes and behavior. *Journal of Marriage and the Family, 48* (August), 503–512.

Miller, S., & Miller, P. A. (1997). *Core communication: Skills and processes.* Littleton, CO: Interpersonal Communication Programs.

Miller, B. C., & Moore, K. A. (1991). Adolescent sexual behavior, pregnancy, and parenting: Research through the 1980s. In A. Booth (Ed.), *Contemporary families: Looking forward, looking back* (pp. 307–326). Minneapolis: National Council on Family Relations.

Miller, S., Wackman, D., Nunnally, E., & Miller, P. (1988). *Connecting with self and others.* Littleton, CO: Interpersonal Communication Programs.

Miller, S., Wackman, D., Nunnally, E., & Miller, P. (1989). *Connecting: Skills workbook*. Littleton, CO: Interpersonal Communication Programs

Mindel, C. H., Habenstein, R. W., & Wright, R., Jr. (Eds.). (1988). *Ethnic families in America: Patterns and variations* (3rd ed.). New York: Elsevier.

Mirandé, A. (1977). The Chicano family: A reanalysis of conflicting views. *Journal of Marriage and the Family* (November), 747–756.

Mirandé, A. (1979). A reinterpretation of male dominance in the Chicano family. *Family Coordinator* (October), 473–479.

Montagu, A. (1964). *Man's most dangerous myth: The fallacy of race*. Cleveland: World.

Montaigne, M. E. (1980). *Essays III* (Chapter 1, p. 5). In E. M. Beck (Ed.), *Familiar quotations: John Bartlett*. Boston: Little, Brown. (Original work published 1595.)

Moore, K. A. (1998). What a difference a dad makes. *Child trends report*. Washington, DC: Child Trends.

More high schoolers abstaining from sex. (1998, September 18). *Lincoln [NE] Journal Star*, p. 3A.

Mroczek, D. K., & Kolarz, C. M. (1999). Happiness in older men. *Journal of Personality and Social Psychology, 75* (5), 1333–1349.

Mulsow, M. H., & McBride Murry, V. (1996). Parenting on edge: Economically stressed, single, African American adolescent mothers. *Journal of Family Issues, 17* (5), 704–721.

Murstein, B. I. (1980). Mate selection in the 1970s. *Journal of Marriage and the Family, 42* (4, November), 52–54.

Murstein, B. I. (1987). A classification and extension of the SVR theory of dyadic pairing. *Journal of Marriage and the Family, 42*, 777–792.

Mussen, P. H. (1969). Early sex-role development. In D. A. Goslin (Ed.), *Handbook of socialization theory and research*. Chicago: Rand McNally.

Nadelson, C., & Sauzier, M. (1986). Intervention programs for individual victims and their families. In M. Lystad (Ed.), *Violence in the home: Interdisciplinary perspectives*. New York: Brunner/Mazel.

Nakonezny, P. A., Shull, R. D., & Rodgers, J. L. (1995). The effect of no-fault divorce law on the divorce rate across the 50 states and its relation to income, education, and religiosity. *Journal of Marriage and the Family, 57* (2), 477–488.

National Council on Alcoholism. (1989). *Facts about alcohol*. New York: Author.

National Council on Alcoholism and Drug Dependence (NCADD). (1995). *If someone you love is an alcoholic*. New York: Author.

Nation's legal drugs may be its worst drugs. (1986, November 23). *Lincoln [NE] Sunday Journal Star*, pp. 1D, 3D.

National Opinion Research Center. (1994). *Survey on sexual behavior*. Storrs, CT: Roper Center for Public Opinion Research.

National Opinion Research Center. (1996). *General social survey*. University of Chicago.

Neubeck, G. (1999). *Minnesota new poems*. 1465 Raymond Ave., St. Paul, MN 55108.

Neugarten, B. (1968). The awareness of middle age. In B. Neugarten (Ed.), *Middle age and aging*. Chicago: University of Chicago Press.

Neugebauer, R., Kline, J., O'Connor, P., Shrout, P., Johnson, J., Skodol, A., Wicks, J., & Susser, M. (1992). Determinants of depressive symptoms in the early weeks after miscarriage. *American Journal of Public Health, 8* (October), 132.

Newman, I. (1990). *Adolescent tobacco use in Nebraska* (Tech. Rep. No. 20). Lincoln: Nebraska Prevention Center for Alcohol and Drug Abuse, University of Nebraska.

Niebuhr, R. (1988). Serenity prayer. In G. Carruth & E. Ehrlich (Eds.), *Harper book of American quotations*. New York: Harper & Row. (Original work published 1951).

Nilsson, L. (1990). *A child is born*. New York: Delacorte/Lawrence.

Nock, S. L. (1995). A comparison of marriages and cohabiting relationships. *Journal of Family Issues, 16*, 53–76.

Norem, R. H., Schaefer, M., Springer, J., & Olson, D. H. (1980). *Effectiveness of premarital education programs: Outcome study and follow-up evaluations*. Unpublished manuscript, University of Minnesota, Department of Family Social Science, St. Paul.

Norris, C. (1990). *What's wrong with postmodernism: Critical theory and the ends of philosophy*. Baltimore: Johns Hopkins University Press.

Norton, A. J., & Mooran, J. E. (1987). Current trends in marriage and divorce among American women. *Journal of Marriage and the Family, 49* (February), 5.

O'Farrell, T. (1992). Families and alcohol problems: An overview of treatment research. *Journal of Family Psychology, 5* (March/June), 339–359.

O'Farrell, T. J., & Birchler, G. R. (1987). Marital relationships of alcoholic, conflicted, and nonconflicted couples. *Journal of Marital and Family Therapy, 13*, 259–274.

Okimoto, J. D., & Stegall, P. J. (1987). *Boomerang kids: How to live with adult children who return home*. Boston: Little, Brown.

Olds, L. (1981). *Fully human*. Englewood Cliffs, NJ: Prentice-Hall.

Olds, S. B., London, M. L., & Ladewig, P. W. (1996). *Maternal-newborn nursing* (5th ed.). Redwood City, CA: Addison-Wesley Nursing.

Olson, D. H. (1989). *Alcoholic families and the Circumplex Model.* Unpublished manuscript, University of Minnesota, Department of Family Social Sciences, St. Paul.

Olson, D. H. (1992). Marriage in perspective. In F. D. Fincham & T. N. Bradbury (Eds.), *Psychology of marriage: Basic issues and applications* (pp. 402–419). New York: Guilford Press.

Olson, D. H. (1993). Circumplex model of marital and family systems: Assessing family functioning. In F. Walsh (Ed.), *Normal family processes* (2nd ed., pp. 104–137). New York: Guilford Press.

Olson, D. H. (1996). Clinical assessment and treatment using the Circumplex Model. In F. W. Kaslow (Ed.), *Handbook in relational diagnosis* (pp. 59–80). New York: Wiley.

Olson, D. H. (1997). *PREPARE/ENRICH counselor's manual.* Minneapolis, MN: Life Innovations.

Olson, D. H., & Cromwell, R. E. (1975). Power in families. In R. E. Cromwell & D. H. Olson (Eds.), *Power in families* (pp. 3–11). Newbury Park, CA: Sage.

Olson, D. H., & DeRubeis, F. (Eds.). (1987). *Inventory of marriage and family literature.* Beverly Hills, CA: Sage.

Olson, D. H., Fournier, D. G., & Druckman, J. M. (1989). *PREPARE, PREPARE-MC and ENRICH inventories* (3rd ed.). Minneapolis: PREPARE/ENRICH.

Olson, D. H., & Fowers, B. J. (1993). Five types of marriage: An empirical typology based on ENRICH. *The Family Journal, 1* (3), 196–207.

Olson, D. H., Fye, S. & Olson, A. (1999). *National survey of happy and unhappy married couples.* Minneapolis, MN: Life Innovations.

Olson, D. H., & Kilmer Hanson, M. (Eds.). (1990). *2001: Preparing families for the future* (NCFR Presidential Report). St. Paul, MN: National Council on Family Relations.

Olson, D. H., McCubbin, H. I., Barnes, H., Larsen, A., Muxen, M., & Wilson, M. (1989). *Families: What makes them work* (2nd ed.). Los Angeles, CA: Sage.

Olson, D. H., Portner, J., & Bell, R. (1986). *FACES II.* St. Paul: University of Minnesota, Family Social Science.

Olson, D. H., Russell, C. S., and Sprenkle, D. H. (1989). *Circumplex Model: Systemic assessment and treatment of families.* New York: Haworth Press.

Olson, J. S., & Wilson, R. (1984). *Native Americans in the twentieth century.* Chicago: University of Illinois Press.

Ooms, T. (1998a) *Strategies to strengthen marriage.* Washington, DC: Family Impact Seminar.

Ooms, T. (1998b) *Toward more perfect unions: Putting marriage on the public agenda.* Washington, DC: Family Impact Seminar.

Orr, C., & Van Zandt, S. (1987). The role of grandparenting in building family strengths. In H. G. Lingren, L. Kimmons, P. Lee, G. Rowe, L. Rottmann, L. Schwab, & R. Williams (Eds.), *Family strengths 8–9: Pathways to well-being* (pp. 259–272). Lincoln: University of Nebraska, Department of Human Development and the Family, Center for Family Strengths.

Orwell, G. (1951). *Animal farm.* New York: Penguin.

Osmond, M. W., & Thorne, B. (1993). Feminist theories: The social construction of gender in families and society. In P. G. Boss, W. J. Doherty, R. LaRossa, W. R. Schumm, & S. K. Steinmetz (Eds.), *Sourcebook of family theories and methods* (pp. 591–622). New York: Plenum.

Padgett, D. (1997). The contribution of support networks to household labor in African American families. *Journal of Family Issues, 18* (3), 227–250.

Parker Pen Co. (1985). *Do's and taboos around the world.* Elmsford, NY: Benjamin.

Parkerson, G. R., Broadhead, E., & Tse, C. J. (1995). Perceived family stress as a predictor of health-related outcomes. *Archives of Family Medicine, 23,* 357–360.

Parkman, A. M. (1992). *No-fault divorce: What went wrong?* Boulder, CO: Westview Press.

Parsons, T. (1955). The American family: Its relations to personality and the social structure. In T. Parsons & R. F. Bales, *Family socialization and interaction process* (pp. 3–21). Glencoe, IL: Free Press.

Parsons, T. (1965). The normal American family. In S. M. Farber, P. Mustacchi, & R. H. L. Wilson (Eds.), *Man and civilization: The family's search for survival* (pp. 31–50). New York: McGraw-Hill.

Parsons, T., & Bales, R. F. (1955). *Family socialization and interaction process.* Glencoe, IL: Free Press.

Pasley, K., & Ihinger-Tallman, M. (Eds.). (1994). *Stepparenting: Issues in theory, research, and practice.* Westport, CT: Greenwood Press.

Pearce, J. K. (1980). Ethnicity and family therapy. In J. K. Pearce & L. J. Friedman (Eds.), *Family therapy: Combining psychodynamics and family systems approaches.* New York: Grune & Stratton.

Peele, S. (1985). *Love and addiction.* Lexington, MA: Lexington Books/Heath.

Pence, E., Duprey, M., Paymar, M., & McDonnell, C. (1989). *The justice system's response to domestic assault cases: A guide for policy development.* Duluth, MN: Domestic Abuse Intervention Project.

Peplau, L. A., & Amaro, H. (1982). Understanding lesbian relationships. In W. Paul (Ed.), *Homosexuality: Social, psychological, and biological issues.* Beverly Hills, CA: Sage.

Peplau, L. A., Cochran, S. D., & Mays, V. M. (1997). A national survey of the intimate relationships of African American lesbians and gay men: A look at commitment, satisfaction, sexual behavior, and HIV disease. In B. Green (Ed.), *Ethnic and cultural diversity among les-*

bians and gay men: Psychological perspectives on lesbian and gay issues, Vol. 3 (pp. 11–38). Thousand Oaks, CA: Sage.

Peplau, L. A., Padesky, C., & Hamilton, M. (1981). Satisfaction in lesbian relationships. *Journal of Homosexuality, 8,* 23–35.

Peplau, L. A., Veniegas, R. C., & Campbell, S. M. (1996). Gay and lesbian relationships. In R. C. Savin-Williams & K. M. Cohen (Eds.), *The lives of lesbians, gays, and bisexuals: Children to adults* (pp. 250–273). Ft. Worth, TX: Harcourt.

Perls, F. (1969). *Gestalt therapy verbatim* (p. 4). Lafayette, CA: Real People Press.

Peters, M. F. (1981). Strengths of Black families. In N. Stinnett, J. DeFrain, K. King, P. Knaub, & G. Rowe (Eds.), *Family strengths 3: Roots of well-being* (pp. 73–91). Lincoln: University of Nebraska Press.

Peters, S., Wyatt, G. E., & Finkelhor, D. (1986). Prevalence. In D. Finkelhor (Ed.), *Sourcebook on child sexual abuse* (pp. 15–59). Beverly Hills, CA: Sage.

Peterson, K. S. (1992a, March 12). Adults should know status of parents. *USA Today,* p. 1D.

Peterson, K. S. (1992b, March 12). Parents hand down financial attitudes. *USA Today,* p. 4D.

Peterson, K. S., & Lee, F. (1985, March). Most find the single life isn't lonely. *USA Today,* p. 1B.

Pink, J. E. T., & Wampler, K. S. (1985). Problem areas in stepfamilies: Cohesion, adaptability, and the stepfather-adolescent relationship. *Family Relations, 34,* 327–335.

Pittman, F. S. (1985). Children of the rich. *Family Process, 24* (December), 461–472.

Pittman, F. (1993a, June). Beyond betrayal: Life after infidelity. *Psychology Today,* 32–38, 78, 80, 82.

Pittman, F. (1993b). *Private lies: Infidelity and the betrayal of intimacy.* New York: Norton.

Pittman, F. (1997). Just in love. *Journal of Marital and Family Therapy, 23* (3), 309–314.

Pittman, F., & Wagers, T. P. (1995). Crises of infidelity. In N. S. Jacobson & A. S. Gurman (Eds.), *Clinical handbook of couple therapy* (pp. 295–316). New York: Guilford Press.

Pittman, J. F., & Blanchard, D. (1996). The effects of work history and timing of marriage on the division of household labor: A life-course perspective. *Journal of Marriage and the Family, 58* (February), 78–90.

Planned Parenthood Federation of America. (1985). Five ways to prevent abortion (and one way that won't). In *Family matters* (Spring 1989, p. 2). Lincoln, NE: Planned Parenthood of Lincoln.

Poinsett, A. (1988, April). A crusade against sexual myths. *Ebony,* 108, 110, 112.

Popenoe, D., & Whitehead, B. D. (1999). *Should we live together? What young adults need to know about cohabitation before marriage.* New Brunswick, NJ: National Marriage Project, Rutgers University.

Popenoe, D. & Whitehead, B. D. (1999). *The state of our unions.* New Bunswick, NJ: National Marriage Project, Rutgers University.

Popenoe, D., Elshtain, J. B. & Blankenhorn, D. (Eds.), (1996). *Promises to keep.* Lanham, MD: Rowman and Littlefield Publisher.

Porter, J. (1999, January 10). It's time to start thinking about electing a female president. *Lincoln* [NE] *Journal Star,* p. 6D.

Poussaint, A. (1982, August). What every Black woman should know about Black men. *Ebony,* 36–40.

Pyke, K., & Coltrane, S. (1996). Entitlement, obligation, and gratitude in family work. *Journal of Family Issues, 17* (1), 60–82.

Raeburn, P. (1995, September 23). Drugs may alter drop in abortion availability. *Lincoln* [NE] *Journal Star,* p. 3A.

Raffaelli, M., Bogenschneider, K., & Flood, M. F. (1998). Parent-teen communication about sexual topics. *Journal of Family Issues, 19* (3), 315–333.

Raven, B. H., Centers, R., & Rodrigues, A. (1975). The bases of conjugal power. In R. E. Cromwell & D. H. Olson (Eds.), *Power in families* (pp. 217–232). Newbury Park, CA: Sage.

Reeder, J. (1992). Freud's narrative: From case history to life story. *International Forum of Psychoanalysis, 1* (1), 51–60.

Rettig, K. D. (1986). *Social decision making.* St. Paul: Minnesota Extension Service, University of Minnesota.

Rettig, K. D., Christensen, D. H., & Dahl, C. M. (1991). Impact of child support guidelines on the economic well-being of children. *Family Relations, 40,* 167–175.

Rettig, K. D., & Hogan, M. J. (1993). Educating for family resource management. In M. Arcus, J. Schvaneveldt, & J. Moss (Eds.), *Handbook of family life education, Vol. 2* (pp. 115–154). Newbury Park, CA: Sage.

Richards, L. N., & Schmiege, C. J. (1993). Problems and strengths of single-parent families: Implications for practice and policy. *Family Relations, 42* (July), 277–285.

Ridley, C. A., Peterman, D. J., & Avery, A. W. (1978). Cohabitation: Does it make for a better marriage? *Family Coordinator* (April), 129–136.

Risman, B. J., Hill, C. T., Rubin, Z., & Peplau, A. (1981). Living together in college: Implications for courtship. *Journal of Marriage and the Family* (February), 77–83.

Risman, B. J., & Johnson-Sumerford, D. (1998). Doing it fairly: A study of postgender marriages. *Journal of Marriage and the Family, 60* (February), 23–40.

Robbins, C. C. (1987, May 25). Expanding power for Indian women. *New York Times,* pp. III, 1.

Robinson, I. E., Ziss, K., Ganza, B., Katz, S., & Robinson, E. (1991). Twenty years of the sexual revolution,

1965–1985: An update. *Journal of Marriage and the Family*, *53* (February), 216–220.

Rodgers, R. H., & White, J. M. (1993). Family development theory. In P. G. Boss, W. J. Doherty, R. LaRossa, W. R. Schumm, & S. K. Steinmetz (Eds.), *Sourcebook of family theories and methods* (pp. 99–116). New York: Plenum.

Rodick, J. D., Henggler, S. W., & Hanson, C. L. (1985). An evaluation of Family Adaptability and Cohesion Evaluation Scales (FACES) and the Circumplex Model. *Journal of Abnormal Child Psychology*, *14*, 77–87.

Rogler, L. H., & Cooney, R. S. (1984). *Puerto Rican families in New York City: Intergenerational processes.* Maplewood, NJ: Waterfront Press.

Roosa, M. W., Tein, J.-Y., Groppenbacher, N., Michaels, M., & Dumka, L. (1993). Mothers' parenting behavior and child mental health in families with a problem drinking parent. *Journal of Marriage and the Family*, *55* (February), 107–118.

Root, M. P. P. (Ed.). (1992). *Racially mixed people in America.* Newbury Park, CA: Sage.

Roscoe, B., & Benaske, N. (1985). Courtship violence experienced by abused wives: Similarities in patterns of abuse. *Family Relations*, *34*, 419–424.

Rosenblatt, P. C., Karis, T. A., & Powell, R. D. (1995). *Multiracial couples: Black and White voices.* Thousand Oaks, CA: Sage.

Rosenfeld, J. A. (1991). Bereavement and grieving after spontaneous abortion. *American Family Physician*, *6* (May), 1679.

Rosenstein, H. (1973, May). On androgyny. *Ms.*, 38.

Ross, C. E., Mirowsky, J., & Goldsteen, K. (1991). The impact of the family on health: The decade in review. In A. Booth (Ed.), *Contemporary families: Looking forward, looking back* (pp. 1059–1078). Minneapolis: National Council on Family Relations.

Rubin, L. B. (1985). *Just friends: The role of friendship in our lives.* New York: Harper & Row.

Rueter, M. A., & Conger, R. D. (1995). Antecedents of parent-adolescent disagreements. *Journal of Marriage and the Family*, *57* (May), 435–448.

Russell, D. E. H. (1986). *The secret trauma: Incest in the lives of girls and women.* New York: Basic Books.

Rybash, J. W., Roodin, P. A., & Santrock, J. W. (1991). *Adult development and aging* (2nd ed.). Dubuque, IA: Brown.

Sable, P. (1989). Attachment, anxiety, and loss of a husband. *American Journal of Orthopsychiatry*, *59* (October), 550–556.

Sable, P. (1992). Attachment, loss of spouse, and disordered mourning. *Families in Society*, *73* (5), 266–273.

Safilios-Rothschild, D. (1976). A macro- and micro-examination of family power and love: An exchange

model. *Journal of Marriage and the Family*, *37* (May), 355–362.

Salholz, E. (1990, February 26). Politics and the pill. *Newsweek*, 42.

Sanchez, L., & Kane, E. W. (1996). Women's and men's constructions of perceptions of housework fairness. *Journal of Family Issues*, *17* (3), 358–387.

Satir, Virginia. (1988). *The new peoplemaking.* Palo Alto, CA: Science and Behavior Books.

Scarr, S. (1998). American child care today. *American Psychologist*, *53* (2), 106.

Schaninger, C. M., & Buss, W. C. (1986). A longitudinal comparison of consumption and finance handling between happily married and divorced couples. *Journal of Marriage and the Family*, *48* (February), 129–136.

Schepers, C. J. (1991, November 17). Proof mounting: Passive smoke kills. *Lincoln* [NE] *Journal Star*, p. 1J.

Schickedanz, D. I., Hansen, K., & Forsyth, P. D. (1997). *Understanding children and adolescents* (3rd ed.). Mountain View, CA: Mayfield.

Schickedanz, J., Schickedanz, D., Hansen, K., & Forsyth, P. (1993). *Understanding children* (2nd ed.). Mountain View, CA: Mayfield.

Schmich, M. (1997, June 1). Advice, like youth, probably just wasted on the young. *Chicago Tribune.*

Schnaiberg, A., & Goldenberg, S. (1989). From empty nest to crowded nest: The dynamics of incompletely launched young adults. *Social Problems*, *36* (June), 251–269.

Schoen, R. (1992). First unions and the stability of first marriages. *Journal of Marriage and the Family*, *54* (May), 281–284.

Schuchardt, J., & Guadagno, M. A. N. (1991). A comparison of lower middle income two-parent and single-mother families. *Family Economics Review*, *4* (2), 9–17.

Schultz, N. C., Schultz, C. L., & Olson, D. H. (1991). Couple strengths and stressors in complex and simple stepfamilies in Australia. *Journal of Marriage and the Family*, *53*, 555–564.

Schwartz, J., Raine, G., & Robins, K. (1987, May 11). A "superminority" tops out. *Newsweek*, 48–49.

Schwartz, P. (1994, September/October). Peer marriage: What does it take to create a truly egalitarian relationship? *Family Therapy Networker*, 57–61, 92.

Schwartz, P. (1995). *Love between equals: How peer marriage really works.* New York: Free Press.

Sedlak, A. J., & Broadhurst, D. D. (1996). *Third national incidence study on child abuse and neglect.* Washington, DC: U.S. Department of Health and Human Services.

Selle, R. (1998, May). People in the news: Feminism's matriarch. *The World & I*, 51.

Seltzer, J. A. (1991). Relationships between fathers and children who live apart: The father's role after separation. *Journal of Marriage and the Family, 53,* 79–101.

Selye, H. (1974). *The stress of life* (2nd ed.). New York: McGraw-Hill.

Sheehy, G. (1976). *Passages: Predictable crises of adult life.* New York: Dutton.

Sheehy, G. (1992). *The silent passage: Menopause.* New York: Random House.

Sheehy, G. (1995). *New passages: Mapping your life across time.* New York: Random House.

Shorris, E. (1992). *Latinos: A biography of the people.* New York: Norton.

Shostak, A. (1987). Singlehood. In M. Sussman & S. Steinmetz (Eds.), *Handbook of Marriage and the Family.* New York: Plenum.

Silverstein, L. B. (1995). Fathering is a feminist issue. *Psychology of Women Quarterly, 20,* 3–37.

Simmons, P. E. (1998). Wild things. *World: The Journal of the Unitarian Universalist Association, 12* (6, November/December), 26.

Simons, R. L., Johnson, C., Beaman, J., & Conger, R. D. (1993). Explaining women's double jeopardy: Factors that mediate the association between harsh treatment as a child and violence by a husband. *Journal of Marriage and the Family, 55* (August), 713–723.

Simpson, J. C. (1989, March 27). Beware of paper tigers. *Time,* 104–105.

Skolnick, A. S., & Skolnick, J. H. (1977). *Family in transition.* Boston: Little, Brown.

Somers, M. S. (1993). A comparison of voluntarily child-free adults and parents. *Journal of Marriage and the Family, 55* (August), 643–650.

Spanier, G. S., & Thompson, L. (1984). *Parting: The aftermath of separation and divorce.* Newbury Park, CA: Sage.

Spitze, G., Logan, J. R., Deane, G., & Zerger, S. (1994). Adult children's divorce and intergenerational relationships. *Journal of Marriage and the Family, 56* (May), 279–293.

Sprey, J. (1990). Theoretical practice in family studies. In J. Sprey (Ed.), *Fashioning family theory: New approaches* (pp. 9–33). Newbury Park, CA: Sage.

Springer, J. S., Fournier, D., & Olson, D. H. (1985). *Commitment and conflict across premarital relationship stages.* Unpublished manuscript, University of Minnesota, Department of Family Social Science, St. Paul.

St. Pierre, T. L., Mark, M. M., Kaltreider, D. L., & Aikin, K. J. (1995). A 27-month evaluation of a sexual activity prevention program in Boys and Girls Clubs across the nation. *Family Relations, 44,* 69–77.

Staples, R., & Mirandé, A. (1980). Racial and cultural variations among American families: A decennial review of the literature on minority families. *Journal of Marriage and the Family, 42,* 887–903.

Stark, E. (1985, June). Androgyny makes better lovers. *Psychology Today,* 19.

Stark, E. (1986, October). Young, innocent and pregnant. *Psychology Today,* 28–30, 32–35.

Stark, E., & Flitcraft, A. (1985). Woman-battering, child abuse and social heredity: What is the relationship? *Sociological Review Monograph, 31,* 147–171.

Starr, S. L. (1998, November/December). [Letter to the editor.] *World: Journal of the Unitarian Universalist Association, 12* (6), 10.

Stauss, J. (1986). The study of American families: Implications for applied research. *Family Perspective, 20* (4), 337–350.

Steinberg, L., Lamborn, S. D., Darling, N., Mounts, N. S., & Dornbusch, S. M. (1994). Over-time changes in adjustment and competence among adolescents from authoritative, authoritarian, indulgent, and neglectful families. *Child Development, 65,* 754–770.

Steinmetz, S. K. (1987). Family violence. In M. B. Sussman & S. K. Steinmetz (Eds.), *Handbook of marriage and the family* (pp. 725–765). New York: Plenum.

Sternberg, D., & Beier, E. G. (1977). Marital communication: Changing patterns of conflict. *Journal of Communications, 27,* 97–99.

Sternberg, R. J. (1986). A triangle theory of love. *Psychological Review, 93,* 119–135.

Sternberg, R. J., & Barnes, M. (Eds.). (1988). *The psychology of love.* New Haven, CT: Yale University Press.

Stets, J. E., (1990). Verbal and physical aggression in marriage. *Journal of Marriage and the Family, 52,* 501–514.

Stets, J. E., & Henderson, D. A. (1991). Contextual factors surrounding conflict resolution while dating: Results from a national study. *Family Relations, 40,* 29–36.

Stets, J. E., & Straus, M. A. (1989). The marriage as a hitting license: A comparison of assaults in dating, cohabiting, and married couples. In M. A. Pirog-Good & J. E. Stets (Eds.), *Violence in dating relationships* (pp. 33–52). New York: Greenwood Press.

Stewart, K. L. (1988). Stress and adaptation: A multi-system model of individual, couple, family, and work systems. (Doctoral dissertation, University of Minnesota, Family Social Science, St. Paul). *Dissertation Abstracts International, 49,* 8A, p. 2410. (University Microfilms No. 88-23570).

Stewart, K. L., & Olson, D. H. (1990). *Predicting premarital satisfaction on PREPARE using background factors.* Unpublished manuscript, PREPARE/ENRICH, Inc., Minneapolis.

Stierlin, H. (1972). *Separating parents and adolescents: A perspective on running away, schizophrenia, and waywardness.* New York: Quadrangle.

Stinnett, N., & DeFrain, J. (1985). *Secrets of strong families.* Boston: Little, Brown.

Stinnett, N., Sanders, G., & DeFrain, J. (1981). Strong families: A national study. In N. Stinnett, J. DeFrain, K. King, P. Knaub, & G. Rowe (Eds.), *Family strengths 3: Roots of well-being* (pp. 33–42). Lincoln: University of Nebraska Press.

Stinnett, N., Stinnett, N., DeFrain, J., & DeFrain, N. (1997). *Good families.* New York: Doubleday.

Stinnett, N., Stinnett, N., Defrain, J., & DeFrain, N. (1999). *Creating a strong family.* West Monroe, LA: Howard.

Straus, M. A. (1989). *Physical abuse of children and spouses.* Paper presented at the annual meeting of the National Council on Family Relations. University of New Hampshire, Family Research Laboratory, Family Violence Research Program, Durham.

Straus, M. A. (1990). The national family violence surveys. In M. Straus & R. J. Gelles (Eds.), *Physical violence in American families* (pp. 3–16). New Brunswick, NJ: Transaction Books.

Straus, M. A. (1994). *Beating the devil out of them: Corporal punishment in American families.* New York: Lexington Books.

Straus, M. A., & Gelles, R. J. (1986). Societal change and change in family violence from 1975 to 1985 as revealed by two national surveys. *Journal of Marriage and the Family, 48,* 465–479.

Straus, M. A., Gelles, R. J., & Steinmetz, S. (1980). *Behind closed doors: Violence in the American family.* Garden City, NY: Doubleday/Anchor Press.

Straus, M. A., & Mathus, A. K. (1996). Social change and trends in approval of corporal punishment by parents from 1968 to 1994. In D. Frehsee, W. Horn, and K. Bussman (Eds.), *Violence against children* (pp. 91–105). New York: de Gruyter.

Straus, M. A., & Sweet, S. (1992). Verbal/symbolic aggression in couples: Incidence rates and relationships to personal characteristics. *Journal of Marriage and the Family, 54* (May), 346–357.

Stroup, A., & Pollock, G. E. (1994). Economic consequences of marital dissolution. *Journal of Divorce and Remarriage, 22* (1/2), 37–54.

Stuart, R. B. (1980). *Helping couples change.* New York: Guilford Press.

Study: 1 of 3 women are abuse victims. (1995, November 15). *Lincoln* [NE] *Journal Star,* p. 6A.

Study says economy hurts young parents. (1997, September 17). *Lincoln* [NE] *Journal Star,* p. 5A.

Stull, D. E., Bowman, K., & Smerglia, V. (1994). Women in the middle: A myth in the making? *Family Relations, 43,* 319–324.

Surra, C. A. (1991). Research and theory on mate selection and premarital relationships. In A. Booth (Ed.), *Contemporary families: Looking forward, looking back* (pp. 54–75). Minneapolis: National Council on Family Relations.

Sweeney, J. (1982, June 21). Taking the long view of marriage: Why do some endure? *Los Angeles Times,* pp. 1, 21–23.

Swift, C. (1986). Preventing family violence: Family-focused programs. In M. Lystad (Ed.), *Violence in the home: Interdisciplinary perspectives.* New York: Brunner/Mazel.

Tannen, D. (1990). *You just don't understand: Women and men in conversation.* New York: Morrow.

Tannen, D. (1993). *Gender and conversational interaction.* New York: Oxford University Press.

Tannen, D., & Aries, E. (1997). Conversational style: Do women and men speak different languages? In M. R. Walsh (Ed.), *Women, men, and gender: Ongoing debates* (pp. 79–100). New Haven, CT: Yale University Press.

Taylor, P. (1988, March 20). It's time to put warnings on alcohol. *New York Times,* p. B2.

Teen moms sexually abused as kids. (1987, September 16). *Lincoln* [NE] *Star,* p. 40.

Theroux, P. (1996). *My other life: A novel.* Boston: Houghton Mifflin.

Thomas, V., & Olson, D. H. (1993). Problem families and the Circumplex Model: Observational assessment using the clinical rating scale. *Journal of Marital and Family Therapy, 19* (2), 159–175.

Thompson, L., & Walker, A. J. (1995). The place of feminism in family studies. *Journal of Marriage and the Family, 57* (4), 847–865.

Thomson, E., & Colella, U. (1992). Cohabitation and marital stability: Quality or commitment? *Journal of Marriage and the Family, 54* (May), 259–267.

Thoreau, H. D. (1962). *Walden.* New York: Time. (Original work published in 1849.)

Thorn, B. L., & Gilbert, L. A. (1998). Antecedents of work and family role expectations of college men. *Journal of Family Psychology, 12* (2), 259–267.

Thorne, B. (1982). Feminist rethinking of the family: An overview. In B. Thorne (Ed.), *Rethinking the family* (pp. 1–24). New York: Longman.

Thornton, J., & Lasswell, M. (1997). *Chore wars: How households can share the work and keep the peace.* Berkeley, CA: Conari Press.

Tiesel, J. W. (1992). *Family system and adolescent development: A meta-analysis.* Unpublished manuscript, University of Minnesota, Family Social Science, St. Paul.

Timberlake, E. M. (1980). The value of grandchildren to grandmothers. *Journal of Gerontological Social Work, 3,* 63–76.

Touliatos, J. (Ed.). (1993). *Inventory of marital and family literature.* Minneapolis: National Council on Family Relations.

Troll, L. E. (1989). Myths of mid-life intergenerational relationships. In S. Hunter & M. Sundel (Eds.), *Mid-life myths: Issues, findings, and practice implications.* Newbury Park, CA: Sage.

Troll, L. E. (1994). Family-embedded vs. family-deprived oldest-old: A study of contrasts. *International Journal of Aging and Human Development, 38* (1), 51–64.

Troll, L. E. (1997). Growing old in families. In I. Deitch, & C. Ward (Eds.), *Counseling the aging and their families* (pp. 3–16). Alexandria, VA: American Counseling Association.

Trotter, R. J. (1986, September). The three faces of love. *Psychology Today,* 46–54.

Turnbull, C. (1983). *The human cycle.* New York: Touchstone/Simon & Schuster.

U.S. Advisory Board on Child Abuse and Neglect. (1990). *Child abuse and neglect: Critical first steps in response to a national emergency.* Washington, DC: U.S. Government Printing Office.

U.S. Bureau of the Census. (1989). *Statistical abstract of the United States* (109th ed.). Washington, DC: U.S. Government Printing Office.

U.S. Bureau of the Census. (1991). *Statistical abstract of the United States* (111th ed.). Washington, DC: U.S. Government Printing Office.

U.S. Bureau of the Census. (1994). *Statistical abstract of the United States* (114th ed.). Washington, DC: U.S. Government Printing Office.

U.S. Bureau of the Census. (1995). *Statistical abstract of the United States* (115th ed.). Washington, DC: U.S. Government Printing Office.

U.S. Bureau of the Census. (1997). *Statistical abstract of the United States* (117th ed.). Washington, DC: U.S. Government Printing Office.

U.S. Department of Health and Human Services. (1997). *Healthy people 2000 review 1997.* (DHHS Publication No. PHS 98-1256.) Hyattsville, MD: Centers for Disease Control and Prevention, National Center for Health Statistics.

U.S. Department of Justice. (1989). *Crime in the United States, 1988* (p. 13). Washington, DC: U.S. Department of Justice, Federal Bureau of Investigation.

U.S. House of Representatives. (1996). *Personal responsibility and work opportunity reconciliation act of 1996* (Conference Report H.R. 3734, Report No. 104–725). Washington, DC: U.S. Government Printing Office.

Van Zandt, S., Mou, R., & Abbott, D. (1989). Mental and physical health of rural bereaved and nonbereaved elders: A longitudinal study. In D. A. Lund (Ed.), *Older bereaved spouses: Research with practical applications.* New York: Hemisphere.

Veevers, J. (1980). *Childless by choice.* Scarborough, Ontario: Butterworth.

Vega, W. A. (1991). Hispanic families in the 1980s. In A. Booth (Ed.), *Contemporary families: Looking forward, looking back* (pp. 297–306). Minneapolis: National Council on Family Relations.

Vega, W. A. (1995). The study of Latino families: A point of departure. In R. E. Zambrana (Ed.), *Understanding Latino families: Scholarship, policy, and practice, Vol. 2* (pp. 3–17). Thousand Oaks, CA: Sage.

Vega, W. A., Patterson, T., Sallis, J., Nader, P., Atkins, C., & Abraham, I. (1986). Cohesion and adaptability in Mexican American and Anglo families. *Journal of Marriage and the Family, 48* (November), 857–867.

Veniegas, R. C., & Peplau, L. A. (1997). Power and the quality of same-sex friendships. *Psychology of Women Quarterly, 21* (3), 279–297.

Veroff, J., Douvan, E., & Kulka, R. A. (1981). *The inner American: A self portrait from 1957 to 1976.* New York: Basic Books.

Visher, E. B. (1989). The Stepping Ahead Program. In M. Burt (Ed.), *Stepfamilies stepping ahead* (3rd ed., pp. 57–89). Lincoln, NE: Stepfamilies Press.

Visher, E. B., & Visher, J. S. (1988). *Old loyalties: New ties.* New York: Brunner/Mazel.

Visher, E. B., & Visher, J. S. (1992). *How to win as a stepfamily* (2nd ed.). New York: Brunner/Mazel.

Visher, E. B., & Visher, J. S. (1996). *Therapy with stepfamilies.* New York: Brunner/Mazel.

von Bertalanffy, L. (1968). *General system theory: Foundation, development, applications.* New York: Braziller.

Voydanoff, P. (1991). Economic distress and family relations: A review of the eighties. In A. Booth (Ed.), *Contemporary families: Looking forward, looking back* (pp. 429–445). Minneapolis: National Council on Family Relations.

Voydanoff, P., Donnelly, B. W., & Fine, M. A. (1988). Economic distress, social integration and family satisfaction. *Journal of Family Issues, 9,* 545–564.

Waite, L. (1995) "Does marriage matter?" *Demography, 32,* (4), 483–507.

Waite, L. (1998). "Why marriage matters." In T. Ooms (Ed.), *Strategies to strengthen marriage* (pp. 1–22). Washington, DC: Family Impact Seminar.

Waite, L. and Gallagher, M. (1999). *The case for marriage.* Cambridge: Harvard University Press.

Walker, A. J., Pratt, C. C., & Oppy, N. C. (1992). Perceived reciprocity in family caregiving. *Family Relations, 41* (January), 82–85.

Walker, A. J., Shin, H.-Y., & Bird, D. N. (1990). Perceptions of relationship change and caregiver satisfaction. *Family Relations, 39* (April), 147–152.

Walker, A. J., & Thompson, L. (1984). Feminism and family studies. *Journal of Family Issues, 5* (4), 545–570.

Walker, L. (1979). *The battered woman.* New York: Harper & Row.

Waller, W. (1951). *The family* [revised by R. Hill]. New York: Dryden.

Wallerstein, J. S. & Blakeslee, S. (1996) *Second chances: Men, women, and children a decade after divorce.* New York: Ticknor & Fields.

Walsh, F. (1998). *Strengthening family resilience.* New York: Guilford Press.

Walsh, F., & Olson, D. H. (1989). Utility of the Circumplex Model with severely dysfunctional family systems. In D. H. Olson, C. S. Russell, & D. H. Sprenkle (Eds.), *Circumplex Model: Systemic assessment and treatment of families.* New York: Haworth Press.

Warmbrod, M. T. (1982). Alternative generation in marital problem solving. *Family Relations, 31,* 503–511.

Waters, H. F. (1985, September 2). Cosby's fast track. *Time,* 50–56.

Watson, R. E. L. (1983). Premarital cohabitation vs. traditional courtship: Their effects on subsequent marital adjustment. *Family Relations, 32* (January), 139–147.

Watzlawick, P. (Ed.). (1984). *The invented reality.* New York: Norton.

Weiss, R. S. (1973). *Loneliness: The experience of emotional isolation.* Cambridge: Massachusetts Institute of Technology.

Weitzman, L. J. (1985). *The divorce revolution: The unexpected social and economic consequences for women and children in America.* New York: Free Press.

Weitzman, L. J., & Dixon, R. B. (1980). The transformation of legal marriage through no-fault divorce. In A. Skolnick & J. H. Skolnick (Eds.), *Family in transition.* Boston: Little, Brown.

West, M. O., & Prinz, R. J. (1987). Parental alcoholism and childhood psychopathology. *Psychology Bulletin, 102,* 204–218.

Whelan, E. (1995, August 31). Some Republicans want more regulations on tobacco. *Lincoln* [NE] *Journal Star,* p. 4B.

Whishman, M. A., Dixon, A. E., & Johnson, B. (1998). Therapists' perspectives of couple problems and treatment issues in couple therapy. *Journal of Family Psychology, 11* (3), 361–366.

Whitam, F. L. (1983). Culturally invariable properties of male homosexuality: Tentative conclusions from cross-cultural research. *Archives of Sexual Behavior, 12,* 207–226.

White, G. L. (1980). Physical attractiveness and courtship progress. *Journal of Personality and Social Psychology, 39,* 660–668.

White, L. K. (1991). Determinants of divorce: A review of research in the eighties. In A. Booth (Ed.), *Contemporary families: Looking forward, looking back* (pp. 141–149). Minneapolis: National Council on Family Relations.

White, M., & Epston, D. (1990). *Narrative means to therapeutic ends.* New York: Norton.

Whitehead, B. D. (1997). The divorce culture. New York: Knopf.

Whiteside-Mansell, L., Pope, S. K., & Bradley, R. H. (1996). Patterns of parenting behavior in young mothers. *Family Relations, 45* (July), 273–281.

Whitman, C. T. (1995, May 31). Wheaton College commencement address. *Good Morning America.* New York: CBS Television.

Wiener, N. (1956). *I am a mathematician.* New York: Doubleday.

Wilhelm, M. S., & Ridley, C. A. (1988). Unemployment induced adaptations. *Lifestyles, 9,* 5–20.

Willie, C. V. (1988). *A new look at Black families* (3rd ed.). Dix Hills, NH: General Hall.

Wilmot, W. W., & Hocker, J. L. (1998). *Interpersonal conflict* (5th ed.). Boston: McGraw-Hill.

Winch, R. F. (1958). *Mate selection: A study of complementary needs.* New York: Harper.

Winch, R. F. (1971). *The modern family* (3rd ed.). New York: Holt.

Winston, M. R. (1994). Dealing with depression and anger: Reactions of family caregivers. *Caring, 13* (8), 52–54.

Woehrer, C. E. (1989). Ethnic families in the Circumplex Model: Integrating nuclear with extended family systems. In D. H. Olson, C. S. Russell, & D. H. Sprenkle (Eds.), *Circumplex Model: Systemic assessment and treatment of families.* New York: Haworth Press.

A woman's fertility window opens six days each month. (1995, December 7). *Lincoln* [NE] *Journal Star,* pp. 1A, 7A.

Woodman, S. (1986, February). How important is sex? *Self,* 130–131.

Woodward, J. C. (1988). *The solitude of loneliness.* Lexington, MA: Lexington Books/Heath.

Wright, H. N. (1980). *Premarital counseling: A follow-up study.* Unpublished manuscript, Christian Marriage Enrichment, 8000 East Girard, Denver, CO.

Wrobel, G. M., Ayers-Lopez, S., Grotevant, H. D., McRoy, R. G., et al. (1996). Openness in adoption and the level of child participation. *Child Development, 67* (5), 2358–2374.

Wuerffel, J., DeFrain, J., & Stinnett, N. (1990). How strong families use humor. *Family Perspective* (Fall), 129–142.

Wynne, L. (1958). Pseudo-mutuality in the family relations of schizophrenics. *Psychiatry, 21,* 205–222.

Yarrow, P. (1972). River of Jordan. *PP&M Lifelines.* Mary Beth Music, ASCAP. Burbank, CA: Warner Bros. Records.

Yi, S. (1984, October). Women progress. *World Press Review, 31,* 58.

Zaslow, M., & Eldred, C. (1998). Parenting behavior in a sample of young mothers in poverty. *APA Monitor.* Washington, DC.

Zigler, E., Rubin, N., & Kaufman, J. (1988, May). Do abused children become abusive parents? *Parents,* 100–104.

Zill, N., Morrison, D. R., & Coiro, M. J. (1993). Longterm effects of parental divorce on parent-child relationships, adjustment, and achievement in young adulthood. *Journal of Family Psychology, 7,* 91–103.

Zuckerman, E. J. (1982). Viral hepatitis. *Practical Gastroenterology, 6* (16), 21–22.

Credits

Explorer/Photo Researchers, Inc.; p. 201L, © Susan Van Etten/Photo Edit; p. 208, © Spencer Grant/Photo Researchers, Inc.; p. 215, © Rhoda Sidney/Photo Edit; p. 224, © Suzanne Arms

Chapter 8 p. 234, © Suzanne Arms; p. 240, © Robert Brenner/Photo Edit; p. 242, © Robert Ginn/Photo Edit; p. 244, © Joseph Nettis 1993/Photo Researchers, Inc.; p. 250, © 1996 James Schnepf; p. 252, © Michael Newman/Photo Edit; p. 256, © Frozen Images/The Image Works; p. 263, © Rob Crandall/Stock Boston

Chapter 9 p. 266, © Joel Gordon 1991; p. 272, © Gary Conner/Photo Edit; p. 275, © Jeff Greenberg/Photo Edit; p. 279, © Cynthia Dopkin/Photo Researchers, Inc.; p. 282, © Blair Seitz/Photo Researchers, Inc.; p. 288, © Robert Brenner/Photo Edit

Chapter 10 p. 296, © Robert Ullmann/Design Conceptions; p. 301, © D. Littell Greco/Stock Boston; p. 307, © Amy C. Etra/Photo Edit; p. 308, © Gary A. Conner/Photo Edit; p. 313, © Robert Brenner/Photo Edit; p. 320, © Fabricius & Taylor/Stock Boston

Chapter 11 p. 324, © Frank Siteman/Stock Boston; p. 331, © Bob Daemmrich/The Image Works; p. 335, © Tony Stone Images/Zigy Kaluzny; p. 339, © Joe Sohm/The Image Works; p. 340, © Martin A. Levick; p. 350, © D. Young-Wolff/Photo Edit

Chapter 12 p. 360, © Cleo/Photo Edit; p. 365, © Esbin-Anderson/The Image Works; p. 380, © David Young-Wolff/Photo Edit; p. 381, © Spencer Grant/Photo Edit; p. 383, © 1995 Strauss/Curtis

Chapter 13 p. 392, © Elizabeth Crews; p. 397, © Susan Lapides 1992/Design Conceptions; p. 404, © Myrleen Ferguson/Photo Edit; p. 407, © Robert Brenner/Photo Edit; p. 410, © Myrleen Ferguson/Photo Edit

Chapter 14 p. 426, © Joel Gordon; p. 431, © Bob Daemmrich/The Image Works; p. 433, © Myleen Ferguson/Photo Edit; p. 437, © Bill Bachmann/Stock Boston; p. 440, © Joel Gordon; p. 443, © Rebecca Cooney/Actuality, Inc.; p. 446, © S. O'Rourke/The Image Works; p. 448, © Jonathan Nourok/Photo Edit

Chapter 15 p. 454, © Dennis MacDonald/Photo Edit; p. 460, © Tony Freeman/Photo Edit; p. 465, M. Antman/The Image Works; p. 467, © Peter Menzel/Stock Boston; p. 473, © Bob Daemmrich/Stock Boston; p. 477, © David Young-Wolff/Photo Edit

Chapter 16 p. 484, © M. Siluk/The Image Works; p. 490, © Patrick Ramsey/Stock International; p. 493, © Will Hart/Photo Edit; p. 500, © Steven Ferry/P&F Communications; p. 501, © Robert Llewellyn; p. 503, © Tom Prettyman/Photo Edit; p. 507, Courtesy of the Ad Council; p. 508, D. Greco/The Image Works; p. 511, © Dan Habib/Impact Visuals; p. 515, © Mary Ellen Mark/Library; p. 520, © Joel Gordon 1984; p. 528, David Young-Wolff/Photo Edit

Chapter 17 p. 534, © Tony Freeman/Photo Edit; p. 538, © Tony Freeman/Photo Edit; p. 539, © Michael Newman/Photo Edit; p. 545, © Will Hart/Photo Edit; p. 547, © Bachmann/The Image Works; p. 553, © April Saul

Chapter 18 p. 558, © Mitch Diamond/International Stock; p. 563, © Bachmann/Photo Edit; p. 569, © Michael Newman/Photo Edit; p. 575, © F. Pedrick/The Image Works; p. 579, © Russell Schleipman/Offshoot Stock

Name Index

Subject Index